Contemporary Issues in Financial Reporting

With the collapse of Enron in 2001, and other similar scandals, financial reporting and its relation to corporate governance has become a contentious issue. In this book Paul Rosenfield involves the reader in exploring contemporary financial reporting, highlighting the deficiencies in current methods.

Contemporary Issues in Financial Reporting challenges the reader to critically think through the issues and arguments involved in the practice of financial reporting. The book goes to the heart of the most difficult and controversial problems, presenting the major issues and commenting upon the solutions that have been offered in the financial reporting literature. The grave defects in current accepted accounting principles are demonstrated and exposed, and Paul Rosenfield offers alternative solutions.

Paul Rosenfield is a CPA for the state of Illinois and worked for the AICPA for 30 years, during which time he was Director of the Institute's Accounting Standards Division. He taught financial reporting at Hunter College, New York, and has published widely on the subject, including co-editing the tenth edition of the *Accountants' Handbook* (2003).

Accounting students and professors, as well as regulators and accounting professionals in firms and companies, can profit immensely from this refreshing and fearless analysis of the major issues of the day in financial reporting.

Stephen A. Zeff, Herbert S. Autrey Professor of Accounting
at Rice University, USA

Routledge new works in accounting history

Edited by Garry Carnegie (Melbourne University Private, Australia), John Richard Edwards (Cardiff University, UK), Salvador Carmona (Instituto de Empresa, Spain) and Dick Fleischman (John Carroll University, USA).

Contemporary Issues in Financial Reporting

A user-oriented approach

Paul Rosenfield

Routledge
Taylor & Francis Group

LONDON AND NEW YORK

First published 2006
by Routledge
2 Park Square, Milton Park, Abingdon, Oxon OX14 4RN

Simultaneously published in the USA and Canada
by Routledge
270 Madison Ave, New York, NY 10016

Routledge is an imprint of the Taylor & Francis Group, an informa business

© 2006 Paul Rosenfield

Typeset in Garamond by Wearset Ltd, Boldon, Tyne and Wear
Printed and bound in Great Britain by TJ Digital, Padstow, Cornwall

British Library Cataloguing in Publication Data
A catalogue record for this book is available from the British Library

Library of Congress Cataloging in Publication Data
A catalog record for this book has been requested

ISBN10: 0-415-70206-2 (hbk)
ISBN10: 0-203-08815-8 (ebk)

ISBN13: 978-0-415-70206-5 (hbk)
ISBN13: 978-0-203-08815-9 (ebk)

To my children Mark, Keith, Valerie, Brian, and Kevin, with love

... the betterment of accounting must begin in the classroom ... our undergraduate curricula consist almost entirely of present practices. ... The undergraduates go into practice and implement what we taught them; the graduate students go into academia and advance the research; the gap between research and practice grows wider and wider. Young and rising accounting practitioners cannot view both sides of the question with impartiality because we teachers do not present both sides of the question. Instead, we pass along and thereby reinforce the inherited dogma. Thus, the long-run reform of accounting practice requires the reform of accounting curricula. My suggestion is that we teach both— we consider alternatives to present practices with the description of present practices.

(Sterling, 1989, 82; 1979, x)

... students ... are being sent out into a world where they will be leaders in 20 years more or less; but in that time it will be a different world. How are they equipped to meet that ... knowing only the current dogma of their time? ... the teacher ... should ... present the very best of what is being done in ... the studies of the researchers, for there is a distinct probability that some of it, heresy today, will become orthodox and accepted in practice in the students' lifetimes. ... To be in the vanguard of advances in knowledge and technology is at once a duty and a source of deep satisfaction to educators.

(Chambers, 1969, 691, 692; 1987, 106)

... [to] provide students not just with a knowledge of current practice, but with the knowledge to evaluate critically that practice and seek its reform.

(West, 2003, 162)

... teaching little except GAAP not only neglects the investing public but may also prepare students poorly for long-run careers, because critical thinking is so important in some the high positions in the profession.

(Staubus, 2004b)

Contents

PART III
Broad issues in financial reporting

Figures

Tables

Foreword

Paul Rosenfield has written an intelligent book on financial reporting, which insists that readers think through issues and arguments and make up their own minds. In a literature dominated by soulless textbooks and how-to-do-it manuals, Paul has crafted a book that challenges the readers' intellect and demands that they take positions. He extensively, sensitively and critically reviews previous writings, and is quick to skewer fallacies and illogic. He goes right to the heart of the most difficult and controversial issues. Accounting students and professors, as well as regulators and accounting professionals in firms and companies, can profit immensely from this refreshing and fearless analysis of the major issues of the day in financial reporting.

Paul Rosenfield is richly qualified to write this book. An accounting graduate of the University of Illinois and a CPA, he has devoted his entire professional career to studying issues and problems in the standard-setting sphere. In the 1960s and early 1970s, following a stint with Price Waterhouse, he served on the research staff of the AICPA's Accounting Principles Board (APB). From 1973 to 1975, he was the first full-time secretary of the International Accounting Standards Committee (IASC), based in London. During the remainder of the 1970s and into the 1980s, he directed the AICPA's accounting standards division, and he was the staff support to the U.S. delegation to the IASC. While at the Institute, he drafted the APB's *Statement on Basic Concepts and Accounting Principles Underlying Financial Statements of Business Enterprises*, published in 1970, which was a forerunner of the FASB's conceptual framework project. Under Paul's influence, the Statement was comprehensive, perceptive and deeply analytical. He has written numerous provocative articles and co-edited the tenth edition of the *Accountants' Handbook*. Paul has never been reluctant to challenge doctrine and to propose his own resolution of accounting controversies.

Paul's book is well suited for the capstone accounting theory or accounting issues course in a professional accounting program. Most accounting programs are devoted almost totally to the indoctrination of students in settled practice, as if there were no raging controversies in the field. Yet, as future professionals, they will be called upon to opine on proper practice and on the principles underlying that practice, whether as audit firm partners, chief accounting officers, accounting consultants, expert witnesses, or authors of articles, and they may also find themselves contesting the opinions of the FASB, the SEC, or the IASB. This book is an excellent vehicle for enlivening their critical faculties at the tail-end of their program of studies.

Stephen A. Zeff
Rice University

Preface

The readers and the author of a book on issues in financial reporting should all struggle toward solutions to the issues. I have tried to emulate Goldberg in making this book ". . . a joint adventure to be undertaken by both writer and reader . . ." (Goldberg, 1965, 24) The book provides information and analysis on all the issues to help you readers make up your minds; my only request is that you orient your approach to solutions of the issues, as this book does, toward the needs of the users of financial reports. The results of my own struggle toward solutions to the issues are also presented as conclusions in this book.

Financial reporting breakdowns

The 2001 Enron collapse was accompanied by the worst financial reporting breakdown in decades, if not the worst ever. The collapse and the breakdown at Enron destroyed Arthur Andersen & Co., one of the five largest international CPA firms, leaving what some call the "final four." The Enron breakdown was accompanied by other reported large-scale breakdowns, for example at WorldCom—whose reported breakdown was called ". . . the most sweeping bookkeeping deception in history . . ." (Kadlec, 2002, 21) and was accompanied by the largest bankruptcy thus far in the U.S.—and others, for example Adelphi Communications, Cendant Corporation, Global Crossing, Qwest Communications, Rite Aid, Waste Management, The Baptist Foundation, Tyco International, Vivendi Universal (a French company), Xerox, and HealthSouth. Levitt, a former SEC chairman, testified before Congress that "What has failed is nothing less than the system for overseeing our capital markets" (Alter, 2002, 25). Thomas said in the *Journal of Accountancy* that "the Enron implosion has wreaked more havoc on the accounting profession than any other case in U.S. history" (C. William Thomas, 2002, 44). Quindlen wrote in *Newsweek* that "In a post-Enron economy . . . [t]he American people are afraid . . . that huge corporate entities that once promised secure employment and investments are hollow at the core" (Quindlen, 2002, 64). The headline of an article by Eichenwald and colleagues stated that Enron "rotted from within" (Eichenwald *et al.*, 2002). *Accountancy Today* said that "corporate financial statements are being perceived as having the authenticity of a sidewalk game of three-card monte" (*Accountancy Today*, 2002). Rossant and colleagues stated that "Shareholder deception, supine boards, and Special Purpose Entities seem to have rendered the U.S. corporate governance model a Swiss cheese of loopholes" (Rossant *et al.*, 2002, 80), and Kadlec said that "a fat slice of corporate America . . . has been ethically bankrupt for years. We're only now getting a look at the red ink on the moral balance sheets . . ." (Kadlec, 2002, 21).

Reform efforts are underway at this writing. The first fruits of those efforts are the Sarbanes–Oxley Act of 2002 and the formation under it of the Public Companies Accounting Oversight Board (PCAOB).

Attention is devoted to the financial reporting breakdowns in a number of the sections of the book, especially in Chapters 2, 3, and 17.

Greater problems

The financial reporting breakdowns at Enron and others demonstrate to everyone involved that there has been something seriously wrong with financial reporting. However, the breakdowns are only part of the story—financial reporting has greater problems:

> Willens, an accounting and tax analyst at Lehman Brothers [said] "At the end of the day, I believe the problem lies in the accounting principles themselves. . . ."
>
> (Henriques, 2002)

This book concludes that the issuers of financial reports don't have to fiddle with the numbers or omit or disorder disclosures to mislead the users of the reports; it holds that all they have to do is conform fully with generally accepted accounting principles (GAAP). That's because the book concludes that the parties to financial reporting that currently have the most power in the design of financial reporting standards, the issuers, have collectively skewed the standards to their benefit and to the detriment of the users and of society. It concludes that in the process, the issuers have turned financial reporting under GAAP into a Wonderland portrayal of the products of their imaginations[1]—"financial reports . . . are often based on imaginary concepts" (West, 2003, 174)—rather than a neutral portrayal of the current financial condition and past financial progress the reporting entity has thus far achieved, and of current factors the users should consider in evaluating the reporting entity's prospects for further financial achievement.

Another fatal kind of problem with GAAP is a requirement in FASB Statement No. 52 to violate the single-unit-of-measure rule, discussed in Chapter 22.

---

1 This is stated forthrightly. See the Prologue about stating positions forthrightly.

This book also concludes that those developments prevent successful auditing of the amounts in financial statements prepared in conformity with current GAAP, which is necessary to provide the credibility essential to using the statements. For amounts in financial statements to be audited successfully, they have to represent aspects of the world outside financial reporting and its underlying documentation and outside the thoughts of the issuers of the statements about the future, and they have to be verifiable. Most amounts determined under current GAAP don't represent such aspects, and they therefore aren't verifiable.

You readers should judge whether those conclusions are supported in this book, in addition to forming your own conclusions.

Detour

The issues discussed in this book were debated more in preceding decades than in the most recent one. The financial reporting literature has taken a detour away from issues concerning optimum financial reporting for the benefit of the users of financial reports. For example, those issues had been a major topic of the *Journal of Accountancy*, the flagship publication of the American Institute of Certified Public Accountants. However, in recent years the *Journal* has run few articles on those issues, preferring instead to give its readers, for example, advice on the best income-tax software programs. Zeff stated that "in 1982, the *Journal of Accountancy* ... announced that it was encouraging the submission of 'practical' articles, code language for the avoidance of controversy ..." (Zeff, 2003a, 200). Further, the major initiative of the profession in the 1990s to study the overall area, the American Institute of Certified Public Accountants (AICPA) Special Committee on Financial Reporting, concentrated on disclosures rather than on determining the amounts on the face of the financial statements.

The direction of the detour has been towards positive accounting (discussed in Chapter 2) and instrumentation rather than objectives: "the discourse of accounting researchers has come to focus on the behaviour of those involved with accounting, and sophistication in method has taken precedence over the significance of discovery" (West, 2003, 113).

One reason the profession's course was set on the detour was the failure of the experiment with price-change reporting in Financial Accounting Standards Board (FASB) 1979 Statement of Financial Accounting Standards No. 33 (SFAS No. 33), which was officially interred in 1986 by SFAS No. 89. Chapters 11 and 13 state why SFAS No. 33 failed and why, because it was flawed, that was a good thing. Nevertheless, for those such as I who have as their first priority increasing the help financial reports can give to their users and society, and who believe that the help those reports currently provide falls woefully short of the help they could provide, being diverted that way was a deplorable development.

Zeff contends that another reason was the transfer of the authority to establish financial reporting standards from the AICPA to the FASB. He referred to the profession's loss of its accounting standard setter and the impact of that loss on the vitality of professional discourse ... [the] repositioning of the big firms from the center to the margin of standard setting soon served to dampen their interest in actively participating in the public dialogue on accounting principles, which should be a *sine qua non* of professional discourse.

(Zeff, 2003a, 190, 198)

It is time for the profession to get back on track for the benefit of the users.

Requests for comments

This book quotes and critically analyzes all the significant positions I could find in the literature on all the issues dealt with. To try to make sure that the analyses are as sound as possible, I sent drafts of the material in which each of those positions is quoted and analyzed to those who stated them in the literature, requesting that they comment. Of those who responded, some simply agreed, some had some differences. I made changes in the manuscript for a few of those differences. I corresponded with those with whom I disagreed. One or two simply said the analyses or conclusions were wrong, but didn't say why and didn't respond to my requests to tell me why.[2]

I would welcome comments from you readers.

---

2 For example, Beresford (see footnote 13 in Chapter 21).

Acknowledgments

I pay homage to the pioneers of thought on financial reporting on whose shoulders I stood to try to see at least a little of the light, especially Philip W. Bell, Raymond J. Chambers, Edgar O. Edwards, Louis Goldberg, Henry Rand Hatfield, Loyd C. Heath, A. C. Littleton, Leonard Lorensen (who was the inspiration for a central idea in the book, that allocation is essentially a device for stabilizing reported income), Fra Luca Paciolo, William A. Paton, Robert R. Sterling, Henry Sweeney, Arthur M. Thomas, William J. Vatter, Ross L. Watts, and Jerold L. Zimmerman.

I am especially grateful to the following persons who provided help and counsel above and beyond the call of duty (that doesn't necessarily mean any or all agree with any or all of what is said here): Denny Beresford, William Bergman, Eugene Flegm, Dale Gerboth, Henry Hill, Vernon Kam, Thomas Kelley, Donald Kirk, Donald Rosenfield, Rudy Schattke, Walter Schuetze, Ross Skinner, George Staubus, Arthur Thomas, and Stephen Zeff; to Keith Rosenfield, my computer guru; and to Terry Clague, Katherine Carpenter, Sue Armitage, and Georgina Boyle, who gave me so much help and encouragement. I accept sole blame for any errors that remain and sole responsibility for the conclusions I express.

Note on assignments

(This note is for those of you who use this book as a textbook.)

One half of the education of English-speaking accountants as financial reporters should be on financial reporting, one half should be on English, and the rest should be on everything else.[1] Financial reporters are professionals. A hallmark of every English-speaking professional is a mastery of English. Progress in a career in any profession is difficult or impossible without such mastery. That's why the assignments for Chapters 5 to 26, which contain issues, include preparing essays. In approaching the assignments, you should take to heart the request stated in the Prologue that you think rather than merely learn—and use the exercise to improve your written English. Even authors of books like this need to continually[2] improve our written English.

Essays could be on subjects such as:

- The author's main conclusions on the issues in this chapter are sound/unsound because . . .
- Observer xyz was particularly astute on issue abc because . . .
- Observer uvw was way off the mark on issue def because . . .
- No firm conclusions can be reached on the issues in the chapter because . . .
- The strongest and the weakest arguments given in this chapter are . . .
- The author completely missed the point because . . .
- The issues discussed are insignificant because . . .; the significant issues in this area are . . .
- Financial reporting couldn't possibly be as off the mark as made out in this chapter because . . .
- Here's what I really think about the issues in this chapter: . . .

The end of each section includes questions to discuss during the class sessions for the Prologue and Chapters 1 to 4, which don't involve issues, and

---

1 Chapter 22 indicates that the FASB says it's okay for us financial reporters to violate an inviolable rule of arithmetic.
2 Yes—split infinitives are okay.

points to debate during the class sessions for the remainder of the chapters and the Epilogue. The debates will give everyone a taste of the stimulation of dealing with issues in financial reporting. The best time to write an essay on the issues in a chapter is after the class has debated them.

Selecting some of the sources listed in the bibliography to read in their entirety should keep those who become caught up in this material out of trouble.

Prologue

Thinking independently

One truth is clear, Whatever is, is right.[1]

(Pope, 1688–1744, Epistle i, Line 289)

Most issuers[2] of financial reports believe that whatever is, is basically right in financial reporting. For example, Flegm, a prominent issuer, referred to "The discipline, reliability, yes, even the artistic beauty of [the double-entry, historical cost-based financial reporting system]..." (Flegm, 1989, 95). This conforms with the view stated in several places in this book, that we financial reporters[3] in effect currently paint pretty pictures[4] rather than report.

1 Contrast this:

> in Voltaire's satire, Candide ... In the face of repeated and horrendous catastrophes, [Dr.] Pangloss keeps insisting that "all is for the best in this best of all possible worlds." Voltaire's point ... is that Pangloss is a fool and that this is the worst of all possible worlds.
>
> (Wallace, 1969, 138)

Voltaire was a contemporary of Pope.

Also, Veblen said that

> the law of natural selection, as applied to human institutions, gives the axiom: "Whatever is, is wrong." ... the institutions of to-day ... are the result of a more or less inadequate adjustment of the methods of living to a situation which prevailed at some point in the past development ...
>
> (Veblen, 1899, 207)

2 The term *issuers* is emphasized in this book rather than the more commonly used term *preparers* to focus on those who have the authority to issue financial reports and are therefore responsible for their contents—management and the board of directors—not merely those who draw up the reports: "Originating these communications are identifiable members of the management and the board of directors" (Herman Bevis, 1965, 8). The SEC also refers to them as "issuers," for example in Rel. No. 33–8039. The quality of the management of the reporting entity by the issuers is implied by the reports, as discussed in Chapter 2.

3 Here the term *financial reporter* is emphasized to focus on those who prepare, issue, and audit financial reports, and to de-emphasize the other functions of those commonly called *accountants*. Chapter 1 discusses the related functions of bookkeeping, accounting, and financial reporting and, by implication, the related functions of bookkeepers, accountants, and financial reporters. Newspeople who write about financial reporting are referred to as *financial journalists*.

Some issuers emphasize "pragmatism," which can be taken to mean whatever is, is basically right. For example, the Business Roundtable, whose members are the chief executive officers of major U.S. corporations, stated that "A more pragmatic, *preparers-oriented*[5] approach is needed" (Business Roundtable, 1998, 13, emphasis added). This contrasts with the *user-oriented* approach emphasized in this book and in some courses on financial reporting: "The focus of many accounting curricula is evolving from a preparer approach to a ... user orientation" (Bline and Cullinan, 1995, 307). An executive of the American Stock Exchange agrees: "we have been pleading for what we would call a user-orientation in developing principles and practices of accounting and financial reporting" (Kopp, 1973, 54). Sterling pleaded for "decision oriented financial accounting" (Sterling, 1972).

Financial reporting apparently is the only activity in which the providers of products or services look to the needs and desires of the providers rather than the needs and desires of the consumers to determine how to design the products or services. Why can't the issuers of financial reports adopt, for example, a slogan similar to Siebel's "EBusiness for a customer-driven world," or follow the example of the AICPA Special Committee on Financial Reporting, which titled its report "Improving Business Reporting—A Customer Focus"?

Other issuers say changes proposed are "too conceptual, not practical, too academic" (Wyatt, 1989a, 126)—for example, "[the FASB] should be independent, but not in an ivory tower manner that doesn't take into account the practical effects of its decisions" (Hansell, 1997, D9, quoting a spokesman for Reed, chairman of Citicorp and chairman of the Business Roundtable), or " 'unnecessary' and 'confusing' " (Petersen, 1998c, D2), which appears simply to mean they don't want to change. Livingston, who in 1999 became President of the Financial Executives Institute, the organization of leading financial executives in business, was quoted as saying that " 'the United States has a great [financial reporting] system, and we hope there isn't too much tinkering with it' " (*Journal of Accountancy*, 1999a, 13). (I wonder if you will agree with Livingston after you finish reading this book.)

A few teachers of financial reporting also say that we should look to what we do to see what we should do, for example, "theory-building ... in accounting [is] abstracting from a mass of observations of accounting practices ..." (Ijiri, 1971b, 5). However, if theory building in transportation, for example, were abstracting from a mass of observations of transportation

---

4 Lowenstein and Brown said about the Enron collapse in 2001 that

> If auditors understood that their true client is ... the investing public—they
> would see their interest is in disclosing a true picture, not a prettified one ...
> hundreds of companies have used the gray areas of accounting to paint prettier
> pictures of themselves than they deserve...
>
> (Lowenstein, 2002, A22; Ken Brown, 2002, C1)

5 Also, "During the 1980s, ... companies and trade associations racheted up their lobbying of the FASB for preparer-friendly standards" (Zeff, 2003b, 273).

practices at the beginning of the nineteenth century, jet planes would never have been invented:

> If customers who took the long coach ride from London to Edinburgh around 1800 were asked how service could be improved, they would be likely to mention the need for fresh horses, better springs on the coach and improved inns along the way. Few, if any, would have suggested inserting the passengers in a metal tube and flinging them through the air at 500 mph in the direction of Scotland.
>
> (Burton and Sack, 1991, 118)

Financial reporters in practice have to apply current GAAP: "To obtain general acceptance of the 'rules of the game' is desirable; otherwise chaos would ensue" (Kam, 1990, 526). Most also support it:

> history records no unwillingness quite so persistent as the unwillingness of mankind to abandon time-honored principles.
>
> (MacNeal, 1970, 184)

> Attempts to depart from [traditional] conventions run into opposition similar to that encountered by any violation of long-established traditions— people automatically assume that the conventional practices are correct.
>
> (Arthur L. Thomas, 1975a, 13)

> All change in habits of life and thought is irksome.
>
> (Veblen, 1899, 199)

> No system smiles on the challenging of its axioms. . . . It develops sincere intolerance.
>
> (Durant, 1950, 930; 1963, 70)

> When all around take fundamental ideas for granted, these must be the truth. For most minds there is no comfort like it.
>
> (Barzun, 2000, 23)

Financial reporters are generally too busy to question current GAAP. They have all they can do to apply it. They don't think about whether their product is information. Were they to think about it, they would probably assume it is; after all, people pay them a lot of money for it. In 1932, the AI[CP]A Special Committee on Co-operation with Stock Exchanges stated that "There is no need to revolutionize or even to change materially corporate accounting..." (AICPA, 1963, 11). (In fact, for example, Chapter 10 discusses how amounts, such as depreciation, that result from allocation aren't information, and Chapter 22 discusses how amounts that result from application of SFAS No. 52 aren't information.)

However, some don't support it. For example, a president of the AICPA said that "the continued preparation of useless [acquisition cost—also called 'historical cost'] data is intolerable. In fact, it is downright suicidal" (Marvin L. Stone, 1971, 146). (As chairman of his firm of outside auditors,[6] he had to engage in such "suicidal" behavior every day.) MacNeal describes such data as "deceptive, and frequently quite meaningless, figures ..." (MacNeal, 1970, 180). Another president of the AICPA, Chenok, tells the following story:

> A pilot made an emergency landing and asked someone where he was. After the person told the pilot he was in a corn field, the pilot told the person he must be a CPA. The person was astounded and asked how he knew. The pilot said because the person's answer was completely reliable but absolutely irrelevant.

That president was instrumental in establishing the AICPA Special Committee on Financial Reporting and drafted its charge, which called for a "consideration [of] the need for ... value[7] based information ..." (AICPA, 1991, 1).

Students have to learn current GAAP and know that they will eventually have to apply it. They don't necessarily have to agree with it. To be sure, the theory section of the CPA examination requires new financial reporters to defend current GAAP, but that's a requirement only to repeat the conventional wisdom, not necessarily to believe it. In fact, ferment characterizes financial reporting thought, especially among those who teach it. Issues abound:

> One is left ... with a sense of bewilderment that a discipline that appears so mundane and practical to some can be so ... ridden with issues ...
>
> (Riahi-Belkaoui, 1993, 41)

> Interminable and inconclusive debates on alternative solutions to controversial issues seem to be a hallmark of the accounting discipline ...
>
> (Lemke, 1982, 287)

---

6 Those commonly called "independent auditors" are called "outside auditors" here because, as discussed in this book, especially in Chapter 2, the extent to which outside auditors are actually independent of their clients is currently in question.

7 *Value* is a chameleon term with multiple and usually undefined meanings and should be used with utmost care if at all: "Accountants have ... attached conflicting meanings to 'value'" (Baxter, 1966, 23).

We fight fierce battles over them:

> Contemporary financial accounting displays ... unresolved disputes over fundamentals, warring schools of thought ...
>
> (Arthur L. Thomas, 1979, 24)

> The relative advantages of the different measurement bases have been ... bitterly debated ...
>
> (Revsine, 1973, 10)

Durant was pessimistic: "On the high seas of reason, on the battlefield of ideas, [r]efutations never convince" (Durant, 1961; Durant and Durant, 1975). I, in contrast, believe that at least in financial reporting, the issues can at length be solved. If nothing else, we may need to change the questions we are asking.

This book discusses the major issues in financial reporting.

The necessity for financial reporters to think independently

> Defined doctrines ... put the mind to rest instead of to work. [We need] a sense of humor to question [our] ideas. [But we should] be skeptical even of our skepticism.
>
> (Durant, 1950, 929; 1939, 22; Durant and Durant, 1975, 492)

This book is purposely controversial, because controversy is the essence of issues. Instilling a habit of independent thinking about financial reporting to help get away from supporting the conventional wisdom in financial reporting without reflection is a primary objective of this book.[8]

There's nothing wrong with supporting the conventional wisdom as long as it's not done without reflection. (I believe that reflecting on the conventional wisdom in financial reporting would result in abandoning it, as indicated throughout this book.) You should support nothing without struggling with it, both the conventional wisdom and challenges to the conventional wisdom, "to throw off the yoke of the inherited dogma and reexamine the fundamentals" (Sterling, 1979, ix). Those of you who are or will become financial reporters should be prepared to practice the conventional wisdom in financial reporting but question it and work to change it whenever and wherever you can and believe it should be changed.

Books on financial reporting generally ask readers to *learn* what current

8 Similarly, in the "Preface to the Japanese Translation" of his *Theory*, translated into English, Sterling urged teachers of financial reporting "not [to] just mindlessly teach and use the conclusions (GAAP or standards) supplied to you by somebody else."

concepts are and what we are currently *required* to do. But "learning [may be] a formality unrelated to understanding" (Chambers, 1969, 150). In contrast, I ask you to *think* about what the concepts *should* be and what we *should* do. Though people are unhappy to be asked to learn, they are even more unhappy to be asked to think. Philosophers, for example Bertrand Russell, have said that: "Most people would sooner die than think; in fact, they do so" (quoted in Robert Byrne, 1988, 14). Durant said that "only a small proportion of any generation . . . think their own thoughts instead of those of their forebears or their environment" (Durant, 1953, 525). Rousseau bemoaned "the weary effort of thought" (Rousseau, 1953, 593). In commenting on the effect of extreme specialization in industry, de Tocqueville said that "men are so busy acting that they have little time to think" (de Tocqueville, 1969, 642).

Some financial reporters have said the same—for example: "Once a certain notion is accepted and used, it is extremely difficult to drop procedural and mental patterns associated with that notion" (Vatter, 1955, 373, quoted in Melcher, 1973, 108). And a financial journalist had a piece in the *Wall Street Journal* with the heading, "Mean Old FASB: Forcing Us to Think" (Holman W. Jenkins, Jr, 1999).

In this book, in addition to the views of others, I have forthrightly stated my own views, some of which may change in the future, and in some areas I have added my own solutions to the issues for which I have provided support. In contrast, a wait-and-see attitude about issues in financial reporting may sometimes be seen in the financial reporting literature. For example, Kam stated the following: "Whether we agree with [Thomas] or not, it is to his credit that he has made us more conscious of the need for real-world evidence to support what we do in accounting"[9] (Kam, 1990, 296). I don't share that attitude. I would rather be wrong than uncertain,[10] unless I have no basis on which to choose—I feel I can always change my mind. Contrast this from a review of another book on financial reporting issues: "edition . . . presents a maximum of useful, factual, traditional material with a minimum of analysis, supported criticism, or innovation" (Sorter, 1983, 655).

In a mode opposite to my forthrightness, for example, Henderson and Peirson observed, "It is difficult to see how a cash outflow can be interpreted as a cash inflow" (Henderson and Peirson, 1980, 183). (That's comparable to saying that "it's difficult to see how up can be interpreted as down.") Skinner observed, "It seems probable that . . . capitalizing all leases . . . would not be readily accepted"[11] (Skinner, 1987, 96). Roberts and colleagues said, "Presentation of the . . . equity section in the balance sheet could be reduced to a single line item" (Roberts *et al.*, 1990, 35), and Lipe said that

9 He was referring to Thomas' views on allocation, discussed in Chapter 10.
10 Similarly, "it [is] worse to be irresolute than to be wrong" (White, quoting Strunk, in Strunk and White, 1979, xvi).
11 Chapter 25 describes the strenuous opposition that would likely ensue.

"financial statement users need to exercise caution if the recognition of gains on debt at the onset of financial distress becomes accepted practice" (Lipe, 2002, 179). Here is a comment on such mild kinds of expressions: "There is a widespread phobia about being positive or definite or unequivocal about statements of principle and rules" (Chambers, 1969, 595). I have no such phobia,[12] and my strongly stated views provide you with grindstones on which to sharpen your swords to use against me. Would you be interested in contesting views stated meekly?

Though I have attempted to be evenhanded (except in the Epilogue), bias is bound to creep into any book such as this, through selection of references, emphasis, and the like. You should challenge the proponents and opponents of every side of every issue, including me. Your attitude should be that I may be as wrong as anyone else; you should trust your own judgment. My views are obviously no more worthy of uncritical acceptance, of the bandwagon effect

---

12 Observers in other fields also have no such phobia. For example, de Tocqueville stooped to arguing *ad hominem* against a political opponent:

> on becoming a minister [M. Hébert] remained attorney general to the marrow of his bones, and he had the icy character and face for it. You must picture a narrow, shrunk, weasel face compressed at the temples; forehead, nose and chin all pointed; cold, bright eyes and narrow, drawn-in lips; add to this a long quill usually held across his mouth, which at a distance looked just like a cat's bristling whiskers, and you have the portrait of a man more like a carnivorous animal than any other I have seen.
>
> (de Tocqueville, 1979, 25)

(Compare that description to Hubbard's description of an auditor in footnote 6 in Chapter 24.) Also, de Tocqueville quoted a newspaper reporter as saying:

> "In this whole affair the language used by Jackson [the President] was that of a heartless despot exclusively concerned with preserving his own power. Ambition is his crime, and that will be his punishment. Intrigue is his vocation, and intrigue will confound his plans and snatch his power from him. He governs by corruption, and his guilty maneuvers will turn to his shame and confusion."
>
> (de Tocqueville, 1969, 182)

A professor of ecology and evolution said this about views that Professor Behe, a molecular biologist, stated in a book on Darwin's theory: "Behe's 'scientific' alternative to evolution ultimately becomes a confusing and untestable farrago of contradictory ideas" (Coyne, 1996).

Also, consider the forthrightness of the title of one of my articles: "Current Replacement Value Accounting—A Dead End," and of the title of a draft article of mine: "How the Defects of Current Generally Accepted Accounting Principles Prevent Successful Auditing of Amounts in Financial Statements" (which is taken from material in Chapter 10), and of this conclusion of another of my articles: "the information provided under the replacement price principle [is unintelligible, uncorroborable, and irrelevant]..." (Rosenfield, 1969b, 797).

Of course, being forthright and unequivocal doesn't necessarily mean you're right. Behe may still be right and de Tocqueville, the newspaper reporter, Coyne, or I may be wrong.

described below, than are those of any others. "Contradiction is not always refutation; a new theory does not necessarily denote progress" (Freud, 1939, 169). With Thomas, "this [book] will . . . rais[e] as many questions as possible about its own validity" (Arthur L. Thomas, 1969, 105).

Rosenthal wrote that

> Before I left for California, a friend asked if I was going with an open mind about the anti-immigration movement. Yes, like a car with a sliding roof panel, open but not really convertible.
>
> (Rosenthal, 1995, A31)

My mind, in contrast, is not only open but convertible (in a few places in this book, such as on page 270, changes in my positions have been noted), and yours should be too. Vested interests in one's own views is fatal to intellectual integrity and growth.

However, long-considered views shouldn't be abandoned lightly:

> An open mind is all very well in its way, but it ought not to be so open that there is no keeping anything in or out of it. It should be capable of shutting its doors sometimes, or it may be found a little drafty.
>
> (Samuel Butler, quoted in Auden and Kronenberger, 1981, 354)

And the following has been characterized as an invaluable saying: "Let us not keep our minds so open that our brains fall out."

The following are among the ideas to which I subscribe that color my discussion of issues in this book. Each of these ideas isn't conformed with—at least occasionally—today in financial reporting or in the financial reporting literature (please correct me in areas in which you believe the ideas are unsound, if any):

1 Financial statements should

   a Contain only information that represents phenomena that have existed or occurred external to the reports and their underlying documentation[13] and external to the thoughts of the issuers about the future (246).[14]

   b Report the financial effects of all events and transactions that have affected the reporting entity that meet reasonable criteria (241).

---

13 The last four words were added to avoid the FASB's position concerning, in Sterling's terms, a blob of ink representing another blob of ink. See the discussion in Chapter 3.

14 The references are to the pages in the text on which examples of the nonconformances are discussed.

c Reflect nothing that didn't happen or that's fictitious by definition (289, 403, 436, 478).

d Reflect the use of only those formulas that track the financial effects of events that have occurred (244).

e Reflect the existence of the reporting entity apart from all other entities with which it's associated (187, 189).

f Not incorporate false assumptions (188, 384, 433).

g Report only the reporting entity's side of each of its transactions and relationships with other entities (195, 196).

h Not affirm and deny the same thing (218).

i Reflect inflation and deflation (228, 260).

j Emphasize the needs of the users of the statements if the needs or desires of other parties to financial reporting conflict with the needs of the users (237, 243, 246, 383, 440, 449).

k Obey the rules of arithmetic (446).

2 Financial statement amounts that can't be audited successfully shouldn't be represented as having been audited successfully (247).

3 Financial reporters shouldn't play tricks on the users (58).

4 The events that have occurred and have affected a reporting entity should be analyzed to determine the financial effects they have had on the reporting entity to decide how to report on those effects; the causes of the events should be ignored in making such decisions (the causes of assets and liabilities may need analysis to determine when they came into existence) (16, 77, 385, 428, 463, 476, 481, 484).

5 Issues that have long evaded solution in financial reporting should be solved or reformulated (75, 186, 452, 504).

6 We financial reporters shouldn't be required to act as though something important to financial reporting is the opposite of what it is (121, 153).

7 The map isn't the territory (124, 205, 221, 231, 233, 251, 437).

8 A cause and its effect only either occur simultaneously or a cause precedes its effect in time (161, 167, 281).

9 The future is only a helpful concept that exists only in the mind (165, 282).

10 Nothing about the future need be considered in order to determine and report history (168).

11 Financial reporters shouldn't represent as assets things that aren't assets, especially if they're losses (205, 484).

12 The equity of a reporting entity is only a helpful concept that exists only in the mind (211).

13 Accrual covers a variety of bases other than the cash basis (273).

14 Costs aren't assets (235).

15 The balance sheet[15] shouldn't, in effect, be turned into a footnote to the income statement (236).

16 Financial reporting standards setters shouldn't prohibit issuers from providing the most current and most relevant information in the reporting entity's financial statements (472).

17 Financial reporting shouldn't be designed merely as a ritual (256).

18 Users shouldn't be forced to tolerate the intolerable (262).

19 Misleading names and misleading shorthand descriptions of concepts and principles shouldn't be used in financial reporting (287).

20 The government as an income-taxing agency is no friend of yours (431).

21 Bookkeeping by the reporting entity can't be a cause of events outside the bookkeeping records, such as creating liabilities (437).

22 We financial reporters shouldn't be required to do anything we can't do (460n2).

23 Incurring liabilities causes costs, not vice versa (474)).

24 Unsuccessful operations can't eliminate liabilities (433).

25 Discharging employees can't eliminate liabilities (478).

26 Active leases aren't executory contracts (493).

27 One can't forfeit what one doesn't have (though one can forfeit an opportunity one does have to obtain what one doesn't have) (478).

You should develop tentative views of your own on the issues (a person's views should always be tentative: "Certainty is not necessary for life ... a high degree of probability suffices" [Durant and Durant, 1975, 144]), test them, think them through, and adjust them with new knowledge and new thinking of your own and of others. You should never allow anyone to lead your thinking down the garden path about financial reporting (or, for that

---

15 The name *balance sheet* refers to only technical aspects of the statement: (1) it reports the balances of the so-called real accounts after they have been closed and (2) the totals of the amounts on the two sides of the statement are equal: the statement balances. It doesn't refer to the information it reports or should report, as the names *income statement* and *statement of cash flows* do. The statement is sometimes called by its other name, the *statement of financial position*. However, as discussed in Chapter 10, the balance sheet as currently designed doesn't report the financial position of the reporting entity at the reporting date (nothing we now do does, though the outside auditor's standard report says that we do). It's justifiably described there as a mere footnote to the income statement. So, calling it a *statement of financial position* is inaccurate:

> The balance sheet ... is scarcely a statement of financial position within the usual meaning of that term...
>
> (Chambers, 1969, 65)

> the balance sheet has little claim to being a statement of financial position at the accounting date. It does not realistically represent the resources employed in the business.
>
> (American Accounting Association, 1991, 92)

When and if the defects of the balance sheet are rectified, the name *statement of financial position* would be justified.

matter, about any other area of life[16]). You should never succumb to "the bondage of tradition and authority" (Durant, 1950, 1004). My point is to urge you not to sacrifice your judgment, your reason in considering issues in financial reporting, but, in considering them, "to engage in the labors of the mind . . . the trouble of thinking. . ." (de Tocqueville, 1969, 458, 692).

In contrast:

> Heaven's Gate [whose 39 members voluntarily departed this life to go to the "level above human"] was a cult with strict mind control . . . In one posting on the Internet, Heaven's Gate listed some of the "offenses" members should avoid: trusting one's own judgment [and] having private thoughts . . . "We wanted our brains washed," said a former Heaven's Gate member. "There's a lot of joy in it."
>
> (*The Record*, 1997a, L-12)

The issues, positions, analyses, and arguments presented in this book are used as sources of debating points at the end of each chapter on issues to help you think independently. I would appreciate receiving for revisions of this book the results of debates you might have that contain

- analysis or arguments contesting analysis or arguments presented on positions presented
- analysis or arguments not presented for or against positions presented
- positions not presented on issues presented, together with analysis or arguments for or against them
- major issues not presented of interest to you, including positions on those issues plus analysis or arguments for or against them.

Why consider issues?

> in order to be of increased service, accountants must maintain a lively interest in emerging developments in accounting and must be prepared to adapt to meet new challenges.
>
> (Editor's Notebook, 1973, 39)

16 At a dialogue among three clergymen of three different faiths I attended, the host clergyman spoke last and said that when the first clergyman spoke, he was so eloquent that if you had heard only him, you would have surely agreed with him. The host said that when the second clergyman spoke and said the opposite of what the first clergyman said, he was so eloquent that had the dialogue ended then, you would have surely changed your mind and agreed with him instead. The host then proceeded to say what he presented as the truth of the matter. You should take my word for what I say simply because I say it no more than you should have taken the host clergyman's word for what he said simply because he said it.

Why should financial reporters consider issues in financial reporting anyway? Because, among other reasons, knowing current practice isn't enough to practice well.

First, practice isn't cut and dried. There is much room for judgment. Areas exist in which current rules are unclear or ambiguous. Sound application of current rules requires thorough understanding of the reasons given in support of and in opposition to them and of practices that are proposed to replace current rules and the reasons given in support of and in opposition to them.

Second, economic activities and conditions change (as discussed below in "Forces for change"), and current rules must be adapted or new rules adopted to report on the new circumstances. Before the changed or new rules are available, practitioners must practice. They must act as practitioners did before profession-wide rules were issued, individually inventing practices to fit the circumstances:

> knowledge [of concepts used with care] may ... provide guidance in resolving new or emerging problems of financial accounting and reporting in the absence of applicable authoritative pronouncements ... in dealing with situations not yet clearly covered by standards.
>
> (FASB, 1980b, introduction and par. 11)

Financial reporting is a learned profession, and its practice, as with the practice of any such profession, requires knowing more than simply its rules. A responsibility of any financial reporter is to keep current on challenges to those rules, to the status quo. Financial reporting is always in a state of change, and those who are involved in that process should have a voice in the changes that are made. But that voice will be heard only if it's articulate and soundly based.

Financial reporting affects people's fortunes, or at least they act as though it does. They therefore attempt to influence the development of financial reporting practices. Some favor maintaining the status quo; they contend with others who favor change. And those who favor change in one direction contend with those who favor change in other directions.

Forces for the status quo

> inertia and a reluctance to think through possibilities for improvements in reporting are powerful impediments to change.
>
> (Skinner, 1987, 513)

Strong forces for maintaining the status quo cause financial reporting practices as a whole to resist sudden or broad changes:

> In both the accounting profession and the corporate community, potent

forces exist which oppose any serious rethinking of traditional accounting conventions—even at the expense of the relevancy of the financial
data which those conventions yield.

(Harold Williams, 1989, 45)

it has been asserted that changing the accounting for [stock-based
compensation, pension liabilities, postretirement benefits, derivatives,
and business combinations] would be the end of Western Civilization.

(Foster, 2003, 3)

We financial reporters fear to "plunge into the unknown" (AICPA, 1994b,
II, 4, 7); we have an "aversion to change" (Adkerson, 1978, 32).

Conservative issuers, outside auditors, standard setters, and regulators

One such force is the natural tendency of the practitioners of any practical
art and their leaders to be conservative and to resist change. They don't like
to modify practices practitioners use, especially if they have used them for a
long time: "Accountants are unlikely to decide unilaterally that their hard-
earned expertise is obsolete and submit themselves to a painful retraining
process" (Henderson and Peirson, 1980, 31). Also, contemporary financial
reporting practices are rules of the game, and people don't like to have rules
changed in the middle of the game: "Any accounting standard that changes
the score keeping will change the way the game is played, and people who
have been playing the game will scream foul at the rule changes..." (Harold
Williams, 1989, 45).

The FASB itself is essentially conservative. The FASB went out of its way
to say as much in its conceptual framework:

> The recognition criteria and guidance in this Statement are generally
> consistent with current practice and do not imply radical change...
> The Board emphasizes that the definitions in this Statement neither
> require nor presage upheavals in present practice.
>
> (FASB, 1984a, par. 3; 1985a, par. 170)

A committee of the American Accounting Association holds that that
conservative conceptual framework is the ideal against which standards
should be judged: "we believe a high quality standard should be consistent
with the FASB's 'Conceptual Framework'..." (American Accounting
Association, 1998, 162). The remainder of this book demonstrates a belief
that that framework is far from ideal.

The former conservatism of the SEC is exemplified by the response of
Barr, its chief accountant, when told in 1969 that the AICPA had just published the APB's Statement No. 3, "Financial Statements Restated for

General Price-Level Changes" (see Chapter 11). His response was blunt, simple, and unequivocal: "We're against it."

Practice, education, and research

The current relationship among financial reporting practice, education, and research also contributes to maintenance of the status quo. That kind of thing has long existed. For example, Kepler complained in 1618 that "academies . . . are concerned not to have the program of teaching change very often . . . frequently . . . the things which [are taught] are not those which are most true but those which are most easy" (Kepler, 1618–21). Tabori reports that

> In 1624, the followers of Copernicus and Galileo were banished from Paris and those who stayed behind were forbidden under penalty of death to "teach tenets differing from those of the old and accepted authorities."
>
> (Tabori, 1993, 156)

And in the nineteenth century,

> people clung to . . . the idea that a star like the Sun might keep hot for long enough to explain events on Earth simply by shrinking very slowly under its own weight, turning gravitational potential energy into heat as it did so. It was Eddington who finally squashed this idea . . . : "Only the inertia of tradition keeps the contraction hypothesis alive—or rather, not alive, but an unburied corpse."
>
> (Gribbin, 1999, 185)

Education in financial reporting is designed mainly to prepare students for practice. Further, practice determines education in financial reporting, perpetuating the status quo. Hatfield says that "Accountants . . . rely on reiteration in lieu of argument"[17] (Hatfield, 1927, 273). Having been taught contemporary practices, the students later apply them in practice and many are unaware of possibilities for change. One purpose of this book is to cut into that circle and foster such awareness.

The reciprocal interaction of education and practice on us financial reporters provides a strong barrier to adoption of the results of research in financial reporting. A former member of the FASB noted examples of barriers to the acceptance in practice of research conclusions: simple inertia, resistance to change, the research was undertaken by an academic, and the need to accommodate the views of constituents to gain acceptability (Wyatt,

---

17 He contradicts himself on the next page, however. "The arguments adduced in favor of valuing at cost or market, whichever is lower, are [a] brilliant . . . instance of flabby thinking. . ." (Hatfield, 1927, 274).

1989a, 125). To a considerable extent, the researchers talk to each other but not to students or practitioners: "the impact of accounting research on courses is negligible. Its impact on the practice of accounting is less" (Burton and Sack, 1991, 122).

Professional users' resistance to change

Professional users of financial reports also tend to be generally conservative and not eager to have financial reporting changed, except for the addition of information (see "Demands for more disclosure" below):

> Even though data contained in historical cost financial statements are largely ignored, "users" of financial statements will still feel more comfortable with the status quo than with the unknown. Financial analysts and other users will undoubtedly express grave concern over a whole new set of unknown complexities.
>
> (Marvin L. Stone, 1971, 149)

For example, the Financial Accounting Standards Board's experiment in its SFAS No. 33 (see Chapters 11 and 13), which required large companies to present supplementary information incorporating changes in prices while assets are held and changes in the general level of prices—inflation[18] or deflation—and which might have been the first step to incorporating that information in the main financial statements, didn't excite the enthusiasm of financial analysts.

Chapters 10 and 17 discuss views expressed by investors and creditors interviewed by the AICPA Special Committee on Financial Reporting and their resistance to significant change to financial statement design.

Forces for change

> only those professions that adjust their institutional underpinnings to the needs of society survive.
>
> (Bedford, 1971, 137)

Significant forces for change in financial reporting practices also exist.

---

18 This term is unfortunate. "Inflation" sounds like something good, building something up, like inflating a tire. The emphasis would better be placed on the *debasement* of money. People would then refer to the debasement rate rather than the inflation rate. No one could confuse that with something good. People might then work harder to prevent it.

Changes in the environment

Changes in the environment in which the reporting entities operate are the strongest force for change in financial reporting practices. The stockmarket crash of 1929 and the inflation of the late 1970s in the U.S. are two examples.

Before the crash, many companies increased the amounts at which they reported their assets, mainly their land, buildings, and equipment,[19] to make them more current, based on the belief that investors were influenced by reported asset amounts more than by reported income amounts, in contrast with the opposite belief today. After the crash, the write-ups were reversed and many companies even wrote their assets down below acquisition cost.

Many said those increased asset amounts contributed to the increase in prices of common stocks leading up to the crash; for example, Clifford D. Brown referred to "The speculative orgy of the predepression days based on frequent and optimistic revaluations of assets, dividend distributions based on inflated values, and heavy reliance on book values of stock..." (Brown, 1993, 69). Investors who had lost money rightly or wrongly placed part of the blame on us financial reporters who had made or permitted the write-ups. Thus burned, we financial reporters changed rules, instituted new rules—"in the United States ... upward revaluation was virtually outlawed in the 'thirties..." (Chambers, 1979a, 40)—and vowed we would never again permit assets to be reported at amounts greater than their acquisition costs: "few people wish to see enterprises and accounting tangle again with the revaluation approach often used in the 1920's and 1930's" (Littleton, 1953, 213). It was said that the financial reporters of that day would all have to die before reporting of assets at greater than acquisition cost would again be permitted. Kuhn is quoted as saying that "Conversions will occur a few at a time until, after the last holdouts have died, the whole profession will again be praticing under a single, but now different, paradigm" (Kuhn, 1970, quoted in West, 2003, 137). Likewise, the economist Samuelson said, "knowledge advances 'funeral by funeral'" (Samuelson, quoted in Wade, 1998, F6). The historian Barzun agrees: "old resisters could be gradually argued into their graves" (Barzun, 2000, 38). Even today, issuers feel much the same. For example,

> It was common practice in the 1920s to "create" values through such questionable practices as writing up one's assets, but the 1929 stock

---

19 The literature commonly refers to these assets as "property, plant, and equipment," based on outdated terminology. *Property* in that expression refers to only land, and *plant* refers to buildings. Also, the expression is ambiguous, because *property* can be real property or personal property. This book refers instead to land, buildings, and equipment.

market crash and the subsequent congressional hearings which resulted in the establishment of the SEC ended such "voodoo accounting."

(Flegm, 1986, 48)

After more than a generation, double-digit inflation plus a nudge from the Chief Accountant of the SEC caused us financial reporters to reconsider. First the SEC in 1976 (Securities and Exchange Commission, 1976, Accounting Series Release 190) and then the FASB in 1979 (FASB, 1979b) temporarily required large companies to present supplementary information reflecting current prices of assets held—often higher than their acquisition costs—and reflecting the financial effects of inflation (see Chapters 11 and 13). For the moment, though, the primary financial statements reflect the Depression mentality of acquisition cost now and evermore. The AICPA Special Committee on Financial Reporting reflected that mentality in 1994: "Despite the periodic call to do so, [standard-setters] should not pursue a value-based accounting model"[20] (AICPA, 1994a, 95). That's ironical, because the Special Committee also stated that "Complete information provided by the best sources enhances the probability that the best decisions will be made" (AICPA, 1994a, 1). The incompleteness of acquisition cost information is its worst defect (as discussed in Chapter 10).

Only time will tell whether the breakdowns of financial reporting that accompanied the Enron collapse and the breakdowns in other companies discussed in the Preface will result in fundamental changes in financial reporting.

Changes in activities reported on

Some changes in the activities reported on in financial reports have caused changes in financial reporting practices. An example is the increase in the 1960s in business combinations of previously separate reporting entities arranged through transfers of ownership securities among the parties involved. Such combinations were reported on by the pooling-of-interests method.[21]

That formerly accepted method minimizes the amounts at which assets are stated at the time of a combination. It thereby permits reporting of income after the combination, when the assets are used or sold, larger than

20 The Committee stated that, in spite of my imploring it, as AICPA staff to the Committee, not to do so.

21 Illustrating that what goes around comes around, the Chairman of the FASB stated at the end of 1998 that "The issues surrounding the [FASB's] project [on business combinations] are particularly important because the growth of mergers has brought greater attention to perceived flaws and deficiencies in existing accounting standards" (FASB, 1998e, 1). This renewed concern resulted in SFAS No. 141, *Business Combinations*.

permitted by the method of reporting on business combinations now permitted, the purchase method (see Chapter 23). Proliferation of combinations reported on that way led to the perception that abuses were occurring and resulted in APB Opinion No. 16 with its twelve criteria that had to be met to report on a combination by the pooling-of-interests method. APB Opinion No. 17, "Intangible Assets," requiring amortization of goodwill related to business combinations, accompanied APB Opinion No. 16.

As indicated below and as discussed in Chapter 23, renewed concern over the results of applying those two Opinions resulted in their reconsideration. The result, SFAS No. 141, eliminated the pooling-of-interests method and eliminated amortization of goodwill related to business combinations. Instead, such goodwill not being amortized that's subsequently determined to have a finite useful life is tested for impairment. If it's found to have been impaired, an impairment loss is reported currently.

Curbing abuses

Financial reporting rules have been changed to curb practices that, though desired by the issuers because of their incentives (see Chapter 2), were considered abuses and therefore harmful to the interests of the users of financial reports.

An example is the rule requiring an all-inclusive income statement. Before the rule was established in 1966 (AICPA, 1966b, par. 17), some items of revenue, expense, gain, or loss were excluded from the income statement and charged or credited directly to equity, on the grounds that they were unusual in some way and including them in reported income would give an unclear view of the earning power of the entity.[22] That practice was often called *dirty surplus*.

Because issuers of financial reports usually like to report income of the reporting entities as high as possible, consistent with avoiding large fluctuations in reported income from period to period (see Chapter 2), they tended to report more charges than credits outside the income statement. A rule was therefore established requiring all items of revenue, expense, gain, and loss to be reported in the income statement with the exception of prior

---

22 The FASB has since said that presentation of earning power isn't part of financial reporting:

> procedures such as averaging or normalizing reported earnings for several periods and ignoring or averaging out the financial effects of "nonrepresentative" transactions and events are commonly used in estimating "earning power." However, both the concept of "earning power" and the techniques for estimating it are part of financial analysis and are beyond the scope of financial reporting.

> (FASB, 1978, par. 48)

That quotation is also used in Chapter 5.

period adjustments (AICPA, 1966b, par. 17). That practice was often called *clean surplus*.

Recently there has been some erosion of clean surplus, with items of gain or loss pertaining, for example, to investments in securities and to reporting on foreign operations now required to be reported outside net income. And the AICPA Special Committee on Financial Reporting has recommended an addition to the list. Those of us who were there when the clean surplus rule was established thought the barn door had been locked. It hadn't.[23]

Responses of standard-setters and regulators

Though standard-setters and regulators are among the conservative parties in financial reporting, as discussed above, some changes in practice have been responses of standard-setting bodies or regulators to perceived problems, to reduce the number of available alternative reporting practices, or to establish what they consider sound practice: "In spite of the oft-quoted quip that no one ever erected a statue to a committee, it is not impossible for committees to innovate" (Solomons, 1986, 196).

Two key examples concern reporting on income taxes and reporting on oil- and gas-producing activities.

Starting in the 1940s, companies began to report on income taxes supposed to be related to certain types of transactions in the periods in which the transactions occurred instead of the periods in which the income taxes appeared in their income tax returns. By 1967, there was considerable diversity in the types of transactions to which the procedure was applied and in the ways in which it was applied.

By issuing APB Opinion No. 11 in 1967, the Accounting Principles Board (the predecessor of the FASB) not only eliminated alternative practices in reporting on income taxes but also extended to all current transactions the practice of reporting income taxes related to the transactions currently, by requiring comprehensive interperiod income tax allocation (see Chapter 21).

Also, the FASB in its SFAS No. 19 required all oil- and gas-producing companies to report on their exploration costs using the successful efforts method of reporting, one of the two methods then in use. It prohibited the full cost method of reporting, the other method then in use. However, the SEC forced the FASB to rescind that prohibition (see Chapter 19).

Demands for more disclosure

Financial analysts want more disclosure. For example, they have become specialists: some concentrate on retail businesses, some on railroads, some on steel companies, and so on. With the arrival of conglomerates—businesses

---

23 See the discussion of comprehensive income in Chapter 9.

in a variety of industries combined into single companies or groups of companies—financial analysts became frustrated, because the information reported on undifferentiated jumbles of many kinds of activities. In consequence, a rule was established that requires disclosure of information by segments along industry lines, and recommendations have been made to strengthen the rule.

Strange results = more change

Rules for translating foreign money amounts have changed several times (see Chapter 22). No matter what we financial reporters have done in this area, people have considered the financial statement results to be strange. When enough people complain about the rules in effect and the financial statement results they give, we change the rules again, always in the hope that the latest change will be the final answer.

Research

Several kinds of research are performed for financial reporting, including that carried on by the FASB for its projects. They are generally described as conceptual or empirical, which are best done in combination, as in any other kind of research. That's often called *hypothesis formation and testing*. Some researchers emphasize one kind and others the other, as do, for example, theoretical and experimental physicists. In recent years, the academic financial reporting literature has emphasized mathematical research. As indicated above, academic research in financial reporting hasn't thus far had much effect on practice.

Felt need for a common set of international financial reporting standards

The professional financial reporting organizations and the standards-setting bodies in many countries have voiced a need for a common set of international financial reporting standards recognized by all. Achieving such standards would be mainly choosing among the financial reporting standards required in the various countries on which to standardize rather than developing new standards. The movement in the U.S. that recently resulted in its elimination of the pooling-of-interests method of reporting after business combinations reflects that development. Herz, Chairman of the FASB, and Tweedie, Chairman of the IASB, recently voiced support:

> In order to make [global] markets work better, we need ... common, high-quality accounting standards ...
>
> (Herz, in FASB, 2002d, 2)

Let's not mess about with preserving our existing standards. If the U.S. has the best answer, change the international standard and vice versa.

(Tweedie, in FASB, 2002d, 2)

Broad principles versus detailed rules

A continuing controversy has been over whether standard-setters and regulators should issue broad principles or detailed rules. Broad principles permit us financial reporters to attempt to tailor the reporting to the particular circumstances, but can lead to inconsistent treatments. Detailed rules promote consistency but foster the loophole mentality in which some seek to avoid the effects of detailed rules once they are spelled out. Observers complain about that:

> professional auditors ... seek ... loopholes in ... standards to exploit for client benefit.
>
> (Wyatt, 1989b, 96)

> Every new rule breeds a profusion of finagles, and time is on the side of the finagler ... The mark of a profession is a commitment to excellence ... that commitment ... will not long survive ... the notion that the job of the professional is to search out and exploit the loopholes in his own standards.
>
> (Gerboth, 1987b, 98, 99; 1988, 107)

> FASB has bogged down in the specifics ... The predictable result has been that creative Big Five accountants and chief financial officers have simply structured ever more ingenious ways around them, [Professor] Carmichael says. "FASB has had all along an unwillingness to specify the objectives of their pronouncements,"[24] [Professor] Carmichael contends.
>
> (Liesman, 2002)

> instead of complying with the letter of the law, [Professor Lev] wants auditors to delve deeper into ... deals [creating special purpose entities] and dig out their true ramifications ... Could the liabilities come back to the company attempting to get them off the books?
>
> (Nanette Byrnes, 2002b, 36, 37)

> certain of the FASB's standards have been rule-based, as opposed to principle-based ... all constituencies must make concerted efforts to report transactions consistent with the objectives of the standards.
>
> (Herdman, 2002, 5)

---

24 However, it occasionally does so. For example, it did so in its SFAS No. 52, but with strange results. See Chapter 22.

Standard-setters and regulators have recently opted for detailed rules. However, SEC Chief Accountant Herdman recently stated that "We have been working with the FASB to change its style to be more principle-based" (Herdman, 2002, 5).

Chapter 17 discusses how the issue has come to the fore in the wake of the Enron collapse.

In December 2002, the FASB issued a "Proposal for a Principles-Based Approach to U.S. Standard Setting." That initiative is part of the effort discussed in the preceding section on "Felt Need for a Common Set of International Financial Reporting Standards" to close the gap between FASB standards and international standards.

On July 25, 2003, the SEC issued an "SEC Study on Adoption by the U.S. Financial Reporting System of a Principles-Based Accounting System," in which the SEC staff recommends that accounting standards should be developed using a principles-based approach.

Bandwagons

> We accountants have a tendency to allow our course to be influenced by the fickle winds of fashion.
>
> (Sterling, 1990b, 132)

A new point of view on financial reporting of some thinkers sometimes becomes popular and is accepted quickly by other thinkers, who jump on the bandwagon. That's flattering to the original thinkers, but does their cause no good. (Nevertheless, Chambers, one of the two leading exponents of current selling price reporting [discussed in Chapter 14], said to me, perhaps jocularly, that he wouldn't mind if the profession started chanting his views.) The only worthwhile proponents of one's views are those who have wrestled with the issues enough to come to the same conclusion independently. (All such proponents may still nevertheless be wrong.)

A bandwagon developed, for example, in favor of current cost reporting with the publication in 1961 of a book[25] advocating it: "Edwards and Bell['s] ... proposal ... resulted in a growing number of followers" (Kam, 1990, 414). Current cost reporting was popular with reformers for about ten years, but it was replaced with a bandwagon for current replacement value reporting (see Chapter 13). With the failure of SFAS No. 33, fervor for current replacement value reporting has dissipated.

The largest bandwagon may be considered to be the one for the most influential book ever written about financial reporting, *An Introduction to Corporate Accounting Standards*, by Paton and Littleton, published in 1940. It provided justification for then current practice, which has hardly changed

25 Edwards and Bell, 1961.

since that time. It is still used as the basic justification for current practice (this is discussed more fully in Chapter 10).

Some nonstandard points of view that have been strongly supported haven't attracted a crowd, such as current selling price reporting (see Chapter 14). That says nothing about the merits of those points of view.

Discussion questions

1 Have you ever previously considered whether current GAAP in general or in particular are sound?

   a If not, was this because
      i You were previously too busy learning the principles and their application to think about whether they are good, bad, or indifferent?
      ii You revered authority too much to think about that question?
   b If so, did you consider the principles in general or in particular?
   c If in particular, which principles did you suspect might not be the best?

2 Do you now care whether current GAAP are sound?
3 Are you willing to think about whether current GAAP are sound?
4 Do you feel that current GAAP is the best guide to the design of GAAP?
5 Should the design of GAAP emphasize the desires of the issuers of financial reports, or the needs of the users of financial reports?
6 Who would you trust more to guide your thinking about the soundness of GAAP—issuers of financial reports, independent accountants, teachers of accounting, or none of the above?
7 Do you now feel confident that you can evaluate the soundness of GAAP in general or in particular, and defend your evaluation?
8 Are you willing to learn to better evaluate the soundness of GAAP in general or in particular?
9 Are you willing to suspend judgment about the views of others cited in this book?
10 Are you willing to suspend judgment about the conclusions reached in this book?

   a Are you offended by conclusions stated forthrightly?
   b Do you think you will be influenced by the forthrightness of the statements of conclusions reached in this book?

11 Do you now have opinions on the items in the list of ideas that color the discussion of issues in this book?
12 Do you now in general favor the status quo or significant changes in financial reporting?

Part I

Setting the stage

1 The nature of financial reporting

> the role of financial . . . reporting in the economy [is] to provide evenhanded financial and other information that, together with information from other sources, facilitates efficient functioning of capital and other markets and otherwise assists in promoting efficient allocation of scarce resources in the economy.
>
> (FASB, 1978, Prologue)

To begin consideration of contemporary issues in financial reporting, it is helpful to set the stage with discussions that provide background for successfully dealing with the issues. This chapter begins that task.

A clear understanding of the nature of financial reporting is essential to the sound solution of issues in financial reporting.

Issuers and users

> Only recently has the report user become the subject of serious attention in accounting circles.
>
> (Lee, 1979, 36, 37)

Financial reporting is a two-party transaction, in which (1) the issuers of a financial report (discussed in Chapter 7), who control its preparation, provide it to (2) the users of the report, who use it in the hope that it will help improve their financial decisions about the reporting entity as a whole.

That financial reporting involves users is often lost sight of by issuers, outside auditors, and standard-setters. In 1961, the AICPA Director of Accounting Research, in a study of the fundamentals of financial reporting, purposely didn't explore the needs of the users: "anyone who stresses 'usefulness' as a criterion, in accounting or elsewhere, must answer the two pointed questions—useful to whom and for what purpose? And herein lies the danger" (Moonitz, 1961, 4). Weetman and Gordon commented: "Most of the arguments against Sprouse and Moonitz [a related study] mentioned usefulness in their criticisms" (Weetman and Gordon, 1988, 25). The issuers of the financial statements of Enron and of the other companies that had financial reporting breakdowns discussed in the Preface apparently didn't make the welfare of the users of the statements their primary concern—Klein quoted Goldwasser as saying that "Andersen [Enron's outside auditors] . . . lost sight of their duties to the public" (Klein, 2002).

The needs of the users of financial reports weren't formally explored in the official financial reporting literature until the end of the 1960s, in American Accounting Association, 1966 and AICPA, 1970c. That revolution hasn't yet fully reached the consciousness of the profession. Some still decry the shift in emphasis to the needs of the users; for example, Anton recently complained about "a decided shift in emphasis in external reporting to providing data primarily for decision making by present or potential equity share holders. This emphasis . . . has had some pernicious effects" (Anton, "Foreword," in Flegm, 1984, vii). Yet, as Solomons pointed out, "Before designing a product . . . it is necessary to consider what purpose or purposes the product is to serve" (Solomons, 1989, 9).

Though the FASB's CON1 and CON2, issued in 1978 and 1980, centered on the users, the FASB has rarely referred to the users since they issued those Statements. The Financial Accounting Standards Advisory Council, which advises the FASB, was asked the following in 1994 in a questionnaire sent to the Council to help it prepare for considering the recommendations of the AICPA Special Committee on Financial Reporting: "What interim steps can the Board take to incorporate the user focus . . . into current projects and forthcoming standards?"—in effect confessing that the Board had forgotten the users. (And Scott forgot that the AAA and the AICPA were the first official organizations to emphasize usefulness: "The earliest . . . statement [of the decision-usefulness approach] comes from the FASB in its Conceptual Framework project" [Scott, 1997, 58].)

In 2002, Pitt, Chairman of the SEC, stated that ". . . in the long bull market we enjoyed, some in . . . corporate America grew complacent and forgot their responsibility of single-minded devotion to the needs and interests of American shareholders" (Pitt, 2002, 2). On the contrary, corporate America has not given much evidence that it ever recognized that responsibility. That is the central lesson of the current financial reporting breakdowns.

As the Prologue states, the users are the parties whom the whole endeavor of financial reporting should benefit.

Functions of records and reports

Financial reporting is the most recent variant of a process that began in antiquity,[1] with records being kept of resources, obligations, and transactions

---

1 "The earliest reference to accounting in the Library of Congress . . . is an exhibit of Sumerian administrative documents dating from 3945 BC" (MacNeal, 1970, 58).

involving money, such as assessments and collections of taxes. Millennia passed before the adoption of double-entry bookkeeping, some time before its first detailed written description, by Paciolo in 1494[2] (Brown and Johnston, 1963).

Management

Until the separation of ownership and control of businesses and the development of credit markets involving participants who don't know one another, the records were kept to help persons and organizations manage their personal and business affairs. Some of those persons kept their own records; other people and organizations had servants or employees keep the records for them.

Financial statements

Littleton observed that "Paciolo ... [made] no provision for financial statements" (Littleton, 1933, 84). However, summary reports eventually began to be produced from the records for the use of the persons or organizations whose affairs were the subject of the records, to help them appraise and better manage those affairs.

Financial statements are the heart of financial reports (see Chapter 17): "Financial statements are the center of business reporting ... few suggest the current framework should be scrapped and a new one developed" (AICPA, 1994a, 5, 26). Of course, it's possible to drape many kinds of architecture on a given framework. Most of the issues in financial reporting pertain to financial statements.

Accountability

If agents were entrusted in any way with those affairs, the records and reports could also be used by the principals periodically to determine how the agents had fulfilled their accountability responsibilities—honesty in dealing and success in operations, also sometimes called *stewardship*, though *stewardship* is sometimes more narrowly construed as merely custodianship of the assets. As late as 1964, a leader of the profession defined financial statements solely in terms of accountability: "The financial statements discussed here are the general-purpose, accountability statements designed to report on the position and progress of a business enterprise..." (Miller, 1964, 43). Some still define financial reporting solely in terms of accountability—for example: "stewardship reporting of managers to absentee owners is the foundation of today's financial reporting" (Flegm, 1989, 94). Also, it is

2 "Records have been discovered of a thirteenth-century Florentine banking house which describe various business transactions during ... 1211. The entries ... were of the cross entry type which later gave rise to double entry" (MacNeal, 1970, 59, 60).

correct that "accountability is the cornerstone of all financial reporting in government" (GASB, 1987).

Economic decisions

In contrast with the emphasis on accountability, the AICPA and the FASB defined financial reporting in terms of making economic decisions, which conforms with the definition of financial reporting in the third paragraph of this chapter:

> The basic purpose of financial accounting and financial statements is to provide quantitative financial information about a business enterprise that is useful to statement users, particularly owners and creditors, in making economic decisions.
>
> (AICPA, 1970c, par. 73)

> Financial reporting is ... intended to provide information that is useful in making business and economic decisions ... [Its] objectives ... stem largely from the needs of those for whom the information is intended ... the stewardship role of accounting may be viewed as subordinate to and a part of the decision making role, which is virtually all encompassing.
>
> (FASB, 1978, par. 9; 1980b, par. 28)

Armstrong reported that "only 37 percent of the responses to the discussion memorandum on the objectives supported this user orientation" (Armstrong, 1977, 77)

May stated the importance of the difference between the use of financial reports for accountability and dividend decisions and their use for making economic decisions:

> "Whether the experience of a company in the recent past is likely to be repeated in the near future is practically immaterial if financial statements are to be considered as reports of stewardship or as guides to the profits that may properly be distributed.[3] It is of paramount importance

---

3 Issues in financial reporting are too complex to tolerate such colloquial terminology. Profits aren't distributed. Assets, mainly cash, are distributed:

> Profits are not a physical "thing" that can be disposed of, retained, or paid out. Profit is the name given to the change in a company's net assets that results from selected operating, financing, and investing activities during a period ...
>
> (Heath, 1978, 101)

May's thought here, soundly stated, is: "guides to the cash that may properly be distributed based on reported profits." Further, Chapter 9, footnote 9, discusses the use of the term "net assets."

if they are to be used as a guide in determining whether to buy, hold, or sell securities."

(May, 1951, 21, quoted in Sprouse, 1963, 688)

Controversy exists today between those who emphasize the accountability function of financial reporting and those who emphasize its function in helping make economic decisions, reflected in diverse conclusions on the issues in financial reporting and therefore diverse policy recommendations. For example,

> Some present-day accountants seem to assume automatically that "accountability" means accountability in terms of [acquisition] costs . . . Thus, by invoking the word "accountability" they somehow invoke a defense for [acquisition] cost and a weapon to be used against [other measurement bases].

(Devine, 1985a, 71)

Regardless of whether financial reports are intended to serve economic decisions or merely for accountability, users use them for economic decisions, and their design therefore needs to accommodate that. Thus, on the arrival of the separation of ownership and control, of markets for ownership shares, and of debt instruments with parties acting through impersonal exchanges, the reports that had been used for management and accountability were and are also used with little or no change for economic decisions by persons operating in those markets. Thus, current financial reporting is the progeny of unconscious adoption of record-keeping methods and reports invented for purposes—management and accountability—other than its current central purpose involving economic decisions by persons not involved in the running of the reporting entity.

That's not an unknown kind of progression. The first automobiles were "horseless carriages" with fringes and buggy whip holders, but the purposes and uses of automobiles were and have been studied, and they have been redesigned to better meet those purposes and uses (though their power is still rated in terms of horses). Most products and services except financial reports, regardless of their origin, are currently designed and improved mainly to serve and better serve the users of the products and services. Financial reports, in contrast, continue to provide buggy whip holders in the days of Formula One racing cars, as discussed throughout this book. And "the persistence of an accounting technique is [not] proof of the utility of the resulting information. It is feasible . . . that business firms have prospered in spite of accounting, rather than because of it" (Chambers, 1969, 72).

Though airplanes were invented by bicycle-makers, they weren't first made as fancy bicycles. They were designed from scratch with the purpose of flight in mind. The additional need of financial reporting to serve the economic decisions of its users is relatively new. If there had been no history of management and accountability reporting, devices would have been invented from scratch to serve that need too. That didn't happen.

Those who consider issues in financial reporting should bear in mind the baggage it carries from its ancestors serving other needs:

> Like all human institutions, [accounting principles] have tended to remain static while conditions have been steadily changing.
>
> (MacNeal, 1970, 70)

> the passing on of practices as traditions disregards the shifts in the context of practice . . . A practical art may, thus, come to be practically artless, though ancillary functions may secure its persistence.
>
> (Chambers, 1966, 346)

They should compare current practices with those that might have been developed from scratch to serve the new need. Part of the charge to the AICPA Special Committee on Financial Reporting from the AICPA Board of Directors in 1991 in effect was to do just that: "to recommend . . . the nature of the information that should be made available to others by management" (AICPA, 1991). This charge in effect acknowledges the remarkable fact that the organized profession hadn't previously carefully considered the nature of the information needed by the users of its product for decision-making.

Financial reporting as mapping

The FASB has noted an analogy that has been made between preparation of financial reports and map-making:

> An analogy with cartography [map-making] has been used to convey some of the characteristics of financial reporting . . . symbols (words and numbers) in financial statements stand for . . . economic things and events pertaining to an entity existing and operating in what is sometimes called the "real world."
>
> (FASB, 1980b, par. 24; 1985a, par. 6)

In financial reporting, the financial statements, the underlying records, and the thoughts of the issuers of the statements that have been incorporated into the statements (as discussed in Chapter 7) are analogous to the map; the conditions of the reporting entity that exist and existed and the financial effects of events that have occurred to the reporting entity outside the financial reporting system are analogous to the territory. Others have observed the same, for example,

Financial statements are . . . in essence, maps of economic territory.

(Heath, 1978, 97)

accounting is compared to financial map-making, where maps have to be accurate and faithful.

(Riahi-Belkaoui, 1993, 76)

Accounting is financial mapmaking.

(Solomons, 1978, 7)

Mapping is a helpful metaphor for representativeness (see Chapter 3): data in the minds of the issuers of the financial statements as portrayed in the line items of financial statements, in the financial reporting map, should purport to represent external phenomena—financially related events and conditions that occurred, existed, and exist external to the reports, phenomena in the financial reporting territory.

Chapter 4 discusses abuses of the concept of mapping in financial reporting.

Venture reporting versus time period reporting

The preceding section describes the first of three ways in which financial reporting didn't evolve completely in fundamental areas, in that case from accountability reporting to reporting for accountability and economic decisions. This section discusses the second, not evolving completely from venture reporting to time period reporting. Chapter 8 discusses the third, not evolving completely to the concept of the reporting entity as the sole focus of attention.

Venture reporting

Venture reporting was used for ventures, for example, one in which a ship was bought and provisioned and hands hired to start the voyage, and, if the ship returned (many didn't), the ship and cargo were sold and the hands were paid at the end of the voyage and the venture. The costs of the voyage were matched with—subtracted from—the revenue, and the excess was deemed to be income. Because the risks were great, profits for successful ventures were great.

Time period reporting

Only historians make divisions; time does not.

(Durant, 1935, 138)

Staubus observed that "[under] venture accounting . . . periodic reporting was not used" (Staubus, 1977, 397). However, reporting entities generally no longer operate discrete ventures, so periods of time have been substituted for ventures as the units that the reports cover:

> *Time periods.* The financial accounting process provides information about the economic activities of an enterprise for specified time periods that are shorter than the life of the enterprise. Normally the time periods are of equal length to facilitate comparisons. The time period is identified in the financial statements ... decision-makers need ... information about the enterprise's degree of success[4] periodically. . . .
>
> (AICPA, 1970c, par. 119; 1973b, 21)

Venture reporting links the financial effects of two classes of events, characterized as efforts and accomplishments. In contrast, pure time period reporting analyzes and reports separately on the financial effects on the reporting entity of each event. As discussed next, current financial reporting retains vestiges of venture reporting in the concept of matching.

Incomplete evolution

> The switch was not complete. . .
>
> (Sterling, 1968, 501)

The evolution wasn't complete. Some didn't mind; they thought that the reports should cover hybrids between ventures and time periods. For example, Goldberg said that "A profit and loss statement is merely a summary of ventures related to each other by virtue of their concurrence through a particular period of time" (Goldberg, 1965, 95). The AICPA Study Group on the Objectives of Financial Statements honored such hybrid reporting with a concept: "**Earnings Cycles**: All business enterprises engage in related activities aimed at goals. These related activities are defined as *cycles*" (AICPA, 1973b, 27). The FASB picked up that concept: "Both an entity's ongoing major or central activities and its incidental or peripheral transactions involve a number of overlapping cash-to-cash cycles of different lengths" (FASB, 1984a, par. 36).

The matching concept, popularized by Paton and Littleton in *Standards*, which "easily qualifies as the academic writing that has been most influential in accounting practice" (Storey, 1999, 1, 21), incorporates that hybrid. Revenue is now tallied at the end of what are considered to be identifiable operations ("ventures"), when it's said to be "realized," and the costs considered to be attributable to the operations that are considered to have ended are tallied and matched with—again, subtracted from—revenue to

4 This refers to what this book calls "achievement" already achieved, especially in Chapter 16. Chapter 16 states that decision-makers also need information to help them judge the reporting entity's current prospects for future achievement.

determine the income for the reporting period in which the identifiable operations ended. Matching is based on associating causes and effects of events (see Chapter 9).

In fact, Paton and Littleton believed venture reporting was still the ideal and time period reporting only a "substitute": "Time periods are a convenience, a substitute, but the fundamental concept is unchanged. The ideal is to match costs incurred with the financial effects attributable to or significantly related to such costs" (Paton and Littleton, 1940, 15). They thought that time period reporting may be an unfortunate tradition: "Fortunately or unfortunately the tradition of annual reckonings has become firmly established..." (Paton and Littleton, 1940, 77). Gilman agreed: "the third major convention of accounting ... one which has proved most troublesome ... the convention of the ... accounting period" (Gilman, 1939, 73).

Matching is a vestige of venture reporting.

Supporters of time period reporting criticized such hybrid reporting:

> the accounting period ... has been flouted...
>
> (Chambers, 1989, 15)

> the disavowal of the venture concept necessitated periodic reporting ... however ... only the variation in quantities was accounted for.... Since the value of the components is a product of two coefficients [the quantity and the price], the concept should be extended to cover the [price] as well as the quantities.
>
> (Sterling, 1968, 500, 501)

Adoption of the conclusion in Chapter 14 would complete the evolution from venture reporting to time period reporting. With the current limbo between the two, the dates and periods stated at the tops of financial statements can't be relied on to indicate the contents of the statements, and the users are fooled as to those contents. For example, improvements in current possession of or access to consumer general purchasing power (see Chapter 11) that occurred in previous periods is often reported as income of the current period. Also, expected expense of future periods is sometimes reported as actual expense of the current period (this is discussed in, for example, Chapters 21 and 24).

Financial accounting versus financial reporting

The process that's the subject of this book has been thought of as *financial accounting* (thus the name **Financial Accounting** Standards Board), simply preparing accounting documents seemingly with the only purpose to recite history: "nearly all of our current GAAP were solidified before the profession became interested in objectives" (Staubus, 1977, 16). Even the names of the processes involved in financial reporting given by the FASB perpetuate that misconception. The FASB calls the two main processes *measurement* and *recognition*. Assets, liabilities, revenues, expenses, and the like are "measured"—often simply calculated (see Chapter 6)—and then "recognized" in, incorporated "into," financial statements: "Recognition is the process of formally recording or incorporating an item into the financial statements of an entity as an asset, liability, revenue, expense, or the like" (FASB, 1984a, par. 6). Issuance by the issuers and use by the users isn't suggested. Such a process may involve only one party, the issuers in their role as preparers, who look inward (as discussed above, the FASB in effect has forgotten about the users):

> We accountants are doing accounting for accountants' sake, not for use by investors, creditors, underwriters, analysts, boards of directors, and regulators who are the people that we accountants should aim to please ... Accounting should not be done for the benefit of accountants.
>
> (Schuetze, 2001, 4, 16)

On the contrary, the issuers (including the preparers) of financial reports aren't simply in the business of *accounting*—of measuring and recognizing—which requires only one party; they are essentially in the business of *reporting*, which requires two parties, the issuers and the users:

> If the [FASB] were to be renamed today, it might well be called the ... Financial Reporting Policy Board ... The word "reporting" rather than "accounting" better conveys the breadth of [the] subject.
>
> (Heath, 1988, 110)

The SEC now issues "Financial Reporting Releases." Until 1982, they were referred to as "Accounting Series Releases" (Sutton, 1997, 97, 97n). Also, on April 1, 2001, the trustees of International Accounting Standards Committee changed the name of International Accounting Standards to International Financial Reporting Standards (http://www.iasc.org.uk/frame/cen1_13.htm).

Issuers essentially *report* assets and liabilities and changes in them rather than merely measure and recognize them. Thinking inward about measuring and recognizing permits financial reporters to forget that there are users out there with needs that have to be served for which financial reports should be designed, which is the only excuse for the activity of financial reporting.

Further, as *reports*, financial statements should

- Report solely information about phenomena pertinent to the reporting entity outside the reports and the reporting system (this is considered in Chapters 3 and 4).
- Report information about the financial effects of events, changes in conditions that occurred to the reporting entity, not financial effects of

events that one believes might occur later to the reporting entity or financial effects of events that might have occurred to the reporting entity but didn't (this is considered in Chapter 7).

In sum, financial statements need to report what is and what happened, outside of thoughts of the issuers about the future. (Measurement problems may make determining what is and what happened difficult or impossible in specific circumstances. Approximations or surrogate measures may sometimes help [see Chapter 6].)

Functions of bookkeeping, accounting, and financial reporting

Thus the separate but related functions of bookkeeping, accounting, and financial reporting need to be kept in mind by those who would consider issues in financial reporting.

Functions of bookkeeping and accounting

Bookkeeping and accounting serve management, by providing both of the following:

*   Help for control and management, i.e. the means to help control and manage the operations of the reporting entity. Flegm calls control *"the principal goal of accounting..."* (Miller and Flegm, 1990, 40). His reference to accounting apparently means financial reporting, because the article in which he stated that was about how the FASB should set standards, and the FASB is concerned only with financial reporting. But the principal goal of financial reporting isn't control; that's one of the principal goals of management accounting. The principal goal of financial reporting is providing information for outsiders. The support by Flegm, a management accountant, for the acquisition cost basis, shown, for example, in the first paragraph of the Prologue, is compatible with underrating the goal of providing information for outsiders.
*   Developing information for financial reporting, i.e. help in developing some of the information financial reporting provides.

Outside auditors are concerned with both functions. They, along with internal auditors, are concerned with the control function, to prevent and detect fraud. Their contribution in this area is substantial and growing. They are also concerned with the information financial reporting provides. However, as discussed in Chapter 10, the defects of current GAAP mainly prevent efforts of outside auditors to contribute in connection with this function.

Functions of financial reporting

As indicated above, financial reporting, in contrast, serves the users, by providing both

- *Help for appraising accountability*, i.e. providing users with information to use in judging how the management and the board of directors have discharged their accountability responsibilities.
- *Help for economic decisions*, i.e. providing users with information to use to attempt to help them make economic decisions, especially investment and credit decisions, about the reporting entity as a whole.

Because this book considers issues in financial reporting, it emphasizes the functions of financial reporting. It deals with the functions of bookkeeping and accounting only peripherally, as they relate to financial reporting.

Conflict of functions of financial reporting in the issuers' minds

The two functions of financial reporting are somewhat complimentary. After judging how management and the board of directors have discharged their accountability responsibilities, the users of financial reports can better determine what actions to take, if any, concerning both

- Management and the board of directors, the issuers of the reports
- Making and retaining investments and credit positions in the reporting entity:

> Unless stewardship means mere custodianship ... stockholders need essentially the same information for that purpose as they do for making investment decisions.
> (Storey and Storey, 1998, 98, citing FASB, 1978, pars 50–53)

However, because financial reports are issued by management and the board of directors and report on the discharge of their own accountability responsibilities, the two functions of financial reporting conflict in the minds of the issuers and color their behavior concerning the reports. The issuers are naturally concerned primarily with the actions the users might take concerning them based on the reports (their incentives [see Chapter 2] are to a considerable extent based on the possibility of such actions). The issuers are concerned only secondarily with making the reports serve well their function of helping the users decide whether to make and retain investments and credit positions in the reporting entity. That conflict of functions in the minds of the issuers is the cause of most of the issues, the controversies, and, especially, the current inadequacies of financial reporting in serving its functions.

To solve the conflict of functions, a suggestion is sometimes made to move the authority to issue financial reports from the current issuers, the management and the board of directors, toward others, such as the reporting entity's outside auditors (for example, in Miller, 1964). Though that suggestion has mainly fallen on deaf ears, and implementing it would indeed cause major problems of its own, it deserves study because of the extent to which the current conflict of functions in the minds of the issuers harms the quality of financial reporting. (The lobbying issuers do on individual issues [see Chapter 2] would be nothing compared with the lobbying they would do against this suggestion if an attempt were made to put it into effect.)

Financial statements versus economics

Financial statements and economics have in common a concern with economic resources. They have fundamental differences, however. Financial statements should contain solely verifiable representations of the financial effects on the reporting entity of events involving economic resources that have occurred to the reporting date. In contrast, economics deals mainly with thoughts of people about the future concerning economic resources. Concepts of income in financial statements and economics should therefore differ. That they don't do so completely has harmed financial reporting, as discussed in Chapter 12.

Financial reporting versus financial analysis

> what information the accountant should supply and what should be left to the decision maker who has access to accounting and other information deserves careful consideration.
>
> (Hanna, 1982, 269n)

In contrast with financial reporting, financial decisions are made based on comparisons of personal opinions that concern the strengths and prospects of improving the strengths (see Chapters 16 and 17) of the entities in which investments or loans may be made or retained. The opinions may be formed by the persons making the decisions or by the persons' advisors. In any case, the personal opinions may be improved if they are based on factual information in financial statements. The process of turning information in financial reports and other information outside of financial reports concerning status, progress, and prospects into personal opinions on which to base financial decisions is called *financial analysis*:

> [The] perspectives [of financial reporting and financial analysis] are diametrically opposed ... Because assets and liabilities are both the result of past transactions and events, so is the accounting measure of net

worth. Financial analysis, on the other hand, assesses, estimates, and gauges value solely in terms of expectations [thoughts] of the future.

(Association for Investment Management and Research, 1993, 17)[5]

Financial statements should be (but aren't) free of opinions, expectations, and other thoughts of the issuers about the future (this is discussed above and in Chapter 7). Therefore,

The point at which the accountant's responsibility should end and that of the analyst begin is neither clear nor fixed . . . There are many examples. Preparation of statements of changes in financial position . . . earnings per share data . . . forecasts of earnings . . . classification of assets and liabilities as current . . .

(Heath, 1978, 72)

In a number of areas, diverse positions are taken on issues depending on where those taking the positions draw the line between financial reporting and financial analysis. For example, "Mr. Halvorson dissents to the Opinion because he believes the subject matter [of earnings per share] is one of financial analysis, not accounting principles . . ." (AICPA, 1968, Dissent). The American Accounting Association agrees: "earnings per share . . . is a naive measure . . . 'performance,' even in a business context, is too complex and multidimensional a concept to be reduced to any single indicator" (American Accounting Association, 1991, 89).

This book concludes overall that present GAAP is over the line, that to a considerable extent it presents analysis rather than reports, especially concerning prospects (see Chapter 16). It also concludes (in Chapter 5) that injecting financial analysis into financial statements in order to stabilize income reporting is a pervasive fault of current GAAP.

Financial reporting versus income tax accounting

in so far as taxation rules are allowed at all to influence reported results and financial positions they interfere with the proper function of financial statements. . . .

(Chambers, 1969, 239)

Income taxes grew out of financial reporting, with its concept of income. Their purposes differ, the one to raise revenue and serve certain social objectives and the other to inform. But income tax accounting nevertheless hobbles the development of financial reporting. The most prominent example in the U.S. is the LIFO booking requirement: "the history of LIFO

---

5 This passage is also quoted in Chapter 12, in another context.

[shows] that as early as 1938 an accounting principle became generally accepted by act of Congress" (Moonitz, 1974, 34).

LIFO is often considered an advantageous income tax treatment. The U.S. Congress required taxpayers to use it in their financial reports in order to be permitted to use it in their income tax returns, though one has nothing to do with the other. The likely reason was that Congress had some doubt that LIFO would be a good income determination procedure for any purpose and felt reassured only by seeing financial reporters use it in their reports.

Worse, the alternative minimum tax incorporates all of financial reporting's income statement choices in determining income tax liabilities, and by a feedback effect influences those choices. In many other countries, the income tax laws also have pervasive effects on financial reporting.

As indicated by the quotation that begins this chapter, the quality of financial reporting affects the quality of decisions about the allocation of resources in a private enterprise economy such as ours, and therefore affects the well-being of us all. Congress shouldn't hamper financial reporting through the income tax laws. Devine even suggests that "the many special needs of the taxing authorities merit a new concept that may be so different that it no longer should be termed income" (Devine, 1999, 236).

A science or an art?

It was formerly fashionable to debate whether financial reporting is a science or an art. Those who wanted it to be relatively free of rules and to leave much to the judgment of the issuers presumably promoted its classification as an art, and those who wanted more discipline in it promoted its classification as a science. The debate bore no fruit, and is no longer engaged in.

If the activity of financial reporting has to be classified, it perhaps should be considered a practical art, like engineering, carried out to serve people's needs. Chambers thought so: "Accounting has generally been regarded by its practitioners as a practical art..." (Chambers, 1966, 342). Like engineering, it should be based at least partly on knowledge of the way the world operates, that is, scientific knowledge, and should conform with relevant scientific insights. But also like engineering, it will always require the ingenuity and creativity of its practitioners.

Discussion questions

1   Do you agree with the definition given for *financial reporting*?
2   What are the implications of the analogy between mapping and financial reporting?
3   Do you consider the primary function of financial reporting to involve accountability or economic decisions?
4   Describe the evolution from venture reporting to time period reporting.

5   State the relationship between the matching concept and venture reporting.
6   How are bookkeeping, accounting, and financial reporting related, and how do they differ?
7   Describe the conflict of functions of financial reporting in the issuers' minds. How does it harm financial reporting?
8   Describe how financial reporting is related to and differs from economics, financial analysis, and income tax accounting.

2 The incentives of the parties to financial reporting

> It may simply not be feasible for the FASB to properly implement the objectives contained in the conceptual framework until incentives are in place for its constituencies to acquiesce to the necessary standards.
>
> (Ronen and Sorter, 1989, 72)

When financial reporting practices have been advocated, reasons for the choices made have usually been given, but many seem like only good reasons in place of real reasons. Self-interest rules:

> pressures [are] applied by powerful business lobbies, elements in the financial community, departments of the Government, and members of Congress to promote one or another accounting practice that would favor special interests.
>
> (Zeff, 1994, 15)

A Chairman of the FASB noted the "conflicting ... interests of those affected by the financial reporting process" (Kirk, 1989b, 85). In contrast, P. R. Brown is almost Utopian: "Each constituent potentially affects formulation of the FASB decisions by providing thoughtful and theoretically sound input..." (Brown, 1982, 283).

A former issuer of financial reports commented that contending that parties to financial reporting attempt to serve their own self-interest is a challenge to their integrity and honesty. However, the great majority of the parties to financial reporting are dedicated, honest professionals whose integrity can't be questioned. Nevertheless, it's natural for each class of party to financial reporting to look out for themselves.

Of course, people don't confess in their arguments that they are essentially serving their self-interest: "the protracted arguments ... have not generally overtly recognized the vested interests that stand to gain or lose by how the argument goes..." (Solomons, 1986, 231). Issuers criticize rules that don't serve their self-interest with terms such as "aren't effective" and "too costly," for example:

Individual members of the Business Roundtable, a powerful lobbying group, have been criticizing the FASB ... Roundtable members have told the SEC that some rules of the chief rule-making body aren't effective and are too costly for companies to implement.

(Berton and Ricks, 1988, 4)

Positive and normative research

A full understanding of issues in financial reporting requires a consideration of the reasons we financial reporters advocate one solution or another to the issues. Two related avenues of research are concerned with the reasons for choices we financial reporters make among existing and proposed financial reporting practices.

One avenue, positive accounting theory (PAT), a relative newcomer, is said by its proponents to be the only scientific kind of financial reporting theory: "the concept of positive theory [is] the concept used in science..." (Watts and Zimmerman, 1986, 8). PAT has as its objective "to *explain* and *predict* accounting practice" (Watts and Zimmerman, 1986, 2)—that is, to see why the issuers choose the practices they choose and to predict the practices they will choose. The proponents of PAT describe "Another popular view ... that the objective of accounting theory is the provision of prescriptions for regulation of accounting and corporate disclosure [that is] **normative**..."[1] (Watts and Zimmerman, 1986, 4, 350). (Normative issues in general concern not what people do but what they should do, which is the main subject of this book: "it is the role of professional knowledge to generate ... normative propositions pertaining to human conduct" [West, 2003, 117].) Watts states that "...positive research in accounting [has] supplanted normative research"[2] (Watts, 1994, 33). PAT proponents believe a normative approach isn't a theory: "By itself, theory ... yields no prescriptions for accounting practice. It is concerned with explaining accounting practice" (Watts and Zimmerman, 1986, 7). Sterling retorts that

it *is* normative to say that accountants ought to make their numerals correspond to some phenomena, but it is *not* unscientific. On the contrary, the correspondence concept is often described as the *basic scientific norm* since it is indispensable to the requirement that scientific research be verifiable.

(Sterling, 1990b, 12)

1   Two authors straddle the issue. They first state that "*Normative theories* explain what should be, whereas *positive theories* explain what is." They then contradict themselves, saying that "The goal of accounting theory is to provide a set of principles and relationships that provide an explanation for observed practices and predict unobserved practices," which rules out normative theories (Schroeder and Clark, 1998, 1).
2   This contrasts with his statement quoted below in the text.

Rather than being concerned with what is or isn't a theory, this book is concerned simply with how to make financial reporting better serve the purposes it should serve, that is, not only with what the issuers do and why they do it but also with what they should do. This book is about issues concerning what the issuers should do, about improving financial reporting.

Proponents both of PAT and of improving financial reporting agree that research in financial reporting should start by determining what the issuers do currently. Such an inquiry is presented in general in Appendix B to Chapter 3 and in Chapter 10 and in particular in various other chapters. There is no apparent reason why the two kinds of research should start with different descriptions of what the issuers do currently, so proponents of PAT presumably could start with the same inquiry.

PAT goes from the description of what the issuers do currently to an inquiry as to why the parties at interest make the choices they do in selecting or recommending financial reporting practices in each of the various areas: "a precondition of a positive theory of standard-setting is understanding management's incentives"(Watts and Zimmerman, 1978, 113). In contrast, the effort to improve financial reporting follows up the description of current practice by

1 Setting up goals for financial reporting
2 Seeing to what extent current financial reporting meets the goals
3 Recommending revisions in what financial reporting does in an attempt to help it better meet the goals.

The goals have been stated by various observers recently in terms of the needs of the users of financial reports.

Like science, PAT can't help in setting priorities: "Science . . . is silent on ultimate . . . values and aims . . ." (Durant, 1953, 14). The issuers of financial reports have their own foremost priority for financial reporting, which is their own welfare: "Corporation management . . . is invariably interested primarily in its own situation . . ." (Skinner, 1987, 28). That conflicts with this book's foremost priority for financial reporting, which is the welfare of the users of financial reports and of society in general. Those conflicting priorities lead to conflicting answers to the issues in financial reporting about what the issuers should do, as discussed throughout this book.

Though PAT doesn't directly work toward improving financial reporting, it might have the indirect result of inciting others to work toward improving it. Positive theorists concede that "a positive theory can have normative implications once an objective function is specified" (Watts and Zimmerman, 1990, 148, citing Jensen, 1983), and Watts states that "positive accounting theory is demanded for the normative prescriptions that can be generated from it" (Watts, 1999). Jensen stated that "In the end, of course, we are all interested in normative questions; a desire to understand how to accomplish goals motivates our interest in . . . positive theories" (Jensen,

1983, 320). He explained that that includes predicting how the various parties would react to a proposal to change financial reporting practices and how they would react to the changed information if it's produced.

Conflicting incentives

> the magnitude of political costs imposed by the improper alignment of incentives.
>
> (Ronen and Sorter, 1989, 74)

Financial reporting affects the parties to financial reporting, especially the users, the issuers, and the outside auditors, and that gives them strong incentives to influence the design of financial statements. The incentives of the issuers and the outside auditors may conflict with the needs of the users. The proponents of PAT are deeply concerned with the incentives of the parties. Observers of financial reporting other than the proponents of PAT rarely if ever inquire into those incentives, into their motives (perhaps they think it unseemly). However, it's helpful for normative research in financial reporting—in the effort to improve financial reporting—to consider those incentives, to help see why current financial reporting is what it is and to facilitate the design of a political course to move more effectively toward improvement of financial reporting for the benefit of the users. Other reasons for an inquiry into the incentives of the parties in normative research include seeing their legitimate concerns and providing some help in appraising the quality of the arguments they put forth on their positions on the issues.

PAT and the effort to improve financial reporting therefore have a common interest in the reasons the parties support the financial reporting practices they support—to inquire into their incentives.

The parties other than the users have had the most influence in establishing financial reporting practices and standards. Those parties may say they act disinterestedly, for the benefit of the users, an efficient market, or an optimum allocation of resources in the economy, but that's often not what they do. Instead, there's a "traditional unspoken doctrine of user subordination and management and accountant domination" (Staubus, 1977, 277). Schmitt calls the users "Wall Street's second-class players" (Schmitt, 2001, 40). Much of the contention on issues in financial reporting is caused not by differences of opinion on how the world works or how to make it work better, but by striving by the parties other than the users to achieve their incentives. Because those parties have the power to influence the resolution of issues in financial reporting, because financial reporting standard-setting currently is essentially a political rather than a technical process, their incentives and the sources of their power need to be understood by those who would consider the issues. The Epilogue discusses this further.

The main classes of parties are users—typified by investors, creditors, and employees—issuers, outside auditors, citizens, standard-setters and regulators, elected government officials, and teachers of financial reporting. Incentives differ within and between the classes.

The material that follows on incentives is necessarily speculative, because people typically don't divulge their private desires. You are obviously free to speculate for yourself. One test of the soundness of this material is its compatibility with what the parties do, which unfolds in subsequent chapters.

Incentives of users

Until shocks such as the Enron collapse and the financial reporting breakdowns in other companies discussed in the Preface hit the fan, users probably believed the other parties to financial reporting were looking out for their interests satisfactorily. So the users haven't been active in shaping financial reporting: "financial statement users [are] badly outspent and outnumbered in the 'due process' activities of the FASB" (Association for Investment Management and Research, 1993, 78). That's odd, considering their stake in it. The AICPA Special Committee on Financial Reporting recognized that lack in 1991, and centered its study on direct contact with professional users in attempting to determine their needs (see Chapter 17). It also recommended that standard-setting bodies and regulators should henceforth include users of financial reports in their memberships and actively seek their input in their deliberations (AICPA, 1994a, 113, 114).

Issuers and outside auditors have always been active in shaping financial reporting, in both the reporting and standard-setting functions, so their incentives have been addressed. It's up to all to address the needs of the users, towards which the whole effort of financial reporting should be directed.

The incentive of individual investors and creditors as users generally is only to obtain the best information to help them make their financial decisions. They would probably want real income instability shown and evenhandedness—not feigned stability in income statements (see Chapter 5) and one-sided reporting based on conservatism in balance sheets (see Chapter 10). And they dislike complexity: if anything, they would like financial reports to be easier to read and understand. Hermanson said

> As investors, we simply want clear, truthful information on how a company has performed, how management expects it to perform in the future and what key risks face the company.
>
> (Hermanson, 2002, 14)

But financial reports are used intensively for financial decisions mostly by a special kind of user—professional analysts and advisors as users serving the decision-makers. Those users have some incentives that could influence financial reporting if acted on, for example if their views as expressed to the

AICPA Special Committee on Financial Reporting and used as the basis of its report are given weight. Their incentives are to have a good track record in advising clients on investments compared with other advisors, and to have to put in only a reasonable amount of effort doing so.

Analysts and advisors might forego the addition of some useful information in financial reports because their competitors would receive the same information and they might believe they can obtain a monopoly on it by obtaining it privately. Or they might object to changes because they would have to change their methods of analysis. An analyst who trains other analysts told me he opposes the introduction of inflation reporting (see Chapter 11) because he would have to retrain them all.

Finally, stockholder users wear two hats. One is as investors, who, as users of financial reports, want the best information to make the best decisions concerning whether to increase, retain, or decrease their investments in the reporting entity, and whether to support the current management and board of directors. The other is as an interested insider, because of the effects the success or failure of the reporting entity has on their interests. Wearing this hat, they aren't users of financial reports. Their interests are similar to those of the issuers: they want any kind of reporting that will help the reporting entity succeed as well as possible, for example by obtaining a lower cost of capital, and they want any kind of reporting that will cause the unit price of their stock to be as high as possible: "shareholders ... benefit from managers' choices of 'loose' accounting standards" (Revsine, 1991, 18). Those desires are independent of and may compete with their desire as investors for the best information.

For example, a spokeswoman for AOL was quoted as saying that a certain kind of lease

> "continues to provide a diversified source of tax advantaged, cost-effective financing ... our synthetic leases are disclosed in our financial statements, and we believe they are in the best interest of our shareholders."
>
> (Muto, 2002)

That's perhaps correct concerning shareholders as interested insiders. However, the spokeswoman neglected to inquire as to whether they are in the best interest of the shareholders as investors and in the best interest of nonshareholder investors.

Incentives of issuers

> the management group has an interest of its own to promote and protect ... The concealment or distortion of information may be viewed as one expression of this.
>
> (Chambers, 1966, 282)

The issuers of financial reports are in charge of the operations of the reporting entities and the preparation and issuance of the reports. In a corporation, the issuers are the management and the Board of Directors. Because the management reports to the Board, the management and the Board may have some conflicting incentives unless management controls the Board (which they do in many corporations). However, because they both report to the stockholders, they always have incentives in common.

Report card

Financial reports inescapably serve as a "tell-tale report card" (Loomis, 1989, 6). "Management wants to win . . . it wants to have a good report card" (Sterling, 1973, 65; see Figure 2.1). To that extent, financial reports report on the accountability of the issuers. They have the incentive to influence the messages those report cards send. Those messages may haunt them. For example,

In response to intense pressure from investors, Jeffrey C. Barbakow stepped down yesterday as chief executive of **Tenet Healthcare**, the

Figure 2.1 Permanently grounded (reproduced by permission of Joe Martin).

troubled hospital chain ... many investors have remained impatient with [Tenet's] weak financial performance...

(Abelson, 2003, C1)

A stunning 78% of the CEOs at the worst performing 20% of companies in the S&P 500 have been replaced within the past five years.

(Reingold, 2003, 78)

They want financial reports to paint as good a picture as possible about their administration of the entity, just as students want their report cards to paint as good a picture as possible about their progress in school:

management is strongly motivated to render biased reports on its own performance.

(Staubus, 2004b)

gamesmanship ... is ... played by those who report. They want to put as good a face as possible on their numbers...

(Yager, 1988, 43)

one of the key insights of the modern theory of information is that participants do not always have an incentive to disclose fully and accurately all the relevant information...

(Stiglitz, 2002, A10)

You can ... disguise the cost of restructuring by timing big one-time charges to coincide with gains on the sale of major assets. In 1987, GE played down a $1 billion write-off this way. Last year United Technologies offset a $149 million write-off of slow-moving inventory with a $137 million gain from the sale of subsidiaries.

(Hector, 1989, 24)

They want to avoid "the propagation of unpopular truth through financial reports" (Association for Investment Management and Research, 1993, 77). They cover up that desire by references to *reality*, with statements such as "it is ... a question of tempering ideals with the realities of the competitive world in which we live..." (Ihlanfeldt, 1991, 34). The editor of the *Journal of Accountancy* quotes Mills, director of accounting policy at Merrill Lynch & Co., as saying that "Implementing accounting policy is a combination of reacting to new rules, staying on top of how standards work and trying to protect the corporation" (Rescigno, 2001, 37). That emphasizes the interests of the issuers of financial reports and of the reporting entity, with no evidence of concern for the needs of the users of financial reports.

The conflict discussed in Chapter 1 in the minds of the issuers between fulfilling the two functions of financial reporting, reporting on the discharge of their accountability responsibilities and providing information for economic decisions, causes them to lean toward biasing the reports, toward presenting a good report card, possibly at the expense of the quality of the information.

Further, once the rules of a game are established, the players don't want them changed: "Change the score-keeping and change the game. Change the game and where does one stop?" (Mautz, 1973, 25).

An anomaly in financial reporting is that the management and the board of directors in effect issue report cards on their own activities, which is comparable to students grading themselves or baseball players acting as umpires on their own plays (that's the main reason for the existence of outside auditors): "the baseball batter should not call the balls and strikes..." (AICPA, 1972c, 60).

Even were they to agree with the latter sentiment, the issuers believe they should have a large voice in establishing the rules of the game. For example,

> the business community has a legitimate role in the standard-setting process...
>
> (Ihlanfeldt, 1991, 34)

> logic would seem to indicate that those who faced the subjective choices of various day-by-day transactions would be particularly well-suited to deal with the problem of establishing reasonable principles.
>
> (Flegm, 1984, 82)

(The latter is comparable to saying that logic would seem to indicate that those who as batters face the subjective choices of how to deal with the various kinds of pitches would be particularly well-suited to deal with the problem of establishing the strike zone.) And the AICPA feels that "there is no reason why the batter should not have some say in developing the rules of the game" (AICPA, 1972c, 60). But what if the rules batters would develop would differ from the rules pitchers would develop? Should batters be allowed to write rules that bias against pitchers? Should issuers of financial reports be allowed to influence rules that bias against the users? Sterling, Moonitz, and Schuetze object:

> we ought to get management out of the business of establishing accounting principles...
>
> (Sterling, 1973, 66)

> The organized profession has acquiesced in a situation in which the party to be judged plays a key role in selecting the criteria by which it will be judged ... First and foremost, accountants must curb the power of management to select the principles of accounting by which its performance and stewardship will be judged ... Management most certainly will not willingly and readily give up its power.
>
> (Moonitz, 1974, 64, 68)

"We need to take control of the numbers out of the hands of management of the reporting enterprise by requiring that the numbers for assets and liabilities come from the marketplace."

(Schuetze, 2004)

Higher reported income or lower reported losses

Other things equal, issuers of the financial reports of for-profit entities usually want them to report income as high as possible or losses as low as possible:

[The Chief Accountant of the SEC] police[s] the SEC's efforts to force accountants to remain independent from . . . corporate clients who often demand liberal interpretations of the accounting rules in order to make their profit look more rosy.

(MacDonald and Beckett, 1998, B2)

Their preference for the formerly used pooling-of-interests method of reporting after business combinations over the purchase method reflected that desire (see Chapter 23). However, that desire, as real and as well known as it is, is tempered by fears of attracting increased demands from suppliers of inputs, such as stockholders and employees, and from the government: "Too much flaunting of success may attract . . . possibly unwelcome attention from government regulatory agencies" (Skinner, 1987, 653). It's also tempered by fears of what Evans and Sridhar call "proprietary costs associated with product market competition (a rival's potential entry into the [reporting entity's] product market). . ." (Evans and Sridhar, 2002, 610).

An anomaly is the recent reporting by Freddie Mac. For example, "according to its restatement . . . in the third quarter of 2002, it earned more than $5 billion—over $4 billion more than the company reported at the time . . . representative Christopher Shays . . . of Connecticut, said . . . 'Freddie Mac . . . obviously can't add or subtract. . .'" (Glater, 2002). If correct, that's a problem improving financial reporting standards can't help.

Stability of income reporting

Other things aren't equal, however. Not only do the issuers usually want income reported as high or losses reported as low as possible, they also want reported income to be relatively stable:[3]

3 This is commonly discussed in terms of "smoothing." That sounds bad: making income that's not smooth look smooth. The term is considered pejorative. In contrast, "stability" sounds good; who could be against stability—unstable minds and unstable governments wreak havoc. So promoting stability of income reporting sounds good and "stability" isn't a pejorative term. But Chapter 5 concludes that making unstable income look stable is nevertheless bad. The term "stable" is

CEOs know that investors hate surprises, so they try to keep net income trending up a nice straight slope.

(Hector, 1989, 24)

Most managements like the entities for which they are responsible to show to the outside world steady and increasing prosperity...

(Research Committee of the Institute of Chartered Accountants of Scotland, 1988, 32)

According to the CEO of a *Fortune 500* firm, "[t]he No. 1 job of management is to smooth out earnings."

(Loomis, 1999)

In the zeal to satisfy consensus estimates and project a smooth earnings path, wishful thinking may be winning the day over faithful representation.

(Levitt, 1998)

A consistent trend of reporting growth in quarterly earnings is the key ... Most executives accept this as an article of faith...

(Eccles *et al.*, 2001, 71)

In fact, their desire to avoid significant fluctuations from period to period in reported income exceeds their desire for higher reported income:

One former FASB member told me recently that 95 percent of the comments the Board receives from financial statement preparers fall into one of three categories: don't make any changes, don't move so fast, and don't make income volatile—don't let it fluctuate.

(Heath, 1990, 57; see also the beginning of Chapter 21, and Chapter 24)

Issuers try to avoid instability of reported income for at least two reasons. First, companies with the same reported income trend but different reported income stability are evaluated differently. Users infer that reporting entities with reported income that's more unstable are riskier than reporting entities with similar reported income that's less unstable, and they discount the securities of the former. Stable reported income with the same trend as volatile reported income therefore brings premiums in the market:

---

emphasized in this book over the term "smoothing" in spite of the positive connotation of "stable" simply to avoid biasing the discussion with the pejorative term "smoothing."

tips on how to increase a business' appeal to potential buyers ...
Ensur[e] steady growth in gross and net income from year to year.

(French, 1987, 137)

A company that shows steady growth with few surprises often gets
rewarded with a sweet premium from investors—a high stock price...

(Brown, 2002, C1)

Higher market values are considered beneficial by the issuers because of
their effect on users' appraisal of how well the issuers manage. Also, "Stable
results tend to lower cost of capital, providing an incentive to try to report
stable results to lower the cost of capital" (AICPA, 1994b, I, 42). For
example, at a meeting of the AICPA Special Committee on Financial
Reporting, a member from industry said he would favor reporting any way
that would lower his company's cost of capital. (It's ironical that that position, which ignores the users, was taken by a member of a committee explicitly dedicated to the welfare of the users.)

Second, a volatile reported income trend includes some periods in which
reported income rises more than the trend. It also includes some periods in
which reported income rises less than the trend, doesn't rise, falls, or in
which losses are reported. Issuers like to report high income (within limits),
but that's exceeded by how much they *dis*like reporting lower income
increases, lower income, or even losses. The credit they get for high reported
income doesn't offset the questions they face later when they have to report
lower than average increases in income, or worse. The stockholders have
short memories and ask what the issuers have done for them lately. They
wonder whether this period's reported less desirable results are the start of a
trend rather than just one of the periodic dips in an ongoing upward trend.
Most executives know that:

what [Wall] Street most care[s] about [is] smoothly growing earnings.

(McLean, 2001, 60)

Bossidy has become New Jersey's highest-paid corporate executive ...
by leading [Allied Signal Inc.] to a steady string of record profits.

(Lochner, 1996, A17)

They hate to report declines, but they also want to avoid increases that
vary wildly from year to year; it's better to have two years of 15% earnings increases than a 30% gain one year and none the next.

(Worthy, 1984, 50)

A reporting entity's major defense against hostile takeover is excellent,
steady earnings growth and share appreciation.

The financial reporting literature ascribes actions to stabilize income

reporting to individual issuers, for example: "Income smoothing, or deliber-
ate voluntary acts by management to reduce income variation by using
certain accounting devices..." (Nasuhiyah *et al.*, 1994, 291). However,
actions of standards-setters and regulators in establishing GAAP rather than
individual acts to circumvent GAAP are more responsible for stabilizing
income reporting. Stability of income reporting, the main desire of the
issuers (who are the parties to financial reporting who, at least currently,
have the most influence on the design of financial reports, as discussed
below), is the fundamental goal of traditional financial reporting.[4] The
desire for such stability is the basis of the support for realization and allocation, from which are derived in turn the acquisition-cost basis for reporting
on assets, the current general principle for reporting on liabilities, and most
of the major current principles in reporting on specific areas in financial
statements, for example, on inventories, buildings and equipment, income
taxes, goodwill, and employee benefits:

> the artificial smoothing of real world volatility [is] a common feature of
> FASB standards...
>
> (Wyatt, 1988, 25)

> a lot of smoothing is preengineered into reports by political compro-
> mises imbedded in GAAP.
>
> (Miller and Bahnson, 2002b, 21)

(This is discussed throughout this book, especially in Chapters 10, 12, 13,
15, 19, 21, and 24.) It's the main reason that financial reporters tolerate the
conditions described in the Prologue in the section on "The necessity for
financial reporters to think independently."

In the early 1970s, the Accounting Principles Board subcommittee on
reporting on marketable equity securities concluded that they should be
reported in the balance sheet at their current selling prices and that
changes in their current selling prices should be reported currently in
income. The subcommittee held a public hearing in which various views
were expressed. The subcommittee polled the APB members and found
that a majority favored its view. However, when the APB met, it voted
the proposal down. The chairman of the subcommittee was mystified; he
said he had no idea what had happened. I didn't either, at the time; I was
equally mystified. I now believe that issuers got to enough members of
the APB behind the scenes to kill the proposal, to avoid the volatility in

---

4 Sterling's view on this is milder. He simply assigns the following as the driving
force in stabilizing income reporting: "it seems that we [financial reporters]
experience uneasy feelings when income and expenses are not smooth" (Sterling,
1979, 222). He thereby minimizes the effects of the desires and political power of
the issuers in skewing financial reporting.

income reporting that would have resulted. This attempt to improve financial reporting contributed to the death of the APB (see Chapter 23).

The issuers usually disguise their strong desire for stable income reporting as discussed throughout this book, often referring to their brand of "objectivity" (see Chapter 10) or to the supposed superior reliability of allocated acquisition costs (though, as demonstrated in Chapter 10, allocated amounts are completely unreliable). Devine said that "accountants tend to deny—with indignation—that they smooth anything (least of all income...)" (Devine, 1985a, 79n). Issuers and their friends sometimes acknowledge the depth of their desire for and their power to achieve stable income reports by the design of GAAP, however. At a public hearing on reporting on defined benefit pensions, Kirk, the then Chairman of the FASB, said a concern of the FASB in drafting the pronouncement was to be sure it contained "an adequate amount of smoothing," apparently to appease the issuers (see Chapter 24). A most naked statement by an issuer of that desire and power is the following:

> field-testing ... sponsored by the Financial Executives Research Foundation ... confirmed that application of the FASB's tentative conclusions would have introduced a high degree of volatility into companies' annual pension expense... This resulted in the Board making changes in the final standard that helped to reduce volatility ... they did listen—but it was not without considerable prodding.
>
> (Ihlanfeldt, 1991, 28; also quoted in Chapter 24)

Notice that all of the concern voiced in that statement is for a desire of the issuers and none of the concern is for the need of the users to have sound income reporting.

Thomas Evans says the "complicated practice procedures" now required are "a result of globalization, exotic securities, downsizing, stock options, write-offs, and other new developments..." (Evans, 2003, v). They are in fact rather the result of the income reporting stabilizing built into current GAAP.

"NONDISTORTION"

An often cited goal in financial reporting is to avoid distortion of reported income. For example, the AICPA stated that

> studies of published reports and other source material have indicated that, where material amounts are involved, recognition of deferred income taxes in the general accounts is needed to ... avoid income distortion...
>
> (AICPA, 1958a, par. 7)

One observer made it a matter of principle:

> THE NONDISTORTION GUIDELINE *From among systematic and rational methods, use that which tends to minimize distortions of periodic net income.*
>
> (Bevis, 1965, 104)

He did hedge his bets:

> [the] discussion of nondistortion accounting methods should be kept in context . . . The discussion should not be considered as suggesting that the effect of unusual gains or losses be hidden . . . nor should it be thought to suggest that fluctuations of revenues and costs directly related to particular periods should be disguised in any way.
>
> (Bevis, 1965, 106)

However, that merely prevented nondistortion from going overboard.

A former chairman of the FASB challenged the guideline: "The [mischievous] 'nondistortion guideline' [became] a rationale for many questionable cost deferrals and accruals" (Kirk, 1989b, 89n, 91). However, reported income distortion is reminiscent of the common expression "bent out of shape." Who could be in favor of bending anything out of shape, especially reported income, a key statistic in financial reporting? So how could nondistortion be mischievous?

The reason is that those opposed to reported income distortion don't imply bending anything out of shape. They refer to wavy reported income trend lines. If a reported income trend line is wavy, according to them it's distorted. The goal is to adopt practices that will tend to straighten out the reported income trend line, to cure the so-called distortion: "If managers are completely successful in their smoothing . . . reported earnings would be *on* the straight line . . ." (Watts and Zimmerman, 1986, 144). Never mind that the incomes of business enterprises actually jump around and that a sound reported income trend line should be wavy. Figure 2.2 indicates the difference: I_1 is the income trend line as it occurs to the reporting entity and I_2 is the reported income trend line applying nondistortion (the figure was provided by Professor Rudy Schattke). Users accept such averaging rather than reporting in financial statements. They don't accept it, for example, for stock indexes. No one advocates presenting the 150-day moving average of the Standard & Poor's 500-stock index to the exclusion of the index itself, and especially not pretending that the 150-day moving average presents the day-to-day movements.

"BIG BATH"

Periodically, issuers can no longer present a nice stable upward-leaning reported income trend line; they have run out of little tricks to maximize

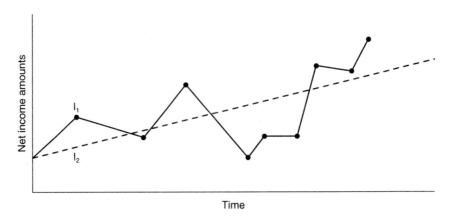

Figure 2.2 The income trend line as it occurs to the reporting entity (I_1) and the reported income trend line applying nondistortion (I_2).

reported asset amounts, minimize reported liability amounts, and minimize "distortion." What can they do? They can play a big trick on the users of their financial reports: they can have a "big bath."

Why do issuers play tricks on the users? Because money talks. Because vested interests at present have more power over financial reporting than those who are supposed to benefit from it, the users, as discussed throughout this book.

In a big bath, assets are reported at their lowest conceivable amounts and liabilities are reported at their highest conceivable amounts. That sounds like something issuers would never do. After all, their basic incentive is to report high and smoothly increasing income, and such a presentation works exactly opposite of that.

In fact, issuers do it gladly:

> The big bath represents the corporate equivalent of two weeks at a fat farm. It rids the company of excess expenses and may eventually firm up profits. New chief executives are especially keen on the tactic because it allows them to blame the bad news on the old CEO.
>
> (Hector, 1989, 196)

(The following quotation has a nice rhythm to it):

> When a firm takes a "big bath," the firm's management changes past, overly optimistic forecasts of its future to a present, more pessimistic forecast of its future for the purpose of changing past profits to losses so that they can change future losses to profits.
>
> (Sterling, 1979, 30)

That gets them points in the securities markets. It "reflect[s] efforts to become lean and mean" (Norris, 1999b, C9). For example,

> Citigroup Inc ... said it expects to take a ... restructuring charge of approximately $900 million after tax ... The size of the ... charge ... gave a boost to Citigroup's shares [which] closed ... up ... 5.8%.
>
> (Beckett, 1998, A8)

Figure 2.3 illustrates the effect and the reasons (the figure was provided by Professor Rudy Schattke).

Occasionally a big bath is actually suspected to be an abuse (which it usually is). For example,

> questions have been raised about the extent to which a large restructuring charge in 1996 may have paved the way for the improved profits last year. Sunbeam has denied that its accounting practices were improper.
>
> (Sterling, 1979, 30)

CONFLICTING VIEWS

Conflicting views on the desirability of stabilizing income reporting are explored in Chapter 5.

Assistance in managing

Issuers have some incentives to have financial reports aid in managing. For example, issuers desire to have the lowest possible cost of capital. Stabilizing income reporting is a means to lower the cost of capital of their reporting entities.

Another means is to keep the debt-to-equity ratio, calculated from

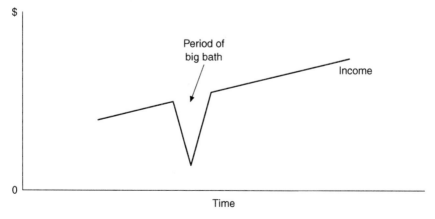

Figure 2.3 The ideal "big bath."

amounts in the balance sheet, as low as possible. To accomplish that, attempts are made to keep liabilities off the statement, so-called off-balance sheet financing: "corporations have concocted so many ways to hide or disguise borrowings that deciphering their true liabilities is often impossible" (Berton, 1983, 1). Norton Simon's principal financial reporting officer was quoted as being ebullient about that ploy:

> "One of the big advantages of off-balance sheet financing is that it permits us to make other borrowings from banks for operating capital that we couldn't otherwise obtain."
>
> (Berton, 1983, 1)

And listen to Willens:

> "As an investment banker, I have found through the years that the principal objective a company and client will have with respect to any transaction or project is to ... keep the debt off the balance sheet. Which is fine with us; that seems to be a legitimate goal."
>
> (Quoted in Fink, 2002, 48)

Norris reported that "many companies have come to view [that they have an] absolute right ... to move assets and liabilities off their balance sheets even though they retain some of the risk and benefits from those assets" (Norris, 2002c).

The collapse of Enron Corporation in 2001 was developing for some time before it became apparent to investors. One reason was that it engaged in off-balance sheet financing by keeping more than 2000 special purpose entities out of its consolidated financial statements:

> a concern at Enron about trying to keep as much debt as possible off the company's balance sheet. Too much debt lowers a company's credit rating, which was a particular worry for Enron, whose vast energy-trading operations relied heavily on its credit standing.
>
> (Emshwiller, 2002, A3)

It also

> hid billions in loans in plain sight ... accomplished using financial contracts called derivatives ... Enron's accounting treatment conformed to existing recommendations from the Financial Accounting Standards Board ... said Timothy S. Lucas, director of research and technical activities at the board ... the group will soon reveal a new recommendation, he said, requiring that such transactions be accounted for as loans...
>
> (Altman, 2002)

Moreover,

> Enron entered into derivative contracts that mimicked loans but could
> be accounted for in less obvious ways ... Citigroup lent Enron $2.4
> billion in ... prepaid swaps ... the transactions, though technically
> derivatives trades ... perfectly replicated loans ... though Enron's
> accounting treatment conformed to accounting recommendations for
> prepaid swaps ... [u]nder forthcoming rules ... a prepaid swap would
> count as a loan as well as an underlying derivative.
>
> (Altman, 2002)

Some other specific kinds of off-balance sheet financing are discussed in
Chapters 25 and 26.

For another example, issuers want to attract highly competent people by
granting them stock options. They previously found that especially advantageous because no cost was formerly required to be reported in connection
with stock options issued to employees. They fought to keep the reporting
that way (this is discussed in Chapter 18).

Flexibility

An incentive that helps issuers achieve their other incentives is their desire
for flexibility in income reporting:

> Those responsible for financial reporting like flexibility in the choice of
> what to report and when to report it. A system that provides a more
> faithful portrayal of economic events might be less open to management
> of results through the choice of transactions engaged in.
>
> (Skinner, 1987, 513)

Earnings management

> Companies report profits now, of course, but many believe they have a
> right to manage those numbers as they wish. There are lots of gimmicks
> that can be used—some of them visible and many not. When account-
> ing rule makers try to do something about it, they must worry that
> corporate America will use political influence to get the rules changed.
>
> (Norris, 1999a, C1)

Because financial reports serve as report cards on management (and the directors), and because, by definition, managing is what managers do, management tries to manage reported earnings. If "events and circumstances [are]
partly or entirely beyond the control of the entity and its management, for
example, price changes..." (FASB, 1985a, par. 32), they try to manage

reported earnings by doing their best to keep the financial effects of those events and circumstances out of the records, and they do that, for example, by supporting retention of realization (see Chapter 10). A user of financial reports decried that: *"to smooth reported earnings is game-playing that not only reduces the quality of earnings but also stains management's credibility"* (AICPA, 1994b, I, 41).

(In fact, price changes aren't outside management's control. The reporting entity became subject to those changes solely because management decided to obtain the assets or incur the liabilities subject to those changes, and it continues to be subject to those changes solely because management decided not yet to dispose of the assets or discharge or fund the liabilities.)

The SEC (and most others) assume that GAAP itself acts as a hindrance to reported earnings management. It has defined *earnings management* as distortion of the application of generally accepted accounting principles. Schipper likewise contends that "GAAP, auditors, audit committees and legal rules—constrain reporting. In addition, economic conditions influence accruals. Some components of earnings are therefore not susceptible to management..." (Schipper, 1989, 98). Healy and Wahlen state that

> Earnings management occurs when managers use judgment in financial reporting and in structuring transactions to alter financial reports to either mislead some stakeholders about the underlying economic performance of the company or to influence contractual outcomes that depend on reported accounting numbers.
>
> (Healy and Wahlen, 1999, 368)

Wolk and colleagues contend that "because [the] use of [income tax allocation] is mandatory where timing differences exist, it cannot be construed as a smoothing instrument—since management has no choice but to use it..." (Wolk *et al.*, 1992, 414).

However, not only may the issuers of the financial reports of individual reporting entities attempt to manage reported earnings by how they apply GAAP, but also, to greater effect, the profession as a whole, through retention of allocation and other means of stabilizing reported income enshrined in GAAP (as discussed throughout this book), manages reported earnings for the benefit of the issuers:

> In some contexts we clearly recognize the inappropriateness of allowing management to smooth income. In other contexts we seem to implicitly justify a smoothing on the basis of some ill-defined notions of "properly matching."
>
> (Sterling, 1979, 226)

Managed earnings is mainly the result not of how GAAP is applied but of sound application of faulty GAAP.

Drucker refers to "the discipline of a financial bottom line..." (Drucker, 1994, 76). However, if the bottom line is managed by management, its discipline is lost. Further, if stabilizing income reporting by management stains management's credibility, what does stabilizing income reporting by the profession through its support of retention of current GAAP do to the profession's credibility?

The costs of financial reporting

> the benefit of rational capital allocation can be far in excess of the relatively small amounts paid to make financial markets efficient.
>
> (Association for Investment Management and Research, 1993, 82)

The issuers are responsible for controlling costs, and financial reporting causes entities to incur costs. Issuers have the incentive to control those costs.

Preparation, issuance, and outside auditing costs

The most obvious costs of financial reporting are those of installing and operating the systems for recording the information, turning it into the reports, and paying for the work of outside auditors involved with the reports. Financial reporting standards overload is one of the concerns here. Issuers prefer simpler to more complex principles, everything else equal, because they are less costly to implement. But everything else isn't always equal here, either. For example, they prefer interperiod income tax allocation, a complex procedure, because it makes income reporting more stable (see Chapter 21).

Issuers also feel that too many financial reporting standards are issued too fast, and they believe that also increases their costs. Suggestions have been made, without effect, for a three-year moratorium on new financial reporting standards. In any event, the following goal in the FASB's *Mission Statement* seems reasonable: "To bring about needed changes in ways that minimize disruption to the continuity of reporting practice" (FASB, 1985c). Others agree:

> those affected will never consent to sweeping changes with all their potential for disaster ... only gradual, step-by-step improvement of accounting practice is feasible, whatever theorists prove or think they have proved.
>
> (Loebbecke and Perry, 1979, 226)

And, in general: "Experience suggests . . . that an old tradition must not be too quickly rejected; our ancestors were not all fools" (Durant, 1944, 556).

Pitt, while Chairman of the SEC, was quoted as saying that "We are incapable of replacing an entire system. . ." (Liesman, 2002, C8). That defeatist attitude is unwarranted. Changes in financial reporting, if desirable, can't and shouldn't all be done at once (except that changing the current unit of measure to one defined in terms of consumer general purchasing power, as recommended in Chapter 11, if done, would have to be done at one time for all amounts in the financial statements). That cure would be much worse than the disease. However, in due time they can all be made.

Legal costs

Users of financial reports sometimes contend that they were misled by the reports and thereby damaged, and should receive compensation from the reporting entities. They may contend that the reports presented misleading pictures of what happened or of what is, or misleading impressions of what might be expected to happen in the future. So-called soft information, information that involves judgment and estimates by those who prepare it, is most susceptible to such charges. Especially vulnerable are forward-looking information (see Chapter 17) and issuers' forecasts of the results of future periods.

Competition

Issuers have information they would prefer the competitors of their reporting entities not to have. They oppose changes that would compel them to disclose additional competitively sensitive information. That was evident in what now seems extreme:

> the [AI(CP)A's] committee on reporting recommended to the SEC [in the early 1930s] that the regulations should not require disclosure of *sales* and *cost of sales* on the grounds of competitive disadvantage.[5]
>
> (Flegm, 1984, 75, emphasis added)

Goldberg pointed out, however, that

> the sort of information [companies] would have wanted to conceal from their competitors has generally been found to have been exaggerated in importance or, as has probably more often been the case, already known to their competitors by other channels of information.
>
> (Goldberg, 1965, 223)

---

5 Nevertheless, "the first regulations promulgated by the newly formed SEC required income statements to disclose sales and cost of goods sold. . ." (Storey and Storey, 1998, 22).

The influence of the issuers

Accounting is what it is today not so much because of the desires of accountants as because of the influence of businessmen.

(Mautz, 1973, 23)

the only special interest that exerts significant influence on the rule-making process is corporate managements ... the motivation to report financial information that makes management look good is built into the system ... corporate management groups and its allies in the American Institute of CPAs and in the U.S. Congress exercise great influence—probably more than all other groups together.

(Staubus, 2003)

The issuers currently have more influence on the shape of financial reporting than any others, because they control the preparation of the reports, they hire and fire the outside auditors (the ability of a client to fire an outside auditor is the central means it has to influence the outside auditor—though that is changing—see the Epilogue), and they actively lobby the standard-setters, the regulators, and appointed and elected government officials:

all GAAP emerged from a political process ... so thoroughly dominated by managers and auditors that the users' and the public's interest have been buried.

(Miller and Bahnson, 2000, 14)

[there is] intense political lobbying against proposals that special inter-ests find to be obnoxious even though the proposed reforms are seen as serving the interests of financial statement users.

(Zeff, 1994, 26)

[Determining principles for] business combinations [was a] steady retreat before the onslaught of management, with the organized profes-sion continually underestimating the ... strength of the opposition.

(Moonitz, 1974, 54; this quotation is also used in Chapter 23)

without the widespread support of industry, significant changes are seldom possible.

(Horngren, 1972, 39)

Because of the power and influence of the issuers in the U.S., those agen-cies respond to the lobbying and the FASB is influenced. The CFA Institute (before May 2004, the AIMR), the national organization of professional users of financial reports, deplored that: "the FASB['s] flagrant departures from theory seemingly [are made] to make [standards] more palatable to ...

members of the business community" (Association for Investment Management and Research, 1993, 81). It gave SFASs Nos 15, 52, 87, 106, and 114 as examples of pronouncements it contends contain such departures.

The Epilogue discusses what, if anything, might be done about this deplorable state of affairs.

In contrast, Anton implied that the FASB hadn't tilted toward the issuers *enough*: "The corporate controller's view . . . has tended to be neglected. . ." (Foreword in Flegm, 1984, vii).

Incentives of outside auditors

> Long before [the Enron collapse] . . . [c]ompanies' desire to produce ever-rosier results for an ever-larger and savvier shareholding public compelled accountants to find ways to put the best possible spin on clients' financial reports.
>
> (Dugan, 2002, A1)

The main incentives of outside auditors are to maintain their professional reputations, to retain and increase their clientele, to increase their returns, and to minimize litigation costs. Outside auditors have considerable influence on the shape of financial reporting because of their influence on specific financial reports through their assurance function, because of their active participation in the standard-setting and regulatory processes, and because of the influence of their professional bodies.

Maintain professional reputations

Outside auditors have reputations for independence, integrity, and competence, which make their assurance function valuable. (The reputation of the profession as a whole has suffered recently because of the current spate of financial reporting breakdowns: "AICPA President Melancon stated [recently] that the accounting profession must restore its most priceless asset: its reputation" [Smith, 2003, 47].) Their professional livelihoods depend on their reputations. They are also motivated by the desire to be part of a profession that people respect. That gives them the incentive to avoid associating themselves with substandard financial reporting or to point out its substandard nature if they are associated with it. That incentive works against associating themselves too closely with the incentives of the issuers.

Retain and increase clientele

Nevertheless, because the issuers hire and fire the outside auditors under the current system,[6] the incentive of outside auditors to retain and increase their

6 See the Epilogue for a discussion of how that's in transition.

clientele gives them some incentive to associate themselves with the incentives of the issuers:

> The auditor is in an awkward position. He makes his living by pleasing management, but his societal justification requires serving investors. The resulting strain should be expected to produce ethical lapses. A ... characteristic behavior in the large, "independent" accounting/auditing firms is intense advocacy on behalf of clients.
>
> (Staubus, 2004b)

> auditors may likewise prefer reporting rules that sometimes distort economic reality. The explanation relates to auditors' obvious preferences for retaining clients: repeat audit engagements are especially profitable owing to the steepness of the learning curve.
>
> (Revsine, 1991, 19)

> The SunBeam Corporation, which last week fired its audit firm, said last night that the auditors had questioned the company's basic method of recognizing revenue as well as two specific transactions.
>
> (Norris, 2003)

> Too often the responses [of CPA firms to FASB proposals] seem to evidence views adapted from those of major clients rather than those flowing from an assessment of conclusions that will best serve the public interest.
>
> (Wyatt, 2004, 24)

Wyatt felt it necessary to state the obvious: "Practicing professionals should place the public interest above the interests of clients..." (Wyatt, 2004, 24). And listen to a Chief Accountant of the SEC:

> The profession will not reach tough unpopular decisions. Why is that? Is it because the profession has become so beholden to its clients that it will not speak to them about realism and relevance and credibility in financial accounting and reporting? Let me list only a few situations where the profession has become a cheerleader for its clients.
>
> (Schuetze, 1992, 10, 11)

Outside auditors have done considerable consulting work for their clients, and that's often cited as a reason their independence is challenged. For example, the outside auditors of Enron received more in consulting fees than in audit fees the year Enron collapsed, and the outside auditors were suspected of overlooking substandard reporting because of that. However, simply because an outside auditor receives audit fees and can be fired by its client is sufficient to challenge its independence, though possible loss of consulting fees adds to the challenge. The *Wall Street Journal* votes for the audit relationship as the culprit:

> Audit failure has an illustrious history that long precedes Enron and long precedes consulting. The problem is and ever was the audit relationship itself.
>
> (*Wall Street Journal,* 2002, A1)

The incentive of outside auditors to associate themselves with the incentives of the issuers contends with the necessity for outside auditors to remain independent of their clients in order for them to properly carry out their assurance function, maintain their reputations, and avoid legal costs. Devine said that "the auditor [is] in an extremely difficult ethical position because in some matters he is an advocate for his client while in others he functions as a representative of the public interest" (Devine, 1999, 64). The expression "between a rock and a hard place" may have been originally formulated to describe "the paradoxical relationship of outside auditors and their audit clients..." (Flegm, 1984, 126). Sterling said that the outside auditor is "in an untenable position" (Sterling, 1979, 16). Gerboth stated in contrast that

> I may be naive ... but I believe that ... [t]he incentives [of professional accountants] are right; we are paid—well paid—to do our best to make sure that financial statements present fairly.
>
> (Gerboth, 1988, 108)

The Chief Accountant of the SEC quoted above tried to improve the situation by some jawboning:

> instead of thinking simply of its clients and itself the profession needs to give some thought to the public that it serves—to the investors and creditors and employees who put up their money and their labor to make investments in the profession's clients.
>
> (Schuetze, 1992, 13)

He implied that if that didn't work, the SEC might need to take stronger action, such as the possibility of the SEC establishing financial reporting requirements or mandating rotation of outside auditing firms, which, because firms couldn't retain their clients in any event, might make them more independent (Schuetze, 1992, 14).

An alternative system that avoids the association of outside auditors with the incentives of the issuers of the financial reports they audit would be for the outside auditors to be employees of the government. That was proposed in 1933 when the SEC was being established. The proposal barely lost, by a vote of two in favor and three against:

> Colonel Arthur H. Carter, senior partner of Haskins and Sells and president of the New York Society of Certified Public Accountants, saved the day for the profession by appearing before a Senate committee

and persuading them that audits performed by private accountants were essential for the proper functioning of the [Truth-in-Securities] Act.

(Hendriksen and van Breda, 1992, 68)

The main objection to government auditors is that audits would become adversarial proceedings and thereby less effective than those conducted by private outside auditors. Nevertheless, in the wake of the Enron collapse

> Ohio Democratic Rep. Dennis Kucinich is drafting legislation that would create a new independent organization that would audit publicly traded companies. The body, operating under SEC authority, would fund itself by charging fees for the audits.
>
> (Liesman *et al.*, 2002b, A8)

Minimize legal costs

The U.S. is currently a highly litigious society—the lawyer jokes attest to that. Litigation reform hasn't yet had much effect;[7] the AICPA and others are active on its behalf. Meanwhile, outside auditors are incurring high costs in defending against and paying for settlements and judgments. In 1993, the six largest U.S. firms paid 19.4% of their gross revenue from auditing for those costs, according to a press release issued by those firms in June 1994.

Users often sue regarding financial reports when reporting entities fail, regardless of the quality of their reports. Though the reporting entities are as liable as any party for misleading financial reports, the only parties that usually have substantial assets when the reporting entities fail are the outside auditors. And the application of joint and several liability can cause the outside auditors to bear the entire cost regardless of their portion of culpability: "Members of the profession . . . cite cases where their 'deep pockets' have been opened to pay for the sins of more culpable, but now insolvent, audit clients" (Schuetze, 1992, 10). In these circumstances, outside auditors have the incentive to be associated with bullet-proof financial reports (though they don't always succeed). They prefer conservatism, treatments that minimize the opportunity for users to complain that they were misled and damaged by over-optimism caused by selection of financial reporting practices, by estimates that underplay risks, or otherwise (see Chapter 10).

---

7 "On December 22, 1995 . . . the Private Securities Litigation Reform Act became [federal] law. [However,] [t]he next step must be state tort reform" (Andrews and Simonetti, 1996, 53). In the wake of the Enron collapse,

> lawmakers want to revisit [the] 1995 law . . . "By forcing through special exemptions for securities, Congress has contributed to the 'Wild West' mentality reflected in Enron's hidden partnerships," said the [Senate's] judiciary panel's chairman, Sen. Patrick Leahy . . .
>
> (Greenburger, 2002, A8)

Users virtually never complain about excessive pessimism in financial reporting.

A new legal incentive of outside auditors has raised its ugly head with the Enron debacle. Because of that episode, Arthur Andersen & Co., one of a handful of international public accounting firms, was virtually destroyed (this is discussed in the Preface). Outside auditors obviously have the incentive to avoid having their firms destroyed.

Incentives of citizens

Citizens have an interest in private enterprise economies operating fairly and efficiently, which requires good information provided by financial reporting. They aren't organized generally to further that interest, however, except in elections, and even then financial reporting issues rarely surface. Citizens generally have to rely on the other parties to financial reporting to serve their incentives.

Incentives of standard-setters and regulators

Standard-setters and regulators of financial reporting actively shape it. Their members, especially the members of the FASB, the SEC, and the PCAOB are charged with the responsibility of protecting the securities markets and the users of financial reports, and thereby the citizens: "[FASB] members are supposed to take a larger view than the sometimes short-sighted views of preparers and their auditors, affected by concern about liability or by perceived immediate self-interest" (Kripke, 1989, 46).

The members of the bodies that preceded the FASB, such as the Accounting Principles Board, worked part time in standard setting and full time in other employment, and "[s]ome asked whether part-time board members who retained affiliations with their accounting firms and corporations were not sometimes motivated by their own self-interests" (Davidson and Anderson, 1987, 122). So the FASB was established with full-time paid members and broad representation: "The FASB was established with the intent of providing a broader representation than the APB of those groups interested in or affected by accounting standards" (Kam, 1990, 39). (Chapter 23 discusses the opposite view, that the FASB was created as a sell-out to the interests of the issuers.)

All standard-setters and regulators, including the members of the FASB, have private incentives beyond the incentive to fulfill their responsibilities to their broad constituencies. They want to maintain their reputations. They have the incentive to avoid too much controversy and not to offend those who provide support. Some believe that standard-setters and regulators lean toward those they regulate:

> standard setters . . . have been "captured" by the intended regulatees and others involved in the financial reporting process.
>
> (Revsine, 1991, 16)

Critics say the FASB's failure to address the off-balance-sheet debt question highlights what is wrong with the private sector body that sets generally accepted accounting principles (GAAP). Rather than being part of the solution, these people say, the FASB all too often is part of the problem, allowing corporations and their auditors to dominate the rule-making, at the expense of clearer financial reporting that would help investors.

(Liesman *et al.*, 2002a, C1)

Levitt and Turner [a former Chairman and a former Chief Accountant of the SEC] said that FASB ... fails to approve needed changes because they are blocked by board members appointed by the securities and accounting industries.

(Schroeder, 2002a, A4)

even accounting regulators often are persuaded to accede to the wishes of corporate managers rather than those of investors.

(Staubus, 2004b)

The Chairman of the FASB said at a public hearing on pension reporting that the FASB wasn't sure it had incorporated enough smoothing, presumably to appease the issuers (as discussed in Chapter 24). In contrast, Gerboth stated the "generous salaries and strict independence requirements add whatever additional incentives [FASB] members may need to decide issues solely on their merits" (Gerboth, 1987b, 7).

Major unanticipated reported losses by the entities that follow their standards and regulations would reflect badly on them, as the failure of the savings and loan association industry reflected badly on the regulators of that industry. They therefore want the reports to lean toward avoiding such unanticipated reported losses, toward conservatism: "Standard setters and regulators are likely to face more criticism if firms overstate net assets than if they understate net assets" (Watts, 2003, 210). They generally feel that unanticipated reported gains wouldn't harm them.

The PCAOB has thus far shown no tendency to introduce the self-interest of its members into its proceedings.

Incentives of elected government officials

Congressional involvement in financial standard-setting has been pure politics, fueled by a system of campaign financing that distorts the pursuit of the nation's legislative agenda. If members of Congress are sincere about identifying and correcting weaknesses in the standards used for financial reporting, then they should investigate the old-fashioned way: follow the money. They are likely to find a trail that leads to the nearest mirror.

(Granof and Zeff, 2002)

Elected government officials in the U.S., especially those in Congress, have the power to shape financial reporting any way they want within constitutional constraints,[8] and they have occasionally exercised that power: "Why did 11 senators crudely strong-arm Levitt [former Chairman of the SEC] on behalf of the accounting firms?" (Alter, 2002, 25).

The greatest exercise of that power was the enactment of the Securities Laws in 1933 and 1934 by the U.S. Congress. (The second greatest exercise of that power was enactment of the Sarbanes–Oxley Act of 2002; see the Preface and Chapter 22.) Those laws established the SEC and gave it the power to specify how registered entities should prepare and issue audited financial reports. The SEC has occasionally exercised that power directly, for example in prohibiting enforcement of APB Opinion No. 2 on reporting on the investment tax credit and of SFAS No. 19 on oil and gas reporting (see Chapter 19). However, the SEC usually delegates its power to the private sector, now especially to the FASB. Ordinarily, the SEC has the best of all worlds: it can sit on the side and let the private standard-setters take the heat (when the APB was the private standard-setter, Horngren said that "most of the time, the APB felt like a lone tree in the midst of 1,000 dogs" [Horngren, 1971, 8n]); nevertheless, whenever it wants, it can have its way almost simply by fiat.

The SEC and the FASB are only in the middle of the pecking order, however, with Congress and the Executive branch of the U.S. government at the top.[9] The Congress and the administration in power can and occasionally do tell them what to do, as discussed next.

Congressmen and presidents, as all elected officials, are pledged to the public interest. That was emphasized by a Chairman of the Subcommittee on Oversight and Investigations of the U.S. House of Representatives: "The best protection to assure that the FASB meets its public responsibilities is informed oversight by the SEC and the Congress" (Dingell, 1988, 2).[10]

However, elected officials want to be re-elected or to have their parties' candidates elected or re-elected. The only group interested in financial reporting that is powerful enough to affect their re-election or the election or re-election of members of their parties is the issuers of financial reports, who threaten to do so when the financial reporting issue is vital enough to them. Lobbying by the issuers on financial reporting issues, of Congress as well as of the FASB, is common. And, in spite of the FASB's pledge to the public interest, it is influenced, mainly through the SEC.

---

8 Also, for example, "The laws that underpin the current accounting standard-setting regimes in both Australia and New Zealand authorize Parliament to overturn the Standards" (Zeff, 2002, 48).

9 See Horngren, 1972.

10 However, see Chapter 18 for a discussion of how politicians bias financial reporting standard setting.

The U.S. Congress has occasionally exercised its power to shape financial reporting directly by enacting legislation on individual issues. For example, when the issue of reporting in connection with the investment tax credit arose again some years after the SEC prohibited enforcement of APB Opinion No. 2, the Congress enacted a law forbidding anyone from requiring the kind of reporting that Opinion called for in reports to agencies of the federal government. And in 1998, legislation was pending in Congress aimed at weakening the power of the Financial Accounting Standards Board. The bills, which didn't become law, were introduced after banks complained to legislators about an attempt to force companies to record the value of financial derivatives in their financial statements. The FASB nevertheless adopted SFAS No. 133, which requires what the bills were designed to fight. Finally, bills were regularly introduced in Congress to attempt to prevent the profession from enacting a standard that requires reporting of expense in connection with stock options issued to employees (see Chapter 18).

Even presidents of the United States have intervened in financial reporting standard setting on at least two occasions. President Kennedy put pressure on the SEC to prohibit enforcement of APB Opinion No. 2, so that entities would more quickly report the benefits of the investment tax credit he sponsored: "the SEC, under pressure from the Administration of President John F. Kennedy, prevented APB Opinion No. 2 . . . from going into effect" (Zeff, 1994, 12). President Clinton spoke out against the FASB's proposal on reporting in connection with stock options, because of its purported prospective negative economic consequences on some start-up companies, especially those in electronics (see Chapter 18; economic consequences of mandated changes in financial reporting are discussed in Chapter 3).

Incentives of teachers of financial reporting

> there is much common ground between practitioners and teachers, most of it quicksand.
>
> (Chambers, 1969, 747)

The main incentives of teachers of financial reporting are to educate their students well, to find time for research and writing, and to obtain tenure and advance in their profession. Involvement in improvement of financial reporting may not be high in their priorities. Nevertheless, educating students well for financial reporting means preparing them to pass the CPA exam and to practice well. Passing the CPA exam and practicing well requires more than knowing current practice. So, to prepare students well, teachers of financial reporting should teach them more than the conventional wisdom (see quotations at the beginning of this book).

Discussion questions

1 How do you feel about inquiring into the motives, the incentives, of the parties to financial reporting?
2 What part do you feel self-interest plays in the establishment of GAAP?
3 Describe the similarities and the differences between positive and normative research in financial reporting.
4 The incentives of which parties to financial reporting should be emphasized by standard setters?
5 Explain why the issuers of financial reports care so much about how GAAP is designed.
6 Do the issuers of financial reports really have an incentive to support stable income reporting?
7 Is a big bath ever justified?
8 How influential would you say the issuers of financial reports now are in the design of GAAP?
9 What role should the issuers of financial reports play in the design of GAAP?
10 How do you feel about earnings management?
11 What are the two most powerful incentives of outside auditors concerning the design of GAAP?
12 What is the relationship between the incentives of the issuers of financial reports and the incentives of outside auditors?
13 What role should government officials play in the design of GAAP?

3 Designing financial statements by starting with desired results or by applying analysis for the benefit of the users

arguments seldom meet on the level of analysis. Instead they meet only at the point of the conclusion...

(Sterling, 1970a, 3)

Two ways of approaching an issue in designing financial statements are (1) to start with desired financial statement results of possible solutions to the issue, or (2) to analyze the events and circumstances surrounding the issue and determine the ways to handle their financial effects based on the qualities that make financial statements best serve their users. Analysis should be used first. The results of using the solutions it derives should then be considered, and if they seem questionable then that should encourage a reexamination of the analysis and its underlying assumptions. (That is done throughout this book, for example, with the results of the temporal and current rate principles of translation; see Chapter 22.) If nothing else works, the issue should be reformulated or replaced by other issues: "If our present formulation of questions prohibits obtaining answers, we must reformulate those questions in order to obtain answers to them" (Sterling, 1979, 5).[1]

One observer, however, says that if a particular analysis is considered sound but its results aren't considered desirable, the analysis should be simply ignored and results considered desirable used:

the decision to classify deferred taxes as liabilities ... is correct because it reaches desirable consequences, not because a definition says so. Sometimes the conceptual framework has so much meticulous theory that it has to be ignored to reach practical results.

(Kripke, 1989, 46)

The observer doesn't say what he considers "desirable consequences" or "practical results," but he presumably means stable income reporting, because that's the result of deferred taxes (this is discussed in Chapter 21).

1 Examples of that necessity are discussed in Chapters 8, 22, and 26.

Starting with desired results in designing financial statements

> Nothing is more likely to undermine the credibility of financial reporting than the suspicion that the results reported were predetermined and the accounting methods used were selected to produce the results desired by the preparers of the report.
>
> (Solomons, 1986, 102)

The incentives of the parties to financial reporting, especially of those who currently have the most power to affect its design, the issuers, are so strong that, in spite of that warning of Solomons and the following similar warning of the FASB, "the predetermination of a desired result, and the consequential selection of information to induce that result . . . is the negation of neutrality in accounting" (FASB, 1980b, par. 100), starting with desired results currently dominates consideration of issues in designing financial statements. The usual route is to start with the financial statement results desired—usually a designer income statement—and to search for reasons afterwards to justify the solution that provides them:

> Feel-good accounting produces numbers for non-cash assets and liabilities that are the result of keeping income smooth or steady, or better yet, steadily increasing, but smoothly. To take what otherwise would be variable, lumpy earnings and smooth the earnings. (Visualize a huge yellow Caterpillar bulldozer pushing the hills of economic change into the valleys of economic change.)
>
> (Schuetze, 2001, 11)

Making the case that desired results are chosen first and reasons are then sought to justify them requires detective work. Such detective work is provided throughout this book. Some, however, has already been done for us—for example, this statement by members of the FASB staff about a formerly accepted practice:

> [Pooling-of-interests reporting] essentially is a means of rationalizing a desired end result, which is to report higher earnings without having to earn them . . .
>
> (Johnson and Petrone, 1999b, 12)

Evidence from the FASB

Storey, a senior member of the FASB staff, told me that a motto around the FASB is: "If you like the result, you will love the theory." (A parody of the results-oriented financial reporter is the tale about one who, when asked how much two and two is, answers, "How much would you like it to be?") Scanning the FASB "Action Alerts" suggests that Storey was right: the FASB avoids analysis in considering an issue; it searches for the reporting result it likes, finds it, determines and promulgates the methods required to reach the reporting result, and then attempts to justify the methods in the "Basis for Conclusions" sections of its SFASs. Evidence from those sections discussed throughout this book further suggests that though the Board usually states what it calls the bases for its conclusions, when it doesn't want to reveal its reasons it invents some other reasons that, at least on the surface, sound good, or that it hopes will never be scrutinized. The Bases for Conclusions thus appear to a considerable extent to be smoke and mirrors rather than dispassionate discussions. Examples follow.

Reporting in connection with the issuance of stock options to employees

(This is discussed in Chapter 18.)

The Board stated explicitly that it didn't do analysis in connection with stock options issued to employees. In its Invitation to Comment, *Accounting for Compensation Plans Involving Certain Rights Granted to Employees*, May 31, 1984, paragraph 155, it stated that the analysis of the transactions involved supplied to it by the AICPA was "beyond the scope of its project." It didn't supply its own analysis. It merely reached for the result it desired. (It later rectified that oversight—see Chapter 18.)

Reporting on income taxes

(This is discussed in Chapter 21.)

SFAS No. 109 requires interperiod income tax allocation with the credit balance in the balance sheet described as a liability. The board had the task of demonstrating that it is a liability. It applied three tests, based on the three characteristics of liabilities outlined by the FASB in CON6, but it didn't complete the job. Test no. 3 requires the amount to be "The result of past events or transactions." The SFAS stated that deferred tax liabilities result from the same past events that create taxable temporary differences, but it didn't say what those events are. One of those events is issuing financial statements prepared a certain way. However, preparing and issuing financial statements by a reporting entity cannot be a cause of the entity incurring a liability; otherwise, restating the financial statements could "pay off" the so-called liability. Real liabilities are serious, sometimes deadly, real-world relationships. They can't be paid off that way.

Foreign operations

(This is discussed in Chapter 22.)

A rule in SFAS No. 52 requires violation of the single-unit-of-measure rule, putting in financial statements the equivalent of the four that results from adding one yard and three feet. The Board then had the obviously impossible task of justifying violation of a rule everyone knows is inviolable.

The Board wrote that it "believes that, for an enterprise operating in multiple currency environments, a true 'single unit of measure' does not, as a factual matter, exist." But no unit of measure exists until it's defined for the purpose at hand. Moreover, if no single unit of measure could be soundly defined for multiple currency environments, sound consolidation or combination involving foreign operations would be impossible.

Defined benefit pension plans

(This is discussed in Chapter 24.)

SFAS No. 87 requires reporting of a liability for pensions to each eligible employee under a defined benefit pension plan with vesting provisions the day the employee starts working, instead of later, when the employee first vests. The Board didn't test the amounts by the requirement that a liability be the result of past events or transactions, probably because it knew or suspected that the amounts would fail the test. No past event or transaction causes a reporting entity to have a liability for pension benefits to an employee who terminates employment before vesting. The work done by the employee before vesting doesn't cause it—the vesting provision of the contract says it doesn't.

SFAS No. 87 refers to such an employee "forfeiting" her unvested pension benefits on termination before vesting. But every employee knows that she doesn't become entitled to benefits before they are vested and that she can't forfeit anything she never had (except for opportunities, such as obtaining vesting in the future if she stays that long—that's one of the things that keeps her there. However, everyone forfeits an infinite number of opportunities every day, and none of them should affect financial statements, being the difference between what happened and what didn't happen, whereas financial statements should report simply what happened).

Leases

(This is discussed in Chapter 25.)

SFAS No. 13 prohibits a reporting entity from reporting a liability if it is a lessee on a certain kind of active noncancellable lease on which some rent is yet to be paid, a so-called operating lease. The Board brought up the irrelevant issue of whether the amount is a legal liability. The issue is irrelevant because the FASB states in paragraph 40 of CON6 that "although most liabilities stem from legally enforceable obligations, some liabilities rest on equitable or constructive obligations..." Worse, an active noncancellable lease *is* legally enforceable and, contrary to some of the literature, not an executory contract, the contract having been fully executed on the lessor's side by transferring possession of the leased property to the lessee at the beginning of the lease. Further, the Board didn't apply the three tests of a liability to the amount. Had it done so, it would have discovered that the amount satisfies the FASB's definition of a *liability*.

Peeking

Starting with desired results is sometimes referred to as *peeking*: "[FASB] members . . . peek under the tent to see if there might be any big surprises" (Heath, 1988, 113). Before they analyze a problem, they peek at the results of each possible solution to see which result they like best. By that label, they seem to confess that they feel it's not completely honorable, that they should instead proceed to wherever analysis leads and then appraise the results. But human nature and the incentives of the parties intercede. Sometimes analysis is simply replaced by peeking, as it expressly was, for example, in the FASB's first treatment of reporting in connection with stock options (see Chapter 18) and its treatment of reporting on employee benefits (see Chapter 24).

Economic consequences

As indicated in the Prologue, financial reporting affects people's or business entities' fortunes, or at least people act as though it does: "a change in accounting standards that makes available more relevant and representationally faithful financial information often will have economic consequences" (FASB, 1995b, par. 84). Skinner observed that "economic consequences . . . favour the interests of one party over another. . ." (Skinner, 1987, 643). The political process, if working properly, should favor the users by making the market for the securities of the reporting entities more efficient (see the discussion of the efficient market hypothesis below). It should thereby work in the direction of achieving optimal distribution of the means for carrying on economic activity in the economy.

Proponents of a solution to an issue may advocate it because they perceive that the economic consequences of its financial reporting results are more beneficial or less harmful to them or those they serve than those of other solutions. For example,

> Some respondents to the Exposure Draft expressed concern that requiring development stage enterprises to present the same basic financial statements and to apply the same generally accepted accounting principles as established operating enterprises might make it difficult, if not impossible, for development stage enterprises to obtain capital.
>
> (FASB, 1975c, par. 48)

That argument didn't carry the day, but a similar argument (here it was more of a brawl) by high-tech companies did originally in the stock option battle (see Chapter 18). Similarly, Merrill Lynch stated that outlawing pooling-of-interests reporting

> "would prove an obstacle to a merger that both parties are eager to consummate. As a result, the wave of consolidations that has enhanced productivity, encouraged innovation, and stimulated dynamism in the U.S. economy may notably decline."[2]
>
> (Quoted in News Report, *Journal of Accountancy*, 1999b, 14)

(Would it be unfair to point out here that Merrill Lynch gets fees from helping companies merge?)

Sometimes we financial reporters or others affected act as though the sky will fall if a particular change in financial reporting standards is enacted. The most egregious case was SFAS No. 15: "In the case of FAS 15 ... I think they peeked, saw Walter Wriston, Arthur Burns, and hundreds of bankers warning of dire economic consequences, and were frightened" (Heath, 1988, 113). It's probably at least a little unfair to damn an FASB Statement by quoting its dissents, but this time I stoop to it:

> [The dissenters] point to the incontrovertible fact[3] that a modification of terms that reduces the face amount or interest rate or extends the maturity date, without equivalent consideration, is a relinquishment of rights by the creditor [and the loss should be required to be reported at the time of the modification].
>
> (FASB 1977a, Dissent of Gellein and Kirk)

A chief accountant of the SEC said that "SFAS 15 has plunged an entire generation of accountants into darkness" (Schuetze, 1992, 11). Wriston was the Chairman of Citicorp and Burns was the Chairman of the Council of Economic Advisors at the time, and they said that the U.S. banking system would collapse were those losses required to be reported currently. The users' need for timely information (discussed below) was ignored. And the efficient market hypothesis (discussed next), if sound, would have prevented such dire results in the unlikely event that such results were actually threatened.

The recent decision by the FASB to require reporting of expense in connection with stock options issued to employees has been criticized by Senator Boxer: "FASB admits that it doesn't take into account the economic impact of its decision" (*Accountancy Today*, 2003, 41). Senator Joseph Lieber-

---

2 Subsequent elimination of the pooling-of-interests method has had no such effect.
3 Would you attempt to controvert an "incontrovertible fact"? (In the history of thought, many so-called incontrovertible facts have turned out to have been nonsense.) Perhaps it's best merely to state what you think is a fact and let it speak for itself, rather than say it's incontrovertible.

man stated concerning that decision that "FASB should adopt the medical principle of 'do no harm'" (BNA Reports, 2004, G-11). However, the economic consequences of financial reporting affect the various parties diversely, and it is usually impossible to avoid doing at least the appearance of harm to one or more of them by a change in financial reporting standards. As stated in the Prologue, financial reporting should emphasize the needs of the users of the statements if the needs or desires of other parties to financial reporting conflict with the needs of the users.

Efficient market hypothesis

Wyatt points out that

> many current considerations in accounting standard setting have relationships to the efficiency of market behavior—the Financial Accounting Standards Board's focus on economic consequences and cost-benefit concerns, the American Institute of CPAs' ongoing concern about accounting standards overload and the historical thrust of standard setters to "narrow the range of accounting alternatives."
>
> (Wyatt, 1983, 56)

Whether choices of financial reporting methods have the economic consequences that proponents or opponents say they do depends, among other things, on the merits of the efficient market hypothesis (EMH), which has many supporters. Under the semi-strong form of EMH, the most relevant form for our discussion is "all public information is reflected in the market price" (Cottle *et al.*, 1988, 24). The information is said to be impounded in the stock prices almost instantaneously. If the market is that efficient, it can't be fooled by the use of one financial reporting method over another as long as all the information is disclosed. The choice of one method over another wouldn't have the economic consequences people worry about. The hypothesis also holds that once the information is impounded in the price, no one can gain further advantage from it.

The verdict's still out on the theory. Though it's supported by much research on the topic, there are some cracks in the armor of EMH. Issuers spend large sums of money to obtain desired financial reporting results:

> If EMH is valid, why do profit-motivated businessmen frequently enter into forms of transactions that aren't very profitable (when compared with alternatives) solely or primarily because those forms will produce financial statement results they believe will make their companies look better?
>
> (Wyatt, 1983, 56)

Such alternatives formerly included business combinations reported using the pooling-of-interests method.

Many investors behave as though they don't believe EMH, trying to outdo each other in using publicly available information. Proponents of the economic consequences view don't believe it, as shown by the way they lobby and report: "The furor over [the investment tax credit, oil and gas, and foreign currency translation] implies ... widespread skepticism about the efficient market hypothesis..." (Solomons, 1986, 229, 230). Moreover, these writers on security analysis don't believe it:

> "slow" ideas may emerge from apparently unrelated developments which investors will not relate to a particular company for an extended period. In essence, there are extramarket returns from analysts' greater diligence and superior understanding which are independent of the timing or breadth of distribution of the information ... To the extent that this occurs, the semi-strong form of market efficiency has not been validated ... the fact that some funds outperform their market sectors consistently by the decade is not by chance but is instead evidence that disciplined security analysis applied across different markets has a logic which can be tested and validated ... one should not assume efficient pricing but should undertake to verify it by disciplined analysis.
>
> (Cottle *et al.*, 1988, 24, 26, 27)

Also,

> "small firm effect, turn-of-the-year effect, low price-earnings ratio, junk bonds (stocks?), low-priced stocks, the Value Line phenomenon, weekend effects, performance of low beta portfolios, sector rotation, and information coefficients ... The question is: How long can the EMH continue, unrevised, against the burgeoning list of idiosyncratic phenomena?"
>
> (*Financial Analysts Journal*, 1984, 9, quoted in Cottle *et al.*,
> 1988, 26, 27)

EMH correlates relative investment success solely to the availability of information concerning reporting entities about conditions at present, about what has happened in the past, and about the opinions of people other than the investors or their advisors, such as the issuers of financial reports, about the reporting entities' prospects and what will happen in the future. It ignores the diversity of the abilities of individual investors or their advisors to use the information to form sound opinions about the reporting entities' prospects or what will happen in the future.

Some who don't agree with EMH apply technical analysis to investing, trying to outguess the market by getting clues as to future price changes from past price changes:

Technical analysis, long scorned by nearly everyone but the few thick-skinned analysts who practice it, now has an unlikely group of new adherents: the die-hard stock pickers, who base their investment decisions on a company's fundamentals rather than the stock charts. Many of these investors have traditionally scorned the technicians (and many still do). But because of the confusing bull market, some of these fundamentalists are conceding that they should adapt the arcane tools of technical research—like "moving averages"—to make sense of it all.

(McGee, 1997, C1)

The irony is that if the semi-strong version of the EMH is correct, it is so only because investors believe it is not so and use all available information as fast as possible to make a killing:

Only if a sufficient number of doubters exists can some degree of efficiency be maintained ... There is ... widespread skepticism about the validity of the EMH ... exponents of EMH are able to turn this skepticism to good account, for, paradoxically, it can be said that by leading the search for abnormal gains skeptics make the market efficient.

(Dyckman *et al.*, 1975, 94, 205)

Applying analysis for the benefit of the users in designing financial statements

after a topic is added to the [FASB's] agenda, the emphasis changes ... to considering how to do it [which] require[s] understanding of the transactions or events underlying an accounting issue, followed by analysis of alternative measurement and recognition methods.

(Van Riper,[4] 1986, 4)

Because of the strength of the incentives of the parties to financial reporting, applying analysis is usually, if anything, an afterthought in designing financial statements. Voices in the wilderness nevertheless still call for application of analysis, such as Van Riper and the following: "Complex business transactions ... call for astute analysis of their elements" (Hill, 1987, 3).

Tools[5] for analysis in the design of financial statements have been established for the benefit of the users, but they are usually promptly forgotten. The tools provided by the APB and by the FASB's conceptual framework include qualitative characteristics of financial statements, definitions of the

---

4 Van Riper was public relations counsel to the FASB. It's too bad the FASB originally explicitly rejected his advice when considering reporting in connection with issuances of stock options. See Chapter 18.
5 "concepts are tools for solving problems" (FASB, 1984a, par. 107).

elements of reporting entities represented in financial statements, operations to design financial statements, classification of events whose financial effects might be reflected in financial statements, and analysis of current GAAP by classes of events. Though the tools are weak in the face of the political forces arrayed against them, they deserve attention if financial statements are to achieve their full potential in serving their users. They are used in this book in considering issues in designing financial statements. Footnote 3 in Chapter 15 discusses why those tools aren't necessarily foolproof and need to be used thoughtfully.

Qualitative criteria

Financial statements have various qualities. The FASB refers to them as "qualitative characteristics." Some of them may be considered beneficial and some of them may be considered detrimental, depending on who is affected. Qualities that are considered desirable for the users may not be desired by the issuers, for example.

User-oriented criteria

According to the FASB:

> The characteristics or qualities of information discussed in this State-ment are ... the ingredients that make information useful. They are, therefore, the qualities to be sought when accounting choices are made. They are as near as one can come to a set of criteria for making those choices.
>
> (FASB, 1980b, par. 5)

Using them as criteria helps sharpen the analysis.

Because financial statements should serve the users as the parties of fore-most concern, the qualities of financial statements that make them most ser-viceable to users should be paramount. Those qualities can be stated as *user-oriented criteria* by which current practices and proposed solutions to issues may be judged.

Though Storey states that the FASB's "conceptual framework helps to ask the right questions" (Storey, 1999, 1, 61), some of the FASB's qualitative characteristics each ask more than one question, as discussed in the section below on "Discussion of user-oriented criteria." Criteria should each ask only one question.

The FASB goes on to state that "The characteristics of information that make it a desirable commodity guide the selection of preferred accounting policies from among available alternatives" (FASB, 1980b, par. 32). However, the FASB doesn't follow its own advice to use them as a guide, as discussed in subsequent chapters, especially in the beginning of Chapter 10.

The American Accounting Association, in its "Theory" (8–18), the AICPA, in its "Basic" (pars 85–109) and *Objectives* (57–60), the FASB, in its CON2 (Figure 1), and the International Accounting Standards Committee, in its "Framework" (pars 24–46) all stated similar lists of user-oriented criteria, variously called, for example, qualitative objectives or qualitative characteristics. Though Sprouse stated that "the final [FASB] Statement . . . of . . . qualitative characteristics . . . [has] not been, and [is] not likely to be seriously challenged," he did say it "may require an occasional polishing" (Sprouse, 1993, 51). The FASB itself said that "[the user-oriented criteria] may . . . change as new insights and new research results are obtained" (FASB, 1980b, par. 2). This book therefore provides its own list, as follows (the criteria listed, including novelties introduced and supported, are discussed after the list is presented).

- *Representativeness.* Data in the line items of financial statements should purport to represent conditions that exist or existed and events that have occurred pertaining to the reporting entity external to the reports and their underlying documentation, to be useful to the users of the reports, just as data in maps should purport to represent territories external to the maps to be useful to travelers, generals, and other users of maps:[6]

    Representativeness . . . the businessman is engaged in the manipulation of real events, real things and real relationships, and symbols are only useful to him if they represent these realities.

    (Chambers, 1969, 76, 77)

    financial statements can only provide *representations* of the phenomena that guide the decision-making processes of investors, creditors and other interested parties.

    (West, 2003, 2)

Diamond refers to representativeness in terms of symbolic communication:

Both chimpanzees and gorillas have been taught to communicate by means of sign language, and chimpanzees have learned to communicate via the keys of a large computer-controlled console. Individual apes have thus mastered "vocabularies" of hundreds of symbols. While scientists argue over the extent to which such communication resembles human language, there is little doubt that it constitutes a form of symbolic communication. That is, a particular sign or computer key symbolizes a particular something else.

(Diamond, 1992, 54)

---

6 See Chapter 4 for a discussion of how financial statements currently don't achieve this result.

If an amount violates representativeness, it doesn't symbolize any "particular something else." Such amounts wouldn't represent, they wouldn't symbolize, anything. Such reporting wouldn't "constitute ... a form of symbolic communication."

- *Relevance.* To be included in the line items of statements, data that represent external phenomena should be information, that is, they should be relevant[7]—they should bear on the financial decisions the users make about the reporting entities. For example, if a person is driving and looking for a place to sleep, a sign about a hotel contains information for the person; a sign about a restaurant doesn't. Data that don't bear on those decisions are useless to the users regardless of whether they represent external phenomena and of whether they conform with the other user-oriented criteria.

- *Neutrality.* Neutrality is a criterion under relevance. Information should be directed to the common needs of users and not the needs or desires of specific categories of users or of other parties: "information ... generally relevant to every ... possible action and end, but particularly relevant [slanted] to none" (Chambers, 1966, 156).

- *Reliability.* Reliability has two aspects:

  I   Each line item in financial statements should represent what it purports to represent, to avoid misinforming the users: they should each be reliable: "Accounting information is reliable to the extent that users can depend on it to represent the economic conditions or events that it purports to represent" (FASB, 1980b, par. 62).

  II For the users to be able to rely on the financial statements as a whole, the reports should conform with all the other user-oriented criteria. In this aspect, *reliable* means about the same as *useful*.

- *Understandability.* Reported information should be understandable to users who are reasonably knowledgeable about the kinds of reporting entities that issue financial statements. It's insufficient for users to believe they understand it when they don't. Information they don't understand is double-talk and useless to them, regardless of whether it's relevant to their financial decisions and conforms with the other user-oriented criteria.

- *Verifiability.* Information reported in the line items of financial statements should be objective in the general sense, that is, capable of being verified—substantially duplicated by independent observers observing the external phenomena being measured:

---

7 The literature is inconsistent on what information is. Some say all data are information; others say only relevant data are information. I choose the latter definition. The inconsistency is of no consequence as long as the intended definition is stated.

verifiability means no more than that several measurers are likely to obtain the same measure.[8]

(FASB, 1980b, par. 89)

An observation is objective [in the general sense] if other persons reasonably well informed would concur with it . . . [if it's] inter-subjectively testable . . .

(Chambers, 1969, 489; 1966, 147)

Another sense of the term *objective* in the design of financial statements is discussed below.

- *Timeliness*. Relevant information should be reported to users in time for them to be able to use it for their financial decisions.
- *Completeness*. Within cost and materiality constraints, all information that's reliable, understandable, verifiable, and timely should be included in financial statements.
- *Consistency*. Financial statement principles applied within and among reporting entities should be consistent and applied consistently, or the inconsistency and the effects on the financial reporting should be disclosed: "Consistency [of] estimates and judgments [is needed] as well as [of] choices from among acceptable accounting practices" (Bevis, 1965, 127).
- *Comparability*. Information should be reported in financial reports that's suitable for the central purpose of financial statements, which is to help users compare the financial status, progress, and prospects (see Chapter 16) of reporting entities in making their financial decisions. To be suitable for that purpose, the information should conform with all the other user-oriented criteria.

Several additional terms have been used to describe qualities that, if characteristic of financial statements, are said to enhance their serviceability to users. For example, in addition to several of those listed above, Herdman, a Chief Accountant of the SEC, recently used "transparent," "full and fair disclosure" (a phrase long in use), "visible," "comprehensive," and "meaningful" in a speech before Congress (Herdman, 2001). And "economic reality" was a term formerly tossed around.

---

8 Because, for example, of that definition and because depreciation is the result of a calculation but not a measurement (see Chapter 10), depreciation can't be verified. The Board contradicts that definition two paragraphs earlier:

when accountants speak of verification they may mean either that an accounting measure itself has been verified or only that the procedures used to obtain the measure have been verified.

(FASB, 1980b, par. 87)

Thus, verification doesn't necessarily mean that a measurement has been verified.

Use of the terms *transparent* and *transparency*, recently introduced into discussions of financial statements, has become a bandwagon such as those described in the Prologue. Their use has even begun to appear in discussions of other areas of communication. Each is a buzzword: those who use them never define them. The term brings to mind a window through which one can see the world. Transparent financial statements thus would be those that permit the users to see the reporting entity clearly. Because much of current GAAP violates completeness and representativeness, discussed below in the section on "Discussion of the user-oriented criteria" and in Chapter 10 (also see footnote 1 in Chapter 10), transparency is the first casualty of current GAAP.

A term that has been used to designate the opposite of transparent is *opaque*. That characterizes much of current financial reporting.

None of the additional terms used by Herdman or other terms that have thus far appeared seems to add anything to the user-oriented criteria listed above, so they aren't included in the analytical tools. Further, the remainder of this book presents reasons for believing that today's financial statements aren't transparent or visible (whatever those terms mean), comprehensive (in the sense of complete), or meaningful (in the sense of representative), and that the disclosures aren't full (in the sense of complete) and that they aren't fair (in the sense of neutral). Those who speak of "economic reality" never define that term, and it is doubtful that they mean that financial statements should be designed as they would be were all of GAAP subjected to testing by and conformed with the user-oriented criteria.

DISCUSSION OF USER-ORIENTED CRITERIA

Representativeness refers to the first of two questions that can be inferred from the characteristic of *representational faithfulness*[9] discussed in FASB, CON2:

1 Do the data purport to *represent* phenomena external to the report pertaining to the reporting entity?
2 If so, do they represent the phenomena *faithfully*?

Paragraph 63 of CON2 does mention that representational faithfulness requires the data to purport to represent phenomena, by referring to "a measure or description and the phenomenon it purports to represent," but it then immediately drops the subject. All the rest of its discussion of representational faithfulness involves faithfulness. The glossary of CON2 states that representational faithfulness is "sometimes called validity." Figure 1 of CON2 makes representational faithfulness only part of reliability.

The reason the FASB doesn't pursue the representativeness portion of rep-

---

9 This concept is also called "correspondence." Sterling concluded that neither students nor teachers of financial reporting understand the concept (Sterling, 1989, 1990a).

resentational faithfulness is that it defines the phenomena the items are supposed to represent to include simply items on worksheets, and it doesn't want to acknowledge that in print. That's demonstrated in the following conversation Sterling had with the members of the FASB when he was on its staff (he emphasizes that "this is a true story," presumably because of how incredible it is):

> [My attempt at the FASB] to draw out the implications of . . . represen-tational faithfulness was a disaster, resulting in the decision to faithfully represent worksheet calculations. As I pointed out to FASB ... this means that "12" on a financial statement would not be a faithful representation of "twelve" on a worksheet, but it would permit "Sterling is 12 feet tall" on a financial statement to be considered to be a faithful representation if "Sterling is 12 feet tall" appeared on a worksheet. I suggested that representational faithfulness should address the question of the correspondence of "12 feet" to my height rather than correspon-dence to a blob of ink on a worksheet. This suggestion was rejected by FASB . . .
>
> (Sterling, 1988, 34, n22)

Financial statements are meaningless under that interpretation of *phenomena*. If the amounts need represent only amounts in worksheets, what-you-may-call-its (see Chapter 9) would pass: "I view the failure to apply the correspondence concept to be a fatal error whereas many accountants see it as a trifling techni-cality" (Sterling, 1979, 213). Such phenomena exist only in the financial reporting map, not in the financial reporting territory (see Chapter 4).

In any event, though the FASB denied to Sterling that the phenomena to be represented have to be anything more than blobs of ink on paper, it knows that they do. In discussing representational faithfulness, it stated that "the phenomena to be represented are economic resources and obligations and the transactions and events that change those resources and obligations" (FASB, 1980b, par. 63). Further,

- Paragraph 18 of its CON1 states that "financial statements involve ... depicting economic things and events."
- Paragraphs 62 and 86 of its CON2 state that "Accounting information is reliable to the extent that users can depend on it to represent the eco-nomic conditions or events that it purports to represent" and "Represen-tational faithfulness of reported measurements lies in the closeness of their correspondence with the economic transactions, events or circum-stances that they represent."
- Paragraph 21 of its CON5 states that "Real things and events that affect a ... business enterprise are represented in financial statements..."
- The Highlights of its CON6 states that "The items in financial state-ments represent in words and numbers certain entity resources, claims

to those resources, and the effects of transactions and other events and circumstances that result in changes in those resources and claims."

Conforming to the criterion of representativeness requires the ability at least in concept to observe the external phenomena purported to be represented.

Representativeness should be the first user-oriented criterion. If some data don't purport to represent external phenomena pertaining to the reporting entity, there's no point in asking whether they're information (that is, whether they're relevant), and therefore no point in asking whether they're reliable, timely, understandable, and so on. When the question is asked (as, for example, in Chapter 10) rather than ignored, it turns out that representativeness is one of the three most violated user-oriented criteria in the design of current financial statements (the other two are timeliness and completeness, as discussed below):

> Definitions are unacceptable which imply that *depreciation for the year* is a measurement . . . of anything that actually occurs within the year.
>
> (AICPA, 1961, 24)

> The difficulty with [the FASB's] definition [of representational faithfulness] is that many of the measures used in accounting have no economic interpretation[10] . . . accounting income is the summation of many positive and negative items, many of which do not have interpretive content . . . net income . . . lack[s] interpretive significance. . .
>
> (Hendriksen and van Breda, 1992, 138, 311)

The latter statement is a sorry commentary on a profession that holds up income reporting as its most important product.

Sterling criticized Watts and Zimmerman for thinking of "financial statements as free-floating collections of words and numerals instead of as representations of things and events" (Sterling, 1990b, 101). That's a sound criticism concerning what financial statements should be, but Watts and Zimmerman were to a considerable extent right concerning what financial statements currently are.

The failure of financial reporters always to apply the concept is attributable to their indoctrination (discussed in Chapter 4), buttressed by their dislike of the results of applying the concept in, for example, reporting on income taxes (see Chapter 21) and on employee benefits (see Chapter 24), and manifest most of all in their affinity for allocation (see Chapter 10).

The faithfulness part of representational faithfulness is covered by the user-oriented criterion of reliability (I).

---

10 Amounts in financial statements that have no economic interpretation aren't "measures," as discussed in Chapter 6.

The FASB states that *relevance* "...is information's capacity to 'make a difference'..." (FASB, 1980b, par. 46), which makes the criteria of timeliness, understandability, and so on a part of relevance. In contrast, relevance is treated here as a single criterion asking one question: do the data bear on the decisions of the users? Whether the data are provided timely, are understandable, and so on, are other questions. For example, a road sign indicating a hazard ahead is relevant to, bears on, a driver's problem about how to drive. However, if it's placed too close to the hazard for the driver to act on it in time, it doesn't provide timely warning, and it's therefore useless. The highway department has to make at least two related but separate decisions concerning the sign: the topic it should cover, such as a hazard, and where it should be placed. Likewise, financial reporting standards setters have to make separate decisions concerning, for example, whether the information bears on the users' decisions and whether it's neutral, reliable, understandable, verifiable, and timely.

Determining *relevance* can involve difficulties: "we know very little about how decisions are actually made. There may be a wide variety of decision models calling for different information inputs" (Skinner, 1987, 639). It's less difficult to determine what's irrelevant—for example, a woman's height is irrelevant when buying her a bottle of perfume. Irrelevant data are discussed in several chapters, above all Chapter 10. Relevant information is discussed in general in Chapters 11, 14, 15, and 17, and in particular in Chapters 18 to 26.

Because the issuers currently have the most influence over financial reporting, the driving force behind the design of current financial statements currently is the incentives of the issuers, the strongest of which is the incentive for stable income reporting. That causes the statements to be slanted towards serving the desires of the issuers and away from serving the needs of the users, and therefore to violate the user-oriented criterion of *neutrality*: "the predetermination of a desired result, and the consequential selection of information to induce that result ... is the negation of neutrality in accounting" (FASB, 1980b, par. 100). That summarizes the basic cause of the defects of current financial statements and the most serious challenge to those who would reform it.

The FASB states that *verifiability* and *neutrality* are both required for information to be reliable (FASB, 1980b, par. 62). However, though verifiable information is best subject to investigation as to whether it meets the user-oriented criterion of *reliability (I)*, subjective information (thoughts), such as plans or predictions of the issuers of the information, which isn't verifiable, may also be considered reliable. Depending on the circumstances, it may be relatively safe to report that the person said they are her thoughts about the future, but such information (discussed in Chapters 7 and 17) should be reported outside the financial statements and labeled as such, so that the users don't take its objectivity for granted and so that it doesn't dilute the messages of the objective information in the financial statements.

(*Objectivity* and *objective* are used in their usual senses here.) Also, information can meet the user-oriented criterion of reliability (I) though not neutral, though slanted.

We financial reporters often refer to *objectivity* in a sense invented for our purposes, not in the usual sense involving *verifiability*. An amount is objective to us financial reporters if it's an aspect of a transaction to which the reporting entity was a party, and it isn't objective if its origin is elsewhere (see Chapters 10 and 14). Also, simply going through motions rather than determining the correspondence between an assertion in a financial statement and a condition or the effect of an event outside the financial statement is sometimes called verification in financial reporting, though it's not:

> merely rechecking the mechanics does not verify the representational faithfulness of the measure . . .
>
> (Storey, 1999, 1, 76)

> "auditing . . . is not a verification of the outputs; instead it is, in essence, a *recalculation* of the outputs . . ."
>
> (Sterling, 1970b, 451, quoted in Solomons, 1986, 92)

> Verification is limited to making certain that the . . . game of accounting is played by the rules.
>
> (Gerboth, 1987b, 98)

> What auditors claimed, with increasing frequency, was a duty of testing the details in accounts for conformity with data processing rules, not for consistency with commercial reality . . . The idea of authenticating the contents of periodical accounts by recourse to independent evidence [has], with the exception of cash, receivables and payables, been submerged.
>
> (Wolnizer, 1987, xi, xii)

The American Accounting Association defined auditing as concerning the correspondence between assertions in financial statements and established criteria, not between the assertions and conditions and the financial effects of events affecting the reporting entity:

> Auditing is a systematic process of objectively obtaining and evaluating evidence regarding assertions about economic actions and events to ascertain the degree of correspondence between those assertions and *established criteria* . . .
>
> (American Accounting Association, 1973, 2)

And the FASB confesses that

empirical investigation has concluded that accountants may agree more about estimates of the market values of certain depreciable assets than about their carrying values. Hence, to the extent that verification depends on consensus, it may not always be those measurement methods widely regarded as "objective" that are most verifiable.

(FASB, 1980b, par. 62)

Objectivity in the special sense (the sense that caused the FASB to place quotation marks around *objective*) is discussed as one of the current broad principles in Chapter 10.

An individual piece of information can violate the user-oriented criterion of *reliability (1)* for at least two reasons. First, it might be knowable but wrong. For example, "If a person asks the direction to a particular place and is told to turn right, whereas the correct direction is to turn left, the statement . . . conveys information, although the information is incorrect" (Goldberg, 1965, 353). Second, information might be unknowable within a required degree of accuracy and therefore unreliable if an attempt is made to state it. For example, information about the quantity of a natural resource beneath a plot of land is relevant to the owner of the land, but the information might be unreliable, and, further, it might be incapable of being made reliable within a useful degree by current technology before extracting the resource.

The response to unreliable information should be either to make it reliable within a useful degree or to eliminate it. Reliability is as essential as relevance.

Reliability and credibility (believability) should be distinguished. Reliability is a financial reporting criterion. Credibility is an auditing criterion:

> **Credibility.** Even if financial statements contain relevant and reliable data, their utility depends on whether users believe the data. This in turn depends on users' faith in the system of financial reporting and the competence and integrity of the auditor. . .
>
> (Cook *et al.*, 1986, 2)

Information can be credible but unreliable, such as that the sun rises[11] in the East (in fact, the Earth sets in the East). Or, information can be reliable but incredible, as exemplified by the information in Sterling's tale concerning blobs of ink related above. Credibility should be added by the outside auditor: the most important criterion for credibility is verifiability.

As indicated above, part of what's required to satisfy the criterion of *understandability* is that the users are reasonably knowledgeable about the

11 "Despite Copernicus the world is still Ptolemaic in its speech . . . The sun will 'rise' and 'set' when Copernicus has been forgotten" (Durant, 1944, 502; 1950, 863).

kinds of entities that issue financial statements and their affairs. However, most people who bother to use financial statements have such knowledge. "Understandability of information is governed [not only] by user characteristics [but also by] characteristics inherent in the information..." (FASB, 1980b, par. 40). In fact, the more important bar to understandability is the defects of the financial statements themselves, so that only people immersed in their arcane lore can try to understand them:

> there are words or phrases that are ... used in accounting in senses more or less at variance with the senses which attach to them in the public mind. (Value, assets, liabilities, surplus, etc.)
>
> (AICPA, 1940, 52)

> mandated financial statements are often arcane and impenetrable.
>
> (Pitt, 2001, A18)

> The literature of accounting is liberally seasoned with assertions that the pubic should be "educated" in the limitations of accounting terms and statements; even if the attempt were made, it is improbable that common sense usages and understandings could be unsettled ... conventional accounting contemplates a privileged class of people who know what the accounts mean, and an under-privileged class of people who, by virtue of common usage and understanding, believe them to be something else; yet it is the latter class—investors and other financial supporters—which the published accounts are intended to inform.
>
> (Chambers, 1966, 171n; 1969, 97)

The AICPA justified the misuse by accountants of words meant to communicate with nonaccountants by a so's-your-old-man argument:

> It cannot be suggested that the special uses in question are chargeable as misuses to the accounting profession, because they are at least as common in governmentally regulated accounting as in accounting not so regulated.
>
> (AICPA, 1940, 53)

In any event, an attempt at educating the public as to our special meanings of the words we use to communicate with them would be unsuccessful, because financial statements as currently presented are in concept not understandable except as to the procedures used to derive them (as indicated in Chapter 10). Schuetze reported that an advertisement in *The Economist* for a seminar promised to "decode published financial statements" and said that "The [financial reporter's] explanation of [the meaning of the representations in financial reports is] understandable ... only to initiated [financial reporters]" (Schuetze, 2001, 3). Hatfield quoted Withers, who said that the balance sheet is an "'impossible cryptogram with an esoteric meaning that is only revealed to an initiated caste, after much fasting and mortification'" (Hatfield, 1927, 270, 271).

Complexity reduces understandability. A central criticism of Enron's financial statements in the wake of its collapse in 2001 was that they were too complex to understand. Reporting on the Enron collapse, Berenson said that "Too often, accounting at big companies is impenetrable, or flat-out deceptive, experts say" (Berenson, 2002, WK1). Byrnes and colleagues, also reporting on the collapse, quoted a complaint of "a comptroller of a major industrial conglomerate" that

> Accounting standards have become so complicated that the challenge is understanding the complicated accounting principles rather than understanding the basic aspects of a company.
>
> (Byrnes *et al.*, 2002a, 48)

Even Pitt, the Chairman of the SEC at the time of the collapse, said, as quoted by Leonhardt, that

> "the agency's financial disclosure regulations ... too often encourage opaque reporting by companies more interested in avoiding liability than in enlightening investors."
>
> (Leonhardt, 2002, BU13)

Representative Dingell said it best, speaking about Enron's financial reports: "'One way to hide a log is to put it in the woods'" (quoted in McLean, 2001, 60).

Timeliness is the second of the three most violated user-oriented criteria in the design of current financial statements, as discussed in Chapter 10.

The FASB makes *completeness* part of relevance: "Completeness of information also affects its relevance. Relevance of information is adversely affected if a relevant piece of information is omitted..." (FASB, 1980b, par. 80). However, all the information reported may be relevant—may bear on the users' decisions—and the omission of other relevant information doesn't adversely affect that. Incompleteness, the absence of some relevant information, rather affects usefulness and can make the information misleading. It relates to the sufficient part of the requirement that necessary and sufficient information be provided (relevance relates to the necessary part). Even the FASB knows that: "A more difficult kind of noncomparability to deal with is the kind that results when ... incomplete data inputs are used to generate information..." (FASB, 1980b, par. 118). Otherwise the report can be a half truth, such as "He picked up a girl and took her home and they drank" (the girl is his daughter and they drank soda pop).

The user-oriented criterion of completeness is usually thought of in connection with the balance sheet and with disclosures. For example, Storey and

Storey illustrated completeness solely with an example from the balance sheet: "Financial statements are incomplete . . . if, for example, an enterprise owns an office structure but reports no 'building' or similar asset on its balance sheet" (Storey and Storey, 1998, 106). Also, completeness is violated by off-balance sheet financing (discussed in Chapters 2, 25, and 26). Hiding by Enron of some of its off-balance sheet financing was said to be a major reason rating agencies, analysts, individual investors, and the SEC became aware of its impending implosion in 2001 only long after it became inevitable.

However, completeness is usually not thought of in connection with the income statement, though it should be. To be sure, the FASB implicitly raised the issue of completeness in the income statement in connection with reliability: "Reliability implies completeness of information..." (FASB, 1980b, par. 79). That's correct in aspect II of reliability, in which it's virtually synonymous with usefulness. However, in aspect I of reliability, which is related to individual elements of the reporting entity represented in financial statements, information can be reliable but not complete.

So, though the FASB confines the user-oriented criteria to understandability, relevance, and reliability (FASB, 1980b, Figure 1), financial statement information can be fully understandable, relevant, and reliable, but misleading because it's not complete. In contrast, the AICPA got it right: "*Completeness.* Complete financial accounting information includes all financial accounting data that reasonably fulfill the requirements of the other qualitative objectives" (AICPA, 1970c, par. 94).

Completeness is the third of the three most violated user-oriented criteria in the design of current financial statements. As discussed in Chapter 10, its violation is the most serious defect of current financial statements other than their defective unit of measure (see Chapter 11).

Completeness is discussed in the auditing literature (SAS 32), but only to see whether all of the requirements of existing GAAP have been included, not as a criterion to test existing GAAP.

Issuers of the reports of an individual reporting entity can control *consistency* in their own financial statements by using consistent practices and applying them consistently and by using consistent estimates and judgments, or by disclosing inconsistencies and their effects on the reporting. They can't control consistency between the financial statements of separate reporting entities, because of the existence of alternative financial statement reporting practices. Only the profession can control that, by reducing the number of available alternatives (see Chapter 19).

Comparability is usually discussed in terms of comparing information:

> Information about an enterprise gains greatly in usefulness if it can be compared with similar information about other enterprises and with similar information about the same enterprise for some other period or some other point in time.
>
> (FASB, 1980b, par. 111)

Comparability is a quality of the relationship between two or more pieces of information . . .

(Storey and Storey, 1998, 114)

That might imply that consistency is all that's needed to achieve comparability. In fact, some say that it is, for example:

Comparability is achieved if similar transactions and other events and circumstances are accounted for similarly and different transactions and other events and circumstances are accounted for differently.

(Storey and Storey, 1998, 114)

comparability and its over-time counterpart, *consistency* . . . if similar things are accounted for the same way, either across firms or over time, it becomes possible to assess financial reports of different entities, or the same entity at different points in time, so as to discern the underlying economic events.

(Schipper, 2003, 62)

However, users compare financial opportunities, not financial information. Miller was the first to make that observation: "financial information . . . should enable users to make valid comparisons between the entities that are reporting" (Miller, 1978, 71).[12] Though comparability is often considered to be achieved solely by consistent use of financial statement reporting principles, comparing financial opportunities based on financial statements of diverse reporting entities that consistently use a principle of reporting the income from one kind of transaction at one dollar and a principle of reporting the income from another kind of transaction at two dollars, for example, would obviously lead the user astray:

If data inputs are ill-chosen or incomplete, the measures that result will not be truly comparable no matter how consistent the procedures are that are applied to them.

(FASB, 1980b, par. 118)

There is nothing to be gained—and much to be lost from consistently applying defective methods of accounting.

(West, 2003, 101)

---

12 The FASB reflected that view two years later in the glossary to its CON2:

Comparability
The quality of information that enables users to identify similarities in and differences between two sets of economic phenomena.

For information to serve comparisons of financial opportunities, all the user-oriented criteria must be conformed with.

Some throw up their hands about the possibility of achieving comparability, for example: "comparability—an ... unfeasible goal" (Riahi-Belkaoui, 1993, 248). Such pessimism isn't warranted. Were it warranted, issuance of financial statements should be abandoned except as accountability reports.

Figure 3.1 presents a flowchart showing how the user-oriented criteria should be applied.

TRADE-OFFS AMONG THE USER-ORIENTED CRITERIA

Many contend that not all of the user-oriented criteria can be fully satisfied at the same time, that some of them conflict, so that increasing conformity with one could decrease conformity with another. For example, "recognition may sometimes involve a trade-off between relevance and reliability" (FASB, 1984a, par. 77). Scott says that that particular trade-off seems impossible to avoid: "it seems impossible to prepare financial statements that are both completely relevant and completely reliable" (Scott, 1997, 27).

Current value is sometimes described as more relevant but less reliable than acquisition cost:

> Inexact measures of contemporaneous economic values generally are more useful than fastidious historic records of past exchanges.
> (Association for Investment Management and Research, 1993, 33)

> The introduction of a value-based system into the formal accounting and reporting system could do great harm. The loss of reliability would open the door for many more extremely subjective determinations...
> (Flegm, 1989, 95)

> analysts ... would not be happy to see historical costs removed from financial statements because they are not convinced that it would result in an increase in relevance sufficient to offset the reduction in reliability of the new data.
> (AICPA, 1994b, I, 35)

That issue is discussed in Chapter 10, which states the view that allocated acquisition cost is completely unreliable, and in Chapter 14, in which a conclusion is reached that no trade-off is necessary between relevance and reliability using current selling price reporting.

In any event, the following views are reasonable:

> any accounting method that scores zero on any one of the ... criteria would be unacceptable.
> (Staubus, 1977, 43)

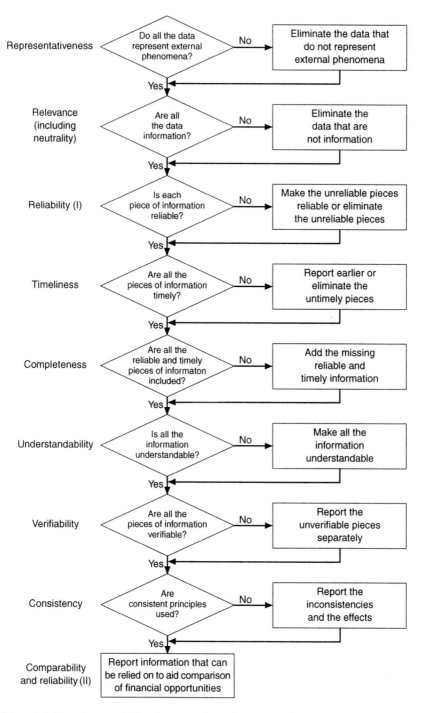

Figure 3.1 Flowchart applying the user-oriented criteria to data.

whether irrelevant numbers are reliable need be of no concern to anyone.
(American Accounting Association, 1991, 94)

Any attempt to cope with the difficulties of measuring a property known to be relevant is preferable to any attempt to measure an entirely different property instead, unless the measure of a different property is the closest possible approximation to the measure of the desired property.
(Chambers, 1966, 231)

A guess at a relevant figure is infinitely more valuable than a precise and objective irrelevancy. If one's decision theory prescribes that length is relevant and radioactivity is not, then radioactivity has zero value regardless of its precision or objectivity. A rough estimate of length has at least some value, no matter how imprecise or unobjective.
(Sterling, 1970a, 303)

Information that's relevant but unreliable, not timely, or not understandable is equally useless.

Issuer-oriented criteria

The issuers are entitled to have their legitimate needs served. They can be stated as criteria to judge the design of financial reports (though the issuer-oriented criteria have been discussed here and there in the literature, only the user-oriented criteria have been previously discussed in an organized fashion):

- *Reasonable amount of disclosure.* Disclosure requirements imposed on the issuers should serve the legitimate needs of the users but shouldn't be excessive.
- *Control of issuance costs.* Financial reports should be designed so that the costs of their preparation and auditing aren't excessive: "The information provided by financial reporting involves a cost to provide and use, and generally the benefits of information provided should be expected to at least equal the cost involved" (FASB, 1978, par. 23).
- *Control of competitive costs.* Financial reports should be designed so that the reporting entities aren't significantly harmed by access to the reports by their competitors (see AICPA, 1994a, 46, 47).
- *Control of legal costs.* Financial reports should be designed so that they don't cause the reporting entities to incur excessive legal costs, for example because forward-looking information reported doesn't turn out to have accurately portrayed the financial effects of events as they subsequently unfolded.
- *Stability in reporting standards.* Financial reporting standards shouldn't be

changed so much and so often that issuers are unable to keep up with the changes: "constituents face ... real and, in some cases, ... significant costs in understanding and implementing the Board's pronouncements" (Scott and Upton, 1991, 2).

Though issuers have incentives for high, stable, and flexible income reporting, those incentives conflict with the user-oriented criteria and are therefore not reflected in the issuer-oriented criteria.

Outside-auditor-oriented criteria

The legitimate needs of outside auditors have also been discussed here and there in the literature, but not in an organized fashion:

- *Verifiability.* The need for the information to be verifiable is as important to outside auditors as it is to the users, because it goes to the heart of the activity of auditing.
- *Control of legal costs.* Financial reports should be designed so that they don't cause outside auditors to incur excessive legal costs, for example, by preventing the reporting entities from using permissive financial statement reporting standards that could result in significantly overstated assets or understated liabilities.[13]

Criteria for the other parties

None of the incentives of the other parties to financial reporting seems worthy to be reflected in qualitative criteria for the design of financial statements. For example, teachers of financial reporting would like to have their pet theories adopted by standard setters and regulators and can't understand why they aren't: "philosophers long to be emperors, and cannot comprehend the stupidity of Providence in withholding from them their rightful thrones" (Durant, 1935, 468). That by itself isn't a sound goal for financial reporting; for one reason, their pet theories conflict, so there would be no way to implement such a criterion.

Definitions of the elements of the reporting entity represented in financial statements

The definitions of the elements of the reporting entity represented in financial statements—assets, liabilities, revenues, and so on—are among the tools for analyzing issues in the design of financial statements. Their content is

---

13 This criterion is related to the desire for conservatism, discussed, for example, in Chapters 2 and 10.

debated, so they are included in Part II (Chapter 9) of this book on issues underlying financial reporting.

Operations to design financial statements

> Understanding the economics of transactions contemplated by a proposed standard is an essential part of the analysis process.
>
> (John T. Smith, 1998, 163)

The APB stated operations to design financial statements (AICPA, 1970c, par. 176),[14] and though they have never been disputed, they have been ignored and violated. Nevertheless, they can help the profession from periodically going astray as it does. Issues whose consideration would be benefited by considering the operations, for example, are reporting on income taxes (see Chapter 21) and reporting on employee benefits (see Chapter 24). The following is the APB's statement of the operations to design financial statements:

1   *Selecting* the events. Events to be accounted for are identified.
2   *Analyzing* the events. Events are analyzed to determine their effects on the financial position of an enterprise.
3   *Measuring* the effects. Effects of the events on the financial position of the enterprise are measured and represented by money amounts.
4   *Classifying* the measured effects. The effects are classified according to the individual assets, liabilities, equity items, revenue, or expenses affected.
5   *Recording* the measured effects. The effects are recorded according to the assets, liabilities, owners' equity items, revenue, and expenses affected.
6   *Summarizing* the recorded effects. The amounts of changes recorded for each asset, liability, owners' equity item, revenue, and expense are summed and related data are grouped.
7   *Adjusting* the records. Remeasurement, new data, corrections, or other adjustments are often required after the events have been initially recorded, classified, and summarized.
8   *Communicating* the processed information. The information is communicated to users in the form of financial statements.

(AICPA, 1970c, par. 176)

Concentrating on events that way, which incorporates time period reporting rather than venture reporting, is a challenge to the matching concept of

14   Goldberg paved the way for the AICPA: "steps ... recognition and selection of the events ... measurement ... recording ... summarizing, classifying and reporting..." (Goldberg, 1965, 54).

Paton and Littleton, which is the basis of much of the thinking about financial reporting today (see Chapters 1 and 10). With individual events emphasized, the implication is that the financial effects of each event selected to be accounted for should be reported when that event occurs. The thrust of matching, in contrast, is to report the financial effects of some of the events selected to be accounted for not when those events occur but later, when other events occur whose financial effects are "matched" with the financial effects of the other events.

Classification of events

The operations are stated in terms of the financial effects of events that have occurred in the financial reporting territory (see Chapter 4) that might be reflected in financial statements. (Operations in the financial reporting map rather than events in the financial reporting territory are sometimes said to be subjects for financial statements, for example, "Internal transactions [adjusting and closing entries]..." [Littleton, 1953, 11].) To put the operations into effect, it's helpful to classify all the kinds of events that might be reported on. First Staubus (Staubus, 1961, 62, 63) and then the APB (AICPA, 1970c, par. 62) did so, and their classifications, though never disputed, have been to a considerable extent ignored. AICPA, 1973a, pars 5, 6, FASB, 1985a, par. 137, and a research report issued by the G4 + 1 Group of standard-setting bodies—*Accounting by Recipients for Non-Reciprocal Transfers, Excluding Contributions by Owners: Their Definition, Recognition and Measurement* (Westwood and Mackenzie, 1999)—did rely on the concept of nonreciprocal transfers developed in the APB's classification, the only three places in which it apparently was used; the FASB at first explicitly avoided using the concept in considering reporting in connection with stock options issued to employees (see Chapter 18). That's unfortunate, because they too can help analyze issues in the design of financial statements and arrive at sound conclusions. The APB's classification appears in Appendix A to this chapter; it's used in this book.

Current GAAP by classes of events

It's also helpful to have current GAAP stated by the classes of events to see how current issues fit in, to see how other similar events are now reported on, and to see how proposed solutions to the issues would change current GAAP. The APB provided such a statement (AICPA, 1970c, pars 181–185), which is presented in Appendix B to this chapter.

Complete and impregnable analysis for the benefit of the users

We shouldn't forget that the most complete and impregnable analysis for the benefit of the users can fall beneath the jackboot of self-interest: "vested interests ... may drown out reasoned discussion" (Skinner, 1987, 62n).

Discussion questions

1   How do you feel about starting the design of GAAP with desired results? If you oppose it, what do you think are its adverse consequences?
2   What attention should standard-setters pay to the purported economic consequences of the standards they propose to enact? What should be the primary economic consequence?
3   Do you subscribe to the efficient market hypothesis? If so, what do you believe the consequences should be for the design of GAAP?
4   Do you believe the power of the issuers of financial reports can ever be overcome sufficiently so that analysis for the benefit of the users can become the major means for determining good GAAP?
5   How important do you consider the criterion of representativeness? Do you think it should be able to be conformed with by a blob of ink representing another blob of ink?
6   Do you believe applying the user-oriented criteria would be helpful in improving the design of GAAP?
7   Should relevance include the criteria of timeliness, understandability, and the like, as the FASB presented them?
8   How important would you now say is the criterion of completeness?
9   How important should be the role of the issuer-oriented criteria and the outside-auditor oriented criteria in the design of GAAP?

Appendix A: classes of events

I   External events: events that affect the enterprise and in which other entities participate.
   A   Transfers of resources or obligations to or from other entities.

   1   Exchanges
      These events are reciprocal transfers of resources or obligations between the enterprise and other entities in which the enterprise either sacrifices resources or incurs obligations in order to obtain other resources or satisfy other obligations. Exchanges occur if each party to the transaction values that which he will receive more than that which he must give up and if the particular exchange is evaluated as preferable to alternative actions. Exchanges encompass many of the economic interactions of entities; they include contractual commitments as well as transfers of goods, services, money, and the exchange of one obligation for another. Some exchanges take place on a continuous basis over time instead of being consummated at a moment of time—for example, accumulations of interest and rent.
   2   Nonreciprocal transfers
      These events are transfers in one direction of resources or

obligations, either from the enterprise to other entities or from other entities to the enterprise.

  a Transfers between the enterprise and its owners

These are events in which the enterprise receives resources from owners and the enterprise acknowledges an increased ownership interest, or the enterprise transfers resources to owners and their interest decreases.[15] These transfers are not exchanges from the point of view of the enterprise. The enterprise sacrifices none of its resources and incurs no obligations in exchange for owners' investments, and it receives nothing of value to itself in exchange for the resources it distributes.[16] Transfers of this type also include declaration of dividends and substituting ownership interest for obligations.

  b Nonreciprocal transfers between the enterprise and entities other than owners

In these transfers one of the two entities is often passive, a mere beneficiary or victim of the other's actions. Examples are gifts, dividends received, taxes, loss of a negligence lawsuit, imposition of fines, and theft.

B External events other than transfers of resources or obligations to or from other entities.

Enterprise resources may be changed by actions of other entities that do not involve transfers of enterprise resources or obligations. Examples are changes in specific prices of enterprise resources, changes in interest rates, general price-level changes, technological changes caused by outside entities, and vandalism. In addition to their direct effects on the enterprise, these types of events also introduce an element of uncertainty into production and exchange activities. Unfavorable effects of these events may at best be insured or hedged against or provided for through policies that promote orderly adaptation to changed conditions.

II Internal events: events in which only the enterprise participates.

A Production.

Production in a broad sense is the process by which resources are combined or transformed into products (goods or services). Production

---

15 Interactions of enterprises with owners acting as customers, suppliers, employees, debtors, creditors, donors, etc., rather than as owners are excluded from this category.

16 The distinction between exchanges and transfers between an enterprise and its owners is important in financial accounting today because resources are normally recorded at the cost (see par. 164) in an exchange; owners' investments have no cost to the enterprise and are recorded at the fair value of the assets received (see par. 182, M-2). Furthermore, revenue and expenses can result from exchanges but not from transfers between an enterprise and its owners.

does not necessarily alter the physical form of the items produced; it may involve simply a change in location or the holding of items over a period of time. Production encompasses a broad range of activities, including manufacturing, exploration, research and development, mining, agriculture, transportation, storage, marketing and distribution, merchandising, and provision of services. Each of these activities is intended to result in a product with an exchange price greater than the cost of the resources used in its production. Production includes all the internal events of an enterprise except casualties. (The term *production* therefore is *not* used in this Statement synonymously with the term *manufacturing*.)

B   Casualties.

Casualties are sudden,[17] substantial, unanticipated reductions in enterprise resources not caused by other entities.[18] Examples are fires, floods, and other events ordinarily termed acts of God. Some events in this category are similar to those in category IB in that they introduce an element of uncertainty and may be insured against.

Appendix B: current GAAP by classes of events

I   External events

A   Transfers of resources or obligations to or from other entities

181. 1. *Exchanges* are reciprocal transfers between the enterprise and other entities that involve obtaining resources or satisfying obligations by giving up other resources or incurring other obligations. Exchanges may take place over time rather than at points of time (for example, accumulations of interest and rent).

S-1. *Exchanges recorded.* Exchanges between the enterprise and other entities (enterprises or individuals) are generally recorded in financial accounting when the transfer of resources or obligations takes place or services are provided.

M-1. *Exchange prices.* The effects of exchanges on assets, liabilities, revenue, and expenses are measured at the prices established in the exchanges.

S-1A.   *Acquisitions of assets.* Resources acquired in exchanges are recorded as assets of the enterprise. Some assets that are not carried forward to future periods are immediately charged to expense (see S-6C).

M-1A.   *Acquisition cost of assets.* Assets acquired in exchanges are measured at the exchange price, that is, at acquisition cost.

17 Casualties also include concealed progressive changes in assets that are discovered after substantial change has taken place, for example, damage from settling of a building foundation.

18 This definition of casualties differs from that in the Internal Revenue Code, which includes some external events as casualties.

Money and money claims acquired are measured at their face amount or sometimes at their discounted amount.

Discussion. Cash, accounts receivable, and other short-term money claims are usually measured at their face amount. A long-term noninterest bearing note receivable is measured at its discounted amount.

M-IA (1). *Fair value.* In exchanges in which neither money nor promises to pay money are exchanged, the assets acquired are generally measured at the fair value of the assets given up. However, if the fair value of the assets received is more clearly evident, the assets acquired are measured at that amount.

Discussion. Fair value is the approximation of exchange price in transfers in which money or money claims are not involved. Similar exchanges are used to approximate what the exchange price would have been if an exchange for money had taken place. The recorded amount (as distinguished from the fair value) of assets given up in a trade is generally not used to measure assets acquired.

M-IA (2). *Acquisition of a group of assets in one exchange.* A group of assets acquired in a single exchange is measured at the exchange price. The total price is allocated to the individual assets based on their relative fair values.

Discussion. Fair value of assets acquired is used primarily as a device for allocating total cost, not as the measurement basis of the assets acquired.

M-IA (3). *Acquisition of a business in an exchange.* A business acquired in an exchange is measured at the exchange price. Each individual asset acquired (other than goodwill) is measured at its fair value. If the total exchange price exceeds the amounts assigned to the individual assets, the excess is recorded as goodwill. If the total amount assigned to individual assets exceeds the exchange price, the difference is recorded as a reduction of the amounts assigned to the assets (also see S-2A and S-2B).

S-1B. *Dispositions of assets.* Decreases in assets are recorded when assets are disposed of in exchanges.

M-1B. *Asset dispositions measured.* Decreases in assets are measured by the recorded amounts that relate to the assets. The amounts are usually the historical or acquisition costs of the assets (as adjusted for amortization and other changes).

Discussion. In partial dispositions, measurement of the amount removed is governed by detailed principles (e.g., first-in, first-out; last-in, first-out; and average cost for inventories) that are based on the presumed "flow" of goods or the presumed "flow" of costs.

S-1C.   *Liabilities recorded.* Liabilities are recorded when obligations to transfer assets or provide services in the future are incurred in exchanges.

M-1C.   *Amount of liabilities.* Liabilities are measured at amounts established in the exchanges, usually the amounts to be paid, sometimes discounted.

Discussion. Conceptually, a liability is measured at the amount of cash to be paid discounted to the time the liability is incurred. Most short-term liabilities are simply measured at the amount to be paid. Discounted present values are often used if the obligations require payments at dates that are relatively far in the future. Pension obligations and liabilities under capitalized long-term leases are measured at discounted amounts. Bonds and other long-term liabilities are in effect measured at the discounted amount of the future cash payments for interest and principal. The difference between the recorded amount of a liability and the amounts to be paid is amortized over the periods to maturity.

S-1D.   *Liability decreases.* Decreases in liabilities are recorded when they are discharged through payments, through substitution of other liabilities, or otherwise.

M-1D.   *Liability decrease measured.* Decreases in liabilities are measured by the recorded amounts that relate to the liabilities. A partial discharge of liabilities is measured at a proportionate part of the recorded amount of the liabilities.

S-1E.   *Commitments.* Agreements for the exchange of resources in the future that at present are unfulfilled commitments on both sides are not recorded until one of the parties at least partially fulfills its commitment, except that (1) some leases and (2) losses on firm commitments are recorded.

Discussion. An exception to the general rule for recording exchanges is made for most executory contracts. An exchange of promises between the contracting parties is an exchange of something of value, but the usual view in accounting is that the promises are off-setting and nothing need be recorded until one or both parties at least partially perform(s) under the contract. The effects of some executory contracts, however, are recorded, for example, long-term leases that are recorded as assets by the lessee with a corresponding liability (see discussion after M-1C).

S-1F.   *Revenue from exchanges.* Revenue is recorded when products are sold, services are provided, or enterprise resources are used by others. Revenue is also recorded when an enterprise sells assets other than products (usually presented as part of a gain or loss—see par. 198).

M-1F. *Revenue measurement.* Revenue from exchanges is initially measured at prices established in the exchanges. The revenue amounts are reduced (or expenses recorded) for discounts, returns, and allowances.

Discussion. Revenue is usually recognized at the time of exchanges in which cash is received or new claims arise against other entities. However, exceptions are made, for example, for certain products that have an assured selling price (see S-6D) and long-term construction type contracts (see S-6E). Revenue is not recognized on purchases.

S-1F(1). *Recognizing revenue and expenses if proceeds are collectible over a long period without reasonable assurance of collection.* The terms of an exchange transaction or other conditions related to receivables collectible over a long period may preclude a reasonable estimate of the collectibility of the receivables. Either an installment method or a cost recovery method of recognizing revenue and expenses may be used as long as collectibility is not reasonably assured.

M-1F(1). *Measuring revenue and expenses on installment or cost recovery methods.* Under both installment and cost recovery methods the proceeds collected measure revenue. Under an installment method expenses are measured at an amount determined by multiplying the cost of the asset sold by the ratio of the proceeds collected to the total selling price. Under a cost recovery method, expenses are measured at the amounts of the proceeds collected until all costs have been recovered.

S-1G. *Expenses directly associated with revenue from exchanges.* Costs of assets sold or services provided are recognized as expenses when the related revenue is recognized (see S-1F).

M-1G. *Expense measurement.* Measurement of expenses directly associated with revenue recognized in exchanges is based on the recorded amount (usually acquisition cost) of the assets that leave the enterprise or the costs of the services provided (see S-6A (1) for a discussion of product and service costs).

Discussion. Revenue is usually accompanied by related expenses. For example, sale of a product leads to recording of revenue from the sale and an expense for the cost of the product sold. If an asset other than normal product, such as a building, is sold, the undepreciated cost of the asset is an expense to be subtracted from the revenue on the sale.

182. 2. *Nonreciprocal transfers* are transfers in one direction of resources or obligations, either from the enterprise to other entities or from other entities to the enterprise.

      a.   *Transfers between an enterprise and its owners.* Examples are investments of resources by owners, declaration of cash or property dividends, acquisition of treasury stock, and conversion of convertible debt.

S-2.   *Owners' investments and withdrawals recorded.* Transfers of assets or liabilities between an enterprise and its owners are recorded when they occur.

M-2.   *Owners' investments and withdrawals measured.* Increases in owners' equity are usually measured by (a) the amount of cash received, (b) the discounted present value of money claims received or liabilities cancelled, or (c) the fair value of noncash assets received.[19] Decreases in owners' equity are usually measured by (a) the amount of cash paid, (b) the recorded amount of noncash assets transferred, or (c) the discounted present value of liabilities incurred.

    Discussion. Measurement of owners' investments is generally based on the fair value of the assets or the discounted present value of liabilities that are transferred. The market value of stock issued may be used to establish an amount at which to record owners' investments but this amount is only an approximation when the fair value of the assets transferred cannot be measured directly.

S-2A.   *Acquisition of a business as a whole through issuance of stock.* The acquisition of a business as a whole by an enterprise through the issuance of stock is recorded when it occurs. (See S-2B for a discussion of poolings of interests.)

M-2A.   *Acquisition of a business through issuance of stock measured.* A business acquired through issuance of stock is measured at the fair value of the business acquired. Each individual asset acquired (other than goodwill) is measured at its fair value. If the fair value of the whole business exceeds the amounts assigned to the individual assets, the excess is recorded as goodwill. If the total assigned to individual assets exceeds the fair value of the whole business, the difference is recorded as a reduction of the amounts assigned to the assets.

S-2B.   *Poolings of interests.* Business combinations effected by issuance of voting common stock that also meet other specified criteria are accounted for as poolings of interests and not as acquisitions of one business by another. A business combination accounted for as a pooling of interests is accounted for when it occurs.

---

19 The fair value of assets received is often measured by the fair value of the shares of stock issued.

M-2B.   *Poolings of interests measured.* The assets, liabilities, and elements of
owners' equity of the separate companies generally become the
assets, liabilities, and elements of owners' equity of the combined
corporation. They generally are measured at the time of
combination by the combined corporation at the amounts at
which they were then carried by the separate companies. The
revenue and expenses of the combined corporation for the period
in which the companies are combined include the revenue and
expenses of the separate companies from the beginning of the
period to the date of combination. Financial statements for prior
periods presented in reports of the combined corporation combine
the financial statements of the separate companies.

S-2C.   *Investments of noncash assets by founders or principal stockholders of a
corporation.* Transfers of noncash assets to a corporation by its
founders or principal stockholders are recorded when they occur.

M-2C.   *Founders or principal stockholders investments of noncash assets measured.*
Transfers of noncash assets to a corporation by its founders or
principal stockholders are sometimes measured at their costs to
the founders or principal stockholders rather than at their fair
value at the date of transfer.

b.   *Nonreciprocal transfers between an enterprise and entities other than
owners.* Examples are gifts and donations, taxes, loss of a
negligence lawsuit, imposition of fines, and theft.

S-3.   *Nonreciprocal transfers recorded.* Nonreciprocal transfers with other than
owners are recorded when assets are acquired (except that some
noncash assets received as gifts are not recorded), when assets are
disposed of or their loss is discovered, or when liabilities come into
existence or are discovered.

M-3.   *Nonreciprocal transfers measured.* Those noncash assets received in
nonreciprocal transfers with other than owners that are recorded are
measured at their fair value on the date received. Noncash assets given
are usually accounted for at their recorded amount. Liabilities imposed
are measured at the amount to be paid, sometimes discounted.

183. B.   *External events other than transfers of resources or obligations to or from
other entities.* Examples are changes in specific prices of enterprise
assets, changes in interest rates, general price-level changes,
technological changes caused by outside entities, and damage to
enterprise assets caused by others.

S-4.   *Favorable external events other than transfers generally not recorded.* External
events other than transfers that increase market prices or utility of
assets or decrease amounts required to discharge liabilities are
generally not recorded when they occur. Instead their effects are
usually reflected at the time of later exchanges.

M-4.   *Retention of recorded amounts.* Assets whose prices or utility are increased
by external events other than transfers are normally retained in the

accounting records at their recorded amounts until they are
exchanged. Liabilities that can be satisfied for less than their recorded
amounts because of external events generally are retained in the
records at their recorded amounts until they are satisfied.

S-4A.   *Some favorable events recorded.* Examples of the few exceptions to
principle S-4 are (1) increases in market prices of marketable
securities held by investment companies and (2) decreases in
the amounts required currently to satisfy liabilities to provide
services or deliver resources other than U.S. dollars, for
example, foreign currency obligations and obligations under
warranties.

M-4A.   *Measuring favorable events.* Recorded increases in market prices
are measured by the difference between the recorded amount
of the securities and the higher market price. Recorded
decreases in liabilities are measured by the difference between
the recorded amounts of the liabilities and the lower amounts
estimated to be required to satisfy them.

S-5.   *Unfavorable external events other than transfers recorded.* Certain
unfavorable external events, other than transfers, that decrease market
prices or utility of assets or increase liabilities are recorded.

M-5.   *Measuring unfavorable events.* The amounts of those assets whose
decreased market price or utility is recorded are adjusted to the lower
market price or recoverable cost resulting from the external event.
Discussion. Recording unfavorable external events other than transfers
varies depending on the type of asset or liability and is governed by
specific rules. The major rules are described below.

S-5A.   *Cost or market rule for inventories.* A loss is recognized by
application of the rule of lower of cost and market to
inventories when their utility is no longer as great as their cost.

M-5A.   *Measuring inventory losses under the cost or market rule.*
Replacement price is used in measuring the decline in price
of inventory except that the recorded decline should not result
in carrying the inventory at an amount that (1) exceeds net
realizable value or (2) is lower than net realizable value
reduced by an allowance for an approximately normal profit
margin.

S-5B.   *Decline in market price of certain marketable securities.* If market
price of marketable securities classified as current assets is less
than cost and it is evident that the decline is not due to a
temporary condition a loss is recorded when the price
declines.

M-5B.   *Measuring losses from decline in price of marketable securities.* The
loss on a price decline of marketable securities is measured by
the difference between the recorded amount and the lower
market price.

S-5C.   *Obsolescence.* Reductions in the utility of productive facilities caused by obsolescence due to technological, economic, or other change are usually recognized over the remaining productive lives of the assets. If the productive facilities have become worthless the entire loss is then recognized.

M-5C.   *Measuring obsolescence.* Obsolescence of productive facilities is usually measured by adjusting rates of depreciation, depletion, or amortization for the remaining life (if any) of the assets. If productive facilities have become worthless, unamortized cost is recognized as a current loss.

Discussion. In unusual circumstances persuasive evidence may exist of impairment of the utility of productive facilities indicative of an inability to recover cost although the facilities have not become worthless. The amount at which those facilities are carried is sometimes reduced to recoverable cost and a loss recorded prior to disposition or expiration of the useful life of the facilities.

S-5D.   *Damage caused by others.* The effects of damage to enterprise assets caused by others are recorded when they occur or are discovered.

M-3D.   *Measuring damage caused by others.* When enterprise assets are damaged by others, asset amounts are written down to recoverable costs and a loss is recorded.

S-5E.   *Decline in market prices of noncurrent assets generally not recorded.* Reductions in the market prices of noncurrent assets are generally not recorded until the assets are disposed of or are determined to be worthless.

M-5E.   *Retention of recorded amount.* Noncurrent assets whose market prices have declined are generally retained in accounting records at their recorded amounts until they are disposed of or have become worthless.

Discussion. In unusual circumstances a reduction in the market price of securities classified as noncurrent assets may provide persuasive evidence of an inability to recover cost although the securities have not become worthless. The amount at which those securities are carried is sometimes reduced and a loss recognized prior to disposition of the securities.

S-5F.   *Increases in amounts required to liquidate liabilities other than those payable in U.S. dollars recorded.* Increases in the amounts required currently to satisfy liabilities to provide services or deliver resources other than U.S. dollars, for example, foreign currency obligations and obligations under warranties, are often recorded. Increases in amounts required currently to liquidate liabilities payable in U.S. dollars because of changes in interest rates or other external factors are generally not recorded until the liabilities are liquidated, converted, or otherwise disposed of.

M-5F. *Liability increases measured.* Recorded increases in liabilities from external events other than transfers are measured at the difference between the recorded amount of the liabilities and the higher amounts estimated to be required to satisfy them.

II Internal Events

184. A. *Production.* Production in a broad sense is the economic process by which inputs of goods and services are combined to produce an output of product which may be either goods or services. Production in this sense is therefore *not* restricted to manufacturing operations, but includes activities such as merchandising, transporting, and holding goods.

S-6. *Production recorded.* Utility added to assets by the internal profit-directed activities of the enterprise is generally not recorded at the time of production. Instead, historical or acquisition costs, including costs of the production process, are shifted to different categories of assets or to expenses as events in the enterprise indicate that goods and services have been used (either partially or completely) in production operations of the period. The costs that continue to appear in asset categories are deducted from revenue when the products or services to which they have been related are sold at a later date (see S-1G).

M-6. *Production measurement.* Utility created by production is generally not measured at the time of production. Instead, previously recorded amounts (usually acquisition costs) are shifted or allocated between asset categories or between activities or periods in a systematic and rational manner.

Discussion. Accounting for production encompasses much of the internal accounting for the enterprise. Accounting to determine costs of manufacturing products and providing services (cost accounting) is a part of production accounting in general. The purpose of production accounting is to relate costs to revenue when the product is sold or services provided or to relate costs to particular accounting periods.

S-6A. *Costs of manufacturing products and providing services.* Costs of manufacturing products and providing services during a period include (1) costs of assets that are completely used during the period in manufacturing products and providing services and (2) allocated portions of the costs of assets that are partially used during the period in manufacturing products and providing services, assigned in a systematic and rational manner to those activities.

M-6A. *Measuring costs of manufacturing products and providing services.* Costs of manufacturing products and providing services are measured at the recorded amounts (usually acquisition costs) of assets used directly and by allocations in a systematic and rational manner of recorded amounts of assets used indirectly. *Discussion.* Cost accounting often involves shifts and allocations of acquisition costs. The shifts and allocations are based on observed or assumed relationships between the assets used and the activities of manufacturing products or providing services. An example of a shift to a different category is the shift of costs from raw materials inventory to work in process inventory. Examples of allocated costs are overhead costs such as power, indirect labor, repair costs, and depreciation of plant and equipment.

S-6A(1). *Product and service costs.* Costs assigned to products and services provided are those costs of manufacturing products and providing services that are considered productive, including direct costs and indirect costs (absorbed overhead). Costs of manufacturing products and providing services for a period that are not assigned to product or service costs are charged to expense during the period, for example, unabsorbed overhead.

M-6A(1). *Measuring product and service costs.* Product and service costs are measured by the sum of productive costs of manufacturing products and providing services assigned to units of product or service in a rational and systematic manner.

S-6B. *Expenses from systematic and rational allocation.* Some expenses are associated with accounting periods by allocating costs of assets over their useful lives.

M-6B. *Determination of expenses by systematic and rational allocation.* These expenses are allocations of the recorded amount of assets in a systematic and rational manner to the period or periods of the assets' lives.

Discussion. If all the benefits of an asset are related to one period, the recorded amount of the asset is charged as expense in that period. If the asset will benefit several periods, the recorded amount is charged to expense in a systematic and rational manner over the periods involved. Depreciation, depletion, and amortization of long-lived assets are examples of amounts allocated to periods as expenses (excluding amounts allocated to costs of manufacturing products and providing services, see S6A).

S-6C. *Expenses recognized immediately.* The costs of some assets are charged to expense immediately on acquisition.

M-6C. *Measurement of expenses recognized immediately.* Expenses from immediate recognition are measured at the acquisition prices of the assets acquired.

Discussion. Enterprises never acquire expenses per se; they always acquire assets. Costs may be charged to expenses in the period goods or services are acquired either under this principle of immediate recognition or, if they only benefit the period in which they are acquired, under the principle of systematic and rational allocation (see S-6B). Examples of costs that often are charged to expense immediately are salaries paid to officers and payments for advertising.

S-6D.   *Revenue at completion of production.* Revenue may be recorded at the completion of production of precious metals that have a fixed selling price and insignificant marketing costs. Similar treatment may also be accorded certain agricultural, mineral, and other products characterized by inability to determine unit acquisition costs, immediate marketability at quoted prices that cannot be influenced by the producer, and unit interchangeability.

M-6D.   *Revenue measured by net realizable value of product.* Revenue recorded at completion of production is measured by the net realizable value of the product.

Discussion. Recognition of revenue at completion of production is an exception to principles S-1F and S-6. The net realizable value of product is its selling price less expected costs to sell.[20]

S-6E.   *Revenue as production progresses.* Revenue from cost-plus-fixed-fee and long-term construction-type contracts is recognized as production progresses using the percentage-of-completion method if the total cost and the ratio of performance to date to full performance can be reasonably estimated and collection of the contract price is reasonably assured. When the current estimate of total contract costs indicates a loss on long-term construction-type contracts, in most circumstances provision is made for the loss on the entire contract.

M-6E.   *Measuring revenue as production progresses.* Under cost-plus-fixed-fee contracts, revenue recognized as production progresses includes either reimbursable costs and an allocated portion of the fee or an allocated portion of the fee alone. Under long-term construction-type contracts, revenue recognized as production progresses is measured at an allocated portion of the predetermined selling price. Product or service cost is subtracted from revenue as an expense as production progresses for long-term construction-type contracts and for those cost-plus-fixed-fee contracts for which recorded revenue includes reimbursable costs.

20 See par. 152, footnote 45, for a discussion of income statement treatment of revenue recognized at completion of production.

> *Discussion.* Recognition of revenue as production progresses is another exception to principles S-1F and S-6.

185. B. *Casualties.* Casualties are sudden, substantial, unanticipated reductions in enterprise assets not caused by other entities. Examples are fires, floods, and abnormal spoilage.

S-7. *Casualties.* Effects of casualties are recorded when they occur or when they are discovered.

M-7. *Measuring casualties.* When casualties occur or are discovered, asset amounts are written down to recoverable costs and a loss is recorded.

4 The indoctrination of financial reporters

> Initial indoctrination and its reinforcement by adherence to so-called generally accepted principles have diverted accountants from seeing for themselves that ... the conventional processes yield ... gibberish.
>
> (Chambers, 1987, 105)

We financial reporters are indoctrinated with the idea that financial reporting is different from everything else, that it's exempt from the constraints to which all other disciplines are subject, as though it resides in a parallel universe:

> accountants ... foster the partition of accounting from other related subjects; their arguments frequently ... seem ... to imply that accounting is an independent discipline or set of operations...
>
> (Chambers, 1969, 17)

> When accounting is based on imaginary concepts—such as cost allocations, future economic benefits and the sums yielded by invalid aggregations—it is segregated from the realm of knowledge-based disciplines and the precepts they provide.
>
> (West, 2003, 65)

> "Accounting practice enjoys a peculiar insulation from the conventional idea in Western law that consumers may presume goods and services to possess the characteristics making them fit for the uses commonly made of them."
>
> (Clarke et al., 1997, 242, quoted in West, 2003, 181; this quotation also appears in the Epilogue)

Both Sterling and Chambers refer to "the isolation of accounting..." (Sterling, 1989, 90n; Chambers, 1987, 105).

We are indoctrinated at the beginning of our education as financial reporters to swallow all the defects of financial reporting without complaint, almost without notice:

our first impressions linger on ... A good accountant will strive to adapt them ... but he cannot shake them off. The child is father to the man ... even when the man is an accountant.

(Baxter, 1966, 6)

I ... resolved to ... try not to be influenced by my accounting upbringing ... Whether I or any other accountant can be successful in this quest is ... questionable.

(Lee, 1979, 35)

Your author was personally subject to this indoctrination and will never be able to fully rid himself of it. Similarly,

Many women pursuing the feminist ideals of our time are painfully aware that much of the value system which they have unequivocally rejected continues to operate within them from their past training and indoctrination. Despite their intellectual commitment to a feminist equality, they still carry these abandoned and despised biases from a past from which few are ever capable of completely freeing themselves.

(Gaylin, 1984, 71, 72)

Only by understanding our indoctrination can we see why we acquiesce to answers currently given to the issues in financial reporting that otherwise defy understanding, as discussed in the section below on manifestations of the indoctrination of financial reporters and throughout this book.

Origin of the indoctrination of financial reporters

the standard textbook and curriculum foist on their consumers a peculiar and in-bred dogma. . . .

(Chambers, 1987, 101)

The origin of our indoctrination in nonsense is a matter of conjecture. The following is my conjecture. Following it is Sterling's conjecture.

In my view, the origin is our training in debits and credits, which now have no counterparts outside record keeping, at the beginning of our education as financial reporters. *Debits* and *credits* used to mean receivables debtors owe to the reporting entity and payables it owes to its creditors:

the terms "debit" and "credit" are thought to have entered the vocabulary of accounting when, during the Renaissance, Genoese and Venetian merchants and bankers recorded the amounts owed to them by debtors and by them to creditors.

(Staubus, 1977, 139)

Now, rather than being representations of anything pertaining to reporting entities, debits and credits take on a disjointed life of their own: simply, an increase in a debit account is a debit and an increase in a credit account is a credit; a decrease in a debit account is a credit and a decrease in a credit account is a debit. A debit amount in a balance sheet is good, but a debit amount in a statement of income is bad. Most credit amounts in a balance sheet are bad, but a credit amount in a statement of income is good. None of it makes any apparent sense, so it has to be memorized.

That's why such a large percentage of first-semester accounting students fail: they rebel against learning nonsense. After the students who stay anyway memorize and accept something that makes no sense, they are willing to accept anything, and nothing after that need make any sense:

> to many accountants there is something hypnotic about debit and credit that sometimes leads to mystical attitudes and expressions.
>
> (Devine, 1985a, 4)

Our training takes us into the arena of debits and credits and financial reports and out of the arena of reporting entities, the arena beyond record keeping, and we never get back in that arena beyond. The landscape of debits and credits becomes reality for budding financial reporters and remains reality for leaders of the profession. Defliese, who was chairman of an international firm of CPAs and president of the AICPA, attempted to prove the worth of deferred taxes by tying it to bookkeeping:

> Our bookkeeping origins tell us that a "balance sheet" is a list of account balances after the year's profit or loss is determined. Are we moving in a completely new direction?
>
> (Defliese, 1983, 96; also quoted in Chapter 7)

That explains, for example, why the financial reporting map (debits, credits, and so on) is treated as the financial reporting territory, as discussed below.

Sterling has a different take:

> In the elementary course we face naive accountants and have some difficulty hammering home the idea that the balance sheet is a statement of unexpired costs, not values. The elementary students have their thinking disrupted and are often confused. In graduate seminars we face sophisticated accountants and have some difficulty hammering home the idea that the balance sheet could be a statement of values, not unexpired costs. The graduate students also have their thinking disrupted and are often confused. We can avoid the second disruption by not teaching current values to graduate students or, for future generations, we can avoid both disruptions by not teaching unexpired costs to

elementary students. If the objective is to minimize disruption, the latter is clearly preferable.

(Sterling, 1979, 88n)

(Chapter 10 discusses the concept of unexpired costs.)

One thing that isn't a matter of conjecture is that we are indoctrinated in nonsense, early in our training: "each of us was trained in ... moonshine chasing..." (Arthur L. Thomas, 1979, 28, 29). That's the only way to understand the oddities discussed in the next section.

Manifestations of the indoctrination of financial reporters

Ordinary folk think that we accountants are practicing a dark art.

(Schuetze,[1] 2001, 24)

Our indoctrination is manifest in a number of ways.

Ideas not observed

Assuming the validity of any or all of the ideas to which I subscribe listed in the Prologue, each of which I state isn't conformed with—at least occasionally—today in financial reporting or in the financial reporting literature (I believe they are all valid), our tolerance of each such nonconformance is a manifestation of the indoctrination of us financial reporters. For example, concerning the violation of a rule of arithmetic referred to there, Chambers said, "In no other discipline is [the] disregard of a basic mathematical rule tolerated" (Chambers, 1969, 257).

Doublethink

Financial reporters are able because of their indoctrination to believe and act on one thing in their personal lives and the opposite in their professional lives. For example,

- Everyone understands in one's personal life that presentation of history is a recitation and analysis of only past events (though the recitation of past events and the interpretation of those events and later events may be relevant to later actions). However, we financial reporters believe in our professional life that presentation of history is a recitation and analysis of both past and future events (as discussed in Chapters 7 and 12). Convincing us of that is a remarkable feat of indoctrination.

---

1 Schuetze was Chief Accountant at the SEC.

- Everyone knows in one's personal life that there is inflation and deflation, sometimes moderate and sometimes more or less severe. However,

> U.S. accountants have ... pretended for decades, if not an entire century, that inflation does not cause the value of the dollar to decay as time passes.
>
> (Miller and Banhson, 2002b, 245)

> most accountants and users of financial statements have been *inculcated* with a model of financial reporting that assumes stability of the [general purchasing power of the] monetary unit...
>
> (FASB, 1986, [SFAS No. 89] Lauver dissent, emphasis added; also quoted in Chapter 6)

That model assumes that there is never any inflation or deflation in the economy.

The thesaurus shows *indoctrinated* and *brainwashed* as synonyms of *inculcated*. West states that students are initially inculcated:

> accounting procedures are taught while the means for evaluating them are withheld until the procedures have been thoroughly inculcated.
>
> (West, 2003, 2)

Schuetze says that financial reporting shouldn't be based

> on ... inculcation. The way it is now, however, to be fully conversant with all of the financial accounting and reporting requirements means that one has to live in a medieval, unheated, stone building in the Pyrenees, wear a brown robe with a rope belt, a skull cap, and clogs, and memorize accounting literature (dogma).
>
> (Schuetze, 2001, 3, 4)

- Everyone knows in one's personal life that the single-unit-of-measure rule, which forbids, for example, putting four as the sum of one yard and three feet into the design of a bridge (or the bridge will fall down), is inviolable. However, financial reporters don't object to being required by SFAS No. 52 to violate the rule throughout financial statements that involve foreign operations, making the statements meaningless and worthless (this is discussed in Chapter 22).
- Though financial reporters predict in preparing financial statements (which are supposed to be historical reports [see Chapter 7], and therefore should be prepared without prediction) and know that they predict, they deny it to themselves and to the world:

Accruals and deferrals are necessary for proper accounting for assets, liabilities, earnings, etc., but they often require allocations and estimates of future transactions. Care must be taken to see that their use not be extended to permit "normalization" of earnings between periods. Normalization, like forecasts and projections, is the province of financial analysis and should not be incorporated into financial reporting.

(AICPA, 1994b, I, III, 2. c, 43)

What are "estimates of future transactions" if not "forecasts"—predictions? (See the discussion of the term *estimate* in Chapter 6.)

- We financial reporters contend that financial statements should be transparent. Herdman, a Chief Accountant of the SEC, recently used "transparent" in a speech before Congress (Herdman, 2001). The term brings to mind a window through which one can see the world. Transparent financial statements thus would be those that permit the users to see the reporting entity clearly. Nevertheless, the FASB defined an element, "willing parties," of a key concept, *fair value*, as hypothetical, fiction:

  Willing parties are all hypothetical marketplace participants (buyers and sellers) that have utility for the item being measured and that are willing and able to transact, having the legal and financial ability to do so.

  (FASB, 2003b; see also Chapter 14)

  There is no way to see the reporting entity clearly if an element of them is defined as fiction.
- The FASB incorporated contradictory ideas into a single phrase: "credit-adjusted risk-free rate" (FASB, 2001c, par. 8), though they know that a risk-free rate by definition doesn't involve credit risk.
- In its SFAS No. 5, paragraph 8, the FASB defines a "loss contingency" as one in which "a liability *had been incurred* by the reporting date" (emphasis added), though they know there is nothing contingent about such a loss or liability (see also footnote 1 in Chapter 15).
- The FASB requires a reporting entity to report a liability if it has issued a guarantee that obliges the reporting entity "to stand ready to perform over the term of the guarantee in the event that the specified triggering events or conditions occur..." which it describes as a "noncontingent aspect ... even [if] it is *not* probable that payments will be required under that guarantee" (FASB, 2002a, pars 8, 9). That requirement violates the FASB's own definition of *liabilities*:

  probable future sacrifices of economic benefits arising from present obligations of a particular entity to transfer assets or provide services to other entities in the future as a result of past transactions or events.

  (FASB, 1985a, par. 35)

First, the requirement holds that the triggering events may be "not probable," so the future sacrifices involved, if any, may not be "probable future sacrifices." Second, the future sacrifices, if any, wouldn't be simply the "result of past transactions or events." They would be partly the result of events to occur after the reporting date, the "triggering events." Though standing ready to perform isn't contingent, the future sacrifices are contingent, not noncontingent, but the definition requires the sacrifices to be noncontingent.

Orwell called such behavior "doublethink" in his novel *1984*. Sterling refers to it as "cognitive dissonance . . . the cognition of a particular problem was completely insulated from a similar problem . . ." (Sterling, 1967, 109), so you are able to hold contradictory beliefs. How much service can a profession provide if its practitioners hold contradictory beliefs, if they engage in doublethink?:

> laymen with no knowledge of accounting may be deceived or, if they know the truth, may tend to regard accounting as the weirdest of professions.
>
> (MacNeal, 1970, x)

> "When you come out of a liberal arts background, you want to know why something is the way it is. [In financial reporting,] there is no reason why. There is no fundamental truth underlying it. It's just based on rules."
>
> (Bethany McLean, quoted in Barringer, 2002)

The map *is* the territory

An analogy between financial reporting and mapping is apt (as discussed in Chapter 1). A key rule of map-making, which should be observed in preparing financial statements as elsewhere, is that *the map is not the territory*: "The mistake of confusing the map with the territory is well known in economics and science . . ." (Sterling, 1990b, 101).

However, under current GAAP, that rule isn't observed consistently. We often observe this rule instead: *the map is the territory*:

> there is a tendency for people who work closely with models to begin to confuse the symbols in models with the phenomena that those symbols represent.
>
> (Sterling, 1987, 53)

> The analogy between cartography and accounting is apt, but the essential implications of it for accounting appear to have eluded the FASB.
>
> (Wolnizer, 1987, 3)

accountants . . . often failed to distinguish assets in the real world from the entries in the accounts and financial statements . . . Just as a cartographer cannot add roads, bridges, and lakes where none exist, an accountant cannot add imaginary items to financial statements without spoiling the representational faithfulness, and ultimately the usefulness, of the information.

(Storey and Storey, 1998, 62, 105)

Behaviors such as costs flowing, costs attaching, cost recovery, and costs expiring that occur only in the financial reporting map, not in the financial reporting territory, are examples of such "imaginary items"; they occur only in the minds of accountants (see Chapter 10).

We are so mesmerized by the flowing, attaching, matching, and allocating that goes on only in our minds that we think it's the reality we are reporting on. Assets and liabilities are thought of as in the map in addition to the territory: the APB and the FASB referred to them as elements of financial statements in addition to elements of the reporting entities represented in financial statements (see Chapter 9). With assets, liabilities, revenue, and expenses thought to exist and occur in the records and the statements—the map—it's easy to see how we could accept that costs behave and are assets (see Chapter 10), neither being outside record keeping. The financial statements seem to be the reality we report on in the financial statements (see Figure 4.1); the reporting entity itself seems beside the point.

During a discussion of the deferred method of interperiod income tax allocation at a meeting of the APB, the AICPA Director of Accounting Research said that there is no such thing as a deferred credit to expense. A member of the APB, the chairman of his international firm of CPAs, said, "Oh, yes there is. Most of my clients have them, right in their balance sheets." Again, the map is the territory.

In the financial reporting territory, in the real world, cause and effect either works simultaneously or forward in time. However, in the current

Figure 4.1 Dilbert in accounting department (copyright 1990 United Feature Syndicate, Inc., reproduced by permission).

financial reporting map, in the minds of present-day financial reporters, future events can cause current conditions—cause and effect can work backwards in time, the future can change the past! For example, Kirk, a former chairman of the FASB, said of pension benefits that "future salary increases have retroactive effects on the benefit earned..." (Kirk, 1990, 89)—though a future event in the financial reporting territory (such as a future salary increase) can't be the cause of, can't affect, can't have a retroactive effect on, a present condition (such as a liability for a benefit earned) (see Chapters 7 and 24). Financial reporters think that way because they have allowed the make-believe world of economists to contaminate financial reporting (see Chapters 1, 7, and 12).

Because the future doesn't exist at present except as a useful concept in people's imaginations (see Chapter 7), thoughts about the future, the foundation of much of today's financial reporting, exist only in the financial reporting map and map nothing about reporting entities. So the foundation of much of today's financial reporting tells us nothing about the financial reporting territory, about the reporting entity.

Crooch and Upton state that "The residual interest—the stockholders' equity—can approach, but can't go below, zero" (Crooch and Upton, 2001, 6; also quoted in Chapter 15). That passage confuses the map and the territory. Stockholders' equity is in the balance sheet (see Chapter 9), the map, and it can go below zero. The residual interest of a limited liability corporation, the interest of the stockholders, is in the territory, and it ordinarily can't go below zero.

Today, the territory isn't the territory; the map is the territory. We are mapping the maps:

> Of course, cartographers have sometimes amused themselves by drawing maps of fictitious countries, like Erewhon or Atlantis, an activity which, too, has had its accounting counterparts.
>
> (Solomons, 1978, 72)

Littleton extolled mapping the map:

> highly useful analytical rearrangements of accounting data can be made after the transaction facts have initially entered the accounting system.
>
> (Littleton, 1953, 62)

The most ubiquitous example of such rearrangements, of mapping the map, is systematic and rational allocation (see Chapter 10).

Some current GAAP use the financial reporting map as a stage on which to present the products of the imaginations of the issuers of financial reports not representative of the events and conditions of the reporting entities (discussed throughout this book, especially in Chapters 3 and 10), which is tolerated because of our indoctrination. This book rather addresses issues in financial reporting by focusing first on the financial reporting territory, on the financial effects of events on the reporting entity. It seeks to determine which financial effects should be represented in financial statements and how to best represent them.

The belief in the supernatural power of bookkeeping

> Remember that accounting debates are arguments about nothing, in the sense that nothing in the real world changes just because you slap a different label on it.
>
> (Jenkins, 1999, A27)

It's amazing what supernatural power some financial reporters and financial journalists believe bookkeeping has, a belief that is a natural result of treating the financial reporting map as the financial reporting territory:

> When an amount is transferred to a reserve, it is thought by many people that by some *magical* process this serves to strengthen the financial position of an enterprise.
>
> (Goldberg, 1965, 268, 269, emphasis added)

> "almost 45 percent of the sample firms conveyed the impression that they had acquired capital assets with depreciation money, financed growth through depreciation, or engaged in similar forms of *black magic*."
>
> (Spiller and Virgil, 1974, 131, quoted in Heath, 1978, 128n, emphasis added)

> To assure business continuity it is necessary to maintain capital, which is accomplished by charging revenue with the sacrifice value of resources used or sold.
>
> (Backer, 1973, 40)

> "Recovering funds to provide for replacement of the asset" was one of the principal reasons [given in answer to a survey question] for choosing allocation methods mentioned by both management and users. That will be disappointing news to those who decry perpetuation of the *myth* that bookkeeping entries provide funds.
>
> (Lamden et al., 1975, 21, emphasis added)

> "Inappropriate revenue recognition can frequently lead to serious cash flow problems . . . or cause a company to go out of business entirely."
>
> (McConnell, quoted in MacDonald, 2000, B10)

AOL Time Warner ... said that it would take a charge of $40 to $60 million ... because of a change in accounting rules ... AOL's move will sharply reduce its total assets.

(*New York Times*, 2002, A1)

The nation's accounting rule makers have tentatively approved new financial reporting standards for the film industry that could cost some Hollywood studios hundreds of millions of dollars.

(Petersen, 1998d, C1)

Ann Moore, the chief executive of Time Inc.... said in a memo to employees ... [that] new financial reporting standards, ... which will require companies to treat stock options as expenses, "make it prohibitively expensive" to continue the practice for all employees.

(Dash, 2005)

O'Brien reported that a bookkeeping "charge" set aside "an additional 184 million euros ($229 million) to pay for any adverse judgment in a price-fixing investigation by the United States Justice Department" (O'Brien, 2004). That's a way to pay for misbehavior on the cheap.

Reporting depreciation and the like in a column with a total labeled *cash provided* in a statement of cash flows prepared using the indirect method leads some to believe that it's a source of cash:

"funds realized through depreciation or depletion ... "

(Herrick, 1944, 54, quoted in Heath, 1978, 49)

Determining the amount of cash flow from depreciation.

(Lamden *et al.*, 1975, 33)

Some people see depreciation as providing funds for the replacement of an asset.

(Henderson and Peirson, 1980, 185)

in what way can a bookkeeping entry for ... depreciation insure against the impairment of capital?

(Zeff, 1961, 119)

adequate depreciation is neither a necessary nor a sufficient condition to the provision of appropriate financial resources for replacement of plant. But common parlance assumes a connection...

(Kripke, 1989, 29n)

A controller once told me in all seriousness that his plan is to spend his company's depreciation each year on fixed assets. The author of the *Dilbert* cartoon recognized such a belief:

FUN THINGS TO SAY TO ACCOUNTING PEOPLE:

Is it okay if I spend my depreciation budget on travel?

(Adams, 2000, Vol. 3, 64)

The bookkeeping process of discounting is said magically to change future changes into current conditions (see Chapter 12).

Bookkeeping, which affects *reported* income, *reported* expense, *reported* performance, and the like, which exist only in financial statements, in the financial reporting map, is often nevertheless said to affect income, expense, performance, and the like, which only occur to the reporting entity, in the financial reporting territory, for example:

The resort to methods such as replacement cost to . . . create . . . profits to be realized in the future.

(Marple, 1963, 478)

field-testing . . . sponsored by the Financial Executives Research Foundation . . . confirmed that application of the FASB's tentative conclusions would have introduced a high degree of volatility into companies' annual pension expense . . .

(Ihlanfeldt, 1991, 28)

investors and analysts were optimistic in the wake of [an] announcement [of a $1.4 billion pretax charge against earnings], saying they thought that Boeing was on the mend and that management was putting the worst behind it so that the company could improve its performance this year.

(Zuckerman, 1998, D5)

SFAS No. 87, the currently effective pronouncement on reporting on defined benefit pension plans, indicates that bookkeeping results in the emergence of assets and liabilities (see Chapter 24). Also, doom was predicted because of the FASB's project on post-retirement benefits other than pensions. Reporting entities would be forced to report mammoth new liabilities, supposedly driving them out of business. (Only ink on paper was to be changed.)

In contrast, Walsh got it right:

A year shaved off an estimate here, a decimal point's difference there can significantly reduce a company's pension obligations *on paper*.

(Walsh, 2003, emphasis added)

Melcher felt she had to say that "Accounting cannot alter facts. . ." (Melcher, 1973, 2). Similarly, the FASB found it necessary to tell us that "Accounting accruals . . . have no effect on an enterprise's cash flow" (FASB, 1975a, par. 61). The reason the FASB had to say that was that

> Accrual of a loss related to a contingency does not create or set aside funds to lessen the possible financial impact of a loss . . . [though] some respondents to the Discussion Memorandum and the Exposure Draft argued to the contrary.
>
> (FASB, 1975a, par. 61)

It described the anguish of some financial reporters at the thought that prohibiting "accrual of so-called 'self-insurance reserves' . . . [would take away] the 'protection' afforded by the accrual. . ." (FASB, 1975a, par. 62). It found it had to say that "Those accruals . . . in no way protect [anything]" (FASB, 1975a, par. 62). A member of the FASB found it necessary to say that "underlying cash flows and economics [are] unaffected by the accounting method employed" (Victor H. Brown, 1991, 67).

However, the FASB itself isn't immune to ascribing supernatural power to bookkeeping. For example, "Recognition of depreciation always reduces a company's profit or increases its loss" (FASB, 1995b, par. 99). The FASB also thinks a reporting entity doing its own bookkeeping a certain way rather than another way is an essential cause of the reporting entity incurring an enormous liability (see Chapter 21).

Virginia[2] and financial reporting

> When people accept . . . the absurd as normal, the culture is decadent.
>
> (Barzun, 2000, 11)

No, Virginia, financial reporting isn't different from everything else. We just act as though it were. When we violate a rule of arithmetic everyone else obeys, for example, we come out with the same kind of nonsense everyone else would come out with.

Financial reporting should be subject to the same general constraints to which other disciplines are subject, and should look to other disciplines for insight. However, care must be used in borrowing concepts from other disciplines for financial reporting, because the nature and purposes of financial reporting differ from those of other disciplines: "Advancing knowledge through . . . borrowing of ideas is conditional on those ideas being carefully and accurately transported between disciplines" (West, 2003, 74). Care

---

2 Apologies to Frank P. Church of the *New York Sun*, 1897. See http://www.barricksinsurance.com/virginia.html.

wasn't taken, for example, in borrowing the concept of present value from economics and management for financial reporting (see Chapter 12) and in borrowing the concept of forfeitures from actuarial science for financial reporting (Chapter 24).

Discussion questions

1   Consider this appraisal of Chapter 4:

> Dump the entire chapter. It comes across as merely an ill-tempered tirade against those who disagree with you—Abe Briloff with hemorrhoids.[3]
>
> > (Dale Gerboth, former colleague of the author at the accounting research division of the AICPA, in a letter to the author)

2   Can you seriously consider that an entire profession is mired in indoctrination in nonsense?
3   If so, what are the forces that led to this result?
4   Do the list of the manifestations of our indoctrination seem forced to make a point?
5   Are hallowed concepts in financial reporting such as costs flowing, costs attaching, cost recovery, and costs expiring really imaginary items that occur only in the minds of accountants?
6   Are you a fan of A. C. Littleton?
7   Is the characterization of our belief that bookkeeping has supernatural aspects strained?
8   How should concepts in allied disciplines be incorporated in financial reporting?

3 Abraham Briloff is currently the foremost critic of the work of outside auditors.

Part II

Issues underlying financial reporting

5 Views on the desirability of stabilizing income reporting by the design of GAAP

> Financial statement users have indicated . . . that information about earnings variability is important to them . . . The Board recognizes that some investors may have a preference for investments in enterprises having a stable pattern of earnings, because that indicates lesser uncertainty or risk than fluctuating earnings. That preference . . . is perceived by many as having a favorable effect on the market prices of those enterprises' securities . . . [But e]arnings fluctuations . . . should be reported as they occur.
>
> (FASB, 1975a, pars 64, 65)

Having set the stage, we go on to the first set of Chapters considering issues in financial reporting, those underlying financial reporting.

As discussed in Chapter 2, stability of income reporting is the fundamental goal of traditional financial reporting. Stabilizing income reporting by selecting principles deliberately to reduce what would otherwise be reported changes from period to period in net income pervades the design of current GAAP, also as discussed in Chapter 2 and throughout this book. Its desirability is therefore of vital concern in considering issues in financial reporting.

Views differ on whether stabilizing reported income by the design of GAAP is desirable.

Views of official organizations

The SEC, the FASB, the AICPA, and the CFA Institute (before May 2004, the AIMR) have stated positions on the desirability of designing GAAP to stabilize income reporting.

Views of the SEC

The SEC's stated position is clearly against stabilizing reported income:

> "Any volatility is a product of a financial institution's investment port-folio. Accounting standards ought not to conceal the reality they are established to portray," the [SEC] said in [a] letter.
>
> (Salwen and Block, 1990, C14)

> The zeal to project smoother earnings from year to year casts a pall over the quality of the underlying numbers.
>
> (Levitt, 1998)

> Earnings management is perhaps too polite a term—others refer to it as accounting irregularities, accounting hocus-pocus, or financial reporting fraud.
>
> (Morrissey, 2000)

Views of the FASB

The FASB has been equivocal on the desirability of designing GAAP to sta-bilize income reporting. In general statements on the subject, it has opposed it, as indicated in the quotation at the beginning of this chapter and in the following:

> procedures such as averaging or normalizing reported earnings[1] for several periods and ignoring or averaging out the financial effects of "nonrepresentative" transactions and events are commonly used in esti-mating "earning power." However, both the concept of "earning power" and the techniques for estimating it are part of financial analysis and are beyond the scope of financial reporting.
>
> (FASB, 1978, par. 48)

Kirk, one of its Chairmen, reiterated that position:

> "the Board has rejected 'smoothing' or 'normalization' as part of the concept for measuring income, thereby more sharply delineating the boundary between accounting and financial analysis ... if normalization is needed, that is the analysts' responsibility ... No matter how well-intentioned the standard setter may be, if information is designed to indicate that investment in a particular enterprise involves less risk than

---

1 See below in the text about the AICPA's onetime endorsement of normalizing reported earnings.

it actually does ... financial reporting will suffer an irreparable loss of credibility."

> (Kirk, 1983, 4, quoted in Solomons, 1986, 167, 233
> [also quoted in Chapter 24])

Beresford, Kirk's successor, agreed: "Volatility is a natural result of business activity. Accounting practices that obscure volatility are not faithful representations" (Beresford, 1991, attachment).

However, Kirk said at a public hearing on reporting on defined benefit pension plans that a concern of the FASB in drafting a pronouncement on the subject was to be sure it contained "an adequate amount of smoothing" (also stated in Chapter 24). An official document of the FASB reiterated that:

> The [FASB] believes that the [pension reporting] method should be more effective in reducing income statement volatility than the method proposed in the Preliminary Views...
>
> (FASB, 1984b, 3)

The FASB didn't say there why designing GAAP to stabilize income reporting is desirable.

In spite of its avowed general opposition to stabilizing income reporting by the design of GAAP, the FASB hasn't eliminated the income stabilizing involved in the GAAP it inherited from predecessor bodies, and it has added GAAP that stabilizes income reporting, as discussed throughout this book.

Views of the AICPA

The AICPA has also been equivocal on the subject. It stated its general opposition to designing GAAP to stabilize income reporting:

> An important objective of income presentation should be the avoidance of any policy of income equalization ... Users believe businesses that are volatile should report that volatility faithfully and should not smooth earnings to appear less volatile than the underlying business. Some pre-parers believe stable results tend to lower the cost of capital. Users need to be apprised of the true volatility to make correct judgments in allo-cating capital. Companies that report significant swings in earnings are more difficult to analyze. However, if that is the nature of their business or industry and, therefore, a risk that needs to be understood, a user needs to understand that fact.
>
> (AICPA, 1947, 259; 1994a, 33)

However, it stated that stabilizing reported income, normalization, is needed in reporting on income taxes:

studies of published reports and other source material have indicated that, where material amounts are involved, recognition of deferred income taxes in the general accounts is needed to ... avoid income distortion ... the income tax legally payable may not bear a *normal* relationship to the income shown in the income statement and the accounts therefore may not meet a *normal* standard of significance.

(AICPA, 1958a, par. 7, 1967, 1944a, 185 and 186, emphasis added; this quotation also appears in Chapter 21)

The AICPA didn't say why avoiding reported income distortion (in the sense of reported income volatility, discussed in Chapter 2) or normalization of reported income is desirable.

Views of the CFA Institute (before May 2004, the AIMR)

The CFA Institute, the national organization of financial analysts, is unequivocal in its opposition to designing GAAP to stabilize reported income:

a primary benefit of mark-to-market accounting is that real volatility would be revealed ... financial managers have much discretion [under the current broad principles] over the recognition of changes in value by astute timing of exchange transactions and by the adoption of artful allocation procedures. Mark-to-market accounting would take away much of that discretion ... it has the propensity to make earnings exceedingly unpredictable, a disconcerting fact for enterprises trying to minimize their capital costs by reporting smooth and growing earnings ... If there is smoothing to be done, it is the province of analysts to do it.

(Association for Investment Management and Research, 1993, 43, 44, 58)

Reasons that have been given in favor of stabilizing income reporting by the design of GAAP

Reasons that have been given that GAAP should be designed to stabilize reported income include the following:

Public policy concerns

Bevis gave the classic reason—a public policy reason—for the profession to support designing GAAP to stabilize income reporting:

Fluctuations in [corporate profits] ... have a psychological effect on the economic mood of the nation ... given a free choice between steadiness and fluctuation in the trend of aggregate [reported] corporate profits, the economic well-being of the nation would be better served by the former.

(Bevis, 1965, 30)

Hepworth said much the same:

the maintenance of a relatively stable level of reported periodic income [in the entire economy] might do much to reduce the effect of "waves of optimism and pessimism" on the level of business activity.

(Hepworth, 1953, 34)

Miller reported that a survey showed that

Eighty-one percent of 133 responding chief executive officers and 81% of 142 chief financial officers said public policy concerns should be considered [in setting accounting standards].

(Miller, in Miller and Flegm, 1990, 36)

In contrast, Johnson and Petrone of the FASB staff and Miller and Bahnson stated their opposition to the public policy argument:

The [FASB] has from time to time heard . . . arguments that accounting standards should assist in achieving certain public policy goals. However, it observed that there would have to be agreement on what those goals should be. Moreover, since those goals often change with changes in government or for other reasons, there would be questions about whether accounting standards should change every time public policy changes. Perhaps most important, if accounting standards were to become a tool for facilitating or implementing public policy, their ability to help guide policy and measure its results would be impaired. For those reasons, the [FASB] concluded long ago that the only public policy position that can be sustained is to maintain and enhance the integrity of accounting information so that capital market participants are on an equal footing.

(Johnson and Petrone, 1999a, 10)

To pursue . . . policies [other than achieving fully informed capital markets] by shaping financial statement content simply means that the policy makers are vainly hoping that they can fool the markets into believing untruthful reports so that the investors and creditors will make decisions that benefit someone else besides themselves.

(Miller and Bahnson, 2002b, 64)

Benefiting investors

The FASB reported that

> Some respondents to the Discussion Memorandum and the Exposure Draft [for SFAS No. 5] took the position that ... financial statement users may be misled by ... report[ed] net income that fluctuates widely from period to period.
>
> (FASB, 1975a, par. 63)

Freund reports that

> German companies argue that their investors have benefited from accounting practices that average out earnings over years ... focusing management attention on longer-run earnings performance.
>
> (Freund, 1993, A6)

German financial reporting has permitted the use of secret reserves to stabilize reported income. Secret reserves aren't unknown in the U.S.:

> the SEC is ... concerned that Microsoft may have set up an accounting system that held back revenue in the form of certain ... reserves during some quarters, and then applied the reserves to future quarters to smooth out earnings ...
>
> (Buckman, 2002, A6)

Gains or losses may be reversed

A participant in the research conducted by the AICPA Special Committee on Financial Reporting stated that

> Running changes in the value of a bond portfolio through the income statement is going to make that statement incredibly volatile, and it may be a faked volatility because those quarterly gains or losses may or may not be realized.
>
> (AICPA, 1994b, II, 2b, 14)

Facilitating financial analysis

As quoted above, the AICPA states that unstabilized reported income makes financial statements more difficult to analyze. In addition, Williams, a former Chairman of the SEC, stated that issuers feel that reducing the stabilizing effects of GAAP "would make it more difficult to maintain an orderly and predictable pattern of earnings growth..." (Williams, 1989, 45).

A participant in the research conducted by the AICPA Special Committee on Financial Reporting stated that "Fair or market values would introduce an unacceptable level of volatility ... which is not useful to users in assessing a company's future performance and prospects" (AICPA, 1994b, I, 52). Wilson referred to the same:

> "Some people would say maybe smoothing makes sense because it gives the best indication of the future and the long-term trend," says Peter Wilson ... at the Sloan School of Management at Massachusetts Institute of Technology.
>
> (Smith *et al.*, 1994, A6)

Seligman is forthright in his support of that position: "when all is said and done, what's wrong with honest smoothing? Why shouldn't companies encourage investors to look at longer-term trends, rather than reacting to sequential bumps on the road?" (Seligman, 2000, 340). Welch, Chairman of General Electric, was hyper about that:

> To smooth out fluctuations, GE frequently offsets onetime gains from big asset sales with restructuring charges; that keeps earnings from rising so high that they can't be topped the following year ... Chairman Jack Welch ... said investors prize GE's ability "to deliver strong consistent earnings growth ... Having this reprehensible [bond-trading] scheme [at Kidder] ... break our more-than-decade-long string of 'no surprises' has all of us damn mad."
>
> (Smith *et al.*, 1994, A1)

Benefiting the reporting entity

As quoted above, the AIMR states that the issuers of the financial reports of reporting entities are disconcerted by the effects of unpredictable reported income on their costs of capital caused by volatility in reported income. Hendriksen and van Breda refer to the same: "adverse consequences perceived by corporate executives include anticipated increases in the cost of capital resulting from a greater fluctuation in reported earnings" (Hendriksen and van Breda, 1992, 81). A participant in the research conducted by the AICPA Special Committee on Financial Reporting stated much the same: *"Volatility in reported numbers could create unnecessary volatility in securities—potentially disrupting capital raising activities"* (AICPA, 1994b, 4, 71).

Producing a favorable effect on the market prices of the reporting entity's securities

As quoted above, the FASB states that many favor designing GAAP to stabilize income reporting because it has a favorable effect on the market prices of the reporting entity's securities.

Avoiding yo-yo reporting

During a public debate, Cason, while Chairman of the AICPA Accounting Standards Executive Committee, described my opposition to stabilizing reported income by deferred taxes as favoring yo-yo reporting. Also: "Many recent popular statements of preference for [stability of income reporting] have included pejorative references to 'yo-yo accounting'" (Staubus, 1985, 66).

Reasons that have been given in opposition to stabilizing income reporting by the design of GAAP

Reasons that have been given that GAAP shouldn't be designed to stabilize reported income include the following:

Violating representational faithfulness

As quoted above, Beresford stated that designing GAAP to stabilize reported income violates the number one user-oriented criterion, representational faithfulness.

Violating neutrality

Designing GAAP to stabilize reported income is an example of starting with financial statement results of possible solutions to issues desired by the issuers (see Chapter 3). It runs afoul of this warning of Solomons:

> Nothing is more likely to undermine the credibility of financial reporting than the suspicion that the results reported were predetermined and the accounting methods used were selected to produce the results desired by the preparers of the report.
>
> (Solomons, 1986, 102; also quoted in Chapter 3)

Designing GAAP to produce results desired by the issuers violates the user-oriented criterion of neutrality.

Obscuring risk

As quoted above, both the FASB and the AICPA state that designing GAAP to stabilize reported income obscures the relative amounts of risk involved in investing in various reporting entities. Also, Chambers stated that

> Censorship is not ... one of the functions of the accountant ... no one should presume to foretell that a shift in one direction will be remedied in due course by a shift in the other direction ... there can thus be no basis on which manipulative elimination of the effects of fluctuations

can be justified. . . [concealing] fluctuations in income . . . conceal[s] . . . risk . . .

(Chambers, 1966, 261, 271)

Sprouse agrees:

> "it is especially important that, where it actually exists, volatility be revealed rather than concealed by accounting practices. Otherwise, financial statements do not faithfully represent the results of risks to which the enterprise is actually exposed."
>
> (Sprouse, 1987, 88, quoted in Storey and Storey, 1998, 65)

Nondisclosure

Chambers stated that

> Of all principles ["smoothing" profits] is one of the most vicious; for its effect is non-disclosure. If profits in fact fluctuate, this is a piece of information which an intelligent investor will wish to know . . .
>
> (Chambers, 1969, 200)

Falsifying information

As quoted above, the SEC referred to earnings management as fraud. Moreover, the National Commission on Fraudulent Financial Reporting stated a relationship between stabilizing income reporting and perpetration of fraud: "the effect of the . . . actions [of the perpetrators of fraudulent financial reporting] is almost always to inflate or 'smooth' earnings or to overstate the company's assets" (National Commission on Fraudulent Financial Reporting, 1987, 24).

Solomons characterized designing GAAP to stabilize reported income in order to influence behavior in the economy as falsifying information, by comparing it mockingly to other possible kinds of information falsification:

> One can think of other measuring devices that could be falsified to produce supposedly beneficial effects on behavior. Speedometers could be made to overregister to discourage speeding, thermometers could be made to overregister in winter and underregister in summer to save energy . . .
>
> (Solomons, 1986, 232)

Improperly injecting financial analysis into financial statements

As quoted above, both the FASB and the AIMR state that designing GAAP to stabilize income reporting improperly injects financial analysis into financial statements. The FASB states that estimating earning power is part of financial analysis, and that devices to portray earning power rather than simply income should be avoided in financial statements. Solomons agrees: "If it is ever useful to smooth income, the process is best left to financial analysts and other users of financial reports; it is not a job for accountants" (Solomons, 1986, 167).

Skewing the allocation of capital

As quoted above, the AICPA states that designing GAAP to stabilize income reporting can tend to skew the allocation of capital in the economy.

Harming the credibility of financial reporting

As quoted above, Kirk and Solomons state that designing GAAP to stabilize income reporting harms the credibility of financial reporting.

Conclusion on the desirability of stabilizing income reporting by the design of GAAP

As Beresford and Solomons state, stabilizing reported income by the design of GAAP violates the user-oriented criteria of representational faithfulness and neutrality. Further, the main devices used to stabilize reported income by the design of GAAP, realization and allocation, result in violation of the user-oriented criteria of representativeness, relevance, reliability, understandability, verifiability, timeliness, completeness, and comparability (discussed in Chapter 10). All the other reasons stated above that have been given in opposition to stabilizing income reporting by the design of GAAP are sound.

Conformity with the user-oriented criteria is necessary for financial statements to serve well their purposes as reports. Strong reasons are required to justify their wholesale violation by stabilizing reported income by the design of GAAP.

The reasons that have been stated in favor of stabilizing reported income are grouped above in these categories:

- Gains or losses may be reversed
- Public policy concerns
- Benefiting investors
- Facilitating financial analysis
- Benefiting the reporting entity
- Producing a favorable effect on the market prices of the reporting entity's securities.

Possible reversal of gains or losses in future periods is irrelevant, because time period reporting should ignore possible reversals of events in future periods. Investors are misled by financial statement data that aren't representationally faithful; they aren't misled by reported net income that is representationally faithful and that fluctuates accurately.

All the other stated reasons besides public policy concerns involve serving parties other than the users—the issuers, the current owners or creditors in their roles as interested outsiders, not as investors, financial analysts as income-seeking business people, and the reporting entity—at the expense of the users. As stated in the Prologue, financial reports should emphasize the needs of the users of the statements if the needs of the users conflict with the needs or desires of other parties to financial reporting. Violation of neutrality by stabilizing reported income by the design of GAAP for the benefit of the issuers is the single worst and most pervasive cause of deficiencies in current GAAP.

The least obviously faulty reason given in favor of stabilizing reported income by the design of GAAP is public policy concerns. For such stabilizing to be considered desirable, the advantages to the public would have to outweigh the disadvantages to the users (who to a considerable extent are the same people).

The public policy reason has two bases. First, stabilizing reported income by the design of GAAP is said to focus management's attention on longer-run income performance. However, only inept managements would manage with a short-run income performance perspective if they had to avoid stabilizing reported income by the design of GAAP, and such inept managements could be rescued by preparing special management reports in which reported income is stabilized. Users wouldn't have to be denied high-quality financial statements to avoid the ill effects of their ineptitude.

Second, stabilizing reported income by the design of GAAP is said to benefit the economic mood and well-being of the nation by reducing the waves of optimism and pessimism on the level of business activity. That's the most plausible reason in its support, and one with which you might at least initially be sympathetic.

It's not persuasive. To be sure, the business cycle is a serious defect of a private enterprise economy. Bubbles and downturns have caused untold suffering, and eliminating the stabilizing of reported income now built into GAAP would cause the reported income of individual reporting entities to fluctuate more than it now does. However, even with the current built-in stabilizing, bubbles and downturns have occurred. Further, there is no reason to believe that reported income of all reporting entities would fluctuate more on average than now were the stabilizing currently built into GAAP eliminated. Finally, users of financial reports would be provided with information of a character different from that of what they now receive. They would adjust to it and benefit more from it, because it conforms more with the criteria that make it useful to them.

The waves of optimism and pessimism aren't caused by the numbers in financial statements anyway. They are caused by changes in views about the prospects of the economy, which aren't portrayed in financial statements. Economists are developing improved macroeconomic tools to dampen the business cycle, and depriving users of financial reports of high-quality information isn't necessary for that purpose. (The main proponent of the public policy concern, Bevis, who was at the time he made his statement the chairman of one of the largest CPA firms, may have been more concerned about the desire of his clients for stable income reporting than about the public, though he would have denied that.)

Finally, pejorative terms such as yo-yo reporting shouldn't be used to address a serious issue such as the desirability of stabilizing income reporting.

Stabilizing reported income by the design of GAAP is undesirable. It undermines the serviceability of financial statements to the users in order to serve the special interests of the issuers. It's a contradiction of the missions of the FASB and the SEC to protect investors and other users.

Lip service

If stabilizing income reporting by the design of GAAP were desirable, the official organizations should stop paying lip service to the user-oriented criteria. (Or they could adopt what may have been a tongue-in-cheek suggestion of Wyatt: "the FASB needs to consider adding to its conceptual framework qualitative characteristics the notion of smoothing volatility found in real world transactions and events" [Wyatt, 1989a, 126]. If this suggestion is ever taken seriously and adopted, the other user-oriented criteria [qualitative characteristics] would have to be abandoned and not merely violated, as they are today.) They should stop objecting to such stabilizing and start defending it, and not merely with indirect defenses, such as support for practices such as realization and their brand of objectivity (see Chapter 10). Most of all, they should stop objecting to it while condoning it and promoting it.

Debating points

1   Income reporting should be stabilized by the design of GAAP (German accountants, especially, believe this, passionately).
2   No income reporting stabilization should be incorporated in the design of GAAP.
3   The profession should openly debate whether GAAP should be designed to stabilize income reporting rather than do it covertly.
4   The official organizations have done themselves proud by their stated views on whether income reporting should be stabilized by the design of GAAP.

6   Measurement in the preparation of financial statements

> the study of measurement theory has not been widespread in accounting
> even though accountants purport to measure things.
>
> (Sterling and Bentz, 1971, vii)

The FASB implies that measurement is an essential process in preparing financial statements, both in the title of its concepts statement, "Recognition and Measurement," and in the following passage from that Statement:

> Measurement involves choice of an attribute by which to quantify a recognized item and choice of a scale of measurement (often called "unit of measure"). The Statement notes that different attributes are currently used to measure different items in financial statements and the Board expects the use of different attributes to continue.
>
> (FASB, 1984a, par. 3)

That measurement is an essential process in preparing financial statements is a sound view.

Measurement, observation, quantification, and calculation

Measurement requires observation and quantification, determining numerical amounts: "a measure is a quantified empirical observation for a present time and conditions" (Collins and Mock, 1979, 207). It sometimes also requires calculation:

> In addition to directly measurable attributes, there are calculated attributes, sometimes called "derived measurements" ... Density—the quotient of weight and volume—and area—the product of length and width—are examples.
>
> (Sterling, 1979, 91)

Measurements of changes that have taken place over time, such as a change in a person's weight, are also derived measurements.

Not all quantifications or calculations result in measurements. First, it's possible to quantify something without doing any observing—for example, to decide the number of soldiers to be designated a platoon. Also, quantifications involving what might happen in the future don't involve observation, as discussed below. Second, two numbers neither of which are the result of measurement, such as simply two and four, may be subject to calculation. The result may be valid according to the rules of arithmetic, but it's not a measurement. Third, some calculations involve numbers that are the result of measurement but don't result in measurements—for example, the result of multiplying a person's height by the person's age (Hempel calls that "hage" [Hempel, 1952, 46]) isn't a measurement.

We financial reporters don't always observe the distinction between measurement and mere quantification or calculation:

> Perhaps quantification and measurement in accounting are synonymous.
> (Staubus, 1977, 131)

> accounting texts use "calculation" as a synonym for "measurement" and accounting laboratories are rooms where students calculate but where they do not measure...
> (Sterling, 1989, 88n)

The FASB also uses the terms "quantification" and "measurement" loosely. For example, in discussing *measurability*, it states that "The asset, liability, or change in equity must have a relevant attribute that can be *quantified* in monetary units with sufficient reliability" (FASB, 1984a, par. 65, emphasis added), and in a footnote to that paragraph it states that "*Attribute* refers to the traits or aspects of an element to be *quantified or measured*..." (emphasis added in last three words). Also, the FASB links measurement to the future, for example, in a passage quoted in the next section, though no aspect of the future can be measured because none can be observed. Finally, the FASB discusses allocated acquisition cost as a measurable attribute of assets (FASB, 1984a, par. 67a), and states that "allocation methods are ... representations..." (FASB, 2000b, par. 93), though allocation involves quantification by calculation, but not measurement or representation of anything (see Chapter 10). (In the same paragraph, it contradicts its statement that allocations are representations and corrects its position that allocated acquisition cost is a measurable attribute of assets: it states that "allocation methods ... are not measurements of an asset or liability.") An allocated amount has these in common with Hempel's hage: they both are the result of calculation but not of measurement, and neither represent anything in the real world.

Time of measurement

> All measurements are made at a point in time. The purpose . . . is to dis-
> cover the magnitude at that point in time without regard to what has
> gone before or what will come after . . .
>
> (Sterling, 1979, 223)

Measurement generally consists of applying a unit of measure to a measurable attribute of something, such as applying a yardstick to the length of
something, at a point in time. The measurable attribute must be observed
by the measurer at the time of measurement. The ability to observe the
external phenomenon is essential to conform with the first user-oriented criterion, representativeness—data in the line items of financial statements
should purport to represent external phenomena—and therefore to conform
with all the rest of the user-oriented criteria. However, we financial reporters
don't have a lot of practice in observing. We do observe physical inventory-
taking and the responses to circularizations of bank balances and receivables
and sometimes payables, and we do look at some productive assets, but we
don't get far into observing prices. We mostly merely look at acquisition
prices on invoices in the reporting entity's files. Chapter 14, for example,
discusses evidence for the measurement of current selling prices that we
might observe.[1]

For something to be observed it must exist, of course. Many of us financial reporters contend that aspects of the future can and should be involved
in measurement (though nothing about the future can be observed; indeed,
the future doesn't even exist currently; this is discussed in Chapter 7). For
example:

> measurements of *future cash flows* . . .
>
> (Staubus, 1971a, 52)

> measures of future net cash inflows or future net cash outflows . . . mea-
> suring progress reliably involves determining whether uncertainty about
> future cash flows has been reduced to an acceptable level.
>
> (FASB, 1978, par. 41; 1984a, par. 49)

> Present value and expected present value: The current measure of an
> estimated future cash inflow or outflow, discounted at an interest rate
> for the number of periods between today and the date of the estimated
> cash flow.
>
> (FASB, 2000b; Glossary)

---

1 Also see the discussion of green eyeshades in Chapter 14.

a future measure . . . a measure of a future event.

(Riahi-Belkaoui, 1993, 27)

Also, Staubus states that "direct measurements of [the present value of the firm's future cash receipts and payments] are seldom feasible. . ." (Staubus, 1971a, 62), implying that such direct measurements are occasionally feasible (he doesn't explain how).

However,

> Accountants have often been accused of looking at the past . . . Unfortunately, those who have been most critical have given no instructions and no procedures for observing the future . . . not even the most accomplished clairvoyants have ever learned anything from observing the future or by taking their clues for present action from the future . . . the past is the only segment available for observation . . .
>
> (Devine, 1985a, Vol. I, 25)

> One is not *required* to peer into the future in order to make a present measurement. In fact, that is a contradiction in terms: Measurement is the discovery of an extant condition and requires a present act.
>
> (Sterling, 1968, 498)

A self-described "future-oriented [financial reporter]. . ." (Staubus, 1977, 186) challenged the position in the latter passage:

> Sterling has . . . argued (1968, 498) that accountants cannot measure future cash flows or discounted future cash flows because a magnitude that lies in the future cannot be measured. The answer to this point is that the use of present contractual and market evidence that is relevant to future events is not the measurement of a nonexistent object. When space scientists base their calculations of the distance between heavenly bodies as of a future date on current and past evidence, the usefulness of such a calculation depends upon the bodies continuing in the orbits as predicted. Similarly, when an accountant reports discounted future cash flow, NRV, or the historical cost of an asset, the value of these data to decision makers depends on the relationship between the amounts reported by the accountant as of the balance sheet date and the future cash flows of the firm . . . The accountant who accepts contractual evidence of future cash flows and discounts them at the current market rate of interest is not "predicting" in any sense different than that in which the accountant who reports current market value is "predicting."
>
> (Staubus, 1977, 209, 210)

However,

- The reference to "space scientists," apparently intended to demonstrate the contention that "the use of . . . evidence relevant to future events" is measuring "a magnitude that lies in the future . . . not the measurement of a nonexistent object," involves current observations, prediction, and calculation, not measurement of a magnitude that lies in the future.
- No one can "report . . . discounted future cash flow," because a report is about events that have occurred and their effects (see Chapter 1), not about events that might occur in the future and their supposed effects. (A prediction is a current thought about such possible future events and their supposed effects—a prediction can be reported, as a prediction, but a report about a prediction of discounted future cash flows is a report about a prediction, not a report about discounted future cash flows.) Further, discounting doesn't magically change the supposed effects of supposed future events into anything else, such as a current condition (see Chapter 12).
- There is no such thing as "contractual evidence of future cash flows," because, as most people know (not, apparently, we financial reporters), there is no knowledge of or evidence of any future event (see Chapter 7), and the financial reporter "who accepts" it isn't, as the passage correctly states, "predicting"—the financial reporter is accepting fiction. Instead, contractual evidence is merely about currently existing promises. No one knows and there's no evidence about whether time will even continue after the present (see Chapter 7, footnote 15) and, if it does, that those promises will later be fulfilled, regarding whether there will be future cash receipts or payments or, if so, about their amounts and timing. Predictions about those possible future events and their financial effects are merely current fallible thoughts as all predictions are, not knowledge or evidence of such events:

> It is difficult enough for the human mind to trace some sort of great circle around the future, but within that circle chance plays a part that can never be grasped.
>
> (de Tocqueville, 1969, 357)

> most forecasts are bravado and bluff.
>
> (Samuelson, 2001, 49)

Evidence about whether similar promises have been fulfilled in the past may relate to the current probability of the currently existing promises being fulfilled (see Chapters 7 and 14), not about what actually will occur in the future, the "future cash flows."

In any event, the passage ends by conceding that Sterling's point might be valid: "If these procedures are not measurement, it is clear that accountants

must not be limited to reporting measured amounts. They certainly constitute useful quantification" (Staubus, 1977, 210). The nature and usefulness
for financial reports of such quantifications and calculations that involve prediction but don't involve measurement (because they don't involve observation of currently existing phenomena), and therefore don't conform with the
user-oriented criteria, especially the criteria of representativeness and
verifiability, are explored above and in other chapters, especially Chapters 7
and 12.

Measurable attributes and units of measure

The objective of a measurement is to find the magnitude at the time of measurement of a measurable attribute of a thing. Things have more than one
measurable attribute, so the measurable attribute being measured has to be
specified, in addition to the thing, the unit of measurement, and the time of
measurement (FASB, 1984a, par. 3). Which measurable attribute and which
unit of measure to use are separate issues, but they are nevertheless related;
for example, a measurement in the inches scale of measurement has to be of
a distance attribute of a thing. The amount of a measurable attribute, such
as the volume of something, can change over time, for example with changes
in conditions such as temperature.

The result of a measurement is a number together with an indication of
the unit of measure, stating how many of the unit of measure are in the measurable attribute at the time of measurement. It's a report on an aspect of
the thing that's measured at the time it's measured in the conditions in
which it's measured.

Choosing the measurable attribute to measure and report in financial
statements is discussed in Chapters 10 and 12–16. Choosing the unit of
measure to use in financial statements is discussed in the next section of this
chapter, and in Chapters 10 and 11.

Defining the unit of measure in terms of the powers of money

> Money is the root of all civilization.
>
> (Durant, 1953, 68)

The unit of measure in a set of financial statements is defined in terms of the
unit of the money of a country (or of much of a continent, in the case of euros).
Money has three kinds of powers in terms of which the unit of measure for
financial statements can be defined. The first is its debt-paying power,[2] which
U.S. paper money implies is its primary or only power: "This note is legal
tender for all debts, public and private." U.S. dollars have only one kind of
power, to discharge debts denominated in U.S. dollars, which never changes.
Tendering one U.S. dollar always discharges one U.S. dollar of debt.

The second kind of power of money of interest in financial reporting is its specific purchasing power. Money can be used to buy specific things: most things for sale in a country are exchangeable for the money or promises of the money of the country. A specific purchasing power of a given quantity of money is its power to buy a single specific kind of good or service. That power depends on the price of that good or service. There is one kind of specific purchasing power for each kind of good or service money can buy. Prices, ratios of exchange, are stated in numbers of units of money. The prices of specific kinds of goods and services can change, so the specific purchasing powers of the quantity of money can change. A financial report may be issued in one country using the money of another country to define its unit of measure, perhaps because the economy in the first country is highly inflationary. The report uses a unit of measure defined in terms of a specific purchasing power of the unit of money of the first country, the power to buy the money of the other country. The price of the money of the other country in terms of the money of the first country (exchange rate) changes.

The third kind of power of money of interest in financial reporting is its general purchasing power. A general purchasing power of a given quantity of money is its power to buy a specified group of diverse kinds of goods and services, often called a "basket of goods and services." A quantity of money at a point in time has one kind of general purchasing power for each kind of basket that can be specified. Skinner observed that "Some people argue that an index of prices in general has no meaning" (Skinner, 1987, 554), but specifying a basket specifies a general purchasing power; it exists because it's a power that exists to buy a selection of things that exist. The prices of the goods and services in the basket can change, so each kind of general purchasing power of the quantity of money can change.

Nevertheless,

> most accountants and users of financial statements have been inculcated with a model of financial reporting that assumes stability of the [general purchasing power of the] monetary unit...
>
> (FASB, 1986, Lauver dissent)

---

2 In contrast, some say the only power of money people are interested in is its purchasing power, for example the FASB: "Money's 'command over resources,' its purchasing power, is the basis of its value..." (FASB, 1985a, par. 29), and Chambers: "the control of monetary units is sought only because it gives control over other things in general" (Chambers, 1969, 570). Chambers' later reference to "debt-paying and general purchasing power..." (Chambers, 1991a, 14) contradicts that quotation. Someone who owes a lot of money wouldn't think money's purchasing power is its only power of interest. As early as 1908, Sprague recognized that money is useful both to buy things and to pay debts: "Cash ... can ... be used ... to extinguish liabilities or to acquire assets..." (Sprague, 1908).

3 By saying that LIFO and FIFO *measures* are simply *calculations*, these authors don't

> U.S. accountants have ... pretended for decades, if not an entire century, that inflation does not cause the value of the dollar to decay as time passes.
>
> (Miller and Banhson, 2002b, 245)

Financial reporters aren't entirely to blame for this. Veblen reported in 1904 that "in the routine of business throughout the nineteenth century the assumed stability of the money unit has served as an axiomatic principle..." (Veblen, 1904, 103).

We financial reporters shouldn't act as though something important to financial reporting is the opposite of what it is.

A specified quantity of money, such as the amount of money held by a reporting entity or the amount of money specified in a price, thus involves debt-paying power, specific purchasing power, and general purchasing power. When money is spent (sacrificed), the holder of the money gives up powers (incurs costs) of those kinds. When money is received, the recipient receives powers of those kinds.

The current broad principles use a unit of measure defined in terms of the debt-paying power of the unit of money (discussed in Chapter 10). Proposals to define the unit of measure in terms of the general purchasing power of the unit of money, inflation reporting, are discussed in Chapter 11.

Surrogate measures

> The attributes specified in accounting principles often are not measurable in practice ... and accountants are justified in resorting to "surrogates" ... to approximate or estimate the desired but unmeasurable attribute. Indeed, they have no alternative short of nonmeasurement.
>
> (Storey, 1973, 318)

We financial reporters sometimes turn that sensible thought of Storey on its head. If we can't or don't want to measure and report a particular variable, we look for one we can and want to measure and report, regardless of whether it approximates a relevant variable, violating the user-oriented criterion of relevance. But

> Surrogates are an appropriate response to lack of data, but *not* to a lack of theory ... ease of calculation alone will not usually be a sufficient defense of an approximation ... The reader is reminded of the old anecdote about the gentleman who dropped his watch when returning home at night from the tavern (the light being poor where he dropped his watch, he proceeded to the next street light before searching for it).
>
> (Arthur L. Thomas, 1969, 12, 21)

The proper use of a surrogate therefore requires these steps:

- To find an attribute that's measurable in general and that's relevant in the circumstances but that can't be measured directly in those circumstances
- To find a variable that approximates the measurable attribute adequately in the circumstances that can be measured in those circumstances
- To measure that variable and use that measurement in place of a direct measurement of the measurable attribute.

Measurement and calculation in financial statements

There is a number for each line item in each financial statement. Virtually all of those numbers are the result of calculations, if for no reason other than that they are the result of summarization, addition of component numbers. And at least some of the elements of most of the calculations are measurements, such as the acquisition cost of an asset, the total of the amounts promised to be paid in a liability, the amount contracted to be received in a receivable, or the amount of revenue paid or promised in a sale. The amount of equity, the difference between the total assets and the total liabilities, though not itself the result of a measurement, is the result of many calculations, most of which have elements that are measurements.

The FASB implies that every one of the numbers in financial statements is the result of measurement. However, as stated, not all numbers are the result of measurement. And under the current broad principles, not all numbers in financial statements are the result of measurement:

> LIFO and FIFO measures . . . are simply . . . calculations . . . The distinction between measurements and calculations is important and should be kept in mind . . .[3]
>
> (Wolk *et al.*, 1992, 13.)

Conventional accounting processes are not all measurement processes. For example, conventional calculations in respect of the historical or current "cost" of inventories, the "depreciated" (written-down) historical or current value of plant and equipment, the "unamortized" amount of goodwill, research and development expenditure, and so on, do not constitute measurement. The inputs to such calculations, apart from initial prices, are arbitrary and privately determined. That the products of those calculations are a common feature of conventionally prepared

take their own advice to keep the distinction between measurements and calculations in mind. It's an easy trap to fall into (LIFO and FIFO amounts aren't measures), especially because of our indoctrination.

4 Another interpretation could be that those who invent or support such practices

financial statements is evidence that the skills of double-entry bookkeeping and financial ratio analysis are not always founded on knowledge[4] of the nature of measurement, quantification or instrumentation.

(Wolnizer, 1987, 168)

The allocations involved in the acquisition cost basis (see Chapter 10) are calculations based on measurements of acquisition cost. But that's all they are. They aren't, except perhaps by coincidence, measurements of anything in the world. They can't be verified by going to the world at the reporting date or at any other time and applying a scale of measurement based on observation. That's a corollary of the conclusion in Chapter 10 that the results of allocation don't represent external phenomena.

So we may say we are reporting measurements in financial statements, but often all we are doing is presenting nonrepresentative results of calculations designed to stabilize reported income.

Measurement and estimation in financial statements

Financial statements are often said by financial reporters to involve estimation. The term is used in two senses in referring to financial statements, but their usage usually isn't distinguished.

First, *estimation* can refer to rough and ready measurement. John Dewey described the weighing of hogs in Texas this way:

> They would get a long plank, put it over a cross-bar, and somehow tie the hog on one end of the plank. They'd search all around till they found a stone that would balance the weight of the hog and they'd put that onto the other end of the plank. Then they'd guess the weight of the stone.

The guessing may be called *estimation*. Using a scale is more accurate and usually isn't called *estimation*. The difference is only of degree: "All measurement processes yield approximations" (Chambers, 1966, 229); "All measures are imprecise to some degree" (Sterling, 1987, 39). Determining a quantity of mineral reserves, for example, usually requires rough approximation, measurement that can reasonably be called *estimation*.

Second, *estimation* can refer to forming a thought about the magnitude of something that may exist or occur in the future, such as when the economic serviceability of a machine might end: "Weather predictions are estimates

may know "the nature of measurement, quantification or instrumentation," but that they prefer the practices because the practices further achievement of their incentives.
5 Such usage is appraised in Chapter 12.

... of incalculable use to aviation. Dependable estimates in accounting ... are similarly invaluable aids in the conduct of business" (Littleton, 1953, 10).

Determining depreciation in financial statements, for example, involves such thoughts about the future. The FASB states that "accountants quite often must use estimated future cash flows as a basis for measuring an asset or a liability"[5] (FASB, 2000b, Highlights). Because such thoughts don't involve observation and the future doesn't exist at present (see Chapter 7), such thinking isn't measurement. That meaning of *estimation* is called *prediction* in everyday life. However, we financial reporters don't like to admit that prediction is part of the process of obtaining amounts for financial statements, which are supposed to report information about the past and the present: "To say that accounting information has *predictive value* is not to say that it is itself a *prediction*" (FASB, 1980b, par. 53). That's why we use the euphemism *estimation* instead of prediction—for example, "In other cases, the nature of the estimation of the future events is more explicit" (Beaver, 1991, 122). I once broke the code at a meeting of the AICPA Accounting Standards Executive Committee and referred to a prediction as a *prediction* rather than as an *estimate*. I was almost thrown out of the room.[6] Nevertheless, supporters of depreciation reporting sometimes explicitly acknowledge that prediction (forecasting) is involved—for example: "In view of the difficulty of forecasting the approximate date of retirement for the typical unit of plant, it cannot be expected that the program of apportionment adopted will be precisely validated by the course of future events" (Paton and Littleton, 1940, 86).

The use of prediction in preparing financial statements is discussed in several chapters, especially Chapters 7 and 12.

Debating points

1 Financial reporting is too practical an endeavor to be subject to the rigid requirements of measurement theory.
2 Adhering to conventional measurement theory is essential to the improvement of financial reporting.
3 Not so much should be made of the distinctions between calculation and measurement and between quantification and measurement in a practical art such as financial reporting.
4 Aspects of the future can and should be involved in measurement.

6 Tom R., a financial analyst, warned me that analysts' predictions should be called *estimates*, not *predictions*, because analysts don't like to be thought of as "examining tea leaves." When pressed, he acknowledged that they predict. (This footnote is also used as part of footnote 3 in Chapter 17.)

5   The distinction between units of measurement and measurable attributes is vital.

6   Only the number of dollars involved, not what they can buy, should be incorporated in financial reports.

7   Though we financial reporters incorporate estimates in financial statements, we don't incorporate predictions in financial statements.

7 Historical report[1]

Historian[s have] penetrating hindsight.

(Durant, 1935, 505; 1953, 307)

As we financial reporters commonly state, and as the AICPA and the FASB stated, financial statements are supposed to be historical reports (this expression is redundant, because all reports are historical, as discussed in Chapter 1; the expression is nevertheless used in this book because it's in common usage and for emphasis):

> the information [financial statements] contain describes the past, while decision making is oriented toward the future.
>
> (AICPA, 1970c, par. 37)

> a financial statement . . . displays either financial position of an entity at a [current] moment in time or one or more kinds of changes in financial position of the entity during a [past] period of time . . . financial statements . . . are historical.
>
> (FASB, 1984a, par. 5; 1978, par. 21)

Financial analysts expect financial statements to be historical reports: "analysts . . . look to the past record of earnings to give us some kind of a clue" (Norby, 1973, 53); "assets and liabilities are both the result of past transactions and events. . ." (Association for Investment Management and Research, 1993, 17).

For financial statements to be historical, they should report the financial effects of events that occurred during the reporting period and the cumulative financial effects of the events that occurred from the inception of the reporting entity to the reporting date. They shouldn't present fiction.[2] In particular, they shouldn't report the supposed financial effects of events that haven't occurred, either because they might occur in the future or because they might have

---

1 Much of this chapter is taken from Rosenfield, 2003.

occurred in the past but didn't. (Parts of financial reports other than the financial statements may present material to help the users in contemplating such supposed financial effects; see Chapter 17.) The main changes to current financial statements that would result from conforming with those goals would be to add information about the present and take away data about the future.

However, we financial reporters find those restrictions too binding, and we violate them.

Pertinent characteristics of time

> Time is nature's way of preventing everything from happening at once.
>
> (Saying on wall plaque)

Time has some characteristics pertinent to the violation by us financial reporters of the restriction of financial statements to historical reports.

One direction

> Backward, turn backward, Oh, Time, in your flight!
>
> (Elisabeth Akers Allen, "Rock Me to Sleep")

Time goes in only one direction, forward.[3] Though that's obvious to people

---

2 A correspondent supplied this "notion gleaned from Milton Friedman's *Essays in Positive Economics*":

> There is nothing wrong with fictions in describing the world; many such fictions are quite useful (the economist's notion of the rational man might be an example). One who objects to them must bear the burden of showing that they do harm.

I attempt to bear that burden here by distinguishing financial statements, which should portray what is and what happened (someone has tell the users what is and what happened uncontaminated with fiction; if not we financial reporters, then who?) from the remainder of financial reports, which may contain analysis (including useful fictions, if any, identified as fictions), from management reports, which may contain conjectures about the effects of actions not taken or of future courses of events, and from the musings of economists, epitomized by one who, asked what she would do if marooned on a desert island with a case of canned tuna, said she would assume a can opener.

3 I feel that here we can ignore Plato's statement: "simultaneously with the reversal of the world the wheel of their generation has been turned back, and they are put together and rise and live in the opposite order..." (*Statesman*), the observation by the White Queen in Lewis Carroll's *Through the Looking Glass*: "there's one great advantage in [living backwards], that one's memory works both ways," and even Deutsch's and Lockwood's statement in *Scientific American*: "The laws of physics do not forbid [time travel]" (Deutsch and Lockwood, 1994, 68). (The latter involves multiple universes.) And Hawking reassures us: "[The best evidence against time travel is that] we have not been invaded by hordes of tourists from the future" (quoted in Stone, 1998, 8). If you disagree, consider all the implications for financial reporting.

Figure 7.1 Time travel (copyright 1990 United Features Syndicate, Inc., reproduced by permission).

who aren't financial reporters, Chambers felt it necessary to remind financial reporters of that: "the passing of time is irreversible..." (Chambers, 1966, 46) (see Figure 7.1).Virtually all believe that (except we financial reporters, as demonstrated, for example, in the statement by Kirk discussed below, in Chapter 12 in the section on "The reversal of cause and effect," and Chapter 24 in the section on "FASB's treatment of the liabilities"). As Omar Khayyám says in a quotation that opens the next section, all the regret, remorse, contrition, and repentance in the world can't change the past, which can be brought back only in memory, that cause and effect, if it occurs,[4] goes in only one direction, forward;[5] that the past and the present can't be affected by events that might occur later.

In spite of this statement by Kirk: "future salary increases have effects on the benefit earned..." (Kirk, 1990, 89; see also Chapter 24), a future event (such as a future salary increase) can't be the cause of or affect a present condition (such as a benefit earned)[6]—events don't have retroactive effects: they can't change the past. (However, retroactive *calculations* [thoughts that may or may not be written down] or retroactive *laws* or *agreements* [which have only prospective, not retroactive, effects: they can't and don't change the past] can be and are made.) Also, Beaver gave a common example of a

4 Some philosophers, especially Hume, doubt that we can know that events can in fact cause other events—but even Hume had doubts about his doubt (Popkin and Stroll, 1956, 140–147).
5 A correspondent wrote that this "is true only of the immanent, not of the transcendent, but that shouldn't affect your book." Mathews and Smith (1921, 452) define *transcendent* as "a reality or being existing in a realm beyond the reach of human experience." That describes much of current financial reporting, as discussed throughout this book.
6 I feel that here we can ignore Sagan's thought that "few of us spend much time wondering . . . if time will one day flow backward and effects precede causes . . ." (Sagan, 1988, ix). If you disagree, see where that leads.

statement that in financial reporting, the future can affect the present and the past!: "the estimated effect of future events on existing assets and liabilities" (Beaver, 1991, 125). Chambers felt it necessary to remind financial reporters that that too is false: "we cannot experience the consequences . . . of an event before the event occurs . . . we always estimate the future from the present, never the other way round" (Chambers, 1989, 7; 1979a, 52).

The present and the past

> The Moving Finger writes; and having writ,
> Moves on; nor all your Piety nor Wit
> Shall lure it back to cancel half a Line
> Nor all your Tears wash out a Word of it.
> (Omar Khayyám, *Rubáiyát*, Stanza lxxi)

Though Sprouse and Moonitz (1962, 27) stated that "people act in the . . . future . . ." in addition to stating that "people act in the present . . . ," events such as actions of people occur in only the present, not the future (this is a tautology, because the definition of the present is the moment in time during which events occur[7]), a moment in time that occurs and moves— "The Moving Finger": "All thoughts and actions occur in some specified present moments" (Chambers, 1991a, 7).

The past is prior moments in time during which events occurred during what was then the present.

The future

> The Future Ain't What It Was.
> (Yogi Berra)

The future is a concept about moments in time and events that haven't yet occurred: "If something in the future is canceled, what is canceled? What has really happened? Something that didn't occur yet is now never going to occur at all. Does that qualify as an event?" (Carlin, 1997, 42).

---

7 An event occurs over a moment, a period of time; no event occurs at a timeless instant. A moment is usually a short period of time, but it can be a period of time of any length. For example, the extinction of the dinosaurs was an event that apparently occurred over an extended period of time. To state that Earth at present is between ice ages is to discuss a ten to twenty thousand year present, according to current scientific evidence (Gribbin, 1999, 158). To discuss the time it takes light to move ten feet is to discuss a fleeting moment. A moment and the present are therefore elastic concepts, depending on the context. Constant are that the past preceded the present and that the future, if it comes into existence as a new present, will follow the present present.

We financial reporters often state that the future is uncertain and that such uncertainty hobbles financial reporting: "measuring progress reliably involves determining whether uncertainty about future cash flows has been reduced to an acceptable level" (FASB, 1984a, par. 49). Some observers state that such uncertainty should be ignored initially to study issues in financial reporting, for example:

> the concept of earnings, given certainty, is useful as an abstraction.[8]
>
> (AICPA, 1973b, 32)

> The basic nature of the periodic income determination problem may best be studied by eliminating the most disturbing factor—i.e., uncertainty.
>
> (Storey, 1960, 449)

But it's not the future that's uncertain; it's people who are uncertain, about what events might occur later.

However, it's worse than that for people. Some financial reporters say we can know the future:

> The normative investor decision model developed [earlier] requires information about future dividend payments.
>
> (Revsine, 1973, 118)

> the known future cash receipts ... and the known future cash disbursements[9] ... Future cash inflows from customers are rights provided for in the contract of sale...[10]
>
> (Staubus, 1961, 58; 1977, 138)

> information about the future events...
>
> (Beaver, 1991, 128)

8 Ignoring uncertainty involves the assumption that everyone knows all of the future, which isn't an abstraction—it's fiction. That assumption makes financial reporting, which provides information about the past to help people plan for a future about which they are uncertain, unnecessary.

9 This observer apparently was ambivalent about this. He also stated:

> The current value approach requires that the "known" future cash movements be discounted to the measurement date ... When he is accounting for monetary assets and equities, the accountant usually "knows" the future cash movements that will be connected with the item.
>
> (Staubus, 1961, 34, 58)

The quotation marks around *known* and *knows* indicate doubt that the future can be known. (Also, some current value approaches, such as current selling price reporting, discussed in Chapter 14, don't involve future cash movements or discounting.)

10 Contracts of sale in fact merely provide *promises* of future cash receipts.

Obviously,[11] to know the past . . . one must know the future. . .

(Lev, 2001, 82)

But no one can know the future and there is no such thing as information about the future:

future conditions cannot be known . . .

(FASB, 1980b, par. 53)

Accountants have long held the belief that our reporting problems would be solved if we knew the future . . . People will continue to yearn for future knowledge . . . Accountants may be able to provide them with some sympathy, but we cannot provide them with future knowledge.

(Sterling, 1979, 26, 130)

all information is about the past . . .

(Devine, 1985a, 25)

"We are here and it is now. Further than that all human knowledge is moonshine."

(H. L. Mencken, quoted in Robert Byrne, 1988, 109)

If you want to make God laugh, say what you will do tomorrow.
(Old Proverb, revived after the terrorist attacks of September 11, 2001)

Gamblers would nevertheless love to have information about the future. Most of the rest of us prefer to do without it (especially information giving the date and cause of our death); life wouldn't be very exciting otherwise.

What's even worse, except as a useful concept in people's imaginations,[12] *the future doesn't exist*[13] *at present*:

[The] future does not yet exist.

(Arthur L. Thomas, 1975, 75)

[The argument] that one cannot measure future phenomena . . . may take the form that measurement is not possible when the subject does not . . . exist . . .

(Vatter, 1971, 115)

---

11 What is obvious to this observer is nonsense to me.
12 And perhaps in the mind of God. I feel we can ignore that possibility here.
13 White describes the treacherous terrain: "The word 'exists' is one of the most pivotal and controversial in philosophy . . . There is . . . a tendency among some philosophers to insist that the word 'exists' is ambiguous and therefore some of the disputes [about the word] are not disputes at all but merely the results of mutual misunderstanding . . ." (White, 1957, 118, 119). Nevertheless, I stick with the position in the text that the future doesn't exist at present.

imagination ... has been defined by Jean-Paul Sartre as *the ability to think of what is not*. Human beings are the only animals who have the capacity to envisage something that ... does not yet exist but which is merely possible.[14]

(Armstrong, 1994, 233)

We financial reporters would do well to distinguish the products of our imaginations from the conditions that exist and the financial effects of events that have occurred in the world around us, which should be the only subjects of financial statements.

What's worst, the future never occurs—comes into existence—as such. Time always comes into existence as the present:

> TOMORROW IS ANOTHER DAY. Not true. Today is another day. We have no idea what tomorrow is going to be. It might turn out to *be* another day but we can't be sure. If it happens, I'll be the first to say so. But you know what? By that time, it'll be today again.
>
> (Carlin, 1997, 136)

Though a common expression is, "when the future becomes the present..." (Sterling, 1982, 55), the imagined future doesn't become the real present. The present moves. People can think about events that might occur later: "an imagined future..." (Chambers, 1989, 17), but if events do occur later,[15] they will be real present events in what's then the present, and

---

14 Perhaps other animals do have that capacity. Our household pets, for example, may not be ruled solely by instinct and anticipate nothing. Consider a dog playing frisbee.
15 We people have no guarantee even that time itself will continue for us. Consider, for example, the ever-present hazards to our home planet, for example, the possibility (likelihood?) of nuclear terrorism:

> Massive stockpiles of enriched uranium and plutonium—the critical ingredient in a nuclear weapon—are literally lying around [in Russia] in poorly guarded facilities. A small chunk of this stuff could make Osama bin Laden's day.
>
> (Zakaria, 2001, 29)

> Harvard ... Prof. Graham Allison ... writes ... that it is only a matter of time before a terrorist detonates a [nuclear] bomb in America... Six *known* [nuclear] thefts in Russia have been intercepted abroad. Once they have the material, terrorists have the bomb. It takes only enough enriched uranium or plutonium to fill a soft-drink can. (Since the U.S. cannot prevent tons of narcotics from getting in, the best place to hide it would be in a bale of marijuana.)
>
> (Rosenthal, 1995, A31)

Our quiet confidence that it won't happen likely is based on the idea that it's unthinkable. The problem is that terrorists think the unthinkable. Further,

after that they will be past events. Imagined events occur in the mind; real events—other than the event of imagining, which occurs in the mind—occur outside the mind; imagined events don't become real events by some magical process; in financial reporting, real events occur only outside the mind, in the financial reporting territory. *There are no future events*, except in imagination and science fiction,[16] for example: "In 2200, the world again began to grow cold" (Silverberg, 1964, 26).

Nevertheless, it has been said that:

> What role future events should play ... is a question that ... pervades accounting ... because virtually every accrual and deferral contains an explicit or implicit assumption about the occurrence or outcome of future events.
>
> (Johnson, 1994, 6; see also footnote 15)

The view that there are future events is so imbedded in the minds of most of us financial reporters that a Conference of Standard-Setting Bodies was held in London in November 1993 under the auspices of the International Accounting Standards Committee to discuss the role of future events in financial statements (Johnson, 1994, 6), and Beaver published a commentary on the "Problems and Paradoxes in the Financial Reporting of Future Events."

The view stated here, that the future doesn't exist at present, involves the age-old dispute between those who believe in free will and those who believe in determinism. If determinism is correct, the future is preordained and therefore in effect exists at present. Current financial reporting literature and practice are deterministic. Most people agree: "they ... believe in scientific

---

> Today, germ and other asymmetrical threats, not missiles, tend to be seen as the dark wave of the future. Last Wednesday, when George J. Tenet, director of central intelligence, told the Senate about "things that threaten the lives of Americans," his first topic was not missiles but terrorism. "The threat," he said, "is real, it is immediate and it is evolving."
>
> (Broad, 2001, WK 18)

That was written exactly seven months before September 11, 2001.
Further, consider the worldwide effort to spot and presumably try to counteract asteroids that might strike the Earth and end life here.

16 Johnson, a senior member of the FASB staff and principal author of *Future Events: A Conceptual Study of Their Significance for Recognition and Measurement*, published by the FASB, said that he agrees with the statement in the text to which this footnote is appended. He said the term "future events" is shorthand for people's current thoughts about the effects of events that might occur later. Its use as shorthand isn't clear from a simple reading of the literature every time it's used. According to his definition and the title of his book, his book considers basing financial reporting on people's thoughts about the future, a slender reed on which to base them, as discussed below in the text.

determinism—the unbreakable sequence of cause and effect..."[17] (Barzun, 2000, 29). The conundrum of free will, to which I subscribe, is that though it denies determinism, it doesn't deny in general the operation of cause and effect.

We financial reporters disregard these characteristics of time, as discussed throughout this book, especially in this chapter and in Chapter 12.

Reflecting in financial statements the financial effects of supposed future events

> *past performance can only be judged when the future is known.*
> (American Accounting Association, 1991, 90)

We financial reporters in effect state directly or indirectly that it's impossible to determine what past events and their financial effects were and what current conditions are for the purpose of preparing financial statements without knowing about events that supposedly will occur in the future and their financial effects.

Support for the view that knowledge of the financial effects of supposed future events is needed to prepare financial statements

The quotation that opens this section is an example of a direct statement of the position that the financial effects of supposed future events need to be known to know the past and the present in preparing financial statements.

A commonly stated view is that the income of a reporting entity is the entire increase in its equity over its life, including its life that may occur later than any particular time, exclusive of the financial effects of transactions with its owners, and that income can be sliced up into only arbitrary portions such as for individual years. For example, the AICPA said that: "The achievement of the primary goal [of business enterprises of maximizing wealth] can be measured meaningfully only over relatively long periods of time, and, with precision, only when the enterprise is ultimately dissolved" (AICPA, 1974, 21). An individual observer said that the view is clear: "Clearly, uncertainty about the future precludes the ascertainment of a true value for the assets (and, conjointly, a true net income) of a continuing concern—except at the termination of the enterprise" (Zeff, 1961, 89).

However, as of any reporting date, the only part of the success or failure of the reporting entity that has occurred has occurred in the past, up to the present. The future doesn't then exist, and nothing about the reporting entity's conjectural success or failure in the future has any effect on its actual success or failure to date—again, cause and effect doesn't work backwards in time.

17 Compare Wheeler's statement: "In the small-scale world [of quantum physics] ... when events are examined closely enough, uncertainty prevails; cause and effect become disconnected" (Wheeler, 2000, F1). Also see footnote 4.

Income determination shouldn't be an attempt to slice up the combination of success or failure that has occurred and supposed future success or failure that might later occur. It should merely determine what has happened to date.

Even more common are indirect statements of the position that the financial effects of supposed future events need to be known to know the past and the present in preparing financial statements: they hold that evidence of the financial effects of supposed future events is required. The evidence would be required only if knowledge of the financial effects of supposed future events is needed.

Some say such evidence should be sought by looking for surrogate measures of the financial effects of such supposed future events:

> Our observation that the significance of assets and liabilities lies in the future means that they can never be measured with absolute certainty. Surrogate measures must be found, and therein lies the essential problem of accounting.
>
> (Skinner, 1987, 635)

(Surrogate measures are discussed in Chapter 6.) That seems at best circuitous: to know something about the past and the present, the future must be known; to know that future, something else about the present must be known.

Others say such evidence may be obtained simply by thinking about the future: by forming predictions—usually called *estimates* by us financial reporters (see Chapter 6), sometimes called *forecasts*, *expectations*[18] ("the product of weighing up fuzzy feelings about fuzzy things" according to a correspondent), *assumptions*, or *assessments* (though thinking about the future provides no evidence about the future; as discussed below, it provides evidence only about the person doing the thinking). Every professional organization to which this book refers says that.

- FASB:

> Accrual is . . . the accounting process of recognizing assets or liabilities and the related . . . revenues, expenses, gains, or losses for amounts *expected* to be received or paid, usually in cash, in the future.
>
> (FASB, 1985a, par. 141, emphasis added)

- AICPA:

> Financial statements should include an explanation that the preparation of financial statements in conformity with GAAP requires the use of management's *estimates*.
>
> (AICPA, 1994c, par. 11, emphasis added)

18 The term "expectancy" is sometimes used in a sense that differs from the sense of *expectations* as thoughts, such as in the expression "life expectancy." In that sense, it refers to a scientific probability, not the thought of an individual. Such probabilities are discussed below in the text.

- American Accounting Association:

  > [to] faithfully represent [the] resources and obligations [of an enterprise] ... it will often be necessary to *estimate* the outcome of future transactions and events.
  >
  > (American Accounting Association, 1991, 89, emphasis added)

- CFA Institute (before May 2004, the AIMR):

  > It is self-evident[19] that reporting on the past always requires the use of *estimates* and other *assessments* of future events...
  >
  > (Association for Investment Management and Research, 1993, 18, emphasis added)

Many individuals say the same, for example:

> the essential characteristic of an asset ... is an *expectation* [of future economic benefit] ...[20] measurement can rest upon ... an *estimate* involving the future such as that of an asset's economic life.[21]
>
> (Skinner, 1987, 633, 664, emphasis added)

> The need to *estimate* and project future events is not unique to pensions. Accounting unavoidably involves many *estimates*...
>
> (Lucas and Hollowell, 1981, 63, emphasis added)

One observer referred to the use of both thoughts about the future and surrogates for those thoughts! "a ... view is that values are inherently future-oriented, and, therefore, they ought to be stated to reflect the present value of *expected* future cash flows—even if we must use *surrogates* to quantify such data" (Vatter, 1971, 115, emphasis added).

Opposition to the view that knowledge of the financial effects of supposed future events is needed to prepare financial statements

Others state that nothing about the future should be included in the preparation of financial statements:

> The anticipation of a future state ... can provide no basis for ascertain-

---

19 Imagine how a person such as I feels about the expression "It is self-evident," meaning "it is self-evidently true," followed by a statement the person considers self-evidently false.
20 Here, an asset isn't an economic resource; it's a thought.
21 This is equivalent to saying, "I can measure my two-year-old child's height sixteen years hence by thinking about it." Calling that operation measurement rather than prediction corrupts the language.

ing [the] present state... There is no such thing as accounting for the future.

(Chambers, 1966, 156; 1969, 581)

records can only be of the past...

(Devine, 1985a, 26)

Our generation was conditioned ... to *define* noncash asset magnitudes as *necessarily* dependent upon the future. Therefore, it looks strange when someone makes the suggestion, *which would be obvious in other contexts*, that a present magnitude depends upon the present, not the future.

(Sterling, 1979, 28n, final emphasis added)

Consider this picturesque statement of that view by a financial analyst:

I agree with this notion of December 31st. That is what it looked like as of December 31st if you are going to take photographs at a point in time it is that photograph. Now maybe somebody ages dramatically two days later and starts to look like a prune well you take a photograph at that time.

(AICPA, 1994b, II, 4, 128)

Defliese apparently didn't agree with that notion of December 31st:

the asset-liability approach to income determination ... emphasizes that the beholder is viewing the balance sheet's year-end position at the split-second of midnight. Our bookkeeping origins tell us that "balance sheet" is a list of account balances after the year's profit or loss is determined. Are we moving in a completely new direction?

(Defliese, 1983, 96)

Watts stated that "capitalized ... future cash flows in financial reports" are "unverifiable" (Watts, 2003, 207), thus violating the user-oriented criterion of verifiability.

Some state their opposition by countering the contention that measurement should involve the financial effects of supposed future events, for example,

The literature ... lament[s] the fact that future events have to be considered before present valuations can be made. [However, o]ne is not *required* to peer into the future in order to make a present measurement. In fact, that is a contradiction in terms: Measurement is the discovery of an extant condition and requires a present act.

(Sterling, 1968, 497, 498)

Conclusion on the view that knowledge of the financial effects of supposed future events is needed to prepare financial statements

Knowledge of the financial effects of supposed future events isn't needed to prepare financial statements, which report past performance and current position, for the reasons stated in the preceding section, and, above all, because outside the minds of people the future doesn't exist at present and there are no future events, so past performance and current position can in no way depend on or be affected by supposed future events—cause and effect doesn't work backwards in time.

(In contrast, the *significance* of the past for the future often can't be known until time passes—the significance of Columbus' discovery wasn't immediately apparent. Reporting history and interpreting history are separate activities. Financial statements should report, and the users should infer significance—financial reports should present information outside the financial statements to help the users do so [see Chapter 17]. Current GAAP suffers from trying to combine the reporting of history with providing interpretations of its significance.)

The purpose of using the financial effects of supposed future events to prepare financial statements

The notion that the future must be known in order to determine and report history is seen in other contexts as obviously false, as Sterling points out above. Someone who isn't a financial reporter and who therefore hasn't been subject to the indoctrination to which we financial reporters have been subject (discussed in Chapter 4) might wonder why we financial reporters act on that notion.

That notion was derived from the concept of present value, which was developed outside financial reporting in contexts that don't involve reporting, without consideration of its suitability for reporting, and which isn't suitable for reporting. The concept of present value involves the definition of the past in terms of the future (see Chapter 12). With the past defined that way, the past indeed can't be known without knowing something about the future. The past should not be defined that way in the design of financial statements,[22] or in any other context.

The notion is retained for the purpose of facilitating the stabilizing of reported income, the primary incentive of the issuers (see Chapter 2), by the use of allocation, which should be rejected because it violates every user-oriented criterion and because it isn't measurement (see Chapter 10). That conclusion concerning stabilizing income reporting is amplified in

---

22 This is similar to Sterling's statement, discussed in Chapter 10, that though financial reporting is now defined as a process of allocating costs, it need not be defined that way.

Chapter 10 in the section on "Stable income reporting" in connection with a general discussion of allocation (including depreciation and inventory reporting) and in connection with discussions of the following—for example,

- The so-called ideal basis of valuation, in Chapter 12 in the section "The ultimate form of allocation"
- The use of current buying prices, in Chapter 13 in the section "Current buying prices"
- Current reporting on liabilities in general, on the investment tax credit, on income taxes in general, and on employee benefit plans, in Chapter 15 in the section "Current broad principle for reporting on a liability," in Chapter 19 in the section "Investment tax credit," in Chapter 21 in the section "The rationale," and in Chapter 24 in the sections "FASB's treatment of the liabilities" and "Postretirement benefits other than pensions"

each of which also involves allocation.

Reflecting in financial statements current conditions that indirectly involve the future

At least three kinds of current conditions indirectly involve the future: (1) current *probabilities* about the effects of events that may occur in the future; (2) people's current *thoughts* concerning the supposed effects of events that may occur in the future; and (3) current *prospects* of financial achievement in the future beyond that achieved to date (discussed in Chapter 16). Those current conditions are part of history (in contrast with the discussion in the preceding section), and to that extent should be considered for possible reflection in financial statements.

Current probabilities

Current probabilities about the financial effects of events that may occur in the future, in the sense stated in SFAS No. 5, paragraph 4: "The future event or events are likely to occur," is the only one of the three kinds of current conditions that indirectly involve the future that should be reflected in financial statements. Even so, only a limited number of this kind should be reflected.

Analogies with the weather and with gambling can help distinguish current probabilities about the effects of supposed future events from the effects of supposed future events and from predictions of the effects of supposed future events.

A 60 percent chance of rain

Some time ago, meteorologists started giving part of what they call weather forecasts in terms of percentages. Formerly they might have said, for example, that it will rain tomorrow. Now they might say that there is a 60 percent chance that it will rain tomorrow. The first way of saying it is in fact a forecast, a prediction. It says what the meteorologist thinks will happen tomorrow. It could turn out to be right or it could turn out to be wrong. The common view was that meteorologists always turned out to be wrong. Meteorologists probably got tired of being second-guessed all the time, so they started stating probabilities about future weather. For them, the beauty is that they can't turn out to have been wrong if they got the probabilities right. If yesterday they said that there is a 60 percent chance that it will rain today and it rains today, they were right. If yesterday they said that there is a 60 percent chance that it will rain today and it doesn't rain today, they were right.

By stating tomorrow's weather in terms of percentages, meteorologists are stating current probabilities, (falsifiable) scientific statements of what is and what happened, based on their knowledge of meteorology, on current weather reports, and the rules of probabilities. They aren't stating predictions, current subjective thoughts about what the future will bring. A statement that there is a 60 percent chance that it will rain tomorrow is really a statement that 60 percent of the time when the weather patterns similar to those leading up to today and the weather similar to current weather occurred and existed in the past, it rained the next day. Such a statement is part of a weather report.

A maverick meteorologist might predict weather that disagrees with the probabilities, perhaps because she has a hunch. The prediction could turn out to have been right or wrong. Or, an inept meteorologist might say there is a 60 percent chance of rain tomorrow though according to current meteorological science, to current weather reports, and to the rules of probability, there is a 20 percent chance of rain tomorrow. That meteorologist can't later be shown to have been wrong because it did or didn't rain, but she can be shown to have been wrong—to have misjudged the probabilities—because of inept application of meteorological science and the rules of probability.

The wrong move at the right time

Edward G. Robinson played a character who won the culminating poker hand in the film *The Cincinnati Kid* by successfully drawing to an inside straight flush (he drew a nine of diamonds holding an eight, ten, jack, and queen of diamonds) to beat a full house held by the Kid. Robinson's character said, "Gets down to what it's all about, doesn't it—making the wrong move at the right time."

Two things about the future were involved in that statement. First, the current probability of successfully drawing to an inside straight flush was small, based on known laws of chance (only two players stayed to the end)—

"making the wrong move." The probability, however, as all probabilities, had nothing to do with what would actually happen in the particular case. That was dramatized by what did happen. Second, he predicted that he would successfully draw to an inside straight flush and made his bet based on the prediction. The prediction, which was what he thought would actually happen, could have turned out to have been wrong but, by dramatic license, turned out to have been right—"at the right time."

A *nearly* 100 percent probability

Some events seem to us to be certain to happen in the future, such as that the sun will appear to rise in the east tomorrow. But even they aren't certain; they're merely nearly 100 percent probable. The sun might not appear to rise in the east tomorrow—any number of astronomical events could prevent it, for example, a collision of an asteroid with the earth that reverses its direction of rotation.[23] (The direction of rotation of Venus and Uranus is opposite to that of the other solar system planets, presumably because of collisions with asteroids or planetoids; Gribbin, 1999, 167.) Also, there's the old story about the chicken that awoke every day for 100 days to sunshine and good food and drink and concluded that it would always be thus. The next day it had its neck wrung. And that something in the future is nearly 100 percent probable doesn't mean we should put it in a report on history. It's nearly 100 percent probable that General Motors will make some sales next year, but next year is soon enough to report them.[24]

Some predictions seem to be at least in part nearly 100 percent probability statements. For example, this weather forecast was actually once given: "It will be dark and rainy tonight."

Current probabilities and intentions of the issuers

Current probabilities exist concerning the financial effects of supposed future events affecting reporting entities.

Most such probabilities involve plans or intentions of the issuers. What's currently probable about what will happen to a machine owned by a reporting entity, for example, depends, among other things, on the issuers' current intentions for the machine. If they currently intend for the reporting entity to use the machine, it probably will. If they currently intend to have the reporting entity sell the machine, it probably will. (Of course, intentions can

---

23 Compare this: "If a donor pledges to give to a charity 'if the sun rises tomorrow,' that is not an uncertain event; the sun will rise tomorrow, at a known time" (Larkin, 1999, 29, 23).

24 "MacNeal makes it abundantly clear that he is not interested [even] in 'certainties'" (Zeff, 1982, 535; the statement is taken from MacNeal, 1970, 146).

change,[25] and they often aren't achieved—"The best laid schemes o' mice and men Gang aft a-gley" [Robert Burns, "To a Mouse"]). Current financial statements reflect current probabilities based on intentions of the issuers. A recent example is FASB, "Impairment" (par. 15), which requires financial reporters to determine whether the issuers are committed to selling an asset they now use. Such current probabilities shouldn't be reflected in financial statements, because intentions (commitments) of the issuers shouldn't be reflected in financial statements, as discussed below.

The FASB's definitions of the elements of the reporting entity that should be represented in financial statements involve current probabilities of the financial effects of supposed future events: its definition of *assets* refers to "probable future economic benefits"; its definition of *liabilities* refers to "probable future sacrifices of economic benefits"; *revenue* and *expenses* are defined in terms of assets and liabilities. The implication is that all current probabilities concerning assets, liabilities, revenue, and expenses, including current probabilities involving the issuers' intentions, should be reflected in financial statements. However, as just stated, current probabilities involving the issuers' intentions shouldn't be reflected in financial statements.

Other current probabilities involved in financial statements

The financial effects of most other events that probably will occur in the future aren't a direct part of a reporting entity's current position, such as the probability that our solar system will continue operating in much the same way as it has done for the foreseeable future.

In at least two areas, current probabilities concerning the financial effects of supposed future events that don't involve plans or intentions or any other kind of thoughts of the issuers about the future, because they are outside the issuers' control, should be considered for reflection in financial statements. One such area is current probabilities that currently held short-term receivables will be collected in the future (see Chapter 14, footnote 7). Another such area is the probable future amounts and timing of payments required on currently outstanding variable loans and certain other kinds of liabilities (this is discussed in Chapters 15 and 24).

Issuers' current thoughts about the future

Historical cost is used for debt securities provided management has the intent and ability to hold those assets on a long-term basis or to maturity, so called accounting by psychoanalysis.

(Schuetze, 1992, 3)

25 For example, in a "Peanuts" cartoon, Lucy pulled the football away, causing Charlie Brown to fall, though she had had programs printed up in advance saying she would hold it for Charlie to kick. She said, "In every program, Charlie Brown, there are always a few last minute changes!"

> The absurdity of having to record a presumably sound investment as if it were a loss ... simply because the assets invested in have no resale value results from a refusal to recognize, for accounting purposes, that values depend on expectations.[26]
>
> (Solomons, 1966, 208)

People have various kinds of current thoughts that involve the future, including predictions (estimates, forecasts, expectations, assumptions, assessments), suppositions, evaluations, pessimism, optimism, wishful thinking, plans, intentions, hopes, dreams, worries, fears, and faith. Although the FASB says that "Investors, creditors, and other users of the information [in financial reports] do their own evaluating, estimating, predicting, [and] assessing..." (FASB, 1978, par. 48), current financial reporting reflects predictions, plans, and intentions of the issuers, for example as discussed above, and evaluations, hopes, and dreams of the issuers, for example, as discussed in general in Chapter 14 in connection with Class B aspects of assets, in Chapter 17 in the section "Supplementary disclosure," and in Chapter 23 in the section "Goodwill." Further, objections are made to current selling price reporting and to reporting liabilities as recommended in Chapter 15 because those treatments don't reflect what those who object believe are the intentions of the issuers, as discussed in Chapter 14 in the section "Intentions" and Chapter 15 in the section "Current early repayment amount," or the expectations of the issuers, as indicated by the statement of Solomons quoted above.

Current thoughts of the issuers about the future shouldn't be reflected in financial statements for at least three reasons.[27]

First, thoughts about the future aren't verifiable and reflecting them violates the user-oriented criterion of verifiability. Skinner said that

> The best we can do is measure and report expectations about the future... Since it is expectations about the future that influence market prices, it is inevitable that market prices will form an important part in the portrayal of representational faithfulness.
>
> (Skinner, 1987, 642)

However, an expectation lacks the most important characteristic required for something to be measurable—it isn't observable. The expectations of issuers of entities operating in markets aren't measurable; the only thing the purchase of a resource by an entity shows about the expectations of the people

---

26 This refers to reporting resources that can be used but can't be sold at their scrap amounts, discussed in Chapter 14.

27 As discussed in Chapter 8 in the section "Perspective of the users," current thoughts of the *users* in general as demonstrated by their behavior, their perspective, should be incorporated into the design of financial statements

running the entity, if they are sensible, is that they expected the net future cash flows of the entity to be enhanced by the purchase compared with not purchasing it, but it doesn't show by how much they expected them to be enhanced. The same transaction shows that the people running the entity selling the resource expected that keeping the resource would have resulted in decreased net future cash flows of that entity compared with selling it, but it doesn't show by how much they expected they would have been decreased. Market prices don't measure people's expectations.

Evidence isn't available to verify someone's thoughts about the future: no one other than a person doing some thinking about the future has any chance of being sure what that person's thinking, still less of measuring it. Though all who aren't financial reporters know that, Kam felt he had to remind us financial reporters of it: "we cannot be expected to read people's minds" (Kam, 1990, 525). Johnson said that "intentions are inherently unknowable by others..." (Johnson, 1994, 6). If the issuer says what she's thinking about the future, she might be lying for her own benefit—some people are wonderful liars. What's worse, the issuer might not even know what she's thinking about the future—people are wonderful at self-deception. She might believe she's thinking one thing but her behavior might demonstrate that she's thinking something else. For example, people often hide their intentions even from themselves. A user understated the problem: "I don't know how much work [it] is ... to verify management's intent" (AICPA, 1994b, II, 5b, 8). Pallais said that "management's intentions ... cannot be examined..." (Pallais, 1999, 34, 24). Sterling didn't beat around the bush: "[thoughts] are impossible to verify" (Sterling, 1987, 22).

Thomas described assertions that are impossible to verify or falsify as incorrigible (giving credit to Sterling as the first to suggest that some elements of financial statements are incorrigible). He gave examples, such as "The spirit of our ancestors live in these skulls," "Beans make me melancholy," and "When the going gets tough, the tough get going" (Arthur L. Thomas, 1975, 51).

Second, current thoughts of the issuers about the future are states of the issuers' minds. The user-oriented criterion of representativeness is intended to include representations of states of and happenings to the reporting entity, not of persons' states of mind: "Accounting depictions must be representations of [things and events that exist outside the mind]..." (Sterling, 1987, 22). Reporting on the current thoughts of the issuers about the future is reporting not on the reporting entity but on the issuers: "What we expect or hope an asset will yield, by use or by sale, is not a characteristic of the asset. What we expect or hope is a characteristic of ourselves" (Chambers, 1979a, 49). As discussed in Chapter 1, thoughts of the issuers about the future are part of the financial reporting map (financial statements are merely thoughts of the issuers written on paper), not part of the financial reporting territory to be mapped. The reporting entity, the financial reporting territory, is where it is and has achieved financially what it has achieved financially regardless of what the issuers or anyone else think about what might happen in the future: "a company's financial position [is] ascertainable . . . independently of wishes . . . neither goals nor expectations can influence a present state" (Chambers, 1969, 609; 1971, 85).

Third, issuers' current thoughts about the future shouldn't be reflected in financial statements because one use of financial statements should be to help guide actions of the issuers in operating the reporting entity. Predictions, plans, and intentions of issuers on the conduct of its operations should be formed based, among other things, on the information in the financial statements, and they should therefore be formed after the financial statements are prepared:

> Financial position [should be] independent of expectations, expectations being formed on the basis of the facts represented by a statement of financial position . . . a system of measurement is quite unconcerned with the intentions of those it serves. Its purpose is to enable people to *form* intentions.
>
> (Chambers, 1966, 366; 1969, 567)

Nevertheless, Demski contends that "Expectations are the centerpiece of accrual accounting . . ." (Demski, 2003, 10).

Because thoughts about the future violate the user-oriented criteria of representativeness and verifiability, financial statement amounts that incorporate them can't be successfully audited (this is discussed further in Chapter 10).

Forward-looking information

Financial reports should include "forward-looking information" (a term used by the AICPA Special Committee on Financial Reporting [AICPA, 1994a, 25]) presented outside the financial statements, disclosures of current conditions and current thoughts of the issuers not portrayed in the financial statements that involve what the future might hold (see Chapter 17).

Reflecting in financial statements the financial effects of events that might have occurred but didn't

> What might have been is an abstraction
> Remaining a perpetual possibility
> Only in a world of speculation . . .
> Footfalls echo in the memory
> Down the passage which we did not take
> Towards the door we never opened
> Into the rose garden.
>
> (T. S. Eliot, "Burnt Norton")

We financial reporters would probably vehemently deny that we reflect in financial statements what might have been, the financial effects of events that might have occurred in the past but didn't. We do, nevertheless.

For example:

- A writedown under current GAAP of inventories from acquisition costs to current costs is intended to reflect the supposed waste supposedly caused by buying the inventories when they were bought rather than buying them later, when they might have cost less (see Chapter 13 in the section "Presenting fiction" for a discussion of supposed cost savings and cost wastes).
- To the extent that so-called compensation cost is reported in connection with the issuance of stock options, it reflects what might have happened but didn't, the issuance of the stock involved to someone else who might have contributed cash (as discussed in Chapter 18 in the section "The analysis").
- Spreading the financial effects of the investment tax credit involves reflecting the difference between what happened—incurrence of the income tax liability the reporting entity incurred—and what might have happened but didn't—incurrence of the income tax liability the reporting entity might have incurred had the investment tax credit not been available for use in calculating its income tax liability, as discussed in Chapter 19 in the section "Investment tax credit." In fact, deferred taxes in general reflects what might have happened but didn't, what the reporting entity's current tax liability might have been had it been calculated based on the principles used in its financial statements (as discussed in Chapter 21 in the section "Deferred taxes").
- The concept of forfeitures in pension reporting is based on the difference between what happened—the employee didn't become vested—and what might have happened but didn't—the employee became vested (as discussed in Chapter 24 in the section "Forfeitures").

Further, two proposed systems of financial reporting using supposed current buying prices are based on reflecting what might have happened but didn't, one popularized by Edwards and Bell and one based on so-called deprival value, both of which are discussed in Chapter 13.

Sterling once held, I believe incorrectly, that current selling price reporting reflects the financial effects of events that might have happened but didn't, but he seems to have since changed his mind, as discussed in Chapter 14 in the section "Evidence for the measurement of current selling prices."

The FASB recently inserted hypothetical participants to events in a measurement rule, parties that in reality didn't participate in the events. In its Project Updates updated August 2, 2003, under "Fair value measurement," it indicated that the reference to "willing parties" in the revised definition of *fair value* means this:

Willing parties are all hypothetical marketplace participants (buyers and sellers) that have utility for the item being measured and that are willing and able to transact, having the legal and financial ability to do so.

This measures events as they might have occurred, not as they did occur (this is also discussed in Chapter 14).

Because might-have-beens aren't part of history, because they are part of a parallel universe invented in our minds, we financial reporters should leave them to novelists, poets, dreamers, managers, and evaluators, and to the preparation of information to be included in financial reports outside the financial statements.

Going concern

The going-concern concept, one of the most venerable in financial reporting and probably the first concept that has been taught to beginning financial reporting students and therefore taken by them as gospel, is that the reporting entity should be considered to be able to continue in operation in the foreseeable future (at least one year) in the absence of evidence to the contrary: "Past economic experience lays the foundation for an assumption as to the future, namely, that the corporation will *continue* to have an indefinitely long life" (Bevis, 1965, 26).

Because such an assumption is a prediction, Sterling objects: "A strong case can be made that the accounting reports ought to show something about the likelihood of the firm continuing instead of the reports being prepared under the assumption that it will continue ... the going concern concept: purge it" (Sterling, 1968, 494, 497).

Another interpretation of the going concern concept, one to which I subscribe, is that, though the continuance of the reporting entity shouldn't be assumed in the preparation of financial statements, after the financial statements are prepared and audited the issuers and the outside auditor should review them and previous financial statements and other available information to see whether they believe they provide evidence that continuation of the reporting entity is *currently* in serious jeopardy (all reporting entities are always in some danger, and those whose managements and boards of directors don't realize that and therefore aren't vigilant are shortly not going) and therefore soon might be a stopping concern. If the evidence shows that it's in effect currently stopping, the issuers might revise the financial statements to a basis assuming liquidation of the reporting entity, such as the statement of affairs. AcSEC Statement of Position No. 90–7 prescribes reporting for entities in Chapter 11 bankruptcy and following emergence from Chapter 11 bankruptcy. Short of that, in accordance with SAS No. 59, the notes to the financial statements and the outside auditor's report should note the serious jeopardy the reporting entity appears to face currently. Those are the only responses that should be called for by the going-concern concept.

However, the going-concern concept has been said to inform us financial reporters of how we should design financial statements other than to consider revising them to a basis assuming liquidation of the reporting entity. The concept is often said to justify the current broad principles discussed in Chapter 10: "the assumption of the going concern ... rules out the use of liquidation values ... and ... forms the basis of depreciation accounting ... It ... requires asset valuation according to intended use" (Storey, 1959, 232, 237). However,

- If a concern is going, it's liquidating its assets through use or sale: "Unless a firm is in the process of orderly liquidation it can scarcely be described as 'going'" (Chambers, 1966, 204).
- As stated above, allocation, including depreciation reporting, violates every user-oriented criterion and therefore shouldn't be used for any concern, going or stopping.
- Intentions of the issuers shouldn't be reflected in financial statements.
- Current selling price reporting is a variety of what has been called current value reporting. Chapter 14, in the section "Intentions," contests the position sometimes stated that current selling price reporting should be used only by reporting entities that are currently going out of business.

Also, Baxter says that "so long as all is going well, sale price has little relevance..." (Baxter, 1967, 212, quoted in Chambers, 1979a, 52). Chambers responds: "We are required to suppose that all is going well, when we are preparing statements to show whether or not all is going well!" (Chambers, 1979a, 52).

Debating points

1 Some aspects of financial statements should have characters other than those of historical reports.
2 Kirk was wrong, events don't have retroactive effects.
3 Of course events have retroactive effects.
4 The future does exist at present, so financial reporters should incorporate aspects of future events in financial statements.
5 The AAA was right; past performance can only be judged when the future is known.
6 The common expression that the income of a reporting entity can be measured with precision only after the entity has been dissolved is right.
7 Income of a reporting entity can be measured just fine up to the reporting date, ignoring what might come later.
8 Evidence of one kind or another about future events is available for use in preparing financial statements.
9 The purpose of incorporating information about the future in financial statements is to stabilize income reporting, an unworthy purpose.

10 If the probability of something happening in the future that is vital about a reporting entity is nearly 100 percent, it should be reflected in its current financial statements.

11 Intentions, expectations, and other thoughts about the future of the issuers of financial reports should be reflected in financial statements.

12 Intentions, expectations, and other thoughts about the future of the issuers of financial reports shouldn't be reflected in financial statements.

13 Some analytical information on what might have been should be reflected in financial statements.

14 The going-concern concept should be incorporated in decisions on the design of GAAP.

8   The focus of attention in financial reporting[1]

what is the focus of interest in the report?

(Skinner, 1987, 43)

Financial reporting, as distinguished from national income reporting, focuses on micro-economic entities, such as persons, families, sole proprietorships, partnerships, branches, divisions, corporations, groups of related corporations, joint ventures, not-for-profit organizations, and national, state, and local governmental units. The first choice in designing a financial report is selection of the *reporting entity*, of the *focus of attention*:[2] you can't report on the whole world.

A handy fiction?

Zeff pointed out that, "[during the Middle Ages t]he separate existence of the reporting entity was in effect denied..." (Zeff, 1961, 57). Some still believe that the reporting entity doesn't exist separately, that it's a handy fiction, as, for example, the following statement implies:

> What we should comprehend in such expressions as "corporation," "company," and the like is a series of relationships between individual human beings; that is, each of these terms is, in a sense, a shorthand expression for a complex of human beings and relationships between human beings.
>
> (Goldberg, 1963, 162)

Based on that, General Motors Corporation doesn't exist. But a creation isn't its creator; a building isn't its builders; a reporting entity isn't merely those

---

1   Much of this chapter is taken from Rosenfield, 2005.
2   Similarly, Stewart called the reporting entity "the subject ... of financial reporting" (Stewart, 1989, 106), and Vatter called the reporting entity "the center or the area of attention" (see quotation on page 187).

who create or support it or the relationships between or among them. Paton was ambivalent on this. He said on the same page both that "the business enterprise [is] . . . an extension of the fiction of the corporate entity. . ." and that "The business enterprise is a *reality*. . ." (Paton, 1922, iv).

The reporting entity does exist. A reporting entity is a principal, with its directors, management, and employees as its agents; it acts through its agents; it can be sued and, through its agents, it can sue; its assets and its liabilities pertain to it (see below); it can succeed or fail—it can become insolvent or go bankrupt. However, because a reporting entity isn't alive, it doesn't think or feel (see below in the section "Reporting entities as persons").

The act of selecting from elements of existence on which to focus gives the reporting entity its existence: it "can be defined as any area of economic interest that has a separate existence of its own" (Kam, 1990, 306). For example, in consolidated financial statements, selected members of a group of related companies are the reporting entity, which is used because the issuer chooses to focus on it, presumably based on the needs of the users of the statements. It exists because those members of the group of companies exist. That selection is known as consolidation policy (see Chapter 26).

Selection of the reporting entity as classification

The selection of a reporting entity on which to focus is an example of classification, which, as discussed in Chapter 20, is a purposive activity. In this case, two classes are selected: (1) the reporting entity, and (2) everything else. As there are no natural classes, there are no natural reporting entities— reporting entities are selected because they best serve the purposes at hand: "the choice of accounting entity is a matter of convenience" (Skinner, 1987, 43).

The original focus of attention

The original focus of attention for financial reporting, the original reporting entity, was the proprietor. A proprietor is a person (or persons) who is the greatest risk-taker involved with the entity, who is the ultimate beneficiary of success or sufferer of failure of the business, and to whom duties of the business to transfer resources to them are discretionary. Originally, a business was identified with its proprietor for record-keeping purposes. In the first printed treatise on double-entry bookkeeping, Paciolo included accounts for the proprietor's household goods, his personal liabilities, and his personal transactions in addition to business accounts (Brown and Johnston, 1963); financial reports weren't yet prepared. Personal accounts were gradually eliminated, leaving only business accounts. Nevertheless, "[During the Middle Ages it was thought that] the business enterprise should be viewed as a part of the proprietor's person. . ." (Zeff, 1961, 46, 53).

The incomplete evolution of the concept of the focus of attention

The focus of attention for financial reporting gradually evolved away from the proprietor and towards the enterprise: "a new concept of a business as an entity with an existence separate from that of the owners began to take root" (Skinner, 1987, 8). However, the evolution has been incomplete, as discussed in the remainder of this chapter. A report should have a single, unified, internally consistent focus of attention. Either the proprietor or the enterprise (or conceivably something else) should be the sole focus. The incomplete evolution of the concept of the focus of attention caused it to be fragmented and internally inconsistent, and that caused disagreements about the nature of the reporting entity for financial reporting. The disagreements center on the debate between the proprietary theory and the entity theory, discussed next.

Theories about the reporting entity

> there are two different schools of thought which are made to serve as [the] integrating framework for accounting theory[:] the "proprietary" ... theory [and] the "entity" [theory]...
>
> (Vatter, 1947, 2)

> one of the most important and as-yet-unresolved problems in financial reporting concerns ... whether ... an enterprise or proprietary approach ... should be applied to income and capital measurement.
>
> (Lee, 1982, 190)

> two essentially irreconcilable accounting theories—the proprietary theory and the entity theory.
>
> (Robbins, 1987, 98)

> there is no surer way to create mass confusion than to set a group of accountants to discussing the logical consequences for accounting of the entity concept.
>
> (Skinner, 1982, 129)

> People still cite the [entity theory versus proprietary theory] debate as if it were important, but I think it's a non-issue.
>
> (Zeff,[3] 1995)

3 It's ironical that Zeff once considered the issue important enough to be the subject of his doctoral dissertation (Zeff, 1961), but by the time he had finished studying it he found it mainly a waste of time, as he indicated at the end of his dissertation and in the quoted letter.

The proprietary and entity theories about the reporting entity (and occasionally other such theories, such as the fund theory advocated by Vatter in *The Fund Theory of Accounting and its Implications for Financial Reports*) attempt to provide solutions to a series of issues in financial reporting. In the quotations above, one calls such a theory the integrating framework for theory in financial reporting; another calls selection of such a theory one of the most important and not yet resolved issues. Still others call it unresolvable and a creator of mass confusion, and another calls it a non-issue. What's going on here?

What is going on is that we are mired in the incomplete evolution of the concept of the focus of attention.

As discussed at the beginning of Chapter 3, this is an example of dealing with an unnecessary issue: should the proprietary theory or the entity theory (or one of the other theories that have occasionally been proposed) be applied in organizing the study of improvement in financial reporting? It's unnecessary because, as discussed below, (1) it deals with the wrong level of abstraction, and (2) it involves contradictions, fictions, and false assumptions, which shouldn't be used in the design of financial statements.

Financial reporters who pay attention to the theories generally feel they have to apply one of them and all it entails for any particular issue, that they can't pick and choose aspects of more than one. Thus in the first quotation that opens this section, Vatter refers to the theories as "schools of thought." In the second, Lee asks whether one of the theories or the other should be applied, presumably to the exclusion of the other. In the third, Robbins refers to them as "essentially irreconcilable," and in the fifth, Zeff refers to a debate between the theories, not between aspects of them.

We should apply neither. The issue between the proprietary theory and the entity theory has been the most intractable issue in financial reporting. It's the result of the incomplete evolution of the concept of the focus of attention, and it should be abandoned. Issues concerning what characteristics the concept of the focus of attention should have with the evolution complete should be considered instead. They are considered below in the section "A complete evolution of the concept of the focus of attention."

The proprietary theory

The proprietary theory gives lip service to the idea that a business enterprise as a reporting entity is the focus of attention: "in the proprietary theory, as well as in the entity theory, the business firm is the center or the area of attention . . . the area of attention for a given set of records and reports must be limited" (Vatter, 1947, 3). However, its concepts tend to contradict that idea and focus on the financial effects on its proprietors of the events reported on:

> to define the area of attention in terms of an enterprise merely restricts the scope of a set of books or a series of reports; the way in which mater-

ials are dealt with within them is quite another matter. For the proprietary theorist the proprietor is the person to whom and for whom reports are made, and the concepts of net worth and profit are personal ideas, in that the proprietor's interest is the axis around which the processes of accounting revolve.

(Vatter, 1947, 3)

Under the proprietary theory, "the . . . proprietor . . . [is] seen as owning the firm's assets and owing its liabilities. . ." (Zeff, 1961, 105). That leads to the unsound view, for example that General Motors doesn't own its factories. Besides, "ownership . . . is a nebulous concept and is extremely difficult to define. . ." (Goldberg, 1963, 162). In any event, who *owns* the assets and who *owes* the liabilities shouldn't even necessarily be determinative for financial reporting: "legal title is not the determinant of asset existence" (Vatter, 1947, 17). To whom the assets and liabilities *pertain* should be determinative for that purpose:

> [With the enterprise as the focus of attention] the principal accounting focus of interest is upon the resources *entrusted* to the entity itself and the changes in them over the accounting period. . .
>
> (Skinner, 1987, 44, emphasis added)

For example, the partners of a partnership ultimately owe its liabilities, but the liabilities pertain to the partnership for purposes of its financial statements. A sole proprietor owns the assets and owes the liabilities of the sole proprietorship, but the assets and liabilities pertain to the sole proprietorship if it's selected as the focus of attention, as the reporting entity. Branches and divisions of a company don't own their assets or owe their liabilities, the company does, but the assets and liabilities pertain to the branches and divisions for purposes of their financial statements. Even for purposes of personal financial statements, the assets and liabilities pertain to the reporting entity, though they are owned and owed by the person or persons. And reporting entities don't have title to and therefore don't technically own some of the assets that pertain to them, because, for example, they obtained them by conditional purchase or lease.

Because the assets and liabilities are considered those of the proprietor under the proprietary theory, the income reported in financial statements is considered that of the proprietor:

> whose is the bottom line? . . . whose income and whose wealth are we reporting? . . . [under the] proprietary [theory] . . . the focus of interest in the income statement [is] the profit accruing to the proprietor after all other claims on revenues are satisfied.
>
> (Vatter, 1947, 43, 44)

Dividends don't in concept take place under this theory, because they are in effect transfers from one pocket of the proprietor to another.

The implication of the proprietary theory that the proprietors are "the focus of interest," the focus of attention, is contradicted by the references in the headings of the financial statements and the outside auditor's report to the financial position and results of operations of the reporting entity, not of the proprietors. Revsine objected:

> the firm ... not its shareholders ... makes a product or delivers a service ... is regulated, taxed, and controlled by a wide array of government agencies and courts of law ... it is potentially misleading to combine the interests of the firm and its shareholders in accounting reports...[4]
>
> (Revsine, 1982, 77)

The entity theory

The entity theory treats all the outside parties associated with a business enterprise defined as the reporting entity, including the proprietors, as essentially the same: "The 'entity theory' ... implies that ... the proprietor [is merely] one of the several financially interested parties..." (Zeff, 1961, 2). Similarly, the FASB pointed out that "employees, suppliers, customers or beneficiaries, lenders, stockholders, donors, and governments are ... 'other entities' to a particular entity" (FASB, 1985a, par. 24). While the proprietors should indeed be treated as outsiders to the focus of attention, they should be treated as "other entities," the proprietors are special outsiders and shouldn't be treated the same as the others. The reporting entity's duties to the stockholders are ordinarily discretionary on the part of the reporting entity.

Considering the proprietors as essentially the same as all the other outsiders under the entity theory leads to unjustifiable views, for example that the reporting entity's equity is a liability: "one English writer in 1910 ... implied the entity viewpoint when he advised his student-readers as follows: 'For the purposes of book-keeping treat capital ... just as if it were a debt payable'" (Goldberg, 1965, 111, quoting Snailum, 1910, 24). It doesn't represent a liability, which is a noncontingent, nondiscretionary duty (FASB, 1985a, par. 54) of the reporting entity to pay money, distribute nonmonetary assets, provide services, or forgive debt. It also leads to the unjustifiable view that taxes and interest aren't expenses: "From an entity point of view, taxes and interest represent distributions of its income from operations like dividends, rather than expenses required to earn entity income" (Skinner, 1987, 45). As late as 1966, the AICPA Director of Accounting

---

4 This would rule the interests of the owners, the "owners' equity," and the "minority interest" out of financial statements. See below in the text, and Chapter 9 in the section "The concept of equity," for a recommendation to do just that.

Research stated, "Whether income taxes are conceptually expenses or distributions of income has not really been resolved by the profession" (Storey, 1966, vii). They should be reported as expenses, however, because they result from profit-directed activities (AICPA, 1970c, par. 78) and are noncontingent, nondiscretionary payments. The users are helped by distinguishing (1) noncontingent, nondiscretionary payments of resources caused by profit-directed activities from (2) discretionary payments of resources that aren't caused by profit-directed activities, such as dividends. Further, rather than defining expenses as costs "required to earn entity income," as Skinner does as quoted above, they should be defined as costs incurred in the process of earning income. Defined that way, they include taxes and interest but not dividends.

Reporting entities as fictitious persons

The theories involve the additional error that a reporting entity is a fictitious person:

> Whose wealth and income should we attempt to measure? The concepts of wealth and income must refer to a specific person or a specific group ... The firm ... in its corporate form is known to be a fictitious person.
>
> (Sterling, 1979, 155, 156)

The law burdened financial reporting with that idea: "because of the ascent of the Stuarts (with James I in 1603) ... the crown could grant special privileges and monopolies to corporations, which would come to be viewed as fictitious legal persons..." (Zeff, 1961, 32). Goldberg pointed out the danger in "the widespread practice of attributing personal attributes to impersonal things. This is properly ... the domain of the poet—and the maker of an animated cartoon" (Goldberg, 1965, 121).

Not only is "a corporation ... not a real person..." (Arthur L. Thomas, 1975a, 96), it's *no* kind of person, fictitious or otherwise. A person is a human being. A reporting entity bears no resemblance to human beings. Sure, both persons and reporting entities are subject to the law, but that doesn't make reporting entities fictitious persons. Rain falls on houses and cars, but that doesn't make cars fictitious houses. Considering a reporting entity, something that exists, as a fiction is harmful to both the law and financial reporting. Were corporations fictitious anythings, they should have no place in financial statements, which should report information on reality, not fantasy (unless they are, say, financial statements of Alice's Wonderful Company in Wonderland and identified as fiction):

> We reject as fundamentally unsound and obsolete the thesis that a corporation can be regarded for any purpose as a mere fiction of the law. To reduce it to fiction is to make it nothing. Then to disregard it as a

fiction is to disregard nothing. A fiction cannot sue or be sued, make and perform contracts, own property, commit torts and crimes. A corporation can do all that, and so is not fiction. So to consider it, is to blind thought to large and important reality.

(Justice Stone, 1953, 41)

A complete evolution of the concept of the focus of attention

The debate between the theories of the reporting entity resulted from the incomplete evolution of the concept of the focus of attention. To completely evolve the concept of the focus of attention to the enterprise as the reporting entity it needs to have the following characteristics, most of which are discussed throughout this chapter, with the rest discussed in other chapters as indicated (because of the novelty of the list that follows, please let me know about differences you might have regarding it, together with your reasons):

- *Reality.*[5] The overriding characteristic is that completely evolved concepts concerning the reporting entity reflect the nature of financial statements as historical reports that map financial aspects of the reporting entity as it exists and as it has changed (see Chapters 4 and 7). Completely evolved concepts concerning the reporting entity avoid contradictions, fictions, and false assumptions.
- *Separate existence.* The enterprise selected as the reporting entity exists, its existence is separate from the existence of all other entities, including its proprietors if any, and it is under the control of one management team[6] (which may report to a higher management team) or one board of directors.
- *Scope of the reporting entity.* The scope of the reporting entity chosen, for example, by the consolidation policy adopted, depends on the needs of the users: "an entity is whatever recipients of reports wish it to be" (Arthur L. Thomas, 1975a, 14). Whatever scope is selected, attention should be focused on it and on it only.
- *Effects on outside parties.* A financial report is about the effects of events on the financial position, results of operations, cash flows, and prospects of the reporting entity, not on any aspects of any other entity.
- *The reporting entity's side of its transactions and relationships.* Only the reporting entity's side of each of its transactions and relationships with other entities is reported.

---

5 The philosophical depths of the nature of reality aren't explored here. All that's meant by this designation is that matters that are contradictory, fictitious, or false by definition should be avoided in designing financial statements.
6 Professor George Staubus suggested this.

- *Assets and liabilities of the reporting entity.* The assets and liabilities of the reporting entity are treated as pertaining to the reporting entity, not to its proprietors if any.
- *Equity of the reporting entity.* The numerical difference between the total of the reporting entity's assets and the total of its liabilities is treated as its equity, *its* interest in its assets net of its liabilities.
- *Income of the reporting entity.* The increase or decrease from profit-directed activities in the equity of a business enterprise selected as a reporting entity, its net income, is treated as pertaining to the reporting entity, not to its proprietors. Further, "All investors are interested in the change in the residual equity due to operations during the period" (Staubus, 1959, 10).
- *Absence of thoughts and emotions.* Because a reporting entity isn't alive, it has no thoughts or emotions.
- *Perspective of the users.* The definition of success of a business enterprise selected as a reporting entity and reported on in its financial statements is based on the perspective of the users of its financial statements.

Effects on outside parties

The restriction of the domain of financial statements to effects of events that affect the focus of attention, the reporting entity, is sometimes ignored. For example, as discussed in Chapter 15, in attempting to support its position that a reporting entity should report a gain when its credit standing declines and a loss when its credit standing increases(!), the FASB referred to supposed changes in the economic positions of outsiders, of its shareholders and creditors:

> A change in credit standing represents a change in the relative positions of the ... shareholders and creditors ... a change in the position of borrowers necessarily alters the position of shareholders, and vice versa.
>
> (FASB, 2000b, par. 87)

Changes in the economic positions of the stockholders and creditors may be relevant to reporting on them, but they are irrelevant to reporting on the reporting entity.

Further, an exposure draft of a proposed FASB Statement of Concepts, "Proposed Amendment to FASB Concepts Statement No. 6 to Revise the Definition of Liabilities, an amendment of FASB Concepts Statement No. 6," dated October 27, 2000, would change and SFAS 150, "Accounting for Certain Financial Instruments with Characteristics of Both Liabilities and Equity," dated May 2003 in effect changed the definition of a *liability* to include a duty of the reporting entity to issue its own equity securities whose value to the recipient at the date of issuance is predetermined. However, at the time the duty comes into existence, the stockholdings of the existing stockholders are fixed, and total 100 percent of the outstanding stock. The reporting entity is unaffected by the identity of the stockholders and the distribution of their stockholdings within the 100 percent. (Voting power for the Board of Directors and on other issues that come before the stockholders are affected, but those are matters we don't and can't report on in the financial statements.) When the reporting entity incurs the duty, it becomes bound to issue some quantity or other of its own equity securities sometime in the future. When the time comes, it issues those equity securities.

Neither of those aspects of the events in which they occur affects the reporting entity's assets or liabilities.

Those aspects, rather, affect the existing stockholders and the prospective stockholders. The first aspect threatens the existing stockholders with having their stockholdings diluted; it turns some entities other than the existing stockholders into prospective stockholders. The second aspect dilutes the stockholdings of the existing stockholders; it turns the prospective stockholders into stockholders. Only the existing stockholders and the entities turned into prospective stockholders are affected by the aspects of the events causing reporting entity to incur and discharge the duty. The reporting entity's assets and liabilities are never affected by those aspects of the events, any more than they are affected by transactions in its stock in the stockmarket.

The Board's justification for the change in the definition of liabilities was that obligations that settle with equity should not be classified as equity unless they *expose the holder* to risks and benefits that are similar to those to which an owner is exposed (FASB, 2003a, par. B42). That justification fails, because the effects on the holders are irrelevant to the reporting of the duty by the reporting entity. Only effects on the reporting entity are relevant to its reporting on itself.

We should be reporting solely on financial effects of events on the reporting entity, the sole focus of attention. We shouldn't account for and report on the incurrence or discharge of a duty that never affects the reporting entity, but only affects outsiders: entities being made into prospective stockholders, entities that are prospective stockholders, and existing stockholders.

The Board issued these documents to avoid what it considers an abuse of the following kind: an attorney provides legal services to the reporting entity and prepares to bill it $1000. The reporting entity asks the attorney whether she would instead accept a promise of stock of the reporting entity in a quantity to be determined at the date the stock is issued to equal $1000 worth of stock. The attorney agrees. The purpose of the arrangement would be to avoid reporting the attorney's fee as an expense. Reporting the duty as a liability would provide that the fee is reported as an expense.

Promising an attorney stock in a set dollar amount is intended as an abuse. The attorney wants money for her services. This is a roundabout way to pay the fee, engaged in solely to keep her fee off the income statement. The FASB established the rule to stop the intended abuse.

However, the FASB's solution, rather than avoiding an abuse, would create an abuse where none exists:

- The abuse the FASB would be creating is requiring reporting entities to report as liabilities duties that do not affect the reporting entities' assets or liabilities.
- The reason not reporting the duties as liabilities would not permit an abuse is that in the illustration, the reporting entity would still be required to report on the receipt and using up of the attorney's services, with the using up reported as an expense. That is essentially identical to the necessity of a reporting entity to report as a capital contribution the receipt of fixed assets received as a capital contribution from a new stockholder and to report the using up of the assets as an expense. It would be recorded as follows:

Attorneys' services (an expense)	1000.00	
Additional paid-in capital—		
attorneys' services		1000.00

To record the receipt and using up of services received from an attorney as a contribution to the capital of the company, to be compensated by the issuance of $1000 market value of unissued common stock of the company.

That is similar to the first entry in SFAS No. 123, paragraph 293,[7] to record the receipt and using up of employee services in connection with the issuance of stock options to employees.

The issuance of the common stock would be recorded by this kind of journal entry at the date the stock is issued according to current GAAP:

Additional paid-in capital		
—attorneys' services	1000.00	
Common stock		1000.00

To record the issuance of common stock in compensation to an attorney for receipt of services.

However, if the recommendation made in Chapter 20 to present equity as a single amount in the balance sheet is adopted, a single entry at the date the services were received would suffice:

7 In that entry, "Compensation cost" is used in place of "Employees' services (an expense)" and "Additional paid-in capital-stock options" is used in place of "Additional paid-in capital–employees' services." This agrees with this statement of the FASB: "... issuances of equity instruments result in the receipt of ... services, which give rise to expenses as they are used in an entity's operations" (FASB, 1995, par. 89).

Attorneys' services (an expense)   1000.00
   Equity   1000.00

> To record expense for the receipt and using up of services from an attorney received as a contribution to the capital of the company, in the amount of the market value of unissued common stock to be issued to the attorney in compensation for the services.

A correspondent brought up different possible patterns of discharging the duty to issue stock to the attorney, say discharge in three years or discharge with options to acquire stock. However, they all seem moot, because it would be hard enough to get the attorney to agree to a simple pattern of discharge, no less a complex pattern. Anyway, if such an arrangement were made, it would merely complicate the measurement of the dollar value of the services received. It is similar to the case of stock options issued to employees in connection with the receipt of employee services. An issue there is how to measure the dollar amount of the services received and used up (the literature disguises the issue by asking how to measure compensation cost[8]). If the FASB were to retract its rule that a liability should be reported here, and made it clear that an expense would have to be reported regardless, the abuse would likely not be attempted. If such an abuse, and a complex one at that, were nevertheless attempted and if the FASB is then issuing principles-based standards, the issuer and the accountant would have to figure out how to measure the services received and used up.

The reporting entity's side of its transactions and relationships

No reporting entity is an island. A reporting entity has transactions and relationships with other entities. Each of those transactions and relationships has two or more sides, the reporting entity's side and the other entity's side or other entities' sides. For example, an exchange may be a purchase by one entity and a sale by another entity. A choice needs to be made as to which side to report. The choice should be obvious: with the focus of attention of financial statements on the reporting entity, a reporting entity should report its side of each transaction or relationship with another entity or other entities, not the other entity's side or other entities' sides, even though they are opposite sides of the same thing.[9]

For example, the issuers of the financial reports of a reporting entity need to know which side of an exchange it's on to be able to report it properly as a purchase or a sale. Being an exchange, a purchase or a sale is a reciprocal

---

8 See Chapter 18.

9 The opposite ends of the Albany–Susquehanna Railroad were owned by J. Pierpont Morgan and Jim Fisk. Heilbroner reports that "[Their] controversy was ... resolved by each side mounting a locomotive on its end of the track and running the two engines, like gigantic toys, into one another" (Heilbroner, 1972, 207).

transfer as defined by the APB (as discussed in Appendix A to Chapter 3 and in APB Opinion No. 29), an event in which the reporting entity sacrifices something of value to it and receives something of value to it. In contrast, the issuance by a reporting entity of its own stock on the receipt of a contribution of money by a stockholder is a nonreciprocal transfer as defined by the APB (also as discussed in Appendix A to Chapter 3 and APB Opinion No. 29), an event in which the reporting entity receives something of value to it and sacrifices nothing of value to it (a reporting entity's own stock isn't an asset to it; see SFAS No. 135, par. 4b), in contrast with an exchange. The issuance of additional stock by a reporting entity has no effect on the reporting entity (except for a counterfactual—fictitious—effect, which is no effect, as discussed in Chapter 18). It affects only the recipients of the stock and the other stockholders. Therefore, the common expression of a sale of the stock of a reporting entity by the reporting entity is misleading: as to the reporting entity, it isn't a sale; it's simply a receipt of a capital contribution. The FASB disagrees. It discusses "transactions in which an entity acquires goods or services from nonemployees in *exchange* for equity instruments [which is] consideration *paid* for goods or services..." (FASB, 1995a, par. 2, emphasis added).

Similarly, a common expression refers to a purchase of the stock of a reporting entity by the reporting entity, for example:

> The McDonald's Corporation said today that it would buy back $3.5 billion of its common stock by the end of 2001 in a repurchase plan...
> *(New York Times*, 1998, C20)

> A corporation may purchase its own shares...
> (Benis, 1999, 22·14)

That expression is also misleading. As to the reporting entity, it isn't a purchase—it's "a distribution to owners" (FASB, 1985a, par. 69), a partial, nonproportional, liquidating dividend.

Ignoring the choice of the side of a relationship the reporting entity is on leads, for example, to unsound descriptions of receivables—as the *duties*, the *debts* of outsiders, of the debtors—and of liabilities—as the *rights*, the *claims* of outsiders, of the creditors, for example: "An enterprise's liabilities ... are ... claims to ... the enterprise's assets by entities other than the enterprise..." (FASB, 1985a, par. 54). Others attribute receivables properly to the reporting entity, as its rights, *its claims* against the debtors and liabilities properly as its duties, *its obligations* to the creditors. The differences lead to diverse positions on issues in financial reporting.

Some completely de-emphasize the reporting entity and its duties, and stress outside parties and their claims. For example, Bricker and Previts suggested revising the balance sheet equation to the following: "**RESOURCES = RESOURCE CLAIMS**" (Bricker and Previts, 1992, 20).

Worse, Bricker and Previts "oriented" the entire reporting on outsiders, those who hold claims on the reporting entity, not on the reporting entity itself: "Accounting should have . . . a claimholder orientation. . ." (Bricker and Previts, 1992, 21). At one point, however, they acknowledged that the reporting entity and its duties (responsibilities), rather than outsiders and their claims, are involved: "Our model is similar in some ways to Hendriksen's . . . Enterprise Theory, which views the corporation as [an] organization having . . . responsibilities. . ." (Bricker and Previts, 1992, 20).

The following passage provides another example:

> If a party exchanges something of value for the sole "ownership" of a firm, then that party has acquired a property right in that firm's resources . . . A similar case could be made for creditors. In both instances, a cost is incurred in a contractual arrangement in order to obtain the property right. The cost incurred and the contractual arrangement are used as the justification for including the property rights of these parties as owners' equity or a liability in the accounting model.
>
> (Bricker and Previts, 1992, 12, 13)

In each case the "cost" is incurred and the "right" is held by the outside parties, not by the reporting entity. Though Bricker and Previts contend that such costs and rights are relevant to the design of the reporting entity's financial statements, costs incurred and rights held by parties other than the reporting entity, in fact, anything that happens to, belongs to, or is owed by any parties other than the reporting entity, are irrelevant to that design.[10] Other than the perspective of the users, discussed below, only events that happen to the reporting entity, resources that belong to the reporting entity, or resources that are owed by the reporting entity are relevant to the design of its financial statements.

Further, Bricker and Previts use the common expression "owners' equity" (Bricker and Previts, 1992, 13). But anything that belongs to the owners, such as their equity in the reporting entity, though relevant to the financial reporting of the owners, is irrelevant to the financial reporting of the reporting entity (see Chapter 9).

---

10 Some contend that current selling price reporting incorporates in the design of the reporting entity's financial statements the financial effects on outside parties of transactions to which the reporting entity isn't a party, transactions that don't affect the reporting entity. They use that contention to reject current selling price reporting. However, current selling price reporting doesn't incorporate the financial effects of those transactions in the design of the reporting entity's financial statements. It uses those financial effects as part of the evidence on which to determine the financial effects of other events, events that change the selling prices of the assets of the reporting entity, events that do affect the reporting entity (see Chapter 14).

The kinds of costs incurred by parties other than the reporting entity to which Bricker and Previts refer are relevant, as they contend, to the reporting entity's contractual duties to the other parties to provide information to those parties. Bricker and Previts are also right in contending that the reporting entity has duties to provide information to certain noncontracting parties. In each case, however, Bricker and Previts emphasize the outside parties and their rights to receive information rather than the reporting entity and its duties to provide information, once again taking attention off the focus of attention.

Thoughts and emotions of the reporting entity

Kam states that "[t]he newer interpretation sees the entity as . . . interested in its own survival" (Kam, 1990, 306). However, not being alive, a reporting entity can't have thoughts or emotions. It can't be interested in anything. It can't care whether it makes income or loss or even what's thought about as income or loss. It can't even care whether it survives: "The entity is as soulless and automatic as a slot machine . . . [It] is incapable of enjoyment, sorrow, greed, or other human emotions which influence those who direct it" (Gilman, 1939, 52). Any caring about the reporting entity has to be done by the people associated with it. That's developed in the next section.

Perspective of the users

> theorists failed to address the perspective from which accounting reports [should] be prepared.
>
> (Stewart, 1989, 98)

Much of the preceding discussion might make it seem that the only place to look to decide on financial reporting issues is the reporting entity. However, looking solely to the reporting entity to see what should be considered good, to define what is income of the reporting entity, is inadequate, because, as the preceding section discusses, the reporting entity can't care about anything, including what's good for it. The users of the financial reports of the reporting entity can care, and they do, about what they consider to be good for the reporting entity:

> If . . . it is asserted that in accounting for an entity the interpretations and judgements of its supporters may be disregarded, the very nature of the entity is therefore disregarded; for any entity exists by virtue of the cooperation of its supporters . . .
>
> (Chambers, 1969, 101)

The "perspective," "the interpretations and judgements," of the users of the financial statements of a reporting entity on what's good for the reporting entity need to be incorporated in the design of financial statements.

A fable about a farm illustrates that. At the beginning of the year, the farm had 1000 cows and no other assets and no liabilities. At the end of the year, the farm had 1000 sheep and no other assets and no liabilities. The proprietors had no transactions with the farm during the year. Based solely on that information, did the farm have a good year or a bad year?

The answer is that it depends. The farm itself couldn't care whether it had cows or sheep or something else or nothing at all. The only ones who could care are people. Let's say that some people love cows and hate sheep, and other people love sheep and hate cows. From the perspective of the people who love cows, the farm had a disastrous year. From the perspective of the people who love sheep, the farm had a great year. The same farm during the same period had both a disastrous year and a great year. How can that be? It's because people add something to circumstances when judging them, and the disastrousness or greatness isn't simply in the farm's year but in the perspectives of the people associated with it. It's like the famous game ending with a score of UConn 77 and Duke 74. Was that a good result or a bad result? Again, it depends.

Because income is so important in financial reporting and because it can be reported on in so many different ways, it's essential to determine what the users consider income and loss in designing financial statements.

The perspective of the users applies, for example, in determining the kind of money to use in defining the unit of measure to use in a set of financial statements. A great majority of the users of the financial statements of most companies reside in and are interested in the money of single countries. Most U.S. users are interested in U.S. dollars, most British users are interested in British pounds, and so on.[11] However, significant groups of the users of the financial statements of some companies reside in more than one country, and the perspective of each group is likely to be based on the money of the country in which it resides. To apply those perspectives, a separate set of financial statements can be prepared for each user group, stated in the money of its country:

> A possible solution for companies having difficulty choosing a currency for reporting purposes is for them to express their statements in more than one currency, in more than one language and with more than one format to correspond to those conditions which various shareholder groups regard as "domestic." This raises the obvious practical question of what percentage shareholding would be necessary for a shareholder group to qualify for reports expressed in terms of its own environment.
>
> (Henderson and Peirson, 1980, 323)

11 In some countries, people are interested in the moneys of other countries. For example, Ecuador, Panama, and, in effect, Argentina, use the U.S. dollar as their currencies (Rohter, 1999, TR3). The users in those countries are interested in financial reports with the unit of measure defined in terms of U.S. dollars.

A company issuing financial reports to users in foreign countries may
... [p]repare two sets of financial statements, one using the home
country language, currency, and accounting principles, the second using
the language, currency, and accounting principles of the foreign
country's users.

(Schroeder and Clark, 1998, 277, 278)

For example, because the Royal Dutch Shell Petroleum Corporation has
significant groups of users of its financial statements in both Britain and
Holland, it presents two sets of financial statements, one in terms of British
pounds and one in terms of euros.

Because of changes in the exchange rate between the two moneys, it's
possible for one of two such sets of financial statements to report net income
for a year and the other to report net loss for the same year. The following
illustrates that possibility:

- At January 1, Year 1, the exchange rate between the British pound and
  the euro was 1:1. At December 31, Year 1, that exchange rate was 2:1.
- At January 1, Year 1, RDS, Inc. had 150 British pounds, no other
  assets, and no liabilities.
- At December 31, Year 1, RDS, Inc. had 100 euros, no other assets, and
  no liabilities.
- RDS, Inc. had no transactions with its owners during Year 1.

In terms of British pounds, RDS, Inc. had income during Year 1 of
$(£2 \div €1 \times €100) - £150 = £50$. In terms of euros, RDS, Inc. had a loss
during Year 1 of $€100 - (€1 \div £1 \times £150) = -€50$.

If significant numbers of the users of RDS's financial reports live in both a
sterling area and a euro area, it should consider issuing two reports, one in
terms of pounds and one in terms of euros.

Whether a reporting entity presents more than one set of financial statements depends on the significance of the groups of users residing in more
than one country, on regulations governing reporting by the reporting
entity by organizations or governments with the power to affect its reporting, on the desires of the users, and on the inclinations of the issuers.

Incorporating the perspective of cow-loving, sheep-hating people or
sheep-loving, cow-hating people or of sports fans doesn't challenge the farm
or the game as sole focus of attention. Incorporating the perspective of the
users in the design of financial statements similarly doesn't challenge the
reporting entity as the sole focus of attention, as assigning a central place to
the proprietors does in the proprietary theory. The perspective of the users of
financial statements is focused on the reporting entity, not on the users.

The most pervasive needs to consider the perspective of the users besides
in the selection of the unit of money with which to define the unit of
measure, as just discussed, are in considering inflation reporting, the

physical operating capacity variety of maintenance of capital, and reporting on foreign operations, as discussed in Chapters 11, 13, and 22.

Debating points

1   A reporting entity is a fiction.
2   The conflict between the proprietary and the entity theories of the firm can't be solved.
3   The sounder theory is the proprietary theory.
4   The proprietor should not be part of the concept of the reporting entity.
5   The conflict between the proprietary and the entity theories should be abandoned.
6   The effects of events on entities other than the reporting entity should be considered in designing GAAP, as the FASB does.
7   The effects of events on entities other than the reporting entity should be ignored in designing GAAP.
8   It's silly to suggest that "owners' equity" should no longer be presented in balance sheets.
9   A reporting entity's feelings should be considered in designing GAAP.
10   There is a true state and a true income of a reporting entity, each of which is independent of the perspectives of the users of its financial statements.
11   A farm with cows or sheep has nothing to do with financial reporting.

9 The elements of the reporting entity represented in financial statements

> the Federal Home Loan Bank Board proposed allowing associations to retire mortgage receivables and delay the reporting of the losses . . . any loss on such a transaction would be set up as an asset . . .
>
> (Ketz and Wyatt, 1983, 35)

Financial statements report on the financial elements of the reporting entity: its assets, liabilities, revenues, and expenses.

The elements are in the financial reporting territory, not in the financial reporting map (see Chapter 4); assets, for example, exist outside the financial statements, not in the financial statements. Financial statements present merely representations of the elements. No balance sheet contains any cash, for example—it's merely represented in that statement; cash exists in, for example, strongboxes and bank accounts. The outside auditor's standard report erroneously states that the financial statements present the financial position and results of operations of the reporting entity. They don't. The financial position and the results of operations, whatever they are, pertain to the reporting entity and exist and occur in the financial reporting territory. They aren't presented in the financial statements, the financial reporting map. Instead, they are *represented* in the financial statements.

In one place the FASB got that right: "Items that are recognized in financial statements are financial representations of . . . assets . . . liabilities . . . and changes in [them] . . ." (FASB, 1984a, par. 5). But in another place the FASB said the elements exist in the financial statements, in the financial reporting map: ". . . elements of financial statements . . .—assets, liabilities . . . revenues, expenses, gains, and losses . . ."[1] (FASB, 1985a, par. 1). Also, the APB referred to "The basic elements of financial accounting—assets, liabilities, owners' equity, revenue, expenses . . ."[2] (AICPA, 1970c, par. 130).

1 The FASB said that it used the term "elements" in both senses because it's a "common practice" (FASB, 1985a, par. 6). Instead of doing so, it should have confined the term to things in the financial reporting territory and referred to their representation in the financial reporting map.
2 I confess that I drafted that expression for the APB. I have since repented. See Chapter 10.

Thinking of the elements as existing in the financial statements or in financial accounting has contributed to the belief by us financial reporters that the financial reporting map is the financial reporting territory.

The focus is on the elements, not on the reporting entity as a whole. Criticism is sometimes erroneously leveled at current value reporting, for example, because it doesn't provide a good indication of the market price of the reporting entity as a whole, though financial statements aren't intended to do so and can't do so: "...financial accounting is not designed to measure directly the value of an enterprise" (FASB, 1978, par. 41).

Economic resources

The entire subject matter of financial statements is economic resources, which are items that are scarce and have utility to those entities to which they pertain. To that extent, financial statements are similar to economics, whose entire subject matter is also economic resources. However, financial statements and economics have different orientations (see Chapters 1 and 12), that is, economics mainly involves thoughts about the future concerning economic resources, while financial statements should be based solely on reliable measurements of the financial effects of relevant events affecting economic resources pertaining to the reporting entity that have already occurred outside of financial reporting. Financial reporting and economics should differ because of those different orientations:

> many accountants ... appear to have lost themselves [in the] confusion of accounting and economic ideas and terminology ... concepts and terms entirely valid in one field cannot be transferred to the other without, at any rate, very careful qualification.
>
> (Paton, 1922, v, vi)

The elements of the reporting entity represented in financial statements are generally defined in terms of economic resources. A reporting entity may hold or owe economic resources, and the amounts it holds or owes may increase or decrease over time. Most economic resources are severable—disposable separately from the reporting entity or a significant portion of the reporting entity, such as cash or items that may be sold separately for cash. Some aren't severable, such as goodwill; views differ on whether such economic resources should be part of the elements of the reporting entity represented in financial statements, as discussed below. Some severable economic resources, such as land, buildings, and equipment, are commonly used rather than held for sale, but they may be sold at any time the reporting entity finds that advantageous. Reporting on such economic resources under current selling price reporting is subject to especial disagreement, as discussed in Chapter 14.

Articulation

Amounts of economic resources held or owed by the reporting entity at the end of a period of time are the results of the amounts of economic resources held or owed at the beginning of the period plus or minus the amounts of increases and decreases in them during the period. The balance sheet and the income statement reflect that. They are said to articulate with each other:

> The financial statements of an entity are a fundamentally related set that articulate with each other and derive from the same underlying data ... "Double entry," the mechanism by which accrual accounting formally includes particular items that qualify under the elements definitions in articulated financial statements, incorporates [that] relation[ship].
>
> (Hill, 1987, 14)

The reason is that "the phenomena articulate" (Sterling, 1987, 51). Further, articulation reflects the so-called accounting equation, which is in essence not an equation but the definition of *equity*, as discussed below.

Articulation disciplines the reporting of income:

> The importance of articulation is that it requires use of the same principles of determining carrying value for both income measurement and determination of asset and liability carrying values. [It embodies] the discipline imposed on financial reporting by the accounting equation.
>
> (Hill, 1987, 14)

However, articulation occasionally leads to income statement results that one or another of the classes of parties to the financial reports considers not to conform to their incentives (see Chapter 2). So,

> [o]ne proposed solution was to abandon the requirement that the balance sheet and income statement articulate ... Those who proposed this claimed that articulation was an outmoded constraint that should be abandoned ... Many accountants still believe that one must choose which statement one wants to be accurate and, as a result, the other statement will be inaccurate ... Accountants even get classified as "balance-sheet theorists" versus "income-statement theorists." My view is exactly the opposite. Since income and wealth are inextricably entwined, an incorrect measure of one yields an incorrect measure of the other and vice versa.[3]
>
> (Sterling, 1979, 195, 196)

---

3 An exception is that the statement of income can be correct if the beginning and ending balance sheets are incorrect in the same direction and in the same amount.

Ways to avoid articulation's discipline on income reporting are discussed below in the section "Nonarticulation."

Definitions of the elements

The basic financial statements are the balance sheet and the statements of income, cash flows, and equity. The elements of the reporting entity represented in the balance sheet at the end of a period are its assets and its liabilities. The equity of the reporting entity is the difference between the total of the assets and the total of the liabilities represented in the balance sheet. The elements of the reporting entity represented in the statement of income for a period are its revenues, expenses, gains, and losses, which are some of the increases and decreases in the reporting entity's equity during the period—those resulting from its "profit-directed activities," as discussed below. Income or loss for a reporting period is the amount by which total revenues and gains are more than or less than total expenses and losses for the reporting period. The definition of *income* may thus be stated as the following:

$$\text{income} = (\text{revenue} + \text{gains}) - (\text{expenses} + \text{losses})$$

The statement of cash flows reports increases and decreases during a period in cash, an element of the reporting entity represented in the balance sheet. The statement of equity reports increases and decreases in equity during the period. Statements of increases and decreases in other elements of the reporting entity represented in the balance sheet can be presented, but they aren't basic financial statements.

The definitions of the elements of the reporting entity, once established well, can serve as tools of analysis (though, in the current results-oriented climate, they rarely do and when they are used, they are often twisted to results-oriented purposes). This is discussed in, for example, Chapters 21 and 24.

Though Sprouse said that "the [FASB] Statement of . . . elements [has] not been, and [is] not likely to be, seriously challenged," he did say it "may require an occasional polishing" (Sprouse, 1993, 51). (Nevertheless, when the FASB found that its definition of *liabilities* prevented a result it desired, it changed the definition [FASB, 2003a]; see Chapter 8).

The FASB's definitions of the elements of reporting entities represented in financial statements are challenged in this book, in this chapter and in various other chapters (especially Chapters 7 and 14).

Definitions of an asset

The concept of an *asset* seems simple, something valuable that pertains to the reporting entity, but views of us financial reporters on the concept differ. The APB defined *assets* as economic resources of an enterprise that are recognized and measured in conformity with generally accepted accounting principles. Assets also include certain deferred charges that are not resources but that are recognized and measured in conformity with generally accepted accounting principles.

(AICPA, 1970c, par. 132)

Though nominally tied to economic resources, the final portion of that definition makes an asset anything we financial reporters treat as assets, including what-you-may-call-its,[4] which are aspects of the financial reporting map that have no counterpart in the financial reporting territory[5] and therefore aren't elements of the reporting entity represented in the financial statements (they aren't, as the definition contends, "measured").

The definition was criticized for including what-you-may-call-its (Staubus, 1972, 39). However, the APB stated that its definitions were intended to be merely descriptive, ones that say what the elements are, and the criticism applies only to prescriptive definitions, ones that say what the elements should be. (The APB included prescriptive material rather in its discussions of objectives [AICPA, 1970c, Chapter 4].)

The FASB presented a prescriptive definition of *assets*: "probable future economic benefits obtained or controlled by a particular entity as a result of past transactions or events" (FASB, 1985a, par. 25). In a discussion of the definition, the FASB said an asset may be usable but not severable. The latter contradicts the view of some that to be an asset, a resource must be severable—for example, "An asset is defined as any severable means in the possession of an entity" (Chambers, 1966, 103) and "assets ... CASH, contractual claims to CASH, and things that can be sold for CASH..." (Schuetze, 1991, 116).

Some even include losses in the category of assets(!) to achieve desired income statement results:

Assets ... cover ... unamortized losses deferred.

(Littleton, 1953, 19)

illustrations in actual practice were found where companies in the development stage had deferred start-up costs including initial operating losses...[6]

(Sterling, 1973, 63)

---

4 This term was first used by Sprouse in his "Accounting for What-You-May-Call-Its."
5 Defliese said that certain what-you-may-call-its, "deferred debits and credits ... are mixtures of asset and liability effects" (Defliese, 1983, 94), but he didn't explain how that's possible.
6 This practice was later prohibited by SFAS No. 7.

> Under [the Competitive Equality Banking Act of 1987], agricultural banks may be permitted for regulatory purposes to defer . . . loan losses for up to seven years . . .
>
> (Arnold, 1988, 2)

(See also the quotation at the beginning of this chapter.)

Figures don't lie, but liars figure (old Chinese proverb, modified).

Definitions of a liability

The concept of a *liability* also seems simple, owing something valuable, but views of us financial reporters on this concept also differ. The APB defined *liabilities* as

> economic obligations of an enterprise that are recognized and measured in conformity with generally accepted accounting principles. Liabilities also include certain deferred credits that are not obligations but that are recognized and measured in conformity with generally accepted accounting principles.
>
> (AICPA, 1970c, par. 132)

Though nominally tied to economic resources, the final portion of that definition makes a liability anything we financial reporters treat as liabilities, including what-you-may-call-its, which are aspects of the financial reporting map that have no counterpart in the financial reporting territory and therefore aren't elements of the reporting entity represented in the financial statements (they aren't, as the definition contends, "measured").

That definition was also criticized for being a poor prescriptive definition, though it was stated to be only a descriptive definition.

The FASB presented a prescriptive definition of *liabilities*:

> probable future sacrifices of economic benefits arising from present obligations of a particular entity to transfer assets or provide services to other entities in the future as a result of past transactions or events.
>
> (FASB, 1985a, par. 35; this definition is also discussed in Chapter 15)

The FASB abuses that definition, as discussed below.

Discussion of the definitions of an asset and a liability

The APB mainly defined assets and liabilities properly in terms of economic resources currently held or owed, which are current conditions. In contrast, the FASB defined them in terms of probabilities of supposed financial effects of events that might take place in the future concerning economic resources—"future benefits" and "future sacrifices." Those are definitions of possible ways to quantify assets and liabilities, not of assets and liabilities, which should be defined in terms of economic resources:[7]

> Defining assets in terms of . . . resources . . . provides a . . . test for establishing what is, and what is not, an asset . . . Specifying that liabilities are . . . obligations of an entity. . . would, similarly, provide a more objective criterion . . . than . . . present rules which mandate speculations on the likelihood and magnitude of future dispositions of economic benefits.
>
> (West, 2003, 107)

The references in the FASB's definitions of *assets* and *liabilities* to "the result of past transactions and events," are essential—otherwise, next year's salaries, for example, would be this year's liabilities. The definitions don't say an asset or a liability can be *partly* a result of past events or transactions and *partly* a result of future events or transactions. That would cause *contingent assets and contingent liabilities* (which aren't assets or liabilities) to conform with the definitions. To be an asset or a liability, an item has to be *solely* the result of past events or transactions.

The restriction to items that result from past events and transactions is sometimes overlooked (perhaps sometimes merely carelessly). For example,

> no credit may be deferred unless there is good evidence it represents a probable future sacrifice.
>
> (Skinner, 1987, 50)

> liabilities . . . are the reporting enterprise's future cash outflows.
>
> (Schuetze, 2001, 20)

Issuers find those references to be an unwelcome impediment to achieving relatively stable income reporting in several areas concerning liabilities today. To get around those references, the FASB has on occasion contended that the references are complied with when they aren't, with the result that liabilities are required to be reported before they are incurred, when only contingent liabilities have been incurred (see examples in Chapters 21 and 24). It's instructive that the issuers accept treatments that require them to report liabilities before the reporting entities incur them in order to make reported income more stable.

Beaver states that

> the term based on past transactions and events, is not necessarily constraining . . . the issue is—what types of past transactions and events are

---

7 The FASB hedged its bets here. It later admitted that "The kinds of items that qualify as assets . . . are commonly called economic resources" (FASB, 1985a, par. 27). Its formal definition of *assets*, however, is merely a way to quantify assets.

considered acceptable as a basis for conditioning beliefs about the future.

(Beaver, 1991, 124)

The expression "considered acceptable as a basis for conditioning beliefs about the future" appears to me to be unintelligible, double-talk, simply an attempt to avoid the restriction on what may be an asset or a liability by the phrase "based on past transactions and events." The expression leads Beaver to accept, for example, estimates of future salary progression in pension reporting (Beaver, 1991, 124; compare the discussion in Chapter 24).

Beaver bemoans that *"Currently we do not have a well articulated statement as to what types of estimates of future events are within the current system of financial reporting versus what types are beyond"* (Beaver, 1991, 124). While it's true that there isn't such a statement and one perhaps would be needed were we to stick with "the current system of financial reporting," the more important issue is whether we need such a statement in a *better* system of financial reporting. (The conclusion in Chapter 10 is that we do need a better system of financial reporting.) The conclusions in Chapters 7, 14, and 15 lead to the view that we don't need such a statement in such a better system.

The FASB discussed assets and liabilities not, as in its definitions, in the plural, but in the singular. The discussions show that the FASB believes that each can be caused by no more than one transaction or event:

> An asset has three essential characteristics: . . . (c) the *transaction* or other *event* giving rise to the entity's right to or control of the benefit has already occurred . . . A liability has three essential characteristics: . . . (c) the *transaction* or other *event* obligating the entity has already happened.
> (FASB, 1985a, pars 26 and 36, emphasis added)

However, an asset or a liability can be caused by more than one event:

> "no event can be wholly and solely the cause of another event. The whole antecedent world conspires to produce a new occasion."
> (Whitehead, Lecture Eight, Modes, quoted in White, 1957, 96)

> [There is] . . . a significant discrepancy between the nature of our thinking-apparatus and the organization of the world which we are trying to apprehend. Our imperative need for cause and effect is satisfied when each process has one demonstrable cause. In reality, outside us this is hardly so; each event seems to be over-determined and turns out to be the effect of several converging causes.
> (Freud, 1939, 152)

The FASB in effect acknowledges that fact elsewhere: "an item does not qualify as a liability . . . if . . . the *events* or *circumstances* that obligate the entity have not yet occurred..." (FASB, 1985a, par. 168, emphasis added). Whether a liability can be caused by only one event or by more than one event is discussed further in Chapter 15, and is critical in the use of the definition, as discussed, for example, in Chapters 21 and 24.

Causes of conditions and events

Considering the causes of *conditions* is important in determining when they came into existence. The FASB definitions of *assets* and *liabilities* properly refer to what they are "a result of," that is, what caused them and when. In determining sound financial reporting on assets and liabilities, among the important issues are when they are obtained or incurred, the amounts at which they are obtained or incurred, the financial effects the obtaining or incurrence have on the reporting entity, and when the assets and liabilities are disposed of or discharged.

Some hold that the causes of *events* should also be considered, in determining how to report their financial effects. Melcher states that

> a transaction must be analyzed to determine why it occurs ... [For example, c]orporate aims and intended results of treasury stock transactions for operating purposes are of first importance. [Also, t]he purposes of a concession granted by a governmental unit ... should govern the accounting.
>
> (Melcher, 1973, 138, 251, 281)

The AICPA committee on accounting procedure similarly based its recommendation on reporting in connection with stock options issued to employees on the following:

> Stock option plans in many cases may be intended not primarily as a special form of compensation but rather as an important means of raising capital, or as an inducement to obtain greater or more widespread ownership of the corporation's stock among its officers and other employees.
>
> (AICPA, 1953b, Chapter 13b, par. 4)[8]

In fact, the concept of matching is based on cause and effect. Matching is a vestige of venture reporting, as discussed in Chapter 1.

Designing financial statements shouldn't involve consideration of the *causes* of events. When events occur is virtually always obvious (and when the timing of their occurrence is unknown, such as when a mineral deposit formed, the timing of the discovery that the event had occurred is also virtually always obvious), and determining their causes isn't needed for any purpose in the design of financial statements. Only the *financial effects* of the

---

8 Another example of considering the causes of events is discussed in Chapter 19.

events that occurred matter; why the events occurred as they did and why other events didn't occur as they didn't occur don't matter. Even if all the reasons were discovered for why the events occurred as they did and why they didn't occur as they didn't (an infinite number of reasons in the latter case), none of those reasons should influence the reporting. It's enough to know that the events occurred, when they occurred, and how they affected the reporting entity. For example:

> Prices and changes in prices are the resultants of mass causes; for any single buyer or seller they are given as part of his environment, and he must adapt himself to them. It is sufficient that the accounting system concerns itself with direct effects on the entity ... the entity may act in response to proximate stimuli even though it has little or no knowledge of distant causes.
>
> (Chambers, 1966, 68, 126)

As to the incurrence of liabilities, reporting entities should keep them at the lowest possible amounts and have them come due at the latest possible dates by whatever legitimate devices they have available, but when they have, only the actual incurrence of the liabilities and the financial effects of their incurrence require and deserve consideration in designing financial reporting on the financial effects of those events.

Financial reporting should and can successfully deal only with the raw circumstances faced by reporting entities. Entities should try to buy at the lowest possible prices, borrow at the lowest possible rates, sell at the highest possible prices, and lend at the highest possible rates, but when they have cut their best deals, regardless of why the prices, rates, price changes, and rate changes turn out to be what they are and not what they aren't, reporting entities are free to operate in markets only at those prices and rates.

Considering the causes of the events whose financial effects are reported on in financial statements should be part of financial analysis, not financial reporting.

The concept of equity[9]

The APB defined *owners' equity* in two different ways: "the interest of owners in an enterprise" and "the excess of an enterprise's assets over its liabilities" (AICPA, 1970c, par. 132). The FASB defined *equity* or *net assets*[10] also in two different ways: "equity or net assets ... is the difference between the entity's

---

9 Much of this section is taken from Rosenfield, 2005.
10 Also, "[Assets minus liabilities may be] describe[d] as net assets" (Chambers, 1966, 113). That's an unfortunate expression. It implies that net assets is a set comprised of net asset 1, net asset 2, net asset 3, and so on, but there is no such thing as a net asset. However, Staubus finds even that term helpful: "The term

assets and its liabilities" and "equity is the ownership interest. It stems from ownership rights (or the equivalent) and involves a relation between an enterprise and its owners" (FASB, 1985a, pars 50, 60). The definitions relating to the interest of owners involve the financial reporting territory; the definitions relating to the difference between the assets and the liabilities involve the financial reporting map.

The concept of equity exists in everyday life. Home-owners discuss their equity in their houses (as in "home-equity loan"), which in each case is probably the value (in some sense) of the house less the outstanding principal balance of the mortgage loan (or loans) on it. The house exists, an asset. The mortgage loan exists, a liability. However, the equity doesn't exist, except in thought, as an inference. It's a useful concept, but it doesn't represent anything that exists outside of thought: "equity . . . is merely a name given to the result of a mathematical operation comparing the amounts of assets and liabilities" (Skinner, 1987, 634).

The equity of a reporting entity is an amount presented in financial statements, in the financial reporting map, but isn't an element of the reporting entity represented in financial statements: it isn't assets, it isn't liabilities. It doesn't exist in the financial reporting territory. Its amount, like the person's equity in the house, is the excess of the total of the reported amounts of the reporting entity's assets over the total of the reported amounts of its liabilities, merely a concept, apparently invented for financial reporting as a by-product of the invention of double-entry bookkeeping: "double-entry . . . introduces an account for proprietorship. . ." (Solomons, 1971, 108).

Because equity doesn't exist in the financial reporting territory, it isn't strictly a part of financial reporting—it doesn't report on anything. Though equity is a vital concept, financial statements need not present its amount: the users could calculate it for themselves, using what's often called the accounting equation:

equity = assets − liabilities

Strictly speaking, it isn't an equation. It contains an equal sign, but that isn't its essential purpose. It essentially is a *definition* of *equity*.

Another way of stating what has been called the accounting equation is:

assets = liabilities + equity

'net asset item' will be used to mean any component of net assets, that is, an asset or a specific equity" (Staubus, 1961, 30n). Further, the expression *net assets* implies that it's helpful to think of a liability as a negative asset, though that expression is misleading, as discussed in the beginning of Chapter 15. Thus the term *net assets* can be misleading and shouldn't be used.

That way of stating the accounting equation is merely an algebraic restatement of the definition of *equity* and adds nothing fundamental in financial reporting.

The simple nature of equity is reflected in the term ascribed to it in the first set of consolidated financial statements issued by the U.S. federal government—"net position" (*Journal of Accountancy*, 1998, 15).

The definitions of *equity* given above and sometimes elsewhere make it appear to exist outside of mere concept, as the interests of the owners: "[the term] 'residual equity' [means] the interest of stockholders in the assets of the company..." (Chambers, 1966, 270) in contrast with the equity in the person's house. Another difference is that for the person, it's the *person's* equity in the *person's* asset, but for reporting entities, it's said to be the "*owners'* equity," the equity of other parties, the owners, not of the reporting entities. The definitions of *equity* thus look through the reporting entity and report on aspects of others, the interests of the proprietors. However, financial reporting should be confined to aspects of the reporting entity (discussed in Chapter 8), which should be the focus of attention. It shouldn't be the *owners'* equity in the assets; it should be the *reporting entity's* equity in its assets:

> An entity's financial capacity to enter into exchanges generally consists in money and is determined by the equitable interest *it has* in its assets. For any entity, this interest is calculated as the monetary difference between the aggregate money equivalent of its assets and the aggregate monetary obligation imposed by its outstanding debts...
>
> (Wolnizer, 1987, 71, emphasis added)

That permits seeing that positions such as the following involve nonissues: "the Committee recommends that [definition of *equity*] be refined to clarify [it] in terms of existing or existing and potential shareholders" (American Accounting Association Financial Accounting Standards Committee, 2004, 69).

Though *equity* is merely a concept, it's a useful one: "residual equity holders and other investors ... are concerned about the amount of the residual equity" (Staubus, 1961, 59).

The distinction has application, for example, in reporting on the equity section of the balance sheet (see Chapter 20). Though representations of liabilities portray the reporting entity's duties to pay money or provide goods or services to its creditors, its equity, the excess of its assets over its liabilities, doesn't portray its duties to its owners. Those duties are more abstract:

> What rights does a stockholder acquire by investing? ... A proportionate vote in the conduct of the firm's affairs; a proportionate share in the firm's dividends ...; a proportionate share in ... a liquidating dividend ...
>
> (Arthur L. Thomas, 1975a, 7 and 8)

The reporting entity also has duties to provide information to stockholders, as Bricker and Previts emphasize in "Rights." In contrast with the reporting entity's duties to its creditors, which are "nondiscretionary" (FASB, 1985a, par. 54), its duties to provide resources to its owners are discretionary.

Some even contend that part of the concept of equity is an asset, as if a reporting entity could own part of itself! For example: "treasury stock required for operating purposes should be shown as an asset of a corporation" (Melcher, 1973, 254). Even the APB said the same, in 1965: "When a corporation's stock is acquired for purposes other than retirement ... in some circumstances [it] may be shown as an asset..." (AICPA, 1965, par. 12.b). That rule wasn't rescinded until February 1999, in SFAS No. 135.

Definitions of revenue *and* expenses

The APB and the FASB define both *revenue* and *expenses* in terms of assets and liabilities, that is, in terms of economic resources (except to the extent that assets and liabilities don't involve economic resources in the APB's definitions of them).

The APB defines *revenue* and *expenses* as

> gross increases or decreases in assets or liabilities recognized and measured in conformity with generally accepted accounting principles that result from those types of profit-directed activities of an enterprise that can change owners' equity.
>
> (AICPA, 1970c, par. 134)

The FASB defines *revenue* and *expenses* as

> inflows or other enhancements of assets of an entity or settlements of its liabilities (or a combination of both) from delivering or producing goods, rendering services, or other activities that constitute the entity's ongoing major or central operations ... out-flows or other using up of assets or incurrences of liabilities (or a combination of both) from delivering or producing goods, rendering services, or carrying out other activities that constitute the entity's ongoing major or central operations.
>
> (FASB, 1985a, pars 78 and 80)

The FASB defines other inflows, settlements, outflows, and usings up of assets or liabilities as gains and losses (FASB, 1985a, pars 82, 83).

Knowledge about revenues, expenses, gains, and losses, which are grounded in assets and liabilities, is derived from inferences:

> An income statement is derived, fundamentally, by inference from two

successive statements of financial position ... Income is the result of a calculation, an inference...

(Chambers, 1966, 118, 342; 1969, 437)

"meaning can be given to assets without first defining income, but the reverse isn't true."

(Gellein, 1992, 198, quoted in Storey and Storey, 1998, 79)

Analysis can't deal with revenues or expenses in isolation, because they are dependent, being defined in terms of assets and liabilities. But assets and liabilities aren't dependent on revenues or expenses, so analysis should concentrate on assets and liabilities when they and revenues and expenses are involved. That conforms with the so-called asset and liability approach to considering issues in financial reporting, as discussed in FASB, 1976a, par. 33. That approach contrasts with the so-called revenue and expense approach, which has in effect been discarded with the publication by the FASB of its Conceptual Framework. That's good:

revenue–expense proponents are primarily concerned with stabilizing the fluctuating effect of transactions on the income statement and are prepared to introduce deferred charges and deferred credits in order to smooth income measurement.

(Wolk *et al.*, 1992, 265)

FASB member John March complained about the change to the asset and liability approach: "Mr. March dissents from this Statement [CON6] because ... [it] uses a concept of income that is fundamentally based on measurements of assets, liabilities, and changes in them..." (FASB, 1985a).

The definitions of *revenue* and *expense* of the APB and FASB have been largely forgotten or rarely incorporated in current GAAP. Revenue and expenses take on lives of their own, and their grounding in assets and liabilities is usually ignored. The prevailing thought is that "the idea of income is more fundamental in accounting than the idea of ... assets..." (Littleton, 1953, 20; see Chapter 10).

The concept of income

As stated above, the numerical difference between the revenues and gains on the one hand and the expenses and losses on the other hand reported for a period is called *income*: "the computed profit residual..." (Chambers, 1979a, 53). It doesn't occur in the financial reporting territory, as revenues, gains, expenses, and losses do; like equity, it's merely a concept, an inference, part of the financial reporting map, though, also like equity, a useful concept. Like equity, income need not be presented in financial statements; the users could calculate it for themselves.

Elements of financial statements

As indicated above, the elements of the reporting entity represented in financial statements are its assets, liabilities, revenues, expenses, gains, and losses. In contrast, the elements of its financial statements are (1) representations of its assets, liabilities, revenues, gains, expenses, and losses, and (2) its net income and equity.

Possibly incomplete financial statements

The APB implied that only some economic resources of a reporting entity are assets: those that are reported as assets in conformity with GAAP. To similar effect, the FASB implied that all economic resources of a reporting entity are assets but that GAAP indicates which assets to report. And the APB's definitions of *revenue* and *expenses* include only certain changes that might go in income statements, those that conform with GAAP, whereas the FASB's definitions of *revenue* and *expenses* include all such changes but leave selection of which revenues and expenses to report to GAAP. The possibility therefore exists under both kinds of definitions that both the balance sheet and the income statement are incomplete. That the statement of income is in fact seriously incomplete under current GAAP is discussed in Chapter 10.

Accrual basis

> There are some things you just don't do … you don't tug on Superman's cape, you don't spit into the wind, and you don't mess around with accrual accounting … Accrual accounting is the tribal god of the accounting profession, it's the equivalent of motherhood, apple pie, and the American flag.
>
> (Gerboth, 1989, 42, 44)

The balance sheet and the statements of income and equity are said to be prepared on the *accrual basis*. The APB and the IASC got that concept right:

> Determining periodic income and financial position depends on measurement of noncash resources and obligations and changes in them as the changes occur rather than simply on recording receipts and payments of money … This is the essence of accrual accounting.
>
> (AICPA, 1970c, par. 121; see footnote 10)

> Under [the accrual basis of accounting], the financial effects of transactions and other events are recognised when they occur (and not as cash or its equivalent is received or paid)…
>
> (IASC, 1989a, par. 22)

All that means is that they aren't prepared on the cash basis. Receivables, nonmonetary assets, and liabilities and changes in them are reported in addition to cash and changes in cash. The FASB also got it right in one place:

> The goal of accrual accounting is to account in the periods in which they occur for the financial effects on an entity of transactions and other events and circumstances, to the extent that those financial effects are recognizable and measurable.
>
> (FASB, 1985a, par. 145)

Some individual observers also get it right, for example:

> An accounting system in which events and transactions are recognized and made the subject of entries in the record, when cash is received or paid is said to be conducted on a cash basis . . . An accounting system in which events and transactions are recognized and made the subject of entries in the record, when they effect changes in assets and equities, even though cash is received or paid at other dates, is said to be conducted on an accrual basis.
>
> (Chambers, 1966, 132)

There are several ways to report on the accrual basis; this book considers the merits of the varieties. However, "[s]ometimes accrual accounting is used as a synonym for income accounting under the historical cost model; at other times it is used differently. The result is undesirable confusion" (Skinner, 1987, 48). Thus, in two places the FASB confined the concept of accrual solely to the current way of reporting:

> The sole result of accrual, for financial accounting and reporting purposes, is allocation of costs among accounting periods . . . matching of costs and revenues, allocation, and amortization . . . [are at] the essence of using accrual accounting to measure performance of entities.[11]
>
> (FASB, 1975a, par. 63; 1985a, par. 145)

Others have done the same, for example:

> allocations . . . are the basis of accrual accounting . . .
>
> (Riahi-Belkaoui, 1993, 421)

> market value accounting may result in much greater fluctuations in income than . . . an accrual process . . .
>
> (Bedford, 1971, 144)

---

11 Note how differently the APB and the FASB perceive the "essence" of accrual.

the principal goal of accrual accounting is to help investors assess the entity's economic performance during a period through the use of basic accounting principles such as revenue recognition and matching.

(Dechow and Skinner, 2000, 237)

When . . . Enron [signed a large power contract it entered into in 1997 with the Tennessee Valley Authority, it] relied on a form of accounting known as mark-to-market, which allowed it to book immediate earnings of $50 million. By mid-1998 . . . energy prices had changed enough that, under the accounting treatment, Enron would have to report huge losses. To avoid that, the complaints say, Enron shifted the contract from mark-to-market to accrual accounting—a change that avoided reporting the loss.

(Eichenwald, 2003)

Those ideas shouldn't but do rule other styles of financial reporting discussed in this book out of the accrual community with a stroke of the pen, without argument.

Elsewhere the FASB tied accrual solely to current thoughts of the issuers about the future, their expectations about cash receipts and payments:

Accrual is concerned with expected future cash receipts and payments; it is the accounting process of recognizing assets or liabilities and the related . . . revenues, expenses, gains, or losses for amounts expected to be received or paid, usually in cash, in the future.

(FASB, 1985a, par. 141)

The American Accounting Association, Beaver, and Demski did much the same:

Accrual accounting, by its very nature, involves looking into the future.
(American Accounting Association, 1991, 1989–90, 83)

Accruals can be viewed as a form of forecast about the future based on current and past events, and accrual accounting can be viewed as a cost-effective way of conveying expectations about future benefits or sacrifices.

(Beaver, 1991, 123)

Accrual accounting, of course, is a formalized anticipatory statement of stocks and flows.

(Demski, 2003, 10)

Beaver also referred to "a comparison between market value accounting versus accrual accounting" (Beaver, 1991, 129). Simply by definition, therefore, they rule conclusions in Chapters 7 and 14 out of the accrual bounds.

The concept of accrual has also been held to be essentially a means to stabilize income reporting! "Corporate reported net income for short periods of time shouldn't be distorted ... This is the basic mission of accrual accounting" (Bevis, 1965, 34).

Nonarticulation

Suggestions are sometimes made to explicitly detach the balance sheet from the income statement so that they don't articulate, for example:

> there is no self-evident reason why net assets need to be measured the same way for both balance sheet and income statement purposes ... articulation exists only by custom...
>
> (Wolk *et al.*, 1992, 266)

> Forcing an articulation between the [balance sheet and the income statement] ... is likely to decrease the ability of the information to achieve its objective.
>
> (Burton and Sack, 1991, 120)

But, as discussed above, the articulation of the two statements reflects the nature of the elements of the reporting entity:

> the recurring argument that we should measure flows and forget about stocks, often stated as articulation being an artificial constraint that impedes progress, overlook[s] the relationship between stocks and flows.
>
> (Sterling, 1982, 54n)

It provides a needed control against reports that are self-contradictory—for example, by affirming something such as a gain in one statement but denying it in the other—or that provide products of the imagination of the designers of the reports rather than information. Income can be reported as whatever the issuers care to report it to serve their incentives if the statements don't articulate:

> determining income more or less independently of balance sheet changes has the great advantage of giving management more control over the number that emerges as earnings. It facilitates income smoothing...
>
> (Solomons, 1986, 132)

> [Income] ... cut loose from association with ... financial position ... [can be smoothed]...
>
> (Chambers, 1989, 14)

The strain on articulation always results from the desire to manage the news by stabilizing income reporting.

Explicit nonarticulation has never (or at least not yet) caught on. Ways to achieve the same result implicitly, without having the balance sheet, the income statement, and the statement of equity look like they are detached, are used instead. They have included dirty surplus, what-you-may-call-its, and abuse of the FASB's definition of *liabilities*.

Dirty surplus

Dirty surplus was the original means of nonarticulation of choice, before it was temporarily prohibited (see Prologue). Increases in assets not accompanied by increases in liabilities or vice versa and not the result of transactions between the reporting entity and its owners were sometimes reported not in income but directly in equity: "deduct[ing value changes] from retained income, thereby decreasing the reported income since the inception of the firm without decreasing the reported income of any particular period" (Sterling, 1970a, 251). But if increases in equity don't come from contributions by owners or from success (and vice versa), where do they come from?

This form of nonarticulation has recently been reintroduced, for example, in reporting on marketable equity securities (FASB, 1993a, par. 13) and in reporting on pensions (see Chapter 24). Also, the AICPA Special Committee on Financial Reporting recommended in 1994 that what it called *noncore assets* and *noncore liabilities* should be reported at their current amounts in the balance sheet and that "changes in unrealized appreciation or depreciation of [them] should be charged or credited directly to shareholders' equity" (AICPA, 1994a, 87). That proposed practice reflects ambivalence about whether to report such current amounts.

The CFA Institute (before May 2004, the AIMR) objects:

> The FAPC [Financial Accounting Policy Committee of the Association for Investment Management and Research] has consistently supported the all-inclusive income statement format, known colloquially as the "clean surplus" approach ... We have profound misgivings about the increasing number of wealth changes that elude disclosure on the income statement.
>
> (Association for Investment Management and Research, 1993, 63)

Recently the FASB has reacted to this kind of objection with a concept called *comprehensive income* (FASB, 1997a). It moves the items that have been charged or credited directly to equity to the income statement, in a separate portion following net income called *other comprehensive income*, or to a separate statement called *statement of comprehensive income,* which starts with net income. It requires the amount of other comprehensive income for a reporting period to be transferred to a separate component of equity with a title such as *accumulated other comprehensive income*. Johnson and Petrone, members of the staff of the FASB, state that "virtually all companies report [other comprehensive income] in the statement of changes in equity..." (Johnson and Petrone, 1999b, 7). Miller and Bahnson said that that practice made them "speculate that at least some managers want to make it harder for users to know what happened by making their statements as opaque as possible" (Miller and Bahnson, 2002b, 249).

The American Accounting Association's Financial Accounting Standards Committee stated that it "believes comprehensive income reporting provides a more complete and transparent framework for reporting on all changes in net assets arising from transactions from non-owner sources" (American Accounting Association, Financial Accounting Standards Committee, 1997, 117). But comprehensive income is still simply nonarticulation by dirty surplus, with new names and new geography, adopted by the FASB to perpetuate the stabilizing effect of nonarticulation.

What-you-may-call-its

After dirty surplus was temporarily outlawed, what-you-may-call-its were the means of choice to achieve the results of nonarticulation, before the FASB's Conceptual Framework supposedly defined them out of existence.[12] Prominent among the what-you-may-call-its were deferred credits and debits to income reported in balance sheets under the deferred method of interperiod income tax allocation. Others, outlined by Sprouse, include gains arising in sale-and-leaseback transactions and deferred investment tax credits (Sprouse, 1966, 46).

The defense of what-you-may-call-its has occasionally approached the farcical. For example, if neither peeking nor analysis convince, you can try mockery: "The deferred credit figure [is] an item much misunderstood by the unsophisticated ... balance sheet purist..." (Defliese, 1983, 94).[13] Also, when someone objected that companies don't have such things as deferred credits to expense, during the APB's discussion of one, a member of the

---

12 This was supposedly done in CON5 and CON6. March dissented from CON5 because of it. However, a little erosion has since occurred. Some interpret paragraph 83.b. of CON5 to sanction what-you-may-call-its. FASB Technical Bulletin 90-1 refers to that paragraph to support its presentation of a what-you-may-call-it, the credit balance resulting from reporting receipt of cash in exchange for incurring a contingent liability for defects in a product under an extended warranty contract that may come into existence after the cash is received. Also, in its Action Alert of September 25, 2002, the FASB stated that a revenue reporting "approach that focuses on an earnings process that *overrides* changes in assets and liabilities [is] consistent with FASB Concepts Statement No. 5" (FASB, 2002c, emphasis added).

13 He was reacting to an article of Bill Dent and me. I confess that I am an unsophisticated balance sheet purist, that I subscribe to the asset and liability approach, as discussed in the text of this chapter.

APB, the Chairman of one of the largest CPA firms, said most of his clients do, right in their financial statements (again, the map is the territory).

What-you-may-call-its may come back. See the next section

Return of what-you-may-call-its?

The FASB may be about to go back to outright what-you-may-call-its. FASB staff members reported that

> the revenue recognition criteria in Concepts Statement 5 sometimes override the definitions in Concepts Statement 6 . . . application of [the] criteria [in CON5] may cause revenue to be deferred, with the deferred revenue being reported in the balance sheet as a liability even though no obligation—and thus, no liability—exists . . . the Board plans to amend the Concepts Statements to eliminate those inconsistencies.
>
> (Johnson and Such, 2002, 4)

It should eliminate the inconsistencies by conforming CON5 to CON6. Otherwise, it would eliminate the single most beneficial improvement caused by the conceptual framework project.

Abuse of the definition of liabilities

Once the FASB defined what-you-may-call-its out of existence, it had to remove them from acceptable practice. That's virtually the only reason, for example, that it abandoned the deferred method of interperiod income tax allocation in its SFAS No. 109. The FASB still liked the income statement results of the deferred method. They dealt with the problem by adopting another of the current means for nonarticulation, abuse of the definition of *liabilities* (discussed in Chapter 21; see also Chapter 24). That's accomplished by requiring some liabilities to be reported before they are incurred. That way, income statement results considered desirable are achieved without detaching the balance sheet from the income statement, without resorting to what-you-may-call-its (except that the liabilities reported before they are incurred are modern-day what-you-may-call-its), and without reporting income items directly in equity.

To avoid the discipline of articulation

By one means or another, issuers continue to find ways to avoid the discipline of articulation when it interferes with relatively stable income reporting.

Debating points

1 Balance sheets do have assets and liabilities in them; every balance sheet I've ever seen has them.
2 We shouldn't question the FASB's definitions of the elements.
3 Assets and liabilities shouldn't be defined in terms of the future.
4 Beaver is right; the reference to past transactions and events in the definitions of assets and liabilities isn't really constraining, and his reasoning isn't double-talk.
5 Melcher is right; the causes of events are sometimes important in designing reporting on them.
6 Equity is just as real as assets and liabilities and is an element of the reporting entity.
7 Get real. The accounting equation is simply an equation.
8 March was wrong in his reason for dissenting to CON6.
9 I, along with Defliese, have no use for balance sheet purists.
10 Income is not only an element of the reporting entity, it's the most important element.
11 Equity and income are merely concepts with no counterpart outside concept.
12 Articulation is outmoded; it stifles financial reporting.
13 Articulation is an essential safeguard in financial reporting.
14 Comprehensive income is more of the same.
15 Comprehensive income is a major advance in financial reporting and not a means to continue stabilizing income reporting.

Part III

Broad issues in financial reporting

10 The current broad principles

> the accounting standards in the United States are recognized widely as the best and most comprehensive in the world. No other accounting system provides comparable transparency to a reporting entity's underlying economic events and transactions. In that sense, the quality of our accounting principles is a national asset that helps set our securities markets apart from those in the rest of the world.
>
> (Turner,[1] 1999, 1, 2)

> the high level and quality of financial reporting and disclosure, which enable investors to confidently compare investment alternatives, have attracted the suppliers of capital, making our markets the premier markets of the world...
>
> (Foster,[2] 2003, 3)

> regardless of how honest or accurate or conscientious an accountant may be, he must almost of necessity prepare false and misleading financial statements if he follows accepted accounting practice.
>
> (MacNeal, 1970, 22)

Having set the stage and discussed issues underlying financial reporting, we now go on to consider issues concerning GAAP. In this section we consider the current broad principles and proposed replacements for the current broad principles of financial reporting.

Financial statements are prepared using practices that developed over many years by the issuers of the statements and later by standard-setters and

---

1 Turner was chief accountant of the SEC when he wrote this. Miller and Bahnson say that

> our assessment of GAAP makes us lean toward describing it as barely translucent instead of transparent ... the last thing the SEC ... should do is rest on their laurels after hearing those oft repeated claims of greatness in financial reporting (especially the ones coming from their own lips).
>
> (Miller and Bahnson, 2002b, 40, 41)

2 Foster was a member of the FASB when he wrote this.

regulators, mainly in response to specific problems. Their development was for the most part not guided by overriding concepts or principles:

> accounting principles originated spontaneously as an unconscious and direct outgrowth of [existing] conditions ... like Topsy, they just "growed."
>
> (MacNeal, 1970, 70)

> Accounting was born without notice and reared in neglect.
>
> (Sterling, 1979, ix)

> [In] the early twentieth century[,] each accounting firm had its own set of standards, which it applied to its client work.
>
> (Eccles *et al.*, 2001, 251)

Schipper in effect contradicted that: "U.S. GAAP is based on a recognizable set of principles derived from the FASB's Conceptual Framework..." (Schipper, 2003, 62). The discussion below in the section "Evaluation of the current broad principles" demonstrates that current GAAP bears little relationship to the framework.

Alternative financial statement reporting practices for the same circumstances resulted from their decentralized development, some of which standard-setters and regulators haven't yet been able to prune (see Chapter 19).

We financial reporters have tried to make sense of those practices. The most effective way to do that would be to discover sound concepts and sound broad principles independently and then use them to appraise current practices and develop improved practices. (The AICPA Special Committee on Financial Reporting was in effect charged in 1991 with doing that, and to some extent it succeeded, mainly in the area of disclosure; see Chapter 17). However, as to broad principles, we financial reporters have turned the procedure on its head. We have extracted broad principles from a consideration of current practices. Catlett called it "reverse logic, by summarizing a wide variety of customs and practices, many of which need to be changed and improved, and then rationalizing back to principles..." (AICPA, 1970c, Catlett dissent). It's nevertheless instructive to consider the broad principles uncovered that way.

Standard-setting bodies have stated tools for evaluating those principles, especially in the FASB's conceptual framework (see, for example, Chapter 3). In 1978 the FASB promised in the foreword to its CON1 (FASB, 1978) to use those tools to evaluate the principles:

> The Board recognizes that in certain respects current generally accepted accounting principles may be inconsistent with those that may derive from the objectives and concepts set forth in the Statement and others in the series. In due course, the Board expects to reexamine its pro-

nouncements, pronouncements of predecessor standard-setting bodies, and existing financial reporting practice in the light of newly enunciated objectives and concepts.

However, in the ensuing 28 years to this writing it hasn't used those objectives and concepts to evaluate the most important principles in GAAP—realization, allocation, and matching—by applying the tools, and there is no sign that it will do so in the foreseeable future. It has had no major project on the two most pervasive subjects in financial reporting, depreciation and inventory reporting (neither did the Committee on Accounting Procedure, nor the Accounting Principles Board). In 2000 in its CON7, paragraph 16, the Board stated that it "does not intend to revisit existing accounting standards and practice solely as result of issuing this Statement." Kripke noted "the [FASB]'s failure to attempt to make progress ... by applying its own qualitative characteristics..." (Kripke, 1989, 25). The reason likely is that the issuers favor the income statement results of those principles and the FASB does not want to apply evaluations they suspect will find the principles to be unsound and offend the issuers.

Schipper contends that such a project couldn't be accomplished, that research can't reach a conclusion on whether a particular practice is consistent with the FASB's conceptual framework: "research cannot provide objective evidence on whether a given proposed standard is close to, or far from, consistency with the Conceptual Framework" (Schipper, 1994, 68). (That statement in effect contradicts her statement quoted near the beginning of this chapter that "U.S. GAAP is based on a recognizable set of principles derived from the FASB's Conceptual Framework.") That's too pessimistic. For only one of many possible examples, the FASB included the following statements in its conceptual framework indicating that the single-unit-of-measure rule must be obeyed:

> financial statements involve adding, subtracting, multiplying, and dividing numbers depicting economic things and events and require a common denominator ... If valid comparisons are to be made ... the unit of measurement used must be invariant.
>
> (FASB, 1978, par. 18; 1980b, par. 114)

Research can easily determine objectively that the current-rate method of translation, which the FASB mandates in its SFAS No. 52, violates that requirement. The FASB itself states that it does; indeed, the FASB defends the violation, strenuously (see Chapter 22). So, research that compares that method with the FASB's conceptual framework would "provide objective evidence" that it isn't consistent with the framework.

The FASB's omission to evaluate GAAP using the tools provided by its conceptual framework is rectified here. The current broad principles are stated and then evaluated, by analyzing them, applying the tools discussed in Chapter 3, and by considering their financial statements results.

Statement of the current broad principles

> The wish to stand off from the hurly-burly of economic change implies the abdication of responsibility: it leads to what one may call Accounting in Wonderland.
>
> (Chambers, 1969, 20)

The current broad principles are stated in the following and then discussed:

- *Definition of the unit of measure in terms of the debt-paying power of the unit of money.* The unit of measure is defined in terms of the debt-paying power of the unit of money. Changes in the general purchasing power of the unit of money (inflation and deflation) are ignored.
- *Objectivity (in a special sense).* Inputs from transactions to which the reporting entity is a direct party are considered to be objective and inputs from other events are considered to be not objective: "Transactions . . . that have not been determined by the bargaining of independent parties in contact with the given enterprise . . . lack . . . objective determination. . ." (Littleton, 1953, 217). (The classic defense of this position is presented and challenged in Chapter 14.) The financial effects of only such so-called objective events are represented in financial statements. (This contrasts with the general sense of *objectivity* as discussed in connection with verifiability in Chapter 3.)
- *Realization.* Increases in assets are reported only when they are realized in transactions between the reporting entity and entities independent of the reporting entity.[3]
- *Matching.* Costs incurred, as causes, are matched with the realized revenue resulting from incurring the costs, as effects, and reported as expenses in the same income statement as the revenue.
- *Systematic and rational allocation.* If costs and revenues can't be matched based on cause and effect, costs and revenue are assigned to income by systematic and rational allocation (SARA). Depreciation, depletion, and amortization, reporting on inventories using acquisition costs, and the current broad principles for reporting on bonds and other liabilities are prime examples of SARA.

The unit of measure in current financial statements in the U.S.

Current financial reporting in the U.S. uses a unit of measure defined in terms of debt paying power, the power of the U.S. dollar to discharge U.S.

---

3 This principle was enshrined in a rule adopted by the AICPA membership in 1934, as quoted in Chapter 19. This book advocates eliminating this principle, among others. Would it take an act of Congress (the AICPA membership) to achieve that?

dollars debts, which is that tendering one U.S. dollar discharges debt of one U.S. dollar and never changes (see Chapter 11 for evaluation of that principle).

The acquisition-cost basis

accounting is primarily based on cost...

(AICPA, 1953b, Chapter 4, par. 5)

The acquisition (historical) cost basis is the major result of the current broad principles:

[the amounts] used for centuries by ... accountants ... were based on [acquisition] costs ... Later, when free and competitive markets [came] into existence, the practice of exhibiting assets at [acquisition] cost was so ancient and so completely embedded in the accounting mind that theories were invented to justify this practice...

(MacNeal, 1970, 179)

In 1936, a committee of the American Accounting Association in effect called that basis part of a "fundamental axiom":

Accounting is ... not essentially a process of valuation, but the allocation of [acquisition] costs and revenues to the current and succeeding fiscal periods.

(American Accounting Association, 1936, 188)

Hatfield called this a "criminal assault on the English Language," first because it's described as "not merely an axiom but a fundamental axiom (if one knows the difference)," and second because an axiom is supposed to be "a self-evident truth" and he demonstrated that this isn't (Hatfield, 1937, 1, 2). Nevertheless, that statement has been the cornerstone of financial reporting ever since. Sterling commented: "We now account for costs because we have defined 'accounting' as a process of allocating costs. We could define it some other way" (Sterling, 1979, 81). Lee states that "Ideas from cost accounting with respect to allocations for matching purposes were available and slowly incorporated into accounting for external reporting" (Lee, 1990, 91, quoted in West, 2003, 60).

The implications of that definition were worked out by Paton and Littleton in the most influential book ever written about financial reporting, *An Introduction to Corporate Accounting Standards* (Paton and Littleton, 1940), which incorporates that view and underlies most of GAAP to this day:

Paton and Littleton, more than anyone else, furnished the logical framework for conventional accounting. The matching concept is one of the key features in this framework. It is so highly regarded that any procedure that is advanced on the basis of proper or better matching usually receives a favorable response.

(Kam, 1990, 287)

[*Standards* is] the definitive explication (and, in large measure, defense) of conventional financial accounting...

(Zeff, 1982, 541)

Standards has been so influential because the principles it espouses result in reporting that serves the incentives of the issuers. A prominent issuer recently stated that "I conclude ... that ... I [do] not believe [the FASB] could improve upon Paton and Littleton's work..." (Flegm, 1990, 157). In contrast, some believe *Standards* has harmed the profession:

"'inductively' derived theories of accounting commit the fallacy of getting *ought* from *is* ... Littleton is the foremost proponent of this methodology, and we agree with Goldberg when he says that Littleton 'got somewhat out of his depth...' in his discussion of the nature of theory."

(Sterling, 1970a, 305, quoting Goldberg, 1963, 462)

The profession is hanging its hat on someone "somewhat out of his depth." Even one of the authors of *Standards*, Paton, has disavowed it:

For a long time I've wished that the Paton and Littleton monograph had never been written, or had gone out of print twenty-five years or so ago. Listening to Bob Sprouse take issue with the "matching" gospel, which the P&L monograph helped to foster, confirmed my dissatisfaction with this publication...

(Paton, 1971, in Willard Stone, 1971, quoted in Storey and Storey, 1998, 61)

West agrees about matching: "Guided by only such vagaries as 'matching' ... conventional accounting practice is a disordered activity" (West, 2003, 108).

A few have written in support of the acquisition-cost basis recently, for example:

What is proposed ... is that we should abandon a proven concept of income, an established procedure that lends itself to known controls, a quality of information that has served well and whose limitations are well known, and accept in their place a vague prescription for current values whose usefulness is not established, for which there is very little expressed demand from those who use accounting data, and for which no known controls are available.

(Mautz, 1973, 27)

The accrual basis . . . attempts to match revenues with related costs where a physical relationship is identifiable and to establish a logical, systematic, and objective method of apportionment where the direct connection cannot be established.

(Bevis, 1965, 31)

the process of income determination [should be] a process of systematic calculations.

(Ijiri, 1971a, 5)

Given that [acquisition] cost accounting for major classes of assets and liabilities is firmly fixed in practice, the next question is: How can financial statements based on [acquisition] cost be made more *useful*?

(Scott, 1997, 37)

Others include Flegm (see the second quotation in the Prologue) and March (see p. 214). Most of its other supporters may feel that Paton and Littleton said it all.

Standards elaborated on the American Accounting Association's axiom: "it is the task of accounting to make the most truthful and significant . . . possible . . . allocation of costs and revenues between the present and future. . ." (Paton and Littleton, 1940, 11). It invented (or at least was the first to articulate) the matching concept and made it the central principle: "Accounting . . . match[es] . . . efforts and accomplishments . . . comprehended within the terms 'costs and revenues' and 'accrual accounting'" (Paton and Littleton, 1940, 16).

Costs on hold

When some costs are incurred, they are recorded and then kept on hold in the balance sheet, ready to be matched with revenue considered to be accomplishments resulting from the efforts in which the costs were incurred and reported in the income statement as expenses in the periods in which the revenue is reported. That's facilitated by the current broad principle of realization.

To keep costs on hold, concepts were invented, mainly by Paton and Littleton in *Standards* (Paton and Littleton, 1940), that have come to be regarded as relationships and processes that exist as to the reporting entity and occur to the reporting entity in the financial reporting territory (though they actually exist only in the minds of us financial reporters, in the financial reporting map). Costs are thought about, talked about, and written about as living entities with "destinies" (Paton and Littleton, 1940, 14). They are described as social butterflies: they are said to "identify with the group," to form "relationships," to "associate," and to have an "affinity" for each other (Paton and Littleton, 1940, 14, 69, 71). They are even said to become intimate: to make "contact," to "cling," to "attach," to "cohere," and to "unite" (Paton and Littleton, 1940, 13, 14, 15, 71). But they are fickle and their attachments may change, several times, during their lifetimes.

Costs metamorphose into a liquid state, in which they are said to form "pools," to "stream," and to "flow" (Paton and Littleton, 1940, 16, 77).

The most striking manifestation of the idea that costs flow is the so-called LIFO (last-in, first-out) flow of costs. AICPA, "Restatement," Chapter 4 (AICPA, 1953b) requires reporting on inventory to follow an "assumption ... as to the flow of cost factors." The cost flow assumed needn't conform with the goods flow. No beer warehouse, for example, could stay in business if its goods followed a LIFO flow, because it would soon pile up some very flat beer. In fact, few if any businesses could stay in business with a LIFO movement of goods. Now, where is the financial reporter supposed to look for the flow of costs when applying LIFO? To the flow represented by the LIFO method. That makes the process a circle. It would support any cost-flow assumption, because method A would look to the flow assumption implied by method A to see how the costs flow and would follow it.

A cost-flow assumption is a systematic and rational allocation formula. Such formulas are discussed below.

Then, in a transmogrification to the military, costs are said to be "mobile" and to be "assembled," "marshaled," and "regrouped" (Paton and Littleton, 1940, 13, 14). Moreover, in a feat akin to prestidigitation, costs are said to become assets (see below).

Finally, the costs become exhausted, grave questions are asked about whether they are "recoverable," and in the end they "expire" (Paton and Littleton, 1940, 16, 33, 77): "accountants ... have held appropriate rites over expired costs" (Devine, 1985a, 4). They are eventually laid to rest in the income statement.

That's all poetry, of course:

> The Paton and Littleton monograph was ... a landmark ... It was also a folly, creating colourful imagery which may well have reinforced misleading concepts, and presenting eloquent, abstruse, but fundamentally flawed, arguments...
>
> (Thompson, 1991, 90)

> "'Expired cost' is ... mumbo jumbo..."
>   (Bonbright, 1961, 196, quoted in Storey and Storey, 1998, 63)

> some unobservable fiction ... such as an "unexpired cost"...
>   (Sterling, 1979, 18)

To return to prose: Though Barden refers to "the observable flow of cost..." (Barden, 1973, 94), costs flow, attach, expire, and do all the other marvelous things they are said to do only in our minds, in the financial reporting map, not in the financial reporting territory, and their so-called behavior isn't observable.

Outside financial reporting, in the financial reporting territory, a cost is a sacrifice, a detrimental effect incurred in an event that occurred at a particular moment in time. Once time passes and the event passes into history, the cost, the sacrifice, also passes into history:

> [Acquisition] costs don't change for the same reason Napoleon doesn't change: both are dead.
>
> (Arthur L. Thomas, 1975a, 519)

> it gives most of us little comfort to know that the [acquisition] cost of every asset now held by business firms throughout the world has not changed since its acquisition.
>
> (Edwards, 1975, 237)

Costs don't flow or do anything else; nothing happens to them after they are incurred, except in the imagination of financial reporters. The resources expended are gone; the costs have been sunk; bygones are bygones. No events occur in the financial reporting territory involving costs except for the events in which they are incurred.

Though the issues in financial reporting are too vital and too complex[4] to tolerate the inaccuracies of poetry, acquisition-cost based financial reporting persists in its devotion to it:

> esthetes ... might be impressed by the similarity of accounting work to, say, the practice of writing poetry ... Both construct symbolic representations of events and situations. Both abstract from what has been dubbed "reality" and form impressionistic patterns that promise to convey their messages. These messages have "meaning" in the sense that users have formed habitual responses that are in some part predictable. Both groups have *avant garde* members who experiment with new forms of expression and encourage users to adopt new responses.
>
> (Devine, 1985a, 114)

Similarly, "Modern economics is in many respects metaphor run wild..." (Kuttner, 1985, 83).

The poetry is part of the ritual that is current financial reporting, discussed below.

---

4 In contrast, see footnote 12.

Costs attach

The acquisition costs of the factors of production are allocated by cost accounting and said to attach to the resulting intermediate or final products, such as work in process or finished goods: "The concept of . . . costs attaching [is] fundamental to accounting. . ." (Paton and Littleton, 1940, 16).[5] The acquisition costs of the factors of production are said to become the acquisition costs of the products. Labor costs, for example, instead of being reported as expense when incurred, are associated with the products on which work was expended.

Advocates of "costs attach" imply that they attach in the financial reporting territory. However, acquisition costs attach by financial reporting convention only, only in the financial reporting map, not in its territory. Outside financial reporting, the acquisition cost of an asset or a service is the cost of acquiring it—that is, the value (in some sense) of the assets or services sacrificed to obtain it. Most factors of production are acquired in exchange for money or promises of money, and their total acquisition costs can be measured in terms of money, at the amounts of money sacrificed (basket purchases make assignment of cost to individual assets impossible except by convention). Products and services resulting from production processes are obtained by sacrificing the factors of production—material, labor, and overhead—used. The costs outside financial reporting of acquiring the products thus are sacrifices of alternative uses of the nonmonetary assets or services that are used in production. For example, the cost of using steel to make cars is the sacrifice at the time it's used of alternative uses of the steel, which is at least the price at which the reporting entity could have sold the steel at that date, not the price it paid to acquire the steel in the past:

> The use of . . . materials . . . is . . . an event separate from their acquisition.
>
> (Staubus, 1961, 60n)

> the cost of *using* an asset varies from time to time.
>
> (Chambers, 1966, 206, emphasis added.)

> I have never seen a cost attach. I never hope to see one. Of those who say they have, I can't myself believe one.
>
> (Coughlan, 1965, 470)

---

5 Paton himself foreshadowed that endorsement of the costs attach concept in his 1922 book: "It is the essential task of the accountant to follow market prices as, attached to *specific property items*, they become affected by the business process" (Paton, 1922, 9).

One observer recently referred to "the outmoded doctrine of 'cost attachment'..." (Paul F. Williams, 2001, 696). Rather than being outmoded, however, it is a cornerstone of today's financial reporting, as discussed in this chapter.

Costs flow, attach, and expire only in the minds of financial reporters. To that extent they are like thoughts of the issuers about the future discussed in Chapter 7. The results of applying those concepts prevents reporting on inventory from complying with the user-oriented criterion of representativeness, which isn't intended to include representations of states of minds of financial reporters. They are simply one more way to rationalize treatments that promote stable reported income rather than treatments that conform with the user-oriented criteria.

The balance sheet under the acquisition-cost basis

> If one claims that the profit and loss account is the more important statement, one can make light of the defects of the conventional balance sheet.
>
> (Chambers, 1969, 103)

The current broad principles primarily serve to result in the kind of income reporting desired by the issuers. But the balance sheet is also presented, and it's supposed to articulate with the income statement. In the process, the balance sheet is debased. It presents acquisition costs, which, because they don't represent financial achievement to date, are irrelevant, except perhaps sometimes as a surrogate, for any current decision. The American Accounting Association, which, in 1936 made presentation of acquisition cost co-equal with financial reporting, as discussed above, more recently still understated the irrelevance: "The relevance in today's market of the acquisition cost of a building bought 20 years ago is, to say the least, dubious" (American Accounting Association, 1991, 89).

A position sometimes taken is that current values are also old and irrelevant: "[current value information] would be stale by the time it is released" (AICPA, 1994b, I, 53). That contention is so obviously defective that I leave it to you readers to fault it.

In the same vein as financial reporters' poetical discussion of the behavior of costs described above, they tend to talk about costs not as sacrifices, bad things that occur, or even as measures of assets, but as assets themselves, good things that exist, for example:

> assets are costs ... costs are properly included ... in the total of assets ... inventories and plant are ... cost accumulations ... awaiting their destiny ... a large part of the total resources of the typical concern consists of a pool of unabsorbed costs in the form of plant, materials, and a complex of current services.
>
> (Paton and Littleton, 1940, 9, 14, 25, 33)

Product costs continue to be recognized as assets until the products that embody them are sold...

(Solomons, 1989, 45)

An entity should report film costs as a separate asset on its balance sheet.

(AICPA, 2000, par. 29)

Schuetze calls this "the cost-per-se-is-the-asset syndrome" (Schuetze, 2001, 13). The FASB acknowledged that "Inventories ... property, plant, equipment ... natural resource deposits, and patents ... have commonly been described in accounting literature as 'deferred costs'..." (FASB, 1985a, par. 177). It found it had to say the obvious, that "costs ... are not ... assets" (FASB, 1985a, par. 179).

Those who call costs "assets" may not mean literally what they say, but the usage can lead to fuzzy thinking. Improving financial reporting is challenging enough without applying fuzzy thinking. This book is intended rather to help you sharpen your thinking.

Also, it's been stated that assets, which most people consider good things to have, are merely aspects of bookkeeping!: "most assets are, in economic effect, deferred charges to future revenue" (Littleton, 1953, 32).

The balance sheet thus is subservient to the income statement: "the amounts at which many assets and liabilities are stated in the balance sheet are a by-product of methods designed to produce a fair periodical net income figure" (Bevis, 1965, 107). For example, the famous dictum of the AICPA on reporting on inventories, first stated in 1947 in ARB No. 29 and saluted to this day, is that

the major objective in selecting a method [of reporting on inventories in the balance sheet] should be to choose the one which, under the circumstances, most clearly reflects periodic income.

(AICPA, 1953b, Ch. 4, Stmt 4)

The income statement reports income statement items, and *the balance sheet also reports income statement items*, items that may appear in future income statements: "[the] function [of the balance sheet is] as one of the income-determining elements of the next period..." (Littleton, 1953, 31).

The balance sheet has fallen so low that its function is as "a list of account balances after the year's profit or loss is determined" (Defliese, 1983, 96), or as "the connecting link between successive income statements" (AICPA, 1939a, 2) or, worse, as "a kind of a gigantic footnote to the income statement" (Bevis, 1965, 57) or, still worse, as "a dimly lit basement parking garage for a collection of antique costs," or "a holding pen for expenditures to be released to expense sometime in the future when the time is right ... ([v]isualize a pen full of sheep awaiting their turn to be sheared)" (Schuetze,

2000, 6; 2001, 10) or worst of all, as "a mausoleum for the unwanted costs that the double-entry system throws up as regrettable by-products" (Baxter, 1950, Introduction, quoted in Storey and Storey, 1998, 58).

The purpose of debasing the balance sheet is in effect to avoid the discipline that articulation of that statement with the income statement places on the reporting of income, to facilitate stabilizing reported income.

Emphasis on income

We financial reporters are sensitive to the debasement of the balance sheet, and have rationalized it by saying that that statement isn't very important (though it is, for many purposes, including ratio analysis, and for disciplining the design of income reporting, and it could be made more useful than it is—this is discussed in Chapters 14 and 15), or at least not as important as the income statement. We have made its debasement a matter of principle:

> *Emphasis on Income* ... Accounting principles that are deemed to increase the usefulness of the income statement are ... sometimes adopted by the profession as a whole regardless of their effect on the balance sheet ...
>
> (AICPA, 1970c, par. 172)

Income reporting is vital; it may in fact provide the most useful information provided by financial reporting. But emphasizing income in solving issues in financial reporting without the discipline of sound reporting of assets and liabilities can lead to income statements designed to paint a picture the issuers want to present rather than to report.

Acquisition costs and reliability

Acquisition costs are often said to conform with the user-oriented criterion of reliability (I) more than current selling prices (discussed in Chapter 14), and are defended on that ground. However, current selling prices can often be determined more reliably than acquisition costs if the acquisition cost records are less than perfect. Also, after allocation, the costs violate the user-oriented criterion of representativeness, as discussed below, because they don't purport to represent anything outside themselves—for example, they don't purport to represent anything about the reporting entity. Because the first requirement for items to be reliable is that they purport to represent something outside themselves (see Chapter 3), *allocated costs are completely unreliable.*

That's demonstrated by a position of the FASB and a position of the AICPA. First, the FASB states that "Accounting information is reliable to the extent that users can depend on it to represent the economic conditions or events that it purports to represent" (FASB, 1980b, par. 62; also quoted in Chapter 3). That means, among other things, that to be reliable, information has to purport to represent external conditions or effects of events. Second, the AICPA states that "Definitions are unacceptable which imply that *depreciation for the year* is a measurement ... of anything that actually occurs within the year" (AICPA, 1953a, 24; quoted in Chapter 3). So costs allocated by depreciation [and, by extension, all allocated costs] don't purport to represent anything.

Acquisition costs and relevance

Acquisition cost has never been supported as benefiting the balance sheet; it's supported solely for its purported benefits to the income statement. Because most costs were incurred at dates earlier than the balance sheet date, they don't except by coincidence pertain to anything about the reporting entity at that date[6] and therefore are *irrelevant* to the choices made by the users as of that date: "Initial money cost means literally nothing to [anyone] ... He is the steward of what he has, not of what he spent to acquire what he has" (Chambers, 1969, 580).

Evaluation of the current broad principles

> Financial reporting rules ... often ... mislead ...
>
> (Revsine, 1991, 16)

Applying the tools of analysis the profession so lovingly developed (see Chapter 3) and then so promptly ignored, shows that the worst things about the current broad principles other than the defective principle defining the unit of measure (discussed at the beginning of Chapter 11) is that they commit a grave sin of omission and a grave sin of commission.

Sin of omission

The sin of omission results in violation of the user-oriented criteria of completeness and timeliness.

The user-oriented criterion of completeness has been stated but rarely applied. It's a wonder anyone bothers to state it—maybe they do so just because it sounds good. Nevertheless, it's vital.

The balance sheet is reasonably complete, other than for resources that can't be sold apart from the reporting entity, such as goodwill and, in many cases, research and development and other intangibles other than good-

---

6 And even if the asset was acquired on the reporting date, its cost doesn't except by coincidence report anything about the relationship between the reporting entity and its environment at that date. See Chapter 14, footnote 8.

will—but some people (including I) believe such resources shouldn't be reported as assets anyway (this is discussed in Chapter 14). (The balance sheet presents amounts that result from allocation, which aren't information, as discussed below. But that only harms the measurement of the assets and liabilities and doesn't by itself make that statement incomplete.)

In contrast, the income statement is incomplete, the single gravest fault of current financial reporting besides using an unsound unit of measure:

> To compare . . . performance by comparing only realized gains implies a definition of performance that many people would regard as incomplete and, therefore, as an unreliable representation.
>
> (FASB, 1980b, par. 118)

> The most general criticism to be leveled at financial statements in their present form is that they are seriously *incomplete* . . . One respect in which financial statements are now incomplete is that, because they are substantially transaction-based, they fail to recognize some value changes occurring during a period that aren't associated with a transaction.[7]
>
> (American Accounting Association, 1991, 83)

It generally presents the results of allocation, which aren't information, or amounts only when the quantities of assets or the set of liabilities change— "Accounting rules are designed to . . . track the flows of assets into and out of a corporation" (Blair and Wallman, 2001, 16)—generally when the reporting entity has transactions with other entities, which to some extent is information. But the amounts of assets and liabilities reported in balance sheets are the products of quantities and prices. Price changes are generally not reported in income statements apart from quantity changes—that's the sin of omission: the FASB acknowledges that "some assets and liabilities . . . are affected by events, such as price changes or accretion, that are not recognized" (FASB, 1984a, par. 27).

A correspondent referred to changes other than changes in quantities caused by transactions as "non-events" (Flegm, 2000), apparently being so indoctrinated by the realization convention that he thinks that transactions with other entities are not only the only events whose financial effects we mainly report on under the current broad principles, but also the only events that occur in the financial reporting territory that affect reporting entities. But price changes can affect the fortunes of reporting entities as much as or more than quantity changes. For example, the exchange of ten shares of a widely traded stock worth $150 a share for $1500 doesn't affect the

---

7 The American Accounting Association certainly has changed since 1936 (see text above concerning a fundamental axiom).

reporting entity much if at all, but a prior change in its price from $100 to $150 a share while held did affect the reporting entity, as anyone who holds such stock can testify (are you indifferent about increases in the current selling prices of your stocks?).[8]

In contrast:

> Does appreciation represent recognizable income? A negative answer to this query is fully justified. Without doubt the movement of prices has an important bearing on the economic significance of existing business assets, but there is little warrant for the view that sheer enhancement of market value, however determined, represents effective income. Appreciation, in general, does not reflect or measure the progress of operating activity; appreciation is not the result of any transaction or any act of conversion; appreciation makes available no additional liquid resources which may be used to meet obligations or make disbursements to investors; appreciation has little or no legal standing as income.
>
> (Paton and Littleton, 1940, 62)

That passage has several fatal defects of concept, for example,

1   "Appreciation ... does not reflect or measure the progress of operating activity" is a truism that has nothing to do with the issue debated by the passage.
2   "Appreciation is not the result of any transaction" is merely a restatement of the issue and not an argument.
3   The additional availability of liquid resources shouldn't be the only change considered to be an achievement worthy of being called income (and, besides, that's just a restatement of the realization convention, not a justification for it).

---

8 SFAS No. 115 (FASB, 1993a) eliminated the sin of omission for debt and equity securities bought and held principally for the purpose of selling them in the near term (but no one but the issuers, if them, can tell what purpose the issuers had in buying and holding the securities for the reporting entity, so that criterion isn't auditable). By requiring unrealized gains and losses to be excluded from earnings and reported in a separate component of shareholders' equity (now through the device of comprehensive income—see Chapter 9) for certain debt and equity securities to be reported in the balance sheet at fair value, it didn't eliminate the sin of omission for those securities. (The FASB defines "earnings" essentially as net income; FASB, 1984a). On June 30, 1999, the FASB announced that it had "decided that if all financial instruments are eventually measured at fair value in a full set of financial statements, all changes in the fair value of financial instruments should be included in earnings when they occur" (FASB, 1999c). If and when that occurs, reporting on major portions of the assets of reporting entities will still be subject to the sin of omission, including reporting on virtually all of their inventories, land, buildings, equipment, and other investments.

4 "Legal standing as income" should have nothing to do with financial reporting

and several defects of draftsmanship, for example,

1 What does "A negative answer to this query is fully justified" say that "No" doesn't say; or better yet, why not start with just "Appreciation shouldn't be recognized as income"?
2 Does an expression as weak as "little warrant" convince you of anything?
3 What's the difference between "sheer enhancement" and "enhancement," and between "effective income" and "income"?

I almost didn't list those defects, because listing them was tedious, and, because they should have been obvious, a waste of paper, of my time writing them, and of your time reading them. Nevertheless, that passage is *from the most influential book in the financial reporting literature.*

Ignoring changes in prices while assets are held and liabilities are owed permits the issuers to manage earnings, by timing the realization of gains or losses, to give, with the other income statement items, the desired bottom line, and permits allocation, discussed next in the section, "The sin of commission." Alternatives to ignoring changes in prices of assets while they are held and price changes related to liabilities while they are owed are discussed in Chapters 12 to 16.

The financial effects of price changes are incorporated and reported later in amounts realized, so their net financial effects aren't permanently ignored; their reporting is delayed; their amounts are combined with the financial effects of other price changes, and they are reported in income statements in the wrong periods. That's how the current broad principles violate the criterion of timeliness.

In contrast with the foregoing, the AICPA Special Committee on Financial Reporting stated without comment the following, which implies that the acquisition-cost basis reports income statement items in the right periods so as to properly identify trends: "Users ... would retain the [acquisition-cost basis] because ... [i]t provides users with a stable and consistent benchmark that's highly useful for ... identifying trends..." (AICPA, 1994a, 94). That was based on comments the committee received from users at focus group meetings it held, for example:

[There is t]oo much variability in a world of constantly changing prices, interest rates, and economic environments. The variability and the way the numbers jump around makes it very difficult to determine what caused what change. So at least there is some stability in the [acquisition] cost and you can place some reliance on that ... that record of actual historical transactions ... that's the benchmark...
(AICPA, *Database*, 4, 84; 4, 87. Also see AICPA, 1994b, I, 52.)

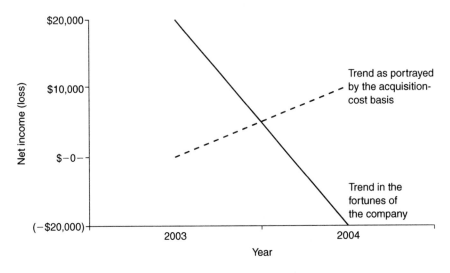

Figure 10.1 Fortunes trend.

The following illustration tests the Special Committee's contention:

> A company buys 100 shares of stock for $20,000 on January 1, 2003, its
> only asset at December 31, 2003, and its only transaction in 2003. On
> December 31, 2003, it can easily sell the stock for $40,000, though it
> doesn't. It sells the stock on December 31, 2004, for $30,000, its only
> transaction in 2004. It has no liabilities in 2003 or 2004. The acquisi-
> tion cost basis would require the company to report no gain or loss in
> 2003, though it doubled its resources, and it would require the
> company to report a gain of $10,000 in 2004, though its resources had
> declined by 25%.

Figure 10.1 illustrates the trend in the fortunes of the company and the
trend portrayed by the acquisition-cost basis.

What's the "stable and consistent benchmark" in the illustration? There
is none. Does the acquisition-cost basis help here in "identifying trends"?
No.[9] (Caution should be applied in relying too heavily on views expressed by
users, such as those expressed to the Special Committee in favor of current
GAAP. Chapter 17 discusses pitfalls of doing so.)

9 I suggested to the Special Committee that it quote the contention of the users at
   the focus group meetings but challenge the contention, based on the illustration
   in the text, which I had provided to the Special Committee during its deliberations. The Special Committee must have disagreed that the illustration demonstrates what I say it does, because it didn't adopt my suggestion. I nevertheless
   stand by my conclusions in the text.

Worse than reporting overall income in the wrong periods, though, is reporting overall income at unsound amounts using an unsound unit of measure, discussed in Chapter 11.

Sin of commission

> the principles of allocation . . . lie at the root of all accounting.
>
> (AICPA, 1944a, 186)

Systematic and rational allocation, the sin of commission, results in violation of the user-oriented criteria of representativeness, reliability (I), verifiability, and relevance.

In a study published by the FASB, Storey and Storey state that

> The distinguishing characteristic of accounting measures whose representational faithfulness normally cannot be verified because only the procedures used to obtain the measures[10] are verifiable is that they result from allocations...
>
> (Storey and Storey, 1998, 109)

But allocation is worse than that: allocated amounts not only can't be verified (simply verifying procedures doesn't meet the user-oriented criterion of verifiability); they don't purport to represent anything outside themselves, they violate the user-oriented criterion of *representativeness*, as discussed next.

Allocation is typically described as presenting the diminution of the service potential of an asset whose cost is allocated. Accounting Research Study No. 3 [ARS 3] defines depreciation:

> with utilization and the passage of time, there is a diminution in the remaining useful services which items of plant and equipment are capable of providing. This diminution when expressed in financial terms is referred to as depreciation.
>
> (Sprouse and Moonitz, 1962, 32)

ARS 3 then addresses determining depreciation: "Depreciation for any given accounting period, then, is the cost or other basis of the services used up[11] in that period" (Sprouse and Moonitz, 1962, 34). Allocation can also be the periodic reporting of the interest cost involved in the total of the payments to be made under a liability, which is amortized, a form of allocation (see also Chapter 15). That sounds like it purports to represent measurements of the financial effects of events occurring external to the reports

---

10 Such amounts aren't measures, as discussed in Chapter 6.
11 Costs are not used up in the financial reporting territory. Nothing happens to them there after they are incurred.

during the reporting periods over which the cost or interest is allocated, as required by representativeness and the operations to design financial statements (discussed in Chapter 3).

However, even allocation's best friends suggested that it doesn't result in representations of external phenomena:

> The method of calculating periodic depreciation expense is of minor concern so long as it does not conflict with the concepts of embodied services, of cost attaching, of matching effort and accomplishment. It does not matter that the simple and convenient straight-line depreciation may not accord with observed physical deterioration nor reflect fluctuating prices for similar equipment.
>
> (Paton and Littleton, 1940, 17)

And though the AICPA referred to measurement in connection with allocation: "measurement problems . . . [f]or example . . . allocations of sacrifices or benefits over periods of time" (AICPA, 1973b, 36), the FASB stated that "allocation methods . . . are not measurements of an asset or liability" (FASB, 2000b, par. 93; quotation also appears in Chapter 6).

The varieties of allocation available challenge their results as being representational. What kinds of changes occurring external to the reports and affecting the reporting entities can be represented by all of the three accepted alternative depreciation methods—straight-line, sum of the years' digits, and declining balance, or all of the 3,628,000 accepted alternative inventory allocation methods (discussed in Chapter 19). The acquisition cost of a depreciable asset minus its accumulated depreciation, an amount presented in contemporary balance sheets, for example, purports to represent nothing outside itself. Anyone who doubts that should attempt to demonstrate what it does purport to represent outside itself. (The usual response to an objection like that is that financial reporting is conventional. This book, in contrast, is intended to open up thinking, rather than close it off that way.)

An allocation formula is selected at the beginning of the period of allocation, before any of the events whose financial effects it supposedly represents occur. Financial reporters can't be that prescient about events that may occur in the future, after we select the formulas. And events don't occur as regularly as the formulas imply. Moreover, allocation doesn't even represent financial effects of underlying economic events. It merely takes amounts from the financial reporting territory, such as costs, enters them in the financial reporting map, and massages them there. It requires costs to behave in the financial reporting territory, though they don't:

> Assets are required, in some circumstances, to be stated after acquisition [at amounts adjusted for amortization or other allocations] . . . such an amount can be described only as an amount calculated under the rules of

amortization or allocation; it cannot be described in terms of a phenomenon outside of financial reporting.

(Lorensen, 1992, 14)

annual [depreciation] is simply a fraction of the total ... cost ... [and] has no necessary relation to ... occurrences within the year ... [it] has no real world connotations.

(Hendriksen and van Breda, 1992, 527, 528)

Auditors do not ... have to measure allocations ... they merely recalculate what their clients have calculated. The results may be rubbish, but they are generally accepted rubbish ...

(Arthur L. Thomas, 1979, 30n)

Thomas, the foremost critic of allocation (in Arthur L. Thomas, 1969 and 1974, which have never been seriously challenged in the literature), at first in effect considered whether allocation resulted in the best matching of incurred cost with realized revenue. He found after thorough study that it doesn't:

if an allocation method is to be theoretically justified, it must be defended completely ... all of [the] allocation approaches lead to arbitrary results if inputs interact ... The inputs interact, and their interaction prevents [them from being defended completely and therefore prevents] theoretical justification from being given to the input allocations employed in financial accounting.

(Arthur L. Thomas, 1969, xiii, 13)

The FASB agrees: "all allocation systems [are] arbitrary ... [t]hat is, [they] cannot be demonstrated to be superior to other methods" (FASB, 1997c, par. 58).

Thomas' conclusion didn't convince many (it obviously didn't convince the FASB to abandon allocation, because, in spite of the preceding quotation, it continues to require allocation), and he felt it necessary to go farther. He in effect abandoned the acquisition-cost basis, implying that even a perfect matching of incurred acquisition (or replacement) cost with realized revenue is still unsatisfactory if it violates representativeness. He concluded after an even more thorough study (at least, a study published in more pages) that allocation necessarily violates representativeness:

[Though a]llocation assertions are almost universally believed to refer to the firm's real world [phenomena] ... financial accounting's allocations actually do not reflect the real-world economic states and activities of the firms to which they purport to refer. Instead, these allocations are merely subjective constructs in accountants' and readers' minds ... We should ... stop allocating for the same reasons that, as they learn to communicate, babies stop babbling.

(Arthur L. Thomas, 1974, 49, 65; 1979, 29)

The conclusion that allocation violates representativeness is buttressed by the conclusion reached above that costs do all of the marvelous things we financial reporters say they do only in the financial reporting map, not in the financial reporting territory. Financial statements should be representations of an external reality, like photographs, not, as today, abstract expressions of financial reporters' fancy, like modern art:

historic cost, replacement cost, and discounted value ... define conventions instead of laws; they define allocations instead of measurements; they define abstractions instead of representations of reality...

(Sterling, 1979, 69, 70)

The presentation of representational faithfulness as a single criterion was thus a fatal defect in the FASB's approach. By not separating the characteristic into its two component criteria, the Board never asks the first question, does the amount represent anything outside financial reporting? It asks only whether the amount represents something faithfully, not realizing that some of the amounts in current financial statements represent nothing, faithfully or otherwise. Asking whether the amount represents anything leads to the question, what does an amount resulting from allocation represent? The answer is that it represents nothing

Based on the view that allocated amounts don't represent phenomena outside financial reporting (outside financial reporting, a cost doesn't "expire" or do anything else except occur, once, and that's the end of it), they are merely signs, devoid of meaning; as stated in Chapter 3, they don't constitute symbolic communication. Not being information, they violate the user-oriented criterion of relevance. As stated above, they violate the user-oriented criterion of reliability (I). That allocation violates four of the primary user-oriented criteria of financial reporting—representativeness, verifiability, relevance, and reliability—is especially distressing because, as stated above, contemporary financial reporting is *defined* as a process of allocation.

Violating the criterion of representativeness to that extent prevents the presentations from being reports, and thus prevents financial reporting from fully being reporting and turns it at least partially into presenting managed earnings (see Chapter 2). The violation helps turn financial reporting into a ritual, as discussed below.

Though "Abandoning allocations would be a drastic departure from what accountants understand, believe in, and are accustomed to presently" (Kam, 1990, 293), what's wrong with a drastic departure from such biased reporting?

Not all commentators believe allocation is all bad. Sixteen years before Thomas issued his objection, the AICPA stated (perhaps at least partly accurately for the time) that "no one suggests that allocations based on imperfect criteria should be abandoned..." (AICPA, 1953b, Chapter 10 [B], par. 4). Devine, who describes Thomas as "one of the more articulate and distraught critics of allocation" (Devine. 1985e, 85n), says (distraughtly) that

> all elements of accounting worthy of cognitive attention involve allocations. Practically all accomplishments and sacrifices are joint endeavors from any viewpoint, and accountants are supposed to *account* for (explain) them in terms of antecedents, sources, responsibilities, influences, decisions, actions, periods, environmental conditions, etc. For the allocation process we make all sorts of judgments and apply all sorts of formulas. But regardless of the machinery for making the required judgments or the rules for making the required measurements, and regardless of the joy or reluctance with which we perform the operations, *allocate we must*!
>
> A word of warning! All explanation is allocation; all causation is allocation; all antecedent-consequent relations are allocations; all marginal imputation is allocation; and all attempts to *account* for outcomes are allocations ... Regardless of the diverse judgments and arithmetics employed, all assignments, all distributions, and all imputations *are* allocations—all judgments and all decisions *require* allocations.
>
> (Devine, 1985e, 79 and 84)

He said his attitude is like that of the noted economist Boulding: "'the allocation of profit among various ... periods is the principal task of the accountant—otherwise accounting would be mere arithmetic'" (Boulding, 1955, 852, quoted in Devine, 1985e, 85n). In fact, it's allocation that's mere arithmetic.

Impossibility of successfully auditing amounts in financial statements

Because amounts that result from allocation don't conform with the user-oriented criteria of representativeness and verifiability, they can't be audited successfully. Because issuers' current thoughts about the future also don't conform with those criteria (see Chapter 7), amounts resulting from GAAP that incorporate such thoughts also can't be audited successfully. Because most amounts resulting from application of current GAAP either result from allocation or incorporate issuers' current thoughts about the future, most amounts in financial statements prepared in conformity with current GAAP can't be audited successfully: "Accounting methods that are not based on the observation of phenomena do not yield outputs that can be independently verified" (West, 2003, 65). A former chief accountant of the

SEC agrees: "Today's financial statements of most companies are not auditable" (Schuetze, 2003, 1). That's remarkable, since the SEC is responsible for seeing that the financial statements of its registrants are soundly audited (that former chief accountant told me that he came to this conclusion after he was no longer in that position). (In contrast, as discussed in Chapter 1, auditing is generally successful in its concern with the control function of bookkeeping and accounting and with the prevention and detection of fraud.)

The relationship between the sins

The sin of omission, by which changes in prices of assets held or in prices related to liabilities owed are ignored when they occur, and the sin of commission, by which amounts are presented that aren't information, are related. If the noninformation is eliminated, assets and liabilities would have to be reported at their original amounts the entire time they are held or owed (an obviously unsatisfactory result) unless price changes are reported when they occur.

Understandability, verifiability, comparability, and reliability (II)—no

The current broad principles also cause financial statements to violate the user-oriented criteria of understandability, verifiability, comparability, and reliability (II).

Users likely believe that all the amounts in financial statements represent external phenomena. If told otherwise, they may realize that they don't understand what purports to be but isn't information. They may also know that mechanical repetition of calculations under systematic and rational allocation by outside auditors is merely going through motions and not verifying correspondence between assertions in financial statements and external phenomena: the FASB states that "the amount of depreciation for a period is normally only indirectly verifiable by verifying the depreciation method, calculations used, and consistency of application" (FASB, 1980b, par. 87). That comment applies equally to all amounts derived from allocation, because they don't conform with the user-oriented criterion of representativeness, as discussed above, and thus can't be verified. Such so-called indirect verification, which is no more than fancy verbal footwork by the FASB, has nothing to do with the user-oriented criterion of verifiability.

Because they don't satisfy the other user-oriented criteria, financial statements don't satisfy the user-oriented criteria of comparability and reliability (II). Comparing investment and credit opportunities using them is hindered. Especially pernicious is the incompleteness of the income statement: when economic events occur in one period but reporting entities report their financial effects in other periods, comparisons are likely to be dangerous.

Also, the users can't rely on the amounts presented, because they include half truths and amounts that aren't information.

Strange timing in current financial statements

In spite of the FASB's assertion that "Earnings ... for a period ... to the extent feasible excludes items that are extraneous to that period..." (FASB, 1984a, par. 34), the current broad principles result in items in the balance sheet and the income statement whose timing doesn't agree with the timing in the headings of the statements.

Conformity of the current broad principles with the incentives of the issuers, outside auditors, standard-setters, and regulators

Because of their defects, the current broad principles other than the principle defining the unit of measure cause financial statements generally to conform with the incentives of issuers, outside auditors, standard-setters, and regulators, and that's why they fight so hard to retain them. Many financial reporting revolutionaries have attempted to convince financial reporters and their standard-setters to rectify the sins of current financial statements. One reason they haven't yet been successful is that they haven't understood the tenacity with which they are defended based on the incentives of the issuers.

Stable income reporting

Systematic and rational allocation is the primary means to achieve stable income reporting, the primary incentive of the issuers:

> depreciation is only part of a broader scheme whose purpose is to equalize charges between different years.
>
> (Hatfield, 1916, 134)

> The very purpose of measurement is to discover variations in empirical phenomena. By contrast, it seems that the purpose of allocation is to make the empirical phenomena appear to be smooth regardless of the actual variations.
>
> (Sterling, 1979, 226)

> allocations [are] designed to produce smoothed income flows.
>
> (Lee, 1979, 45)

The key to the principle of allocation is the "systematic" part; a predetermined, smooth formula is used to determine financial statement amounts:

> Allocation is the accounting process of assigning or distributing an amount according to a . . . formula.
>
> (FASB, 1985, par. 142)

> amortization of old amounts by a predetermined pattern . . .
>
> (Staubus, 1977, 217)

> the pseudo-scientific formulae which have been developed for the apportionment of common costs.
>
> (Chambers, 1969, 84)

But for reporting to avoid derision, the allocation method must also be "rational." The AICPA gave a tautological meaning to that expression: "the allocation method should appear reasonable to an unbiased observer . . ." (AICPA, 1970c, par. 149). So, obviously ludicrous allocation methods are avoided, such as basing the formula on the numbers on the license plates of the first ten cars crossing the Brooklyn Bridge every morning. That seems to be all the rational part of SARA entails. It doesn't seem to mean, as it seems to imply, that the allocation has been determined to best serve the legitimate purposes of financial reporting. Nevertheless, the following somewhat more charitable views have been taken: "the requirement that the method be rational probably means that it should be reasonably related to the expected benefits in each case" (Hendriksen and van Breda, 1992, 527). "[In 'systematic and rational,'] rational . . . is . . . based on internally consistent reasoning" (Lamden *et al.*, 1975, 42). Do those sentiments speak to you?

Not all allocation methods that avoid derision are permitted. Increasing charge depreciation methods, which have some reasoning behind them, aren't permitted by the SEC, for example, probably because they aren't conservative:

> Depreciation accounting using a compound interest . . . method—either the annuity or the sinking fund method—has long had the approval of theorists but has had little acceptance in practice, possibly because its relatively small charges during the early years of the asset's life with increasing charges thereafter seem to make cost recovery more uncertain.
>
> (American Accounting Association, 1991, 95)

Perhaps we shouldn't search too hard for a meaning for "rational" in the term "systematic and rational." Such a word originates by a staff person thinking it up one day. She comes to the office to do a day's work for a day's pay. She is faced with selecting or inventing a term to use in a first draft she is working on, and none is obvious. One pops into her mind, she likes it, and she uses it in the draft. What she uses isn't too important at this stage—after all, it's only a first draft, and first drafts get rewritten numerous times. For the word to become embedded in our authoritative language, it has to survive all the scrutiny of experienced and capable people that such drafts go through.

I was occasionally faced with such a situation. For example, I had to invent terms when preparing the first draft of APB Statement No. 4, *Basic Concepts and Accounting Principles Underlying Financial Statements of Business Enterprises* (AICPA, 1970c), which, among other things, contrasted two kinds of transactions: (1) transactions in which the reporting entity both received something of value to it and gave up something of value to it, and (2) transactions in which the reporting entity either received something of value to it or gave up something of value to it but not both. The terms "two-way transfer" and "one-way transfer" popped into my mind. I thought they were neat and did the job, so I put them in the draft. The Chairman of the APB Subcommittee dealing with the Statement wasn't as enraptured by them as I was, but he didn't immediately have a substitute. We had an extended conversation, during which the word "reciprocal" popped up. That's how, by accident, the terms "reciprocal transfer" and "nonreciprocal transfer" entered our authoritative literature, and they have become embedded for the 36 years since APB Statement No. 4 was published.

For another example, I was faced with selecting or inventing a term to refer collectively to assets, liabilities, equity, revenue, expense, and net income in drafting APB Statement No. 4 (AICPA, 1970c). The term "basic elements of financial accounting" popped into my mind and I put it into the draft. It survived all the reviews of the pronouncement and was part of the final statement published in 1970. It became embedded in the authoritative literature and remained so until 1980, when the FASB changed it to "elements of financial statements" in its CON3 (FASB, 1980c). That has remained to this day, now embedded in its CON6 (FASB, 1985a).

On taking over the term, the FASB rectified the less serious of its two defects, the redundancy between the words "basic" and "elements" (all elements of things are basic; I don't know what I was thinking when I included the word "basic"). It didn't rectify the more serious defect of the term. They are *not* elements of financial accounting or of financial statements. They are elements of the reporting entity. This is another case of confusing the map and the territory. (See footnotes 1 and 2 in Chapter 9 and the text at those footnotes, including my statement of repentance.)

There is nothing profound about selecting or inventing a term to put into a first draft of an authoritative pronouncement. The drafter needn't worry that the term might not survive; it probably won't. Drafting authoritative pronouncements (and books like this) is grunt work, not rocket science.[12]

12 This is based on high authority: Schuetze, a former Chief Accountant of the SEC, said that "Financial ... reporting ... is not rocket science" (Schuetze, 2001, 3). (Mundane occupations such as financial reporting used to be compared to "brain surgery" rather than to "rocket science." Besides, most people who work on rockets are engineers, not scientists.)
   In contrast, Devine stated that "accounting ... is not the only area worthy of intellectual effort, but it is one such area" (Devine, 1985e, 186).

The undistinguished origins of the words we use should prevent us from giving them uncritical approval. They have become embedded, it's true, but not necessarily for good reasons. The word "rational" in the term "systematic and rational" had the same inglorious origin as all such words: it popped into someone's mind, sounded good, got drafted, and stuck. Those in the business of reviewing drafts of authoritative pronouncements are busy, even harassed people. They may not think too carefully and critically about a word that makes them feel good. Perhaps it stuck simply because it sounds good and doesn't make us think too much. Perhaps it doesn't mean *anything*.

In fact, as discussed above, allocation is *ir*rational, in the sense that its results don't conform with *any* of the criteria that make financial statements valuable to their users.

To get back to the substantive word in the expression, "systematic:" to be sure, SARA prevents manipulating amounts to easily overstate income or achieve completely stable results by certain unsystematic methods, such as providing depreciation at times and in amounts decided by the Board of Directors, a practice that preceded SARA: "As recently as the 1890s, the amount provided for depreciation by a number of large corporations was considered to be a function of profits" (Flegm, 1984, 75). Zeff reports that "as a result of the Revenue Acts of 1913 and 1918, many company executives came to appreciate the importance of recording depreciation, because it was deductible for tax purposes" (Zeff, 2003a, 190, 191). However, an alternative to allocation itself, current selling price reporting (discussed in Chapter 14), can better prevent manipulation.

Being sytematic, allocation avoids arbitrary decisions on the amounts of expense to report in connection with long-lived assets. But the systematic aspect is also what got us into trouble: it appealed to the issuers' desire for stable income reporting, so that aspect was a double-edged sword. And *simply* because a new method, such as allocation, can better prevent manipulation than the method it replaced, depreciation decided annually by the Board of Directors doesn't make it a sound method. Those who initiated the use of allocation in the late nineteenth century might have but didn't notice that it doesn't purport to provide information about any aspect or any change in any aspect of the reporting entity, that it violates the criterion of representativeness, and is therefore completely unsound. It prospered not because of its soundness but because it has the result of contributing to stabilizing income reporting, the usual reason principles have prospered to date in financial reporting. The users of financial reports in the twenty-first century deserve better than that.

Thomas recently told me that he wished that he had similarly "homed in on the issuers' desire for smooth . . . stable-appearing profits. . ." That's allocation's unstated but only honest justification.

Scott even said that the ability of the acquisition-cost basis to stabilize income reporting is a virtue:

[acquisition]-cost based earnings are a way to "smooth out" cash flows for the current period into a measure of the longer-run or persistent earning power that is implied by these cash flows.

(Scott, 1997, 28)

It's ironical that the foremost supporters of allocation, Paton and Littleton, said that

There are lean years and fat years in business operation and it is a function of accounting to disclose this condition sharply, not to cover it up ... the remedy is to supplement the annual statement by cumulative and average reports covering longer periods, rather than to issue "doctored" yearly exhibits.

(Paton and Littleton, 1940, 77)

Allocation is the primary means to doctor yearly exhibits.

Stable reported income is also facilitated by the realization principle: "[acquisition] cost ... permits management of reported gain or loss by advancing or delaying realization" (Skinner, 1987, 529). Income is generally reported when revenue or gains are said to be realized. Changes in prices except below cost are generally ignored when they occur; they are reported only to the extent that they are incorporated in the amounts of realized revenue. Were they reported when they occur, they could cause reported income to fluctuate more than it does under the current broad principles. Further, though reporting entities generally want to realize income as soon as possible, they are able to affect the timing of its realization to some extent, especially the timing of realized gains, and therefore of reported revenue, and are able to some extent thereby to smooth out the wrinkles in the reported income trend. Also, the realization principle permits the acquisition-cost basis and thereby allocation, with its powerful stabilizing effect on reported income.

I communicated these views on the harmful nature of realization and allocation to the SEC (and in an article in the October 2000 *Journal of Accountancy* [Rosenfield, 2000]); the Epilogue (footnote 2) states the result.

It's true that reporting entities can tend to stabilize reported income by timing their incurrence of items charged directly to expense, such as advertising and research and development. But first, that's a bad business practice and therefore self-limiting, and second, such expenses could be required to be analyzed in the notes to the financial statements so the users could see their stabilizing effect and make allowances for it.

The current broad principle of objectivity is a smoke screen:

objectivity has a long, ignoble history ... objectivity [is] one of the most slippery concepts in accounting ... it was used to support both sides of diametrically opposed positions.

(Sterling, 1979, 6, 7)

We have cut the meaning of "objectivity" down to a size that suits us, regardless of its meaning in other fields of discourse and in the ordinary everyday world.

(Chambers, 1969, 689)

that "sacred cow" of accounting—the "objectivity principle."

(Philip W. Bell, 1971, 32)

Issuers would never admit to directing their most powerful principles toward stabilizing reported income, their greatest desire. So instead they take an estimable concept, objectivity, which means that the observations of independent observers of phenomena that exist outside the minds of the observers and outside record keeping would be much the same, a good quality for financial reporting and an essential one for auditing (not to mention science), and redefine it, backwards, as the result of the principle of realization, confining reporting of the financial effects of events mainly to the financial effects of transactions to which the reporting entity is a party in order to stabilize reported income, and then making that result a matter of principle.

The issuers' allegiance to the acquisition-cost basis and their opposition to reporting so-called unrealized gains demonstrate the view stated in Chapter 2 that they prefer stable income reporting to high income reporting when the two conflict.

Minimize legal costs and criticism

Both issuers and outside auditors want to minimize their exposure to legal costs should financial reports with which they are involved be called into question, and they, standard-setters, and regulators want to avoid being criticized even if it doesn't involve legal costs, because it could involve their reputations. But issuers aren't as eager to avoid those woes as outside auditors, standard-setters, and regulators. Issuers usually want to report higher income or lower losses (as long as that doesn't interfere with reporting stable income), so they generally tend to overoptimism in financial reporting. If they have financial reversals severe enough to be sued on the grounds of inadequate financial reporting, the reporting entities generally don't have any money then to pay for legal costs anyway, and their reputations aren't as much involved. In contrast, outside auditors don't have quite the same incentive for high reported income, except by association with their clients, their reputations are vital to them, and they have the deep pockets when lawsuits are filed. Standard-setters and regulators have no incentive for those they regulate to report high income. Outside auditors, standard-setters, and regulators therefore desire balance sheets that lean over backwards not to attract complaint, that minimize reported asset amounts, that is, that are *conservative*: "auditors['s] own situation leads to a . . . bias toward . . . conservatism" (Skinner, 1987, 659). That's facilitated, for example, by the realization convention:

> [outside auditors] produced the convention that unrealized gains are not part of earnings ... because auditors don't want to be sued ... this ... approach keeps users from being fully informed.
>
> (Miller and Bahnson, 2002b, 248)

The Chairman of a leading firm of outside auditors once told me that it's better to have financial statements understated nine times out of ten than to have them overstated one time out of ten. He neglected to say that it's better for outside auditors, standard-setters, and regulators, not for the users.

It's sometimes said that it's impossible to be consistently conservative, that a conservative balance sheet leads to an unconservative income statement. The AICPA committee on accounting procedure decried such a result: "conservatism in the balance-sheet is of dubious value if attained only at the expense of a lack of conservatism in the income account, which is far more significant" (AICPA, 1939b, 13). But conservatism is mainly a goal only for balance sheets. Outside auditors, standard-setters, and regulators are generally not concerned if income statements aren't conservative, as long as balance sheets are conservative. For example, the pooling-of-interests method of reporting on business combinations, which until recently was part of GAAP and widely used, produced conservative balance sheets and high income reporting, the best of both worlds for issuers, outside auditors, standard-setters, and regulators (but not for users).

Conservatism violates the user-oriented criterion of neutrality: "a conservative view [or] a confident or optimistic view ... any such modification involves (subjective) tampering with the objectivity [in the general sense] of the statements" (Chambers, 1966, 154).

Financial reporting as ritual

> [R]itual ... instructs, nourishes, and often begets, belief ... it charms the senses and the soul with drama, poetry, and art; it binds individuals into fellowship and a community by persuading them to share ... the same thoughts.
>
> (Durant, 1935, 742)

> Perhaps investors *are* naive.
>
> (Solomons, 1986, 230)

Do we financial reporters believe that the users are "naive"? Is financial reporting after all only a ritual?

Financial reporting as we now know it may in fact be largely ritual: Coughlan asks:

What is the declining balance but ritual? Surely the sum of the digits from ten to one (namely 55) is just a magic number on a par with 3, 5, 7, 11 and various other numbers that have played a part in witchcraft, fraternal organizations and poetry. Surely the term *systematic and rational* as applied to contemporary depreciation is just an euphemism for *arbitrary and ritualistic*.

(Coughlan, 1965, 436)

Thomas says "our allocations ... are mere rituals—solemn nonsense—and our beliefs in them are fallacies" (Arthur L. Thomas, 1975b, 68).

One has his doubts:

It is conceivable that financial reports might ... be a mere customary ritual. It hardly seems likely, however, that a mere ritual would have persisted as long as financial reports have or would generate so much heated argument as they sometimes do, if they were not thought to have important practical uses.

(Skinner, 1987, 635, 636)

Similarly, Thomas referred to the rationalization of some that "The accounting rituals that we use would not have survived had they not been good" (Arthur L. Thomas, 1979, 30n). Those sentiments are wishful thinking. The acquisition-cost basis results in data that violate all the user-oriented criteria. The two worst paragraphs in the financial reporting literature—(1) paragraph 88 of SFAS No. 52 (see Chapter 22) and (2) paragraph 79 of SFAS No. 109 (see Chapter 21), under which the FASB on the one hand knowingly and purposefully forces us financial reporters to present amounts throughout financial statements that don't mean anything and on the other hand forces us to present enormous amounts as representations of liabilities that the reporting entities don't have—are met by CPAs with indifference. Also, consider these confessions by the AICPA and the FASB:

it is a universally accepted practice to add the cost ... of one asset to the market value of another, and to deduct from the sum the amount of a liability to arrive at a net figure. This procedure, although open to obvious criticism of its mathematical propriety, possesses so many practical advantages and is so well established that it is not likely to be abandoned.[13]

(AICPA, 1953a, 8)

13 Ruth J., who isn't a financial reporter, said the following about this statement: if she had written four as the sum of two plus three, her second grade school teacher would have asked her to do it over.

The Board acknowledges that the delayed recognition included in ...
Statement [No. 87] results in excluding the most current and most relevant information from the employer's statement of financial position.

(FASB, 1985b, par. 104)

In the FASB's statement, the Board is implying that the issuers have the
most current and most relevant information but the Board won't let them
provide it to the users! Similarly,

Accountants ... routinely perform and sanction aggregations of
financial quantifications that represent different attributes ... and are
expressed in different monetary units ... This ... defies a basic principle of arithmetic. The origins and persistence of the practice must be
explained by custom, ignorance, convenience or some other factor.

(West, 2003, 39)

That's not to say that financial reporting wouldn't be useful were it
merely ritual, but only that it wouldn't provide useful information. Its ritual
function perhaps would be worth the cost. Some helpful activities, such as
marriage ceremonies, obviously are rituals. Boulding took the position that
the ritual nature of financial reporting doesn't make it worthless and that it
should be acknowledged:

Ritual is always the proper response when a man *has* to give an answer
to a question, the answer to which he cannot really know. Ritual under
these circumstances has two functions. It is comforting ... and it is also
an answer sufficient for action. It is the sufficient answer rather than the
right answer which the accountant really seeks ... The wise business-
man will not believe his accountant[14] ... provided that the accounting
rituals are well known and understood, accounting may be untrue but it
is not lies...

(Boulding, 1962, 53, 54, 55)

Similarly,

It may be said that in commercial or investment banking or any business extending credit, success depends on knowing what not to believe
in accounting.

(Justice Jackson, 1954, 652)

Other rituals, for example those of "the primitive medicine man [who]
performs artistic rituals" (Sterling, 1979, 11) (and often of modern MDs),

14 To my knowledge, financial reporters are the only professionals about which
such a statement has been made.

depend for their efficacy on the belief of persons subject to the rituals that they aren't merely rituals, that they change undesirable conditions, such as illness or lack of information, not merely states of mind. If the financial reporting ritual is of this kind, its usefulness would depend on the belief of persons at whom the ritual is directed that it's not a ritual, that it in fact cures lack of information: "[Myths] are the truth to the people who believe in them and live by them" (Hamilton, 1988, ix). It would be similar to the faith the Russian people had in the military ability of Russia's commanding general Kutuzov, who defeated Napoleon, though he has been said to have had no such ability.[15] His ritual function has been said to have carried the day. Mattessich, who discussed Kutuzov's function, contends that "Likewise the effectiveness of traditional accounting lies not in the preciseness of information . . . but in its authoritative character" (Mattessich, 1964, 414).

If financial reporting to a considerable extent serves a ritual function today, we should work to tip the scales so it more serves an information function. Or, as Jenkins said in the *Wall Street Journal*,

> When a ritual has so emptied itself of real meaning as to become positively dangerous to its participants, it's time for a rethink.
>
> (Holman W. Jenkins, Jr., 2002, A17)

Debating points

1 Turner and Foster are right about the quality of financial reporting in the U.S.
2 The FASB has more important things to do than to test current GAAP against its ancient conceptual framework.

---

15 A biographer agreed that some held that view of Kutuzov:

> He has been condemned as lazy, incompetent, cowardly, a lecherous imbecile too fat to ride a horse, who sought only fresh virgins and other comforts for his dissipated body.
>
> (Parkinson, 1976, 1)

That's an unflattering comparison for financial reporting. However, that biographer quoted Tolstoy as saying that Kutuzov was ". . . a . . . truly great figure, who could not be cast in the lying mould invented in history" (Parkinson, 1976, 2). And the biographer described Kutuzov's "strategic principles" as

> the avoidance of unnecessary battles, the preservation of his army, the reliance upon the power of manoeuvre, the appreciation that psychological victory over the enemy could be equally devastating as defeat inflicted upon the battlefield itself . . . Not even Napoleon could match Kutuzov's clarity of strategic vision and his awesome tactical coolness . . . No man played a greater single part in Bonaparte's downfall than Kutuzov. . .
>
> (Parkinson, 1976, 1, 120, 234, 235)

That's a view of Kutuzov that could better inspire financial reporting.

3 The acquisition-cost basis is the bedrock of sound financial reporting.

4 Mautz was right; it would be better to stay with the devil we know than go to an unknown devil.

5 The acquisition-cost basis should be junked.

6 *Standards* is one of the worst books ever published on financial reporting.

7 *Standards* is the best book ever published on financial reporting.

8 A book used in a university course on financial reporting shouldn't mock serious concepts such as cost flow and costs attach.

9 The balance sheet under the acquisition-cost basis isn't worth the paper it's printed on.

10 Income should be emphasized over financial position in the design of GAAP.

11 Acquisition costs, with or without allocation, are the most reliable amounts in financial statements.

12 Scott was right; the ability of the acquisition-cost basis to stabilize income reporting is a virtue.

13 Financial statements under the acquisition-cost basis are hopelessly incomplete.

14 Paton and Littleton were right about appreciation.

15 Allocation in financial reporting is hoodoo-voodoo.

16 Devine is right about allocation.

17 Financial statement amounts based on current GAAP can be successfully audited; auditors do it all the time.

18 Conservatism is a legitimate response to the overoptimism of the issuers of financial reports.

19 Current financial reporting is nothing more or less than ritual.

11 Inflation reporting

"the [APB] agreed that the assumption in accounting that fluctuations in the value of the dollar may be ignored is unrealistic..."

(Minutes of APB meeting, April 28, 1961, quoted in Sprouse and Moonitz, 1962, 17)

Units of money used in money measurement are not in one significant sense—their command over goods and services—invariant over time ... A 10-year summary of sales revenues covering a period when the purchasing power of the monetary unit has been declining may convey an exaggerated picture of growth ...

(FASB, 1980b, pars 114, 121)

The current broad principle of defining the unit of measure in terms of the debt-paying power of the dollar can result in strange information. To illustrate, an investment was bought in 1945 for $10,000 and sold in 1995 for $15,000. Defining the unit of measure that way and applying the realization principle results in reporting income of $5000 in 1995. The general purchasing power of the dollar, measured by the Consumer Price Index, fell about 88 percent from 1945 to 1995. In terms of general purchasing power, each dollar received was worth about 12 percent of what each dollar paid was worth. $10,000 was considerable wealth in 1945. It would buy a new house. $15,000 was a lot less wealth in 1995. It would barely buy a new car. So we financial reporters would report income of $5000 in circumstances in which people who aren't financial reporters would say that the investor lost her shirt. (People who aren't financial reporters aren't imbued with the idea that inflation doesn't matter. To test that, ask someone who isn't a financial reporter what she would say to her financial reporter friend who bragged about a 20 percent raise she got at the end of a year in which there was 50 percent inflation. That's no worse than her reporting the $5000 income.)

The AICPA and the FASB each once felt the same, as indicated in the opening quotes. This sentiment agrees with that sound view:

To the extent that growth of the corporation is overstated because it is reported in dollars without measurement of their decline in value, then society, corporate management, and the stockholder are all misguided.

(Bevis, 1965, 40)

(It's possible for the reported growth to be understated for the same reason.)

Defining the unit of measure in terms of the debt-paying power of the dollar forces presentation of amounts characterized as gains and losses that don't conform with the ordinary understanding of the users of financial statements of gains and losses as improvements and reductions of economic well-being. The amounts therefore violate the user-oriented criterion that the financial statements be understandable to the users.

Defining the unit of measure in terms of general purchasing power

When the rate of inflation gets high enough, we financial reporters sometimes see the light. The high inflation rate in Mexico recently moved the financial reporters there to adopt inflation reporting, that is, to change the unit of measure used in their financial statements from one defined in terms of debt-paying power of their money to one defined in terms of the general purchasing power of their money (McConnell and Pegg, 1995). Inflation reporting has recently also been required in Chile and Venezuela (Schwartz, 1998, 9), and the IASC requires that definition in highly inflationary economies (IASC, 1989b). (The events that occur in such economies may differ from ordinary events. For example, debt may bear very high interest rates or be indexed. The financial effects of the events that do occur are the ones that need to be reported, even if that means devising novel treatments for novel financial effects.)

A former Chief Accountant of the SEC pooh-poohed purchasing power units by abbreviating them as PuPUs (Burton, 1975, 70).

Many think that inflation reporting might be a good thing when there is high inflation but it isn't needed when inflation is low or even moderate—for example, the FASB:

> as rates of change in general purchasing power increase, financial statements expressed in nominal units of money become progressively less useful and less comparable. The Board expects that nominal units of money will continue to be used to measure items recognized in financial statements. However, a change from present circumstances (for example, an increase in inflation to a level at which distortions became intolerable) *might* lead the Board to select another, more stable measurement scale.
>
> (FASB, 1984a, pars 71 and 72, emphasis added)

(The message is that the Board likely would force users to tolerate the intolerable.)

However, a study conducted by the APB in the 1960s demonstrated that even the low inflation rates of those years, in only the 2 percent to 3 percent range over a period of many years, can result in income reported in a unit of measure defined in terms of the debt-paying power of money different from income reported in a unit of measure defined in terms of the general purchasing power of money (the study and its results were reported in Rosenfield, 1969a), with the differences considerably above the SEC's materiality threshold (Securities and Exchange Commission, 1999a). That's caused by the result of cumulative inflation over a period of years affecting the amounts reported in any one year: "Although the current inflation rate in the United States is relatively low in the context of recent history, its compound effect through time is still highly significant" (FASB, 1986, Mosso dissent), and the magnification of a small effect of inflation on individual revenues and expenses on the smaller net income: "greatly magnif[ies] the net results..."[1] (Littleton, 1953, 21). In contrast, the FASB stated that "At low rates of change in general purchasing power (inflation or deflation), nominal units of money are relatively stable" (FASB, 1984a, par. 71).

The low rates of inflation during the study period are presented in Table 11.1, and the results of the test in Table 11.2.

We get excited about material differences caused by misapplication of reporting principles other than the principle that defines the unit of measure, but we ignore the material differences caused by misdefining the unit of measure. If you think it isn't bad in financial reporting, perhaps you would think it's bad if required to pay income tax on the nonexistent income of $5000 discussed above. The U.S. tax laws require payment of such taxes:

> What ... purports to be a tax on income is, during a period of rising prices, potentially a levy on capital as to part of the tax liability.
>
> (Chambers, 1966, 336)

> an inflation neutral tax system ... would [remove] the federal government ... as a profiteer of inflation...
>
> (Cheeseman, 1975, 51)

> The [C]ontract [with America] would increase—or index—for inflation the adjusted [tax] basis of certain capital and other assets for purposes of determining the gain or loss on sale.
>
> (Willens and Phillips, 1995, 34)

---

1 Also see Rosenfield, 1969a, 47–48.

Table 11.1   Inflation in the United States as measured by Gross National Product Implicit Price Deflators, 1945–67

Year	Index number (1958 = 100)	Rate of inflation (deflation) (%)
1945	59.7	2.6
1946	66.7	11.7
1947	74.6	11.8
1948	79.6	6.7
1949	79.1	(0.6)
1950	80.2	1.4
1951	85.6	6.7
1952	87.5	2.2
1953	88.3	0.9
1954	89.6	1.5
1955	90.9	1.5
1956	94.0	3.4
1957	97.5	3.7
1958	100.0	2.6
1959	101.6	1.6
1960	103.3	1.7
1961	104.6	1.3
1962	105.7	1.1
1963	107.1	1.3
1964	108.9	1.7
1965	110.9	1.8
1966	113.9	2.7
1967	117.3	3.0

Source: United States Department of Commerce, Survey of Current Business, issued monthly. Copyright 1969 by AICPA, reproduced with permission.

Unfortunately, that part of the Contract, a program of the 1994 Republican Congress, wasn't adopted.

AICPA, "General Price-Level Changes," and SFAS No. 89 illustrate restatement to a unit defined in terms of general purchasing power.[2]

2 The information before restatement is based on GAAP developed for financial statements stated in units of debt-paying power. Perhaps those aren't the best GAAP for financial statements stated in units of general purchasing power. The issue is similar to the issue of whether GAAP for the financial statements of a subsidiary in a particular country whose unit of measure is defined in terms of the money of that country are the best for use when including information on the subsidiary in consolidated financial statements whose unit of measure is defined in terms of the money of its parent company country, an issue considered in Chapter 22. That issue in the context of inflation reporting has never been considered in the literature. You might consider it.

Table 11.2 General price-level accounting field test: highlights of results

Company	Net income difference* (Column 1)	General price-level gains and (losses) % of restated net income (Column 2)	Effective federal income tax rate Restated (Column 3)	Historical (Column 4)	Cash dividends (% of net income) Restated (Column 5)	Historical (Column 6)	Rate of return on owners' equity Restated (Column 7)	Historical (Column 8)
A	4%	4%	39%	38%	61%	58%	14.2%	16.7%
B—1st year	0%	19%	44%	43%	52%	50%	(not available)	(not available)
2nd year	0%	22%	44%	44%	49%	48%	12.0%	13.0%
C—1st year	5%	3%	49%	47%	36%	33%	(not available)	(not available)
2nd year	14%	5%	50%	47%	50%	44%	13.2%	15.8%
D—1st year	233%	(271%)	75%	46%	(no dividends)		(not available)	(not available)
2nd year	434%	(542%)	82%	46%			0.7%	3.7%
E—1st year	(30%)	50%	31%	38%	54%	74%	9.3%	10.3%
2nd year	(25%)	52%	25%	30%	52%	69%	8.1%	9.7%
F	10%	3%	(not available)		49%	44%	(not available)	(not available)
G	8%	(1%)	12%	11%	66%	61%	12.5%	15.9%
H—1st year	20%	(5%)	39%	34%	90%	72%	7.5%	10.3%
2nd year	18%	(3%)	41%	37%	86%	72%	7.9%	10.5%
I—1st year	11%	8%	50%	46%	63%	54%	(not available)	(not available)
2nd year	15%	22%	50%	46%	58%	50%	15.1%	18.1%
J—1st year	15%	5%	50%	46%	37%	32%	11.4%	13.9%
2nd year	29%	8%	56%	49%	65%	50%	6.4%	8.8%

K	12%	7%	41%	38%	49%	43%	12.6%	16.1%
L	13%	9%	36%	34%	92%	80%	(not available)	(not available)
M—1st year	(10%)	13%	35%	38%	21%	22%	(not available)	(not available)
2nd year	(9%)	22%	30%	31%	29%	32%	14.0%	15.0%
N—1st year	4%	(7%)	50%	48%	(not available)		(not available)	
2nd year	12%	(7%)	48%	45%				
O	28%	(11%)	57%	50%	78%	60%	(not available)	(not available)
P—1st year	(26%)	49%	31%	36%	48%	62%	(not available)	(not available)
2nd year	(31%)	59%	21%	27%	56%	79%	4.9%	5.8%
Q	(12%)	36%	37%	39%	24%	27%	(not available)	(not available)
R—1st year	21%	20%	52%	46%	37%	29%	(not available)	(not available)
2nd year	15%	6%	50%	46%	46%	39%	13.0%	15.6%

Source: Copyright 1969 by AICPA, reproduced with permission.

Note
*Percent that historical-dollar net income is higher (lower) than restated net income in terms of restated net income.

The Chairman of the APB subcommittee that drafted AICPA "General Price-Level Changes" said that he was certain that if financial statements were originally stated in a unit of measure defined in terms of general purchasing power and a suggestion was made that they be changed to financial statements stated in a unit of measure defined in terms of debt-paying power, as today, the suggestion wouldn't have been adopted.

Which general purchasing power?

A unit of money has one general purchasing power for each basket of goods and services that can be specified (see Chapter 6). The APB recommended that for inflation reporting, the unit be defined in terms of a basket of producer and consumer goods and services that mirrors the U.S. economy, using the Gross National Product Implicit Price Deflators, simply because it's the broadest index of general purchasing power (AICPA, 1969, par. 30). Others said that that index "seems" to be or "is probably" best:

> because money has command over any good or service, it seems reasonable to use as general an index as possible, which would be the GNP Deflator Index.
>
> (Kam, 1990, 204)

> in terms of measuring the extent of overall price changes, the [Gross National Product Implicit Price Deflator] is probably more relevant.
>
> (Riahi-Belkaoui, 1993, 317)

That sounds good until you ask what's so special about the broadest kind of basket.

Defining the unit of measure defines the notion of income. With the unit of measure defined in terms of the debt-paying power of the unit of money, income is an increase in debt-paying power. The 5000 U.S. dollars gain discussed above is such income. But if you end up with more debt-paying power after a period in which a given amount of debt has become much less burdensome, that's nothing to write home about, or report income about.

Income should be defined according to the perspective of the users of the financial statements (see Chapter 8). People are interested in consumption. They may invest in producers' goods and services, but not to use them. Their investments in such goods and services are merely deferred consumption: "The ultimate objective of all investment activities is consumption of goods by people"[3] (Staubus, 1977, 239). Just as defining whether the farm's year referred to in Chapter 8 was a good year or a bad year depends on the feelings of people about cows and sheep, and just as defining whether the

---

3 Staubus presumably includes services in his reference to goods.

game referred to in Chapter 8, which ended with a score of UConn 77 and Duke 74, is a victory or a defeat depends on the feelings of the fans, income should be defined in terms of what people care about: consumption. The income of reporting entities should be defined in terms of an increase in the ability of people to consume, currently or later, not merely to pay given amounts of debt whose burden may increase or decrease with changes in the general purchasing power of money. The unit of measure in financial statements should be defined in terms of the consumer general purchasing power of the unit of money, one involving a basket of consumer goods and services.

In the U.S., applying the Consumer Price Index results in such a unit of measure. SFAS No. 33 required the use of a consumer price index, though simply because it's revised less often than the Gross National Product Implicit Price Deflators, not because of its relevance to users.

Some believe that inflation affects different reporting entities diversely and that the index of general price-level changes to be used in inflation reporting should reflect that: "Using the same general price level index to adjust the statements of all firms assumes that the effects of price changes are uniform across firms" (Revsine, 1973, 58). However, the only price changes that affect firms are changes in the prices of the *specific* goods and services they buy and sell. Inflation not only doesn't affect reporting entities diversely—it doesn't affect them at all. Inflation reporting pertains instead to the financial effects of inflation on the perspective of the people who use the financial reports.

Using an index that corresponds to the specific purchases of the reporting entity affects the attribute being measured; issues concerning the attribute to be measured are discussed in Chapters 10 and 12–16. Such a use doesn't pertain to inflation reporting, which involves rather the unit of measure used in financial statements.

Gains and losses on monetary items

Inflation reporting reports a class of gains and losses that reporting entities experience but that they can't otherwise report: gains and losses of general purchasing power on monetary items. Monetary items are assets and liabilities denominated in the money of the country whose general purchasing power is used to define the unit of measure in the financial statements. For example, an entity reporting in terms of U.S. dollars holds 1000 U.S. dollars cash continuously during a period in which the general price level in the U.S. doubles. During the period it has thereby lost one-half of the general purchasing power represented by the cash at the beginning of the period. Similarly, if it owes 1000 U.S. dollars continuously during the period, it has gained one-half of the general purchasing power represented by the debt at the beginning of the period—the burden of the debt in terms of general purchasing power decreased. Severe inflation can virtually eliminate liabilities: "[German i]ndustry ... wiped out its debts in the [hyper]inflation [of

1923]..." (Shirer, 1960, 61, 117). The assets represented by the gain, if any, were received in advance, when the debt was incurred.

Some have occasionally advanced the argument that if inflation was or could have been predicted at the beginning of the period and inflation occurred during the period, the reporting entity didn't have such a gain or loss during the period. For example, "anticipated inflation can never give rise to gains on debt" (Revsine, 1982, 78n). However, anticipating an event such as a tornado or inflation doesn't cause the effects of the event not to occur when and if the event occurs; the anticipation takes place in the mind, the event takes place outside the mind.

Arguments against inflation reporting

The following is an argument against inflation reporting by the most committed supporter of the acquisition-cost basis in the financial reporting literature and one of the authors of the most influential book in the literature:

> the sweeping rise in price levels that characterized the 1920's ... the collapse of prices late in 1929 [followed by] a severe depression ... during most of the 1930's ... these two decades showed how little real usefulness would appear if accountants tried to make their accounts keep pace with changing conditions outside the enterprise concerned ... The data would lose their prior significance every few days.
>
> (Littleton, 1953, 212)

Applying the so's-your-old-man argument, also known as the pot-calling-the-kettle-black argument, how soon does acquisition cost lose its prior significance? At least the information produced by inflation reporting would have a single unit of measure in terms of general purchasing power relevant to the users current at the reporting date. (Wouldn't not keeping pace with the changing conditions prevent the data from *ever* having significance?)

Here are other arguments against inflation reporting:

Users do not believe information in units of general purchasing power would be more helpful than information in units of money.

Several surveys, including those by Backer, Estes, Dyckman, and Barker, have suggested that users do not believe ... information [from inflation reporting] would be more helpful.

Information in units of general purchasing power would be confusing to users.

This argument was advanced by Stickney and Green ... who said in 1974 that "...users might be confused as to the meaning of the adjusted statements." They admitted, however, that "an educational program could help."

Changing to units of general purchasing power does not make a material difference.

This argument was advanced by Stickney and Green, because rankings based on rate of return seem to remain unchanged.

People are interested in information in terms of money, not in terms of general purchasing power.

Revsine and Weygandt ... implied that argument, citing the "objective of cash flow predictions" ...

General price level indexes are not sufficiently reliable.

Stickney and Green wrote that "substantial uncertainty regarding the accuracy and reliability of the price indices seems warranted."

(Rosenfield, 1981, 24, 32)

The following thoughts apply in connection with those arguments:

- Users usually respond to surveys based on past habits without opening their minds to new possibilities (see discussion in Chapter 17).
- Just because we financial reporters don't seem to understand the financial effects of inflation, that doesn't mean that users of financial reports who aren't financial reporters don't understand them.
- People usually make investment decisions based on earnings-per-share information, not on rate-of-return information. Further, rate-of-return information based on equity derived from the acquisition-cost basis is notoriously unreliable.
- Only we financial reporters think that people are interested in comparisons simply of money amounts regardless of changes in its general purchasing power.
- General price-level indexes are considered reliable enough, for example, for use in adjusting Social Security payments. Besides, not using the imperfect indexes is equivalent to assuming that the rate of inflation is zero, which gives much more unreliable results.

Another counterargument sometimes given is that the users can restate conventional statements for themselves and issuers needn't do it for them. However, those who argue this way have never illustrated how to do it. That isn't surprising, because it's impossible, which is clear to anyone (such as I) who has restated financial statements for inflation.

Some contend that inflation reporting presents the financial effects of events as they didn't occur, as fiction: "GPLA [general price-level accounting] would restate firms' accounts *as though* past transactions occurred at current price levels using the Consumer Price Index" (Watts and Zimmerman, 1986, 271, emphasis added). However, remeasuring the effects of events that do occur from one scale of measurement to another doesn't change the events that occurred or their measured effects to events and effects that didn't occur, just as remeasuring the height of a door that exists from inches to centimeters doesn't change it to the height of a door that doesn't exist.

Failure of SFAS No. 33

The FASB conducted an experiment in its SFAS No. 33 (FASB, 1979b) in which certain companies were required to present supplementary information stated in a unit of measure defined in terms of the general purchasing power of the dollar. The FASB thought that "Supplementary financial statements, complete or partial, may be useful, especially to introduce and to gain experience with new kinds of information" (FASB, 1984a, footnote 5). Solomons and I said as much:

> The easiest way for the board to innovate is through requirements to provide supplementary information. That way, change—even radical change—can be introduced for a trial period without disrupting GAAP.
>
> (Solomons, 1986, 196)

> One thing I know is that we cannot get the general price-level statements to be the only statements now. That would be absolutely[4] impossible, considering the educational job that would be required for both accountants and users, to cite just one problem.
>
> (Rosenfield, 1971a, 162)

Experience with SFAS No. 33 has caused me to repent of that sentiment.

People said they didn't know what to do with the information, so the FASB terminated the experiment. An unfortunate effect of the failure of SFAS No. 33 is that interest in reflecting changing prices in financial statements in the periods in which they change has, at least temporarily, diminished since then.

An opponent of inflation reporting celebrated SFAS No. 33's failure: "One of the challenges that academics should address . . . is why SFAS No. 33 was such a dismal failure..." (Flegm, 1989, 95). That challenge is accepted here.

The reason people didn't know what to do with the supplementary information was that it competed with the usual financial statement information stated in a unit of measure defined in terms of the debt-paying power of the dollar, which pertained to the same things as the supplementary information but gave different amounts. The debt-paying power information was familiar; the supplementary information was unfamiliar:

> the presentation of financial statements on the traditional basis supplemented by statements on any contemporary basis will only increase, not diminish, confusion . . . where the supplementary information is contradictory of the principal information . . . recipients know not what to do with it.
>
> (Chambers, 1969, 440; 1987, 195)

4 This experience has cured me of being absolutely absolute about anything.

The competition was too much for the supplementary information. That was the best way to condemn inflation reporting. Miller and Bahnson concluded that "there wasn't much else the board could have done to ensure that it would fail to produce results" (Miller and Bahnson, 2002b, 238).

Inflation reporting shouldn't be toyed with. One set of financial statements should be presented. The unit of measure in the financial statements should be defined in terms of the consumer general purchasing power of the unit of money. (As stated above, Mexico, Chile, and Venezuela, for example, did that.) People would know what to do with such financial statements— the same things they do with current-style financial statements, only better.

The failure of SFAS No. 33 is also discussed in the beginning of Chapter 13.

Inflation reporting and current value reporting

> The two approaches are ... attempted solutions ... to two entirely different problems.
>
> (Coughlan, 1965, 45, 46)

Inflation reporting involves the definition of the unit of measure. Current value reporting, discussed in Chapters 12 to 14, involves selection of attributes to measure. The matrix in Figure 11.1 illustrates the relationship (taken from Rosenfield, 1972, 66).

They are separate responses to separate problems:

> A common misconception is that the results [of restatement for inflation] represent current values ... the question of current cost is one of "value," and the question of general price level adjustments is one of "scale." These are two separate issues.
>
> (Kam, 1990, 205, 449)

	Historical Cost	Current Value
Units of money	1	2
Units of general purchasing power (general price level restatement)	3	4

Figure 11.1 Relationship between general price-level restatement and current value reporting (copyright 1972 by AICPA, reproduced with permission).

However, the separation is often disregarded, for example:

> general price level accounting and current-value accounting are competing alternative measures for dealing with problems created by inflation.
>
> (Riahi-Belkaoui, 1993, 305)

> Past approaches have taken one of two competing tracks. Constant dollar accounting, whereby financial statements are adjusted for changes in the purchasing power of the reporting currency ... [and c]urrent cost data...
>
> (White and Sondhi, 1999, 12, 16)

The effect on income statements in general of changing the attribute that's measured is merely to change the periods in which income is reported:

> [the] choice of attributes to be measured ... do[es] not affect the amounts of comprehensive income ... over the life of an enterprise but do[es] affect the time and way parts of the total are identified with the periods that constitute the entire life.
>
> (FASB, 1985a, par. 73)

Changing the unit of measure, in contrast, changes the amount of overall reported income.

Inflation reporting and reporting on foreign operations

Inflation reporting and reporting on foreign operations involve similar issues, and care is required when they are both applied (as discussed in Chapter 22).

Debating points

1   Only kooks believe financial statements should reflect inflation or deflation.
2   The nonreflection of inflation and deflation in financial statements is one of their worst defects.
3   If inflation and deflation are to be reflected in financial statements, they should be based on a general index of changes in consumer prices.
4   The failure of SFAS No. 33 shows that price changes shouldn't be reflected in financial statements before they are realized.

12 Presenting discounted future cash receipts and payments in financial statements[1]

the . . . ideal basis of valuation [is] the present value of . . . future cash flows.
(American Accounting Association, 1991, 93)

Obviously,[2] to know the past . . . one must know the future . . .
(Lev, 2001, 82; also quoted in Chapter 7)

The AICPA and the FASB listed the following three concepts that they said could be considered as measurable attributes of assets of reporting entities alternative to acquisition cost for use in financial statements:

- Discounted future cash receipts and payments
- Current buying prices
- Current selling prices

(AICPA, 1973b, 41; FASB, 1976a, par. 390)

For a single asset, the amounts based on those three concepts and acquisition cost can all differ substantially. A reporting entity may have paid $50,000 to acquire a machine suitable for only its own operations a year ago. The issuers of its financial statements may think that in the future, before the machine wears out, it can be applied to materials, labor, and overhead costing $35,000 to make products that can be sold for $145,000. That could make the future cash receipts and payments from the machine that they predict, assuming that all of the cash receipts and payments pertain to the machine and the conversion efforts, discounted at 10 percent, equal to, say, $90,000. What the FASB considers the current buying price of the asset might have risen to $75,000 for reasons, for example, of supply and demand or increases in the costs of manufacture. In contrast, because the machine is

1 Much of this chapter is taken from Rosenfield, 2003.
2 It is striking that what is obviously true to some people, here to Lev, is obviously false to other people, here to me. Compare Chapter 7.

suitable for only the reporting entity's operations, it may be able to sell the machine currently only for scrap at a current selling price of $1000.

In addition, some have stated or implied that *prospects* for future financial achievement should be the alternative to acquisition cost to use in presenting assets and liabilities in financial statements.

This chapter discusses the use of discounted future cash receipts and payments as an alternative to acquisition cost, and Chapters 13, 14, and 16 discuss alternatives that involve current buying prices, current selling prices, and prospects, respectively.

The "ideal basis"

A blue-ribbon committee of the AICPA agrees with the assertion of the American Accounting Association quoted at the beginning of this chapter that the "present value of . . . future cash flows" is the "ideal basis" for all "valuation" in financial statements, by stating that

> if one could reduce the future cash flows to a single number at various times through an appropriate discounting process, earnings for a period could be determined by comparing changes in present value . . .
>
> (AICPA, 1973b, 32)

Staubus made the same kind of statements:

> [the] discounted present value [of an asset is] the theoretically best measure of asset worth . . . The current value of the residual equity is equal to the total of all assets measured on the basis of present values minus the total of the specific equities measured at present values.[3] . . . discounted future cash flow is a *relevant attribute* of any asset . . .
>
> (Staubus, 1961, 32, 33; 1977, 140)

Scott defined relevance in terms of this basis: "relevant financial statements [are] ones which [show] the discounted present values of the cash flows from the firm's assets and liabilities" (Scott, 1997, 60).

The current condition of the reporting entity as to an asset is thus asserted (everywhere without support, to my knowledge) to ideally be the *present value* of the asset, defined as the discounted amount of future cash receipts and payments supposedly obtainable from it and caused by it. (Each

---

3 In a later document, Staubus stated that potential for future cash receipts and payments rather than the incremental effect on the net discounted amount of the reporting entity's future cash receipts and payments is the attribute we seek to measure (see Chapter 16). Further, present value can't be measured, as discussed below in the text.

liability would ideally be the discounted amount of the net cash payments it supposedly will cause.)

Three questions emerge. First, does *present value* defined that way exist as a current measurable condition of the reporting entity? If not, the amount violates the user-oriented criterion of representativeness. Second, if so, is it a relevant measurable condition of the reporting entity? Third, if so, is it the best relevant measurable condition of the reporting entity to measure and report in financial statements?

The approach of this chapter is to inquire about the answers to those questions by seeing what affirmative responses to them would require, and thereby to form a conclusion about the soundness of the view that the present value of future cash flows is the ideal basis for the measurement of assets.

Not only is present value recommended to be the attribute in concept to replace acquisition cost in general in financial statements, but it is also widely used in current requirements and practices. CON7, "Using Cash Flow Information and Present Value in Accounting Measurements" states in its Highlights that "accountants quite often must use estimated future cash flows as a basis for measuring an asset or a liability." The analysis and conclusions in this chapter apply equally to these uses of the concept of present value.

The existence of present value

The present value of supposed future cash receipts and payments is said to be the ideal basis of valuation of assets. The term "ideal" isn't intended to mean that present value doesn't exist outside people's thoughts. It's intended to mean that present value exists outside people's thoughts and is the best attribute to use, but that it is difficult or impossible to measure directly. The main reasons given for the view that present value is difficult or impossible to measure directly are:

- The inputs to the cash receipts and payments interact: "What part of the firm's receipts are earned by the office typewriter?" (Baxter, 1966, 9)—making assignment of the cash receipts and payments to the inputs arbitrary.
- It is hard to know future events.
- It is hard to specify the discount rate to use. However, some minimize this problem—for example the AICPA, in a quotation above, a portion of which refers without discussion merely to "an appropriate discounting process." Also, Staubus stated without elaboration that "There are several possible sources of discount rates . . . all [of which] are likely to have useful applications in the measurement of [assets and liabilities] by discounting future cash movements" (Staubus, 1961, 35). In fact, such specification is impossible:

  there are . . . as many . . . discounted values as there are participants in

> the market ... The discount rate is personal to each individual decision maker.
>
> > (Sterling, 1979, 132, 138)

> Subjective value is a personal evaluation ... the receipts expected by a person discounted at a rate of interest which that person expects to be the appropriate rate.
>
> > (Bedford, 1965, 25, 28)

If an attribute that exists is difficult or impossible to measure directly it might be measurable indirectly, for example by surrogates. But if it doesn't exist, surrogates don't solve its lack of existence (as discussed in Chapter 6).

The first question this chapter addresses is the first issue—whether present value exists currently.

The parentage of the concept

> Present value is one of the foundations of economics and corporate finance, and the computation of present value is part of most modern asset-pricing models ...
>
> > (FASB, 2000b, par. 19)

The parents of the concept of present value were economics and management.

Economics is the father of the concept: "Accounting is ... strongly rooted in economics..." (Paton and Littleton, 1940, 13); "Accounting is a branch of economics" (Staubus, 2003, 193).

Both economics and financial reporting deal with economic resources (see Chapter 9). Further, they both have concepts called "income," and an assumption has been made, without demonstration of its soundness or even inquiry into its soundness, that the concepts should refer to much the same thing. The AICPA made that unsupported assumption:

> With perfect knowledge,[4] economic and accounting earnings as measures of [improvement in well-being] would be readily determinable and would be identical. With such knowledge, earnings for a period would be the change in the present value of future cash receipts and payments, discounted at an appropriate rate...
>
> > (AICPA, 1973b, 22)

---

4 This means perfect knowledge of the future. Perfect knowledge of the future doesn't exist, of course; if it did, financial reporting would be unnecessary. Further, as discussed in Chapter 7, the future doesn't even exist at present.

Financial reporting is said to represent the *value* of assets in one sense or another, and "present value" contains that term.

Individuals made the same kind of statement:

> Since concepts of income ... hold a prominent position in economics, ... accountants ... can expect some aid from discussions in economic literature.
>
> (Schattke, 1960, 698)

> Economic income is the ideal indicator of enterprise performance, because it reflects current cash flows and changes in future cash flows[5] ...
>
> (Carsberg, 1982, 70)

> it is possible to reconstruct from the literature a justification for the dissemination of replacement cost reports to investors. This justification is based on the assumption that replacement cost income is a surrogate for economic income.[6]
>
> (Revsine, 1973, 93)

Ronen said that "According to the [economic income] view, there exists an underlying 'true' state of the world and changes therein" (Ronen, 1974, in AICPA, 1974, 143), which economic income purportedly presents.

The idea is so ingrained in the minds of academic accountants that the first time I submitted a paper to a journal challenging the idea, the editor, a professor of accounting, rejected it apparently for the simple reason that it challenged the idea. In his letter of rejection, he said: "I doubt that you will find many people who support your views on present values ... I do not believe [your position] can be supported in any substantive way."[7]

An assumed intimate relationship between financial reporting and economics became ingrained in academic accountants' minds early:

5 It blows my mind to think about something in the future changing (that observer wasn't referring to changes in people's opinions about what might happen in the future).

6 As discussed below in the text, economic income occurs only in people's minds, and can be anything people think. Replacement cost income can be defined so as to occur in the world outside people's minds. One cannot therefore be a surrogate for the other, and the assumption isn't justified.

7 You should rather struggle with ideas with which you might initially disagree. In any event, I stand by the conclusion I present below in the text in the section "Conclusion on whether present value is a current condition of the reporting entity" and by the evidence I present for it. (The paper was subsequently published in another journal—see Rosenfield, 2003.)

When accountants initially received academic training, it was in the area of economics. Understandably, as their teachers had obtained an economics degree, accountants tended to follow methods of economics and attempted to develop accounting income concepts accordingly.

(Stewart, 1989, 111)

Paton reported that in 1912, he "enroll[ed] in an accounting principles course at the University of Michigan. The instructor . . . was . . . a professor of economics who knew nothing about accounting" (Paton, 1972).

The reason for the retention of that thought in their minds is a matter of speculation. Here is my speculation:

Economics is considered to be an ancient, highly honored, intellectual endeavor. Financial reporting started with none of those attributes. Even now, financial reporters (as all accountants) are known as bean counters; there is no Council of Accounting Advisors in the federal government to match its Council of Economic Advisors and no Nobel Prize in Accounting as there is in economics. Financial reporters had and continue to have an inferiority complex in relation to their brothers the economists. So they emulate them and borrow their concepts without reflection to convince themselves they are just as good.

There is no reason for that attitude now, if there ever was.

Management is the mother of the concept. Finance is a vital part of management: "the present value concept of securities values has [long] been recognized by students of finance" (Staubus, 1971a, 48). Management also involves choices in other areas, for example the following: "The times and amounts of future cash flows are the principals for some managerial decisions involving an asset, such as the sell-or-hold decision" (Staubus, 1971a, 60). Management may hold or acquire resources if the present values management believes the resources involved exceed their acquisition costs by more than such excesses in opportunities to acquire other resources.

Both economics and management involve a variety of decisions concerning the effects of events the decision-makers believe may occur in the future.

Edwards and Bell noted that "economists have approached [income measurement] with essentially subjective concepts derived from expectations concerning future events. . ." (Edwards and Bell, 1961, viii). Economists imagine policy choices, predict what they suppose the outcome of each will be, and advise policy-makers on which policy to choose to attempt to obtain the best results or the least bad results.

Management of finances, among other things, involves pricing in possible future transactions. It informs investors, for example concerning contemplated transactions (such as in capital budgeting decisions or contemplated purchases of fixed income securities), about the amount that should be spent in exchange for an expected or promised series of repayments in order to obtain an expected or promised given overall rate of return, or about the overall rate of return that would be involved in paying a given amount for a given expected or promised series of repayments: "net present value is the common criterion for choice among options..." (Chambers, 1989, 15). Management also involves a variety of additional decisions concerning the effects of supposed future events, for one example, personnel decisions.

Neither economics nor management is concerned with reporting financial conditions of the reporting entity as they exist and existed and financial effects of events as they occurred to the reporting entity, to which the preparation of financial statements should be confined:

> the economist is concerned with what [people] think; the accountant is concerned with measuring the results of what [people] have done.
> (Goldberg, 1965, 252)

> [The] perspectives [of financial reporting and financial analysis] are dia-metrically opposed ... Because assets and liabilities are both the result of *past* transactions and events, so is the accounting measure of net worth. Financial analysis, on the other hand, assesses, estimates, and gauges value solely in terms of expectations of the *future*.
> (Association for Investment Management and Research, 1993, 17; this passage is also quoted in Chapter 1 in another context)

Because economics and management involve actions that have supposed future consequences while financial reporting involves reporting on the financial effects of past events, the parentage of the concept of present value should by itself raise doubts as to whether it refers to a current condition of the reporting entity, the first question we are dealing with. The origin of the concept doesn't, however, by itself conclusively answer the first question. Financial reporting theorists did borrow the concept of present value without consideration of its suitability in the new setting of financial report-ing (see Chapter 4 for a discussion of borrowing from other disciplines). Chambers commented:

> Awareness of the necessity of preparing accounting statements which shall be relevant to the future is not lacking. But the end is not achieved by simply borrowing economic concepts which have an independent function in the making of choices different from and complementary to the results of a well designed accounting system.
> (Chambers, 1966, 351, 352)

However, they presumably borrowed it in good faith assuming that it's serviceable there. We can't simply discard that assumption without evaluating it.

The magic of discounting

> discounting *into the present* the value of future fixed payments or
> receipts . . .
>
> (Ronen and Sorter, 1989, 73, emphasis added)

To implement the concept, the financial effects of supposed future events are
thought to be discovered, either by thinking about them or by using surrogates (see Chapter 6). The amounts involved in the financial effects of those
supposed future events are discounted, multiplied by fractions less than one.
Discounting is held to *move those effects of events backwards in time*, as Ronen
and Sorter say, as quoted above, "into the present," and *to change the effects of
the events into conditions*. Others refer to the same startling process:

> The stream of net expected values . . . is still *future* in time, and thus
> each item in the stream must be discounted before it can be treated as
> an element in *present* valuations.
>
> (Edwards and Bell, 1961, 81, emphasis added)

> [discounting] techniques . . . convert *future* amounts (for example, cash
> flows or earnings) to a single *present* amount . . .
>
> (FASB, 2004b, 3, emphasis added)

That process is said to result in the present value. Discounting, we are asked
to believe, magically changes both the timeframe and the nature of the
amounts of the financial effects of the supposed future events: supposed
future changes are somehow transmuted into supposed *current conditions*. The
process is said to purport to result in representing conditions of the reporting entity in the financial reporting territory, not merely the imaginings of
economists and managers or the doodles of financial reporters.

We are asked to believe in magic. Many of us financial reporters do
believe in it, because we are indoctrinated.

Perhaps you can tolerate your financial reporter believing in magic. Could
you tolerate your doctor believing in magic?

There is no such thing as magic—sorry, boys and girls[8] (but there are
laws of physics, including those related to time).

In fact, "a discounted value is [merely] an arithmetically adjusted
forecast . . ." (Sterling, 1979, 171).

---

8 An infant receives food, warmth, affection, and the like from where it knows not.
  It takes it for granted that its needs will be supplied with no effort on its part.
  Everything seems magical to it. As infants grow, they find that not everything
  necessarily comes with no effort. That saddens them. They therefore like to think
  that at least some magic remains. But it doesn't, not for children, and not for
  financial reporters.

The reversal of cause and effect

> So little disciplined by the irreversibility of time are some processes and
> their rationalizations that time sequences have become inverted.
>
> (Chambers, 1989, 14)

If "past performance can only be judged when the future is known" (as
quoted in Chapter 7) and, as implied in the quotation by the American
Accounting Association that opens this chapter, past performance and
current conditions can't be known at present—we must await future events
to occur to know them:

> Time present and time past
> Are both perhaps present in time future
> And time future contained in time past
>   (T. S. Eliot, "Burnt Norton")

But that's poetry again. Getting back to prose, a present value of an asset is
supposed to be a current condition of the reporting entity. The way it's
defined, as the discounted amount of the future cash receipts less the discounted amount of the future cash payments attributable to the asset, makes
those future receipts and payments the *causes* of the current condition: as of
time T_1, the time the current condition of present value is said to exist, there
have been no such future receipts and payments (only prospects of them), so
there is as of yet no present value. Later, at times T_2, T_3, and so on, some
receipts and payments occur. The definition says that there is now a present
value at T_1. Those receipts and payments at times T_2, T_3, and so on, therefore
caused the present value to come into existence at time T_1. *Cause followed
effect*. The future affected the past!

   To illustrate: a current condition of the reporting entity supposedly
might be the present value of a car factory possessed currently. Future cash
movements concerning the factory, if they occur, depend, for example, on
what might be future actions of car buyers. If Ms A buys a car built at the
factory later, we are told to conclude that the current condition of the
reporting entity was one thing. If Ms A considers buying the car later but
doesn't, we are told to conclude that the current condition of the reporting
entity was something else. Based on that, if Ms A buys the car later, that's a
cause of a current condition of the reporting entity, because, had Ms A
passed up buying the car later instead, the current condition of the reporting
entity would have been different. A cause, we are thus asked to believe, can
follow its effect in time.

   Even financial journalists aren't immune to such thinking (or at least such
writing):

A company's *value* today depends on its *future* profits and cash dividends and assets. It doesn't depend on a company's past numbers, because we can't revisit the past.

(Sloan, 2002, 94, emphasis added)

Perhaps what Sloan meant was that what people *think* a company's value is today depends on what they *think* its future profits and cash dividends and assets will be. But that's not what he wrote.

A cause can't follow its effect in time; the future can't affect the past (except in the minds of financial reporters, and, as just indicated, apparently in the mind—or the pen—of at least one financial journalist).

Presenting solely the financial effects of supposed future events

By holding that the current condition of the reporting entity is present value and defining *present value* as the discounted amount of supposed future cash receipts and payments, we need to somehow know *only* those supposed future events. Once we somehow know them, we multiply the amounts of their financial effects by fractions less than one.

The APB and the FASB have given lip service to the view that financial statements should be historical reports, that they should report on the financial effects of past events, not presentations of the financial effects of supposed future events (as stated in Chapter 7). But here we are in effect told we needn't know anything about the past or the present (other than perhaps the current cash balance). We are told to present the financial effects of those supposed future events (arithmetically adjusted), rather than use the financial effects of supposed future events merely as evidence, and we thus are told to violate the restriction of financial statements to historical reports.

In fact, based on the concept of present value, we present the opposite of historical reports. Rather than presenting reports whose raw material is confined to the financial effects of past events, the raw material of what we present is virtually confined to the financial effects of supposed future events.

Nonexistent future events

[The substance of a] net present value is a figment, a compound of imagined future events or sequences of events, and discounting factors.

(Chambers, 1989, 15)

Finally, the future doesn't exist at present except in imagination (as discussed in Chapter 7). But the current condition of the reporting entity does exist and the past did occur to the reporting entity. The current condition of the reporting entity and the past of the reporting entity therefore can in no way depend on the future. The supposed future events whose financial effects we are told constitute the raw material of financial statements exist at present only in the minds of the issuers, in the financial reporting map, and don't pertain to the reporting entity. Barton, Sterling, and Bedford correctly referred to the subjective nature of present value, that it resides solely in the mind of the subject, the person, considering it:

> Present values are subjective and are in the eye of the decision maker.
>
> (Barton, 1974, 678)

> discounted values are . . . subjective.
>
> (Sterling, 1979, 126)

> Subjective value is a personal evaluation . . . The subjective value of an asset . . . is the present value of the expected receipts which [it] will yield . . . the receipts expected by a person discounted at a rate of interest which that person expects to be the appropriate rate.
>
> (Bedford, 1965, 25, 28)

The reason we can believe that cause and effect can work backwards in time is that we fool ourselves into believing that the whole process, which takes place solely in our minds, actually takes place outside our minds, outside financial reporting. We can imagine future cash movements, multiply them in our minds by fractions less than one, which we call discounting, and arrive at amounts we think exist currently. But the process has nothing to do with a system whose number one user-oriented criterion is representativeness, a system that is supposed to hold a mirror up to the reporting entity rather than to our minds.

Conclusion on whether present value is a current condition of the reporting entity

> One cannot measure achievements in terms of [present value] data, notwithstanding the human failing in some people to confuse their pipedreams with their achievements.
>
> (Barton, 1974, 679)

To summarize: Use of the concept of present value in the preparation of financial statements violates these conclusions reached in this chapter:

1   The future doesn't exist at present except in imagination, so the past and the present can in no way depend on the future.
      Use of the concept of present value in the preparation of financial statements requires the past and the present to depend on the future.
2   The future doesn't exist at present except in imagination, so there can be no information or evidence about the future and no surrogates of information or evidence about the future.

Use of the concept of present value in the preparation of financial statements requires evidence or surrogates of evidence about the future.

3   Discounting doesn't change a supposed future event or events—a supposed future cash receipt or payment or a series of supposed future cash receipts or payments—into a current condition.

Use of the concept of present value in the preparation of financial statements is based on the view that discounting changes supposed future events into current conditions.

4   Cause and effect operates either simultaneously or forward in time. An effect can't precede its cause in time.

Use of the concept of present value in the preparation of financial statements incorporates the view that an effect can precede its cause in time.

Because of those violations, the answer to the first question under consideration in this chapter is no, present value defined as the discounted amount of the supposed financial effects of supposed future events doesn't exist as a current condition of the reporting entity (so the second and third questions need not be answered): "[a] discounted value [is] not [a] measurement ... [It has] no present empirical referent" (Sterling, 1979, 126). Present value violates the number one criterion for the design of financial statements, that the items represent phenomena external to the financial statements and their preparation, and it therefore violates all the rest of those criteria. The primary reason given for the need to know supposed future events in preparing financial statements, which is to determine the past and the present, is invalid. Contrary to the statements of the AICPA and the FASB referred to above, the discounted amount of supposed future cash receipts and payments doesn't exist outside of imagination and therefore isn't an attribute of assets, no less the ideal attribute, for the measurement of assets. It shouldn't be considered a viable alternative to acquisition cost for use in presentation in financial statements.

The fundamental problem with using the concept of present value in the design of financial statements is that it defines the past in terms of the future. The past shouldn't be defined in terms of the future in the design of financial statements (or anywhere else).

Appendix: the ultimate form of allocation

Having reached that conclusion, the major conclusion of this chapter (and one that disagrees with most of the financial reporting literature, so beware), I append this consideration of the relationship between the concept of present value and allocation.

The so-called ideal basis of valuation—the present value of supposed future cash receipts and payments—is held to be impractical, as the term "ideal" implies. Supporters nevertheless call the present value of what they suppose to be future cash receipts and payments the ideal against which all other bases should be judged. Solely to test that position, it's appraised here ignoring the reasons it's impractical and not a condition of the reporting entity.

We are told that, ideally, the amounts and timing of all supposed future cash receipts and payments are somehow known. They are supposedly discounted backwards in time to determine financial position at the dates at which they were caused, using the compound interest formula and a discount rate. Income for a period is held to be determined by comparing the financial positions determined that way at the beginning and end of the period and excluding transactions between the reporting entity and its owners.

The compound interest formula is a "systematic and rational allocation" formula, which, as all formulas used in allocation, is predetermined without consideration of events as they occur period by period. The so-called ideal basis is the ultimate form of allocation, because it determines all amounts by allocation. The result, as usual, is to stabilize income reporting.

Debating points

1 If so many authorities say the equivalent of "the . . . ideal basis of valuation [is] the present value of . . . future cash flows," it must be right.
2 The parentage of a concept is irrelevant.
3 The editor who rejected a manuscript that avowed the thesis of this chapter was right.
4 Discounting is a fine, hallowed practice in preparing financial statements.
5 Amounts taken seriously by virtually all academic accountants shouldn't be referred to dismissively as doodles.
6 Discounting incorporates magic into what is supposed to be a serious activity, the preparation of financial statements for investment decisions.
7 It's nonsense to think that financial reporters believe that a cause could follow its effect in time.
8 Present value is used in the preparation of financial statements solely to stabilize reported income.

13 Proposed broad principles for reporting on assets using current buying prices

> the main thrust of replacement-cost proponents is a desire to update accounting reports. They want to present current data instead of past data.
>
> (Sterling, 1979, 145)

SFAS No. 33 (FASB, 1979b) required certain companies to present supplementary information applying current duplication-replacement price reporting,[1] one of the kinds of alternative reporting principles using current buying prices, discussed in this chapter, but the FASB terminated that experiment because of apparent lack of interest by users. That was good because, as discussed below, reporting using current buying prices is even worse than reporting using the current broad principles, bad as that is. (It was a mixed blessing because, though the experiment also required use of a unit of measure defined in terms of a general purchasing power of the dollar, which is good, the experiment demeaned that unit, as discussed in Chapter 11.)

Current buying prices

> In general, authoritative recommendations for the presentation of current value information have been based on entry values of assets rather than on exit values.
>
> (Skinner, 1987, 601)

---

1 This is usually called simply "current replacement value reporting." However, when an asset is held and is valuable, it may be duplicated, but it can't be replaced; this can be done only when it's worn out or gone. To report in the balance sheet a valuable asset that's held, the principle uses a duplication price. To report in the income statement an asset that has been sold, the principle uses a replacement price. Considering the basis of reporting the asset a replacement price injects into the reporting the fiction that an asset represented in the statement of position doesn't exist as an asset of the reporting entity. The design of financial statements shouldn't incorporate fictions.

The titles *current buying prices* and *current selling prices* are shorthand. The literature rarely writes them out longhand, but that's necessary to appraise soundly the principles that apply them (they are written out longhand in this chapter and Chapter 14). Even worse is the common use in the literature of the terms *entry price* in place of *buying price* and *exit price* in place of *selling price* after being popularized by Edwards and Bell (Edwards and Bell, 1961, 75). By their abstractness, those usages conceal that real-world buying and selling are being referred to. We have to be mindful of that fact to understand principles that apply those prices.

Though principles using current buying prices aren't fashionable now among reformers in the U.S., at least no one there seems to be writing in their favor currently, they have appeared to many to be sensible alternatives to the current broad principles and should be considered if for no reason other than to put them finally to bed (as if anything could ever be made final in financial reporting). And they continue to be recommended for optional supplementary information in FASB, "Changing Prices" (FASB, 1986), and they might be required again.

A complaint about the current broad principles is that they make the balance sheet report out-of-date amounts based on costs incurred to acquire assets before the statement date. Current buying price reporting, in contrast, as the name implies, presents amounts that are current as of the reporting date and seem to be related to the assets. As Sterling states in the quotation that opens this chapter, that's enough for many.

Current buying prices have appealed to reformers who wanted to improve financial statements but not take too many chances by deviating too far from the current broad principles. Because they resemble costs, current buying prices retain three old friends: realization, systematic and rational allocation, and matching. In contrast, "current cost advocates believe that using exit price deviates radically from the basic nature of the accounting process as it is known today" (Kam, 1990, 449). (What's wrong with deviating radically from so defective a basic nature?)

Though some old friends are retained, objectivity (in the special sense) and conservatism are sacrificed: prices in transactions to which the reporting entity isn't a party are used as evidence and, being current, they are often higher than acquisition prices. Those two sacrifices are too much for many of us financial reporters to accept, and many of us fall off at this point. The following is for those who are willing to continue to suspend judgment.

Current buying prices are all one kind or another of asking prices: the least amounts others do or would ask in order to sell goods to the reporting entity. They aren't bid prices: the amounts the reporting entity does or would bid for goods of others; such prices aren't part of the reporting entity's environment—they could be any amounts the issuers of the financial statements care to say.

There are three ways to express current buying prices longhand, all of which are discussed in this chapter. Not considering those longhand expressions has misled their proponents. All such expressions make it clear that current buying prices don't belong in financial statements. (Some have suggested that current buying prices may be helpful as surrogates for or predictors of the financial effects of supposed future events or as surrogates for other attributes; their possibilities are discussed in Chapters 12 and 14).

The overriding reason they don't belong in financial statements is that once a reporting entity buys an asset, it's finished with the buying market for the asset. It can't buy an asset it owns while it owns it (obviously); as Sterling states, there are "entry values of *unowned* assets..." (Sterling, 1979, 101, emphasis added). Nevertheless, Sterling stated that "I mean by 'entry values' the process of valuing assets at their current purchase price ... [But] the relevance of entry values of owned assets escapes me" (Sterling, 1979, 124). That's understandable, because it's impossible to "valu[e] assets at their current purchase price" and there is no issue of whether current buying prices of owned assets are or aren't relevant. *Such prices don't exist.* This exemplifies the trap of referring to "entry price" or "entry value" rather than to "the price at which the reporting entity can currently buy an asset it owns," which, when thus written out longhand, can be seen as obvious nonsense (note that this doesn't refer to the price at which the reporting entity can currently buy an asset *similar* to an asset it owns; that kind of price is considered later, in the section "Using the price of an asset not owned or sold"). Others fell into the same trap:

> A given asset [owned by a firm] may have several different market prices [including] what it would cost [the firm] to purchase [it] now...
> (Arthur L. Thomas, 1975a, 36)

> A current ... price for an asset [owned by a firm] can be obtained from ... markets ... in which the firm could buy the asset...
> (Edwards and Bell, 1961, 75)

> Current costs represent the exchange price that would be required today [for an entity] to obtain the same asset or its equivalent.
> (Hendriksen and van Breda, 1992, 495)

Edwards and Bell even state that a reporting entity can buy an asset it owns from a competitor! "If the asset being valued is a good in process or a finished good ... the cost to purchase it from a competitive firm would..." (Edwards and Bell, 1961, 91).

Like time, and cause and effect, assets go in only one direction; for assets, that direction is from purchase, to use (if any), and to sale. After an asset is bought by a reporting entity, the entity can only either use it or to send it to its selling markets for the asset or its products (if a reporting entity has to dump an asset it holds it may sell it in the same place it bought it, but that's still a selling market for the reporting entity, and it sells it for its selling price in that market). But we financial reporters spin theories to avoid that conclusion, though current buying prices are even worse than acquisition costs, because acquisition costs at least are attributes of the assets. Current buying prices violate the number one user-oriented criterion, representativeness, because they purport to represent nothing about the assets held by the reporting entity. They therefore violate all the rest of those criteria.[2]

The use of current buying prices by those who would reform financial reporting follows the law of the hammer, which states that if you give a four-year-old a hammer she will discover that everything needs hammering. "It is the 'Seek and ye shall find' principle which affects so much of social-science research" (Gaylin, 1984, 50). If you give a financial-reporting theorist current buying prices, she will discover that financial statements can't do without them. That's opposite to the way advances in technology should proceed. A technical problem should first be identified and analyzed and a mechanism then sought to solve it, rather than vice versa.

Because methods that use current buying prices involve allocation, they serve to facilitate the stabilizing of reported income as all allocation methods do.

Presenting fiction[3]

> For of all sad words of tongue or pen,
> The saddest are these: "It might have been!"
> (John Greenleaf Whittier, "Maud Muller")

Current buying prices of the first kind became popular among reformers for a time. However, they involve might-have-beens. The first kind of current buying price of an asset owned or sold is the amount of money it might have taken the reporting entity currently to buy the very asset it owns now or just sold, with not only its model number if it has one but also its serial number if it has one (not merely an asset of the kind it owns now or just sold—with the same model number but a different serial number, if it has those numbers—such assets are discussed below in the section "Using the price of an asset not owned or sold")—had it not bought it previously (though it did).

That kind of current buying price is a counterfactual, because it relies on an assumption that's contrary to fact, that is, fiction: that the reporting entity didn't buy the asset previously. The reporting entity obviously did buy it previously, otherwise it wouldn't have to figure out how to measure it

---

2 As stated above in the text, FASB, 1986, par. 3, nevertheless encourages reporting entities to present supplementary financial statements based on current buying prices.
3 Much of this section is taken from Rosenfield, 1969b.

to report it in its balance sheet or income statement.[4] So, being fictitious, that kind of a current buying price isn't an attribute of the asset owned or sold (or of any thing else). Balance sheets should report factual measurements of attributes of assets it owns and sells, not fictitious measurements of nothing else. They shouldn't use current buying prices of the first kind.

Proponents of current buying prices of the first kind have defended them because of their income statement effects. The defense doesn't hold water, as one would expect, because the method involves a factor that's fictitious, that isn't part of the history of the reporting entity, though income is supposed to be part of its history.

The description and defense of the income statement results of the first kind of current buying prices were popularized by Edwards and Bell[5] and picked up in a bandwagon effect, as discussed in the Prologue. They said that it divides net reported income into two components, "operating profit or loss" and "holding gains or losses."

It reports so-called operating profit, when it's said to be realized, as the excess of the selling price over the buying price current at the date of sale. They don't mention that the buying price is fictitious, what it might have cost to buy the asset when the reporting entity sold it had it not bought the asset before (though it did): "Current replacement costs measure opportunities forgone" (AICPA, 1973b, 43). The operating profit is merely pro forma.

It reports so-called holding gains or losses while assets are held, in the amounts of the increases or decreases in the fictitious buying price during the reporting period. Edwards and Bell take pains to point out that such a gain isn't realizable, because it involves a cost, not revenue:

> It cannot be called a realizable capital gain because the excess is a difference between entry values, not exit values. A realizable capital gain would imply that it could be realized by selling the asset. When current cost figures are being used, it is not at all clear that a sale of the asset would convert the excess current cost into a realized value.
>
> (Edwards and Bell, 1961, 93)

---

4 Similar counterfactuals are involved in the "but-for" world of litigation consulting services:

> In discussing damages, we rely on the concept of the "but-for" world. The but-for world is the economic and physical environment that would have existed "but-for" the actions of the defendant.
>
> (Kinrich *et al.*, 1999, 40, 16)

5 It's ironic that Edwards and Bell say that ". . . of all the alternative courses of action considered in past decisions, the most important one, of course, is the alternative that was in fact adopted" and that ". . . current cost is a . . . summary of actual events. . ." (Edwards and Bell, 1961, 3, 92).

Instead, they contend that it's "a cost saving [or cost waste],[6] a saving attributable to the fact that the input used was acquired in advance of use" (Edwards and Bell, 1961, 93). Similarly,

> a company may purchase excess fixed-asset capacity and justify the extra investment on the grounds that it represents a "good buy," because the resources are expected to increase in price and will be needed at a later date.
>
> (Bedford, 1965, 130)

The reporting entity supposedly saved money by buying the asset in the past when it did rather than currently when it might have cost more (though no one can ever know what might have been had the past been different from what it was: "we can never know, with certainty, whether a profit gained from particular activities would ever have been different in other circumstances, since those circumstances did not, in fact, apply" [Goldberg, 1965, 252]). Such supposed savings supposedly are gains—"making gains in anticipation of higher prices" (Edwards, 1975, 237)—that are a component of net income, as the so-called operating profit or loss supposedly is.

Such a supposed saving has been called a *subjunctive gain*, because the subjunctive mood of the verb is required in describing something contrary to fact—that is, fictional. It's the difference between the current position of the reporting entity and what its current position might have been had (subjunctive mood) the past been different from what it was. The ordinary kind of gain has been called an *intertemporal gain*, because it's the difference between the current position of the reporting entity and its past position. The operating profit under the first kind of current buying price reporting has been called a *subjunctive intertemporal gain*, because it's an intertemporal gain that might have been earned had the past been different from what it was. The amount reported in the balance sheet under the first kind of current buying price reporting has been called a *subjunctive cost*, because it's the amount it might have cost to acquire the asset had the past been different from what it was (Rosenfield, 1969b, 788, 789, 795).[7]

Edwards and Bell's analysis, as groundbreaking as it was, stopped short. It neglected to draw conclusions from the fictional nature of both supposed components of net income. The so-called operating profit is the income the reporting entity might have earned had it bought the asset currently rather

---

6 A writedown of inventories under current GAAP to the lower-of-cost-and-market based on replacement cost reflects a might-have-been, a supposed cost waste, supposedly caused by buying the inventories when they were bought rather than buying them later, when they might have cost less. In contrast, a writedown under current GAAP to the lower-of-cost-and-market based on *net realizable value* doesn't involve a might-have-been.

7 Also see Revsine, 1973, 87–90.

than when it did, in the past. And the cost savings are the differences between what the reporting entity paid for the asset and amounts it didn't pay for the asset but might have under circumstances and events that didn't exist or occur. Even two observers with whom the conclusions of this book mostly disagree said that "cost savings are in no sense revenue. If the business buys well, costs are simply on a lower level than would otherwise be the case" (Paton and Littleton, 1940, 64). Neither the operating profit nor the cost savings is part of history, and for that reason neither is a component of net income as Edwards and Bell and their followers contend. Their amounts approximately add up to net income over a period of years as calculated under the current broad principles, but that's only an arithmetical coincidence.

To be sure, gains and losses of that kind are real to those who enjoy or suffer them:

> Don't even think about saying that you have only paper losses, not real losses. Your loss consists in having paid a high price for something that you could have bought a lot cheaper if you had waited a month or two.
>
> (Sloan, 1996, 49)

> computer virus attacks—last month's dual assault cost billions of dollars in lost productivity alone.
>
> (Harmon, 2003)

For example, a business interruption loss or a loss of personal income through illness is the difference between what is (the fortunes of the business or the person at the end of the interruption or illness) and what isn't (what those fortunes might have been then had the business not been interrupted or had the person not been ill).

Such a loss can be insured against, though it's not an ordinary kind of loss but a different kind of loss, a subjunctive loss, because one part of the calculation is fictional. It's not history, and a loss of that kind doesn't belong in income statements, which should present history. Also, if we let such amounts in, where should we stop? There's an infinite number of differences between what happened and what didn't happen, one for each of the infinite number of things that didn't happen, and the fictional differences under current buying price reporting are no more pertinent to the users of financial reports than any other fictional difference: "the cost . . . of replacing [a producer's good] is . . . no different in principle from the cost of any investment alternative to his existing investment" (Chambers, 1969, 585).

This is reminiscent of an old story:

> I walked instead of taking the bus and saved 10¢.
> Why didn't you walk instead of taking a cab and save $1.00?

It's also reminiscent of a recent true story: I shopped for a particular kind of wrought iron and wooden bench. At one store it was on sale for $70, marked down from $100. At another store, it was on sale for $70, marked down from $90. I bought the one marked down from $100, because, would you believe it, it represented the larger saving.

The income statement results of the first kind of current buying price reporting are the reverse of what one would expect. It presents gains simply when the reporting entity's buying prices go up. Did you ever meet a businesswoman who smiles on buying price increases, on increases in her costs? Quite the contrary, businesswomen should and do resist them. The only thing that happens solely because the reporting entity's buying prices rise is that it's harmed,[8] because those prices are factors solely of its buying opportunities, which are harmed. Gains shouldn't be reported when the only thing that happens to the reporting entity is that it's harmed. (The buying prices for inputs essential to the reporting entity's production processes may rise so much that it can no longer afford them and is forced out of business. Events with that result shouldn't be reported as causing gains.)

Imagine an owner bargaining all night with her employees, all of whom have unique skills she needs, and finally caving in and signing a disastrous contract that doubles their salaries, the buying prices of their services. She would be in no mood to have her financial reporter smile and say she can now report large gains. The financial reporter would have to find another job.[9]

Using the price of an asset not owned or sold

The second kind of current buying price related to an asset a reporting entity owns or sold is the amount of money it would take the reporting entity currently to buy an asset it *doesn't own and hasn't sold* that's similar in form or function to an asset it owns or sold (perhaps it has the same model number, but it doesn't have the same serial number); that is, its current duplication or replacement price. The FASB stated that it's an attribute of the asset the reporting entity owns or sold, but it's not. It's an attribute of

---

8 Its selling prices may coincidentally go up or they may stay the same or they may go down (which is called a cost-price squeeze): "changes in input costs do not necessarily covary with changes in output prices..." (Revsine, 1982, 85). If the selling prices do go up coincidentally, the amounts at which the assets are reported would be increased under current selling price reporting (see Chapter 14), but because of the selling price increases, not because of the buying price increases.

9 Reporting gains simply when buying prices go up has been recommended because "The changes in prices have occurred, they are objectively determined, and the accounting entity is clearly affected" (Sprouse and Moonitz, 1962, 30). To be sure, the reporting entity is clearly affected, but the clear effect is to harm the reporting entity, not to help it. (Moonitz at the time was Director of Accounting Research at the AICPA.)

the asset the reporting entity doesn't own and hasn't sold, and is therefore irrelevant to the financial position and results of operations of the reporting entity. The only connection the asset the reporting entity owns or sold has to that price is as part of a rule of selection. The asset the reporting entity owns or sold helps to select the asset it doesn't own and hasn't sold of which the current buying price is an attribute. It pertains to the reporting entity's buying opportunities, because it's a price of something it can buy:

> replacement prices are related to . . . assets owned, but . . . the relationship is [not] sufficiently close to justify interpreting them as attributes of the assets owned. (Instead, they are attributes of assets not owned— the replacement assets.)
>
> (Lorensen, 1992, 13)

Balance sheets and income statements should present measurements of attributes of assets the reporting entity owns or has sold, not of assets it doesn't own and hasn't sold—that it has merely opportunities to buy.

Chambers presents another argument against using current duplication–replacement prices, which is a corollary of his central argument in favor of using current selling prices (see Chapter 14): "the buying price . . . does not indicate capacity, on the basis of present holdings, to go into a market with cash for the purpose of adapting oneself to contemporary conditions..." (Chambers, 1966, 92). Also, such a price doesn't represent financial achievement to date of the reporting entity as to the asset, which the amount ascribed to the asset should represent (see Chapter 14).

Arguments against current duplication–replacement price reporting[10]

Two kinds of arguments have been given against using the second kind of current buying prices, current duplication–replacement price reporting, in addition to the argument that such prices are not attributes of assets owned or sold by the reporting entity, one concerning maintenance of capital and the other concerning a defective operating profit.

Maintenance of capital

> to buy similar tools of production takes many more dollars today than formerly; to count as profits, rather than as cost, the added sums required merely to sustain production is to retreat from reality into self-deception.
>
> (U.S. Steel, *1947 Annual Report*)

10 The following discussion is taken from Rosenfield, 1975.

Under current duplication–replacement price reporting, changes in the duplication or replacement prices of inventories, land, buildings, and equipment are presented in equity, not in income. Proponents of that kind of reporting have defended it also not because of its effects on the balance sheet but because of its effects on the income statement. They rely on a particular notion of maintenance of capital to defend that treatment.

Virtually all writers on income determination agree that it should be based on the concept of maintenance of capital. The term *capital* has many usages in finance and financial reporting, but in this usage it simply means *equity*. Income should be reported in an amount by which ending equity exceeds beginning equity, excluding the effects of transactions between the reporting entity and its proprietors, the amount by which capital has been more than maintained.

In all current and proposed principles of income determination other than current duplication–replacement price reporting, the equity at the end of the period is compared with the equity at the beginning of the period—the equity at the beginning of the period is the zero point for the comparison. It's similar to determining weight gain by seeing how much current weight exceeds former weight. Figuring a gain in weight of five pounds from 150 pounds to 160 pounds using 155 pounds as the weight at the beginning, an operation similar to the way income is calculated under current duplication–replacement price reporting, would flatter but not inform the person being weighed.

In current duplication–replacement price reporting, the capital to be maintained isn't the equity at the beginning of the period. It's a hybrid: (1) the equity at the beginning of the period related to assets other than inventory, land, buildings, and equipment and to liabilities in the measuring unit used in the balance sheet at the beginning of the period; and (2) the inventory, land, buildings, and equipment at the beginning of the period in physical units. It's called *physical capital maintenance* (though it's so only to the extent of the inventory, land, buildings, and equipment). If capital in physical units has only been maintained but is presented at greater money amounts because of increases in buying prices, no income is presented: the difference is reported directly in equity.

The usual goal of business is to buy low and later sell high. Current duplication–replacement price reporting changes that. It makes the goal to sell high and later buy back low: "it is implied that unexpended future outlays (at current cost levels) rather than past expended costs are to be covered by current revenues" (Lemke, 1982, 322). General objections to this notion of capital maintenance are that it uses more than one unit of measure; that physical operating capacity ignores the perspective of the users, who judge the success or failure of a reporting entity in terms of consumer general purchasing power, not in terms of physical units of anything (as discussed in Chapters 8 and 11), and that it retreats to dealing with physical things while ignoring their financial aspects, which isn't really part of financial reporting.

Defenses of using this notion have been implied. They mainly involve survival and dividends. They don't hold up.

SURVIVAL[11]

The proponents of current duplication–replacement price reporting hold that a reporting entity shouldn't report income during a period in which its survival has been put in jeopardy. They contend that its survival has been put in jeopardy if it hasn't maintained its physical operating capacity. That view has two defects.

First, a *reporting* entity may obtain income at the same time as its survival is threatened. To be sure, "repeated failure to maintain physical capacity can be inimical to the survival of the firm, each failure being a step on the road to extinction" (Lemke, 1982, 291). But it needn't be. That's called living on the edge, on the wild side. The reporting entity takes chances, makes out well, and at the same time totters:

> Ronald Northedge's company is desperately short of cash. But his problems are as different from the liquidity worries facing traditional British engineering groups as chalk is from cheese . . . they are the problems of success.
>
> (Bell, 1974)

"Qualcomm is . . . getting smaller, spinning off division after division. If the future belongs to Qualcomm, it will be on the strength of the company's intellectual creativity . . ." (Romero, 2000, C1). And a single elimination contest threatens survival at the same time it provides an opportunity for gain.

Second, maintenance of physical operating capacity isn't necessary for survival. Some have implied that it is:

> there is a major distinction . . . between (i) a profitable firm putting all of its profits into assets to expand, which has no surplus liquidity but equally no problems, and (ii) an unprofitable firm with insufficient internally generated liquid resources even to maintain its present size . . .
>
> (Merrett and Sykes, 1974)

That begs the question, implicitly defining an unprofitable firm as one not sufficiently liquid to keep its physical operating capacity at least level. However, a reporting entity may downsize for the purpose of surviving, and

11 Solomons is the only author to my knowledge who has indicated, correctly in my view, that at bottom this is the sole interest of creditors: "Creditors . . . are . . . concerned with . . . profitability only to the extent that it is a prerequisite for survival" (Solomons, 1989, 11).

a reducing physical operating capacity in an industry characterized by increasing incomes can be consistent with growing prosperity.

Some proponents of current duplication–replacement price reporting also support it based on the view that income shouldn't be reported in periods in which dividend capacity hasn't been increased: "Which ... accounting alternative ... generates an income figure that reflects the amount of resource inflows that could conceivably be distributed as a dividend without impairing the physical operating level of the firm?" (Revsine and Weygandt, 1974, 72). But obtaining income and increasing dividend ability require different kinds of success: "profitability [versus] viability" (Solomons, 1989, 9). Success in increasing equity belongs in an income statement; survival doesn't—it belongs in the balance sheet and the statement of cash flows. Success in terms of income requires increasing equity; success in increasing viability, of surviving, of increasing dividend capacity, requires increasing cash balances. An operating capacity diminished in physical terms may be increased in financial terms, and portend increasing cash dividends.

Defective operating profit

Another defect of current duplication–replacement price reporting is its defective operating profit. It's based on the view that assets have to be replaced when sold. However, replacement is a separate investment decision, and it might not be the one portending the greatest income, especially if the current buying price has increased so much that it reduces margins too much. Further, it presents the amount given up as the cost of buying another similar asset. But the sacrifice of an asset in an exchange is its opportunity cost—the sacrifice of the opportunity to get some other return from it—not the replacement price.

Deprival value

The third kind of current buying price theory is called *deprival value*, which "comes largely from the work of ... Bonbright" (Baxter, 1966, 27):

> "The value of property to its owner is identical in amount with the adverse value of the entire loss, direct or indirect, that the owner might expect to suffer if it were to be deprived of the property."
>
> (Bonbright, 1937, quoted in Baxter, 1966, 27)

The idea is that an asset should be stated at the amount of money it would cost to make the reporting entity whole were it deprived of the asset. Its use in place of acquisition cost as the attribute of assets to measure has been advocated:

> The value of an asset to the business . . . is the loss that it would suffer if it were deprived of the asset.
>
> (Solomons, 1989, 52)

> Deprival value is arrived at by asking how much worse off would the entity be without the asset in question. This approach to fair value measurement has been adopted by the U.K. Accounting Standards Board, under the label of "value to the business."
>
> (Schipper, 2003, 65n)

Like the first kind of current buying price, this kind involves a fiction, that the reporting entity has been deprived of the asset. That it hasn't is indicated by the need to find an amount at which to represent it in the balance sheet. Again, the amount at which an asset is presented in the balance sheet shouldn't involve a fiction.

The income statement effects of the deprival value theory haven't been discussed, but one effect probably would be to present as a gain or loss the change over the period in the fictional buying price of the asset held, similar to the cost savings in the first kind of buying price theory. Gains and losses involving fictional conditions shouldn't be presented in income statements.

When an asset is sold, the reporting entity is in effect deprived of the asset (though deprival seems a strange concept in the circumstances: the reporting entity is usually not forced to sell the asset). The defense is that to make the reporting entity whole in that circumstance, it would have to buy a replacement asset (though for some assets, such as costly obsolete specialized equipment, that would be the worst investment it could make), so the current buying price used to measure the asset sold under the deprival value theory would be the price at which the reporting entity could buy an asset the reporting entity doesn't hold and has never held but might buy if it judges that to be a good investment, which isn't an attribute of the asset sold. That's the same kind of operating profit that would be reported under the second kind of current buying price theory, and it should be rejected for the same reasons.

Supplementary information on current buying prices

Current buying prices aren't an attribute of assets held or sold by the reporting entity, and therefore don't belong in its financial statements. However, current buying prices of resources the reporting entity doesn't own do affect a reporting entity's buying opportunities. If it wants or needs to duplicate or replace an asset or buy an unrelated asset and the buying price has gone up (a bad thing, not a good thing—right?), information on that could be helpful to the users of its financial statements. It might portend difficulties. At the worst, the reporting entity might have been priced out of its buying markets, and therefore driven out of business (while reporting gains under the first and third kinds of current buying price reporting), even if its selling prices still exceed its buying prices. Financial reporting standard-setters should consider requiring supplementary information on selected buying prices of the reporting entity to warn of such a threat.

Debating points

1   The definitions given for current buying prices are too literal.
2   Edwards and Bell misled a lot of people.
3   Gains and losses that can be insured against should be reported in income statements.
4   Replacement cost reporting has had a lot of support and should be considered a viable substitute for acquisition cost reporting.
5   U.S. Steel was right in its 1947 annual report about increasing costs of tools of production.
6   The cost of a duplicate or replacement asset and changes in its cost should have no place in the design of financial statements.
7   Simply because an amount is a counterfactual is no reason to reject it in preparing financial statements.
8   The real counterfactuals—fictions—in this book are the author's conclusions, however forthrightly stated.

14 Proposed broad principles for reporting on assets using current selling prices

> Information based on current prices should be recognized if it is sufficiently relevant and reliable to justify the costs involved and more relevant than alternative information.[1]
>
> (FASB, 1984a, par. 90)

Current selling price reporting (CSPR), which reports assets at their current selling prices, has less support than any of the other proposed alternatives to acquisition costs as the basis of reporting on assets except for incorporating prospects, discussed in Chapter 16 (though it does have some support[2]). This doesn't necessarily indicate its worth, considering, for example, that the current broad principles with their pervasive defects have the most support.

Current selling prices are all one kind or another of bid prices: the largest amounts others do or would bid to buy goods from the reporting entity. They are part of the reporting entity's environment: "When functioning

---

1 Ironically, the FASB made that revolutionary statement in a concepts statement, "Recognition and Measurement in Financial Statements of Business Enterprises" (FASB, 1984a), which many consider reactionary. For example, Cason, the Chairman of AcSEC when the FASB issued the concepts statement, commented that the FASB had promised to issue a statement on recognition and measurement in financial statements of business enterprises but apparently had decided not to do so. And the Chairman of the FASB at the time said: "[the] recognition and measurement . . . phase of the conceptual framework project had promised more, consumed more time, and delivered less in comparison to what was expected, than any other part of the project" (Kirk, 1989b, 100). Also, Storey said that "Concepts Statement 5 does make some noteworthy conceptual contributions—they are just not on recognition and measurement" (Storey, 1999, 1, 110).

2 Chambers, for example, in Chambers, 1966, and Sterling, for example, in Sterling, 1970a, are the foremost supporters of CSPR. Other supporters are the UK Research Committee, Professor Tom Lee, Dean Peter Wolnizer, Professor Graeme Dean, Professor Frank Clarke, Dr Brian West, Kyle Oliver, and a former Chief Accountant of the SEC, who said the measurement of an asset "ought to be [its] price . . . in a current sale for CASH . . ." (Schuetze, 1991, 116n). This book also supports it.

properly ... financial statements describe in money terms the position of an entity relative to its external environment..." (West, 2003, 2). They aren't asking prices—the amounts the entity does or would ask to sell goods to others. Asking prices aren't part of the reporting entity's environment; they could be any amounts the issuers of the financial statements care to say.

The current colloquial term for CSPR, "mark-to-market" reporting, isn't always used carefully. In the following, it's erroneously used to refer to reporting involving predictions of the financial effects of future events ("forecasts"):

> [One of t]he two accounting rules that Enron abused the most dealt with ... using "mark-to-market" calculations to produce profits based on questionable forecasts.
>
> (Norris, 2002a)

Byrnes used the term correctly:

> As the Enron scandal showed, corporate guesstimates can play a big part in corporate earnings. Managers there estimated what the future demand for their products would be and derived current earnings based on those guesses. This is one step beyond "mark-to-market" accounting, whereby financial instruments are valued based on current worth.
>
> (Byrnes, 2002b, 37)

The only current measurable financial attribute

To introduce CSPR, it would be instructive first to enter the world of people who aren't financial reporters. (The analysis that follows won't appeal to those who believe that financial reporting is or should be apart from every-thing else in life, as discussed in Chapter 4.) In that everyday world, a man with beady eyes and a turned-up collar might whisper to someone who isn't a financial reporter that he has a great deal for her. He will sell her a new car for only $20,000, which she can immediately turn around and sell for $17,000 (see Figure 14.1). She at first thinks she will tell him to get lost, but then she thinks that though she can get only $17,000 back now, she might be able to use the car in the future to get more than $20,000 back, so it might be a satisfactory deal:

> The purchaser of a new car knows that one minute after he drives it out of the showroom, its sale value drops by several hundred pounds; he does not on that account think that the purchase was a mistake, because he did not buy the car to sell it immediately.
>
> (Solomons, 1989, 54)

She buys the car, and a short time afterwards starts to determine her then

**"It's just like they always say — a
new car depreciates 30 percent the
second you drive it off the lot."**

Figure 14.1   New car (copyright 1997 John McPherson, reproduced with permission of Universal Press Syndicate, all rights reserved).

current situation in terms of consumer general purchasing power,[3] including
the car. (It's her current situation she's interested in currently, for the
purpose of making current decisions; she might also be interested in her past
situation for comparison with her current situation; that situation was her
current situation in the past; she can currently only guess as to her later situation.) She wonders what amount to include for the car. She has several
choices that, as someone who isn't a financial reporter, she can easily reject as
not pertaining to anything that could reasonably be called her situation in
terms of consumer general purchasing power at that date but that, were she

---

3 This resource, which is embodied in money, and its relevance are explored in
   Chapter 11.

a financial reporter indoctrinated in the current broad financial reporting principles or in much of the current academic financial reporting literature, she couldn't so easily reject:

- The amount of consumer general purchasing power she paid for the car (the acquisition cost), which pertains to no aspect of her affairs or her relationships with the world at that date. No one who would be interested in her current situation in terms of consumer general purchasing power would have more than idle curiosity about that amount.
- The amount of consumer general purchasing power she might have paid for the car at that date had she not bought it beforehand, which is a phantom.
- The amount of consumer general purchasing power for which she could currently buy another car similar to the one she owns. That's part of her current buying opportunities. She has too many buying opportunities and they are too diverse to be considered part of her current situation in terms of consumer general purchasing power. Moreover, that amount of consumer general purchasing power doesn't represent her ability to operate financially represented by the car she owns, which sounds to her like a reasonable way of thinking about that part of her current situation in terms of consumer general purchasing power.
- The amount of consumer general purchasing power she thinks she will be able to get in the future by using the car, multiplied by a fraction less than one ("discounted"), because that's a thought of hers about the future, part of her, not part of her current situation in terms of the car.
- The amount of consumer general purchasing power she has in prospect from the car, because prospects are indefinite and unmeasurable (see Chapter 16).

Financial achievement to date

> financial achievements to date do not mix with hopes for the future.
>
> (Baxter, 1966, 3)

As much as she hates to admit it, she concludes she should include the car at $17,000, the amount she can sell it for at that date (though she may have no intention to sell it currently). The current selling price of the car represents her financial achievement in terms of current possession of or access to consumer general purchasing power to that date (this contrasts with current possession of consumer general purchasing power, which consists of current possession solely of money rather than current possession of money and means that can currently be sold for money) solely as to the car in the eyes of the world, the only eyes that count for a presentation of her current situation in terms of consumer general purchasing power that's truly objective (in the usual sense)—it's the only current relevant financial relationship she has with the world solely as to the car. (Because the future doesn't exist at present, later financial achievement can't be part of her current situation.) Moreover, current selling price is the only current measurable financial relationship with the world of any kind she has solely as to the car. Current selling price is the only attribute of an asset measurable in terms of consumer general purchasing power at that date in the world outside of her thinking and outside of her preparation of a presentation of her current situation in terms of consumer general purchasing power, the place where attributes of assets exist.[4] (This is a key conclusion. If you doubt that it's correct, convince yourself to your satisfaction that there is another.)

Immediate decline

Her main reluctance is the necessity to include a decline of $3000 soon after buying the car and hardly using it. How can she have suffered a decline simply by buying a car?

In fact, her current possession of or access to consumer general purchasing power has declined (though she believes the increase in her prospects more than compensates for the decline—see the discussion of prospects in the next section). The world shows that, by explicitly or implicitly bidding only $17,000 on it; in other words, $17,000 is the highest amount others are currently willing to pay for it. That made her hesitate to buy the car in the first place.

Class A and Class B aspects

By buying the car, she obtained two classes of aspects of things in terms of consumer general purchasing power (she also obtained transportation, possibly prestige, and so on, but her current situation in terms of consumer general purchasing power includes only the money aspects of things): (A) current possession of or access to consumer general purchasing power, which consists of current possession of consumer general purchasing power and current possession of severable resources[5] that can be sold for consumer general purchasing power; and (B) current prospects of obtaining possession of or access to more consumer general purchasing power in the future. She gave up money, the most flexible and widely desired resource, the resource that provides consumer general purchasing power, and obtained the chance

---

4 Other concepts that have been called current attributes of assets are discussed and challenged in Chapters 12, 13, and 16.
5 Staubus asks "why should we want to require severability? If something will provide measurable service potential to the owners only in its existing setting, why should it not be included as an asset?" (Staubus, 1977, 126). However, financial statements shouldn't reflect or report potential (prospects), and potential isn't measurable. See Chapter 16.

to recoup some of that prized resource currently by selling the car currently for $17,000, plus the chance to recoup more when time moves on. The world currently recognizes the Class A aspect in its bid on the car—at the amount that is the owner's current selling price for the car. The Class B aspect, the prospects, isn't measurable (as discussed in Chapter 16). (If the car were owned by a corporation, the Class B aspect would be measurable as part of the current overall esteem the world has for the corporation as a whole as reflected in the price of its common stock—but financial statements don't, can't, and shouldn't reflect such overall esteem except in reporting on investments in such stock.) It's not yet a verifiable part of her current situation. All assets that are bought and held other than for consumption are bought with the thought that they have prospects of turning out to be good investments, that they have Class B aspects when they are bought or while they are held. If a person doesn't have such thoughts, the person shouldn't buy or hold them: "The sacrifice of market value would be willingly accommodated only if it were compensated for by the increase in subjective goodwill" (Edwards and Bell, 1961, 49). Why engage in a trade or hold an asset other than for consumption that portends no income or even a sure loss? (Goodwill is pure Class B aspect, pure prospects [see Chapter 23].)

She should include the car at the amount she can sell it for currently, the way the world now sees her car in terms of consumer general purchasing power (the only way an outside auditor can currently see it objectively in terms of consumer general purchasing power).

Reporting the Class A aspect and disclosing information concerning the Class B aspect

Similarly, to return to financial reporting by financial reporters, assets should be reported continuously[6] at their current selling prices. *Assets* should therefore be defined as

> Economic resources held by reporting entities that the entities can sell separately from the reporting entities and any subordinate part of the reporting entities.

When and if time moves on beyond the present (see Chapter 7, footnote 15) and current prospects turn into measurable substance, that's soon enough to report the increase based on the prospects. The Class A aspect belongs in the balance sheet. The reporting entity's current possession of or access to consumer general purchasing power has declined by paying for the Class B aspect (meanwhile the Class B aspect, its prospects, may have

6 Chambers describes CSPR as "continuously contemporary accounting," which he abbreviates as COCOA.

improved, but the world doesn't bid on prospects for individual assets—see Chapter 16), and the reporting entity should report that decline. Information helpful to users to appraise the Class B aspect should be part of its disclosure of opportunities (discussed in Chapter 17). There the issuers can say how good they think things portend to be. And the section on investments in prospects recommended for the income statement (see Chapter 17) would give added insight. Everyone would be informed. No one would be misled.

That at first may seem to be "a severe treatment" (Chambers, 1966, 245), especially compared with the mixture of fact and fantasy we now issue:

> many ... do not accept that a business is worse off as soon as it formally takes on a risk that the business was set up to undertake ... most businessmen instinctively think it undesirable ... that income reported should suffer when management makes an investment in specialized equipment based on a capital budgeting analysis that indicates the purchase should be profitable.
>
> (Skinner, 1987, 609, 621)

However, the current well-being and past progress of a reporting entity are partly measurable, by the principles recommended in this chapter and Chapter 15, and partly unmeasurable, consisting of prospects. A report of a decline in the reported equity of a reporting entity accompanied by information, such as the capital budgeting analysis Skinner refers to, that suggests improved prospects, which the reporting recommended in this chapter and Chapters 15 and 17 provides, is balanced reporting, not a severe treatment.

The Brookings Task Force reports that

> [e]conomist Robert Hall has analyzed the rather large discrepancy ... between the value assigned to firms by the financial markets and the value recorded on their books. He concludes that this [demonstrates that] "corporations own substantial amounts of intangible capital not recorded in the[ir] books..."
>
> (Blair and Wallman, 2001, 11, 12)

That agrees with the analysis in this section that Class B aspect intangibles abound, but, contrary to the analysis, it implies that perhaps they are in fact measurable and should be treated as Class A aspect resources. The Task Force acknowledges that

> intangibles are inherently difficult to measure ... one ... must ... rely on indirect measures ... to say something about their impact on some other variable that can be measured.
>
> (Blair and Wallman, 2001, 15)

Such amounts don't conform with the user-oriented criterion of verifiability and should therefore be confined to supplementary information (as discussed in Chapters 16 and 17). The Task Force believes that such disclosure

> implies that the inputs . . . are used up on production in the period in which the [expenditures] are [made], and do not . . . provide an input into future production.
>
> (Blair and Wallman, 2001, 17)

Disclosing such expenditures for prospects in the income statement (see Chapters 16 and 17) prevents such an inference.

When time moves on and the world shows its increased appreciation of a reporting entity's assets by bidding them up individually (bidding them up collectively in the price of the reporting entity's common stock should, as stated above, be outside financial reporting except in reporting on investments in such stock), either because prices change or production changes the time, place, or form utility of the assets or their products, CSPR reports the assets at the increased prices and reports income in the amount of the increases.

To the extent that the world currently explicitly or implicitly bids more for the individual assets of the reporting entity than the reporting entity paid for them, they are reported under CSPR at what we financial reporters would call unconservative amounts. If the world is willing to bid on them, we financial reporters should be willing to report the amounts of the bids. But people will sue anybody for anything, even if it means threatening to deprive users of relevant, verifiable information. Perhaps issuers and outside auditors should be provided safe harbor protection against lawsuits if they present such amounts to the best of their knowledge: "Lawmakers, regulators, and standard setters should develop more effective deterrents to unwarranted litigation . . ." (AICPA, 1994a, 116).

Many intangible assets have no Class A aspect: they can't be sold separately. They have only Class B aspects, providing only prospects of increases in current possession of or access to consumer general purchasing power. Chapters 16 and 23 discuss prospects involved in intangible assets.

Long-term receivables, investments in bonds, and the like would be reported under CSPR at their current selling prices. An issue that the proponents of CSPR haven't addressed is the treatment of short-term receivables under CSPR. A strict adherence to CSPR would report them at their factoring prices. However, they could be reported at the gross amounts of those that, according to evidence of current probabilities (see Chapter 7), will be received. Alternatively, they could be considered as virtually cash, and reported at the estimated gross amounts of those that aren't bad at the reporting date, though implementing that requires considerable judgment. That agrees with the view of the FASB in SFAS No. 5 that losses should not be recognized before it is probable that they have been incurred, even though it may be probable based on past experience that losses will be incurred in the future.

CSPR and the user-oriented criteria

CSPR is the only kind of financial reporting that conforms with all of the user-oriented criteria:

- *Representativeness.* All the individual line items in financial statements under CSPR purport to represent financial effects of events that have occurred to the reporting entity to the reporting date and conditions that exist pertaining to the reporting entity at the reporting date outside financial reporting.
- *Relevance.* CSPR reports amounts that tell the extent to which the reporting entity has achieved to date the overriding goal ascribed to it by the users in terms of consumer general purchasing power, the terms in which financial statements should be prepared and issued: increasing its current possession of or access to consumer general purchasing power. (This is the central argument of this book in favor of CSPR.[7]) Additional disclosures provide information for the users to use to judge the extent to which the reporting entity has achieved its additional goal of increasing its prospects of gaining additional possession of or access to consumer general purchasing power in the future (discussed in Chapters 16 and 17).
- *Neutrality.* CSPR isn't slanted to the desires of any particular group or groups of parties to financial reporting.
- *Reliability (I):* The criterion of reliability (I) requires that the information represent what it purports to represent about the reporting entity. The first necessity in order to conform with that criterion is that the information in fact purports to represent such a thing. Assets have only two attributes that conform with that requirement: gross acquisition price and current selling price. Gross acquisition price is merely a curiosity for assets held, even at the date of acquisition[8] (it doesn't

7 Sterling's central argument in favor of CSPR is the relevance of current selling prices in a wide variety of contexts:

> "selling prices [are] relevant to all three market decision models. They are necessary to define market alternatives, they express the investment required to hold assets and they are a component of a risk indicator. For all of these reasons, I conclude that the items on the balance sheet should be valued at their present selling prices."
>
> (Sterling, 1972, quoted in Staubus, 1977, 529)

Chambers joins Sterling in Sterling's central argument in favor of CSPR: "there is a place for resale prices—in *every one* of the contexts [in which the various attributes of assets are used]" (Chambers, 1979a, 55). That argument hasn't been persuasive to academic or practicing financial reporters (or to me). In contrast, I, for one, find my central argument, given in the text at this footnote, persuasive.

8 A common view, even among those sympathetic with reporting that reflects current prices, is that acquisition price is a sound amount at which to report an asset held at the date of acquisition. Not everyone agrees: "The use of [current

conform with the criterion of relevance); so current selling price is the only relevant attribute that's a candidate for conformity with this criterion. Reliable kinds of evidence for the measurement of current selling prices are discussed below. If reliable evidence for the measurement of current selling prices of particular assets isn't available, the existence and description of the assets should be disclosed but they shouldn't be reported in the balance sheet.

The conclusions that CSPR can conform fully with relevance and reliability means that no trade-off is necessary between them.

- *Understandability.* Everyone understands what it means for the reporting entity to be able to sell or not to be able to sell assets it holds. CSPR doesn't lack the understandability that, for example, partially allocated amounts in the balance sheet and allocated amounts in the income statement lack.
- *Verifiability.* Because the amounts reported under CSPR report on measurable conditions in the world outside financial reporting and outside anyone's thoughts about the future, they are accessible to all observers. They are ordinarily capable of being measured and the measurements are ordinarily capable of being verified. If the selling prices of particular assets are too indefinite to be able to be measured and verified reliably, the assets should be excluded from the number columns of the financial statements and their existence and description disclosed (as indicated in

---

selling prices] suggests that [they] should dominate the accounting records from the original acquisition of inputs ... The initial gain or loss which becomes realizable upon the acquisition of inputs should be recorded immediately ... if ... exit values ... dominate ..." (Edwards and Bell, 1961, 79, 87); "such [a] proposition as 'when property is new, cost and value are normally the same' ... assume[s] an absence of buyer's or seller's surplus which is probably contrary to fact in most cases" (Goldberg, 1965, 324). Those statements are sound. The amount a reporting entity paid for an asset doesn't in the instant when the reporting entity obtains it represent a part of its financial position, of its ability to operate financially. We need only remember the example of the purchase of a new car. A complete analysis of an exchange in which cash is sacrificed and a salable asset is received based on current selling price reporting is that (a) equity (the excess of assets over liabilities) is reduced by the sacrifice of cash and (b) equity is increased by the increase in the current selling prices of salable assets held:

Equity	$1000.00	
(an expense account—"purchases of assets")		
Cash		$1000.00
Asset, at selling price at date of acquisition	$850.00	
Equity		$850.00
(a gain account—"increase in current selling price of assets")		

The difference between the equity amounts would be reported in the income statement as an investment in prospects in conformity with a recommendation in Chapter 17.

the discussion of reliability (I) in Chapter 3). For example, the current selling price of a unique item, such as a painting, an antique, or a parcel of land, may be pure conjecture before sale[9]—the *New York Times* reported that artworks "sold for prices well above their estimates at an auction":

- A Book of Hours (prayer book)—estimated selling price $3.3 million—$4.9 million; actual selling price $13.3 million
- A King Louis XVI Commode—estimated selling price $2.5 million—$4.1 million; actual selling price $10.9 million
- A portrait by Frans Hals—estimated selling price $4.1 million— $5.7 million; actual selling price $12.8 million (*New York Times*, 1999, A1)

- *Timeliness.* CSPR reports achievement in increasing possession of or access to consumer general purchasing power as soon as it occurs, which makes it the most timely kind of financial reporting.
- *Completeness.* CSPR reports all assets that provide current possession of or access to consumer general purchasing power and whose current selling prices are sufficiently reliable and verifiable and reports currently all sufficiently reliable and verifiable changes in such possession or access.
- *Consistency.* CSPR involves no alternative reporting practices, so its application doesn't result in inconsistent practices. It incorporates no predictions or other thoughts about the future of anyone, so it can't apply inconsistent predictions or other thoughts about the future. Nevertheless, application of judgment by financial reporters is unavoidable in all kinds of financial reporting, including CSPR, and we financial reporters must exercise consistent judgments when applying CSPR.
- *Comparability.* All amounts reported under CSPR are derived from the same public markets and conform with all the preceding user-oriented criteria and therefore, together with reporting of liabilities as recommended in Chapter 15 and information on current investments in prospects and with disclosure of other information helpful to users to judge the reporting entity's prospects (see Chapter 17), aid comparisons of investment opportunities.
- *Reliability (II).* Because it conforms with all the other user-oriented criteria, users can rely on the information reported in financial statements under CSPR.

9 One observer stated their conjectural nature this way: "in the cases of (1) unique assets, such as real property, or (2) any asset purchased in an auction market, the purchaser could be the only person in the world who thinks the newly-acquired asset is worth as much as he paid for it" (Staubus, 1977, 215). Sinclair wrote that "The cash value of a work of art is one of the most highly speculative things in the world..." (Sinclair, 1945, 327). (Also see Rosenfield, 1981.) Nevertheless, the acquisition costs of such assets often may be the least informative amounts.

Evidence for the measurement of current selling prices

Sterling stated that the current selling price of an asset a reporting entity holds is the amount at which the reporting entity could now sell the asset: "the amount of money that could be received from an immediate sale of an asset" (Sterling, 1979, 70). Others agree:

> Exit values measure the opportunity to sell assets . . . that continue to be held.
>
> (AICPA, 1973b, 43)

> current net realizable values . . . are the values which the assets could be sold for, if disposed of in an orderly fashion, near the time of the account.
>
> (Research Committee of the Institute of Chartered Accountants of Scotland, 1988, 58)

> market value . . . the amount of cash that could be received.
> (Association for Investment Management and Research, 1993, 33)

That makes current selling price a factual amount and therefore acceptable in financial reporting. In contrast, an amount used in the kind of current buying price reporting advocated by Edwards and Bell—the amount at which the reporting entity could now buy an asset it holds, that is, an amount that doesn't exist, that's by definition counterfactual, fictional—is unacceptable in financial reporting: you can sell an asset you hold but you can't buy it.

However, Sterling previously stated that current selling prices are counterfactual—fiction—too:

> Measurements of this kind are conditionals in which the antecedent is false . . . it specifies an immediate past instant which will never recur. "If I had sold at time t_1" can never be verified *by sale*, because the sale didn't occur at t_1 . . . Subsequent sales are not pertinent.
>
> (Sterling, 1970a, 322)

Similarly,

> The current valuer responds that the land and the investments could have been sold, that management should be held accountable for changes in value which it could have realized. How far should we indulge in such "might-have-been accounting"?
>
> (Mautz, 1973, 25)

When the time interval between trades is large, there can be substantial disagreement as to what the market price *would have been* for a trade that *would have occurred* within that interval (i.e., valuing securities at year-end).

> (Beaver, 1991, 129, emphasis added)

Fair value of a financial instrument should be an estimated exit price—the price that would have been received or paid *if it had been* sold or settled—on the measurement date.

> (FASB, 2002b, emphasis added)

If Sterling were correct here rather than as first quoted in this section, and if Mautz, Beaver, and the FASB were correct, CSPR shouldn't be adopted, because financial statements should exclude fiction. However, no one simply reading the balance sheet can know whether the reporting entity didn't in fact immediately after the date of that statement sell the asset at the current selling price:

> Some contend that, if a firm has already decided to continue possession and use of an asset, its selling price is irrelevant ... But to suppose that decision already to have been made in no way forestalls the potential necessity of revoking it when the full array of data—asset composition, debt dependence, rate of return and so on—are brought under periodical notice.
>
> (Chambers, 1989, 15)

Sterling, Mautz, Beaver, and the FASB likely were led to their conclusion about a counterfactual aspect of current selling prices by assuming that a sale is involved. No sale is involved. The only thing involved is measurement. And the most reliable *evidence* for the measurement of the current selling price of an asset held isn't the price at which a similar asset was sold other than to the reporting entity immediately before the end of the day whose date appears on the balance sheet. An asset held at the end of that day can't be sold on that day, though it can have a current selling price then. Reliable kinds of evidence for the measurement of the current selling price at which an asset can be sold at the reporting date instead is the following, in descending order of quality (to my knowledge, this list is novel; please comment on it):

- The price at which the asset was sold immediately after the date of the balance sheet, which is the first opportunity the reporting entity has to sell an asset held at the reporting date at its current selling price.
- The price at which a similar asset was sold other than to or by the reporting entity about that time.
- Prices bid other than by the reporting entity if available or estimable then.
- The price of a later sale of the asset.

- The price of the next sale of a similar asset other than to or by the reporting entity.
- The price at which a similar asset was sold other than to or by the reporting entity before the end of the reporting date, if conditions are judged not to have changed significantly since then.

The kind of evidence used should be disclosed if such disclosure is needed by the users to properly appraise the quality of the information.

If no reliable evidence is available in time to prepare the financial statements, the resource should be disclosed but not reported as an asset.

If you think obtaining reliable evidence for the measurement of the current selling price of an asset held is sometimes challenging, compare it with the steps the FASB requires us to follow in implementing discounted future cash flow reporting for nonfinancial assets and liabilities for which there is no market for the item or a comparable item:

a Identify the set of cash flows that will be discounted.
b Identify another asset or liability in the marketplace that appears to have similar cash flow characteristics.
c Compare the cash flow sets from the two items to ensure that they are similar. (For example, are both sets contractual cash flows, or is one contractual and the other an estimated cash flow?)
d Evaluate whether there is an element in one item that is not present in the other. (For example, is one less liquid than the other?)
e Evaluate whether both sets of cash flows are likely to behave (vary) in a similar fashion under changing economic conditions.

(FASB, 2000b, par. 44)

Is measuring current selling prices reliably more difficult than that?

Current buying prices are sometimes suggested as surrogates for current selling prices. However, those amounts rarely if ever conform to the approximation criterion of the second of the three steps for the use of a surrogate listed in Chapter 6. Further, if current selling prices can't be measured directly, the first requirement listed there, there is rarely if ever any way even to determine whether the approximation criterion of the second step is met. Current buying prices shouldn't be used as evidence of current selling prices.

Discounted future cash receipts and payments has often been recommended as a surrogate for current selling prices, for example, by the FASB:

for some assets ... management's estimates [of discounted future cash receipts and payments] may be the only available information [to determine current selling price].

(FASB, 2002b, "Highlights")

However, discounted future cash receipts and payments exist only in the minds of the issuers of the financial statements, and therefore don't conform to the measurability criterion of the second step for the use of a surrogate—they could be anything the issuers think they are. Discounted future cash receipts and payments shouldn't be used as evidence of current selling prices.

CSPR and stable income reporting—the foremost objection to CSPR

> present accounting practice ... has a tendency to *smooth* the expenses and income ... exit-value accounting ... has a tendency to "rough" the expenses and income ... This ... is the basis for objections to reporting it. Some use the derisive term "yo-yo profits" to express this objection.
>
> (Sterling, 1979, 200)

The main grounds people have for objecting to CSPR, which they often don't acknowledge, even to themselves, is a practical one, based on reaching for results rather than on analysis for the benefit of the users—that it results in income reporting that's less stable than that of other kinds of reporting:

> financial managers have much discretion [under the current broad principles] over the recognition of changes in value by astute timing of exchange transactions and by the adoption of artful allocation procedures. Mark-to-market accounting would take away much of that discretion ... it has the propensity to make earnings exceedingly unpredictable, a disconcerting fact for enterprises trying to minimize their capital costs by reporting smooth and growing earnings.
>
> (Association for Investment Management and Research, 1993, 43, 44)

> Chase [Manhattan Bank] Controller ... Sclafani said in a ... letter to the [FASB that among] ... the bank's concerns [is] that: "Fair value accounting will result in significant income-statement volatility."
>
> (Sherer, 2000, C16)

The following is presented merely as an example of a fruitless debate on this matter:

> *Participant I-12*: Fair value accounting would just make the volatility of earnings that much worse.
> *Participant I-16*: Does that make it worse or does that just recognize the reality?
> *Participant I-12*: What's reality? (AICPA, 1994b, II, 4, 30)

Chapter 3 concludes that designing financial statements should be based on analysis for the benefit of the users, not on reaching for results that some people, especially the issuers of the statements, consider desirable. And Chapter 5 concludes that income reporting shouldn't be stabilized.

Most of the other objections are rationalizations, good reasons in place of the real reasons. We financial reporters are able to overcome great difficulties when we want to achieve a given result, for example to minimize taxes or to stabilize reported income—consider the grief we go through to implement SFAS No. 109 solely for that purpose. We could overcome the difficulties of CSPR. We don't want to, because the issuers don't want us to.

Foremost conceptual objections to CSPR

Opponents of CSPR have two major conceptual objections to it.

Achievement to date versus prospects of achievement

> "investors ... make judgements about the performance and prospects of companies."
>
> (Chambers, 1973, 144, quoted in West, 2003, 44)

A conceptual objection to CSPR is that it ignores the reporting entity's prospects or potential for future achievement of current possession of or access to consumer general purchasing power beyond such achievement to date. The first quotation in Chapter 16 states that objection. Chapter 16 discusses the objection.

The aggregation (additivity) problem in CSPR

The current selling price of an aggregation of assets is usually ambiguous. An example of the ambiguity is the difference between (1) the total of the current selling prices of the machines and other equipment in a factory and of the factory building and land at which they could be sold separately, and (2) the selling price at which the fully equipped factory plus the land could be sold as a unit. Also, there is "...concern as to whether the price at which a small trade takes place can be extrapolated to the price that would result from a larger order at the same point in time..." (American Accounting Association, 1991, 93). Because CSPR reports the current selling prices of an aggregation of assets (at least the whole collection of the nonmonetary assets of the reporting entity), its opponents charge that the ambiguity makes CSPR unsound for use in financial statements. But is this a reason for rejecting CSPR, or is it a problem to be solved by standard-setting bodies if and when they enact CSPR? A person's answer to that question presumably depends on whether the person is attracted to or repelled by CSPR on other grounds. A person attracted to CSPR on other grounds would believe it's simply a problem to be solved. Some are on the fence, for example:

is the aggregation problem enough of a black hole that financial statements would be more informative without allocation-free, current-
market-value reports than they would be with them? I cannot answer
this...

(Arthur L. Thomas, 1979, 27)

Sterling, who is attracted to CSPR on other grounds, is troubled by the
issue. After dealing with it with what some (such as I) might consider
double-talk:

A most elementary definition [of additivity] might take the following
form: There is an operation of dimensional addition which corresponds
to the operation of arithmetical addition ... the operation of dimensional addition ... is the combination of objects ... not ... only ...
dimensions that are additive are measurable ... but ... [additivity]
makes the measurement *more* useful...

(Sterling, 1970a, 101)

he concluded thus:

I ... am not entirely happy with [my explication of the additivity of
exit values. However,] we must apply [the additivity criterion] with
equal force to its competitors.

(Sterling, 1979, 167)

(*I'm* unhappy with such so's-your-old-man arguments.)
  Larson and Schattke are the most outspoken champions of the view that
the aggregation problem dooms CSPR. Their complaint is essentially a
restatement of the problem, that the total of the selling prices of the items
sold separately doesn't equal the selling price of all the items as a collection:

the [current selling prices] of individual assets ... [must be able to be]
summed without loss of meaning; the resultant summations must equal
the current selling price of the collection of assets ... in the aggregation
... [The sum of the prices of the assets sold separately] would have no
significance relative to a wide variety of possible future market actions
... [using the sum of current selling prices of] individual assets ... pre-
sumes independent sales of those assets ... Our argument rests on the
demonstrable difference between a series of sales of individual assets and
the sale of a package of assets ... the limits of financial action are not
indicated by the property [of the current selling prices sold separately]
and [the] system fails on this ground.

(Larson and Schattke, 1966, 634, 637, 639, 640)

(Though those quotations are representative, in this case only reference to the entire article might do justice to their argument.)

Larson and Schattke's article was in response to Chambers' written support of CSPR. He responded with his characteristic firmness:

> Larson and Schattke['s] alleged refutation of the additivity of [CSPR] ... turns on argument relating to mercantile action, rather than to financial action or even metrological action ... [They] presume ... that the accountant knows what goods will be sold and in what combinations and at what prices before the point of sale is reached ... If the resale price of x and y [whose separate resale prices are \$10 and \$15] together exceeds \$25, the excess is a potential profit which ... the firm ... may not anticipate.
>
> (Chambers, 1969, 612, 615)

Larson wrote the following in refutation with equal firmness:

> Chambers' response to our paper was absolutely false. In no way did we "presume ... that the accountant knows what goods will be sold and in what combinations and at what prices before the point of sale is reached." To the contrary, the presentation of exit value totals has no clear meaning unless Chambers (and others who want to add exit values) *presumes* that the individual assets will be sold separately. Furthermore, the burden of proof that any such additions are meaningful is on those who argue for adding—an insurmountable burden given the obvious existence in most instances of goodwill (or negative goodwill).
>
> (Larson, 2000)

Chambers unfortunately died recently, so his response couldn't be obtained. He likely would have responded that current selling price reporting shouldn't and doesn't report on goodwill. Chapter 23 agrees, as does the CFA Institute (before May 2004, the AIMR): "goodwill ... ought to be removed from the list of assets forthwith ... a goodwill write-off should appear on the income statement..." (Association for Investment Management and Research, 1993, 49).

Goodwill related to business combinations (and all other goodwill for that matter), represents only issuers' thoughts about the future, its hopes and dreams. The gamble in acquiring goodwill should be reported by an immediate chargeoff to income of its cost or its current amount at the date of acquisition. And Chambers would have refused to presume anything about the future in the design of financial statements.

Sterling made a suggestion about attaching meaning to the concept for individual items of inventories:

> The retailer's exit value is the wholesale selling price of carload lots, less

> incidentals. Thus the retailer's entry value is greater than his exit value at least by the amount of the incidentals ... The retailer cannot *immediately* sell the units at the retail price.
>
> (Sterling, 1979, 111n)

Presumably, the current selling prices of inventories would be in wholesale lots. A recent advertisement offered to buy "excess inventory at full wholesale" (Tradewell International, 1998, 79).

This chapter and Chapters 10, 12, 13, and 16 conclude that, outside of this problem, CSPR has everything going for it and that no other system has anything going for it. Overwhelming evidence that this is a fatal flaw has to be presented in order to scuttle this system. Such overwhelming evidence hasn't thus far been presented. Further, we shouldn't in measuring the assets anticipate that the issuers will sell two or more of the individual assets as a collection. For example, a reasonable interpretation of CSPR wouldn't involve Daimler-Chrysler reporting Chrysler's assets at the amount for which Chrysler could be sold currently as a company.

Reporting entities wouldn't ordinarily sell assets in groups if they could get more selling them individually. The total of their current selling prices sold individually should therefore be the floor of the reported total amount. Selling the assets in groups, or selling all the assets and liquidating the reporting entity, would often bring more (except that selling inventories at wholesale in carload lots wouldn't bring more), but reporting the higher amounts would incorporate management's intentions or other kinds of thoughts about the future—which, as discussed in Chapter 7, shouldn't be incorporated in the design of financial statements. So the total of their current selling prices sold individually should therefore also be the ceiling of the reported total amount. The "clear meaning" of the total of the current selling prices of the assets sold individually, in Larson's terms, would be the amount the reporting entity could obtain apart from presumptions about thoughts of the management.

In any event, it's not such a serious problem. Mandatory disclosure can solve it. Users know that selling separately a collection of items would often fetch a total amount different from the amount selling the items collectively would fetch. If and when standard setters mandate CSPR, they should require a uniform policy on how collections of items should be measured (preferably as sold individually except for inventories) and they should require the reporting entities to disclose the policy.

Larson continued to demur:

> Your conclusion that full disclosure of a mandated policy on how collections of items should be measured may be acceptable. However, you retain the burden of explaining why the total of items "sold separately except for inventories" are meaningful disclosure.
>
> (Larson, 2000)

That was before I wrote about the floor and the ceiling. His response to that was that the total price of all the assets on liquidation wouldn't involve intentions. However, it would involve management thinking about liquidating a going concern, and, as stated above after receiving his comment, such thoughts should be excluded from the design of financial statements.

Other conceptual objections to CSPR

Opponents of CSPR raise several other kinds of conceptual objections to it (which they would overcome if they liked the results).

Objectivity

The conceptual objection to CSPR held by most of us financial reporters is that it isn't what we call "objective" because it's said to report the financial effects of transactions to which the reporting entity isn't a party: "Transactions ... that have not been determined by the bargaining of independent parties in contact with the given enterprise ... lack ... objective determination..." (Littleton, 1953, 217; also quoted in Chapter 10). This is the classic defense of that position:

> dependable classification begins with the separation of our transactions from those of everyone else. Unless this is consistently and thoroughly done, any irrelevant, alien facts that get into our accounts will introduce irrelevant (improper) modifications in the statistical story our accounts try to tell of *our* efforts and *our* accomplishments ... A single outside transaction, an average of many outside prices, or a chart of price level change, may be of considerable significance to management for use in studying a company's accounting for its own direct transactions. Yet, no matter how significant, an outside fact is not an inside fact.
>
> (Littleton, 1953, 49, 197)

To be sure, a reporting entity shouldn't report in its financial statements the financial effects of transactions or events to which it isn't a party: General Motors shouldn't report Ford's sales as its own. (The reporting entity shouldn't even report on the financial effects on the other party to a transaction to which the reporting entity *is* a party, as discussed in Chapter 8.) However, those aren't the events that change the selling prices of the assets of the reporting entity. They merely reflect and provide evidence of other events, events that do change those prices, events to which the reporting entity is a party. The FASB agrees that reporting entities are parties to such events:

> all entities are affected by price changes, interest rate changes, technological changes ... and similar events ... some assets and liabilities ...

are affected by events, such as price changes or accretion, that are not recognized.

(FASB, 1985a, par. 218; 1984a, par. 27; also quoted in Chapter 10)

Such an event could be, for example, conversion by a reporting entity of raw materials, labor, and overhead to salable products, a change in the tastes of consumers that affects the prices at which a reporting entity can sell its merchandise, or a change in the assessments by investors of the prospects of companies whose securities the reporting entity holds that changes the amounts at which the reporting entity can sell the securities. CSPR reports on the financial effects of those events, the events that change the selling prices of the reporting entity's assets, not on the financial effects of events to which outsiders are parties that provide evidence of those changes.

Using such evidence is necessary to keep current the prices in the calculations made to derive the amounts at which the assets are reported. We readily accept stale prices. Would we as readily accept stale quantities? (We have been reassured that we wouldn't: "no one has suggested that a quantity that was in existence prior to December 31 be reported on the December 31 financial statement" [Sterling, 1970a, 162]). Keeping both the quantities and the prices current is necessary to conform with several of the user-oriented criteria, especially relevance, timeliness, and completeness.

Intentions

> this Statement ... does not resolve ... [a] most important problem ...
> accounting based on intent...
>
> (FASB, 1993a, Sampson and Swieringa, Dissent)

A common conceptual objection to CSPR is that it reports assets at the amounts at which they could be sold though the opponents of CSPR hold that the issuers don't intend to or plan for the reporting entity to sell some of them, for example:

> the market-selling price system ... give[s] accurate information as to how much better off the company is ... *if* it ... plans to sell its assets at year-end ... If the company plans instead to continue its normal manufacturing and service activities, then that information is totally irrelevant for almost all parties ... management might use such information in considering a decision to liquidate at year-end, but it does not seem realistic to assume that the management of every company makes such a decision on a continual basis.
>
> (Weston, 1971, 101)

[Land, buildings, and equipment] are acquired and held to be used up, not to be sold as stock-in-trade.[10] They do not represent potential revenues, as do the inventories, and therefore are not amenable to treatment as though they were receivables. As a consequence "net realizable value" has no relevance [for them]...

(Sprouse and Moonitz, 1962, 33)

And in making the same point, Littleton ignored the difference, also ignored by Weston in the quotation above, between liquidation of the reporting entity and orderly liquidation of its assets:

if accounting attempts ... to provide values in the financial statements, it would have to do so on the assumption that dissolution was under consideration ... unless dissolution was in view, the fixed assets would not be for sale.

(Littleton, 1953, 210)

However, the intentions or plans of the issuers, for example, as to use or sale of an asset, should be ignored in financial reporting (as discussed in Chapter 7), and liquidation of the reporting entity and orderly liquidation of its assets need to be distinguished.

Thomas Evans says that "current selling prices only apply to assets held for resale or offered in a market" (Evans, 2003, 224). However, most assets of all kinds, including those commonly held for sale and those commonly held for use, can be sold if sale is desired or necessary: "Beyond the level of the stock of means necessary for planned consumption, no stock of goods may be considered irrevocably committed to any purpose ... adaptation is continuous..."[11] (Chambers, 1979a, 40). Sterling made a similar point, which Butterworth challenged:

exit values are said to be "obviously irrelevant" because the firm does not intend to sell its depreciable assets. [But] the purpose of measurement ... is to provide information about the state of the world. That ... may be necessary to a decision ... that may alter our intentions ... to prohibit a measurement on the basis of some previously formulated

10 As discussed below in the text, all assets are eventually sold.
11 This is Chambers' central argument in favor of CSPR. He came on this argument while he "was engaged in the teaching of aspects of management" (Chambers, 1979a, 39). It reflects the interests and behavior of managers. Staubus agrees: "Ray ... liked to think of the decision facing the owner/manager of an asset who was faced with the decision to sell or hold that particular asset" (Staubus, 2003, 179). My central argument in favor of CSPR, in contrast, reflects the interests and behavior of the users of financial statements. See the text at footnote 7. Chambers and I nevertheless come out at about the same conclusion, though Staubus uses Chambers' reasoning as ammunition against CSPR.

intentions is to prohibit a rational decision ... measurements ... provide information about what's possible regardless of intentions ... There is an entire class of scientific terms (called "dispositional terms") ending in "ble" which are quite useful (relevant) but which do not imply anything about intentions. Flexible, soluble, and flammable are examples ... I suggest that we add the term "salable" to this class of scientific concepts and try to measure the number of dollars that assets would fetch if they were sold without regard to intentions ... all assets are sold eventually, if only for scrap. Thus all assets are intended for sale ... Firms regularly replace their owned assets. I have great difficulty understanding the strident assertion "assets are intended to be used and therefore exit values are irrelevant" that's so often encountered in the literature. People who make that assertion must be overlooking the fact that firms adapt to changing technology, changing consumer tastes, and changing prices.[12]

(Sterling, 1979, 74, 74n, 75, 121; 1968, 487)

This is Butterworth's challenge:

The analogy with scientific measurements of properties such as flexibility and solubility is false ... In the scientific environment ... the measurement of the property sought can be objectively established. In the economic environment ... [n]one of the tests available to the scientists are available to the accountant or auditor to verify the hypothetical amount of an incomplete transaction: completion of the transaction is required to provide the necessary evidence.

(Butterworth, 1982, 112)

According to that, the only way to objectively establish in the general scientific environment the measurement (1) of the property solubility of the particular object involved would be to dissolve it, and (2) of the property flammability of the particular object involved would be to burn it. So completion of the "transaction" would be as necessary in the general scientific environment as it would be in financial reporting. No such completion is necessary in either case.

Zeff once stated another formerly popular objection to CSPR related to intentions, that it violates going concern: "The assumption of continuity of enterprise, or going concern, is ... inconsistent with a wholesale application of current-price valuation..." (Zeff, 1961, 121, 122). However, the going-concern concept isn't useful in determining measurement practices for financial statements (see Chapter 7). Further, that position is another example of ignoring the difference between liquidation of the reporting entity and orderly liquidation of its assets.

12 Here, Sterling joins Chambers in Chambers' central argument in favor of CSPR.

Sterling said this about intentions to do what the measurement implies: "[Some] accountants ... say ... it's 'obviously irrelevant' to measure an attribute if one does not intend to do what's 'implied' by the measurement" (Sterling, 1979, 74). But he countered that

> *nothing* is "implied" by measurement ... On several occasions the AEC has gone to some pains to try to measure the number of people that would be killed if an atomic bomb were dropped in various metropolitan areas. I would hope that we would not employ the opponents' "logic" and tell the Atomic Energy Commission that since they have made the measurements, they must intend to drop the bombs.
>
> (Sterling, 1979, 74n)

Specialized assets

Some specialized assets that the issuers consider valuable can be sold for no more than scrap value (such assets are called "nonvendible durables" by Chambers [Chambers, 1966, 243]). Opponents of CSPR object especially to the proposal under CSPR to report such assets at scrap value, for example:

> The fatal deficiency of NRV is the irrelevance of realisable values ... most especially of assets that are specifically adapted to the needs of a particular business, when judging the financial position of a going concern.
>
> (Solomons, 1989, 54)

Other specialized assets might occasionally be work-in-process inventories, if they can't be sold currently as is.

But the purchase or production of an asset so specialized that it can be sold for only scrap value is a considerable gamble, that cash (or assets that can be sold for cash) in excess of scrap value will be recouped in the future. Most assets can be used or sold; these in effect can be only used, and, "inflexibility in a fluid environment detrimentally affects the expectations of security of capital and regularity of income" (Chambers, 1966, 244). When and if time moves on and the gamble has paid off is soon enough to report the current existence of an asset. Meanwhile, specialized assets acquired to retool General Motors factories in the confident belief of the issuers that they will be used to produce next year's models that will be sold should be reported the same way as specialized assets acquired in the confident belief of the issuers of the financial statements of other reporting entities that they will be used to produce perpetual motion machines that will be sold—at their scrap value. To be sure, most people would believe that General Motors' prospects of recouping its investment and making income on it are greater than the prospects concerning the purported perpetual motion machines. But they have this in common: *for both companies, they are prospects.* Anyone who advocates putting prospects into financial statements should consider that proposal in its entirety (considered in Chapter 16).

Skinner uses an extreme illustration:

> Consider a remote paper mill with a well-established customer base that invests in new paper-making equipment, the purchase being completely justified by demand and cost projections ... If the amount realizable from dismantling and transporting that equipment elsewhere for resale would be very small, [CSPR] would ... charge it to income in the year of acquisition ... Most accountants find this difficult to accept as a reasonable way to measure income.
>
> (Skinner, 1987, 625n)

He is correct about how most financial reporters would feel about this, being indoctrinated and steeped in current GAAP. But agreeing with him would require abandoning the idea that financial statements are reports: reports don't involve predicting (as discussed in Chapters 1 and 7)—making "demand and cost projections" (except reports explicitly about what people have predicted, such as a report that "The weatherperson predicted fair weather for tomorrow"). Also, financial statements shouldn't incorporate issuers' current thoughts about the future. The central defect of his argument is that it incorporates not only financial achievement to date but expected future financial achievement.

If the world isn't willing to bid on resources currently, no matter how wonderful the owner thinks they are and how much riches she thinks they will bring her in her thoughts about the future by using them or selling them, or if the world's explicit or implicit bids are too indefinite to be determined reliably and verifiably, the person shouldn't report them as assets until and unless reliable, verifiable explicit or implicit bids for them become manifest. The person shouldn't report the Class B aspects in the number columns of the financial statements until they become Class A aspects. She should merely disclose them. The issuers may also be inclined to present a note to the financial statements concerning assets reported at scrap amount worded somewhat like the following:

> Assets so specialized that they could be sold currently only for their scrap amounts are reported at their scrap amounts, totaling $100,000, in order to avoid anticipating future achievement. At the times they were acquired and now, management expected and expects the company to use them in the future to obtain money in excess not only of their scrap amounts but also of their acquisition costs. The total of the gross acquisition costs of assets currently reported at their scrap amounts, which were acquired at various times in the past, is $5,000,000.

Chapter 17 discusses how the amounts spent on productive assets, especially on specialized assets, in excess of their current selling prices at the dates of acquisition could be highlighted in a new section of the income statement on investments in prospects.

Representativeness

Solomons stated that CSPR violates the criterion of representativeness: "The use of resale prices in this situation leads to . . . failure to measure up to the criterion of correspondence with the . . . economic events which are being recorded" (Solomons, 1966, 208). However, other than unallocated acquisition cost, CSPR is the only kind of reporting that meets the criterion because, among other reasons, it's the only current attribute of an asset measurable in terms of consumer general purchasing power. If changes in selling prices are being recorded, the record corresponds "with the economic events which are being recorded" by definition. Solomons presumably meant that the record doesn't correspond with the financial effects of economic events *he* thought *should* be recorded. This book presents a challenge to that idea.

Other practical objections to CSPR

Some have challenged CSPR on practical grounds besides that it makes reported income unstable.

Reliability (I)

The foremost other practical objection is that CSPR makes it difficult to conform with the user-oriented criterion of reliability (I):

> The introduction of a value-based system into the formal accounting and reporting system could do great harm. The loss of reliability would open the door for many more extremely subjective determinations. . .
>
> (Flegm, 1989, 95)

And consider this tender sentiment:

> As anybody who has been involved with appraisals or merger negotiations knows, there can be wide honest differences of opinions about what constitutes fair value . . . I have a real problem with, to use a phrase, a bunch of green eye shades sitting in a room determining what a value is on PP&E and other categories on the balance sheet.
>
> (AICPA, 1994a, II, 4, 13, 88)

We financial reporters who, at present, mainly simply sit in a room and calculate rather than measure deserve that slur. If we start measuring, we would deserve better. And if we did start measuring, we wouldn't be merely "sitting in a room." We would be gathering evidence, as discussed above in the section "Evidence for the measurement of current selling prices."

Even Chambers acknowledged that "calculations . . . relating to . . . transactions to which the entity was a party can be made with greater certainty than calculations embodying inferences from events of which the entity was only a passive subject." He cautioned, however, that "certainty is relative. . ." (Chambers, 1966, 82).

Sterling's attitude, as indicated by the following, appears sound:

> prices are sometimes difficult to determine in the absence of an exchange. We can all lament this fact, but this does not give us license to report irrelevancies simply because they are easier to determine[13] . . . problems in measuring exit values . . . are those that are common to all measurement endeavors. They are not problems that are fundamentally different nor fundamentally more difficult.
>
> (Sterling, 1970a, 186; 1979, 72)

The task of outside auditing will become more challenging when and if CSPR is adopted. The natural tendency of some of the issuers would be to determine the income they wish to report and back into the current selling prices of the reporting entity's assets to arrive at that income. The outside auditors would have to adhere scrupulously to whatever kinds of evidence the profession determines is required to support measurement of the current selling prices used (see the section above, "Evidence for the measurement of current selling prices"). Improvements would be required in the props outside auditors have for their independence; a start on that is discussed in the Epilogue, and more help perhaps will come as the current spate of financial reporting breakdowns becomes more rectified. Also, issuers might take seriously the position of Miller and Bahnson in *Quality Financial Reporting* (Miller and Bahnson, 2002b), which is that the investment community can become aware of the quality of the financial reporting by the various companies, and it does or would take into consideration that quality in making investment decisions. Those authors believe that self-interest would therefore tend to move the issuers to simply let the evidence speak for itself. Time will tell whether their hopes are realistic or merely pious.

Savagely high charge

Baxter complains about "a savagely high . . . charge in the year of an asset's purchase" (Baxter, 1966, 25). But the charge to income is only half the story. The other half is the enhanced prospects for future financial achievement, which should be suggested by supplementary information (see

---

13 Remember the tale in Chapter 6 of the gentleman who dropped his watch where the light was poor.

Chapter 17) and by the section of the income statement on investments in prospects recommended in Chapter 17.

Gains reversed or losses recouped

Some object to CSPR because it reports gains or losses that might be reversed or recouped by the time the related assets are realized:

> if you'd marked banks' assets to market [a number of years ago when interest rates were high] you'd basically wiped off their government securities portfolio and their net worth. And a year later, interest rates declined and those asset values increased.
>
> (AICPA, 1994b, II, 4, 37)

That, in effect, is an argument against time period reporting.

Motivation

CSPR has been said to be a poor motivator:

> changes in command over resources in the limited sense of *command through disposal* is ... a poor basis for evaluating operating perform-ance—[a] usual function ... of income ... the obvious motivation for managers [under CSPR is] to obtain good performance marks by select-ing assets with the highest [selling prices] even though [selling] is *not* a feasible alternative ... Management might well avoid specialized com-mitments in order to avoid unfavorable reports...
>
> (Devine, 1985c, 75)

> Use of [CSPR] in financial accounts may ... result in ... decisions to buy less suitable but non-specific assets.
>
> (Baxter, 1966, 25)

The few if any issuers that have such a short run point of view of how to manage a business would shortly cut their own throats and wouldn't be around any longer to engage in such self-defeating behavior.

Complete remodeling

The magnitude of the task of changing to CSPR has been said to be a bar to its adoption: "uniform theories are unlikely to be changed because their changes require a complete remodeling of the entire accounting system" (Ijiri, 1971b, 10, 11). But, unlike reflection of inflation and deflation in financial statements, which must be done all at once, CSPR can and should be adopted piecemeal. In fact, it's already creeping in, as discussed below.

Wishful thinking

> we need the humility and stoicism to accept that much that we and
> users of our reports would dearly love to know is in principle unknow-
> able.
>
> (Arthur L. Thomas, 1979, 29)

Underlying the defense of current selling price reporting in this chapter is the
view that much of the financial reporting literature is based on wishful thinking, thinking that financial statements can do more than they can do while
still conforming with reasonable criteria—thinking that current selling price
reporting often doesn't do a lot and it must be possible to do more in financial
statements, such as find numbers to put on the reporting entity's prospects
and put the numbers in its balance sheets. However, though current selling
prices might not always tell users as much as they might want, at least they
tell them something (something important—how far the reporting entity has
thus far achieved the major goal assigned to it by the users). And there's no
satisfactory way to tell more in financial statements.

More can be told in the financial report outside financial statements, to
help the users judge how far the reporting entity has achieved the secondary
goal of improving its prospects. But that judgment is part of financial analysis. We financial reporters go wrong by trying to inject financial analysis or
unverifiable material to facilitate financial analysis into financial statements.

Quiet appeal

With acquisition prices still old and irrelevant (except for diehards), discounted future cash receipts and payments considered impractical (if not
nonexistent), and current buying prices in eclipse (also if not nonexistent),
beleaguered current selling prices have a quiet appeal:

> there is a greater readiness today than formerly to give current values a
> more prominent position in financial statements...
>
> (American Accounting Association, 1991, 94)

> Much as it goes against the grain of those of us who grew up on the con-
> cepts of matching and realization, and their corollary, valuation at his-
> toric cost, it's beginning to appear more and more as if the glory days of
> historic cost are coming to an end. There are too many times that it falls
> so short of depicting economic reality and those instances are growing
> in number.[14]
>
> (Knutson, 1995, 5)

14 "Current values" and "economic reality" are interpreted in those passages as
current selling prices. Satisfy yourself that they can be interpreted otherwise if
you wish and can.

Fair value

Current selling prices are gradually creeping into GAAP, often in the guise of what's called *fair value*, which is usually defined like this:

Fair value of an asset (or liability)
The amount at which that asset (or liability) could be bought (or incurred) or sold (or settled) in a current transaction between willing parties, that is, other than in a forced or liquidation sale.

(FASB, 2000b, Glossary)

That definition is consistent with the definition given in paragraph 42 of SFAS No. 125 (FASB, 1996) and with the definition given in paragraph 4 of an FASB exposure draft issued on June 23, 2004, on "Fair Value Measurements," which states:

Fair value is the price at which an asset or liability could be exchanged in a current transaction between knowledgeable, unrelated willing parties.

The definition of *fair value* is always accepted as stated. But it's remarkable what analyzing it uncovers.

The analysis that follows deals only with assets. Similar conclusions would be reached dealing with liabilities.

The definition refers to "willing parties." That sounds like any entity that's willing to be a party to the transaction. But that can't be. The definition refers to a particular asset that exists and is owned by a particular owner that exists (the reporting entity)—it's not any old asset owned by any old owner, or, worse, any old asset that isn't owned and hangs out in midair or, still worse, an asset that doesn't even exist except in imagination.[15] Ownership adds something to an asset. Only the owner can sell it, of course. So the owner has to be one of the "willing parties" in the definition. The other of the "willing parties" has to be an entity other than the owner, because the owner can't sell an asset to itself, of course. And that other party has to be willing to buy.

Not only that, but the owner that's willing to sell and the other entity that's willing to buy have to be willing to exchange at some particular price. And "Owners of assets often contend that they would not be willing sellers at the prices offered by potential buyers" (Schuetze, 2000, 20). If the owner's lowest asking price is higher than the highest explicit or implicit bidding price of all prospective buyers, there would be no exchange, and the asset has

---

15 Imaginary things such as perfect competition apparently are useful in economic analysis. They don't seem to be useful in analyzing issues in designing financial statements, though financial reporters do use them for that purpose.

no fair value according to the definition. That's probably the case for most productive assets, at least. If an owner of a productive asset could have found a buyer willing to buy it for as much as the lowest price at which the owner would have been willing to sell it, considering that selling a productive asset causes the owner inconvenience at least, the owner would have sold it. Continuing to own it suggests that there is no such price and no fair value according to the definition, at least not currently.

We can now substitute revised language in the definition:

> The fair value of an asset is the highest amount the owner could reasonably expect to receive for it by selling it currently to an outside party that's willing to buy it for at least as much as the least amount for which the owner is willing to sell it.

If there is such a buyer, there would be an exchange. Because for the owner this is a sale,[16] it would be selling the asset at its current selling price. So, if the definition of fair value defines anything, it defines the owner's current selling price.

As we have seen, for many assets it doesn't define anything. However, the large and growing popularity of the concept of fair value must mean that those who use it intend it to define something for every asset it covers. The liberty is taken here of conjecturing that they mean the fair value of each covered asset is the highest price bid by outsiders for the asset, regardless of whether the owner is willing to sell at that price. (Or, it could be the lowest price at which the reporting entity is willing to sell it, regardless of whether any buyer is willing to buy it for that price. Nevertheless, the conjecture is retained.) Having taken that liberty, the definition becomes the following:

> The fair value of an asset is the highest amount bid for it by outsiders.

That's the definition of the owner's current selling price, so, interpreted that way, when the literature refers to fair value, it means current selling price.

The FASB agrees with this in its definition of *fair value* in its Preliminary Views, *Reporting Financial Instruments and Certain Related Assets and Liabilities at Fair Value*, issued on December 14, 1999:

> Fair value is an estimate of the price an entity would have realized if it had sold an asset or paid if it had been relieved of a liability on the reporting date in an arm's-length exchange motivated by normal business considerations. That is, it's an estimate of an exit price determined by market interactions.
>
> (FASB, 1999d, par. 47)

---

16 Chapter 8 discusses the importance of determining the side of a relationship or transaction the reporting entity is on.

Further muddying the water is a definition given in FASB *Status Report*, May 31, 2000, page 6, which is consistent with the definition in the Preliminary Views, and a definition given in FASB *Action Alert*, January 2, 2002, for financial instruments, which is also consistent with the definition in the Preliminary Views.

So, the FASB used one definition in its SFAS No. 125 issued in June 1996, a second, different, definition in its Preliminary Views issued in December 1999, the first again in its CON7 issued in February 2000, and the second again in its *Status Report* issued in May 2000, and, for financial instruments, in its *Action Alert* issued on January 2, 2002. Why the FASB issued two different definitions of *fair value* at about the same time isn't clear.

Of course, the analysis or conjecture may be wrong (after all, the definition does refer to a willing seller). If so, it's unclear what the propounders of this concept mean. The concept probably was taken from a discipline other than financial reporting, such as economics. It seems to have the character of the economist's hypothetical can-opener discussed in footnote 2 in Chapter 7. That speculation was confirmed by the FASB in its Project Updates updated August 2, 2003, under "Fair Value Measurement," which indicates that the reference to "willing parties" in the revised definition of *fair value* means this:

> Willing parties are all hypothetical marketplace participants (buyers and sellers) that have utility for the item being measured and that are willing and able to transact, having the legal and financial ability to do so.

Financial statements are intended to provide transparent factual information about the reporting entity reported on. Inserting hypothetical buyers and sellers in the design of the statements prevents achievement of that objective (this is discussed further in Chapter 7).

Meanwhile, here's a small suggestion: stop referring to fair value and refer only to current selling prices, so everyone knows what everyone else is talking about.

Creeping in

> life maintains itself only by abandoning old, and recasting itself in younger and fresher, forms ... civilization achieves a precarious survival by changing its habitat or its blood.
>
> (Durant, 1935, 218)

Areas in which current selling prices (as such or in the guise of fair value) are creeping in are, for example, the following:

- They have always been essential parts of the rule of cost or market, whichever is lower, for inventories (the net realizable value part; current buying prices are an aberration there (see Chapter 7), which isn't found, for example, in the IASB rule).
- In connection with nonmonetary assets: "distribution of nonmonetary assets ... in a spin-off ... should be based on the recorded amounts ... Other nonreciprocal transfers of nonmonetary assets to owners should be accounted for at fair value..." (AICPA, 1973a, par. 23).
- "The Board concluded that [defined benefit pension] plan investments ... should be measured at fair value ... the Board believes that the relevance of fair value is so great as to override any objections to its use" (FASB, 1980a, par. 103).
- They are the amounts at which SFAS No. 115 requires reporting of investments in debt securities that aren't classified as held-to-maturity and equity securities that have readily determinable prices.
- They are the amounts at which the AICPA Special Committee on Financial Reporting recommended reporting what it called noncore assets (AICPA, 1994a, 79).
- They are the amounts at which derivatives are required to be reported under SFAS No. 133 (FASB, 1998f, par. 334).
- "the Board believes that all financial instruments should be carried in the statement of financial position at fair value when the conceptual and measurement issues are resolved" (FASB, 1998f, par. 334).
- "At its December 19, 2001, meeting, the Board decided that the

  - Fair value of a financial instrument should be an estimated exit price—the price that would have been received or paid if it had been sold or settled—on the measurement date...
  - "The mid-point of a bid-asked spread should be used as the basis for estimating fair value if the bid and asked prices are firm offers to buy or sell in an active market"[17] (FASB, 2002b, 8).

17 Two problems with the Board's decisions stated here are (1) they involve a counterfactual—"if it had been sold or settled," which, as discussed earlier in the text of this chapter and, for example, in Chapters 1, 7, and 13, shouldn't be part of financial statements, and (2) asking prices are involved. As discussed above in the text, asking prices aren't part of the reporting entity's environment; they could be any amounts the issuers of the financial statements care to say. The only prices that involve that environment are bid prices. The decision about asked prices conflicts with an earlier decision of the FASB: "the Board agreed that the fair value of spread-traded instruments should be measured at the bid price for assets..." (FASB, 1998d, 2) and its later reversion to that decision: "The Board decided that the fair value measurement should be determined using bid prices for long positions (assets)..." (FASB, 2003c).

- The Corporate Law Economic Reform Program (CLERP) of the Commonwealth Department of Treasury of Australia enacted in 1999, which calls for the introduction of market value financial reporting.

(Jones *et al.*, 2004, 379–381)

And "What's heresy today could be history tomorrow" (Schwarz, 1998, 4W).

Debating points

1 There is no way the profession will accept current selling price reporting, nor should it.
2 It's far-fetched to say that current selling prices are the only current measurable attribute of assets.
3 An entity can in fact suffer an immediate decline on buying an asset, which may be compensated for by an immediate increase in prospects.
4 Prospects are too indefinite a concept to be considered in thinking about optimum financial reporting.
5 Current selling price reporting is the only kind that satisfies all the user-oriented criteria and it should replace the acquisition-cost basis.
6 Current selling prices are too indefinite for inclusion in financial statements.
7 Achievement versus prospects is mumbo-jumbo.
8 The additivity problem is solved in the text.
9 Good old objectivity is like good old religion: it's good enough for me.
10 Get the intentions bugaboo out of my face.
11 Though the answer on specialized assets is severe, it's right.
12 Amounts under CSPR can be reliable.
13 I like to do wishful thinking; it's better than a reality check.
14 The FASB couldn't be as wrong on fair value as the text says; and it isn't.
15 The author of this book should creep out.

15 Current and proposed broad principles for reporting on liabilities

> Traditionally, the most important of [the objectives of liability valuation] has been the desire to record expenses and losses in the determination of current income.
>
> (Hendriksen and van Breda, 1992, 675)

Those who propose basic reforms in financial statements almost without exception concentrate on asset reporting and related income reporting (as discussed in Chapters 12, 13, 14, and 16). They have almost all neglected reporting on liabilities:

> the proper valuation of assets is the very basis of truthful financial statements.
>
> (MacNeal, 1970, 67)

> Much has been written concerning the measurement of assets in a current value accounting system. Very little, relatively, has been written about the measurement of liabilities.
>
> (Skinner, 1987, 546)

> Accountants typically perceive the measurement of liabilities as less difficult than the measurement of assets.
>
> (Staubus, 1977, 185)

> Discovery of the amounts of ... debts owing ... poses no major problem.
>
> (Chambers, 1989, 12)

It seems that they either don't find liabilities interesting or they think nothing much is wrong with their current reporting. However, "The measurement of liabilities [is] as complex as the measurement of assets" (Henderson and Peirson, 1980, 65).

Further, detailed principles involving certain liabilities have been developed without analysis based on the nature of liabilities, to achieve desired income reporting results, which has led to unsound reporting on the liabilities and on the related income (see, for example, Chapters 21 and 24).

Some contend that a liability should be treated as a negative asset and that its reporting should be congruent with reporting on assets:

> A liability may be regarded as a negative asset.
>
> (Skinner, 1987, 633)

> debt [should] be treated as a negative asset...
>
> (Sterling, 1979, 159)

> valuation of liabilities conceptually is the same as valuation of assets...
>
> (Barth and Landsman, 1995, 103)

Others disagree: "Liabilities may not ... be considered as negative assets..." (Chambers, 1966, 110). That's sound. A liability is no kind of an asset, neither a positive asset nor a negative asset. Instead, it's an anchor around the debtor's neck, and the debtor's freedom of action concerning a liability is considerably more restricted than its freedom of action concerning an asset. Even Skinner, who, as quoted above, believes liabilities may be treated as negative assets, stated that "there is a difference in the flexibility of action available with respect to assets and liabilities" (Skinner, 1987, 547). Further, an asset may directly involve no other entity, but a liability always does. Determining sound financial reporting of liabilities requires that they be considered separately and on their own merits.

This chapter considers current and proposed broad principles for reporting on liabilities. Much of the rest of it is taken from Lorensen, 1992.

Events causing a liability to be incurred

More than one event can cause a reporting entity to incur a liability, as discussed in Chapter 9 (though standards have been established in some areas based on the view that a liability can only be caused by one event; see, for example, Chapters 21 and 24).

For example, the reporting entity can manufacture for inventory a defective product—one event. That product can later be sold to a customer—another event. Both events cause the reporting entity to incur a liability to the customer to repair or replace the product, in the sense that it wouldn't incur the liability in the absence of either event. The date at which it incurs the liability is the date of sale. A liability should be first reported as of the date it's incurred—the date the final event that causes it occurs. Before then, the reporting entity has at most a contingent liability, a relationship between the reporting entity and other entities that's contingent on the occurrence of the final event (in this case, the sale) to become a liability.[1] The reporting entity must pay for the liability if the customer discovers the defect and asks for repair or replacement, but the discovery and the request don't cause the liability to be incurred; they only cause the liability to be paid. Measuring such liabilities involves current probabilities, as discussed below.

Though the events causing the liability must have already occurred, standards have been established in some areas based on the view that liabilities, which are current conditions, can be caused at least partly by future events (see, for example, Chapters 21 and 24). Again, cause and effect is held to work backwards in time.

This analysis leads to conclusions on reporting on specific kinds of liabilities that differ from current requirements (see, for example, Chapters 21 and 24). For example:

> Statement No. 60 [paragraph 21] requires [liabilities to pay benefits for insured events that have not yet been incurred] to be recognized ... the ... liability is recognized [currently] in order to attain certain desired income statement effects...
>
> (Lorensen, 1992, 140)

Names of payments required

What some or all of the payments required on a liability are called—*interest payments, principal payments, combined interest and principal payments*, and so on, or nothing at all—is irrelevant to their current reporting and to proposed principles for their reporting; all of the payments are promised or required and default on any one of them causes the debt to be in default: "[The] future payments include periodic 'interest' payments and all 'principal' payments, whether in installments or in a lump sum at maturity" (Sprouse and Moonitz, 1962, 39).

Events causing a liability to be discharged

A liability is discharged when all the amounts required or promised are paid, when convertible debt is converted, when the creditor forgives the liability, when nonrecourse debt such as certain mortgage loans is assumed by a third party in conjunction with the sale of an asset that serves as sole collateral for that debtor (FASB, 2000a, n5), or when a court discharges the liability in a bankruptcy proceeding. A liability can't be discharged, for

---

1 SFAS No. 5 (FASB, 1975a) requires reporting of "loss contingencies" as liabilities, but, by the definition given in the statement, there is nothing contingent about them. It requires that an asset had been impaired or a liability had been incurred by the reporting date.

example, by having unsuccessful operations (though the current standard on reporting on income taxes involves the view that it can; see Chapter 21), or by firing employees (though the current standard on reporting on pensions involves the view that it can; see Chapter 24).

Current broad principle for reporting on a liability

The current broad principle for reporting on a liability is to state it in each balance sheet at whose date it's outstanding at the total of the amounts of money unpaid on that date, discounted by the so-called "interest method" at the interest rate implicit in the events that caused the reporting entity to incur the liability. (Short-term liabilities aren't discounted for convenience. Also, pension and postretirement liabilities are measured at funding amounts [Lorensen, 1992, 124–126], which are discussed below.) That rate is contained in the compound interest formula that links the total proceeds (if any) that the reporting entity received, the total amounts of money it originally promised or was required to pay, the dates of receipt of proceeds, and the original due dates of the required payments. That rate is used for discounting during the entire life of the liability.

Discounting is used for systematic and rational allocation in reporting on liabilities: "The proposed concepts Statement would . . . address instances in which future cash flows are used as a basis for allocating costs, for example, periodic amortization using the interest method" (FASB, 1997b, 2). The compound interest formula by which liabilities are discounted is a predetermined formula, like all formulas used for such allocation. It results in a constant reported effective interest rate on the outstanding balance of the liability. That has been called the correct rate.

Another advantage has been cited for this method:

> The effect of the interest method is to report a periodic interest expense that represents a level effective rate of the book value of the debt . . . The advantage is . . . that it can be assumed to be the effective rate for which the firm is committed.
>
> (Hendriksen and van Breda, 1992, 677, 678)

It's true that the firm would incur expense at that rate over the life of the debt if the debt isn't discharged or funded early. But it could be discharged or funded early, and a prediction that it won't shouldn't be incorporated in financial statements. Moreover, we don't report on the expense incurred over the life of the debt but the expense incurred reporting period by reporting period, which is incurred at rates that bear no necessary relationship to the rate at which the expense is incurred over the life of the debt:

> To be sure, we can calculate overall discount rates for the [period] *as a whole*. But such average rates are *all* that we know; nothing entitles us to

> assume either that what is true of the [total period] is true of each individual year ... or that it is not.
>
> (Arthur L. Thomas, 1979, 17)

Using the simple interest formula, which results in interest charges that are constant in amount over the life of the liability, is considered wrong simply because it doesn't give a constant rate.

In any event, discounting shouldn't be used in reporting on liabilities, for two reasons. First, discounting shouldn't be used in preparing financial statements, as discussed in Chapter 12. Second, systematic and rational allocation shouldn't be used in financial statements, as discussed in Chapter 10: a predetermined formula for reporting on a liability doesn't result in representation period by period of the financial effects of events that occur during the periods. It only contributes to a relatively stable income reporting trend:

> The general tendency is for discounting to smooth the reported influence of events.
>
> (Devine, 1985e, 114)

> Current practice is supported simply because it causes income statement charges to be presented at a constant rate of return on the reported amount of the liability, not because the amounts faithfully represent events or conditions outside of financial reporting.[2]
>
> (Lorensen, 1992, xiii)

No one explicitly supports it for that reason, but that's its result, a result that meets the incentives of the issuers and thereby of the outside auditors.

The unamortized balance of a liability using the compound interest formula represents nothing about the reporting entity's relationship to the creditor at the reporting date. It's the same kind of amount as the undepreciated balance of a long-lived asset. They are both meaningless amounts, not information, parts of the gigantic footnote to the income statement that the balance sheet now represents (see Chapter 10). Current reporting on liabilities has all the failings of allocation and should be replaced with reporting that meets the user-oriented criteria, especially the criterion of representativeness, which current reporting on liabilities doesn't meet.

The following statement by the Accounting Principles Board disputes that conclusion: "some exchanges take place on a continuous basis over time

---

2 Lorensen's statement led me to the insight that, as discussed in Chapter 10, sytematic and rational allocation is used solely because, by applying smooth formulas, it spreads income statement items over reporting periods smoothly, contributing to meeting the issuers' incentive for stable income reporting.

instead of being consummated at a moment of time—for example, accumulations of interest..."[3] (AICPA, 1970c, par. 62 [I.A.1.]) (FASB's CON5, paragraph 84d, contains essentially the same principle.) That concept is taken for granted by the profession. Were it correct, and if the compound interest formula reliably represented those supposed continuously occurring financial effects of events, the conclusion perhaps would be wrong. However, no such continuous financial effects occur. (The assumption that they occur likely came merely from observing that financial reporters behave as if they occur. Reporting that way conforms with the issuers' incentive for stable income reporting, so that gives standard setters the incentive to look for events to conform with the reporting.) The single event that causes the borrower to become indebted to a lender in a loan before repayment is the transfer of money from the lender to the borrower at the inception of the loan. After that, the lender does nothing but wait around until the money rolls in (sooner or later, depending on the contract and the borrower).

The supposed continuously occurring event has been characterized under the headings of delay, the passage of time, the continuous provision of money, the continuous permission to use money, and the continuous use of money (Lorensen, 1992, 36).

Delay is an inference, not an event. If an entity is required to do something at a particular time but does it not then but later, the entity has delayed doing the act. However, in a loan contract, neither party has the opportunity unilaterally to require deceleration of any of the acts required to be performed under the contract before performance is required, so neither party has the opportunity to delay performance.

The contention has been made that interest accrues over the life of a loan simply because of *the passage of time*. However, no other asset or liability accrues simply because of the passage of time. Obligations that increase over time, such as for wages, do so because the working of employees or other events occur over time, not simply because time passes.

It has been said that the accrual of interest is a continuous exchange (the APB said that in the passage quoted). A lender's continuous act under the exchange could be the provision of money or permission to use money. Let's see.

It has been said that a lender *continuously provides money* to the borrower over the life of a loan and that that's an event that causes interest to accrue

---

3 That statement is contained in the analysis of classes of events presented in Appendix A to Chapter 3. That analysis is one of the tools discussed in Chapter 3 for considering financial reporting issues. This shows that those tools aren't necessarily foolproof and need to be used thoughtfully, just as the statement of the user-oriented criteria provided by various sources, including this book, also such tools, have to be used thoughtfully. That's why a revised list of those criteria is provided in Chapter 3 and why you should use all such lists, including the revised one, thoughtfully.

continuously over its life. However, the lender provides money only once, at the inception of the loan.

It has been said that *continuous permission by a lender* for the borrower to use the money is the event that causes interest to accrue continuously over its life. But permission to use something means refraining from preventing its use. The lender has no right to prevent the borrower from using the money at any time during the term of the loan.

It has been held that the *continuous use by a borrower* of money lent over the period of the loan causes interest to accrue over its life: "The use of money is viewed as a service rendered, over the period of the credit relationship, by the lender to the borrower" (Staubus, 1977, 139). However, the money could be kept idle or used continuously and the same changes would occur in the liability, in the relationship between the borrower and the lender.

None of the events whose financial effects supposedly occur continuously occurs continuously, causing interest to accrue continuously. No exchange takes place on a continuous basis over time, so the justification of the APB and the FASB of current reporting on liabilities is invalid.

Proposed broad principles for reporting on a liability

Alternative reporting on liabilities could use other discount rates, another formula, or other possible attributes.

Other discount rates or another formula

One way to look for alternatives to current reporting on liabilities is to consider other interest rates that may be used to discount them. But the rates would be entered into either the simple interest formula or the compound interest formula, which would perpetuate the unsatisfactory use of discounting and allocation in current reporting on liabilities. So that avenue of inquiry wouldn't be fruitful.

Other possible attributes

Another way to look for alternatives to current reporting on liabilities is to consider their possible attributes, the kinds of amounts at which they may be stated in successive balance sheets. Possibilities, reminiscent of the possible alternative asset measurement attributes described in Chapter 12, are as follows:

- *Gross amount*—the total of the promised or required payments unpaid at the reporting date. The amounts or timing or both of some of the promised or required payments on some liabilities are unknown at the reporting date. For example, only a small percentage of mail-in rebates are usually claimed. And, as discussed above, the number of products sold that are defective and the number of the defective ones that will be presented for recompense can't be known for sure currently. The number of pension payments that will be required to be paid based on a current liability for pensions is unknown at the reporting date.[4] The amounts that are most probable at that date should be considered the gross amount, as discussed in Chapter 7, based on the best evidence then available. (That can be implemented more easily if there are a number of liabilities. How would you measure a single liability in the face of evidence that payment is generally requested for only 40 percent of such liabilities?) Events predicted to occur after the reporting date that might affect the amounts most probable of the liabilities shouldn't be anticipated. If changes in the amounts most probable occur after the reporting date, they should be reported as of the periods in which the amounts change.

In contrast, Lorensen states that both predictions and probabilities are involved: "Determining the ambiguous probable amount ... involves a prediction of future interest rates ... [or] the predicted dates at which the payments making up the liability's probable amount will be made" (Lorensen, 1992, 104, 151).

- *Current early repayment amount*—the minimum amount the creditor will accept for early repayment at the reporting date.
- *Current fictitious borrowing amount*—the amount of proceeds the reporting entity could have received at the reporting date in exchange for promising to make the payments outstanding at that date had it not previously incurred the liability.
- *Current incremental borrowing amount*—the amount of proceeds the reporting entity could receive at the reporting date in exchange for promising to make payments in addition to those required on the existing liability in the same amounts and at the same dates as those still required on the existing liability.
- *Current risky funding amount*—the amount of money the reporting entity could invest in other than risk-free securities whose promised cash payments are the same in amount and timing as the payments required under the liability.
- *Current risk-free funding amount*—the amount of money the reporting entity could invest in risk-free securities (U.S. government securities or U.S. government-backed securities are considered to be risk-free[5]) whose promised cash payments are the same in amount and timing as the payments required under the liability.

4 Lorensen presents other examples in *Liabilities* (Lorensen, 1992).
5 Are they? Confederate debt and the bonds of Tsar Nicholas II, for example, weren't (though Sorkin reported that in 1986 and 1997 to 2000, Russia paid somewhat less than 100 kopecks on the ruble for the bonds, in depreciated rubles [Sorkin, 2000, WK 10]).

At least one observer apparently once held that liabilities should be reported at their *gross amounts*, apparently even zero coupon bonds: "the monetary measure of every liability is the contractual amount of the bargain established at the time of the exchange to which it gave rise" (Chambers, 1966, 106). However, reporting all liabilities at their gross amounts would be unsatisfactory. Investments in two reporting entities each of which has a liability of the same gross amount but that have different payment due dates couldn't be satisfactorily compared by users. For example, one reporting entity may owe $100,000 to be paid one year hence. Another reporting entity may owe $100,000 to be paid ten years hence. The burdens of the liabilities differ, and reporting both at $100,000 would prevent helpful comparisons of investments in the entities.

Liabilities shouldn't be reported at their gross amounts.[6]

Current early repayment amount

Some observers hold that

> If payment in cash now will discharge the liability,[7] that ... is the measure of the liability, even though in fact payment is delayed.
> (Sprouse and Moonitz, 1962, 39)

> financial position is represented by the current cash equivalents of assets and obligations as determined in contemporary markets.[8]
> (Chambers, 1966, 290)

> the debt [should be reported] at the market value of the bonds.
> (Sterling, 1979, 159)

> A liability should be valued at its market purchase price.
> (Baxter, 1966, 16)

The FASB suggested the same: "The Board ... indicated ... that it generally finds no support for measuring the fair value of financial assets and liabilities differently" (FASB, 1998b, 2). In fact, it requires disclosure of the "fair value" of debt securities of the reporting entity, which incorporates the current market price of the securities (FASB, 1998f, par. 10). But it reflected doubt about that: "However, the main issue in that area involves whether to

---

6 Under SFAS No. 109 (FASB, 1992), deferred taxes are said to be liabilities but are presented at their gross amounts. They aren't liabilities, however, as discussed in Chapter 21.
7 Payment in cash will always discharge a liability if enough cash is offered.
8 Compare the text above in the section "Gross amount." Chambers was rarely self-contradictory this way, and in the same publication.

reflect the effect of changes in an entity's own credit risk in the fair value of its liabilities..."[9] (FASB, 1998b, 2).

That doubt is well placed. If such credit risk is incorporated in the measurement of liabilities represented by traded securities by measuring them at their current market prices, it results in a paradox. When the riskiness of the reporting entity would be perceived by the users of its financial statements to have decreased, they would bid up its liabilities. Because of that, the reporting entity would increase the amounts at which it states its liabilities using this attribute. That would make the reporting entity look more risky. The users would then bid its liabilities down, and it would decrease the amounts at which it would report its liabilities, thereby making it look less risky, causing its liabilities to be bid back up again. The circle would perpetuate:

> since investor predictions and risk assessment are, in part, based on the information contained in the financial statements, it would be circular to reflect these composite predictions and assessments in the statements.
>
> (AICPA, 1973b, 31)

> It is intuitively repugnant to many that a decline in debt [if the entity is perceived to have become riskier] should be reported as an increase in equity...
>
> (Skinner, 1987, 547)

> Companies would recognize gains as their credit ratings decline and a later loss if the full face value amount were paid. Gains for doing badly and losses for improving? Come on.
>
> (Beresford, 2001, 39)

Consider this title of an article: "Fair Valuing Debt Turns Deteriorating Credit Quality into Positive Signals for Boston Chicken" (Lipe, 2002). At the extreme, if prospective creditors decide that a reporting entity's debt instruments have become worthless, they will bid them down to near zero. The reporting entity's reported income will skyrocket. There has to be something wrong with that.

The FASB disagrees: "there is no rationale for why, in initial or fresh-start measurement, the recorded amount of a liability should reflect something other than the price that would exist in the marketplace" (FASB, 2000b, par. 85). (That there was such a rationale available at the time the FASB

---

9 The FASB ignored that doubt in a decision reported in its Action Alert, November 25, 1998 (FASB, 1998d), in which it stated that it "agreed that the fair value of [a] spread-traded [liability] ... should be measured at [its] asked price..." It later explicitly stated that credit risk is to be incorporated in the measurement of liabilities, as discussed below in the text.

wrote this—with which the FASB was free to disagree—is shown by the statement of its doubt quoted above.) In footnote 4 to its exposure draft issued on June 23, 2004, on "Fair Value Measurements" (FASB, 2004b), the FASB stated explicitly that the reporting entity's credit standing should be reflected in the amounts assigned to its liabilities:

> For a liability, the estimate of fair value should consider the effect of the entity's credit standing so that the estimate reflects the amount that would be observed in an exchange between willing parties of the same credit quality.

(In general, the FASB appears to have disliked the idea of requiring reporting a loss simply because a liability is incurred, reached for the result it prefers, and afterward tried to defend it. Lipe couldn't even imagine reporting such a loss: "when credit quality is low at *issuance*, initial measurement of the debt must include credit quality; otherwise the credit to bonds payable does not equal the debit to cash" [Lipe, 2002, 179]. [The balancing item is the loss.] A defense of reporting such a loss is given below in the section on risk-free funding amount.)

It disagrees that there is a paradox:

> [In the] view [of some], a fresh-start measurement that reflects changes in credit standing produces accounting results that are confusing. If the measurement includes changes in credit standing, and an entity's credit standing declines, the fresh-start measurement of its liabilities declines. That decline in liabilities is accompanied by an increase in owners' equity, a result that they find counterintuitive. How, they ask, can a bad thing (declining credit standing) produce a good thing (increased owners' equity)?
>
> A change in credit standing represents a change in the relative positions of the two classes of claimants (shareholders and creditors) to an entity's assets. If the credit standing diminishes, the fair value of creditors' claims diminishes. The amount of shareholders' residual claim to the entity's assets may appear to increase, but that increase probably is offset by losses that may have occasioned the decline in credit standing. Because shareholders usually cannot be called on to pay a corporation's liabilities, the amount of their residual claims approaches, and is limited by, zero. Thus, a change in the position of borrowers necessarily alters the position of shareholders, and vice versa.
>
> The failure to include changes in credit standing in the measurement of a liability ignores economic differences between liabilities. Consider the case of an entity that has two classes of borrowing. Class One was transacted when the entity had a strong credit standing and a correspondingly low interest rate. Class Two is new and was transacted under the entity's current lower credit standing. Both classes trade in the marketplace based on the entity's current credit standing. If the two liabili-

ties are subject to fresh-start measurement, failing to include changes in the entity's credit standing makes the classes of borrowings seem different—even though the marketplace evaluates the quality of their respective cash flows as similar to one another.

(FASB, 2000b, pars 86–88)

The main specific objection to the FASB's defense is that it relies on the financial effects on parties separate from the reporting entity: the creditors and the shareholders. A financial report on a reporting entity should be solely about financial effects of events on the reporting entity, not on any other entity (see Chapter 8). Regardless of changes in the values to the creditors of claims or to shareholders of rights, the reporting entity has the same obligation to make the same payments, unchanged by changes affecting the creditors or shareholders.

The FASB states that the reporting entity's reported shareholders' equity "may appear" to increase using the kind of reporting it prefers in the face of a decline in the credit standing of the reporting entity. In fact, it does increase. The FASB says that the increase probably is offset by losses that may have occasioned the decline in credit standing. The message is that it's correct to in effect reverse reporting such losses. No justification for such a reversal is offered or apparent.

Though, as the FASB states, the marketplace evaluates the quality of the respective cash flows of the Class One and Class Two liabilities it illustrates as similar to one another, their promised cash flows are different, because their interest payments are different, reflecting the difference in the credit standing between the times they were incurred. Under the reporting recommended in this chapter, they would appear different. Were their required cash flows the same, they would appear the same under the reporting recommended in this chapter.

A member of the FASB and a member of its staff added to the attempt to defend the view that sound financial reporting results in reporting gains when the price of a reporting entity's bonds decline and reporting losses when the price of a reporting entity's bonds rises:

A balance sheet is composed of three classes of elements—the entity's economic resources (assets), claims against those resources held by nonowners (liabilities) and the residual claims of owners (equity). In a corporation, the value of owners' residual claims cannot decline below zero; a shareholder cannot be compelled to contribute additional assets. When an entity's credit standing changes, the relative values of claims against the assets change. The residual interest—the stockholders' equity[10]—can approach, but cannot go below, zero. The value of

10 Equating these two concepts confuses the financial reporting map and the financial reporting territory, as discussed in Chapter 4.

creditors' claims can approach, but probably can never reach, default risk-free. Traditional financial statements have ignored those economic and legal truisms, so any measurement more consistent with real-world relationships will necessarily be unfamiliar.

(Crooch and Upton, 2001, 6)

Those "truisms" appear merely to state that the price of ownership shares of a reporting entity can never go lower than zero and the price of the bonds of the reporting entity can never rise as high as the price of similar bonds of the U.S. government. That says nothing about the ratio of those prices (their "relative values"). And changes in that ratio demonstrate nothing about whether financial reporting should show the net income of a reporting entity skyrocketing when its bonds are bid down to zero. (Further, stockholders' equity, an amount that exists only in balance sheets, can go below zero.)

If a liability is to a single creditor, the debtor usually wouldn't know how much the creditor would require for early repayment; the creditor is unlikely to say if asked. If the debtor knows for sure, which virtually never occurs, and the amount is less than the current risk-free funding amount (see below), the current early repayment amount should be used to report the liability.

Current fictitious borrowing amount

The current fictitious borrowing amount involves a fictitious assumption: that the reporting entity didn't incur the liability previously, which it did. It's thereby similar to the first kind of current buying price discussed in Chapter 13. A liability shouldn't be presented at an amount that involves a fiction. Liabilities shouldn't be reported at their current fictitious borrowing amounts.

Current incremental borrowing amount

A suggestion has been made to report liabilities at their

Relief value, the burden of a liability to the enterprise, [which] is the mirror image of the "value to the business" of owning an asset . . . [it] is the *higher* of the amount that could be raised currently by an issue of a precisely similar debt security or the cost of discharging the liability by the most economical means (i.e., by repurchase in the market, exercise of call privileges or provision of a fund to service the liability on its due dates).

(Solomons, 1987, 174)

The first of those options (the amount that could be raised currently by an issue of a precisely similar debt security) is the current incremental borrowing amount (the others are discussed elsewhere in this section). But that amount pertains not to the liability owed but to a liability not owed, one that presumably could be incurred currently. It's an attribute of the liability not owed, not of the liability owed, and is thereby similar to the second kind of current buying price discussed in Chapter 13. The amounts of attributes of liabilities not owed shouldn't be reported as the amounts of liabilities owed; they aren't part of the reporting entity's financial position. Liabilities shouldn't be reported at their current incremental borrowing amounts.

The two remaining kinds of attributes involve the concept of funding the liability.[11]

Current risky funding amount

The securities the reporting entity could buy for the current risky funding amount would result in receipts in the amounts and on the dates payments are due on the liability, if the issuers of the securities don't default, though only measurement and not buying is involved. (The current risky funding amount is now implicitly required for pension, post-retirement benefits, and insurance liabilities.) Because they are risky securities, the issuers might default, so the reporting entity couldn't be sure to get the monkey of its liability off its back by buying such securities. The current risky funding amount represents nothing definite concerning the reporting entity, its liability, and its environment at the reporting date. Liabilities shouldn't be reported at their current risky funding amounts.

Current risk-free funding amount

The reporting entity could be as sure to get the monkey of its liability off its back by buying risk-free securities that promise payments in the amounts and on the dates payments are due on the liability as it could be of anything about the liability short of paying it off immediately. The current risk-free funding amount therefore represents something relevant concerning the reporting entity, its liability, and its environment at the reporting date. (A creditor should always be willing to accept the risk-free funding amount, because, if nothing else, the creditor could invest the proceeds in risk-free securities and obtain full repayment with the risk of nonpayment virtually eliminated.)

---

11 Sprouse and Moonitz were early advocates of using this concept (though they didn't distinguish risky and risk-free funding amounts): "If the creditor will not or cannot accept cash now in discharge of the liability, the appropriate amount is that sum which, if invested now (e.g., in a sinking fund), will provide the sums needed at maturity, even though in fact no explicit sinking fund or other investment device is actually used" (Sprouse and Moonitz, 1962, 39).

But reporting a liability when it's incurred at its risk-free funding amount results in reporting a decline in current possession of or access to consumer general purchasing power from borrowing money, the way reporting an asset when it's bought at its current selling price results in reporting a decline in current possession of or access to consumer general purchasing power from buying the asset. For example:

> An immediate loss . . . is suffered because we have borrowed $4,590,000 but would need $4,789,325 to settle the obligation immediately. The current cash equivalent method requires losses of this type to be written off[12] immediately.
>
> (Henderson and Peirson, 1980, 64)

How can a reporting entity suffer such a decline simply by borrowing money?

To see how, we should free our minds of preconceptions concerning reporting on liabilities and income determination and see what's happening outside the reporting system, which the reporting system is supposed to map. Let's again consider the beady-eyed man with the turned-up collar who offered the woman the car for $20,000 in Chapter 14. He now whispers that he has another great deal for her. This time, he tells her he will give her $100,000, and all she has to do is promise to pay him $150,000. Her natural reaction is again to tell him to get lost. The man says, hold on, she doesn't have to promise to give him the $150,000 right away. She can promise to give him $5000 at the end of each of the next nine years and $105,000 at the end of the tenth year.

The woman agrees and takes the $100,000. Later, she asks herself what she has done, agreeing to pay $50,000 more than she received. Then she thinks, maybe she will be able to take the $100,000 she received and use it to earn more than an additional $50,000 over the ten years. But that's in the future. Meanwhile, she figures she is out the extra $50,000. But then she thinks, no, she isn't out the whole $50,000, even now. Suppose she could take the $100,000 she received, add $12,000, and invest it now in risk-free securities and be virtually certain to obtain sufficient returns over the ten years to pay off the liability. If so, she sees that she is actually out currently a maximum of only the extra $12,000.

As far as the world is concerned, she has to pay either the $150,000 total payments or the $112,000 to fund the liability currently at the risk-free funding amount, in order to be virtually certain it will be paid off. No one forced her to incur the debt, and she must face the consequences. She should report the liability the way the world sees it, at $112,000, not at $100,000,

---

12 Losses aren't written off. Asset amounts are written off; losses are reported.

which would incorporate her dreams of future income enough to pay off the whole $150,000.

Not everyone agrees:

> discounting at the ... risk-free rate would ... involve recognition of a loss on issue of the debt, a step that is not consistent with any view of borrowing with which we are familiar,
>
> (Staubus, 1977, 186)

Solely because a view is unfamiliar shouldn't by itself be a reason to reject a measurement attribute. Also,

> Probably the main objection to the current cash equivalent approach to liabilities is that it assumes behavior which is unlikely to eventuate. It assumes that liabilities will be settled on the balance sheet date when they are much more likely to be allowed to run to maturity.
>
> (Henderson and Peirson, 1980, 64, 65)

That argument involves measuring the current amount of liabilities by the issuers predicting future events (assumed behavior), which is a contradiction of the meaning of measurement and which in any event should have no place in financial statements (see Chapter 7). Measurement involves no assumption of behavior—it's an antecedent to behavior.

Reporting entities should report their liabilities at their current early repayment amounts to creditors if known for sure (which is rare) or at their current risk-free funding amounts, whichever is lower, as Henderson and Peirson said (omitting to refer specifically to risk-free funding):

> the amount which, if paid to the creditor on the balance-sheet date, would discharge the obligation in full; or ... the amount which, if invested on the balance-sheet date, would provide sufficient cash to meet the interest and principal obligations as they fall due. The effective current cash equivalent would be the lower of these two amounts.
>
> (Henderson and Peirson, 1980, 64, 65)

Those amounts for reporting on liabilities meet the user-oriented criteria the same way current selling prices for reporting on assets meet the user-oriented criteria (discussed in Chapter 14). That treatment reports declines (and increases) in current possession of or access to consumer general purchasing power in the income statement not now reported. However, the current well-being of a reporting entity is partly measurable, by the principles recommended in this chapter and Chapter 14, and partly unmeasurable, consisting of prospects (as stated in Chapters 14 and 16). A report of a decline in the reported equity of a reporting entity accompanied by information that suggests improved prospects, which the reporting recommended in this chapter and Chapters 14 and 17 provides, is balanced reporting. Additional help can be provided to users by highlighting the excess of the risk-free funding amounts of loan liabilities incurred over the proceeds of the loans at the inceptions of the loans in a new section of the income statement on investments in prospects (discussed in Chapter 17).

Debating points

1   I don't care about how to report on liabilities (I don't really much care about any of the issues discussed in this book)—get a life.
2   I'm fascinated by all the issues in this book; they leave me breathless.
3   Don't criticize the FASB so much, for example, over a little inconsistency on whether a liability can or can't be caused by more than one event.
4   Like good old objectivity in Chapter 14, the way we've always reported on liabilities is good enough for me; and don't lay that allocation bugaboo on me again.
5   Of course interest accrues over time—doesn't the author of this book know anything; or does it?
6   Reporting an immediate loss on borrowing money (ignoring the effects on prospects) is hard to swallow, but I'll try.
7   It's plain nonsense to report an immediate loss on borrowing money.
8   I'm a fan of paradoxes.
9   This author can't believe the profession will adopt a rule for reporting on liabilities as complicated as the one he favors, can he?

16 Reflecting or reporting prospects in financial statements

> The interesting aspect of [current selling price reporting] is that discouraging prospects are reported precisely when subjective value is usually being added, and reported progress is inverse to the change in prospects as perceived by the managers themselves ... [current selling price reporting] make[s] little or no pretense at showing what earnings potential management has at its disposal.[1]
>
> (Devine, 1985c, 76; 1985d, 25)

The current objective (in the ordinary sense) financial situation of a reporting entity depends on the current willingness of the market to buy its assets, on the current selling prices of the reporting entity's assets, and on the current conditions of the market permitting it to fund its liabilities risk-free, on the reporting entity's current risk-free funding amounts, or on the willingness of its creditors to accept less currently. In contrast, assets are sometimes defined in terms of prospects (potential, promise, outlook):

> "assets are service potential..."[2]
>
> (Vatter, 1947, 17, quoted in Staubus, 1961, 29n)

> "[service-potentialities are] the significant element[s] behind accounts..."
>
> (Paton and Littleton, 1940, 13, quoted in Staubus, 1961, 29n)

1 These two statements are contradictory. In the first, Devine states that CSPR reports prospects (discouraging ones). In the second, he states that it doesn't report prospects (potential). The second statement is correct.
2 The expression "service potential" refers to the potential ability of assets to provide any kind of service in the future. One kind is to provide money on the current sale of an asset. That is referred to as current access to consumer general purchasing power in Chapter 14 and various other chapters. Other kinds of potential services promised by the possession of an asset include use of the asset in production and increase in the ability of the asset to provide possession of or access to consumer general purchasing power in the future by, for example, future increases in the selling price of the asset. This chapter discusses those other kinds of potential services.

Also, Devine defines *value* as "income potential" and *assets* as "potentials for adding value"[3] (Devine, 1999, 4, 156). However, "[t]he market does not buy ... potential; it buys ... services, as ... potential becomes an actuality"[4] (Chambers, 1966, 10).

People evaluating a person or a reporting entity may conclude that the person or the reporting entity currently has prospects, potential, of achieving possession of or access to consumer general purchasing power in the future beyond that achieved to date and reported under CSPR and under the principle for reporting liabilities recommended in Chapter 15:

> A company that loses money isn't necessarily a bad investment. I'm more than happy to pay up today if a company's business model promises long-term success.
>
> (Kessler, 2000, A26)

> the endless question of how to properly value a company and its prospects.
>
> (Jenkins, 1999, A27)

Such thoughts are commonplace (though thinking doesn't make it so). Graduation from college is usually thought to improve the graduate's prospects. Reporting entities with specialized assets that can be sold currently for only scrap value are usually thought to have prospects at the dates they are acquired of using the assets to obtain a net return greater than their acquisition costs, no less their scrap value. That's why issuers buy them so regularly. Hiring Iaiccoca was thought by many as improving Chrysler's prospects (they later attributed much of its financial achievement during his tenure to him and to the federal bailout he arranged). *Newsday* announced that "Martha Stewart's Earnings Slump: But Company Touts Prospects" (*Newsday*, 2002, A4).

When the FDA approved Viagra, the prospects of Pfizer, its manufacturer, were thought to have been, well, aroused, and those thoughts were initially found by subsequent movements in its stock price to have been amply warranted. Since then, based on the number of prescriptions written and movements in Pfizer's stock price, its prospects apparently have been thought to have alternatively, well, risen and fallen.

---

3 Nevertheless, Devine stated that "the term potential is delightfully vague and need not be associated with values, costs or physical concepts" (Devine, 1999, 297).

4 An exception is in the market for securities of the reporting entities, which reflect investors' evaluations of the prospects of reporting entities as a whole. As stated several times earlier, financial reporting doesn't, shouldn't, and can't report on aspects of reporting entities as a whole (except in reporting on investments in such securities).

MacNeal states that prospects are paramount: "the ... most important element of the total value of a going business [is] the outlook for its future" (MacNeal, 1970, 232).

Reflecting prospects in financial statements

The prospects of a reporting entity, if any, depend not only on its holding of assets and the burden of its liabilities, whose effects on its prospects are indefinite, but on many other variables, all of which are also indefinite, especially the quality of its management. Butterworth speaks of

> the fatal fallacy, apparently the consequence of some sort of accounting wishful thinking, which holds that current values of assets are adequate predictors of future cash flows. The fallacy arises because future cash flows are a function of all the factors of production and not just of the capital asset factor on which analysts tend to focus. The ability of a firm to generate future cash flows depends on its labour contracts, the quality of its labour relations, its management skills, its technological supremacy, its research capability, its exploration and development resources, its command over output markets, and its command over factor markets other than the market for its capital assets.[5]
>
> (Butterworth, 1982, 106)

One management may be capable of running a reporting entity currently in a particular situation into the ground while another management with the same reporting entity currently in the same situation (except that it has a different management) may be capable of making it soar. Prospects for the reporting entity in those two circumstances differ in respects that can't be known but can only be judged by investors putting their money on the line.

Norris relates a telling anecdote illustrating that prospects don't necessarily or even usually reside in assets:

> In 1915, a young man named Benny Grossbaum told his bosses at a Wall Street firm that an operation called the Computing-Tabulating-Recording Company had a very useful machine and that the stock was undervalued. His boss told him the company's assets were highly suspect, and to stay away from it, which he did. In later years both the man and the company changed their names. Grossbaum became Ben Graham, the father of modern securities analysis. And Computing-Tabulating-Recording became International Business Machines. Its assets were doubtful, but its prospects were phenomenal.
>
> (Norris, 1998, 9; see also Cottle *et al.*, 1988)

---

5 It also depends to some extent on luck; consider, for example, September 11, 2001.

Prospects are conjectural and, not being observable, aren't measurable and therefore are unverifiable. Whether a reporting entity or a person has had prospects can't be judged later by waiting to see how events unfold: prospects of a person may not be realized, for example, because of too abundant an indulgence in whiskey, or of a business because of the untimely death of a key employee, but that doesn't mean they didn't exist. Whether a reporting entity has prospects and the extent to which it has them are solely matters of opinion, of evaluation, and people's evaluations will be diverse.

Such an evaluation has to be made sometimes, for example to settle a business interruption insurance claim which is intended to compensate the claimant for income that would otherwise have been earned during an interruption. It involves the prospects of the claimant for achievement during the period of interruption not realized because of the interruption. Making such an evaluation requires subjective assumptions, which may vary considerably, causing the results to vary considerably. The subjective nature of such an evaluation is exemplified in the following cases:

> [insured] with the assistance of an accountant who had previous experience in U&O ["use and occupancy"—business interruption] claims, filed a 64-page proof of loss supported by 12 exhibits claiming U&O damage of nearly $1\frac{1}{2}$ million ... The adjusters, after consulting competent experts in this business and obtaining accounting and legal advice, arrived at a figure of $80,000 for the loss ... the claim was settled for $110,000.
>
> (Clarke, 1957, 35)

In another case, the witness for the insured, a CPA, determined the loss in gross earnings during the period of interruption to be $102,006.70. The special master in the case, also a CPA, found the loss to be $7735.80, based on the determination of a witness for the insurers, another CPA (*American Alliance Insurance Company* vs. *Keleket X-Ray Corporation*, 248 F. 2nd 920, 1957).

The first subjective evaluation by the Federal Victims Compensation Fund established to compensate victims of the terrorist attacks on September 11, 2001, was the basis of an award to a victim's family of $1,014,000 on August 8, 2002, partly to compensate them for his "unfulfilled economic potential."

Reporting entities regularly invest in prospects, for example when they buy long-lived assets whose current selling prices are lower than their acquisition costs, and especially when they buy or otherwise acquire goodwill, which is pure prospects. Such a purchase doesn't necessarily make the reporting entity worse off or better off. *The current well-being and past progress of a reporting entity are partly objectively measurable, by the principles recommended in Chapters 14 and 15, and partly not measurable, consisting of prospects. The* following is a contrast between objectively measurable financial achievement ("success") and prospects ("potential") in advertising:

> Advertising on the Internet, like most uses of this new medium, is still in the early stages of a long and presumably fruitful evolution. In other words, it is long on potential but, so far, short on success stories.
>
> (Tedeschi, 1999, C6)

Users of financial reports should judge the well-being and progress of reporting entities based partly on their financial positions and incomes reported based on those principles and partly on their own evaluations of the reporting entities' prospects.

The track record of the reporting entity as shown by its financial statements over the years can be of some help to users in judging its prospects—for example, "The General Motors Corporation worried Wall Street today by reporting first-quarter earnings that suggested underlying weaknesses in the company's prospects later this year" (Meredith, 1998, D1). Gu and Lev point out that royalty income on severable and unseverable resources can be "an important signal about [their] prospects..." (Gu and Lev, 2004, 2). And a new section on investments in prospects can be added to the income statement, as discussed in Chapter 17. Finally, the major contribution of the AICPA Special Committee on Financial Reporting was to recommend enhanced disclosures to help users make those evaluations (see Chapter 17).

Reporting prospects in financial statements

> we need the humility and stoicism to accept that much that we and users of our reports would dearly love to know is in principle unknowable.
>
> (Arthur L. Thomas, 1979, 29; also quoted in Chapter 14)

Nevertheless, a conceptual objection to current selling price reporting, voiced in the second of the two quotations that open this chapter, is made that, in its determination of asset amounts, such reporting ignores the reporting entity's prospects for achievement of possession of or access to consumer general purchasing power beyond its achievement to date of such possession or access. Several observers have stated or implied that such prospects are the very attribute of assets that should replace acquisition cost for use in financial statements, that they should be not only reflected but reported in the statements (if they exist, prospects are current conditions [see Chapter 7], and so to that extent are candidates for use as such an attribute):

> the principal attribute that we seek to measure is cash flow potential ...

the present significance, considering prospective timing and amount, of any existing capacity to produce a cash inflow or outflow.[6]

(Staubus, 1977, 162, 163)

the term "income" should be reserved for those instances in which an augmentation of operating flow potential has occurred.

(Revsine, 1973,[7] 115)

information is relevant if it informs users about the ability of an asset or liability to affect the reporting entity's [cash flow potential].

(Miller and Bahnson, 2004a, 14)

(According to those views, achievement in a particular reporting period is an increase in prospects for achievement in later reporting periods!)

Indirect "measurement"

Though the AICPA discussed "measuring prospective cash flows" (AICPA, 1973b, 32), Staubus conceded that "The cash flow potential of most assets and liabilities cannot be measured directly" (Staubus, 1977, 163). (However, none can be measured directly. Further, none can be measured indirectly, as discussed below.) Staubus' solution is to approximate it: "This problem typically is approached by measuring an alternative attribute that has a demonstrable economic relationship to cash flow potential and so can serve as an estimate of it ... a 'surrogate' attribute" (Staubus, 1977, 163). He gave some advice on finding such surrogates:

the selection of a measurement technique is a selection of the most appropriate type of evidence ... regarding the potential service, or disservice, of the item being measured ... the investor must attempt to predict the firm's capacity and willingness to pay, [so] ownership of money must be considered the best evidence of potential service to residual equity holders. Measurement techniques utilizing other types of evidence may be ranked ... For assets which have been acquired very recently and which do not involve definite claims to future cash receipts, original money cost may provide the best available evidence of their

6 In an earlier document, Staubus stated that the incremental effect on the net discounted amount of the reporting entity's future cash receipts and payments rather than its potential for future cash receipts and payments is the attribute we seek to measure (see Chapter 12).
7 In the same document, Revsine stated that the discounted present value of an asset rather than its operating flow potential theoretically is the best measure of the asset (see Chapter 12).

service potential . . . the more specialized an asset is, the more difficult it
is to find evidence of the monetary equivalent of its service potential.

(Staubus, 1961, 39, 40, 50)

He cited future cash receipts or payments, discounted future cash receipts
or payments, discounted promised cash receipts or payments, net realizable
value, and replacement cost as other amounts to be evaluated for their serviceability as such surrogates (Staubus, 1977, 164, 172). Likewise, Revsine
cited replacement cost as such a possible surrogate:

if replacement cost information is to provide a predictive basis for external investors, there must be high covariance between changes in asset
prices and changes in an individual firm's operating flow potential.

(Revsine, 1973, xiii)

Both Staubus and Revsine emphasize that the usefulness of surrogates
needs to be determined:

we must make certain that a relationship exists which justifies the
acceptance of one measure as a surrogate for another . . .

(Staubus, 1977, 163, 164)

the empirical question becomes: How well does this stringent condition
approximate . . . observed real-world conditions . . . Obviously, empirical research is needed to answer this question.

(Revsine, 1973, xiii)

However, neither Staubus nor Revsine have demonstrated how the following
requirements for using surrogates (discussed in Chapter 6) are met by any of
their suggested surrogates:

- To find an attribute that's measurable in general and that's relevant in
  the circumstances but that can't be measured directly in those circumstances.
- To find a variable that approximates the measurable attribute adequately in the circumstances that can be measured in those circumstances.
- To measure that variable and use that measurement in place of a direct
  measurement of the measurable attribute.

The first requirement can't be met, because prospects are in concept not
measurable.

The specific surrogates Staubus and Revsine suggest are nevertheless considered here.

Money

Staubus assumes that an amount of money held is a surrogate for the reporting entity's prospects involved in the money. However, an amount of money held represents achievement to date in gaining possession of or access to consumer general purchasing power. Using it to approximate prospects of gaining more assigns zero to the prospects of a holding of money. No other amount could be used to quantify the infinite variety of possibilities a holding of money promises. An amount of money held isn't a surrogate for prospects.

Acquisition cost

That a reporting entity paid the acquisition cost of an asset when it acquired it demonstrates only that its management then believed that the purchase provided the reporting entity with prospects of recouping more than the acquisition cost and more than an alternative investment. That was solely their opinion. There's no objective way to demonstrate that that opinion was correct or incorrect: no such opinion is verifiable. Further, managements don't formulate opinions on exactly how much more will be recouped, on the extent of the prospects, and, if they did, acquisition cost wouldn't determine it. For those reasons, acquisition cost bears no necessary relationship to the prospects, if any, and isn't a surrogate for them.

Current duplication cost

The amount it would currently cost a reporting entity to buy a duplicate of one of the assets it holds (its current duplication cost; Revsine calls it the "replacement cost") depends, among other things, on demand, which is influenced, among other things, by the competing prospective buyers' opinions on the prospects each can gain by buying such an asset. Those opinions (1) vary widely; (2) involve the view by each buyer that its returns will be greater than the duplication cost, not merely equal to it; (3) aren't specific to the prospects the reporting entity might obtain by buying one; and (4) aren't verifiable.

The current duplication cost is also influenced by matters outside of prospects, such as supply and the cost of manufacture and the like. A reduction in manufacturing cost leading to a reduction in the duplication cost doesn't mean that the prospects of entities that use assets of that type have declined. They probably have increased, because the cost of buying them would have declined.

Using current duplication cost as a surrogate for prospects has effects similar to using it in concept as the attribute to use in place of acquisition cost (as discussed in Chapter 13). Using duplication costs as surrogates for prospects, increases in those costs would be reported as income though such increases are increases in the reporting entity's costs. Such increases, every-thing else being equal, are harmful to the reporting entity, and shouldn't be reported as income. If large enough, such increases could drive the reporting entity out of business (see Chapter 13).

A general principle to report assets at their current duplication costs because prospects supposedly are improved might be partially justified if selling prices increase correspondingly, but there is no reason to adopt that generalization. If adopted, the preferable treatment would be to use current selling prices, not current duplication costs, but that would involve report-ing on achievement, not on prospects.

For all those reasons, current duplication cost bears no necessary relation-ship to the prospects provided by an asset to the reporting entity that holds it, if any, and isn't a surrogate for them.

Staubus counters that conclusion as follows: "assets held for use will affect the firm's future cash position by reducing future cash outflows leads ... to the close surrogate—present replacement cost..." (Staubus, 1971a, 61). However, such an assumed reduction in future cash payments is the dif-ference between the future cash payments that might become required and the future cash payments that might not become required because of the possession of the asset. Involving such events that won't happen incorporates a counterfactual, fiction, in the analysis, putting it outside the domain of financial statements (such a counterfactual use of current buying prices is discussed in Chapter 13).

Future cash receipts and payments and discounted future cash receipts and payments

Neither future cash receipts or payments nor discounted future cash receipts or payments exist at present outside the mind (as discussed in Chapter 12). The amount of a concept that doesn't exist at present outside the mind shouldn't be used to approximate an attribute of an asset for reporting in financial statements.

Discounted promised cash receipts or payments

Long-term receivables would be reported at their current selling prices under CSPR (see Chapter 14). That represents the reporting entity's achieve-ment to date of possession of or access to consumer general purchasing power as to those assets. The only prospects to achieve more with them involves selling them between the reporting date and their maturity dates for more than their current selling prices or to receive the promised amounts when due, if the debtors don't default. Discounting doesn't result in amounts that meet the criterion of representativeness (see Chapter 12). Such a process shouldn't be used with unverifiable forecasts of possible future pro-ceeds to approximate an attribute of these assets.

Net realizable value

This concept sometimes denotes current selling prices. Such prices measure achievement to date in possession of or access to consumer general purchasing power, not prospects of achieving more. This concept sometimes denotes prospective future selling prices less prospective future costs to complete, perhaps reduced by other prospective future costs such as selling costs. Such prospective future amounts aren't verifiable. This denotation of net realizable value therefore shouldn't be used in financial statements to approximate the reporting entity's prospects.

Conclusion on suggested surrogates

The various suggested surrogates are unsatisfactory as amounts to use in concept to replace acquisition costs in financial statements, as discussed in preceding chapters. They are also unsatisfactory to use as surrogates for the use of prospects as the attribute to replace acquisition cost in financial statements.

Reporting on intangibles

Views have recently been expressed that the prospects involved in intangibles should be included in the amounts presented as assets in financial statements. For example, Elliott, former Chair of the Board of the AICPA, was reported in the August 11, 2000, issue of *Dow Jones News Service* as advocating "valuing" intangibles, such as intellectual property. Another Chair of the Board and a President of the AICPA made essentially the same suggestion:

> we have already begun to focus . . . on the benefits that will accrue from a reporting model that is suitable to Information Age companies, whose earning assets are often not accurately valued by traditional, manufacturing-based measures.
>
> (Castellano and Melancon, 2002, 1)

PricewaterhouseCoopers has a concept it calls *ValueReporting*™ under which its representatives contend that

> intangible[s] . . . such as expenditures for R&D, information technology, marketing, branding, and customer loyalty programs, are treated as expenses by today's accounting standards [though they are] . . . really assets[8] . . .
>
> (Eccles *et al.*, 2001, 55, 57)

---

8 No expenditure is an asset. The issue is rather whether the results of R&D, information technology, and the like, are assets. See the discussion on costs as assets in Chapter 10.

The Brookings Task Force on Intangibles

> argues that the large and growing discrepancy between the importance
> of intangible assets to economic growth and the ability to identify,
> measure, and account for those assets is a serious potential problem for
> . . . investors . . .
>
> (Blair and Wallman, 2001, vi)

And Lev states that

> I propose the recognition as assets of all intangible investments with
> attributable benefits that have passed certain prespecified technological
> feasibility tests. [However,] managers should not be expected to disclose
> *values* of intangibles . . .[9]
>
> (Lev, 2001, 124, 125, 127)

In contrast, Bayless, SEC Chief Accountant of the Division of Corporation Finance, states that such prospects shouldn't be presented in amounts in financial statements but disclosed and explained in nonfinancial terms:

> registrants should identify and explain what management does to develop,
> protect and exploit [intangibles]. Operational, non-financial, measures
> can be very effective in explaining to investors the value of a company's
> intangibles.
>
> (Bayless, 2001, 4; also quoted in Chapter 17)

Such intangibles generally can't be sold separately from the reporting entity, and therefore don't agree with the definition of *assets* proposed in Chapter 14—they merely provide prospects. The proposal of Elliott, Castellano, Melancon, Eccles *et al.*, the Brookings Task Force, and Lev should therefore be rejected. Information to evaluate the prospects involved in such intangibles should be disclosed in the notes and in supplementary information, as discussed in Chapter 17.

Likely future achievement

Though current prospects aren't measurable, even were they measurable they shouldn't be reported in financial statements. A good prospect is a current likelihood that progress will be achieved in the future. It isn't certain (nothing about the future is certain), but even if it were certain, the progress involved would be to be achieved in the future. Historical reports such as

---

9 This proposal combines the defects of reporting prospects as assets discussed in this chapter and of measuring them at acquisition cost discussed in Chapter 10.

financial statements should report financial achievement achieved, not financial achievement in prospect, even what seems to be almost certain financial achievement in prospect. General Electric will almost certainly make sales next year. That prospect doesn't belong in this year's financial statements of General Electric.

Conclusion on reflecting or reporting prospects in financial statements

> The cash generating ability of an enterprise involves an evaluation of its present ability to generate cash in the future ... [It] is present prospects, not future accomplishments ... Information should be structured and presented to aid users in forming their own judgments about the cash generating ability of an enterprise.
>
> (Sorter *et al.*, 1974, 113; also quoted in Chapter 17)

Financial statements should reflect and report only financial achievement to date. They shouldn't reflect or report prospects of future financial achievement. Supplementary information provided in financial reports outside financial statements should provide information on current conditions, momentums, plans, intentions, and the like not suitable for reporting in financial statements to help users evaluate the reporting entity's prospects for future financial achievement beyond the help provided by the financial statements (see Chapter 17). Such evaluations are in the domain of financial analysis, not of financial reporting.

Debating points

1 Viagra has nothing to do with financial reporting.
2 Prospective cash flows should be the attribute to replace acquisition cost as the fundamental basis of reporting.
3 Prospects shouldn't be reflected or reported in financial statements; information to help users judge the prospects of the reporting entity for further financial progress should be reported as supplementary information.
4 We shouldn't reject a suggestion of two Chairs and a President of the AICPA.

17 Disclosure in financial reporting

> The desire for secrecy, for the right of privacy of one's affairs, persists to this day...
>
> (Flegm, 1984, 29)

> At Berkshire, full reporting means giving you the information that we wish you to give us if our positions were reversed. What Charlie and I would want under that circumstance would be all the important facts about current operations as well as the CEO's frank view of long-term economic characteristics of the business. We would expect both a lot of financial details and a discussion of any significant data we would need to interpret what was presented.
>
> (Buffett, 2000)

Information in financial reports is disclosed in the financial statements, in the notes to those statements, which are called part of the financial statements, and in supplementary information reported outside the financial statements.[1]

The supplementary information is mainly intended to help users evaluate the current prospects of the reporting entity to remain or become solvent, to retain what it has achieved financially to date, and to achieve financially more than it has to date:

> Cash generating ability ... is present prospects ... Information should be structured and presented to aid users in forming their own judgments about the cash generating ability of an enterprise.
>
> (Sorter et al., 1974, 113; also quoted in Chapter 16)

---

1 Such supplementary information has sometimes been reported in what are called unaudited notes, for example, information provided in conformity with SFAS No. 33 (FASB, 1979b).

Disclosures about a company's condition and prospects are common . . .
(Richtel, 1999, C2)

Two members of the SEC recently stated that supplementary information should be expanded and that some information should be disclosed more frequently than annually or quarterly:

the public and private sectors must partner to produce a sensible and workable approach that includes . . . *disclosure of significant "trend" and "evaluative" data* . . . that begin where line-item and Generally Accepted Accounting Principles disclosures end . . . We will soon propose a significantly extended list of items that companies will be required to disclose at intervals more frequent than the current quarterly and annual reporting requirements.
(Pitt, 2001, A18; 2002, 3)

[Commissioner] Glassman said the goal for each corporation ought to be a clear, compelling, and understandable story about its prospects in the market. This approach needs to be evident in the financial information and in the Management's Discussion and Analysis (MD&A) section of reports.
(Bologna, 2003, G-7)

A tangle of trees

Hiding the forest of disclosure in a tangle of trees is discussed in general in the Prologue in the section "Broad principles versus detailed rules." The problem showed its ugly face especially in connection with the collapse of Enron, WorldCom, and the like:

FASB is too bogged down in the specifics. Rather than agree on a broad principle for what should be disclosed, it has insisted on detailing rules for every possible situation. So, creative Big Five accountants and chief financial officers structure ever more ingenious ways around them, [Professor] Carmichael says.
(Liesman *et al.*, 2002a)

instead of complying with the letter of the law, [Professor Lev] wants auditors to delve deeper into . . . deals [creating special purpose entities] and dig out their true ramifications . . . Could the liabilities come back to the company attempting to get them off the books?
(Byrnes, 2002b, 36, 37)

auditors . . . work to help clients comply with the letter—but not the spirit—of accounting rules, at investors' expense . . . memos . . . show that partners [of the auditors of Boston Chicken] studied the letter of the accounting rules and the technical requirements for passing Securities and Exchange Commission review. But they reflect no discussion about the overall impression [its] results would present to investors.

(Richards and Thurm, 2002, C1)

Glassman, a commissioner of the SEC, said that

Too often ... the SEC sees annual reports featuring complicated and tedious explanations of business issues that are useless to shareholders. The commission also sees reports that are technically correct, but essentially inaccurate with respect to the substantive issues affecting the firm. Other reports seem to create complexity to confuse shareholders. She said none of these results is acceptable, and that firms producing such reports would, at a minimum, be punished in the marketplace. Firms engaged in such disclosures also risk enforcement action by the SEC.

(Bologna, 2003, G-9)

Major reforms of the FASB's approach and of auditing standards are needed in this area.

Information to help users evaluate current prospects

The central tasks of financial analysis are to understand the current strengths and evaluate the current prospects of each reporting entity under consideration and to compare such understandings and evaluations:[2] "when a stock is selling for 50 or 100 times the company's current profits per share, that value has to rest mainly on prospects for the future..." (Krugman, 2001, A17).

Financial statements reporting assets measured based on CSPR and liabilities measured as recommended in Chapter 15 present representations of the current strengths of the reporting entities in the only objective, verifiable ways available, based on the market. Rather than attempt to report the reporting entity's prospects in the financial statement portion of financial reports, a new section should be added to the income statement on investments in prospects, discussed next, and additional information should be

2 Prediction is also commonly said to be part of financial analysis. As stated in footnote 6 in Chapter 6, a financial analyst warned me to call analysts' predictions *estimates*, not *predictions*, because analysts don't like to be thought of as "examining tea leaves." When pressed, the analyst acknowledged that they predict. Though analysts do predict future cash flows, income, and the like, prediction is an arcane art and almost always wrong unless the financial statements are rigged. Analysts base their predictions mainly on their evaluation of current prospects.

provided in financial reports outside the financial statements to help users evaluate the reporting entity's prospects.

Investments in prospects

Adoption of some of the recommendations in this book could sometimes result in lower reported income than by application of current GAAP. That could be offset by information on additions the issuers believe have been made to the prospects of the reporting entity. A new section of the income statement on investments in prospects, indicating amounts charged to expense spent to enhance prospects, by category of expenditure, could help the users obtain a fuller picture of the effects. Examples of such items could include the following:

* The amounts spent on assets in the current reporting period in excess of their current selling prices at the dates of acquisition
* The risk-free funding amounts of loan liabilities incurred in the current reporting period in excess of the proceeds of the loans at the inceptions of the loans
* Investments in intangibles in the current reporting period:

> [My] proposed ... reporting ... would complement the conventional one ... by providing standardized information on ... *intangible investments* ...
>
> (Lev, 2001, 119, 122, emphasis added)

The Brookings Task Force recommends

> breakouts of *expenditures* on basic research, new product development, on-going product and process improvement, the *expenditures* associated with quality assurance programs and service functions, training systems, the development and installation of information technology systems, advertising or brand development, market alliances, distribution networks, and enhancement and renewal of workforce skills, and salaries, bonuses, and incentive compensation systems.
>
> (Blair and Wallman, 2001, 62, emphasis added)

* Expenditures to acquire goodwill in business combinations.

Supplementary information

Additional information to help the users evaluate the reporting entity's prospects may not meet the user-oriented criterion of verifiability, and that should be made clear in the report. Confining the presentation of such additional information to supplementary information would take the pressure off the financial statements to do more than they can do, as suggested in preceding chapters, especially Chapter 10.

As early as 1977, a United Nations group agreed that nonfinancial reporting "should be made an integral part of general purpose reports." It listed these areas for inclusion in minimum disclosure: labor and employment, production, investment programs, organizational structure, and environmental measures (United Nations Economic and Social Council, 1977, 33–38).

The major contribution of the AICPA Special Committee on Financial Reporting was to recommend greatly improved disclosures to help users form opinions on the reporting entity's prospects. Its 1994 report recommended that financial reports contain nine elements besides financial statements:

- High-level operating data and performance measurements that management uses to manage the business
- Reasons for changes in the financial, operating, and performance-related data and the identity and past effect of key trends
- Opportunities and risks, including those resulting from key trends
- Management's plans, including critical success factors
- Comparisons of actual business performance to previously disclosed opportunities, risks, and management's plans
- Information about … directors, management, compensation, major shareholders, and transactions and relationships among related parties
- Broad objectives and strategies [of the company]
- Scope and description of business and properties
- Impact of industry structure on the company.

                                                      (AICPA, 1994a, 52)[3]

In response to the report of the Special Committee, the FASB, on January 29, 1998, "decided to undertake a research project to consider the types of information (in addition to financial statements) that companies should be providing investors" (FASB, 1998a).

An Enhanced Business Reporting Consortium was formed in 2004 whose mission is stated as

> A Consortium of stakeholders collaborating to improve the quality, integrity, and transparency of information used for decision-making in a cost effective, time efficient manner.

It was formed by the AICPA's Special Committee on Enhanced Business Reporting. Its website address is http://www.ebrconsortium.org/who.htm.

---

3 Eccles *et al.* made a similar recommendation in *Revolution* (2001), which it discussed, for example, on pages 123 and 124.

SEC Chief Accountants Turner and Bayless recommended addition of information such as

> backlog, revenues per employee, percentage of revenue dollars spent on research and development, marketing and capital expenditures, the utilization rate and capacity of a manufacturing plant, the amount of revenues generated from new products introduced in the year or from the top ten customers, the number of design wins, and size, nature and type of patent portfolio...
>
> (Turner, 2001, 4)

> registrants should identify [important intangibles] and explain what management does to develop, protect and exploit them. Operational, non-financial, measures can be very effective in explaining to investors the value of a company's intangibles.
>
> (Bayless, 2001, 4)

The Brookings Task Force on Intangibles

> [holds that] the effectiveness of [current] disclosure requirements at ensuring good corporate governance ... is being eroded, because as intangibles become more important relative to tangible assets, this required disclosure reveals less about the ... sources of value inside a firm.
>
> (Blair and Wallman, 2001, 26)

It

> call[s] for the ... SEC and the ... FASB ... to [participate in] identifying reliable performance indicators that should be included in the disclosures required of publicly traded companies...
>
> (Blair and Wallman, 2001, 5)

The Task Force states further that

> the best one can hope for at present is to identify and develop indirect indicators, or clusters of indicators, to help understand [investments] in productivity and wealth creation ... it is irrelevant whether such information is incorporated into the regular financial statements of companies or presented in some other format, for example, in footnotes or the management discussion and analysis or in some other supplementary disclosure material ... In fact, most members of the Task Force concluded that capitalization of ... any ... intangibles ... is a poor proxy for the richer information disclosure that we believe is necessary.
>
> (Blair and Wallman, 2001, 58, 67)

The latter sentiment agrees with the position in this book.

Particular attention should be given to disclosing information on quality enhancement programs and cost reduction measures that are vital to the success of the reporting entity.

Had Enron dutifully followed the report of the Special Committee since its publication and the recommendations of Lev, Eccles *et al.*, Turner, Bayless, and the Brookings Task Force, its outcome may have been different. Further, Bloomberg news reported on April 23, 2002, that

> In 54 percent of the 673 largest bankruptcies of public corporations since 1996, auditors provided no cautions in annual financial statements in the months before bankruptcy ... Major accounting firms routinely certify books with audit opinions that don't inform investors of risks, the 673 cases show. Many of the companies involved were ... suffering from high levels of debt, eroding sales and declining profit margins.
>
> (Bloomberg News Service, 2002)

The FASB should move quickly on the report of the Special Committee and the recommendations of the others.

Nevertheless, not nearly all of the information needed for economic decisions for which information in financial reports is used is or can be reported in financial reports:

> Though the accounting function provides a necessary part of the premises of choice, it does not provide the whole. The factual premises of choice are provided by many streams of information; many of these streams provide information of generically different kinds...
>
> (Chambers, 1966, 372)

Caution about stated views of users

The Special Committee reached its conclusions based on stated views of professional users obtained in focus groups and in surveys. A member of the Special Committee and subsequently Chair of the AICPA warned the Chairman of the Special Committee about that: "I doubt that our customers will demand anything beyond incremental improvements—an insufficient response to our problem" (Elliott, 1992). The Special Committee agreed: "Most users naturally are concerned with current practice and their current problems. Thus, they seldom offer or consider radically new ways or processes by which better decisions could be made" (AICPA, 1994a, 15). A professor stated the same forcefully: "when people have been conditioned to believe something, we learn nothing from polling them except that they have been conditioned" (Arthur L. Thomas, 1974, 85). Two other professors stated the same colorfully:

Perhaps historical cost data are used primarily because they are provided. Some people also follow the practice of rubbing a rabbit's foot every morning, but we need not conclude that such a practice affects subsequent events.

(Staubus, 1977, 217)

my priors were that "sophisticated" (e.g., bankers and financial analysts) users would have been conditioned[4] to ask for a continuation of what they had been getting, that is, historic costs ... and the "naive" (the general public) users, not having been subjected to such conditioning, would want current values ... Surveys have confirmed my priors ... No profession, except the oldest profession, adopts an unqualified policy of giving the customers what they want.

(Sterling, 1979, 88n, 89n)

And remember the tale of nineteenth-century transportation practices related in the beginning of the Prologue. Offhand opinions of users should be used with caution.

Disclosure of contingent liabilities

The section on "Events causing a liability to be incurred" in Chapter 15 defines a *contingent liability* as a duty that's contingent on the occurrence of a future event, that is, not a liability. SFAS No. 5 (FASB, 1975a) requires accrual of "loss contingencies" if

Information available prior to issuance of the financial statements indicates that it is probable that an asset had been impaired or a liability had been incurred at the date of the financial statements.

Such a "loss contingency" isn't a contingent liability (as stated in Chapter 15, footnote 2). The asset had been impaired or the liability had been incurred.

Included in "loss contingencies" in SFAS No. 5 are guarantees of the obligation of the indebtedness of others. FASB Interpretation No. 45 requires that guarantees of obligations of other entities should be reported as liabilities even if it is not probable that payments will be required under the guarantee. Chapter 4 discusses the flaw in that requirement.

Eichenwald and colleagues reported that a central problem in Enron's financial reporting before its collapse was that it had in effect guaranteed huge indebtedness of its off-balance-sheet special purpose entities, which

---

4 Here, Sterling is saying that "sophisticated" users are indoctrinated ("conditioned") the same as financial reporters.

would become liabilities of Enron if the price of Enron stock fell below "trigger" levels, but it hadn't disclosed the contingencies (Eichenwald *et al.*, 2002, L28). In the absence of consolidation, the possibility of such contingencies becoming realities should be disclosed to fully inform the users of financial statements.

Disclosure of duties to classes of equity security holders[5]

Any discretionary duties of the reporting entity

- to provide resources to holders of classes of equity securities (securities or aspects of securities of the reporting entity that do not involve liabilities), such as common or preferred stock
- to provide stock or other equity instruments of the reporting entity to such holders, such as convertible preferred stock or stock options
- to minority stockholders to provide dividends if and when declared by subsidiaries

are not liabilities of the reporting entity and, further, can't and shouldn't be displayed as part of the reporting entity's own equity in its own assets. Those duties should be described in the notes in order to inform the holders of such securities of the priority of their rights to receive resources from the reporting entity under various circumstances.

The disclosures should be in enough detail to inform the users, for example, of conversion clauses, the priority of the duties to the classes, the rates of discretionary dividends if established, any cumulative dividends in arrears, and the percentages of stock held by minority stockholders and changes in those percentages. As usual, a statement of equity should be provided that reconciles the beginning and ending balance of equity, with details of transactions involved, including net income or loss for the reporting period.

"Non-financial" information

The Special Committee recommended that reporting of what it called "non-financial" information be required: "Non-financial information is important to understanding a company, its financial statements, the linkage between events and the financial impact on the company of those events, and for predicting the company's future" (AICPA, 1994a, 147). Though the FASB stated that "the information provided by financial reporting is primarily financial..." (FASB, 1978, par. 18), it has mentioned reporting of so-called nonfinancial information similar to that recommended by the Special

5 This section is taken from Rosenfield, 2005.

Committee: "Corporate annual reports, prospectuses, and annual reports filed with the Securities and Exchange Commission are common examples of reports that include ... nonfinancial information" (FASB, 1978, par. 7). Such information isn't strictly nonfinancial, however, because it bears indirectly on finances. For example, information on geological faults running near the reporting entity's facilities bears indirectly on finances, because of the risk of financial loss not covered by insurance if such a fault causes an earthquake (including losses from business interruption) that damages the reporting entity's operations. Information that has no financial implications isn't part of the Special Committee's recommendations.[6]

Forward-looking information

> the accountant should strive to supplement his report of the amounts of assets and equities with other data that can be of aid to the investor in predicting his future cash returns.
>
> (Staubus, 1961, 52)

Much of the additional disclosure recommended by the Special Committee is called *forward-looking information* (AICPA, 1994a, 29–31), a relatively new term that at first seems to be concerned with only prediction. But prediction, forming thoughts about what's going to happen when time moves on, is in fact not involved in the recommended forward-looking information. The users the Special Committee contacted were unequivocal that they don't want financial reports to include issuers' explicit predictions of income of subsequent periods. They were concerned that if such predictions are included, the issuers would tend to subsequently manage the reporting entity so as to make the predictions come true rather than manage solely in the best interest of the stakeholders of the reporting entity, or they would bias their subsequent reports to make it appear that the reporting entity came close to fulfilling the predictions: "Users do not seek management's forecasts or projections because ... [t]hey encourage management to manage earnings toward previously published projections" (AICPA, 1994b, I, 88, 89). Those concerns would be less for including issuers' explicit predictions of cash flows, because subsequent reporting of cash flows would be less susceptible to management than subsequent reporting of income.

The organization of professional analysts said the opposite of what the individual analysts told the Special Committee: "Financial analysts avidly seek management's forecasts as part of the financial reporting process..."

---

6 The Special Committee called the subject matter of this book "business reporting," not "financial reporting," because so-called nonfinancial information is included. This book continues to call it "financial reporting," however, because all the so-called nonfinancial information recommended has financial implications.

(Association for Investment Management and Research, 1993, 18). And the AICPA equivocated: "Financial forecasts should be provided when they will enhance the reliability of users' predictions" (AICPA, 1973b, 46).

I agree with the analysts who spoke to the Special Committee and have the same concerns they have. In general, predictions should be the responsibility of the users and we financial reporters should provide information about the past and the present to help the users make the predictions. Especially troubling would be for outside auditors to be associated with issuers' explicit predictions of income. Because comparisons of such predictions with subsequently reported results would reflect on the outside auditors, they might be tempted to join with the issuers in making the subsequently reported results look similar to the predictions, diminishing the service they provide to the users by audits.

Rather than consisting of predictions, the recommended forward-looking information relates to current circumstances, developments, momentums, opportunities, intentions, risks, prospects, dangers, and the like that portend future changes in assets or liabilities and the issuers' current views on those matters:

> All existing contracts or conditions that are likely to have a significant impact on future cash flows should be disclosed in notes to the financial statements if capitalized values of such cash flows have not been recognized as assets and liabilities in the balance sheet.
>
> (Skinner, 1987, 517)

Included should be the Class B aspects of assets discussed in Chapter 14 in the section "Class A and Class B aspects," prospects for achievement of access to consumer general purchasing power seen by the issuers but not yet seen enough by the world for it to bid on them individually. The reporting entity should give its views on such prospects, which would make it unnecessary for it to attempt to measure the unmeasurable and enter it in its financial statements.

Noll and Weygandt cautioned that "the nonfinancial and forward-looking information elements [of the report of the Special Committee] are widely recognized as the most challenging disclosures in the proposed model" (Noll and Weygandt, 1997, 60).

Disclosure overload

The Special Committee's recommendations and recommendations made in the wake of Enron and the rest would result in a considerable increase in disclosure, much of it not of the kind we financial reporters have traditionally dealt with, not being the output of the accounting system. For example, after Enron collapsed, "GE said its [2001] report had 30% more financial information than the year before" (Silverman, 2002).

Differences of opinion are voiced on the optimum amount of disclosure to include in financial reports:

We analysts are information junkies.

(AICPA, 1994b, II, 1(b), 43)

[The FASB] constantly treads a fine line between requiring disclosure of too much information and requiring too little.[7]

(FASB, 1980b, par. 36)

Management should not be required to report information that would harm a company's competitive position significantly.

(AICPA, 1994a, 55)

Managers who wish to withhold information have an easy excuse for nondisclosure—the information asked for will be useful to the company's competition. That claim is hard to refute, and it may even occasionally be true ... many of the arguments against [disclosure requirements] are based on what has been called Panglossian economics—everything (absent interference by regulators) is for the best in the best of all possible worlds...[8]

(Solomons, 1986, 188, 189)

Barth and Murphy observed that "Disclosure requirements have increased over time; few have been eliminated" (Barth and Murphy, 1994, 1). For example, Household Finance Corporation's entire 1928 annual report contained four pages, reproduced in Figures 17.1, 17.2, and 17.3. The 2001 annual report of Household International, its successor company, contained 104 pages, with 36 pages of financial statements, including 31 pages of notes to the financial statements.

Borelli fretted about prospective increases in disclosures required:

members of the Financial Accounting Standards Board ... want executives to volunteer some of the same nonfinancial information that they use for management purposes, from statistics on employee turnover to measures of customer loyalty to numbers of defective products ... "The thing that bothers us the most is the volume of data," said Frank J. Borelli ... one of the ... board members [of the Financial Executives Institute].

(Petersen, 1998a, D1, D8)

---

7 This was stated pre-Enron. The FASB will likely now lean towards the "too much" end of the spectrum.

8 In the current environment, few would likely voice this sentiment loudly.

February 15, 1929

To the Stockholders:

On behalf of the Board of Directors, I submit the following report covering the operations of the Corporation for the year ending December 31, 1928:

The Corporation's books and accounts have been audited by Haskins & Sells, Certified Public Accountants, whose report is contained herein.

During 1928 the Corporation transacted a volume of business of over $25,500,000, with satisfactory results. After charging off all bad debts and setting up full reserves for depreciation and the 1928 Federal Income Tax, the year's operations produced a net income of $2,309,405.57. Since the financing in October, 1928, when public offering was made of the Participating Preference Stock, dividends have been paid at the rate of $3.00 per share per annum on the Participating Preference Stock and the Class B Common Stock (there being no Class A Common Stock outstanding). There were charged against the Surplus Account during the year the entire expense of the Participating Preference Stock issue and an additional reserve of $150,000 for possible losses in collection of receivables, leaving a balance in Surplus Account at the close of business December 31, 1928, of $1,230,233.07. Cash on hand, in banks and due from bankers amounted to $3,289,316.40, with no notes payable to banks and only the normal current liabilities and accrued items.

Since the sweeping reduction made in October, 1928, in the rate of interest charged by the Corporation to its borrowers, the aggregate of outstanding loans up to January 31, 1929, has increased by more than $3,200,000 and new loans are being made in satisfactory and growing amounts. The general effect of the reduction of the interest rate has been very good and has tended to stabilize the Small Loan Business and to strengthen the Corporation in its position of leadership therein.

The Chattel Loan Society of New York, Inc., our wholly owned subsidiary corporation, has more than doubled its volume of business since its acquisition by us May 1, 1928, and is in very satisfactory condition.

The branch offices of the Corporation now number seventy-four, located in industrial centers in the states of Illinois, New York, Pennsylvania, New Jersey, Rhode Island, Maryland, Indiana, Michigan, Iowa, Wisconsin and Missouri.

The Corporation has an efficient and loyal organization under capable management and you may look forward with confidence to continued success in 1929.

Respectfully yours,

L. C. Harrison

President

Figure 17.1 President's letter (copyright 1928 by Household Finance Corporation, reproduced with permission).

HASKINS & SELLS
CERTIFIED PUBLIC ACCOUNTANTS

OFFICES IN THE PRINCIPAL CITIES OF
THE UNITED STATES OF AMERICA
——AND IN——
LONDON, PARIS, BERLIN, SHANGHAI, MANILA,
MONTREAL, HAVANA, MEXICO CITY

CABLE ADDRESS "HASKELLS"

HARRIS TRUST BUILDING
CHICAGO

Household Finance Corporation and Wholly-Owned Subsidiary, Chattel Loan Society of New York, Incorporated

CERTIFICATE

We have made general examinations, for the year ended December 31, 1928, of the accounts of the Household Finance Corporation, and, for the eight months ended that date, of the accounts of the Chattel Loan Society of New York, Incorporated, a wholly-owned subsidiary acquired as of May 1, 1928. The accompanying statements include the results of operations of the subsidiary for the period subsequent to its acquisition.

At June 30, 1928, we verified the cash on hand at each of the various branch offices, and comprehensively tested the physical possession of the notes receivable held at those offices. This verification was not repeated at December 31, 1928.

The income, expense, and profit and loss accounts of the companies are kept on a cash receipt and disbursement basis, and that basis has been observed in the accompanying statements. Arising from this practice, a net asset resulting from income and expenses accrued but not collected or paid at December 31, 1928, in the approximate net amount of $215,000.00, is not included in the accompanying balance sheet. A similar net asset existed at January 1, 1928, in the approximate amount of $180,000.00.

WE HEREBY CERTIFY that, in our opinion, the accompanying statements, subject to the foregoing, are correct.

(Signed) Haskins & Sells

Chicago,
January 25, 1929.

Figure 17.2 Auditors' report (copyright 1928 by Household Finance Corporation, reproduced with permission).

Household Finance Corporation
and Wholly-Owned Subsidiary, Chattel Loan Society of New York, Incorporated

Summary of Consolidated Net Income for the Year Ended December 31, 1928

Gross Income from Operations		$ 4,814,462.43
Operating Expenses		2,137,011.92
Net Income from Operations		$ 2,677,450.51
Other Income Credits		52,177.22
Gross Income		$ 2,729,627.73
Income Charges other than Federal Income Tax		97,191.13
Net Income Before Federal Income Tax		$ 2,632,436.60
Federal Income Tax		323,031.03
Net Income		$ 2,309,405.57

Statement of Consolidated Surplus for the Year Ended December 31, 1928

BALANCE, JANUARY 1, 1928			$ 1,427,910.83
NET INCOME FOR THE YEAR, AS ABOVE			2,309,405.57
GROSS SURPLUS			$ 3,737,316.40
CHARGES:			
Capital stock premium and expense (net)		$ 490,340.07	
Provision for possible losses in the collection of receivables		150,000.00	
Miscellaneous		11,927.34	
Dividends—cash:			
Capital stock		$ 1,466,746.00	
Participating Preference stock		94,916.67	
Class "B" Common stock		293,153.25	
Total charges			2,507,083.33
BALANCE, DECEMBER 31, 1928			$ 1,230,233.07

Household Finance Corporation
and Wholly-Owned Subsidiary, Chattel Loan Society of New York, Incorporated

Condensed Consolidated Balance Sheet, December 31, 1928

ASSETS

CURRENT ASSETS:		
Cash on hand and in banks	$ 1,908,967.95	
Loans to bankers	1,380,348.45	
Instalment notes receivable, less reserve of $150,000.00	15,510,501.59	
Sundry notes and accounts receivable	22,581.05	
Total current assets		$18,822,399.04
NOTES RECEIVABLE—sale of capital stock (secured)		192,807.40
INVESTMENTS		5,450.00
FIXED ASSETS, LESS DEPRECIATION		208,251.84
ADVERTISING SUPPLIES		8,380.63
TOTAL		$19,237,288.91

LIABILITIES

CURRENT LIABILITIES:		
Notes payable—individuals	$ 159,755.00	
Employes' thrift accounts	220,688.31	
Dividends payable	397,403.25	
Sundry accounts payable	34,480.46	
Federal income tax—year 1928	323,031.03	
Total current liabilities		$ 1,135,358.05
RESERVE FOR CONTINGENCIES		150,922.79
CAPITAL STOCK:		
Participating Preference—authorized, 400,000 shares of $50.00, par value, each; in hands of public, 139,000 shares	$ 6,950,000.00	
Common, Class "A"—authorized, 580,000 shares of no par value; outstanding, none	Nil	
Common, Class "B"—authorized, 520,000 shares of no par value; outstanding, 390,831 shares at a stated value of $25.00 each	9,770,775.00	
Total capital stock		16,720,775.00
SURPLUS, PER ACCOMPANYING STATEMENT		1,230,233.07
TOTAL		$19,237,288.91

Figure 17.3 Balance sheet and income statement (copyright 1928 by Household Finance Corporation, reproduced with permission).

And Groves urged a halt to the increase in disclosure requirements: "the sheer quantity of financial disclosures has become so excessive that we've diminished the overall value of these disclosures ... in financial disclosure, more is not better" (Groves, 1994, 11, 14).

Sensitive to this situation, the Special Committee searched (without success) for currently required disclosures that could be dispensed with, and it recommended that standard-setters and regulators continue the search (AICPA, 1994a, 91, 92). But businesses are complicated and investment decisions are vital, so caution should be exercised in restricting disclosure of information that could improve those decisions:

> The history of concealment, misinformation and disinformation is as long as the history of mankind. Since so much may be done with wealth and so little without it, financial affairs especially have been considered to be private, confidential—to be disclosed only for clear advantage or under threat of damage, and then only to the extent necessary.
>
> (Chambers, 1989, 17)

> "recently the buzz words 'disclosure overload' have become very popular—talk about an oxymoron. How can anyone who is a thoughtful investor be overloaded with information about his or her investment or prospective investment?"
>
> (Foster, 2003, quoted in Miller and Bahnson, 2002b, 135)

> we cannot in our wildest imaginations come up with a scenario where specialized analysts would cry out to a management, "Stop! Stop! We already know too much! We don't want to know anything else. Just take our money and leave us alone!"
>
> (Miller and Bahnson, 2002b, 172)

Nevertheless,

> there is a sizable number of investors who make investment decisions on the basis of only one statistic about a corporation: its net income per share or, perhaps more specifically, the price-earnings ratio.
>
> (Bevis, 1965, 4)

> what about the floor traders who see only what the broad tape chooses to print?
>
> (Defliese, 1983, 95)

There's no hope for such self-defeating investors.

Reporting in the financial statements versus disclosure in the notes

To achieve their incentives, issuers and their friends sometimes recommend that items that might otherwise be reported in the number columns of the financial statements be simply disclosed in the notes instead. For example, Mautz made that recommendation concerning the general issue of the treatment of increases in market value above acquisition cost: "disclosure of such changes can be made readily without any need for shifting from a historical cost to a value basis of accounting" (Mautz, 1973, 25). Also, as discussed in Chapter 2, everything else being equal, issuers prefer to report higher rather than lower income. One way to do that is to disclose an amount rather than report it as an expense.

For example, in round one of the controversy over reporting in connection with stock options, discussed in Chapter 18, the FASB proposed that companies start reporting an expense in connection with issuing the options. The FASB ended up in that round being forced to permit the amount to be disclosed in the notes rather than reported as an expense. Also, at the beginning of round two, during renewed interest in reporting in connection stock options granted to employees in 2003, a bill introduced in Congress, the Broad-Based Stock Option Plan Transparency Act (which wasn't enacted into law), would direct the SEC to require increased and improved disclosure in financial statements of company employee stock option plans. During the three-year period after its enactment, the SEC would not recognize as a generally accepted accounting principle any new accounting standard on stock options (Hamilton, 2003, 7).

However, "disclosure cannot rectify a wrong or inappropriate treatment" (IASC, 1975, par. 10).

Debating points

1 A major challenge to the profession is to move issuers to make disclosures conform more to the advice of Warren Buffet.
2 No amount of jawboning will force recalcitrant issuers to disclose more than the bare minimum.
3 There is no way to end obfuscation in financial statements.
4 Adding a section in the income statement on investments in prospects would be a major advance in reporting.
5 A section in the income statement on investments in prospects would do little or nothing for the users of financial reports.
6 Evaluating achievement achieved is challenging enough to the users; for them to judge a reporting entity's prospects for future achievement based on any kind of information in financial reports is too much to ask.
7 A textbook writer shouldn't give advice to the FASB, such as to reform

its approach to disclosure requirements, or to point out flaws in its requirements.

8   Sound information on current developments and momentums can significantly help users judge the reporting entity's prospects for future achievement.

9   Groves is right; too much disclosure is already required—it overburdens the users and the issuers of financial reports.

Part IV

Specific issues in financial reporting

18 Reporting in connection with stock options granted to employees

With the stage set, and having discussed the underlying and broad issues, which inform most of the specific issues, we go on to the specific issues.

The battle royal on the issue of reporting in connection with stock options, which took place in two rounds, highlights several shortcomings of financial reporting standard setting today, and that's why that topic is the subject of the first specific issue considered.

Round one

> misleading accounting—an accurate description of the current treatment of stock options...
>
> (Morgenson, 2002, 12)

The first round, which took place from 1982 to 2002, witnessed most of the shortcomings in this area. In that round, the FASB tried to help the users in its way. The analysts did their best. But the issuers of financial reports, the AICPA Accounting Standards Executive Committee, the SEC, the Congress, the President, his advisors, and his appointees, and possibly outside auditors prevented improvement in the area, as discussed below. At the end of that round, we had what the *New York Times* financial journalist called "the fictional accounting permitted by generally accepted accounting principles..." (Norris, 2000b, C1). The second round, discussed below, came out better.

The battle began in 1982, when the AICPA Accounting Standards Executive Committee (AcSEC) presented the FASB with an issues paper[1] (AICPA, 1982) that stated that the then current standard on reporting in connection with stock options, APB Opinion No. 25, "Accounting for Stock Issued to Employees" (AICPA, 1972b), was unsatisfactory. This was because it had several deficiencies, including the requirement for reporting entities

---

1 I and other members of the staff of the Accounting Standards Division of the AICPA prepared this and other issues papers. Perhaps that's how I got the idea to write this book on issues in financial reporting.

to report costs for some plans whose benefits to employees are less than the benefits to employees covered by other plans for which the Opinion doesn't require reporting of costs.[2] The Opinion didn't require reporting entities to report costs for most stock option plans.

Compensation cost

> Valuable financial instruments given to employees give rise to compensation cost that is properly included in measuring an entity's net income.
>
> (FASB, 1995b, par. 75)

In round one, the profession held that if the reporting entity does incur such a cost, it's *compensation cost*, on the assumption that the reporting entity incurs a cost in compensating the employees when granting them stock options. It always merely asserted the assumption, never defended it, except to imply that since the employees get something valuable to them, the reporting entity must give up something valuable to it—that is, incur a cost on granting the stock options. Miller and Bahnson consider that argument to be the final word on the subject: "Options have value and the transfer of value to anyone for services rendered is an expense-period. End of discussion" (Miller and Bahnson, 2004b, 16). The analysis that follows shows that to be false.

Issuers didn't want to start reporting such a cost. To back up their position, issuers contended either that the reporting entities don't incur such a cost or, if they do, that it's unmeasurable. Others, such as AcSEC (an AcSEC later than the one that presented the issues paper), said they do incur such a cost but that it's unmeasurable and they should therefore not report it. Still others, including the FASB initially, said they do incur such a cost, it's measurable, and it should be reported, but the FASB later caved in to pressure brought to bear against it, discussed below, and didn't require that reporting.

Operating in the dark

> [This analysis is] beyond the scope of this project.
>
> (FASB, 1984c, par. 155)

The earlier AcSEC, through its issues paper, was the only group that analyzed the events that occur in connection with employees providing service and being granted and exercising stock options, rather than guess what

---

2 In accordance with the analysis in Chapter 8, that difference in the effects of the plans on the *employees* is irrelevant to financial reporting on the plans by the sponsors of the plans. Their effects on the *reporting entities* are the only ones that matter. Nevertheless, the different effects on the employees gave standard-setters a clue that something was amiss.

was occurring or avoid analysis and decide the income reporting results desired and work back to the bookkeeping entries to accomplish the results. The analysis is discussed in the next section. When the FASB received the issues paper, it stated that it would ignore its analysis, as indicated in the quotation that opens this section. It made that statement though the Board later stated that the project was "complex" (FASB, 1995b, par. 367). That was a strange position, for how could analysis of events be beyond the scope of a complex project to consider how to revise reporting on such events? Don't the operations to design financial statements (discussed in Chapter 3) start with the injunction to select and analyze the events to be reported on? Is there something wrong with those operations (other than they might not serve particular interests other than those of the users)? And when would the FASB consider such events? It had shut down its Conceptual Framework and had no current plans to reopen it. (It subsequently issued CON7, [FASB, 2000b] but that Statement didn't cover the events involved in issuing stock options to employees.)

A Chairman of the FASB said after the first round of the stock option battle was concluded that people who consider the stock option issue should "think more critically about such [a] continuing issue ... as the following: Is an expense incurred when equity securities are issued as compensation for labor services, or is it a capital transaction?" (Beresford and Johnson, 1995, 111). That's the central question considered in the analysis of the issues paper.

The FASB shouldn't have deliberately operated in the dark. If the AcSEC analysis was defective (there is no reason to believe it was), the FASB should have conducted its own. It didn't.

The analysis

> [under] an option plan ... the company parts with no resources ... the compensation is paid for by the other shareholders through dilution of the value of their shares.
>
> (Skinner, 1987, 141)

The following analysis is taken from the issues paper.

The events that occur in connection with the granting and exercise of stock options are extraordinary, directly involving three parties simultaneously, not the usual two:

1 Employees who become prospective stockholders when contributing their services and who become stockholders on exercise of the options
2 The reporting entity
3 The existing stockholders.

Only the financial effects of the events *on the reporting entity* should be reported on by the reporting entity, and if other parties participate in such events, the reporting should be confined to the reporting entity's sides of the events (as stated in Chapter 8). Nevertheless, "the literature ... focuses on the effects *on the employees...*" (AICPA, 1982, par. 32).

Because the issue is complex, as the FASB assured us, the financial effects on the various parties must be carefully distinguished. These events occur:

1 The employees contribute services to the reporting entity.
2 The employees are granted stock options and become prospective stockholders.

- They may also be paid a salary, but here it is assumed that they aren't. That merely simplifies the analysis without biasing it. If you don't think so, drop the assumption and work through the analysis without it.
- One way to highlight the issue of reporting in connection with stock options granted to employees is to consider what the result would be of the then current practice of reporting no expense in that connection by companies that compensate all of their employees only by granting them stock options. That isn't entirely farfetched:.

John N. Lauer, chief executive of Oglebay Norton, a shipping company ... has gained notoriety in corporate circles for his insistence on being paid entirely in options...

(Strom, 2002)

3 The employees vest in their options.
4 The employees exercise their options and become stockholders.
5 The reporting entity uses up the services.

Events (1) through (4) were portrayed graphically by AcSEC in Exhibit 1 (Figure 18.1). All five events and their financial effects on all three parties were presented by AcSEC in Table 18.1. The exhibit and table show these financial effects *on the reporting entity*:

- It receives services from the employees (the employees become prospective stockholders).
- It may receive cash from the employees on their becoming stockholders.
- It uses up the services it received from the employees.

It receives the services and perhaps cash *at no cost* to itself. Do you believe that? It's key to the analysis. The argument supporting that conclusion follows.

The services are contributed to the capital of the reporting entity by employees who become prospective and then actual stockholders in nonreciprocal transfers, in accordance with the analysis of classes of events discussed in Chapter 3 and presented in Appendix A to that chapter, and in accordance with paragraph 5 of APB Opinion No. 29 (AICPA, 1973a):

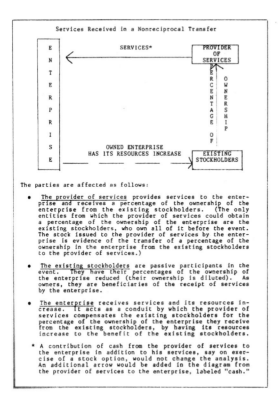

The parties are affected as follows:

- The provider of services provides services to the enterprise and receives a percentage of the ownership of the enterprise from the existing stockholders. (The only entities from which the provider of services could obtain a percentage of the ownership of the enterprise are the existing stockholders, who own all of it before the event. The stock issued to the provider of services by the enterprise is evidence of the transfer of a percentage of the ownership in the enterprise from the existing stockholders to the provider of services.)

- The existing stockholders are passive participants in the event. They have their percentages of the ownership of the enterprise reduced (their ownership is diluted). As owners, they are beneficiaries of the receipt of services by the enterprise.

- The enterprise receives services and its resources increase. It acts as a conduit by which the provider of services compensates the existing stockholders for the percentage of the ownership of the enterprise they receive from the existing stockholders, by having its resources increase to the benefit of the existing stockholders.

* A contribution of cash from the provider of services to the enterprise in addition to his services, say on exercise of a stock option, would not change the analysis. An additional arrow would be added in the diagram from the provider of services to the enterprise, labeled "cash."

Figure 18.1　Exhibit 1 (copyright 1982 by AICPA, reproduced with permission).

"Some ... transactions are nonreciprocal transfers between an enterprise and its owners." That is, when options are granted, the entity doesn't sacrifice assets or incur liabilities, as Skinner states in the quotation that opens this section; it merely makes a contingent commitment to issue shares at a later date. Because "an entity's own stock is not its asset..." (FASB, 1995b, par. 372), it incurs no cost in connection with making that commitment. When and if it issues shares based on its commitment, the issuance as to the reporting entity is merely formal recognition by it of the rearrangement of the proportional holdings of current and new stockholders. Who holds its stock and how those holdings change don't affect the reporting entity's assets or liabilities or cause it to incur costs, just as dealings in its stock on the stock market don't.

The reporting entity compensates the employees for their services by giving them stock options. The compensation doesn't cost the reporting entity anything; it *incurs no compensation cost*. As Figure 18.1 and Table 18.1 show, granting of the stock options constitutes contingent dilution of the rights of the existing stockholders. In other words, *the existing*

Table 18.1 Events and their effects in stock option plans

I. Events (at dates or over the periods indicated)	II. Effects on the enterprise	III. Effects on the employees	IV. Effects related to the plans on the existing stockholders (other than effects on them caused by effects on the enterprise, which they own)
1 At the grant date. Options are granted to the employees.	1 Acquires the prospect of receiving services and cash from the employees.	1 Acquire the prospect of obtaining rights to buy stock at less than the market price and of working for the enterprise throughout the vesting period.	1 Acquire the prospect of dilution of their ownership shares by issuances of stock to the employees on exercise of the options.
2. During the vesting period. a The employees render services to the enterprise and become vested.	2 a Receives the employees' services. Has a change in its prospects of receiving cash from the employees.	2 a Render services to the enterprise. Have a change in the prospect of obtaining rights to buy stock at less than the market price.	2 a Have a change in the prospect of dilution of their ownership shares.
b The market price of the stock may change.	b Has a change in its prospect of receiving cash.	b Have a change in the prospect of obtaining the right to buy stock at less than the market price.	b Have a change in the prospect of dilution of their ownership shares.
3 During the periods the employees' services are used up. The enterprise uses up employees' services. It may use them over the periods received or over other periods	3 Uses up the employees' services.	3 None	3 None
4 During the period between the vesting date and the exercise date. The market price of the stock may change.	4 Has a change in its prospect of receiving cash.	4 Have a change in the prospect of obtaining rights to buy stock at less than the market price.	4 Have a change in the prospect of dilution of their ownership shares.
5 At the exercise date. The employees exercise the options.	5 Receives cash.	5 Pay cash. Receive stock.	5 Have their ownership shares diluted.
6 At the expiration date. Options not exercised expire.	6 Loses the prospect of receiving cash.	6 Lose the prospect of obtaining the right to buy stock at less than the market price.	6 Loses the prospect of dilution of their ownership shares.

Source: AICPA (copyright 1982, reproduced with permission).

stockholders, not the reporting entity, incur the (contingent) cost. When the employees exercise the options, *the existing stockholders* incur a real cost of dilution:

> a portion of the proportionate interests of existing stockholders is transferred to other stockholders.
>
> (Melcher, 1973, 139)

> options ... impose ... additional costs on shareholders; the more options granted, the lower the return for investors, since their holdings are, one way or the other, diluted.
>
> (Strom, 2002)

Meanwhile, "the corporation ... goes on about its own affairs regardless of who owns its shares" (Arthur L. Thomas, 1975a, 8). Reporting the financial effects on the stockholders as compensation cost of the reporting entity violates the injunction stated in Chapter 8 referred to above that only the financial effects on the reporting entity should be reported.

Some contend that the reporting entity itself incurs a cost of dilution, for example,

> segregation or reservation [of securities for stock options] immediately eliminates the opportunity which the issuer would otherwise have of selling, or holding for future sale, the ... securities. The *cost* to the corporation of issuance of the [option] seems to me to be the value of the lost opportunities at the time of issuance.
>
> (Hackney, 1973, 307)

But Melcher decries such might-have-been reporting: "Discussions in those terms introduce irrelevant conditions; the accounting is not a matter of what would have happened if events were different. Rather, the accounting should recognize what did happen..." (Melcher, 1973, 182). (This conforms with a discussion at the beginning of Chapter 7.)

The contribution of services to the reporting entity by the employees who become prospective stockholders is similar to a contribution of assets to a reporting entity by purchasers of unissued stock. "Assets may ... be acquired ... for shares of stock or other equity in the enterprise. In these cases, costs ... do not exist" (Sprouse and Moonitz, 1962, 26). Most financial reporters haven't been able to understand that similarity. They are both nonreciprocal transfers *as to the reporting entity*, costing it nothing.

(They are reciprocal transfers *as to the contributors*, as shown in Figure 18.1 and Table 18.1—unusual ones, because the contributors give something valuable to one party, assets or services to the reporting entity, and get something valuable from another party, a proportionate share in the stockholding of the reporting entity from the existing stockholders—but the reporting entity isn't reporting on the financial effects of the events on the *contributors*.)

When a reporting entity receives a contribution of assets when issuing stock, it reports the assets at their current amounts at the date of receipt. When a reporting entity receives a contribution of services when granting stock options, it should similarly report the services at the dates of receipt at their current amounts at those dates: "employee services represent valuable consideration for which the entity should be accountable..." (Skinner, 1987, 141). In connection with stock options granted to employees, the reporting entity should report its receipt of services as contributions to the equity of the reporting entity at the current amounts of the services when received (dr. resources, cr. equity; no entry to cost or expense). When the reporting entity uses or sells the assets it received on issuing stock, it reports an expense because it sacrificed them. When it uses up the services it received on granting stock options, it should report an expense—of using up services, not of compensation for the receipt of services (dr. expense, cr. resources).

> A corporation may issue additional equity securities for ... services of officers and employees ... A corporation should recognize as additional equity an amount assigned to services received as consideration for securities issued ... measuring the amount to be assigned to services received and accounting for the corresponding ... expense are separate problems. Present accounting practices rarely recognize the services received ... for option stock.
>
> (Melcher, 1973, 153, 171)

The two entries are illustrated as a single entry for the receipt and using up of the services as the first illustrative journal entry in paragraph 293 of SFAS No. 123 (FASB, 1995b), except that the cost of using up the services is called "compensation cost" rather than "employee services used."

Because "making a reliable independent estimate of the value of services received is impracticable..." (Melcher, 1973, 172), a surrogate measure will usually be necessary. The value of the stock options at the date of grant is the most plausible surrogate.

The FASB contended that the *event* whose financial effects should be reported is the granting of the stock options. However, the events whose financial effects should be reported on are the receipt and using up of the services, and the granting of the stock options merely provides *evidence* of the magnitude of the event.

An irony is that though the FASB insisted that a reporting entity incurs a cost by granting options to employees, not by using up the services the employees contribute, in one place it stated the opposite, which is the conclusion of the above analysis: "issuances of equity instruments result in the receipt of ... services, which give rise to expenses as they are used in an entity's operations" (FASB, 1995b, par. 89). Similarly, the FASB published a Special Report authored by a member of its staff that conforms in every respect with the above analysis. For example, the report states:

> the "no cost therefore no charge" argument is unsound because it fails to appreciate that the debit entry made when shares or options are issued is to recognize the resources *received* by the entity, that is, the resources that another party has contributed to the entity ... Any charge to the income statement recognizes the ... *consumption* of those resources.
>
> (Crook, 2000, 10)

The federal government believes so strongly that reporting entities incur a cost in connection with employee stock options (it doesn't say whether that's because they grant the options or because they use up the services) that it permits deductions for them as expenses in their income tax returns. Johnston reported that "Recent annual reports filed by Microsoft and Cisco Systems indicate that they paid no federal income taxes in 1999 because stock options exercised by employees wiped out profits for tax purposes" (Johnston, 2000, C2).

The exposure draft and its fate

The FASB issued an exposure draft on June 30, 1993 (FASB, 1993b), which would have required reporting entities to report compensation cost for the granting of stock options. Though that disagrees with the analysis presented above and ignores the events that occur (as the FASB promised it would in its *Invitation to Comment* [FASB, 1984c]), it would have resulted in reporting costs, which may have been better than under APB Opinion No. 25 (AICPA, 1972b), because the reporting entity eventually incurs costs (as indicated in the above analysis) and application of the Opinion usually results in no reporting of costs.

Whether the exposure draft would have required reporting of costs in the amounts and in the periods implied by the analysis is unanswered. What do you think? At a meeting of AcSEC, a member said that the financial reporting results would be the same regardless of whether a conclusion was reached that (1) the reporting entity does incur a cost when options are granted, or (2) it doesn't incur a cost then but it at least eventually incurs costs some other way. However, though both conclusions can result in reporting costs in connection with granting stock options to employees, there is no way to tell in the absence of analysis whether sound reporting of the costs based on the two conclusions would or wouldn't materially differ in timing or amount or both.

What's worse, by asserting that the reporting entity does incur a cost simply by granting a stock option though it doesn't incur one that way, there is no way to counter those who contend that it doesn't incur a cost that way and that for that reason the reporting entity incurs no costs of any kind. For example, Schuetze stated that

No cash or other asset goes out of the enterprise and no obligation to pay cash arises when a stock option is granted or exercised, so there is no decrease in assets or net assets and *therefore nothing to account for except for the cash received when the option is exercised.*

(Schuetze, 2001, 23)

Similarly, "The Council of Institutional Investors ... agreed that options should not count as an expense because companies do not have to use cash to award them"[3] (Leonhardt, 2002, WK13).

In a recent conversation, the AcSEC member repented.

The expenses reporting entities incur in connection with using services received for which stock options are granted may be relatively small in comparison with most of the other expenses they incur, though, because they haven't been reported, we can't be sure. And Morgenson reported that

Sanford Bernstein & Company ... estimates that if the nation's 500 largest companies had deducted the cost of options from their revenue, their annual profit growth from 1995 to 2000 would have been 6 percent instead of the 9 percent that was reported.

(Morgenson, 2002, 12)

Regardless, compensation received through stock options is a significant part of the total compensation received by many people in the U.S.—for many, the majority of their compensation. They obviously don't want their stock options to be threatened or even to appear to be threatened, and they will do whatever they can to prevent this. And Bryant implied they might be threatened if reporting on them is changed: "One reason options are doled out so freely is that, because of favorable accounting rules, they don't show up as a charge against a company's earnings" (Bryant, 1998, WK2).

Financial reporting in connection with stock options was so contentious, therefore, not necessarily because the magnitudes of the amounts related to them are in the same league as the magnitudes of the other amounts reported by the reporting entities, but because those who receive stock options believed changing the reporting could threaten their stock options:

FASB's chairman ... Dennis Beresford ... says he scoffed at the dooms-day arguments during a heated discussion aboard one corporate jet. The executives he was debating invited him to exit the craft—at 20,000 feet

(Helyar and Lublin, 1998, B5)

the CEO of one of America's most successful companies ... said that if

---

3 Technically, the Council was right: using up the services received, not awarding the options, should count as an expense. But the quotation implies that the Council agreed that no expense should be reported at all in the circumstances.

the FASB was allowed to finalize the draft as proposed "it would end capitalism."

(Beresford, 1997, 83)

They had the muscle to do something about it because they receive so much money from stock options.

They didn't state their case that way, of course. They didn't say that if the rules in the exposure draft are enacted, their stock options would be threatened, they might be personally harmed. That isn't good public relations. They had to appear to be disinterested—and they did manage to appear so. However, their defense didn't extend so far as to contend that the users of financial reports would be harmed by such rules, because they weren't in the habit of considering the users and usually showed little or no awareness even of the existence of the users. And if they contended that, they couldn't have defended that position.

The way they stated their case was to contend that reporting entities would be harmed by such rules. For example:

Counting options as an expense would disproportionately depress the earnings of small companies, making it harder for them to sell stock and attract loans. This would be particularly onerous for Michigan's high-tech companies, which have sufficient difficulty convincing lenders that technology entrepreneurs exist outside California and Massachusetts.

(Crain's Detroit Business, 1994, 6)

The new accounting rule would "destroy the high-tech industry," warned the head of the American Electronics Association.

(Hitt and Schlesinger, 2002, A8)

That such companies would be harmed by such an improvement in information was doubtful, though, because users would adjust for the new reporting, and the efficient market hypothesis (to the extent that it's valid) would make the change irrelevant anyway. Further, if they would have been harmed, the user-oriented criterion of neutrality would have made that irrelevant anyway (their message was—the users, the *raison d'être* of financial reporting, be damned).

Or, they contended that we would be doomed: "The Financial Accounting Standards Board ... tried to end the anomaly. Corporate America protested en masse: Earnings would suffer. Stock prices would slide. Depression would ensue" (Helyar and Lublin, 1998, B5).

They chose the U.S. Congress as one of the audiences for their argument, as part of "an unprecedented lobbying campaign as a result of [the FASB's] proposal on accounting for stock options..." (Beresford, 1995, 56). The result was the preparation of a bill entitled the Accounting Standards Reform Act, which, if enacted, would have required the SEC to pass on all new standards approved by the FASB. The bill stated, in part: "any new accounting standard or principle, and any modification ... shall become effective only following an affirmative vote of a majority of a quorum of the members of the [Securities and Exchange] Commission" (Beresford, 1995, 57). The bill was proposed simply so the U.S. administration could pressure the SEC to prevent the FASB from making this particular exposure draft final. (Neuhausen was quoted as stating that "'The bill is clearly about stock compensation'" [John, 1994, 15]). That shows how strongly those who receive stock options felt their interests would be threatened and how much influence they had. However, they would have gotten more than they asked for:

> the ramifications extend well beyond the stock compensation project ... The SEC would become a sort of appellate accounting court ... Congress could easily step in to set accounting standards ... After being overruled a few times by the SEC the FASB would lose support and motivation ... there would be strong temptation to eliminate the "middle-man" and just have the SEC or another federal agency replace the FASB entirely. The next step might be a government takeover of auditing standards and procedures as well ...
>
> (Beresford, 1995, 57)

Not everyone in Congress was influenced. When the exposure draft was outstanding, "Senators Carl Levin and John McCain offered a bill that would have forced companies to count stock options as an expense against profits ... it died quickly" (Leonhardt, 2002, WK13). Senator Levin offered a similar bill in the wake of the Enron collapse (Hitt and Schlesinger, 2002, A1).

Then others got into the act. As the Chairman of the FASB put it:

> The Secretaries of Treasury and Commerce and the chairman of the National Economic Council spoke out against [the FASB's] proposal [on stock options]. The Senate Banking Committee conducted hearings on it. And one SEC Commissioner[4] condemned the proposal publicly, criticizing the FASB for adopting an attitude of "the truth will set investors free"—an attitude, incidentally, for which I find it hard to apologize ... President Clinton ... not[ed] that "it would be unfortunate if FASB's proposal inadvertently undermined the competitiveness of some of America's most promising high-tech companies."
>
> (Beresford, 1995, 56)

The position of the SEC Commissioner is remarkable considering that the SEC was established to protect investors. The position of the President is also remarkable, putting the needs of special interests above the needs of the users of financial reports and of the economic system that serves those needs.

4 Beresford told me it was J. Carter Beese.

In 2002, when the issue of financial reporting in connection with stock options granted to employees came to the fore again in the wake of the Enron collapse,

> the Senate Finance Committee ... noted that radical changes in the accounting ... for stock options could damage the U.S. corporate economy, and undermine start-up companies that use options as recruitment.
>
> (*Financial Times*, April 19, 2002, reported in AICPA, 2002)

The campaign contributions of people who have so much money because they receive stock options likely influenced members of Congress, the President, his cabinet members, his appointee, and his advisor to oppose the exposure draft:

> the largest contributions [of accountants] went to politicians who were known to oppose accounting reforms ... opposed by corporate management and viewed by others as in the interests of investors.
>
> (Staubus, 2004b)

> Sen. Dodd ... has accepted nearly $500,000 in accounting-industry contributions since 1989, the most of any sitting member of Congress ... He ... has resisted ... efforts in the mid-1990s to toughen standards for stock options.
>
> (Schroeder and Hitt, 2002, A12)

> this problem of candidates selling themselves and legislation to the highest bidder ... The current [campaign contributions] law ... is about who has the money and who has the power...
>
> (Friedman, 1998, A13)

> "Politicians make a profession of appeasing vested interests..."
>
> (Perfect, quoted in Shearer, 2000, 22)

> Since politicians depend on money from private interests to fund their campaigns, there's not much that can be done to reduce radically the influence industry holds over regulators.
>
> (John A. Byrne *et al.*, 2002, 78)

Although he stated no position on what financial reporting should be in connection with stock options granted to employees, the Chief Accountant of the SEC said: "accountants may have become cheerleaders for their clients on the issue of accounting for stock options issued to employees" (Schuetze, 1994, 62). This conforms with the analysis in Chapter 2 in the section "Incentives of outside auditors."

The stock options die was (temporarily) cast:

in the final analysis, the Board decided that there simply isn't enough support for the basic notion of requiring expense recognition [in connection with stock options granted to employees].

(Beresford, 1994, 1)

Bowing to political pressure and corporate opposition, the Financial Accounting Standards Board backed away yesterday from requiring companies to report as an annual expense the value of stock options given to executives and other employees ... Arthur Levitt Jr., the SEC Chairman, issued a statement ... call[ing] the result "evidence that private-sector accounting works well—benefiting investors and the public in general."[5] ... Business opposition to the stock-option proposal has been the strongest of any board proposal, including some that had far greater impact on profit and loss statements ... [FASB Chairman] Beresford said the board backed down in part because it feared the whole process of setting accounting standards "would be destroyed" if it did not.

(Norris, 1994, D1, D2)

Leisenring, the vice-chairman of the FASB, commented wryly: "Why is stock options the only subject on which the FASB is forbidden to act?" (Leisenring, 1994).

The FASB summed up the sorry episode:

the nature of the debate threatened the future of accounting standards setting in the private sector ... The Board chose a disclosure-based solution for stock-based employee compensation to bring closure to the divisive debate on this issue—not because it believes that solution is the best way to improve financial accounting and reporting ... the Board's decision not to require recognition of compensation expense based on the fair value of options issued to employees was not based on conceptual considerations.

(FASB, 1995b, pars 60, 62, 91)

5 It's ironical that a Chairman of the SEC could on the one hand oppose a proposal that one of his fellow commissioners described as resulting from "adopting an attitude of 'the truth will set investors free,'" as quoted above in the text, and which would have gone in the direction of telling the truth, and on the other hand answer his own rhetorical question, "What is the Financial Accounting Standards Board's great sin?" by stating: "It has asked companies to tell investors the whole truth about their financial performances" (Levitt, 1997). Six years after Levitt opposed the proposal, when he was about to retire as Chairman,

he said he regretted his actions in 1994, when he persuaded the Financial Accounting Standards Board to back down on a proposed rule that would have required companies to deduct the value of stock options given to executives and employees from their profits ... In retrospect, he said, he should have stepped aside and let the accounting board act... "I doubt that Congress would have come up with the votes to roll it back."

(Norris, 2000a, C1)

Translated, that means those who receive stock options and the companies that grant them would have taken whatever steps necessary to terminate the FASB had they not gotten their way. As usual, the users were the losers.

Borders, President of the Association of Publicly Traded Companies, later exulted that "'We have to recognize, as FASB did after its stock-option proposal, [that] highly controversial issues like this don't do these organizations any good'" (quoted in Plitch, 2001, C14). The message is that if the issuers put up enough of a stink about a proposal they don't like in order to have the issue labeled "highly controversial," the users are out of luck.

Perhaps the exposure draft would have had a better fate had it been backed by sound analysis. But that isn't likely. As of round one, golden rule II prevailed—those who have the gold make the rules.

The financial reporting standard-setting process should be changed to avoid repetition of such a deplorable result. Wyatt voiced a similar opinion:

> The experience with the stock option issue ... indicates that the preparer community and the auditor community may become so joined together over an issue that the underlying concept on which the FASB was based—diverse group representation that will work for the protection of investors—may be so badly fractured that consideration should be given to a different accounting standard-setting structure.
>
> (Wyatt, 1997, 130)

Round two

Movement on the issue began again with the International Accounting Standards Board. Norris reported about Herz, who was appointed to succeed Jenkins as Chairman of the FASB on July 1, 2002, that

> Herz said that "... conceptually, the right answer is that it is an expense." [Herz] said that if the [International Accounting Standards Board] does adopt such a rule, he would expect the [FASB] to see how users of financial statements reacted before deciding whether to go along with the international rule.
>
> (Norris, 2002b)

On March 12, 2003, the FASB voted to start a comprehensive project on reporting in connection with stock options granted to employees. And in its May 19–June 1, 2003 issue, *Accountancy Today* reported that the FASB

> voted unanimously that stock based compensation should be recognized as an expense in income statements, with amounts recorded at fair value measured at the grant date.
>
> (*Accountancy Today*, 2003, 1)

That treatment agrees with the analysis in this chapter if the services are used at the grant date, except that the expense would be called "compensation expense" rather than cost of services used up.

At first it was only a hope, however, because the Stock Option Reform Act, intended to block the full effect of the decision, was passed in the U.S. House of Representatives and a companion bill was introduced in the U.S. Senate.

Nevertheless, the federal government didn't block issuance of an SFAS on the subject this time, and the FASB issued SFAS No. 123 (revised 2004) (FASB, 2004a) in December 2004 with the provisions reported as quoted above in *Accountancy Today*. In paragraph 9, it basically agrees with the analysis in the issues paper and in this chapter:

> The objective of accounting for transactions under share-based payment arrangements with employees is to recognize in the financial statements the employee services received in exchange for equity instruments issued or liabilities incurred and the related cost to the entity as those services are consumed.

But it refers to the transaction as an "exchange," and it still refers, for example, in paragraph 12, to "compensation cost." Old habits die hard.

Debating points

1   Of course, issuing stock options to employees costs the reporting entity, and it should be reported as compensation cost.
2   The analysis in the text clearly and correctly shows that the reporting entity incurs no cost in issuing stock options to employees.
3   Issuance of stock for cash on the exercise of options should be the only recording in connection with employee stock options.
4   Expense for the using up of the employee services received in connection with the issuance of stock options should be reported when the services are used up.
5   No way exists to soundly measure the expense incurred in using up services received in connection with the issuance of employee stock options.
6   Regardless of the merits of the positions on the issues of reporting in connection with employee stock options, interference by governmental officials in the standard-setting process was detrimental to the interests of the users of financial reports.
7   Reporting entities have to be protected by governmental officials from run-away financial reporting standard setters.
8   The financial reporting standard-setting process worked fine during the entire episode of reporting in connection with employee stock options.

19 Alternative financial statement reporting practices

> The difficulty in making financial comparisons among enterprises because of the use of different accounting methods has been accepted for many years as the principal reason for the development of accounting standards.
>
> (FASB, 1980b, par. 112)

Alternative financial statement reporting practices emerged because of their decentralized development (see Chapter 10). It became conventional wisdom that investment and credit opportunities of companies using the alternative financial statement reporting practices could be meaningfully compared if and only if the alternatives were eliminated. (In spite of the conventional wisdom, eliminating the alternatives wouldn't be sufficient to lead to comparability, as discussed in Chapter 3.)

Standard-setting and alternatives

Financial reporting standard-setting was started because of that concern:

> Since its organization [in 1887] the American Institute of Accountants [now the AICPA], aware of divergences in accounting procedures and of an increasing interest by the public in financial reporting, has given consideration to problems raised by these divergences. Its studies led it, in 1932, to make certain recommendations to the New York Stock Exchange which were adopted by the Institute in 1934. Further consideration developed into a program of research and the publication of opinions, beginning in 1938, in a series of Accounting Research Bulletins.
>
> (AICPA, 1961, 5)

The Special Committee whose report led the Council of the AICPA to set up the APB in 1959 recommended making the reduction of the alternatives one of the Board's two goals:

> The general purpose of the Institute in the field of financial [reporting] should be . . . to determine appropriate practice and to narrow the areas of difference and inconsistency in practice.
>
> (AICPA, 1958b, 62, 63)

The Wheat Commission, whose report in 1972 led to the formation of the FASB, also recommended that reducing alternatives be one of its primary missions (AICPA, 1972c, 84). A president of the AICPA implied that there was no other significant objective of financial reporting standard-setting: "Our overall objective . . . is to reduce the number of alternative practices not justified by actual differences in circumstances. . ." (Trueblood, quoted in Davidson and Anderson, 1987, 118). Wyatt implicitly agreed: "The fundamental nature of standard-setting is to eliminate alternatives and generally to constrain freedom of behavior" (Wyatt, 1988, 20).

The FASB itself has supported that mission:

> The Board has considered the question of accounting alternatives at length . . . and has concluded that differences in accounting may be appropriate when significant differences in facts and circumstances exist, but different accounting among companies for the same types of facts and circumstances impedes comparability of financial statements and significantly detracts from their usefulness to financial statement users . . . Comparable reporting by companies competing for capital is, in the Board's judgment, in the public interest.
>
> (FASB, 1977b, pars 129 and 132)

But its concern for the users and the public hasn't yet moved the FASB to remove a number of such alternatives, such as the 3,628,000 alternative inventory methods allowed in the U.S. in any particular circumstance, discussed below.

Power to reduce alternatives

The committee on accounting procedure, which issued the Accounting Research Bulletins, didn't actually succeed in reducing the number of alternatives. The reason was that no one was obliged to follow the Bulletins, or in fact to pay any attention to them, or even to know about them. They were advisory and stated only preferences—they didn't and couldn't outlaw any practices.

The AICPA membership adopted six rules in 1934, such as:

> Unrealized profit should not be credited to income account of the corporation either directly or indirectly, through the medium of charging against such unrealized profits amounts which would ordinarily fall to be charged against income account.
>
> (AICPA, 1961, 11)

Though they probably were more influential than the ARBs, because the membership had voted on them, they were also not binding because there was no way to enforce them.

In its early years, the APB could also be ignored with impunity. That mocked the fanfare with which it was founded, with its research program and separate budget. So, in 1964, the AICPA Council gave the APB some (fairly dull) teeth with a resolution requiring a member of the AICPA to object to a report that violated an APB Opinion unless the treatment had other substantial authoritative support, and even if so, requiring the member to note the departure.

The meeting of Council at which this resolution was passed was the longest and most acrimonious in its history. Members castigated other members for proposing to restrict their freedom that way. Even advocating a requirement to note the existence of the APB was at the time considered treason. Denunciations rang through the halls of my CPA firm employer at the time at the thought of it: how could one CPA tell another CPA what to do? That year, an observer referred to "Accountants' fear of uniformity— intuitively, instinctively, and emotionally" (Miller, 1964, 44). It's now difficult even to imagine those licentious days.

When the FASB was formed in 1973, the AICPA quietly passed Rule 203 of its Rules of Conduct of its Code of Professional Ethics, requiring its members to object to reports that departed from standards issued by the FASB (except in remote circumstances that virtually never exist). The profession had been so softened up by that time that the furor over having to *note* a departure from a pronouncement of the APB wasn't only not matched when members were required to *object to* a departure from a pronouncement of the FASB; the members acquiesced so meekly that the action was hardly noticed.

Alternatives reduced

Though before Rule 203 members could accept departures from APB Opinions, as long as they noted them, departures were rarely made, so the APB did get down to the business of reducing alternatives. And the FASB continued the work.

A substantial part of the alternatives have by now been eliminated (though there were notorious cases and other significant areas in which they weren't, discussed below). Reporting in the following major areas was made uniform by the indicated pronouncements (though that doesn't mean that the best reporting was necessarily chosen; the opposite conclusion is reached more often than not in this book):

- *Leases*, by APB Opinions Nos 5 and 7 and SFAS No. 13
- *Pensions*, by APB Opinion No. 8 and SFAS No. 87
- *Income taxes*, by APB Opinion No. 11 and SFAS No. 109

- *Earnings per share*, in APB Opinions Nos 9 and 15
- *Intangible assets*, in APB Opinion No. 17 and SFAS No. 142
- *The equity method*, in APB Opinion No. 13
- *Accounting changes*, in APB Opinion No. 20
- *Stock options*, in APB Opinion No. 25 and SFAS No. 123 (revised 2004)
- *Nonmonetary transactions* in APB Opinion No. 29
- *Research and development*, in SFAS No. 2
- *Contingencies*, in SFAS No. 5
- *Foreign operations*, in SFASs Nos 8 and 52
- *Capitalization of interest*, in SFAS No. 34
- *Consolidation*, in SFAS No. 94
- *Other postretirement benefits*, in SFAS No. 106
- *Investments in debt and equity securities*, in SFAS No. 115
- *Business Combinations*, in APB Opinion No. 16 and SFAS No. 141

Alternatives not reduced—notorious cases

The profession tried but didn't reduce alternatives in these two notorious cases:

- Investment tax credit
- Oil and gas exploration

Investment tax credit

> the investment tax credit debate ... made it clear ... that accounting policy issues might at any time be subordinated to political considerations.
>
> (Solomons, 1986, 223)

The investment tax credit is a provision in the income tax law used by taxpayers in calculating their liabilities to the federal government.

As discussed in Chapter 9, in determining sound financial reporting on liabilities, the important issues are

- When the liabilities are incurred
- The amounts at which the liabilities are incurred
- The financial effects the incurrence of the liabilities have on the reporting entity
- When the liabilities are discharged.

Financial reporting shouldn't and can't consider the reasons behind any of the events financial reporting reports on; it should report on the financial *effects* of the events, not on their *causes* (see Chapter 9). It shouldn't and can't successfully consider

- Why the liabilities were incurred when they were
- Why the liabilities weren't incurred when they weren't
- Why the liabilities were incurred at the amounts they were
- Why the liabilities weren't incurred at amounts at which they weren't.

In determining how to report on the incurrence of income tax liabilities, the causes of their incurrence should be ignored. For that purpose, the investment tax credit is irrelevant. It's merely one of the myriad of income tax law provisions that cause what has to be reported on, which are the liabilities.

The argument about the investment tax credit has been between ignoring or paying attention to that particular cause of the amounts of income tax liabilities. Ignoring the investment tax credit is usually called the "flow-through method" of treating it. That terminology misleads, because it considers how to treat a cause of an event that affects the reporting entity—to flow it through—rather than how to treat only the financial effects of the event. All such causes, including that particular cause, should be ignored.

Paying attention to the investment tax credit in determining how to report on income taxes has had the effect of a recommendation to spread the difference between the income tax liabilities incurred and those that would have been (but weren't) incurred in the absence of the investment tax credit, that is, fiction. This treatment is similar to the spreading that is but shouldn't be done in interperiod income tax allocation (as discussed in Chapter 21). Such spreading serves the issuers' incentive for stability of income reporting, but it violates the user-oriented criterion of representativeness, among others, because it factors in what didn't happen.

As stated elsewhere in this book, fictitious assumptions (such as that used to justify spreading in connection with the investment tax credit) should have no place in financial reporting meant to disclose the history that occurred, not history that didn't occur or the difference between the history that occurred and history that didn't occur.

In its Opinion No. 2, "Accounting for the 'Investment Credit'" (AICPA, 1962), the APB chose the opposite conclusion, by requiring such spreading. President Kennedy insisted that that Opinion not stand (as indicated in Chapter 2): "the ultimate decision [on financial reporting for the investment credit was] made by the U.S. Congress ... and President..." (Staubus, 1977, 52). That decision was implemented by the SEC: "the SEC, knowing the government's wishes ... undercut the Board ... in Accounting Series Release 96 ... which stated that either accounting treatment of the tax credit was acceptable" (Solomons, 1986, 223). The infamous investment tax credit affair that followed nearly destroyed the APB when it was just getting started: "As a result of the sharp split in the financial community over the APB's position [in Opinion No. 2], it almost died before it was out of its swaddling clothes" (Moonitz, 1974, 18). The APB finally acquiesced and rescinded its Opinion No. 2 in its Opinion No. 4, which had the same title, and permitted either such spreading or ignoring the credit.

The sound move would have been to permit only ignoring it, for the reasons stated above. Opinion No. 4 was nevertheless an improvement over Opinion No. 2, because it at least permitted the sound treatment, though it didn't require it. But the APB did it for a wrong reason, to further the political goals of a U.S. president rather than to improve financial reporting for the benefit of the users and the economy.

Davidson and Anderson said that the affair led to the 1964 requirement to disclose departures from Opinions of the APB, discussed above: "The investment credit fiasco forced the profession to recognize that additional authority would have to be conferred upon the APB" (Davidson and Anderson, 1987, 118).

The APB tried again in 1971 to eliminate the so-called flow-through method of reporting on the investment credit. Congress put a stop to that. It passed a law forbidding it: "no taxpayer shall be required to use any particular method of account for the [investment tax] credit for purposes of financial reports subject to the jurisdiction of any federal agency or reports made to the federal agency" (Revenue Act of 1971).

Oil and gas exploration

Two methods of reporting on oil and gas exploration costs are now permitted:

- *Successful efforts*, in which the exploration costs of successful drilling are capitalized and expensed as production proceeds and the exploration costs of dry holes are expensed when they are discovered to be dry
- *Full cost*, in which the exploration costs of all holes are capitalized and spread over the production from the wet holes.

The first thing to notice is that the difference wouldn't occur if all the items on all balance sheets were always reported at current amounts. This is an argument about what acquisition cost to use, but acquisition cost itself shouldn't be used, as discussed in several chapters, especially Chapter 10.

Supporters of full cost like it because it serves the incentives of the issuers for stable income reporting. The FASB outlawed full cost in 1977, in its SFAS No. 19, "Oil and Gas" (FASB, 1977b). That seemed to end it.

That didn't end it. The smaller, newer oil- and gas-producing companies would have been made to appear less successful in comparison with the seasoned companies if they had had to switch to successful efforts than they did without switching:

> For an expanding firm, the full-cost method typically increases the level and reduces the variability of reported earnings and increases asset

values and shareholders' equity vis-a-vis successful efforts ... However, the reduction in earnings variability due to full cost is relatively lower, the larger the firm ... and this reduces the incentive of larger firms to select full cost.

(Watts and Zimmerman, 1986, 274)

Those companies got the ears of elected officials: "The new standard was violently opposed by a number of small companies that were using full cost; they used every means at their disposal, including appeals to Congress, to get the standard set aside" (Solomons, 1986, 225). They got to the SEC, which called a halt to SFAS No. 19 in Accounting Series Release 253 (Securities and Exchange Commission, 1978) before it became effective.

The FASB had to suspend the effectiveness of its prohibition of full cost in SFAS No. 19, which it did in its SFAS No. 25, "Suspension of Certain Accounting Requirements for Oil and Gas Producing Companies—an amendment of SFAS No. 19" (FASB, 1979a), in 1979. That suspension has been in effect at this writing for the intervening 27 years and it seems all but permanent now.

Meanwhile, the SEC temporarily muddied the waters. They not only pressured the FASB to suspend SFAS No. 19, they also mandated reserve recognition reporting, in which oil- and gas-producing companies would report their reserves at current amounts every year end rather than at full cost or successful efforts cost. That was a good idea: it conforms with the conclusion in Chapter 14. In their dissents to SFAS No. 19, Litke and Walters in effect agreed: "Conceptually ... it is necessary to account for mineral reserves at fair value ..." And Skinner said that

> both methods [full cost and successful efforts] produce irrelevant information. The information that matters is the physical quantities and qualities of the reserves, where they are situated, the extent to which they have been consumed and replenished over a reporting period, and some indication of their value.
>
> (Skinner, 1987, 452)

The SEC said in its release 33–5969 that reserve recognition reporting would go into effect three years after they promulgated it, but I didn't believe it and no one I knew believed it. Sure enough, the SEC backed down three years later, getting us back to square one, with both full cost and successful efforts permitted. Can one be blamed for suspecting that the whole exercise was the SEC's way of clamping down on the FASB for attempting to protect the users of financial reports without the SEC appearing to do so too blatantly? Listen: "Political interference ... was not motivated by any general sense that ... SFAS No. 19 was contrary to the public interest. It was *private* interests [that] caused the SEC to act" (Solomons, 1986, 226).

Alternatives not reduced—other significant areas

Standard-setters haven't reduced alternatives in such other significant areas as inventories, depreciation, construction contracts, and the cash flow statement.

Inventories

If you think the alternatives in the areas just discussed are bad, have you heard the one about inventories? Chambers once foolishly stated that U.S. financial reporting rules permit only 9100 alternative inventory methods in any particular situation (Chambers, 1969, 186). Because Chambers wasn't an American, Sterling, who is an American, suspected that Chambers might have understated the richness of U.S. inventory-reporting through chauvinism, and Sterling made his own calculation. As an American, I am proud to say that Sterling was right, that U.S. inventory reporting is far richer than Chambers said. Sterling demonstrated that we have 3,628,000 alternative inventory methods (Sterling, 1966, 181). Chambers apologized for being so "wantonly cursory" (Chambers in Sterling, 1966, 183; see Appendix – The author's favorite article).

Nevertheless, these sentiments have been voiced to and by the AICPA Special Committee on Financial Reporting:

> On the inventory side, I don't think there's much of a problem; there aren't that many accounting standards used and they are well understood ... users indicate that the current flexibility [in reporting on inventories and property, plant, equipment] is not a significant impediment for users' analyses, provided the methods used are disclosed.
>
> (AICPA, 1994b, II, 8a, 4; 1994a, 97)

The alternatives are all different ways of allocating acquisition cost. The extremely large number of alternatives makes support of acquisition cost for inventory based on the view that it's objective (regardless of what that term is supposed to mean) seem weak to say the least.

Endless arguments appear in the literature about the superiority of one method of inventory reporting at acquisition cost over another, such as the marvelous benefits or the dreadful detriments of direct costing. They're all arguments about the best way to stabilize reported income. Because there's no such thing as *the* cost of anything that has any jointness to it, which most inventories have, there's no way to demonstrate beyond doubt the superiority of any method over any other: "We believe that [the] problem [of inventory alternatives] reduces to a joint cost allocation and therefore is in principle unresolvable" (Sterling, 1970a, 278). A cost accountant once said to me that if someone selects an item in his inventory and gives him any amount in advance, he would be able to demonstrate that that amount is the cost of the item.

All currently accepted inventory methods conceal production and selling price gains while the inventories are held, and thus don't serve the needs of the users for complete reports.

Depreciation

> The cost of a purchased asset, net of sum-of-the-digits amortization, is not a faithful representation of any economic phenomenon, but instead the result of an accounting computation.
>
> (FASB, 2005, 6)

The variety of depreciation amounts possible under GAAP in any situation is smaller than that of inventory amounts, but the differences between two reports on two different depreciation methods or lives can be as great as or greater than the differences between two reports on two different inventory methods. Nevertheless, at least one user feels that *"If the inventory or depreciation method a company uses is clearly disclosed, there is no reason to restrict management's choice of the method that is most appropriate for the company"* (AICPA, 1994b, I, 67). Again, the argument is simply on different ways to apply the acquisition cost basis to stabilize income reporting: "depreciation is clearly a device for smoothing irregular capital budgeting outlays" (Devine, 1985b, 79n), so I don't care which way the argument goes: "There is no theoretical basis for preferring any one method [of accounting amortization] over any other" (Hendriksen and van Breda, 1992, 528).

Character and quality of arguments for and against the various acquisition-cost based inventory and depreciation methods

The arguments for and against the various kinds of acquisition-cost inventory methods, such as between absorption costing and direct costing, and between acquisition-cost depreciation methods, such as individual asset depreciation and group and composite depreciation, appear to have the same character and quality as the following arguments by Kepler:

> By what arguments do you affirm that the sun is situated at the centre of the world? ... arguments ... drawn from the dignity of the sun ... and from the sun's office of vivification and illumination in the world ... By what arguments is it proved that the sphere of the fixed stars does not move? ... it is not apparent for whose good ... it changes its position and appearances by being moved ... and ... it obtains by rest whatever it could acquire by any movement.[1]
>
> (Kepler, 1618–21, *Epitome*, Part I.2, Part II.1)

---

1 Fairness requires reminding you readers that Kepler was the first to realize and prove mathematically that the shapes of the orbits of the planets around the sun are ellipses, a seminal discovery in astronomy.

And listen to this sentiment of Coughlan:

> No knights of old searched for the Holy Grail with more persistence and devotion than the hundreds of accountants who seek the best method of pricing inventory. No alchemists sought a means of transmuting base metals into gold with more diligence than thousands of accountants now seek the best depreciation method. Compared to contemporary accountants, the knights of old and the alchemists were engaged in promising pursuits.
>
> (Coughlan, 1965, 523)

Carman provides an example of an argument against double-declining-balance and sum-of-the-years digits depreciation that, if nothing else, at least has the merit of being entertaining:

> [Financial reporters] have concocted several bastard schemes [of depreciation]. [They] have no more *raison d'être* than have square wheels. Their origins are as inglorious as are those of a mule. If something must be written in the stud-book then truth compels the statement that they are by Ineptitude out of Ignorance. At least two segmented [depreciation] schemes foaled by these progenitors have been given names ["straight-line" and "double-declining-balance"] and a description of them might well be entitled: Two Little Misbegots and How They Grew.
>
> (Carman, 1956, 456, 463)

And MacNeal condemned the whole exercise of arguing about current GAAP. He called us a profession "relying upon sophistry and specious reasoning to defend its ancient dogmas" (MacNeal, 1970, 176).

Let supporters of such nonrepresentational systems carry on the fight.

Construction contracts

Construction contracts are reported using either the percentage-of-completion method or the completed contract method. They result in significantly different net income trends reported by construction contractors. The percentage-of-completion method is preferred unless

> reasonably dependable estimates cannot be made [to implement the percentage-of-completion method] or ... there are inherent hazards that cause forecasts to be doubtful.
>
> (Schwartz and McElyea, 2002, 28, 36)

However, the percentage-of-completion method requires use of issuers' thoughts about the future, which Chapter 7 concludes shouldn't be used.

Further, both methods are based on the acquisition-cost basis, which Chapter 10 concludes shouldn't be used.

Cash flow statement

Chapter 20 discusses the two alternative methods of display permitted on the statement of cash flows and the misleading nature of one of them, the indirect method. This alternative is perhaps the least harmful, because it's the only one that doesn't affect comparisons of reported assets, liabilities, or income. Its real harm is that one of the alternatives, the indirect method, is not only uninformative but that it leads to such nonsensical ideas as that depreciation is a source of cash (discussed in Chapter 4).

The users yawn

Even the conventional wisdom cited at the beginning of this chapter that the existence of alternative reporting practices applied by two or more companies hinders comparability wasn't borne out by talking to professional users. The AICPA Special Committee on Financial Reporting found that

> Many users believe they can handle differences in accounting among companies, even in the same business, if they can obtain information that enables them to understand the differences and interpret them as clearly as possible. Differences in the way companies apply accounting rules should be allowed as long as there is disclosure of the application methods. Many users value information that is consistent over time more highly than information that is comparable among companies because they consider themselves capable of adjusting information to compensate for non-comparabilities resulting from use of alternative accounting procedures ... However, they usually are unable to adjust for inconsistent information resulting from business combinations accounted for by the purchase method, changes in accounting principles, and the like.
>
> (AICPA, 1994a, 34)

Maybe the users yawn because they feel, though perhaps they don't know, that contemporary financial statements don't represent much of anything outside themselves anyway.

The FASB said that though "comparing liquidity between two enterprises by comparing their current ratios would usually not be valid if one enterprise valued its inventory on a last-in, first-out basis while the other valued inventory on first-in, first-out..." (FASB, 1980b, par. 117), it said that "That kind of noncomparability ... is relatively easy to diagnose and, with sufficient disclosure, can be rectified by a user of the information" (FASB, 1980b, par. 118). If users say they are indifferent about interentity inconsistency, maybe they are. But why? Here is the opposite view:

It is commonly supposed that if companies disclose the bases of valuation and the methods used, any user of financial statements will be able to make due allowance for the differential effects when comparing statements having different bases. He may notice that they are different, but he has no means whatever of knowing the effects of the differences.

(Chambers, 1969, 190)

In any event, most alternatives are the result of the use of the acquisition-cost basis, of different ways to paint pretty pictures on the financial reporting map that don't correspond to anything in the financial reporting territory. That makes a mockery of the periodic call for tailoring alternatives to circumstances: none of them tied to acquisition cost correspond to any circumstances.[2] If and when the acquisition-cost basis is soundly supplanted, many of the alternatives will simply go away, and those bars to comparability will disappear.

Debating points

1   The only alternatives that can be reduced are the ones the issuers of financial reports don't care enough about.
2   The existence of alternative financial reporting practices is no big deal in such a practical endeavor.
3   The existence of alternative financial reporting practices is a travesty and a condemnation of the profession.
4   As long as the acquisition-cost basis rules GAAP, the existence of alternative financial reporting practices is inevitable; it's the basis, not the existence of the alternatives, that's the culprit.
5   Mocking alternatives the way Coughlan and Carman do doesn't further the improvement of financial reporting.

2 Though Sterling agrees that "there are no observations which could be used to confirm or disconfirm [any allocated amount]..." he was more circumspect than I in his conclusion: "I am unable to discover any particular circumstances which imply any particular method" (Sterling, 1979, 23n).

20 Display on financial statements

[The project on] reporting about the financial performance of business enterprises will be limited to the display of items and measures in financial statements . . . [It] will focus on form and content, classification and aggregation,
and display of specified items and summarized amounts on the face of all
basic financial statements . . .[1]

(FASB, 2002b, 6)

Specific issues exist in display on the balance sheet, the statement of income,
and the statement of cash flows.

Display on the balance sheet

Issues concerning display on the balance sheet involve classification of
certain assets and liabilities as current and subclassification of equity.

Classifying certain assets and liabilities as current[2]

The current practice of identifying [certain] assets and liabilities as
current . . . should be discontinued.

(Heath, 1978, 8)

The practice of classifying certain assets and liabilities as current and presenting their subtotals on the balance sheet began at the end of the 19th
century:

certain economists in the eighteenth and nineteenth centuries . . . made
a distinction between two types of assets. . . . long-term assets as "fixed

---

1 Can we hope that that project will rectify some or all of the faults discussed in
this chapter? I have given the FASB a copy of a draft of this chapter.
2 Much of this section is taken from Heath, 1978.

> capital" . . . money . . . tied up for only a short period . . . as "circulating
> capital."
>
> (Kam, 1990, 71, 72)

> Sometime in the last few years of the 1890s there arose the practice of
> comparing current assets of an enterprise to its current liabilities.
>
> (Horrigan, 1993, 287)

Such classification permits, for example, the calculation of working capital
and the current ratio. (The other assets and liabilities—presumably noncurrent ones—are generally simply listed and not subtotaled.)

The practice is still considered important. For example, the APB fought an
extended battle over the classification of deferred tax credit balances related to
current assets, resulting in a provision in AICPA, "Income Taxes" (AICPA,
1967), paragraph 57, that required that the balances be classified among the
current liabilities (even though that paragraph stated that they aren't liabilities!). Issuers would have preferred to classify them outside current liabilities,
to improve their calculated working capital amounts and current ratios.

The practice is sometimes held to be based on the nature of the assets and
liabilities classified as current and therefore essential and beyond challenge:

> in 1776 . . . Adam Smith . . . recognized [in *The Wealth of Nations*] that
> some of the assets of a business are purchased by the business for use and
> consumption in its operation and others are acquired to be modified in
> some way and then sold[3] and replaced so the process can be repeated.
> Accountants call these . . . current and fixed, or capital, assets.
>
> (Hill, 1987, 3, 4)

But

> there are no natural classes . . . no classification . . . is an end in itself . . .
> Classification is a purposive mental action . . . Objects *may* be classified
> only if they are perceived to have some property in common. Objects *will*
> be classified only if classification promotes the attainment of some purpose.
>
> (Chambers, 1966, 10, 85)

Therefore, no system of classification is beyond challenge. Items aren't classified if there is no purpose to it; they are simply listed.

If there is a purpose, the attribute of the items on which to base the classification is selected to achieve the purpose. A group of people may be
classified, for example by age, by gender, by height, or in many other ways,
or not classified at all, simply listed. If the practice of classifying certain

---

3 As discussed in Chapter 14, all assets are eventually sold.

assets and liabilities as current is to be justified, it can't be justified because it's a natural class. It must be justified on the basis that there is a purpose to that classification and that that classification serves the purpose best.

The purpose of classification of assets and liabilities as current is thought to be to help users determine whether the reporting entity currently has enough resources to pay its liabilities as they come due: "The balance sheet classifications should be appraised on the basis of whether they . . . help in the assessment of a firm's solvency" (Kam, 1990, 71). But it can't help them do that, because

- A reporting entity pays its liabilities when due with cash, not with its short-term assets, and it can't divest itself of its short-term assets if necessary to provide cash to use to pay its liabilities when due without gravely harming its business.
- The debt-paying ability of a reporting entity is dynamic, not static:

  neither the amount of working capital nor the working capital ratio is necessarily a good indication of the ability of the firm to pay current liabilities as they come due. This is because working capital is a static concept, and debt-paying ability is dynamic . . . the ability of a firm to meet its debts as they mature depends primarily on the outcome of projected operations; the pairing of current liabilities with current assets assumes that the latter will be available for the payment of the former.

  (Hendriksen and van Breda, 1992, 469)

- Increases in short-term assets don't necessarily indicate improved ability to pay liabilities when due; they might indicate just the opposite, that that ability is impaired, as discussed below.

The underlying concept was *pounce value*: "credit analysis . . . centered on the ability of a company to repay its debts if liquidation were to occur . . . its 'pounce' value" (Heath, 1978, 12). Creditors whose receivables are due supposedly could pounce like birds of prey on the short-term assets of their debtors if they aren't being paid on time. No creditor actually ever did that, but it sounded good.

A debtor entity pays its liabilities with cash. It gets its cash from cash flow, which is dynamic. Solvency analysis should reflect that, mainly by considering its statements of cash flows:

To fully understand a company's viability as an ongoing concern, an auditor would do well to calculate a few simple ratios from data on the client's cash flow statement . . . Without that data, he or she could end up in the worst possible position for an auditor—having given a clean opinion on a client's financials just before it goes belly up.

(Mills and Yamamura, 1998, 53)

and users' predictions of its future cash flows: "Cash flow analysis is critical in all credit rating decisions" (AICPA, 1994b, II, 1c, 77).

If a debtor is having trouble paying its liabilities, it needs to improve its cash flow or it will get into deeper trouble, eventually ending up insolvent. Divesting itself of its short-term assets in a crisis is no way to improve its cash flow. Even factoring its receivables is expensive and hurts its cash flow.

For a creditor to pounce on its debtor, the creditor has to sue it—the creditor can't just come in and pick up some cash, receivables, and inventory; it can't simply pounce on the short-term assets. All the assets are fair game in a lawsuit. Suing it would likely hurt the debtor's ability to pay. And "A creditor forces a company into liquidation only as a last resort ... 'Liquidation under bankruptcy is very costly, very tedious, and invariably disappointing'" (Dewing, 1953, 709n, quoted in Heath, 1978, 19 and 19n).

If the reporting entity is in cash flow trouble, its receivables may be paying more slowly or its inventory may not be selling well, and one or the other or both may therefore be increasing:

> "Then I tried to tell the story of our lovely inventory
> Which, though large, is full of most delightful stuff.
> But the banker saw its growth, and with a mighty oath
> He waved his arms and shouted, 'Stop! Enough!
>   Pay the interest, and don't give me any Guff!'
>
> Though my bottom line is black, I am flat upon my back,
> My cash flows out and customers pay slow.
> The growth of my receivables is almost unbelievable;
> The result is certain—unremitting woe!
> And I hear the banker utter an ominous low mutter,
>   'Watch cash flow.'"
>   (Bailey, 1975, quoted in Heath, 1978)

Also,

> I always check to see if inventories are piling up. With a manufacturer or a retailer, an inventory buildup is usually a bad sign ... FISH (first in, still here) ... is what happens to a lot of inventories ... I once visited an aluminum company that had stockpiled so much unsold material that aluminum was stacked up to the ceiling inside the building, and outside it took up most of the employee parking lot. When workers have to park elsewhere so the inventory can be stored, it's a definite sign of excessive inventory buildup ... On the bright side, if a company has been depressed and the inventories are beginning to be depleted, it's the first evidence that things have turned around.
>   (Lynch, 1989, 215, 216)

Children's Place Retail Stores Inc. investors sued the company ... The complaint claims company officials misled investors ... by failing to reveal its declining sales and burgeoning inventories...

(*The Record*, 1997b, A-13)

An increase in a reporting entity's working capital or in its current ratio, rather than being a sign of improved prospects of paying its bills, could therefore be a sign of increased difficulty in paying them. Current classification of certain assets and liabilities thus not only isn't informative but it could easily mislead. Heath's statement quoted at the beginning of this section that current classification should be discontinued is sound.

The orders of reporting assets and liabilities and additional disclosures recommended in Heath, 1978 (pages 76 to 78), or the following should be considered:

Because, for immediately prospective exchanges, the rate at which cash will become available is relevant, liquidity may be considered to be a generally useful principle of ordering individual items in a list of assets ... To distinguish the temporal priority of liabilities is critical.

(Chambers, 1966, 108, 109)

Subclassifying equity

Hendriksen and van Breda observed that

Classification of stockholder equities ... traditionally presented is an outgrowth of certain assumed legal and economic relationships, rather than being a result of a complete analysis of the needs of the various users of financial statements.

(Hendricksen and van Breda, 1992, 779)

And the FASB has said that

In financial statements of business enterprises, various distinctions within equity, such as those between common stockholders' equity and preferred stockholders' equity, between contributed capital and earned capital, or between stated or legal capital and other equity, are primarily matters of display that are beyond the scope of this Statement.

(FASB, 1985a, footnote 29)

Subclassifying equity has been denigrated even more than by calling it only a matter of display that way. Some have expressed the thought that equity perhaps shouldn't be subclassified on the balance sheet at all:

Presentation of the ... equity section in the balance sheet could be reduced to a single line item ... This article ... offers alternative

accounting presentations that will better inform users of financial statements about (1) corporations' compliance with state laws and (2) their
capacity for making distributions.

(Roberts *et al.*, 1990, 35, 44)

[the ratios at which] fully paid shares [are] initial[ly] issue[d], like . . .
historical [costs], are more likely to be misleading than informative . . .
we envisage a rule . . . to the effect that the stockholders' equity would
be shown at any time as one sum[4] . . .

(Chambers, 1966, 286)

If it's presented as a single amount, many complicated kinds of bookkeeping
entries would be avoided. That would be a boon for those who dislike complicated kinds of bookkeeping entries and for students in general. They
could skip, for example, the 21-page chapter Paton and Littleton devoted to
"Surplus" in *Standards*.

Solely a helpful concept?

Chapter 9 contains a conclusion that the equity of a reporting entity doesn't
exist apart from thinking about it, that it's solely a helpful concept, simply the
difference between the total of the reporting entity's assets, which exist, and
the total of its liabilities, which exist. For those willing to accept that view, it
may be sufficient to convince them that equity has no parts and can't be
divided into components that represent external phenomena. They may agree
with the suggestion not to subdivide equity and join a search for other ways to
accomplish what subclassification of equity attempts to accomplish.

(If any of the classes of stock causes the reporting entity to have noncontingent duties not under the discretion of the management or the board of directors to provide resources other than stock of the reporting entity to holders of
such classes of stock, the reporting entity should classify those duties as liabilities. In contrast, any contingent or discretionary duties of the reporting entity
to provide resources to holders of such classes of stock, such as preferred stock,
or to provide stock or other equity instruments of the reporting entity to such
holders, such as mandatorily convertible preferred stock, should merely be disclosed. Those duties shouldn't and can't be displayed as part of the reporting
entity's own equity in its own assets. The disclosures should be in enough detail
to inform the users, for example, of conversion clauses, of the priority of the
duties to the classes, the rates of contingent dividends if established, and any
cumulative dividends in arrears.)

Others may not be that easily convinced, however. They may agree with

---

4 Actually, equity should be shown as one difference, the difference between total
reported assets and total reported liabilities. Perhaps Chambers was referring to
an algebraic sum.

the following expressions that equity has components: "the components of stockholders' equity..." (Melcher, 1973, 100); "Existing balance sheet presentations of stockholders' equity segregate the various components according to whether they are contributed or earned" (Roberts *et al.*, 1990, 35). The following discussions of sources of equity and restrictions on dividends is for them.

Sources of equity

One of the two objectives that have been attributed to subclassifying equity has been to report its sources: "The two sources of invested funds are essential to understand the means of financing a corporation and to evaluate the existing capital structure" (Melcher, 1973, 127). The two main sources of equity are investments by stockholders (and perhaps governments) and income. (Other amounts added to equity are reported under current principles involving nonarticulation [discussed in Chapter 9], but they aren't sources of equity separate from income.) The purported component amounts reported by corporations in equity consist of paid-in capital (usually common stock and additional paid-in capital) and retained earnings. That sounds good, but it doesn't work. We fiddle with the amounts so much that nothing about sources of equity can be learned from them. The FASB acknowledged that

> transactions and events ... mix the sources and make tracing of sources impossible except by using essentially arbitrary allocations. Thus, categories labeled invested or contributed capital or earned capital may or may not accurately reflect the sources of equity of an enterprise.
>
> (FASB, 1985a, par. 214)

For example, current reporting on stock dividends[5] rearranges the amounts

---

5 These are events with no substance done as a subterfuge—the assets, the liabilities, the stockholders' relative holdings, and everything else except evidence of rights remain unchanged. The directors want the stockholders to think they received something when they didn't:

> The proportionate interests of stockholders [in the assets of a corporation] are not changed by a common stock ... dividend ... the interests ... are the same ... but are represented by more stock certificates, more pieces of paper ... labeling the distribution a dividend hides [its] significance...
>
> (Melcher, 1973, 39, 214, 219)

The AICPA committee on accounting procedure acknowledged the misconception in the minds of recipients of so-called stock dividends and recommended financial reporting to safeguard the recipients from their misconception (AICPA, 1961, 51). The only sound way to safeguard the recipients from their misconception would be to prohibit stock dividends. A dissenter to ARB No. 43 (AICPA, 1953b) disagreed: "stock dividends should be regarded as marking the point at which corporate income is to be recognized by shareholders ... He believes the arguments regarding severance and maintenance of proportionate interest are unsound..." But corporate income should be "recognized" only by the corporations earning it; *shareholder income* should be "recognized" by shareholders.

without changing the sources. Dividends are deducted from retained earnings though the source of the cash can't be identified. Quasi-reorganizations terminate any semblance of source designation. That was demonstrated by the feeble requirement of AICPA, "Restatement" (AICPA, 1953b), Chapter 7(a), paragraph 10, to date earned surplus (retained earnings) from the date of the quasi-reorganization.

The worst aspect of using the balance sheet to depict the sources of equity is that it's a current, static statement and sources are matters of history. If the sources of equity need to be known for any current decisions (no one has demonstrated that they do, and our getting along fine in spite of their current obfuscation shows that they don't), they should be provided by historical reporting of their amounts period by period to show their trends, though in any event such reporting for any more than, say, ten years would be ancient history and not helpful.

Restrictions on dividends

To protect the creditors of corporations, state laws and regulations, court decisions, and agreements restrict the dividends they may pay to their stockholders. Historically, the restrictions have had some relationship to amounts reported on balance sheets. And that relationship has been praised:

> A distinction between invested capital and retained earnings has relevance to stockholders. For example, when cash dividends are distributed, stockholders are entitled to assurance that they are based on current or past profits and do not constitute merely a return of some of the cash or other assets originally invested in the enterprise or of previous earnings converted[6] into invested capital.
>
> (Sprouse and Moonitz, 1962, 42)

But the laws and regulations vary from state to state and their interpretation varies from court to court and from time to time. The laws, regulations, and interpretations aren't tied to changes in financial reporting standards and practices:

> the traditional view is outdated given the recent changes in state corporation codes that govern distributions to stockholders ... According to the 1950 Model [Business Corporation] Act, a corporation was permitted to make distributions to stockholders so long as the corporation was not insolvent ... insolvency is now defined by the 1984 Revised Model Business Corporation Act as either (1) the inability to pay debts as they come due *or* (2) as an excess of liabilities over asset *fair values* ... the

6 Such "conversions" occur only in the financial reporting map.

January 1, 1988 [annual report of] Holiday [Corporation showed a legal] $1.55 billion dividend, financed with borrowed funds, [which] not only exceeded the corporation's retained earnings but total stockholders' equity as well by more than three quarters of a billion dollars ... only Holiday's management had information about the fair values of the assets [on which the dividend was based].

(Roberts et al., 1990, 35, 36, 37, 38, 41)

Simply looking at the amount of retained earnings reported under GAAP doesn't tell anyone whether the reporting entity may legally pay dividends, and, if so, how much. That's a complicated question, and even lawyers with access to all the records of the reporting entity struggle to answer it: "a final determination of stated capital is a legal decision subject to court interpretation and not basically an accounting problem" (Hendriksen and van Breda, 1992, 781).

Disclosure of the factors affecting the legality of dividends would be more informative and less likely to mislead than reporting retained earnings as a so-called component of an indivisible amount of equity for that purpose:

> current financial statement disclosures do not include such basic information as what legal restrictions exist regarding distributions to stockholders..., whether ... a corporation is in compliance with state legal requirements, or the corporation's capacity for making distributions.

(Roberts et al., 1990, 36)

Display on the statement of income

Income and expense items don't all occur regularly. Some have been called unusual, extraordinary, noncore (AICPA, 1994a, 81), and so on. Financial reporting standards have attempted to result in informative reporting of them, but the users of financial reports believe they have been unsuccessful (AICPA, 1994a, 80). The users have developed a concept of core earnings to sort out such items for themselves.

The AICPA Special Committee on Financial Reporting has recommended that we financial reporters specify components of core earnings and its total on the statement of income, based on each reporting entity's view of its items that constitute those components[7] (AICPA, 1994a, 83, 84). Though such classification is really part of financial analysis rather than financial reporting, and additional disclosure could facilitate determination of core earnings by the users rather than by us financial reporters, it conceivably could be a service we financial reporters can helpfully provide to users, and it

---

7 That's one of the relatively few recommendations made by the Committee for changes on the face of financial statements.

will be interesting to see how the recommendation is handled by standard-setters and regulators.

A recommendation is made in Chapter 17 to classify all items involved in enhancing the prospects of the reporting entity that are charged directly to expense as investments in prospects. Such items are currently, for example, most costs of intangibles and research and development costs. If the recommendations in Chapters 14, 15, and 23 are adopted, for example, they would also include the cost of goodwill, the excess of the acquisition costs of assets over their selling prices at the dates of acquisition, and the excess of the risk-free funding amount of liabilities at the date of borrowing over the proceeds of the borrowing.

Display on the statement of cash flows

The two permitted methods of displaying data on the statement of cash flows are called the *direct method* and the *indirect method* (FASB, 1987b, pars 27 and 28). The FASB holds that the direct method is preferable:

> The more comprehensive and presumably more useful approach would be to use the direct method in the statement of cash flows and to provide a reconciliation of net income and net cash flow from operating activities in a separate schedule...
>
> (FASB, 1987b, par. 119)

The GASB now requires the direct method in Statement No. 34 (GASB, 1999), paragraph 105, which eliminates the permission given in its Statement No. 9 (GASB, 1989), to use the indirect method.

Besides, the direct method reports amounts that belong in a statement of cash receipts and cash payments—cash receipts and cash payments. The indirect method reports some amounts that belong in such a statement but others that don't, because they don't affect cash, such as depreciation.[8] The noncash items reconcile the statement of cash flows and the statement of income. Somehow we financial reporters haven't gotten over the idea that a cash flow statement is just some kind of an offbeat income statement, so we put the reconciling items in to make it look more like an income statement. Because it's relatively new, we haven't yet caught on that it's an independent, valuable statement in its own right and has an advantage (under the direct method) over current income statements of not incorporating allocations.

The reconciling items don't belong in a financial statement. They are worksheet adjustments, not information on the subject of the statement (and they duplicate items reported in the income statement). Financial reporters should keep their worksheets to themselves:

8 See Chapter 4 for expressions of the view of some that depreciation does affect cash.

The indirect method is basically a set of work sheet adjustments ... It is analogous to calculating income by subtracting stockholders' equity at the beginning of the year from stockholders' equity at the end of the year, then adjusting the difference [for] nonincome items, such as dividends and [transactions in the company's] capital stock ... if accountants were to prepare income statements in that way ... users ... would begin to describe dividends, for example, as a "source" of profits the same way they now describe depreciation as a "source" of funds ... The indirect method of calculating cash provided by operations is pernicious because it ... reinforc[es] the incredible notion that ... depreciation [is a] source ... of cash.

(Heath, 1978, 126, 127)

An observer (a representative of the CFA Institute [before May 2004, the AIMR]) did state that

it is asserted by many reporting firms that they do not keep their records in such a way as to permit reporting operating cash flows in gross amounts, thereby making the direct method prohibitively expensive to implement.

(AICPA, 1994b, II, 5c, 6)

But that observer said that "the ... argument ... is unpersuasive" (AICPA, 1994b, II, 5c, 6) The AIMR itself agrees. It reports "overwhelming ... support for the direct method by virtually all professional users of financial statements in the United States and Canada..." (Association for Investment Management and Research, 1993, 66).

Financial reporters are capable of remarkable feats when the feats serve their incentives. They could accomplish this, which isn't a remarkable feat, to serve the users were they sincerely interested in the users' welfare.

Only the direct method of display in statements of cash flows should be permitted.

Debating points

1 We shouldn't muck around with time-honored practices such as the current classification on the balance sheet and subclassification of equity.
2 Current classification in the balance sheet and subclassification of equity are insupportable now if they ever were supportable.
3 Current classification is necessary to aid the users in a variety of ways.
4 Subclassification of equity is necessary to present vital information.
5 The indirect method of presenting cash flows in the statement of cash flows is ludicrous.
6 Issuers shouldn't be prevented from presenting the statement of cash flows any way they please.

21 Reporting on income taxes

Deferment of income taxes has become a political issue.

(Kam, 1990, 339)

The AICPA committee on accounting procedure observed in 1944 that

> basic difficulties arise in connection with income taxes where there are material and extraordinary differences between the taxable income on which they are computed and the income reported in the income statement under generally accepted accounting principles ... As a result of such [differences] the income tax legally payable may not bear a *normal* relationship to the income shown in the income statement and the accounts therefore may not meet a *normal* standard of significance ... Such a result ... can readily be shown to be contrary to the principles of allocation which lie at the root of all accounting.
>
> (AICPA, 1944a, 185, 186, emphasis added)

Thus began the *normal*ization of income tax expense. McKnight noted that the "practice of interperiod tax allocation is referred to in the utility industry as normalization"[1] (McKnight, 1999, 27, 29).

Henderson and Peirson objected: "the recognition of future tax ... result[s] in undesirable profit normalization" (Henderson and Peirson, 1980, 435). And a user agreed with them: "Normalization ... is the province of financial analysis..." (AICPA, 1994b, I, 43). Further, if you agree that allocation, rather than being "at the root of all [financial reporting]," shouldn't even ever be used in financial reporting (as concluded in Chapter 10), you might not need to read on. You might immediately decide that income taxes shouldn't be allocated.

---

1 Normalization in financial reporting by reporting entities subject to rate-making is within the scope of this book. However, normalization for rate-making purposes is beyond the scope of this book.

However, such normalization is accepted by most of us financial reporters, for example:

> Proponents of defer[red taxes] state the following . . . [otherwise] the amount of income tax expense would be subject to wide variability . . . Net income would not be representative of the performance of the company . . .

> (Kam, 1990, 337)

Of course, few items that go into an average are representative of the average:

> incomes . . . are subject to fluctuation, from a modest to a marked degree . . . [they] are not representative of the average or long-run effects of operations.

> (Chambers, 1966, 261)

Were they all, for example, a weatherperson would have to report that the temperature was 50°F all day every day in spring if that's the average springtime temperature in the area. To paraphrase the proponents to whom Kam refers, "Otherwise the temperature would be subject to wide variability." Similarly, "We would all recognize it as an error if the weather service 'deferred' a flood and allocated it evenly over a future expected drought" (Sterling, 1979, 226).

One observer asserted that income tax allocation doesn't involve stabilizing income reporting, reducing wide variability: "Interperiod tax allocation isn't a smoothing device. It is an attempt to produce a conceptually sound approach to periodic income" (Defliese, 1983, 98). He didn't attempt to defend that position.

A prime early example of differences between taxable income and GAAP income was caused by certificates of necessity issued during the Korean War under Section 124A of the Internal Revenue Code, covering emergency facilities considered essential to the war effort and discussed in AICPA, "Emergency Facilities," issued in 1952. The certificates permitted the owners of the facilities to depreciate them for income tax purposes over five years. However, the owners predicted that the facilities would last longer, say 20 years, and they depreciated the facilities for financial reporting purposes over those longer lives.

The owners didn't like the income reporting results those certificates caused. For the first five years of the lives of the facilities, they received large income tax depreciation deductions on the facilities and thereby incurred relatively low income tax liabilities in those years. For the rest of the lives of the facilities, they received no income tax depreciation deductions on the facilities and thereby incurred relatively high income tax liabilities in those years. That made their reported income less stable and lower in later years, two characteristics of financial reports that issuers abhor.

Deferred taxes

To save the day, we financial reporters invented interperiod income tax allocation, usually called *deferred taxes*, to make reported income more stable, to normalize the tax rate rather than leave it to the people who should normalize it, the users (an analyst told the AICPA Special Committee on Financial Reporting, "we try to normalize the tax rate" [AICPA, 1994b, II, lb, 47]).

The alternative to deferred taxes is sometimes referred to as cash basis reporting, for example, "Otherwise the sale would be on an accrual basis and related tax effect on a cash basis" (Kam, 1990, 33). However, the alternative requires reporting liabilities for income taxes that have appeared in income tax returns but haven't yet been paid, so it's not cash basis reporting. The view that the alternative to deferred taxes is cash basis reporting reflects the erroneous view that accrual requires allocation—indeed, that accrual is virtually synonymous with allocation (see Chapter 9).

Deferred taxes reports income tax expense for financial reporting the way it would have been reported, for example, had depreciation deductions been taken for income tax purposes in the same amounts and in the same years as depreciation expense was reported for financial reporting (though the deductions weren't in fact taken that way). In the words of Bulletin 23: "the amount of income taxes to be allocated to the income statement should be the amount that *would have been* payable if [events had occurred differently from how they occurred]" (AICPA, 1944a, 187, emphasis added). A dissent to Bulletin 23 complained that:

> No expense other than federal income and profits taxes is allocated on the basis of applying to a given transaction so much of the expense as would not have occurred if the transaction to which the expense is attributed had not taken place.

Such reporting on what might have happened but didn't is dismissed as unacceptable in general in the beginning of Chapter 7.

They invented a slogan for deferred taxes: let the tax follow the income: "What the income statement should reflect under this head ... is the [income tax] expense properly allocable to the income included in the income statement for the year" (AICPA, 1944a, 186). It sounds good: "Many accountants argue that income tax is an expense which is uniquely related in some way to accounting profit"[2] (Henderson and Peirson, 1980, 422). Few question it. (It's questioned below.)

2 That could be read as "many want it to be so."

The differences between the amounts of depreciation deducted for income tax purposes and expensed for financial reporting purposes, for example, were called timing differences. A number of timing differences emerged, some of which resulted in the extension of deferred taxes, and some of which didn't. Further, the methods used to implement deferred taxes differed from financial reporter to financial reporter.

Three methods of deferred taxes developed: the deferred method, the liability method, and the net-of-tax method.

The deferred method

Under the deferred method, the so-called tax effect of a timing difference is excluded from the computation of income for financial reporting for the year and stored in the balance sheet as a deferred credit to expense. Such an amount is a what-you-may-call-it, one of the kinds of liabilities referred to in the definition of *liabilities* in AICPA, 1970c that aren't obligations, that don't represent anything outside the financial statements (see Chapters 4 and 9).

In the depreciation example, income tax depreciation deductions exceed depreciation reported for financial reporting in the early years of an asset's life. In those years, a deferred credit builds up in the balance sheet. Later, the timing difference on the asset reverses, and depreciation reported for financial reporting on the asset exceeds income tax depreciation deductions. In those later years, the deferred credit decreases. But other timing differences usually occur, based on other assets, resulting in other deferred credits more than making up for the ones decreasing.

Under the deferred method, a deferred credit is an amount saved, supposedly part of history,[3] which doesn't change. It's not a liability, which can change. For that reason, amounts deferred aren't subsequently changed for changes in income tax rates. Also, the compound interest formula isn't applied to the deferred credits, as it is for liabilities: the deferred credits aren't discounted.

The liability method

Under the liability method, the difference is called a temporary difference, whose so-called tax effect is also stored in the balance sheet, but this time called a deferred tax asset or a deferred tax liability, supposedly a resource or an obligation. Under the liability method, amounts deferred are subsequently changed for enacted changes in income tax rates. However, whether the amounts should be discounted is up in the air and is not now permitted.

---

3 But, as discussed in Chapter 13, a saving, the difference between what happened and what didn't happen, isn't part of history. History is simply what happened.

The net-of-tax method

Under the net-of-tax method, the so-called tax effect of the timing dif-ference is excluded from the computation of income for financial reporting for the year and added to or deducted from the net amount at which the asset or liability that gave rise to the timing difference is reported. For depreciable assets: "the loss of future deductibility for income-tax purposes of the cost of fixed assets [is reported] by [a] credit to an accumulated amor-tization or depreciation account ... applicable to such assets" (AICPA, 1958a, par. 7). Or an asset may be reported at current selling price in the balance sheet, with an increase in its current selling price during the year reported in the statement of income, but the increase isn't included in taxable income for the year. The so-called tax effect of the resulting timing difference is deducted from the amount at which the asset is reported. The net amount is the current selling price less the portion related to the current selling price of the income tax related to the asset that might in the future be incurred in the year the asset is sold.

Discounting isn't involved, because no liability is involved. Changes in income tax rates apparently aren't reflected currently, but we don't know for sure, because that issue has apparently never been discussed and the net-of-tax method has rarely if ever been used.

Comprehensive interperiod income tax allocation

By the 1960s, deferred taxes was in disarray, as discussed above. Some timing differences were subject to deferred taxes and some weren't, and several methods of deferred taxes were in use.

Accounting Research Study No. 9

The AICPA accounting research division determined that a majority of the members of the Accounting Principles Board favored comprehensive inter-period income tax allocation, that is, they favored deferred taxes, and they wanted all timing differences included. It also determined that the Board members preferred to limit the permitted methods to one.

The division stated that "whether taxes should be allocated or whether the taxes currently payable should be the income tax expense for a period has never been adequately studied" (Storey, 1966, vii). It concluded, however, that that question had in effect been settled by vote, and the only question that remained to be studied was which method of comprehensive interperiod income tax allocation should be required. It considered the three methods discussed above and whether the amounts they produced should be affected by discounting or by changes in income tax rates. The resulting study (Black, 1966) recommended comprehensive interperiod income tax alloca-tion using the liability method for credits and the deferred method for debits on the balance sheet, implied that income tax rate changes should be reflected, and stated that the amounts should be discounted.

The study rejected the net-of-tax method because of its complexity.

APB Opinion No. 11

In 1967, the APB issued its Opinion 11 (AICPA, 1967), which agreed with the study that comprehensive interperiod income tax allocation was necessary: "The APB decided by a mere assertion . . . that comprehensive allocation is an integral part of the determination of income tax expense" (Kripke, 1989, 23). But it disagreed with the study on its preferred method. It required the deferred method for all amounts, acknowledging in paragraph 57 that the deferred debits and credits resulting from deferred taxes aren't assets and liabilities "in the usual sense." (That's its way of saying that they aren't assets and liabilities.) It didn't permit discounting or reflection of income tax rate changes, because it treated the deferred amounts as what-you-may-call-its. As was its custom, the APB didn't give reasons for its choices.

SFAS No. 109

The FASB's Conceptual Framework outlawed the what-you-may-call-its presented by the deferred method: "Only the deferred method [of deferred taxes] that is prescribed by APB Opinion No. 11, *Accounting for Income Taxes*, does not fit the definitions [of the elements of the reporting entity represented in financial statements]"[4] (FASB, 1985a, par. 241). It therefore had to replace its Opinion No. 11 or prohibit deferred taxes. The FASB replaced the deferred method of deferred taxes of APB Opinion No. 11 with the liability method of deferred taxes in its SFAS No. 109 (FASB, 1992) (after briefly issuing SFAS No. 96 [FASB, 1987c] to essentially the same effect), the currently effective pronouncement on the subject.

SFAS No. 109 requires reflection of enacted income tax rate changes but defers consideration of discounting. Were the credit balance amount in the balance sheet based on SFAS No. 109 a liability (the discussion below concludes that it's not), not discounting it would be reporting it like a zero-coupon bond at its gross amount, which would give highly unsatisfactory results (as discussed in Chapter 15). However, discounting it would prevent it from providing the income statement results desired, as discussed below.

The rationale

The slogan cited above, that the taxes should follow the income, incorporates the rationale underlying deferred taxes: income tax expense (taxes)

---

4 The text concludes below that the liability method also doesn't fit the definitions.

should be reported in the same periods (follow) as the events (income) giving rise to the income taxes, regardless of when those events affect taxable income. The purpose is to avoid distortion. For example, the AICPA committee on accounting procedure said that "The cases that are likely to call for allocation are those in which transactions affecting the income tax ... would have a distorting effect on net income..." (AICPA, 1953b, Chapter 10[B], par. 7). It's an application of the nondistortion guideline (see Chapter 2), an income statement device. The purpose is to bring reported income tax expense into a desired relationship with reported income. It serves the issuers' incentive for stable income reporting: "Most analysts have viewed tax allocation as a form of income smoothing and accepted it as such" (Burton and Sack, 1989, 111). It's a product of starting with results rather than analysis for the benefit of the users.

The analysis

Analysis would question the slogan. Why should taxes follow income (besides serving the incentives of the issuers)? That issue is analyzed here,[5] starting with the FASB's own analysis.

The effects on the balance sheet

The issue has always involved *when* income tax expense should be reported in the *income statement*. The effects on the *balance sheet* have always been an afterthought. But the Conceptual Framework not only outlawed what-you-may-call-its, it also said that expenses are incurred by definition only by reducing or giving up assets or incurring or increasing liabilities. So deferred taxes automatically became an issue for the balance sheet. For deferred taxes to be legitimate now, the items reported under it on the balance sheet have to represent assets and liabilities that are resources and obligations.

Are they liabilities?[6]

The author of Accounting Research Study No. 9 offered this reason for his belief that the credit balances from deferred taxes are liabilities: "A postponed tax meets the test of an estimated liability because future payments

---

5 Some of the analysis and the conclusion in this section are similar to the analysis and conclusion in Rosenfield and Dent, 1983.
6 Deferred tax assets also result from the application of SFAS No. 109 (FASB, 1992). The arguments for the view that no deferred tax assets exist are virtually the same as those below in the text for the view that no deferred tax liabilities exist, especially the second fatal defect of the statement in paragraph 79 of SFAS No. 109 (FASB, 1992) in support of test no. 3.

are expected to arise from current and past transactions" (Black, 1966, 46). (The reason is challenged below.) Others countered that "Users simply do not see a tax liability existing when the tax law does not impose an obligation to pay. Such a result is counterintuitive..." (Burton and Sack, 1989, 111). One observer defended its being treated as a liability not because it conforms with the definition of a *liability* but simply because he likes the results of treating it as a liability, as discussed in Chapter 3.

If deferred taxes aren't liabilities, if the reporting entity doesn't now owe[7] any of the taxes that may appear in its future income tax returns and if the amounts presented on the right side of the balance sheet under the liability method of deferred taxes therefore don't satisfy the number one user-oriented criterion of representativeness, the liability method is unsound, and only the net of tax method (which is dealt with below) is left.

"Interest-free loan"?

A general defense of the existence of a liability for deferred taxes is the idea that the government provides an "interest-free loan" by permitting taxpayers to report income later or expenses earlier for income tax purposes than for income statements:

> Messrs. Bows, Broeker, and Burger ... believe ... the Government sponsors a benefit by providing the use of tax funds during the deferment period...
>
> (AICPA, 1972a, Bows, Broeker, and Burger, dissent)

> The reference to deferred taxes as an interest-free loan from the government has become prevalent, and all knowledgeable users now understand it.[8]
>
> (Defliese, 1983, 96)

> the nature of the deferred tax balance is quite clear ... The government has made a deliberate investment in business corporations...
>
> (Hill, 1987, 77)

> The availability of what are effectively interest-free loans, obtained from the U.S. Treasury, reduces the requirements for other sources of capital, thereby reducing capital costs.
>
> (McKnight, 1999, 27, 33)

---

7 Some supporters of deferred taxes might hold that a liability doesn't have to be "owed," at least not currently. If not, such an item exists only in the financial reporting map.

8 This was in reaction to an article Bill Dent and I had published. I guess that means that we're not knowledgeable users.

However, for taxpayers in their roles as taxpayers, the government as tax collector is only bad: sometimes less bad, sometimes more bad, but always only BAD (Figure 21.1) The basis of the interest-free loan concept seems to be, in contrast, that if the government as tax collector has been *less bad* to you than it might *otherwise* have been, then it has been *good* to you. But taxpayers are permitted to follow the rules of the government as tax collector to figure the least amount required and the latest payment date allowed, and when they have, they're required to pay what's required when it's required. The difference between the taxes you pay currently by applying the rule book most prudently (why shouldn't you be most prudent with an organization out to get you?) and the taxes you might have but didn't pay currently had you not applied the rule book most prudently isn't a loan or an investment—it's a phantom. It's a result of incorporating a counterfactual assumption—a fiction—in the analysis: that the government has treated the taxpayers *otherwise*, that is, as it didn't. Nothing fictional should be injected into the design of financial statements, as discussed in Chapter 7.

Except for refunds for overpayments and tax loss carryovers, which are returns of taxpayers' own money, and payments to individuals for the earned income tax credit (which has nothing to do with deferred taxes), the government as tax collector gives taxpayers as taxpayers nothing pertaining to income taxes.

Consider this scenario. There are no financial statements. The government passes an income tax law specifying how taxable income is to be calculated, including a requirement to use double-declining-balance depreciation. Next, the government permits straight-line depreciation in calculating taxable income, but no one uses it, because it accelerates the incurrence of income tax. Next, taxpayers start to prepare financial statements, using double-

Figure 21.1   Ziggy (copyright 1995 Ziggy and Friends, inc., reprinted with permission of Universal Press Syndicate, all rights reserved).

declining-balance depreciation. Next, taxpayers obtain the ability to use either double-declining-balance depreciation or straight-line depreciation in their financial statements. Some taxpayers use straight-line depreciation in their financial statements. After those events occur, the situation is as it actually is now. When, where, and how has the government loaned anybody anything in this scenario?

Though the government may have reasons to enact provisions of the Internal Revenue Code other than to simply raise revenue, the reasons are among the causes of the events that lead to taxpayers incurring obligations for income taxes. Designing financial statements shouldn't involve consideration of the causes of events (see Chapter 9). Only the financial effects of the events that occurred matter; why the events occurred as they did and why other events didn't occur as they didn't don't matter. Reporting entities should keep their liabilities at the lowest possible amounts and have them come due at the latest possible dates by whatever legitimate devices they have available, but when they have, only the actual incurrence of the liabilities and their financial effects require and deserve consideration in devising financial reporting on those effects.

The sole actual (in contrast with counterfactual) effect of the government as tax collector on a taxpayer as a taxpayer is to relieve him or her or it of money; it's not designed to and doesn't give anything away, loan anything, provide the use of anything, make anything available, or invest anything. Whatever the government gives people, it gives it to them as citizens, not as taxpayers, regardless of how much income taxes they pay, of when they pay income taxes, and even of whether they pay income taxes:

> income tax cannot be regarded ... as a payment to the government for the provision of collective goods and services ... essential in order for the company to earn revenue ... for it is not incurred by all companies which use the services but only by those companies which have taxable income.

> (Henderson and Peirson, 1980, 433)

That agrees with the classification of taxes in the APB's classification of events, presented in Appendix A to Chapter 3, as nonreciprocal transfers, not as reciprocal transfers, that is, exchanges.

A blue-ribbon committee of the AICPA disagreed: "An enterprise gets police and fire protection, national security, and other social benefits. In *exchange* for these social benefits, the enterprise makes tax payments" (AICPA, 1973b, 53, emphasis added).

Three tests

The FASB didn't rely on the notion of an interest-free loan in defending its requirement to use the liability method. Instead, to its credit, for once it provided an analysis (though it started with desired results and used the analysis only to try to bolster its case). In paragraphs 75 to 79 of its Statement No. 109 (FASB, 1992) it concluded that deferred taxes are liabilities, using the three tests embodied in its definition of *liabilities* (all from paragraph 36 of its CON6) (FASB, 1985a), all of which must be passed for deferred taxes to result in liabilities:

- *Test No. 1:* Does the item embody a duty or responsibility to one or more other entities that entails settlement by probable future transfer or use of assets at a specified or determinable date, on occurrence of a specified event, or on demand?
- *Test No. 2:* Does the duty or responsibility obligate a particular entity, leaving it little or no discretion to avoid the future sacrifice?
- *Test No. 3:* Has the transaction or other event obligating the entity already happened?

Unfortunately, its analysis fails, as discussed below.

The following discussion is based on the view that only a single liability for income tax may be incurred for each income tax reporting period, which is caused by all the events specified by the tax law and regulations to affect that tax reporting period. For income taxes, there is only a single creditor, and a single calculation is required to determine a liability for each income tax reporting period. That's implied by the FASB: "A government levies taxes on net taxable income" (FASB, 1992, par. 77).

(The view that only a single liability for income taxes may be incurred for each income tax reporting period contrasts with liabilities for defined pension benefits, as discussed in Chapter 24. Such a liability is incurred for each employee. For defined benefit pensions there are multiple creditors, the employees, and defined benefit pension contracts require a separate calculation of a separate liability to each employee.)

A contrary view is that individual transactions, events, or circumstances can cause more than one individual, separable income tax liability for a particular income tax reporting period, which can and should be reported on separately. That view contradicts the income tax law and regulations and is adopted, consciously or unconsciously, simply for the purpose of stabilizing income reporting. Further, neither view invalidates the argument stated below that the statement in paragraph 79 of SFAS No. 109 that Test No. 3 is passed has the second and third of the three fatal defects described there, that Test No. 3 therefore fails, and that deferred taxes therefore doesn't result in liabilities.

Discussion of Test No. 1

The FASB contended that the entity has such a current duty or responsibility because of the following points in paragraphs 76 and 77 of its SFAS No. 109 (FASB, 1992):

Taxes are a legal obligation imposed by a government, and an obligation for the deferred tax consequences of taxable temporary differences stems from the requirements of the tax law ... Temporary differences will become taxable amounts in future years, thereby increasing taxable income and taxes payable, upon recovery or settlement of the recognized and reported amounts of an enterprise's assets or liabilities.

That only says that a duty "will become" involved in the future because of the tax laws and because of events that might occur when time moves on. The duty isn't a current duty, because some events required to happen haven't yet happened but might happen in the future. And the FASB can't know that they "will" become taxable amounts. No one knows the future— the future doesn't even exist currently (see Chapter 7). In fact, the temporary differences may never be associated with taxable amounts, thereby increasing taxable income, so no duty may come into existence in the future, because the reporting entity may go out of business before then or may have tax losses in the future in excess of such amounts that will prevent any taxes from becoming payable then: "[A deferred tax] liability ... could be wiped out if the enterprise ran into a period of losses" (Solomons, 1989, 62). And a liability can't be discharged by unsuccessful operations, as discussed in Chapter 15.

The conclusion in the preceding paragraph is in effect disputed by the FASB in paragraph 78 of its SFAS No. 109 (FASB, 1992):

> A contention that those temporary differences will never result in taxable amounts ... would contradict the accounting assumption inherent in the statement of financial position that the reported amounts of assets and liabilities will be recovered and settled, respectively; thereby making that statement internally inconsistent. For that reason, the Board concluded that the only question is when, not whether, temporary differences will result in taxable amounts in future years.

However, all the assets may be recovered and all the liabilities may be settled in the future at their stated amounts, but the reporting entity may still never incur any income taxes in the future. Many scenarios could lead to that result. Taxes are paid on taxable income, and the reporting entity could go along for years realizing its assets at their stated amounts, settling its liabilities at their stated amounts, and buying high and selling low. Further, the going concern assumption behind the reporting of assets doesn't mean the reporting entity is expected to last forever, usually only at least a year.

And if, as the paragraph emphasizes, "the only question is when, not whether, temporary differences will result in taxable amounts in future years," doesn't that say that taxable amounts haven't yet resulted and that no current duty exists, as the test requires?

Discussion of Test No. 2

The second test involves two questions: Does the duty or responsibility obligate the reporting entity? Does the reporting entity have little or no discretion to avoid the future sacrifice?

The first question implies that the issue isn't only whether the duty or responsibility obligates the reporting entity, but whether it has obligated the reporting entity by the reporting date. If it obligates the reporting entity but after the reporting date, the reporting entity isn't obligated at the reporting date and it has no liability then. The passage from paragraph 78 quoted above is supposed to answer that question, but, as indicated above, the passage doesn't apply to whether the obligation has already been incurred. An answer to that question awaits consideration of Test No. 3.

In answer to the second question, if the reporting entity had already incurred the obligation, it almost certainly would have to pay it, so this part of Test No. 2 is passed conditionally.

Discussion of Test No. 3

The FASB states in paragraph 79 of its SFAS No. 109 in support of its position that deferred tax liabilities meet Test No. 3—Has the transaction or other event obligating the entity already happened?—that "Deferred tax liabilities result from the same past events that create taxable temporary differences."

That statement is key to the FASB's defense of its position that reporting entities incur liabilities for deferred taxes. The statement is false, for three reasons, each of which is fatal.

FIRST FATAL REASON—LIABILITY NOT YET INCURRED

In an omission of key points, the statement doesn't say precisely to what past events the FASB is referring and how those events cause the reporting entity to incur a liability (that demonstrates the offhand way the statement was devised, or, more likely, that the omission was caused by the realization that providing that information would make it clear that the contention that Test No. 3 is passed is wrong), so they have to be inferred. The inference here begins with recognition that the FASB means that a taxable temporary difference is created by preparing a tax return one way and preparing a set of financial statements another way, among other events, because, in the absence of either of those events, no temporary difference is created. For example, the reporting entity deducts depreciation on a new asset in its tax return for the year in which it acquires it using double-declining-balance depreciation. A temporary difference and a purported liability hasn't yet been created. The reporting entity could still go ahead and use double-declining-balance depreciation on the asset in its income statement for the year. The reporting entity then deducts depreciation on the asset in its income statement for the year using straight-line depreciation. That creates a temporary difference, and, according to the passage in paragraph 79, that's enough to cause a deferred tax liability to be incurred.

But it's not enough.

The FASB's definition of a *liability* requires that a liability be a result of past events or transactions—it doesn't say a liability can be *partly* a result of past events or transactions and *partly* a result of future events or transactions. That would cause contingent liabilities to conform with the definition of *liabilities*. To be a liability, an item has to be *solely* the result of past events or transactions.

An income tax liability develops solely through the operation of the income tax law on the operations of the business, as paragraph 76 of SFAS No. 109 states: "an obligation for the deferred tax consequences of taxable temporary differences stems from the requirements of the tax law" and as the FASB also stated before it issued its SFAS No. 109:

> Transactions or events that result in liabilities imposed by law or governmental units . . . are often specified or inherent in the nature of the statute or regulation involved . . . For those imposed obligations, as for obligations resulting from exchange transactions, no liability is incurred until the occurrence of an event or circumstance that obligates an entity to pay . . .
>
> (FASB, 1985a, par. 210)

The income tax law says what events have to occur for the reporting entity to become obligated to pay the federal government. And, according to the law, for the reporting entity to go into debt for the income taxes on its income tax return for a year, an event covered by the law has to occur that year.

So, for sake of argument, the events that create a temporary difference at a point of time may be assumed to be among the events that cause the reporting entity to incur a liability for income taxes (that assumption is challenged below) but neither of them is the *last* event that causes it: "The future obligation arises only in part from the past transaction . . . The main [cause]—the levying of the tax—is a future transaction"[9] (Hendriksen and van Breda, 1992, 718).

The last event causing an income tax liability to be incurred always occurs in the year in which the taxes appear in the tax return, and, by the definition of a cause, no liability is incurred before the last event causing it to be incurred occurs. If anything, only a contingent liability has been incurred before then.

9 See Chapter 15 for a discussion of how a liability can be caused by more than one event though the FASB's discussion of its definition of *liabilities* in its CON6 (FASB, 1985a) implies that it can't.

No income tax liability is ever incurred before the end of the year of the tax return in which it appears,[10] and no reporting entity therefore ever incurs a deferred tax liability. No reporting entity ever currently owes any of the income taxes that might be reported in future income tax returns. That it does was invented only to buttress the ship of deferred taxes with its effect of stabilizing income reporting, which started to sink on the enactment of the FASB's Conceptual Framework and its outlawing of what-you-may-call-its.

That's disputed as follows:

> the opponents of tax allocation object, in no other case is the occurrence of the future event dependent upon future revenue earning activity of the company ... There is a conclusive answer to this argument ... realization of virtually every asset carried at cost or some derivative of cost in the balance sheet ... is dependent upon future transactions and, if a profit cannot be assumed, the assets are written down.
>
> (Skinner, 1987, 254)

However, future taxable income isn't assured regardless of whether future transactions realize the assets at their reported amounts (no profit need be assumed). Further, financial reporting shouldn't incorporate assumptions about the future, as discussed in Chapter 7.

SECOND FATAL REASON—THE SUPERNATURAL POWER OF BOOKKEEPING

What's worse, the assumption adopted in the discussion of the first fatal reason for the sake of argument, that the events that create a temporary difference are among the events causing a deferred tax liability, shouldn't be retained, because it's false. *The events that create a temporary difference do nothing to create a deferred tax liability.* (You may be wondering about that after the FASB has said they're the *only* events needed to cause a deferred tax liability.)

A temporary difference is a difference between two amounts. The FASB itself states that those two amounts are: "the tax basis of an asset or liability and its reported amount in the financial statements..." (FASB, 1992, Appendix E, Glossary). To create a temporary difference, those two amounts must be brought into existence. The amount in the financial statements is

10 If the end of the year for financial statements of a reporting entity differs from the end of its year for income taxes, the income tax expense should be the amount in the tax return for the income tax year that ends within the year for financial statements. No liability for income taxes that might appear on the next income tax return has been incurred by the end of the year for financial statements. By then, such an amount is still only a contingent liability. The contingency can be eliminated by subsequent events reducing taxable income to zero or below. Such events don't discharge liabilities. That result can be avoided by conforming the financial statement and income tax years.

brought into existence by doing bookkeeping a particular way, so one of the past events that creates a temporary difference is doing bookkeeping a particular way. Because of that and the FASB's contention in paragraph 79 of its SFAS No. 109 that deferred tax liabilities are the result of the same past events that create taxable temporary differences, the FASB implicitly contends that doing bookkeeping a particular way is one of the past events necessary to cause a deferred tax liability, a detrimental relationship with another entity, not merely a series of marks on paper or on a computer drive.

Apparently, according to the FASB, if the reporting entity does its bookkeeping a particular way rather than another way, it incurs the liability. The issuers of the reports of a reporting entity don't like it to incur any liabilities it doesn't have to: *real* liabilities—liabilities that exist in the financial reporting territory and not merely on paper or in computers, in the financial reporting map—are harmful. (A real $1.4 billion liability run up by a rogue employee at Barings Bank put that company out of business.) If deferred taxes were real liabilities, not figments of financial reporters' imaginations, the issuers would be inclined to do its bookkeeping the way they prepare its income tax returns. Millions, even billions, of dollars of supposed liabilities are involved. For example, ExxonMobil Corporation presented a deferred tax liability as of December 31, 2004, of $21.1 billion. *The FASB would have us believe that the issuers of ExxonMobil's financial reports would voluntarily choose a bookkeeping method that would cause it to incur a real liability of $21.1 billion rather than another bookkeeping method that would not cause it to incur the liability!* If deferred tax liabilities actually existed, if there actually were such detrimental relationships, even bookkeeping wouldn't be worth that.

What if the reporting entity prepared its books and financial statements to result in a temporary difference and, according to the FASB, incurred a liability, but later restated its financial statements to eliminate the temporary difference?[11] What would happen to the liability? Would it be discharged simply by changing marks on the reporting entity's own pieces of paper? What kind of a liability is that? Do we financial reporters have so much power that we can cause our employers to incur income tax liabilities, detrimental relationships that exist and don't merely appear on paper, some very large, simply by keeping books and preparing financial statements a certain way, and then relieve our employers of the liabilities simply by changing the books and the financial statements? Can making marks on maps raise real mountains in real countries and erasing the marks tumble them?

Rather than by revising financial statements, doesn't a liability have to be discharged by payment of money, by distribution of goods or provision of

11 "Between 1997 and 2000, the number of restatements of reported income of companies that sell their securities in public markets doubled, from 116 to 233" (Byrnes, 2002a, 44). Few if any restatements to eliminate temporary differences likely have thus far been made, but they can be made as easily as any other.

services, by conversion to equity securities, by forgiveness of the indebtedness by the entity to which the liability is owed, by having nonrecourse debt such as certain mortgage loans assumed by a third party in conjunction with the sale of an asset that serves as sole collateral for that creditor (SFAS No. 140, n5), or by discharge by a court in a bankruptcy proceeding? The FASB said that, twice:

> Once incurred, a liability continues as a liability of the entity until the entity settles it, or another event or circumstance discharges it or removes the entity's responsibility to settle it . . . A debtor shall derecognize a liability *if and only if* it has been extinguished. A liability has been extinguished if either of the following conditions is met: (a) The debtor pays the creditor and is relieved of its obligation for the liability. Paying the creditor includes delivery of cash, other financial assets, goods, or services or reacquisition by the debtor of its outstanding debt securities whether the securities are canceled or held as so-called treasury bonds. (b) The debtor is legally released from being the primary obligor under the liability, either judicially or by the creditor.
>
> (FASB, 1985a, par. 42; 1996, par. 16, emphasis added)

But the FASB contradicted that in its SFAS No. 141. A liability for deferred taxes of a business entity that the FASB pretends exists simply disappears if that entity is bought by another business entity: "An acquiring enterprise shall not recognize . . . deferred income taxes recorded by an acquired enterprise before its acquisition" (FASB, 2001a, par. 38).

In fact, bookkeeping doesn't have supernatural power (see Chapter 4), and it can't cause a reporting entity to incur a liability:

> According to any reasonable understanding of the word, obligations are incurred independently of how financial statements are prepared, and they would be incurred *even if financial statements were not prepared.*
>
> (Lorensen, 1992, 159)

THIRD FATAL REASON—REVERSAL OF CAUSE AND EFFECT

Finally, SFAS No. 109 reverses the direction of cause and effect (a general discussion of the reversal of cause and effect is presented in Chapter 12). Consider the reporting entity in the discussion of the first fatal reason that Test No. 3 isn't passed: on January 10, 2003, it deducts depreciation on a new asset in its tax return for 2002, the year it acquired it, using double-declining-balance depreciation. A temporary difference and a purported liability hasn't yet been created as of December 31, 2002. The reporting entity could still go ahead and use double-declining-balance depreciation on the asset in its income statement for 2002. Those who do its final bookkeeping for 2002, on January 15, 2003, in fact consider using double-declining-balance depreciation for its books for 2002 but decide instead to use straight-line depreciation. That creates a temporary difference as of December 31, 2002. SFAS No. 109 requires it to report a deferred tax liability as of that date. Events that occur on January 10 and January 15, 2003, supposedly cause a condition, a liability, to exist on December 31, 2002. If bookkeeping could be a cause of a deferred tax liability (it can't), cause would have followed effect!

This reversal of the direction of cause and effect is another fatal defect of SFAS No. 109.

Blind?

The APB said reporting entities don't incur such liabilities when it wrote its Opinion No. 11, when it didn't need the fact that they do to obtain the income reporting results it desired. The FASB said they do incur such liabilities when it wrote its SFAS No. 109, when, because of its Conceptual Framework, it did need the fact that they do to obtain the income reporting results it desired. Could the APB have been so blind that it overlooked requiring us to report such liabilities? Aren't we financial reporters, especially our leaders such as members of the APB, responsible to see that all liabilities are reported, especially enormous ones? Was the APB as guilty of causing us to conceal huge liabilities as Enron was in concealing other huge liabilities?

Construing the amounts as liabilities

Flegm reported that the FASB's position in August 1977 appeared to be that deferred taxes would disappear completely (Flegm, 1990, 165). It didn't disappear. He reported that at a meeting held by the FASB on July 26, 1978, with selected representatives of various constituencies to thrash out disagreement concerning the Board's Conceptual Framework project:

> the Board and Reed Storey [Director of the FASB Conceptual Framework project] stated that, under the asset/liability view, the . . . [Board] could accept interperiod tax allocation . . .[12] During the discussion, it came out that tax allocation would be permitted under the asset/liability view with the major shift being to *construe* the deferred taxes to be liabilities rather than deferred credits or assets rather than deferred charges.

12 Storey was said to have been the one who first asserted this. Though the conceptual framework superficially eliminated the revenue–expense view (though some modern day what-you-may-call-its remain), changing to the asset–liability view doesn't permit everything. It doesn't automatically make the credit balance in the balance sheet from deferred taxes a liability, as Storey implied. What it does is ask the question: is it really a liability? The text concludes that it's not.

(Flegm, 1990, 156, 163, emphasis added)

So, rather than *investigate* whether deferred taxes involve liabilities, the FASB *construed* that it does. Such a laid-back kind of process is similar to the process Kirk describes as to "consider" that the rendering of service by employees to be the obligating event for defined benefit pension costs, as discussed in Chapter 24. In both cases, a stable pattern of income reporting is the desired reporting result, and the nature of the item is construed or considered to be whatever it takes to achieve that result.

That's a way to obtain desired financial reporting results rather than to design financial statements by analysis for the benefit of the users. Didn't the FASB invent ("construe") the idea that reporting entities have such liabilities simply because it backed itself into a corner with its Conceptual Framework?

In fact, the amounts on the balance sheet under the so-called liability method are the old outlawed what-you-may-call-its as under the deferred method with their fatal defects, simply renamed *assets* and *liabilities*.[13]

Due process of law

What happens to the concept of due process of law when the U.S. government, through its agency, the SEC, forces businesses to report to it that they owe it a great deal of money that they don't owe it? Will the government next start trying to collect the money?

> An obligation to the government [for deferred taxes] does not . . . exist. If it did, the Internal Revenue Service would press its claim for payment . . .
>
> (Hendriksen and van Breda, 1992, 718)

> Clearly such items [are] not liabilities in the strict sense of the word,[14] i.e., the IRS would ask for payment at once of any taxes legally due them.
>
> (Flegm, 2002)

13 Beresford and Brown were members of the FASB when its SFAS No. 109 (FASB, 1992) was issued and each assented to its issuance. On being shown the analysis in a draft of this chapter, Beresford said he disagrees with the analysis, but he didn't say why. Brown said he agrees with the analysis and now agrees with the conclusion in this chapter.

14 This book encourages readers to use and understand words in their strict senses unless there is an overwhelming reason to do otherwise. No such reason appears to exist here.

When Tony Benn, the secretary of state for industry in the Labour Government, openly advocated a gradual nationalization of industry, some companies nervously feared the Government might interpret the large deferred tax balances as amounts owed to the Government that might serve as the pretext for a takeover. The *Financial Times* reported, "The suggestion was that a future Government might call in all the deferred tax, or nationalise companies instead."

(Lafferty, 1978, quoted in Zeff, 2002, 47)

Net-of-tax

Virtually all now agree that the deferred method is unacceptable. If you agree with the above discussion, you agree that the liability method is unacceptable. That leaves the net-of-tax method. That method is unacceptable because it's based on an unjustified assumption that income taxes will be incurred in the future and that even if it's certain that they will (nothing about the future is certain), that such possible future events cause current conditions, again, that cause and effect can work backwards in time.

If no one can come up with another method, that should do it for deferred taxes.

Earnings management

Deferred taxes is just one more way to manage earnings to stabilize income reporting rather than provide information. It should be eliminated and replaced by additional disclosure concerning current circumstances that might later change the reporting entity's effective income tax rate. Reported income might thereby yo-yo more, but that would represent what happened, not what the issuers would like to present had happened.

Debating points

1 I accept interperiod income tax allocation as the way to report income tax expense.
2 The users of financial reports, not the issuers of financial reports, should normalize income tax expense.
3 The alternative to income tax allocation is undesirable cash basis reporting.
4 It makes sense to report income tax expense in relation to income in the income statement.
5 All would be well if we could go back to the deferred method of income tax allocation—the conceptual framework wrongly condemned it; the conceptual framework should be condemned instead.
6 Anyone who doubts that the government grants interest-free loans in connection with income taxes has never had to meet a payroll.

7 The so-called interest-free loan supposedly granted by the government in connection with income taxes is blarney.
8 No reporting entity ever has a deferred tax liability.
9 All reporting entities that do their taxes different from their books have deferred tax liabilities; it's obvious.
10 The reason the government doesn't collect the deferred taxes companies owe is because the government provides them with interest-free loans.

22 Reporting on foreign operations

financial statements involve adding, subtracting, multiplying, and dividing numbers depicting economic things and events and require a common denominator.

(FASB, 1978, par. 18)

Three times the profession has overhauled its translation rules to deal with the problem caused by the need to include amounts for foreign operations in consolidated (or combined) financial statements, resulting in four different sets of translation rules. The origin of the problem is that arithmetic can't be soundly or informatively applied, for example, to the amounts of assets and liabilities and changes in them of a U.S. parent company stated in terms of U.S. dollars and those of its UK subsidiary stated in terms of pounds sterling. But the solution isn't immediately obvious.

Four sets of translation rules

The four sets of translation rules differ in the foreign exchange rates they use, which are the changeable prices at which the moneys of different countries are exchanged. The choice has always been between the current rate and historical rates. The current rate is the rate on the date of the balance sheet. A historical rate is the rate at the date implicit in the basis on which the element of the reporting entity represented in financial statements is stated other than the rate on the date of the balance sheet, for example the rate at the date inventory stated at acquisition cost was acquired.

The four sets of translation rules have been known as the *current–noncurrent method*, the *monetary–nonmonetary method*, the *temporal method*, and the *current-rate method*.

The current–noncurrent method

Under the current–noncurrent method, first advocated in a report issued in 1931 by a special committee on accounting procedure of the AI(CP)A

(Bulletin of the American Institute of Accountants, No. 137, January 11, 1934, reprinted in AICPA, 1939c), current assets and current liabilities are restated using the current rate, while other assets and liabilities are restated using historical rates. No one appears to have ever developed any reasoning in support of the current–noncurrent method.

The monetary–nonmonetary method

Under the monetary–nonmonetary method, monetary assets and liabilities (generally, assets and liabilities denominated in fixed or determinable amounts of money) are restated using the current rate, while nonmonetary assets and liabilities are restated using historical rates. Little reasoning was offered in support of the monetary–nonmonetary method, except for virtual tautologies such as "The argument ... for the ... monetary–nonmonetary [method] ... is ... that a change in the exchange rate will affect monetary and nonmonetary items differently" (Henderson and Peirson, 1980, 331). Hepworth, apparently the first promoter of the method, merely said that the method is "logical": "the logical classification of ... items for the purpose of translation of foreign balances into dollars is a division between those items which represent a contractual right to receive or pay a fixed number of foreign currency units, currently or in the future, and items the value of which may vary in terms of the foreign currency unit" (Hepworth, 1953).

The current–noncurrent method and the monetary–nonmonetary method were used concurrently:

> In 1965, the APB endorsed [the monetary–nonmonetary] method by concluding (APB Opinion No. 6) that long-term receivables and payables were to be translated at current rates "in many circumstances," which is their way of saying "always." Inventories, as a nonmonetary item, were to be translated at historic rates. Translation was not limited to this method, however, thus the current–noncurrent method was still used prior to 1976.
> (Flegm, 1984, 109n)

That was one reason that the AICPA decided to study the area.

The temporal method

The temporal method, adopted by the FASB in its SFAS No. 8 (FASB, 1975d), issued in October 1975, was the result of that study (Lorensen, 1972). The study adopted a definition of *translation* as a measurement conversion process[1] (Lorensen, 1972, 11), in which the amounts are converted from ones stated in one unit of measure to amounts stated in another unit of

---

1 Lorensen took that definition from a statement of it in Rosenfeld, 1971b, 61. That statement had been influenced by the view then held by everyone that

measure. The first unit of measure is defined in terms of the money of the country of the foreign operation. The second unit of measure is defined in terms of the money used in the consolidated or combined financial statements. Chambers stated the same conclusion:

> The rate of exchange is a rule for transforming measurements in one scale into measurements in another scale . . . the foreign currency equivalence law . . . is the same in kind as the laws by which other measurements expressed in one scale are converted to measurements expressed in another, for example 1.62 kilometers = 1 mile.
>
> (Chambers, 1966, 94; 1991a, 4)

The study used that definition to develop its method. It reached the conclusion that foreign exchange rates are serviceable in the conversions. Because the rates change over time, the rate selected for a particular conversion would have to pertain to the timing of the item converted, thus the name *temporal method*. For example, amounts stated at acquisition price and amounts such as depreciation derived from acquisition prices were converted at the rates in effect on the dates of acquisition; amounts such as cash, receivables, and nonmonetary assets stated at current selling price, which all pertain to the date of the balance sheet, were converted at the current rate.

The temporal method has the advantages of being based on some reasoning and of stating all of the amounts it reported in the final financial statements in a single unit of measure. However, it can cause strange results—bad things reported when good things happen and vice versa—as the author of the study admitted:

> A foreign subsidiary that has long-term debt in foreign money outstanding when the U.S. dollar foreign exchange rate for the money changes recognizes a dollar gain or loss on the debt under the temporal principle . . . The foreign subsidiary also has a more or less offsetting dollar loss or gain on the change in the *current value* in terms of dollars, however defined, of the plant and equipment. As some accountants put it, the change in rate results in no "economic" or "overall" gain or loss to the extent that the gains or losses on the two items offset. Accountants that want to recognize in the translated financial statements that no economic or overall gain or loss has occurred are in a dilemma because no acceptable way presently exists to do so . . . The dilemma is . . . unresolvable as long as the historical cost basis of accounting continues to be used.
>
> (Lorensen, 1972, xi, xii)

---

reporting on foreign operations should involve translation, which is the view held virtually unanimously now. Since stating it, I stand by it as a definition of translation, but I have abandoned the idea that reporting on foreign operations should in fact involve translation, as discussed below in the text.

Objections were common: "the so-called yo-yo effect on earnings[, which] could mask the underlying success or failure of a company's operations . . . created so much opposition to SFAS No. 8" (Solomons, 1986, 227).

The cause of the strange results wasn't in the method of translation but a defect in translation itself, discussed below in the section "Stop Translating," and those results were its downfall.[2]

The current-rate method

Under the current-rate method, all assets and liabilities are translated using the current rate. An objective adopted in SFAS No. 52, "Foreign Currency Translation" (FASB, 1981), paragraph 4, issued in December 1981, the currently effective pronouncement (though, as stated in footnote 2, the temporal principle is still in effect required for foreign operations in hyperinflationary economies) which mandated the current-rate method, was to avoid reporting that bad things happened when they didn't and vice versa, as under the temporal method. That was a worthwhile objective. Though the method appears to achieve that objective, in fact it doesn't because, as discussed below, it results in meaningless amounts.

As stated in paragraph 70, the FASB also considered whether to adopt another objective: "To use a 'single unit of measure' for financial statements that include translated foreign amounts." Philip P., who isn't a financial reporter, said that asking whether this should be an objective sounds like a trick question. Asking it was as unnecessary as asking whether to require us financial reporters to use four as the sum of two plus two. What's worse, as stated in paragraph 75, the FASB, inconceivably, rejected it: "[The] objective . . . was not adopted."

How can our profession attract the best and the brightest if we ask them to swallow this? (At least three authors avoided dealing with the anomaly of rejecting that objective by ignoring it, referring to only the objectives the FASB accepted [Schroeder and Clark, 1998, 748; Rubin, 1999, 9, 17]).

When Margaret R., who isn't a financial reporter, was shown paragraphs 70 and 75, she asked, "Are you sure that isn't a misprint?"[3] In contrast, this rejection has been greeted in the financial reporting literature and by the profession and academe complaisantly. For example, Wolk, Francis, and Tearney devote a number of pages to SFAS No. 52, including problems they find with it, without mentioning that it requires us to violate the single-unit-of-measure rule (Wolk *et al.*, 1992, 572 *et seq.*). Financial reporters who realize we are required to violate the single-unit-of-measure rule appear to be complaisant about it, likely because of our indoctrination. (Most financial

---

2 The temporal principle with its defect is still in effect required for foreign operations in hyperinflationary economies in conformity with SFAS No. 52, pars 11, 47–54.
3 Chapter 4 notes what everyone knows, that in no other discipline is the disregard of a basic mathematical rule tolerated.

reporters probably don't realize it; those with whom I've discussed it hadn't read the "Basis for Conclusions" or the dissents in SFAS No. 52 and said they didn't realize it until I pointed it out to them.) Those in business appear to be unaware that we financial reporters regularly violate a rule of arithmetic that everyone else knows is inviolable—the financial press hasn't noted it. If business people were to become aware of it, few likely would be concerned, most caring because of their self-interest for only the (apparent) financial reporting results the violation causes (the apparent results are deceiving—the results are actually meaningless). Most users are also likely unaware of it. How would they react if they became aware of it?

I am aware of no complaint in the financial reporting literature about the requirement to violate the single-unit-of-measurement rule other than in the dissents to SFAS No. 52 and my article in the August 1987 issue of the *Journal of Accountancy* (Rosenfeld, 1987). That's how indoctrinated we are. I feel like the boy who said the king is wearing no clothes.

If the FASB required us to report, for example, that up is down, we might not challenge even that: "In accounting, dogmatism is the basis by which accountants come to accept the validity of rules and procedures ... The issue is whether confidence in the authoritative body is well placed" (Kam, 1990, 493).

The Board stated in its defense in paragraph 85 that it "...believes that, for an enterprise operating in multiple currency environments, a true 'single unit of measure' does not, as a factual matter, exist." (The shouting involved in the expression "as a factual matter" suggests doubts in the mind of the drafter.) But a unit of measure exists if it's defined for the purpose at hand. Moreover, if no single unit of measure could be soundly defined for multiple currency environments, sound consolidation or combination involving foreign operations would be impossible.

Finally, the Board violated the first law of holes—which is, when you are in one, stop digging. In paragraph 88, the Board literally added insult to injury to those of us who object to being required to violate the single-unit-of-measure rule, accusing us of thinking artificially and of harboring illusions: "The Board concluded that for many foreign entities, adhering to a 'single unit of measure' was artificial and illusory."

In reality, everyone learns in elementary school the necessity of conforming with the single-unit-of-measure rule in all arithmetical operations that involve units of measure. Brian and Kevin, two of my children, said they learned it in third grade. Chambers said as much: "mathematical ... laws ... govern ... adding, subtracting and relating ... The brief form of one such law is: unlike magnitudes may not be added" (Chambers, 1991a, 2). The AICPA knows it: "Stating assets and liabilities and changes in them in terms of a common financial denominator is prerequisite to performing the operations—for example, addition and subtraction—necessary to measure financial position and periodic net income" (AICPA, 1970c, par. 165). And even the FASB in fact knows it too. It said so, as quoted at the beginning of this chapter and as follows: "If valid comparisons are to be made . . . the unit of measurement used must be invariant" (FASB, 1980b, par. 114).

Because of the violation of the rule, the inputs to the calculations that result in the amounts in a set of financial statements under SFAS No. 52 aren't all stated in a single unit of measure, so most of the amounts in the statements, including virtually all the subtotals and totals, such as net income, are numbers with a unit of measure sign in front of them that doesn't match the numbers. That constitutes a booby trap in the statements hidden from the users—they expect "$100" to mean one hundred U.S. dollars, but under SFAS No. 52 it not only doesn't mean that—*it doesn't mean anything*. It has no more significance than the four that results from adding one yard and three feet. (Would you walk or drive across or under a bridge built in conformity with BDSB Statement No. 52 of the Bridge Design Standards Board that required the use of four as the sum of one yard and three feet in the design of bridges? I wouldn't, because the bridge would fall down.) The amounts are symbols that seem to mean something but that don't, that are double-talk:

> Form is, itself, a sign. It predisposes the receiver to interpret a message in the manner in which he customarily or habitually interprets messages in the same form. Consider some lines in the "Jabberwocky" of Lewis Caroll:
>
> "Twas brillig and the slithy toves
> Did gyre and gimble in the wabe:
> All mimsy were the borogoves
> And the mome raths outgrabe."[4]
>
> (Chambers, 1966, 173)

For amounts to have meaning, they have to represent something in the financial reporting territory—they have to conform with the user-oriented criterion of representativeness. We financial reporters are in the habit of dealing with amounts in the financial reporting map, such as LIFO inventories or accumulated depreciation, that don't mean anything, that don't conform with that criterion. We are therefore not disturbed by the results of applying SFAS No. 52, which don't mean anything. We, and the members of the FASB who assented to Statement No. 52, must believe in magic. We must believe that numbers that have no meaning gain meaning simply by being put in financial statements—meaning important enough for people to pay attention to them and base their economic decisions on them.

The Chairman of the FASB when it issued its SFAS No. 52, who dis-

---

4 Nicol Williamson insisted, however, that "The mome rath isn't born that could outgrabe me" (quoted in Robert Byrne, 1988, 254). Also, consider this weighty statement by Harry Stanley, double-talking vaudevillian: "But I for one feel that all the basic and sadum tortumise, all the professional getesimus and tortum kimafly will precipitously aggregate so that peace shall reign. I want to make that perfectly clear" (Robert Thomas, 1998, B13).

sented from the Statement, saying it should have adopted a single unit of measure as an objective, agreed, in effect saying that the amounts resulting from application of the Statement don't mean anything:

> multiplying the local currency historical cost of General Motors' European factories by today's exchange rate between each of the European currencies and the U.S. dollar and ... putting a $ in front of the product. *I cannot explain what the product is . . .*
>
> (Kirk, 1989a, 101, emphasis added)

Even so, he said that "it did resolve a very controversial accounting problem— and in a very popular way" (Kirk, 1989a, 101), rather than that financial statements whose amounts don't mean anything are worthless. Hendriksen and van Breda said that "The compromise [in SFAS No. 52] appears to have been satisfactory because the previously loud level of complaints has been muted" (Hendriksen and van Breda, 1992, 434). The muting of the level of complaints isn't a satisfactory criterion of satisfactoriness. They did go on to say that "[w]hether the compromise is theoretically sound is a matter of ongoing debate" (Hendriksen and van Breda, 1992, 434).

Because the amounts don't mean anything and therefore violate the first of the user-oriented criteria, representativeness, they violate all the rest of those criteria.

A requirement to violate the single-unit-of-measure rule throughout application of a standard is a fatal defect in the standard. It's like the fatal defect that resulted in the recent failure of a Mars lander, caused by some of the engineers on the program using the English system of measurement and others using the metric system and combining the measurements without conversion. SFAS No. 52 therefore needn't be considered further to see what merits it might have. Its paragraphs 66 and 68 present the concepts of (1) a net investment in operations that are relatively self-contained and integrated in a foreign country, and (2) a functional currency.[5] They represent simply a

---

5 SFAS No. 52, par. 75, states in defense of the functional currency concept that (emphasis added):

> [Conforming to the single-unit-of-measure rule] reflects in consolidated financial statements the transactions of the entire group, including foreign operations, *as though* all operations were extensions of the parent's domestic activities and all transactions were conducted and measured in the parent's reporting currency.

However, such conformity doesn't have the counterfactual—"as though"—effects described. Such conformity, as discussed in a succeeding section in the text, reflects foreign operations as they are, foreign operations of separate components of the reporting entity, that those operations were conducted in foreign currencies. Such conformity does, nevertheless, measure the foreign operations in the consolidated reporting currency, the currency of the parent company. (Measuring operations conducted in one currency in a unit of measure defined in terms of units of another currency introduces no counterfactual. It is provided for, for example, by SFAS No. 52, pars 15 and 16, for the foreign currency transactions of the parent company.) That is how conformity to the single-unit-of-measure rule is achieved.

vain attempt to avoid the unavoidable fatal consequences of violation of the single-unit-of-measure rule.

The Board's consciousness of its virtually unquestioned authority apparently allowed it to aim for a result it wanted in SFAS No. 52 though it knew that to do so required it to state nonsense and to require us to implement nonsense. Walters, one of the four members of the FASB who assented to issuance of SFAS No. 52 (in fact, the swing vote—three dissented), told me that he assented because he believes that the defects of acquisition-cost reporting are so great that the violation of the single-unit-of-measure rule couldn't make financial reporting any worse (Walters, 2002). But to fulfill his responsibilities as a member of the FASB, which by its mission statement is devoted to "improv[ing] the usefulness of financial reporting" (FASB, 1985c), he should have worked to remove the currently existing defects of financial reporting instead of adding to its defects. His characterization of acquisition-cost reporting agrees with conclusions expressed throughout this book, especially Chapter 10. He also said that he believes that there is no satisfactory method of translation. That agrees with a conclusion stated in the section "Accounting for foreign operations" in this chapter.

The current-rate method of translation should be abandoned.

Catch-22

The fatal defect of SFAS No. 52, along with the fatal defects in other areas of current GAAP, discussed in other chapters of this book, cause the Sarbanes–Oxley Act of 2002 to subject CEOs and CFOs to whom the Act applies to a Catch-22: Section 302 of the Act requires CEOs and CFOs to certify that:

> The financial statements, and other financial information included in the report [to the SEC], fairly present in all material respects the financial condition and results of operations of the issuer as of, and for, the period presented in the report.

That requires CEOs and CFOs to violate the Act, because

- The law requires financial statements filed with the SEC to conform with current generally accepted accounting principles (GAAP)
- Because of the fatal defects of current GAAP, no financial statements included in a report required to be filed with the SEC that conforms with current GAAP fairly present anything
- CEOs and CFOs are therefore required to certify to a false statement.

No CPA is required by generally accepted auditing standards to state simply that financial statements fairly present anything. CPAs are required by those standards instead to state whether, in their opinion, the financial statements fairly present, in all material respects, the financial position and results of operations of the reporting entity in conformity with generally accepted accounting principles. The message is that the financial statements fairly present only to the extent that financial statements that conform with current GAAP fairly present. CPAs never use the expression "fairly present" apart from the expression "in conformity with generally accepted accounting principles."

No CEO or CFO should be required to do something no CPA would think of doing. No CEO or CFO should be punished because an Act of Congress requires the CEO or CFO to violate that Act of Congress.

The reason the drafters of the Act omitted a reference to GAAP in the required certification apparently was to avoid the situation in *U.S. v. Simon* (425 F. 2d 796, Fed. Sec. L. Rep P92,511). In that case, the defendants contended that the financial statements conformed with GAAP and that their audit conformed with GAAS. They asked for instructions to the jury that a defendant could be found guilty only if, according to GAAP, the financial statements as a whole didn't fairly present the financial condition of the company and then only if the departure from professional standards was due to willful disregard of those standards with knowledge of the falsity and intent to deceive. The court declined and stated that the critical test was whether the financial statements as a whole were fairly presented, and if not, the basic test was whether the defendants acted in good faith. It found that an accountant is under a duty to disclose what he knows when he has reason to believe that, to a material extent, a corporation isn't being operated to carry out its business in the interest of all the stockholders but for the private benefit of its president. The ultimate test is whether the auditor has told the truth as the auditor knows it.

The Act avoided that problem, but in doing so it introduced the Catch-22.

In the absence of an amendment of the Act's certification requirement, a CEO or a CFO could append something like the following at the end of the required certification to protect herself from having to certify that a set of financial statements fairly presents something when it does not: "to the extent that the generally accepted accounting principles to which the financial statements conform do not themselves prevent a fair presentation."

Accounting for foreign operations[6]

Along with Lorensen, quoted above, the assenters to SFAS No. 52 called translation a "dilemma," in paragraph 60. (How could the FASB, an all-powerful body, confessing to being mystified, force on a profession a requirement to embarrass itself by doing what no third-grade schoolchild would

6 Much of this material is taken from Rosenfield, 1987.

do?) The dissenters to that statement called translation "an exceedingly difficult problem." But translation isn't a dilemma or a difficult problem; it's an impossible problem. It's an issue that has defied solution for a long time, such as those discussed at the beginning of Chapter 3 and in Chapters 8 and 26. In this case the issue should be abandoned; another method of translation shouldn't be sought. The problem isn't in the various methods of translation; the problem is translation itself. Instead of accounting for foreign operations in terms of the unit of measure in the financial statements in which they are reported, as we do for virtually everything else, we follow a mechanical procedure, translation, without first inquiring into its suitability for the purpose.[7] Inquiry shows that, though the conventional wisdom is the following:

> Many enterprises have investments in branches and subsidiaries that operate in foreign countries and prepare financial statements expressed in the foreign currencies. For purposes of preparing consolidated financial statements it is *necessary* to "translate" those financial statements...
> (Skinner,[8] 1987, 385, emphasis added)

In fact, translation isn't only not necessary but is unsound. It should be abandoned in favor of accounting for foreign operations.

The rule of GIGO

The problem with translation is related to the rule of garbage in, garbage out (GIGO), a rule developed in connection with computer programs but that has wider application. The rule is that a transformation step shouldn't be performed if the input to the step isn't serviceable for the purposes for which the output of the step is to be used. For example, the rule of GIGO is violated by converting the height of a door from inches to centimeters if the width of the door is known in inches but the width in centimeters is needed to be used to determine whether the door can be moved through an opening whose largest dimension in centimeters is known.

Translation is the third of a four-step process that results in including data in consolidated financial statements about a subsidiary operating in a country whose money isn't the money used to define the unit of measure used in the consolidated financial statements. The process has these steps:

---

7 Inflation reporting also uses a mechanical procedure, called *restatement*. The suitability of that procedure should also be considered. See footnote 2 in Chapter 11.
8 When Skinner was shown a draft of this chapter, however, he said that "Owing to my frustration with the problem of finding a fully logical translation method, I am rather receptive to your proposition that the answer lies, in principle, in accounting for the foreign operations directly in the domestic [domestic to the parent company] currency of account."

1   The subsidiary operates.
2   The subsidiary represents those operations in financial statements in a unit of measure defined in terms of the unit of money of the country in which it operates, using ordinary GAAP.
3   The amounts in those statements are transformed by a measurement conversion process, called translation, to amounts stated in a unit of measure defined in terms of the unit of money in which the consolidated financial statements are stated.
4   The converted data are included in the consolidated financial statements.

That process violates the rule of GIGO. Step (3) of the process, translation, is a transformation step: "different units may be used interchangeably by the process of measuring one in terms of the other. The resulting relationship is called ... a 'transformation function'" (Sterling, 1970a, 76). The input to that step isn't pertinent or serviceable for the purpose for which its output is to be used, because Step (2), which provides the input to Step (3), uses the wrong GAAP for the purpose of the output of Step (3), as discussed below. Step (3), translation, therefore shouldn't be performed. It's no wonder we financial reporters have had such grief in this area, trying to determine how best to perform a step we shouldn't perform.

Domestic company GAAP

The problem with the GAAP used in Step (2) is that they are domestic company GAAP, the GAAP that should be used only by a domestic company, a company operating in a country whose unit of money is used to define the unit of measure used in its financial statements. When the subsidiary performs Step (2), for that purpose it's a domestic company preparing domestic financial statements in the domestic unit of measure defined in terms of the domestic unit of money using GAAP pertinent for such a purpose, which can be called "domestic company GAAP." For example, an English subsidiary of a U.S. company is a domestic English company preparing domestic English financial statements in a unit of measure defined in terms of English pounds, the domestic unit of money for the English company, using domestic company GAAP, the GAAP pertinent to such a company preparing financial statements that way. (For purposes of consolidation, the domestic company GAAP it uses is conformed with the domestic company GAAP in the country of the parent country.)

However, the subsidiary isn't a domestic company when included in consolidated financial statements stated in a unit of measure defined in terms of the money of the country of the parent company. For those statements it changes into a foreign company, conducting foreign operations, just as a Canadian crossing the Canadian border into the U.S. changes from a citizen to a foreigner. And foreign operations differ from domestic operations for financial reporting purposes in one decisive respect. All of the elements of such operations are one more market away from the money in terms of which the unit of measure in the consolidated financial statements is defined than are the elements of the operations of the parent company.

The parent company's cash is the kind of money used to define the unit of measure in the consolidated financial statements, and its other monetary items are denominated in terms of that money. The foreign company's cash and other monetary items are each one market away from that money, the foreign exchange market, one market more than the monetary items of the parent company.

The parent company's nonmonetary assets, assets that have to be sold in markets other than a market for money to obtain any kind of money, are each one market away from the money used to define the unit of measure in the consolidated financial statements. The foreign company's nonmonetary assets are each two markets away from that money, one more than the nonmonetary items of the parent company, with the extra market again being the foreign exchange market.

Domestic company GAAP doesn't work for foreign operations because it ignores the financial effects on those operations of the extra market, the foreign exchange market, which financial effects the FASB acknowledges: "If the enterprise operates in more than one currency environment, it is affected by ... changes in relative prices among the several units of currency in which it conducts its business" (SFAS No. 52, par. 57). In that market, monetary-type assets are exchanged for monetary-type assets. Domestic company GAAP, which are designed to deal only with the financial effects of events occurring within a country, aren't designed to deal with operations subject to the foreign exchange market and so don't report on the financial effects of events that occur in that market.

Being merely a transformation step, translation uses information from the foreign exchange market merely to transform data that report on the financial effects of events *outside* the foreign exchange market, not to report on the financial effects of events *in* the foreign exchange market. *Translation thus neglects to report on the financial effects of an entire class of relevant events*, the events in the foreign exchange market. New GAAP are needed to report on the financial effects of those events.

Foreign company GAAP

New GAAP should be designed for foreign operations, which may be called "foreign company GAAP;" it should include rules to deal with the financial effects of the events that occur in the foreign exchange market. Using that GAAP, those operations have in concept to be originally measured in the unit of measure used in the consolidated financial statements, making translation unnecessary. (The bookkeeping can for convenience be done originally in terms of the money of the other country; the fix involves principles, not bookkeeping.) The principles have to be designed to come up with the amounts that would result from originally measuring the foreign operations in that unit of measure, using foreign company GAAP, which reports on the financial effects of all pertinent events, including those that occur in the foreign exchange market. (That isn't as hard as it sounds. A suggestion on how to do so is presented in Rosenfield, 1987.)

The resulting information will all be reported in a single unit of measure and will report gains when good things happen and vice versa.

Reporting on foreign operations and inflation reporting

Issues involved in reporting on foreign operations are similar to issues involved in inflation reporting (see Chapter 11). In a consolidated group involving foreign operations, elements of the reporting entity represented in financial statements are denominated in or exchangeable for more than one kind of money. In inflation reporting, amounts are originally measured in more than one unit of measure in terms of consumer general purchasing power. In each kind of reporting, a goal is to have all the amounts in the final financial statements stated in a single unit of measure. When the two kinds of reporting are combined, that remains the goal.

In combining the two kinds of reporting, SFAS No. 89 (FASB, 1986), paragraph 39, permits factoring in foreign inflation by permitting the use of the so-called restate–translate method. But the only way to achieve the goal described in the preceding paragraph is to ignore foreign inflation. That's sound, however, because, believe it or not, foreign inflation is irrelevant to inflation reporting involving foreign operations.

Foreign inflation is a change in the general purchasing power of the foreign monetary unit. Such a change involves changes in the prices of goods and services bought and sold in the foreign country, most of which the foreign operation doesn't buy or sell and which therefore don't affect it. The only changes in prices in the foreign monetary unit that affect the foreign operations are changes in the specific prices of its inputs and outputs bought and sold with that money and of foreign moneys bought and sold with that money on the foreign exchange market. (Similarly, the only changes in prices in the monetary unit in terms of which the unit used in the consolidated financial statements is defined that affect the parent company's operations are changes in the specific prices of its inputs and outputs bought and sold with that money, as discussed in Chapter 11.)

Inflation in the country of the parent company affects the users of the consolidated financial statements, and it thereby affects the perspective with which they look at the consolidated group. The effect on the users is the only excuse for factoring inflation into financial reporting (see Chapter 11).

The only inflation that affects their perspective is inflation in the country of the parent company, and it's the only inflation that should be factored in.[9]

Further, factoring in foreign inflation for foreign operations and inflation in the country of the parent company for operations in that country in inflation reporting, as SFAS No. 89 permits under restate–translate, still results in amounts not all stated in a single unit of measure in terms of consumer general purchasing power. Restate–translate results in statements in which all amounts are stated in a unit with the same name, but "The mere use of numbers of units bearing a common name does not constitute the named unit a common denominator" (Chambers, 1969, 236).

SFAS No. 89, paragraph 37, does also permit ignoring foreign inflation in inflation reporting involving foreign operations and incorporating only inflation in the country of the parent company, under the so-called translate–restate method. (The FASB doesn't explain why it permits both restate–translate and translate–restate, which result in widely different amounts, when the FASB states that one of its most important functions is to reduce alternatives; this is discussed in Chapter 19.) However, because the amounts under SFAS No. 52 before applying the restate portion of translate–restate aren't all stated in a single unit of measure, they aren't all stated in a single unit of measure in terms of consumer general purchasing power after the restate portion of translate–restate. Either way of applying inflation reporting to amounts resulting from SFAS No. 52 results in amounts not all stated in a single unit of measure in terms of consumer general purchasing power—the very defect inflation reporting is intended to correct.

Inflation reporting should therefore not be applied to amounts resulting from SFAS No. 52. Because inflation reporting is imperative to avoid misleading financial statements (discussed in Chapter 11), this is another fatal consequence of SFAS No. 52.

In contrast, amounts resulting from application of foreign company GAAP to the foreign operations of a consolidated or combined group, as discussed above, are all stated in a single unit of measure defined in terms of the unit of money used to define the unit of measure used in the consolidated financial statements. For inflation reporting, they should be restated the same as the amounts in financial statements covering only operations in the country of the parent company, incorporating only the inflation in that country. That

- Avoids incorporating irrelevant foreign inflation
- Incorporates the perspective of the users of the consolidated financial statements in all the amounts

---

9 Domestic inflation affects the monetary items of the parent company from the perspective of the users; changes in exchange rates and domestic inflation affect the monetary items of the foreign operations from the perspective of the users.

- Ends up with amounts all stated in a single relevant unit of measure in terms of consumer general purchasing power, the goal of inflation reporting.

Debating points

1 A high-powered Board such as the FASB need not be concerned with minutiae such as the single-unit-of-measure rule.
2 FASB 52 must be sound, seeing that it has survived so long.
3 The current-rate method is the best because it gives the best answers.
4 The current-rate method, with its built-in violation of the single-unit-of-measure rule, is a scandal for the profession.
5 It is unseemly to compare the FASB with third-grade school children.
6 Bridge design has nothing to do with GAAP design.
7 The concepts of a net investment in operations that are relatively self-contained and integrated in a foreign country and of a functional currency never passed my smell test.
8 Walters was right—current GAAP is so bad it doesn't matter that SFAS No. 52 added the defect of the violation of the single-unit-of-measure rule; it just became one of a hundred defects, and we have lived with and survived them all.
9 The defects of GAAP put everyone who has to follow Section 302 of the Sarbanes–Oxley Act of 2002 in an impossible position.
10 The solution to the problem translation has been trying to solve is to measure all amounts in the financial statements of all members of the consolidated group originally in the money in terms of which the consolidated statements will be stated.
11 The thought of dealing simultaneously with domestic and foreign operations and with inflation blows my mind.

23 Reporting after business combinations and on related goodwill

The two major issues in reporting after a business combination have been (1) the bases on which the assets and liabilities of the combining companies should be reported after the combination, which has traditionally been called a choice between the pooling-of-interests method and the purchase method, and (2) the treatment of the related goodwill.

The pooling-of-interests method, which is no longer permitted, combined the balance sheet accounts of the combining reporting entities as they were immediately before the combination, without adjustment. No goodwill was recognized because of the combination. Only the purchase method is now permitted to determine the amounts of the assets and liabilities after combination.

SFAS Nos 141 and 142 (FASB, 2001a, 2001b) issued in 2001, are the currently effective pronouncements on those issues. Considering the history of the preceding pronouncements illuminates the issues and provides insight into the quality of the current pronouncements. It also provides insights into the vicissitudes and politics of standard-setting.

Requirements before the battle

> [Determining principles for] business combinations [was a] steady retreat before the onslaught of management, with the organized profession continually underestimating the . . . strength of the opposition.
>
> (Moonitz, 1974, 54; also quoted in Chapter 2)

APB Opinions Nos 16 and 17 (AICPA, 1970a, 1970b), the pronouncements on reporting after business combinations and on the related goodwill that preceded SFAS Nos 141 and 142, both of which were issued in 1970, were born in battle, as discussed below. Before the battle, the history of requirements for pooling versus purchase and for the related goodwill was relatively calm.

Previous requirements for pooling versus purchase

The first pronouncement on pooling versus purchase was ARB No. 40, "Business Combinations" (AICPA, 1950), issued in 1950. It described the two kinds of treatments and stated in general terms the circumstances in which each should be applied. It implied that the two methods were already in existence and that the bulletin was merely tidying things up. ARB No. 40 was incorporated without change in Chapter 7(c) of ARB No. 43. That chapter was superseded in turn by ARB No. 48 (AICPA, 1957), also called "Business Combinations," which tidied things up a little more. ARB No. 48 was in effect at the time APB Opinions Nos 16 and 17 were being considered.

Previous requirements for related goodwill

Reporting on goodwill related to business combinations was covered by two pronouncements before the battle—AICPA, "Intangible Assets" (Bulletin 24) (AICPA, 1944b), and AICPA, "Restatement" (Bulletin 43) (AICPA, 1953b).

Bulletin 24

Bulletin 24, issued in 1944, stated that before it was published, "accounting practices [for goodwill related to business combinations] have varied greatly."

Bulletin 24 indicated that for some goodwill related to business combinations "there is evidence of limited duration." Such evidence might have to do, for example, with an unusually beneficial relationship with a customer or customers that because of current circumstances won't last longer than a determinable length of time,[1] but, for "goodwill generally," there is "no such limited term of existence" and "no indication of limited life . . ." It provided that "the initial carrying value of [both of those kinds of related goodwill] should be [acquisition] cost . . ." After initial recording,

- The cost of the related goodwill for which there is evidence of limited duration "should be amortized by systematic charges to the income statement over the period benefited . . ."
- The cost of the related goodwill for which there is no evidence of limited duration "may be carried continuously [apparently without adjustment]"

  - "unless and until it becomes reasonably evident that [its] term of existence . . . has become limited," or if the reporting entity "decides that [it] may not continue to have value during the entire life of the

---

1 Philip R., who isn't a financial reporter, once had a job with a company that, though independent, had Sears Roebuck & Co. as its only major customer.

enterprise . . . despite the fact that there are no present indications of such limited life" in which cases it "should be amortized by systematic charges in the income statement over the estimated remaining period of usefulness,"[2] or, "if such charges would result in distortion of the income statement, a partial write-down may be made by a charge to earned surplus,[3] and the balance of the cost may be amortized over the remaining period of usefulness," or

- until it "becomes worthless," in which case it "should be charged off either in the income statement or to earned surplus as, in the circumstances, may be appropriate."[4]

The Bulletin stated the following caveat (emphasis added), which acknowledged that the committee was permitting a treatment that "may give rise to misleading inferences"!

the committee recognizes that in the past it has been accepted practice to eliminate [goodwill related to business combinations] by writing [it] off against any existing surplus, capital or earned, even though the value of the asset is unimpaired. Since the practice has been long established and widely approved, the committee does not feel warranted in recommending, at this time, adoption of a rule prohibiting such disposition. The committee believes, however, that such dispositions should be discouraged, especially if proposed to be effected by charges to capital surplus . . . the reduction of the investment, upon which the responsibility and accountability of management is based, *may give rise to misleading inferences* if subsequent earnings are compared with the reduced base.

2 It didn't say how to predict the "remaining period of usefulness" if there are "no present indications . . . of such limited life" (except to say that "where [goodwill related to a business combination is an] important income-producing factor . . . and [is] being currently maintained by advertising or otherwise, the period of amortization should be reasonably long"). There is no basis on which to make the required prediction, so the bulletin required us financial reporters to do something we can't do. Solomons said something appropriate to that: "It hardly needs to be said that financial reporting regulations should never call for information that is not feasible to provide" (Solomons, 1989, 37, 38).

3 Not only did the Bulletin require stabilizing reported income by "systematic charges," thereby preventing the data from being representational, but it also explicitly permitted an additional element of stabilizing by charging some of the cost directly to equity. It attempted to justify the direct charge to equity by stating that "misleading inferences might be drawn as a result of the inclusion of substantial charges in the income statement . . ." But how can users be misled by reporting that simply informs them of what happened? And if this reporting doesn't simply inform users of what happened, why require it?

4 No advice was provided as to how to determine what was "appropriate." "Appropriate" is a common weasel-word in financial reporting regulation.

Skinner commented about the committee's attitude: "The belief that accounting standards could not be imposed but must develop through acceptance made the committee [CAP] timid..." (Skinner, 1987, 31).

Bulletin 43

Bulletin 24 was revised and presented as Chapter 5, "Intangible Assets," of Bulletin 43. It changed some of the rules for reporting on goodwill related to business combinations. It provided that

- For the related goodwill for which there is evidence of limited duration: "If it becomes evident that the period benefited will be longer or shorter than originally estimated, recognition thereof may take the form of an appropriate decrease or increase in the rate of amortization or, if such increased charges would result in distortion of income, a partial write-down may be made by a charge to earned surplus" (paragraph 5)
- "Lump-sum write-offs of [the related goodwill] should not be made to earned surplus immediately after acquisition..." (paragraph 9)
- "[the related goodwill] should [not] be charged against capital surplus" (paragraph 9).

The battle

> Opinions 16 and 17 [dealt with] an intractable problem ... the APB was polarized into two schools of thought whose views were so far apart and so strongly held as to be irreconcilable.
>
> (Hill, 1987, 18)

The pooling-of-interests method was questioned in the 1960s, and that was related to and matched by dissatisfaction with the then current reporting on goodwill related to business combinations. Issuers didn't want to charge the cost of the related goodwill against income (remember that issuers similarly wanted to avoid charges to income in connection with the issuance of stock options and that in that case they succeeded [temporarily]). They didn't have to under pooling. If pooling was to be eliminated, that would make things even worse.

If they had to ever use the purchase method of reporting after business combinations, issuers wanted to be able to either retain the related goodwill on the balance sheet indefinitely without amortization or charge it off against equity on acquisition. Either way would avoid charges to income for the related goodwill.

The research

One AICPA research study at the time recommended the elimination of pooling, reporting goodwill related to business combinations seen to have a life equal to that of the reporting entity without amortization, and the continuance of amortization of such goodwill if it's seen to have a life less than that of the reporting entity (Wyatt, 1963, 105, 106). The AICPA Director of Accounting Research at the time was dissatisfied with the following assumption underlying the analysis in the study:

> regardless of the form, a business combination occurs when one company acquires, assumes, or otherwise gains control over the assets or properties of another company by an exchange of assets or equities, or when two companies of equal size merge to form a new enterprise. Thus a business combination is essentially a particular type of business transaction.
>
> (Wyatt, 1963, 69)

He therefore had another researcher try.

The other researcher applied a different assumption:

> A business combination occurs whenever two or more companies are brought together or combined under common ownership for the purpose of continuing to carry on the previously conducted businesses.
>
> (Holsen, in Wyatt, 1963, 109)

The second researcher said that the first researcher had provided not "a definition of all business combinations ... [but] a definition of a purchase, a particular kind of business combination" (Holsen in Wyatt, 1963, 110). He said that

> In a pooling, one company does not acquire the assets or control of another; rather the shareholders who controlled one company join with the shareholders who controlled the other company to form the combined group of shareholders who control the combined companies.
>
> (Holsen, in Wyatt, 1963, 110)

He concluded that pooling should be continued.

Kam said pooling involves a "fiction":

> two arguments are given to justify the pooling of interests method. First ... this transaction is ... two groups of stockholders uniting (pooling) their interests ... second ... because the two entities ... continue to exist as going concerns, there is no new basis of accountability for the net assets ... The argument that a pooling is only an arrangement between two groups of stockholders is a fiction ... a discontinuity has taken place. Because of this disruption, a new basis of accountability exists.
>
> (Kam, 1990, 376, 377, 379)

Flegm implied the same: "pooling ... permits the earnings history of the old companies to be combined and reported ... for the new company *as though* it had been in existence for as long as the two companies existed" (Flegm, 1984, p, 95, emphasis added).

That is sound. Pooling should never have been permitted, because financial statements shouldn't incorporate fiction.

A second AICPA research study at the time also recommended the elimination of pooling but an immediate charge-off of the related goodwill directly against equity (Catlett and Olson, 1968, 105, 106).

Saving the day

The APB initially considered both pooling versus purchase and reporting on the related goodwill in one project on reporting after business combinations. But assenting votes of 12 of the 18 members of the APB were necessary at the time to adopt an Opinion, and disagreement on the Board was so fierce that no group of 12 members could be found that agreed on any combination of conclusions on both issues. It looked for a while that the APB wouldn't issue an Opinion in this area.

Someone saved the day, by suggesting that the issues be severed and placed into two projects. Having done that, 12 members were found who agreed on conclusions on pooling versus purchase and a different 12 members were found who agreed on conclusions on reporting on the related goodwill. That's the reason the APB issued its Opinions Nos 16 and 17 rather than one Opinion on two such intertwined issues on reporting after business combinations.

The APB's discussions of pooling versus purchase and of reporting on the related goodwill focused as usual on financial statement results and not on analysis, not on the nature of such goodwill, of financial position, or of income or on the needs of the users of financial reports. (I sat through every discussion by the APB on the issues, so I know that not even the existence, no less the needs, of the users was ever mentioned.)

APB Opinion No. 16

The APB issued an exposure draft in which it proposed to eliminate pooling. That was good standard-setting, as discussed in the last section of this chapter, but it was bad politics.

The first result was that the APB was forced by persons with power who have so much to gain by pooling to rescind its exposure draft and to issue its Opinion No. 16, which in effect permitted pooling and purchase as a free alternative (the criteria involved can be met relatively easily). *The second result was that the exposure draft (plus the Board's work on marketable securities [as discussed in Chapter 2]) was the direct cause of the death of the APB.* Though many alleged that the APB died because it failed, for example:

[The APB's] days were numbered. It became increasingly clear that the growing complexity of economic life required a full-time standard-setting group.

(Davidson and Anderson, 1987, 118)

the part-time APB was not equal to the task . . .

(Anton, "Foreword," in Flegm, 1984, vii)

the APB died not because it failed but because it threatened to succeed, to protect the users of financial reports against those who don't put the users' needs ahead of their own interests: "the concept of 'pooling of interests' [was] the rock upon which the Accounting Principles Board . . . founder[ed] in the late 1960s . . ." (Flegm, 1984, 81). That was how strongly the issuers felt about it.

Though Anton said that the APB was replaced by "the *independent* and more broadly based Financial Accounting Standards Board . . ." (Anton, "Foreword," in Flegm, 1984, vii, emphasis added), persons with much to gain from pooling and other principles they preferred thought they could more easily control the FASB, with the standard-setting body taken out of the AICPA and that very kind of person placed on the FASB's supervising Foundation. The creation of the FASB 32 years ago was a sell-out to the interests of the issuers according to a Chairman of the FASB and to a former member of the FASB:

The APB . . . was replaced by the FASB during its most productive period . . . through the efforts of a relatively few determined and vocal individuals who concluded that greener grass grew elsewhere.

(Beresford, 1995, 58)

"The FASB was created out of the ashes of its predecessor burned up in the fires of the . . . political process."

(Mosso, speech, 1, quoted in Solomons, 1986, 243)

The APB was killed, and the FASB, with its mammoth budget, was conceived, merely to shift the locus of power even more to the issuers of financial reports.

After the FASB announced in 1999 a tentative decision to try a second time to outlaw the pooling-of-interests method (*The New York Times*, 1999, C22), Senators Schumer and Shelby called for hearings by the U.S. Senate because, they said, the FASB "has not demonstrated the necessity" of killing "pooling of interests" (*Wall Street Journal*, 1999, B5). Lipe said: "It's certainly possible that, if the FASB pooling plan is defeated, Congress may question whether FASB should continue to be the primary standard-setting body" (quoted in *Journal of Accountancy*, 1999b, News Report, 16).

APB *Opinion No. 17*

The problem the Board faced in considering goodwill related to business combinations wasn't that they couldn't agree on an *analysis* of the events occurring, because they did no analysis; it was that its members couldn't agree even on the *results* they wanted:

- Some of its members wanted such goodwill to be charged off immediately directly to equity, but others didn't, because the reporting entities or their existing stockholders, through dilution, had paid so much for it
- Some of its members wanted such goodwill retained on the balance sheet indefinitely without amortization, but others couldn't accept that
- None of its members could accept large yearly charges against income for amortization of such goodwill.

Those three views appeared incompatible, and it looked for a while that the APB wouldn't issue an Opinion in this vital area.

Again someone saved the day, by suggesting a solution that achieved all three seemingly incompatible desired results:

- Goodwill related to business combinations was placed on the balance sheet
- Goodwill related to business combinations wasn't kept on the balance sheet without amortization indefinitely
- Goodwill related to business combinations wasn't amortized to income with large yearly charges.

All three were accomplished by extending the estimated life of such goodwill long enough so that yearly amortization charges were relatively small. That's where the 40-year life of such goodwill in the Opinion No. 17 came from:

> Permitting goodwill to be amortized over a maximum period of 40 years through the income statement in many instances strains credibility. But the 40-year period takes the sting out of the annual charge for goodwill, and with the effect of inflation over time, reduces the opposition to the rule.
>
> (*World Accounting Report*, 1989)

It didn't come from any studies of the lengths of lives of such goodwill, because such studies are impossible: it's not even possible to define the length of the life of such goodwill. That's acknowledged, for example, by the following:

few, if any, intangible assets last forever, although some may seem to last almost indefinitely.

(Opinion No. 17, par. 23)

Goodwill does not have a demonstrable useful life...

(AICPA, 1970b, Catlett dissent)

goodwill [has an] indeterminate [life]
(AICPA, 1970b, Burger, Davidson, Hellerson, and Horngren dissent)

Goodwill ... has no permanent existence (such as land). It has no definite, measurable life. It has neither limited nor unlimited usefulness.

(Blensly and Plank, 1985, 108)

The IASC understated the problem, saying the impossible is merely difficult: "Because goodwill represents future economic benefits from synergy or assets for which separate recognition is not possible, it is frequently difficult to estimate its useful life" (International Accounting Standards Committee, 1983, par. 46).

No one alleged that any studies had been conducted to arrive at the 40 years; it was just legislated: "The period of amortization should not ... exceed forty years"[5] (AICPA, 1970b, par. 29). (That's reminiscent of the tale, possibly apocryphal, that a state legislator once proposed a law that would have declared that the value of pi is three.) In contrast, the IASC legislated that the amortization period shouldn't exceed 5 years unless a longer period, not exceeding 20 years, can be justified[6] (International Accounting Standards Committee, 1983, par. 46).

Results of reporting after business combinations in conformity with Opinions Nos 16 and 17

There are no best results of reporting after business combinations in conformity with the current broad principles, with the defects of those principles. However, there are worse results of such reporting.

Pooling was the best of both worlds for issuers and outside auditors, as discussed in Chapter 10. It resulted in low reported asset amounts and high reported income: "The purchase method's effect is to reduce an acquiring firm's after combination earnings relative to pooling..." (Watts and Zimmerman, 1986, 296).

---

5 This was amended by SFAS No. 72 (FASB, 1983) to a slightly less arbitrary period for financial institutions.
6 The IASC managed to adopt one standard for both the pooling versus purchase issue and the goodwill issue.

Pooling permitted, even required, reporting entities *to report income they've bought rather than earned:*[7] "[It] essentially is a means of rationalizing a desired end result, which is to report higher earnings without having to earn them..." (Johnson and Petrone,[8] 1999b, 12). For example, "For years ITT was able to manage reported profits by selling stock that had been owned by Hartford Insurance before ITT acquired it" (Norris, 1999a, C1). (Hartford had earned the income ITT reported on the stocks but hadn't had the opportunity to report it yet under the current broad principles; pooling merely highlighted the real culprit, the acquisition-cost basis.)

Even Flegm, a passionate proponent of the acquisition-cost basis (remember, he referred to its "artistic beauty," as quoted in the beginning of the Prologue), acknowledged "instant earnings through poolings... pooled enterprises ... occasionally sell off a significant operating asset ... and obtain a dramatic boost in [reported] earnings" (Flegm, 1984, 94 and 96). Pooling shouldn't have been permitted even under the current broad principles, because it exacerbated the misinformation caused by the acquisition-cost basis.

Because the purchase method conforms with the current broad principles, it's also not beyond criticism, for example: "the purchase method allows the purchaser to distort dramatically in some cases the operating results of the acquired enterprise ... purchase accounting ... allows for more finagling than pooling" (AICPA, 1994b, II, 8b, 2).

The new requirements

As stated above, the requirements for reporting after business combinations were changed with the issuance by the FASB of its SFAS Nos 141 and 142 (FASB, 2001a, 2001b). The preceding discussions are helpful in appraising them.

Those pronouncements eliminated the pooling-of-interests method and terminated the amortization of the stated amount of the related goodwill. Instead, the related goodwill is stated in the balance sheet at the time of combination at its imputed cost, as always under the purchase method, but ordinarily left unchanged. Tests for impairment of goodwill are required annually and sometimes more frequently, usually requiring a present value technique. If a test shows that an amount of goodwill has been impaired, a loss is reported in the income statement in the amount of the impairment.

---

7 This conclusion is based on the view that the contention that no acquisition is involved in combinations reported on by pooling is false. This view agrees, for example, with the view stated by the Chairman of the FASB on March 2, 2000: "all business combinations are acquisitions" (Edmund Jenkins, 2000, 3).

8 These authors were members of the FASB staff, and the quotation is from an FASB publication.

The major improvement in financial reporting caused by those pronouncements is the elimination of the pooling-of-interests method, which,
as stated above, resulted in reporting income the reporting entity had not
earned but had bought. Another improvement is the elimination of the
amortization of the stated amount of related goodwill, a rational and systematic allocation, which, as discussed in Chapter 10, should not be used in
preparing financial statements. Offsetting that improvement is the requirement to test goodwill for impairment. Goodwill is pure prospects, which are
unmeasurable (see Chapter 16). No satisfactory test for the so-called impairment of goodwill is therefore possible. (The test requires predictions of the
issuers of the financial statements of future profitability of the reporting
entity; such thoughts of the issuers about the future shouldn't be used in the
design of financial statements, as discussed in Chapter 7.)

Reporting after business combinations to conform with the user-oriented criteria

Consideration to date by standard-setting bodies of reporting on business
combinations has been in the context of the current broad principles, especially its emphasis on acquisition costs for assets and its requirement to
present liabilities at the total of the amounts of money unpaid on the date of
combination, discounted at the interest rates implicit in the events that
caused the reporting entity to incur the liabilities (though those principles
would permit practical expedients, for instance, immediate write-off to
equity of goodwill related to business combinations, which was considered
during the battle). Presentations in conformity with those principles don't
in general comply with the user-oriented criteria (as indicated in Chapter 10
and elsewhere). Reporting after business combinations that would comply
with those criteria is considered here.

Chapter 14 concluded that to comply with the user-oriented criteria, assets
would have to be severable resources reported continuously at their current
selling prices. Chapter 15 concluded that to comply with those criteria, liabilities would have to be reported continuously at their current early repayment
amounts to creditors if known for sure, or at their current risk-free funding
amounts, whichever are lower. Based on those conclusions, the issue of pooling
versus purchase doesn't exist. (For assets, that issue involves which acquisition
costs to use as at the date of combination: [1] for pooling, the "unexpired" portions of the acquisition costs in the records of each combining company immediately before the combination, or [2] for purchase, the "unexpired" portions of
the acquisition costs in the records of the purported acquiring company then
and the costs incurred by the purported acquiring company to acquire the
assets of the purported acquired company at the time of combination [if the
companies were combined by transfer of stock and the assets therefore acquired
at no cost to the acquiring company, they would be reported at their amounts
current then, which would thenceforth be treated the same as acquisition costs].

For liabilities, that issue involves whether to report assuming [1] that the purported acquiring company incurred the liabilities originally incurred by the
purported acquired company at the date of combination, or [2] that the dates
the liabilities were incurred were the dates at which each combining company
originally incurred them. Neither of those choices is required, based on the
conclusions in Chapters 14 and 15.)

Based on those conclusions, all the severable assets of the combining companies would be reported at their selling prices current as at the date of combination and as at later dates, and all the liabilities of the combining companies
would be reported at their early repayment amounts to creditors if known for
sure or at their risk-free funding amounts, whichever are lower, current as at
that date and as at later dates. Since goodwill related to business combinations
isn't severable from the reporting entity or major components of the reporting
entity and thus has no current selling price, its cost or its current amount at the
date of acquisition would be reported as expense in the income statement of the
period of acquisition, preferably in a new section of the income statement on
investments in prospects (see Chapter 17).

That conclusion on the treatment of such goodwill requires amplification.
Goodwill related to business combinations (and all other goodwill for that
matter) represents only issuers' thoughts about the future, their hopes and
dreams:

> The amount assigned to purchased goodwill represents a disbursement
> of existing resources, or of proceeds of stock issued to effect the business
> combination, in *anticipation* of future earnings.
>
> (Catlett and Olson, 1968, 106, emphasis added)

> [Goodwill is] a quintessential "gain contingency"...
>
> (Schuetze, 2001, 5)

By definition, goodwill can't be sold separately from the reporting entity.
Though the reporting entity may have paid a large amount of money or
issued a large amount of its stock for it, the world doesn't currently show
that it sets any store on it by bidding on it, because it can't bid on it.[9]

---

9 Except as it might bid on an entity as a whole. But, as discussed in Chapter 9,
financial reporting does, should, and can report only on the individual assets and
liabilities of reporting entities, not on reporting entities as a whole (except in
reporting on investments in securities of the reporting entities). Reporting on
entities as a whole would be a new ball game. For example, not only would goodwill related to business combinations have to be considered, but also all goodwill
of all components of a reporting entity. At that stage, we would be outside financial reporting and in the arena of financial analysis: "The investor determines the
value of a business enterprise, based on his appraisal of the earning power of a
company" (Catlett and Olson, 1968, 107). Financial analysis should be informed
by, not inform, financial reporting.

Buying it is a crapshoot—will tomorrow's super income justify the expenditure? The FASB agrees: "assessments of future economic benefits [from goodwill] may be especially uncertain" (FASB, 1985a, par. 175). Issuers' thoughts about the future don't belong in balance sheets (see Chapter 7).

The gamble in acquiring goodwill should be reported by an immediate charge to income of its cost or its current amount at the date of acquisition. The CFA Institute (before May 2004, the AIMR) agrees: "goodwill ... ought to be removed from the list of assets forthwith ... a goodwill write-off should appear on the income statement..." (Association for Investment Management and Research, 1993, 49). So does a former Chief Accountant of the SEC: "the cost of purchased goodwill ... represent[s] an expense at the time the cost is incurred" (Schuetze, 1998, 5). These are the only other places advocacy of the treatment supported here apparently has been given. All other supporters of reporting the acquisition of goodwill related to business combinations by an immediate charge recommend that the charge go directly to equity. In categorizing the possible treatments, Bevis didn't even mention a charge-off to income:

> There are three broad possibilities of accounting for ... goodwill [related to business combinations]: (1) ... carry the amount in the balance sheet indefinitely ... (2) amortize ... (3) write off ... immediately ... *outside ... net income.*
>
> (Bevis, 1965, 143, 144, emphasis added)

Others indicated the defects of the third possibility:

> [An] objection to [writing off purchased goodwill at the date of acquisition against any surplus account that is available] is that if management of an entity has bought an asset, it should be accountable for it.
>
> (Skinner, 1987, 193)

> when you write goodwill off to equity ... it appears that the company's return on equity is phenomenal when in fact it is not.
>
> (AICPA, 1994b, II, 7a, 9)

Charging the cost or current amount of goodwill related to business combinations to income, in the section proposed in Chapter 17 on investments in prospects, when the goodwill is acquired sends a message to the users that the issuers have gambled a great deal of the reporting entity's current possession of or access to consumer general purchasing power or of the current stockholders' proportionate share in the reporting entity's stock on prospects and, being put on notice, the users will be able to decide whether they think that the improvement in the reporting entity's prospects is worth that depletion of its current substance. They should be helped by discussions on prospects in disclosures recommended by the AICPA Special Committee on

Financial Reporting and others in supplementary information, where they belong (as discussed in Chapter 17).

The improvement in the reporting entity's prospects by acquiring goodwill must usually be thought to be worth the cost, because goodwill is acquired so regularly. Besides, you can't make a buck without spending a buck. But tomorrow's hoped-for buck doesn't belong in today's balance sheet. It belongs in supplementary information.

Debating points

1 The history of the pronouncements on the topics of this chapter is boring and a waste of my reading time; just tell me what we have to do now and get on with it.
2 I'm enthralled by the history of the pronouncements in this area.
3 The pooling-of-interests method of reporting after business combinations presented the substance of the events best, and we should go back to it.
4 The pooling-of-interests method was the worst manifestation of the acquisition-cost basis.
5 The APB deserved to die, trying to jerk around the establishment that way.
6 The origin of the FASB was shameful.
7 Again, the author makes the issuers the bad guys for no good reason.
8 Allocation is a shell game; it's good that amortization of goodwill related to business combinations was eliminated.
9 Judging whether goodwill has been impaired is equivalent to holding a séance or patronizing fortune tellers.
10 An immediate charge to income of the cost of goodwill related to business combinations doesn't make any sense.
11 The only sound treatment of the cost of goodwill related to business combinations is to charge it off immediately to the income statement.

24 Reporting on employee benefits

Many employers spend considerable amounts of money on employee benefits in addition to the amounts they spend on salaries and wages. Employee benefits costing 30 percent of salaries and wages aren't unusual. Two major kinds of employee benefits have been the subject of issues in financial reporting—defined benefit pensions and postretirement benefits other than pensions—resulting most recently in FASB, "Pensions" (SFAS No. 87) (FASB, 1985b), and FASB, "Postretirement Benefits" (SFAS No. 106) (FASB, 1990a).

Reporting on defined benefit pensions

> [FASB] Statement [No. 87] retains [a] fundamental aspect . . . of past pension accounting: *delaying recognition* of certain events[—]changes in the pension obligation[s] . . . and changes in the value of assets set aside to meet those obligations are not recognized as they occur but are recognized systematically and gradually over subsequent periods . . . The Board acknowledges that the delayed recognition included in . . . Statement [No. 87] results in excluding the most current and most relevant information from the employer's statement of financial position.
>
> (FASB, 1985b, Summary, par. 104)

Defined benefit pension reporting has been in perpetual development. The FASB said in its SFAS No. 87, paragraph 5, that

> This Statement continues the evolutionary search for more meaningful and more useful pension accounting. The FASB believes that the conclusions it has reached are a worthwhile and significant step in that direction, but it also believes that those conclusions aren't likely to be the final step in that evolution. Pension accounting in 1985 is still in a transitional stage. It has not yet fully crystallized . . .

That's confirmed by the quotation at the beginning of this section and the inquiry that follows.

Focus on cost

> The assumptions and the attribution of cost to periods of employee service are fundamental to the measurements of net periodic pension cost and pension obligations required by this Statement.
>
> (FASB, 1985b, par. 15)

As this quotation indicates, the Statement establishes a focus on defined benefit pension *cost*. That conforms with the titles of both the predecessor of the Statement, APB Opinion No. 8, "Accounting for the *Cost* of Pension Plans" (emphasis added) (AICPA, 1966a) and the accounting research study that preceded it, Hicks, *Accounting for the <u>Cost</u> of Pension Plans* (emphasis added) (Hicks, 1965). The message is that the important thing in reporting on defined benefit pension plans is the income statement amount. Once that amount is determined, the related amounts in the balance sheet fall out:

> A liability . . . is recognized if net periodic pension cost recognized pursuant to this Statement exceeds amounts the employer has contributed to the plan. An asset . . . is recognized if net periodic pension cost [charged] is less than amounts the employer has contributed to the plan.
>
> (FASB, 1985b, par. 35)

Assets and liabilities again are supposed to come into existence solely by the supernatural power of bookkeeping: "pension cost recognized" and "pension cost charged" (discussed in Chapter 4). Hicks even advocated forgetting about assets and liabilities and concentrating solely on cost even in the balance sheet:

> it may be desirable to avoid using words such as *accrued* and *liability* in describing pension cost in an employer's balance sheet. Instead, a descriptive expression such as *Provisions for pension cost in excess of payments* or *Pension cost charged to expense but not funded* may be preferable.
>
> (Hicks, 1965, 85)

Focus on assets and liabilities

The income statement focus can distract attention from determining whether the items required to be reported as assets or liabilities under the Statement represent assets or liabilities and, if so, whether when they are required to be reported and whether the amounts at which they are required to be reported are sound. If not, their required reporting (along with the required reporting of cost) should be changed regardless of the thought given in the Statement to determining cost.

As to a reporting entity, a defined benefit pension contract concerns liabilities (as to the employees, it concerns rights). Costs are inferences from diminutions of assets or incurrences of liabilities. An employer incurs a defined benefit pension cost by incurring a liability for defined benefit pensions under the operation of a defined benefit pension contract; it doesn't incur a liability for defined benefit pensions by incurring a defined benefit pension cost. The sounder way to begin, therefore, is to see whether, when, and in what amounts an employer obtains assets or incurs liabilities under a defined benefit pension contract, not whether, when, and in what amounts the financial reporter finds it convenient to report such assets and liabilities. The assets or liabilities will then be reported soundly, and the cost will be too, being dependent on the assets or liabilities. Starting with the cost, in contrast, without the discipline of independent inquiry into how to report the assets and liabilities soundly, is likely through the political process to derive amounts that satisfy the incentives of the issuers, especially for stable income reporting, rather than reliably represent the operation of the contract. The FASB acknowledged that: "this Statement result[s] in . . . *gradual* . . . recognition of significant liabilities . . ." (FASB, 1985b, par. 152, emphasis added). A former Chief Accountant of the SEC said the same: "A large part of SFAS 87 is devoted to smoothing the hills and valleys of change" (Schuetze, 1991, 113). That's why standards on the subject have emphasized cost.

Strange contracts[1]

A further reason the FASB and others have had so much trouble determining how to report on defined benefit pensions is that "pension contracts with vesting provisions are strange contracts . . ." (Lorensen, 1992, 117), causing strange events with strange financial effects. Pension contracts are designed to be strange on purpose, to bind the employees to the employers. Reliably representing strange financial effects produces strange (though informative) results, but we financial reporters resist producing strange results. SFAS No. 87 is an example of such resistance.

The profession has ignored the strangeness. It thinks one simple pertinent event occurs:

> The critical past event is the rendering of services by employees . . .
> (Kam, 1990, 119)

> The FASB argued that the legal date of vesting serves merely to confirm an event which in substance[2] occurred some years before.
> (Hendriksen and van Breda, 1992, 748)

---

1 Much of this section is taken from Lorensen and Rosenfield, 1983.
2 The APB stated that financial reporting emphasizes the substance of events even though the form may differ from the substance (AICPA, 1970c, par. 25). That was for cases such as documents labeled "lease" that in substance evidenced sales. For example, an FASB EITF stated that "the fact that a contract called a 'trans-

It in effect contends that a reporting entity with a defined benefit pension plan with vesting provisions incurs a liability for pensions to each eligible employee the day the employee starts working instead of later, when the employee first vests. Such wishful thinking serves the issuers' incentives for stable income reporting. The contracts are strange because, contrary to the wishful thinking, the obligations and the increments in the obligations employers incur to the employees under the contracts period by period aren't all directly related to the work performed by the employees in those periods. If they were, that wouldn't encourage the employees to stay. The obligations and the increments in the obligations jump around. It's a wonder employers are able to get employees to agree to such compensation patterns. The employees wouldn't accept the salary and wage component of their compensation jumping around that way if they could help it.

An employee may work a considerable length of time for an employer with a defined benefit pension plan without the employer yet becoming obligated to her for a defined benefit pension benefit.

The conventional wisdom disagrees with that statement. It holds that the employer starts to become obligated to the employee for pension benefits when the employee starts working, before vesting occurs:

> The rendering of service by employees is *considered* the obligating event for pension costs and other postretirement benefits, even if the rights to compensation have not yet vested. This means that employees may have to render future service before they have a right to *any* benefit. However, in such a case, if it is probable that future service will be performed and payment will be made and the amount is reasonably estimable, a liability is to be accrued.
>
> (Kirk, 1990, 89, first emphasis added)

some employees will not receive their pensions because their employment is terminated before vesting. But this is a problem in *estimating* the amount of the employer's liability that can be solved on the basis of past experience and judgment, just like the problem of estimating

---

portation contract' is labeled a 'lease' is not automatically conclusive that the contract is a lease" (FASB, 1991c, par. 5). The concept became controversial when it was found that it was being abused. The presumption in particular circumstances should be that the substance is the same as the form and that convincing evidence is needed to overcome the presumption. Nothing in the pension reporting area provides any evidence, no less convincing evidence, to overcome the presumption that vesting is an event of substance, that the only reason for overcoming the presumption is to stabilize income reporting.

future warranty costs.[3] Only in this way can cost be recorded at the time necessary for *sensible income accounting*.

(Skinner, 1987, 208, emphasis added)

Rather than analyzing the events that occur, we "consider" what events would have to be occurring to justify the income reporting result we desire (see the discussion of the related term "construe" in Chapter 21). The so-called "sensible income accounting" is stable income reporting, regardless of what happens to reporting entities that have such strange contracts. And how about sensible reporting in the balance sheet?

An analysis rather than an offhand consideration of the financial effects of the events that occur follows. This analysis has to be provided because SFAS No. 87 doesn't provide such an analysis.

Analysis

No past event or transaction causes a reporting entity to have a liability for pension benefits to an employee who terminates employment before vesting. The work done by the employee before vesting doesn't cause it—the vesting provision of the contract says it doesn't. After an employee has started working but hasn't yet become even partially vested, the reporting entity has incurred merely a *contingent* liability, one that's contingent on vesting.

After some more time has passed, the employee becomes partially vested, and the employer suddenly incurs an obligation to the employee in two parts.[4] The first is based on the employee's current year's service and current

3 In fact, liabilities involved in warranties cover *existing* conditions (the usual expression is "manufacturing defects") that may come to light as the consumers use the product; they are current, not future costs. Those rare warranties that cover defects caused later by the consumer represent contingent liabilities that shouldn't be reported as liabilities but merely disclosed until the customers cause the defects. Reporting on liabilities for manufacturing defects is discussed in Chapter 15. Similarly, the allowance for doubtful accounts should cover only receivables that are currently bad, as discussed in Chapter 14. Measuring the amount often requires rough estimates. Chambers and Staubus believe, in contrast, that prediction is involved: "provision for doubtful accounts ... are anticipatory and, therefore, not corroborable" (Chambers, 1966, 261); "the estimation of future cash flows requires that consideration be given to bad debts..." (Staubus, 1977, 139).

4 It may be argued that the employer incurs no obligation to an employee for any particular defined benefit pension payment until and unless the employee has retired and lived long enough to collect it. If so, defined benefit pension liabilities are incurred when defined benefit pension payments are due and the employees are alive and not before. Lorensen said he "rejected this ... because attributing a separate obligation to each *payment* promised is not reasonable" (Lorensen, 1992, 116, emphasis added). An additional counterargument is that living to a particular date is a nonevent, the absence of dying, and is therefore not one of the events causing a defined benefit pension liability to come into existence. You should think about this relatively uncharted area.

salary or wage. That isn't strange. The second is based on a retroactive calculation incorporating prior years of service and on the current salary or wage. That's strange. Would a coal-dealer sell you coal that way?

The employer may incur two increments in the obligation to the employee each subsequent year. The first is based on the added year of service and the then current salary or wage. That isn't strange. The second, if any, again is based on a retroactive calculation, caused by a salary or wage increase, if any, that year, which is multiplied by the total of the previously incurred obligation. That's strange. It's an imposition on the employer and a windfall to the employee of a kind that befalls no party to any other kind of contract to my knowledge.

Later, in addition to those two yearly increments in the obligation, the employer suddenly incurs another large increment based on a retroactive calculation whose magnitude is comparable to the first obligation incurred based on a retroactive calculation, caused by the employee receiving an increase in the vesting percentage. That again is strange.

For each subsequent year, the employer may again incur two increments in the obligation to the employee. The first is based on the added year of service and the then current salary or wage. That isn't strange. The second, if any, again is based on a retroactive calculation, caused by a salary or wage increase, if any, that year, which is multiplied by the total of the previously incurred obligation. That's strange.

Next, the employee may become fully vested, which means that the employer suddenly becomes obligated for another large strange increment in the obligation based on a retroactive calculation, again caused by the employee receiving an increase in the vesting percentage.

This kind of analysis has been described as the output of "accountants with a legalistic bent of mind..."[5] (Skinner, 1987, 207). However, the analysis concerns timing, when liabilities are incurred under defined benefit pension plans, and doesn't depend on whether they are legally enforceable. This kind of analysis would apply equally to pledges made to a church that are never legally enforceable. Such an analysis would conclude that such a pledge results in incurrence of a liability by the person who makes the pledge, *but not before the person makes the pledge*. Further, were a vested benefit not legally enforceable, it could still be a liability under certain circumstances.

"Forfeitures"

> The Board believes that the actuarial measurement of the obligation encompasses the probability that some employees will terminate and *forfeit* nonvested benefits.
>
> (FASB, 1985b, par. 149, emphasis added)

5 I was one of the financial reporters he was referring to.

The concept of *forfeitures*, which underlies current defined benefit pension reporting, may be satisfactory in the never-never land of actuarial work, from which financial reporting borrowed it, as paragraph 149 states (see the last paragraph in Chapter 4 for a discussion of borrowing from other disciplines). But financial reporting is supposed to deal with the real world, as paragraph 21 of FASB's CON5 states: "Real things and events that affect a ... business enterprise are represented in financial statements..." In the real world, the concept of forfeitures is misleading concerning the pattern in which the employer incurs obligations and increments in obligations under a defined benefit pension contract. It means that the employer becomes obligated to provide benefits and the employees become entitled to benefits before they are vested, but that if an employee leaves before becoming vested, she forfeits some or all of the benefits to which she previously became entitled and the employer is relieved of the previously incurred obligations.

But every employee knows that she doesn't become entitled to benefits before they are vested and that *she can't forfeit anything she never had*—"You can't lose what you don't have" (Grisham, 2001, 181)—(except for the opportunity she does have of obtaining vesting in the future if she stays that long—that's one of the things that tends to keep her there—but everyone forfeits an infinite number of opportunities every day, and none of them should affect financial statements, being the difference between what happened and what didn't happen (see Chapter 7). For example, she also forfeits the opportunity to continue to be employed by the reporting entity, to be promoted, and so on). As Kirk stated, as quoted above, "employees may have to render future service before they have a right to *any* benefit." They have no rights they would be able to forfeit before they vest, and, likewise, the employer has no such obligation.

That can be seen in bold colors by considering a new reporting entity with new employees and a new pension plan that provides for partial vesting only after employees have been working for the reporting entity for at least three years. SFAS No. 87 would require the reporting entity to report a liability for pension benefits a year after it started, when no employee yet has the right to any future pension benefits—none has any benefits to *forfeit*— and the reporting entity has no obligation for any pension benefits.

Perhaps employers want to try to fool employees into thinking they get something before they get it and that the employer becomes obligated before the employees vest. I doubt that the employees are fooled. And we financial reporters shouldn't let ourselves also be fooled. Aren't we financial reporters supposed to be cold-blooded, clear-eyed skeptics?[6] Reporting shouldn't be based on such fictions.

6 Consider this oft-quoted description by Elbert Hubbard:

The typical auditor is a man past middle age, spare, wrinkled, intelligent, cold, passive, non-committal, with eyes like a codfish; polite in contact but at the same

Employees gain no pension rights before they become at least partially vested—they have nothing yet to forfeit—and their employers incur no liabilities for pension benefits to them before then, only contingent liabilities. The only reason we pretend otherwise is to stabilize the reporting of unstable pension costs and expenses: as quoted above, the FASB acknowledges that (emphasis added):

> changes in the pension obligation[s] ... and changes in the value of assets set aside to meet those obligations are not recognized as they occur but are recognized [by following SFAS No. 87] *systematically and gradually* [read "smoothly"]...

The Board decided to ignore the nature of contractual vesting provisions so it could achieve the result it wanted to achieve for the issuers, a relatively stable reported pension expense trend, rather than the strange reported pension expense trend that actually occurs under pension contracts with vesting provisions, which are strange contracts. Such standard-setting violates the principle against such stabilizing quoted below, established by the very body, the FASB, that stated the principle.

FASB's treatment of the liabilities

SFAS No. 87 doesn't provide such an analysis. It bases its determination of liabilities and cost simply on allocations based on predictions of—thoughts about—salaries and wages and vesting percentages at the times the employees are predicted to retire or leave, as indicated in its definition of *actuarial present value*:

> The service cost component of net periodic pension cost [on which the pension liability is based, as discussed above] is the actuarial present value of benefits attributed by the plan's benefit formula to services rendered by employees during the period
>
> (par. 16)

> *Actuarial present value.* The value, as of a specified date, of an amount or series of amounts payable or receivable thereafter, with each amount adjusted to reflect ... the probability of payment (by means of decrements for events such as death, disability, withdrawal, or retirement) between the specified date and the expected date of payment.
>
> (Glossary)

---

time unresponsive, calm and damnably composed as a concrete post or a plaster of Paris cast; a petrifaction with a heart of feldspar and without charm of the friendly germ, minus bowels, passion or a sense of humour. Happily they never reproduce and all of them finally go to Hell.

That treatment hides the jumpy way defined benefit pension obligations and increments in obligations are incurred. Beresford, a Chairman of the FASB, said as much: "much of the complexity of SFAS 87 is due to efforts to reduce volatility of earnings" (Beresford, 1990). At a public hearing on reporting on defined benefit pension plans, Kirk, the then Chairman of the FASB, said a concern of the FASB in drafting the pronouncement was to be sure it contained "an adequate amount of smoothing," apparently to appease the issuers. That contrasts with other statements he made, also quoted in Chapter 5:

> the Board has rejected "smoothing" or "normalization" as part of the concept for measuring income, thereby more sharply delineating the boundary between accounting and financial analysis . . . if normalization is needed, that is the analysts' responsibility.
>
> (Kirk, 1986, 4, quoted in Solomons, 1986, 167)

> No matter how well-intentioned the standard setter may be, if information is designed to indicate that investment in a particular enterprise involves less risk than it actually does . . . financial reporting will suffer an irreparable loss of credibility.
>
> (Kirk, 1986, 233)

Further, the treatment results in presenting some of the liabilities before they are incurred.

The purpose isn't to arrive at the most faithfully representational amounts for defined benefit pension assets and liabilities (and costs). If that were the purpose, they wouldn't include amounts for salary and wage increases not yet granted and vesting percentages not yet gained. Such amounts have two flaws, each of which is fatal.

First, the future salary and wage increases may not be granted and the future vesting may not occur (in fact, the future may not occur; this is discussed in Chapter 7, footnote 15). The FASB would probably say that's taken care of in the probability work done by the actuaries, implied by the definition of *actuarial present value*. Though I don't agree with that, it's not in any event the more fatal flaw (assuming that there are degrees of fatality).

The more fatal flaw is the violation of the FASB's definition of *liabilities*. The definition requires that all the events causing liabilities have already happened by the date of the balance sheet (see Chapter 9) "as a result of *past* transactions and events," that, in contrast with a contingent liability (which isn't a liability), no event required for the relationship to come into existence is yet to happen. Including future salary and wage increases and future vesting, which by definition haven't yet happened, makes some of the so-called liabilities the retroactive effects of events that haven't yet happened, that may happen later. Kirk said that: "future salary increases have *retroactive effects* on the benefit earned . . ." (Kirk, 1990, 89, emphasis added). However, though retroactive *calculations* (thoughts that may or may not be written down) or retroactive *laws* or *agreements* (which have only prospective, not retroactive effects—they don't and can't change the past) can be and are made, *events don't have retroactive effects* (they also don't and can't change the past—see Chapter 7), as everyone knows. Time marches on. Cause and effect don't work backwards in time. Including such future events in reported pension liabilities doesn't reliably represent the employer's obligations at the reporting date.

Sprouse stated that view in his dissent to SFAS No. 87:

> an employer cannot have a present obligation for pension benefits related to salary increases that are contingent upon future events . . . the decision to grant increases in wages and salaries . . . is an event that has directly related consequences, including increases in employer social security taxes and pension costs, as well as the wages and salaries themselves. Accounting should recognize all of those directly related consequences at the time the event occurs . . . Anticipating the effects of those future events on pension cost in accounting for the current period . . . is no more appropriate than anticipating the future higher wages and salaries themselves in accounting for the current period.

The FASB countered that in SFAS No. 87 (par. 82) by another misuse of the accrual concept (see Chapter 9):

> Any accrual basis of accounting for defined benefit pension plan inevitably requires estimates of future events because those events determine the amount of benefits that will be paid.

But accrual doesn't require "estimates [predictions] of future events"; it requires nothing except the absence of the cash basis. (If it required anything positive, it would be periodic determinations of all financial-related *current* conditions and all changes that *have occurred* in all financial-related conditions. The user-oriented criteria such as representativeness require or prohibit more than accrual does, but the FASB doesn't invoke them, as we have seen.) Once again we are given the incredible proposition that current conditions (in this case, currently existing defined benefit pension liabilities) are caused by or affected by or somehow dependent on future events rather than vice versa. (The issue is when the events occurred causing the obligations to be incurred, not what events determine the amounts.)

Because accrual doesn't require predictions of future events, because in fact that's the antithesis of accrual, which reports what did happen, that quoted passage is rewritten to state what's really meant:

> To report pension cost for a defined benefit pension plan in a stable pattern, predictions of future events are required, because that's the only way to achieve that result.

The only reason SFAS No. 87 adopted such thinking is that it results in presenting incurrence of defined benefit pension liabilities and costs in a stable pattern rather than how they were actually incurred. As an issuer stated,

> field-testing ... sponsored by the Financial Executives Research Foundation ... confirmed that application of the FASB's tentative conclusions would have introduced a high degree of volatility into companies' annual pension expense ... This resulted in the Board making changes in the final standard that helped to reduce volatility ... they did listen—but it was not without considerable prodding.
>
> (Ihlanfeldt, 1991, 28, also quoted in Chapter 2)

That caused the FASB to surrender. It said: "The [FASB] believes that the [pension reporting] method should be more effective in reducing income statement volatility than the method proposed in the Preliminary Views" (FASB, 1984b, 3). Even SFAS No. 87 stated that an alternative considered by the Board was "rejected [simply] because of the volatility that it would introduce..." (FASB, 1985b, par. 155). That contrasts with the FASB's avowed opposition to stabilizing reported income:

> The Board recognizes that some investors may have a preference for investments in enterprises having a stable pattern of earnings, because that indicates lesser uncertainty or risk than fluctuating earnings. That preference ... is perceived by many as having a favorable effect on the market prices of those enterprises' securities ... [But] earnings fluctuations ... should be reported as they occur.
>
> (FASB, 1975a, par. 65, also quoted in Chapter 5)

Even so, a complaint was voiced that the statement allowed too much instability in income reporting to remain, that it doesn't result in a "steady state charge":

> In ... Statement ... No. 87 ... the FASB mandated the projected unit credit (PUC) method ... even though the method was used by less than half the U.S. companies, most of whom favored some variation of the entry-age normal (EAN) method ... The PUC method results in the accrual of a point-in-time liability which ignores the long-term nature of employee relationships ... On the other hand, the EAN method reflects the long-term nature of pension costs and results in a steady state charge to earnings...
>
> (Flegm, 1989, 92)

When this chapter was first drafted, it said that

I don't know what "the long-term nature of pension costs" and "the long-term nature of employee relationships" mean, though I have often heard those expressions. The author didn't explain what they mean (no one has to my knowledge), why this expense or these relationships conform with those expressions, whatever they mean, and why they make any difference in the reporting. Also, the concepts seems to suit what seems to be the purpose of the author—stabilizing income reporting. For those reasons, I tentatively conclude, until and unless I learn more about it, that the concept was invented solely for that purpose and not to make financial statements conform more closely to the user-oriented criteria.

When I showed that to Flegm, he said the long-term nature of the expense and the long-term nature of the relationships are "self-explanatory and reflective of the fact that pension costs accrue over decades of employment." That doesn't address the issue in pension reporting, which is the pattern, period by period, in which pension obligations are incurred, not the total length of time over which they are incurred. Saying that pension costs accrue over decades of employment doesn't help solve that issue, and it doesn't demonstrate that the pattern is a "steady state."

Employers want to keep their employees bound with defined benefit pension contracts, but don't want to report the strange results of the contracts.

Sound pattern of reporting defined benefit pension liabilities and costs

Defined benefit pension liabilities (and related costs) should be reported based on the conclusions in Chapter 15 in the pattern in which the employer incurs defined benefit pension obligations and increments in the obligations, as discussed above. It should report that it has become obligated for each of the obligations and increments when it incurs it, not before. That means that imagined future vesting and imagined future salaries and wages should be ignored in reporting on pensions (as all issuers' thoughts about the future should be ignored in designing financial statements; this is discussed in Chapter 7). SFAS No. 87 should be changed to accomplish that. Current probabilities involved in pension liabilities should be considered in determining their amounts (see Chapter 7).

Other peculiarities

Paragraphs 35, 36, and 37 of SFAS No. 87 contain other examples of how starting with results rather than proceeding by analysis for the benefit of the users got the FASB into trouble in that Statement. Paragraph 36 sets a floor on the liability determined in accordance with paragraph 35 of what it calls the *unfunded accumulated benefit obligation*. If a liability otherwise determined has to be raised to the floor by a given amount, paragraph 37 requires that amount to be also presented as an intangible asset to the extent of the unfunded prior service cost.

However, that amount isn't an asset. It doesn't fit the FASB's definition of an asset, there being no benefit involved: a reporting entity doesn't get anything from a defined benefit pension plan except improved employee morale unless it has excess defined benefit pension assets, and this amount isn't such an excess and it doesn't represent improved morale. A former Chief Accountant of the SEC asked: "What can users do with an intangible asset arising from smoothing out pension expense except to ignore the asset?" (Schuetze, 1991, 117).

The FASB shouldn't permit, no less require, us financial reporters to report as assets things that aren't assets.

Further, paragraph 37 requires the excess of the given amount over the unfunded prior service cost to be presented as a separate component (deduction) in equity, reflecting the FASB's ambivalence about the additional liability. If the reporting entity actually incurred the additional liability, it would be a reduction of income, not an asset or a reduction of equity. It's another example of nonarticulation to achieve the financial reporting results desired rather than to simply reliably represent the financial effects of the events when the events occur.

Postretirement benefits other than pensions

While the FASB project that resulted in its SFAS No. 87 on defined benefit pensions was underway, a rumor circulated that, as much as that project was expected to affect financial reporting, a project on postretirement benefits other than pensions (mainly health-care benefits) was in the wings whose effects would dwarf those of the defined benefit pension project. Doom was predicted because of high and rising health-care costs. Reporting entities would be forced to report mammoth new liabilities, driving them out of business (this again reflects a belief in the supernatural power of bookkeeping).

SFAS No. 106 (FASB, 1990a), the result of the second project, required employers for the first time to report liabilities for postretirement benefits other than pensions before the employees retire and possibly before they become sick or injured. It hasn't brought about doom.

Though the issuers opposed this development vigorously, they didn't take the ultimate step of stopping it by appealing to Congress and the SEC or terminating the existing private sector financial reporting standard-setting body, as they did in connection with reporting on oil and gas exploration costs, pooling of interests reporting, and round one concerning reporting in connection with the issuance of stock options (as discussed in Chapters 18, 19, and 23). They likely were ambivalent about this one: they didn't like to have to start reporting a large liability for postretirement benefits, as they do for deferred taxes, which they support, but the Statement did to some extent serve their incentive for stable income reporting, by reporting the cost of postretirement benefits ratably over the working lives of the employees.

Objective of the statement

> An objective of this Statement is to recognize the cost of an employee's postretirement benefits over the employee's credited service period...
>
> (FASB, 1990a, par. 158)

This quotation reveals what the FASB had in mind in designing reporting for these benefits—stable reporting of the cost involved. Why didn't the FASB, having sworn allegiance to representational faithfulness in its CON2, paragraph 63 (FASB, 1980b), have as its objective instead to represent the compensation cost faithfully in the periods in which it's incurred, rather than to produce a designer income statement that makes some people feel good?

It could have found out when the cost is incurred the same way the timing of the incurrence of any cost should be determined, by determining when liabilities whose incurrence causes the costs are incurred (or when assets decreases occur that cause costs to be incurred). As discussed above, incurrence of liabilities causes incurrence of cost, not vice versa. Instead, under SFAS No. 106, the FASB construed when the liabilities are incurred by fashioning the income reporting that pleased it and letting the liabilities fall out.

Fatal defect

As a result, SFAS No. 106, like SFAS No. 87, discussed above, and SFAS No. 109, requires reporting of liabilities before they are incurred, when they don't exist. The FASB's attempted defense of the existence of the liabilities at the reporting date has the same fatal defect as in Test No. 3 in its defense of deferred tax liabilities (discussed in Chapter 21). It relies on the error in its discussion of a *liability* cited in Chapter 21 and in the discussion of defined benefit pension obligations above, that a liability is caused by only one event.

Since a liability can in fact be caused by more than one event (see Chapter 15) and, by the definition of a cause, isn't incurred until the last event that causes it occurs, we should see whether any events after the reporting date are causes of the liability the FASB requires us to report as of the reporting date. We have to look because the FASB didn't. They had an agenda, indicated by the quotation that opens the section above on "Objective of the statement," about an objective of SFAS No. 106.

The liabilities are mainly for health-care bills incurred for sickness or injury requiring treatment after the employees retire. For most of those bills, the people covered haven't become sick or been injured by the reporting date.

For example, a covered employee who is 20 years old at the reporting date may incur hospital and doctor bills because she may break her arm 50 years after the reporting date, five years after she retires. Breaking her arm, if it happens, is a cause of the liability (in the absence of which the liability wouldn't come into existence) in addition to her working 50 years before. The employer doesn't have a liability to pay those bills 50 years before she broke her arm. FASB, 1975a (pars 29 and 30) says that:

> An enterprise may choose not to purchase insurance against risk of loss that may result from injury to others ... Mere exposure to risks of those types ... does not mean that ... a liability has been incurred ... Losses of those types do not relate to the current or a prior period but rather to the *future* period in which they occur.

In accordance with those paragraphs, it's at most a contingent liability that requires no more than disclosure until she breaks her arm: "Recognizing a liability for postretirement benefits under SFAS No. 106 can ... result in recognizing a liability before it is incurred..." (Lorensen, 1992, 118). A so-called liability for uninsured postretirement benefits for care for health problems that haven't occurred by the reporting date is one of the old, outlawed, reserves for so-called self-insurance.

A source in effect challenged that:

> The assumption that OPEBs [other postemployment benefits] are part of the total compensation package for covered employees clearly stamps them as being attributable to past transactions or events.
>
> (Wolk *et al.*, 1992, 497)

That view implies that because OPEBs are attributable to past transactions or events, they cause expense when they are incurred. However, employers can compensate employees by incurring either liabilities or contingent liabilities. OPEBs cause merely contingent liabilities. Incurring those contingent liabilities is attributable to past transactions or events, as the view states, but it doesn't cause expense, at least not at the times of their incurrence. Expense in such circumstances is caused at the times contingent liabilities become liabilities.

Reporting liabilities for postretirement benefits for health care shouldn't be anticipated. Other postretirement benefits should be similarly analyzed. When such liabilities are incurred, they should be reported based on the conclusions in Chapter 15. The contingent liability should be disclosed.

Exceptions for insurance and pre-existing conditions

If postretirement benefits involve purchase of insurance, expense for such benefits is incurred when the obligation to purchase the insurance is incurred, fulfilling that obligation can't be avoided, and the payments on the obligation for the insurance, if made, can't be recouped. The obligation and the expense should be reported then. Also, if an employee becomes ill or is injured on or before the reporting date and it's probable at that date that the illness or injury will cause the employer to make health-care payments after the employee retires, the employer should report a liability for postretirement benefits in the amounts of those payments that are probable at the reporting date (as discussed in Chapter 7).

Advance funding

Some employee benefits are funded in advance of payments being made to the employees, especially pensions. Such advance funding is making of deposits, which should be shown as resulting in an asset, to be recouped by reversion to the employer or by use for payment of benefits.

Earnings management

Like deferred taxes, the current principles for reporting on employee benefits are just one more way to manage earnings to stabilize income reporting rather than provide information. They should be changed to represent the financial effects of the events that occur period by period. Reported income might thereby yo-yo more, but that would represent what happened.

Debating points

1 The FASB should be complimented for taking a go-slow approach to pension reporting reform.
2 It's a scandal that the FASB requires reporting entities to withhold vital information they have available on their pension plans.
3 Pension costs are the most important thing to get right, so analysis should begin with them.
4 Pension liabilities are the name of the game, and analysis should start with them, even if just to get pension costs right.
5 Reporting on strange pension contracts should reflect that fact.
6 Pension reporting should make us feel good.
7 What's good enough for actuaries should be good enough for us.
8 Actuaries live in their own little world; we shouldn't let ourselves be led around by the nose by them.
9 Unvested pension liabilities is an oxymoron.

10 It feels just as bad to me to lose unvested pensions as to lose vested pensions.

11 Don't snipe at me about the nonexistence of an asset from dealing with an unfunded accumulated pension benefit obligation.

12 It's hard for me to swallow abandoning the standard on postretirement benefits other than pensions.

25 Reporting on leases and executory contracts

To have an asset, an entity must control future economic benefit to the extent that it can benefit from the asset and generally deny or regulate access to that benefit by others, for example, by permitting access only at a price ... Leases ... give a lessee a right to possess and use the property ... the future economic benefits of a particular building can be an asset of a particular entity only after a transaction or other event—such as ... a lease agreement—has occurred that gives it access to and control of those benefits.[1]

(FASB, 1985a, pars 183, 185, 190)

Leases are pervasive in business operations, and how to report on them has occupied much attention by standard-setters.

Capitalize all active noncancelable leases?

A former director of research of the AICPA who was an author of two AICPA research studies (Moonitz, 1961, and Sprouse and Moonitz, 1962) contended that all active noncancelable leases should be reported as providing assets: "the asset ([is] the right to occupy the premises)..." ([Moonitz and Jordan, 1963, 325]) and causing liabilities if some rent is yet to be paid. (Active leases are those in which possession of the leased property has been transferred to the lessee.) Two AICPA research studies themselves contended the same thing:

> [if] the right to use the asset has not been purchased for its full useful life ... it is not incorrect to record ... the smaller asset being purchased for a smaller price ... The fact that the right expires before the asset becomes useless to anyone in the economic sense can hardly make a

---

1 Might one hope that the FASB would some day act on those statements from its Conceptual Framework and require reporting of assets for all active noncancelable leases and liabilities for all active noncancelable leases on which some rent is yet to be paid?

significant difference; it is useless to the lessee at the expiration of the lease.

(Myers, 1962, 37)

In a fixed-payment operating lease, the transfer of control of the property to the lessee is the last event specified in the contract that must occur before all payments become unconditionally required of the lessee. When that event occurs, the lessee incurs a liability . . . in exchange for the right to use the property for a specified period. Such a property right is in conformance with FASB's definition of assets.

(Lorensen, 1992, 75, 76)

Even the AICPA committee on accounting procedure hinted back in 1949 that assets and liabilities should be reported for all active noncancelable long-term leases, in AICPA, 1949, by referring in paragraph 1 to "the practice of using long-term leases as a method of financing..." (It didn't, however, require such reporting; in fact, in paragraph 3 it said this about reporting in connection with leases at the time: "It has not been the usual practice for companies renting property to disclose in financial statements either the existence of leases or the annual rentals thereunder." The SEC did require such disclosure at that time.)

The CFA Institute (before May 2004, the AIMR) agrees: "We would require capitalization of all executory contracts with an initial term in excess of one year. That would eliminate many of the problems attendant on lease accounting" (AICPA, 1994b, II, 8c, 3). Some members of the FASB and some respondents to its drafts also agreed that all active noncancelable leases should be reported as resulting in assets and all with some rent left to be paid as resulting in liabilities:

Some members of the [FASB] hold the view that . . . a lease, in transferring for its term the right to use property, gives rise to the acquisition of an asset and the incurrence of an obligation by the lessee which should be reflected in his financial statements . . . A number of the respondents [argue] that some leases contain clauses that make the lessee's obligation absolute and unconditional, and . . . such clauses should be made the determinant for capitalization of leases containing them.

(FASB, 1976b, pars 63, 70)

Also, the FASB published a study that concluded that "a compelling case can be made that any non-cancelable lease will give rise to assets and liabilities..." (McGregor, 1996, 17). Others have said the same, for example:

In theory . . . all long-term leases ought to be capitalized.

(Hill, 1987, 89)

A lease is equivalent to a purchase except that access to the services is acquired for a limited period of time only, rather than for the asset's lifetime. If the essence of an asset lies in the services it can provide, it is arguable that all leases should be capitalized ... opposition [comes] from those who desire ... off-balance sheet financing ... It seems probable that ... capitalizing all leases ... would not be readily accepted.

(Skinner, 1987, 96)

Nevertheless, they are voices in the wilderness (though they haven't been directly challenged in the literature). As discussed below, the conventional and FASB wisdom is that if a lease doesn't meet any of the conditions for a capital lease in SFAS No. 13 (FASB, 1976b), it's a so-called operating lease, said to be an executory contract. And as long as a contract is executory, it's not reported under current GAAP as providing assets and causing liabilities (unless a loss is involved because the assets to be received are currently worth less than the consideration promised): "The effects of executory contracts ... are generally not recognized until one of the parties at least partially fulfills his commitment" (AICPA, 1970c, par. 146).

The issue is of concern to issuers of financial reports, because they want to keep obligations from so-called operating leases off the balance sheet—they want, as Skinner says as quoted above, to do so-called *off-balance sheet financing*. The reason is that "Other things being equal, the lower the equity–debt ratio, the greater the risk borne by creditors" (Chambers, 1966, 191). Adding them to the statements as assets and liabilities would decrease their reported equity–debt ratios and possibly cause them to incur higher costs of capital. In fact, the rules in SFAS No. 13 can be used to design contracts to avoid that result: "people intent on avoiding capitalization of leases [use the SFAS 13 rules] to do so" (Taper, 1981, 23, quoted in Solomons, 1986, 124). That's the opposite of searching for ways to provide sound information for the benefit of the users.

A proviso is needed: a lease may be cancelable by the lessee: "a company can get out of a lease obligation in some circumstances" (AICPA, 1994b, II, 8c, 7). If so, no liability is involved under any theory (except possibly for past-due rent), and an asset consisting of the right to use the leased resources is involved for only any period for which the rent is paid up.

Definition of an executory contract

Because of the special treatment under GAAP of a contract while it's executory, it's important to know when a contract is executory and when it stops being executory.

There is no single authoritative definition of executory contracts, though there is general agreement on their nature. The following is a typical definition: "commitments call for a future exchange of resources, and until one party to the agreement performs all or a part of the agreement ... [it is an] executory contract" (Danos and Imhoff, 1986, 687). Under that definition, a contract is certainly executory before either party has performed at all on its promise. When one party has completely performed on its promise, the contract is just as certainly no longer executory, and GAAP requires reporting of the resources and obligations involved as assets and liabilities. There may be a gray area between the extremes in which some performance by one party or both parties may or may not terminate its status as an executory contract.

Capitalize all executory contracts?

Some have advocated that GAAP for executory contracts be changed so the promises are reported as creating assets and liabilities for all contracts while they are still executory. In addition to the AIMR, quoted above, one pair of authors support that by quoting AICPA, 1970c, par. 181 (S-1E), that "an exchange of promises between the contracting parties is an exchange of something of value..." (Cramer and Neyhart, 1979, 136). The FASB has been on the fence:

> Although the definitions in this Statement do not exclude the possibility of recording assets and liabilities for purchase commitments, the Statement contains no conclusions or implications about whether they should be recorded.
>
> (FASB, 1985a, n75)

The FASB announced on June 11, 2003, that it would study reporting on executory contracts anew.

Among reasons given against capitalizing all executory contracts are that

> The promises have value, but their value is slight because they are conditional. An exchange of promises of value does not imply that the promises cause obligations to be incurred ... The promises made or received by a party at the inception of a contract may exert some compulsion on the party to perform. However, that compulsion would be too weak to justify the conclusion that the party incurs an obligation at that time.
>
> (Lorensen, 1992, 6, 6n)

If two parties sign a contract, that shouldn't yet be enough to justify requiring reporting of a liability by either party. If anything, it is a contingent liability; the "value" the AICPA referred to is contingent, contingent on performance by the other party.

Are active leases executory contracts?

> Some of the forms of executory contracts are long-term noncancellable leases...
>
> (Cramer and Neyhart, 1979, 135)

It's commonly thought that active leases are executory contracts. The AICPA thought so: "Agreements for the exchange of resources in the future that at present are unfulfilled commitments on both sides are not recorded until one of the parties at least partially fulfills its commitment, except that ... some leases ... are recorded" (AICPA, 1970c, par. 181 [S-1E]). And, as quoted above, the AIMR thinks so.

However, *no noncancelable lease is an executory contract once it's active, that is, once possession of the leased assets has been transferred from the lessor to the lessee.*

Some agree with that conclusion:

> Where a lease contract is not cancelable by the lessor it is probable that a nonexecutory contract exists. The lessor has provided the property for the period of the lease ... The lessor has performed his obligations ... The lease contract would need to be "effectively cancelable" for an executory contract to exist.
>
> (Henderson and Peirson, 1980, 352)

> It can be argued that a lease contract is fully executed by a lessor when possession of the leased asset is transferred to a lessee.
>
> (Wolk *et al.*, 1992, 512)

> The lessor ... turned [the assets] over to the lessee ... The lease is fully performed on the lessor's side...
>
> (Kripke, 1989, 38)

> Leases can be distinguished from executory contracts by the fact that leases cease to be executory when the leased property is delivered or otherwise made available to the lessee.
>
> (Nailor and Lennard, 2000, 20)

However, that position is contrary to the views of most of us financial reporters and needs convincing defense if it's to be accepted.

The defense in outline is that the lessor has promised to do only one thing, to transfer possession of the leased assets to the lessee at the inception of the lease. Once the lessor has done that, the lessor has performed its single promise under the contract; the lessor has nothing left to do. Because a contract in which one party has fully performed is no longer executory under any reasonable definition of that term, the contract is no longer executory.

At that time, the lessee has the control of an asset required by the FASB, as indicated by the quotation that begins this chapter.

The contrary position, that the lessor hasn't fully performed on its promise under the contract when the lessor has transferred possession of the leased assets to the lessee at the inception of the lease, is supported by a statement in the analysis of classes of events presented in Appendix A to Chapter 3. The statement is that

> some exchanges take place on a continuous basis over time instead of being consummated at a moment of time—for example, accumulations of . . . rent.
>
> (AICPA, 1970c, par. 62 [I.A.1])

The message is that the lessor performs not at the inception of the contract when the lessor transfers possession of the assets, but continuously, "over time." That statement is taken for granted by the profession.

However, no one has ever seen a lessor perform continuously over time (have you?), so one wonders where the APB got that idea (it doesn't say where). A possibility is that the APB saw that we financial reporters report rent continuously over time and assumed that the reporting represents the effects of external events. The lessor must be performing continuously over time, the thought must go, or there apparently would be no excuse to report rent continuously over time. Also, reporting that way conforms with the issuers' incentive for stable income reporting, so that gives standard-setters the incentive to look for events in the financial reporting territory to conform with the financial reporting map.

A lender who gives money to a borrower at the inception of a loan and then does nothing but wait around until the money rolls in (sooner or later, depending on the contract) is analogous to a lessor who gives possession of assets to a lessee at the inception of a lease and then does nothing but wait around until the rent money rolls in. The statement quoted above about exchanges taking place continuously over time equally covers loans, referring to "interest." The possibility of events occurring continuously over time during the term of a loan has been explored and dismissed in Chapter 15. They don't occur that way for leases any more than they occur that way for loans.

Reporting on leases

Because active leases aren't executory contracts, all active leases result in the acquisition of assets and all active noncancelable leases result in the incurrence of liabilities unless all the rent is paid at the inception of the lease, and they should be reported as such.

Many loan agreements contain debt covenant clauses that cause the debts covered by the clauses to come due immediately if the total amount of other debt of the debtors exceeds stated or determinable amounts. Currently, many liabilities under leases aren't reported as such in balance sheets. Were they to become required to be reported as such, they could be counted as debt under many of the debt covenant clauses and cause covered debts for many debtors to become due immediately. That's likely the main reason the FASB hasn't required the liabilities under all active noncancelable leases to be reported as such in balance sheets. Its solution to the problem has apparently been to protect the debtors and to deprive the users of financial reports of sound information on the debtors' liabilities. The sound solution would be to require such reporting and thereby force the debtors to have the debt covenant clauses rewritten.

Because "[t]he greater the relationship between the amount of a residual equity and the amount of liabilities, the less is the risk of the creditor" (Chambers, 1966, 107), reporting all active noncancelable leases as resulting in liabilities would make many reporting entities appear riskier than they now appear, which might depress the market prices of their securities. When and if this treatment is considered by standard-setters, issuers would fight to prevent enactment of a requirement to put it into effect because current reporting of operating leases provides so-called off-balance-sheet financing—financing that doesn't result in presentation of liabilities in the balance sheets of their companies—which enactment of the requirement would prevent. Leasing companies would likely join the fight, because part of the justification of the existence of their industry is that they provide so-called off-balance-sheet financing.[2] Past performance of standard-setters shows that they likely would acquiesce to those special interest groups rather than protect the users.

The old saw that disclosure is the way to go instead of reporting the asset and liability, discussed in Chapter 17, is often stated in connection with leases, for example:

> Full disclosure of the obligation under the lease agreement is more meaningful than the way the leases are accounted for on the balance sheet. It is more important to have full disclosure than to account for the lease in a specific way.
>
> (AICPA, 1994b, I, 73)

It's no more worthy here than anywhere else. Were it, few assets and liabilities would need to be reported in the line items of financial statements.

Enron's main fault was leaving some large liabilities out of its balance sheets. SFAS No. 13 permits large liabilities to be omitted legally.

---

2 Even in 1972, "organized lobbying on accounting for leasing was rampant" (Horngren, 1972, 40).

Reporting under the current broad principles

The reporting of assets and liabilities obtained by leases depends on whether the current broad principles are applied or whether reporting is designed to best conform with the user-oriented criteria.

Application of the current broad principles to active noncancelable leases as worked out by SFAS No. 13 and its amendments and interpretations requires rules to determine which of such leases result in assets and liabilities and which don't. Those rules are irrelevant for sound reporting, because no such distinction should be made except for cancelable leases. A problem with those rules is that once they are stated, issuers find loopholes in them to avoid reporting the liabilities they would require, so new rules are required to close the loopholes. The process never ends: "The ... FASB found it necessary to issue twenty-four separate pronouncements on accounting for leases [up to 1987]..." (Hill, 1987, xi), many of which pertain to the distinction.

Rules are provided to measure the assets and liabilities to be reported once the distinction is made. Lease contracts are complex and diverse. Applying the current broad principles to those contracts can be complicated—thus the need for detail rules. The quality of those rules is irrelevant, because, as Chapter 10 concludes, those principles result in data that don't conform with the user-oriented criteria and should be abandoned.

Reporting to conform with the user-oriented criteria

To conform with the user-oriented criteria, the conclusion in Chapter 15 applies to liabilities incurred under active noncancelable leases, because they are in general similar to those incurred under other kinds of arrangements. Special rules may have to be developed to apply that conclusion in special cases, but they aren't considered here (Lorensen considers them in Lorensen, 1992).

The resources acquired under leases, the right to use leased resources, are strange: "a lessee ... has no right to sell the acquired property when it is acquired" (Lorensen, 1992, 83). A lessee can do only two things with resources acquired under active noncancelable leases: (1) use the leased resources, or (2) sell the right to use the leased resources to others (sublease them). Some leases prohibit subleasing, so the lessee can only use the leased resources.

In either case, a lessee takes a gamble entering into a noncancelable lease. The lesser gamble is with a lease that permits subleasing. The greater gamble is with a lease that prohibits subleasing.

Applying the conclusion of Chapter 14 to active noncancelable leases depends on whether subleasing is permitted. If it is permitted, the asset should be reported at the amount for which the leased resource can be sublet at the reporting date (payment is sometimes made by assuming the lessee's obligation). Subleasing is often difficult or impossible even if the contract permits it. A rebuttable presumption should therefore be made that though the contract permits subleasing, it's unlikely that a subtenant could be found as of the reporting date. Strong evidence would be needed to rebut that presumption. The evidence would indicate the amount for which the resources could be sublet, and that would be the current selling price at which the leased asset should be reported.

However, if subleasing is prohibited or not possible, the following applies:

> The current cash equivalent of the asset lease rights is the amount for which they could be sold. If they are not salable then the current cash equivalent is zero and there would be no asset on the books.
>
> (Henderson and Peirson, 1980, 357)

That's similar to the reporting of specialized assets that can be sold only at their scrap amounts at those amounts (as recommended in Chapter 14). But look what the lessee has gotten itself into: it can't get out of paying the rent until the lease term ends, and the only thing it can do with the leased resources is use them. The danger in entering into such a contract was illustrated in the 1930s:

> The ... defect ... lies in the omission of a significant asset and an even more significant debt. The debt is more significant because it is fixed by contract; the tenant cannot get out from under [it] at will. The experience of many companies in the Great Depression caused some doubts to be expressed as to the adequacy of the conventional approach. These companies found that the asset (the right to occupy the premises) had declined substantially in value; the debt ... was however not so easily scaled down. Bankruptcy proved in some instances to be the only way to get out from under the obligations—obligations which had *not* been reflected in their financial statements.
>
> (Moonitz and Staehling, 1952, 318)

An example closer to the home of us financial reporters was a lease entered into by the firm of outside auditors Spicer and Oppenheim for office space it couldn't service and couldn't sublease:

> The New York-based firm ... had the misfortune of opening fancy new headquarters at the World Trade Center only months before the 1987 stock market crash and insider trading scandals sent its core Wall Street clientele reeling...
>
> (Cowan, 1990, D3)

> Spicer & Oppenheim ... said it could disband as early as Friday ... the

firm continued to be hamstrung by costly expenses such as its recent four-story office lease in Manhattan's World Trade Center.

(*Wall Street Journal*, 1990, C17)

The lease was a principal cause of the firm going out of business.[3]

The acquisition of a resource under an active noncancelable lease that the reporting entity can't sublease results in no current achievement of current possession of or access to consumer general purchasing power the same as the acquisition of a specialized asset that can't be sold for other than scrap, and the assets should be reported the same, at scrap or at zero. The liability should be reported as recommended in Chapter 15.

Debating points

1   Lease reporting is just fine as it is.
2   All active noncancelable leases should be reported by lessees as providing assets.
3   Of course all leases are executory contracts; everybody has always said they are.
4   Reporting assets acquired under leases by referring to subleasing clauses would mislead users of financial reports.

3 That may have been lucky for those who worked for Spicer and Oppenheim, considering the events of September 11, 2001.

26 Consolidated financial statements

There is a presumption that consolidated statements are more meaningful than separate statements and that they are usually necessary for a fair presentation when one of the companies in the group directly or indirectly has a controlling financial interest in the other companies.

(AICPA, 1959, par. 1)

Consolidation of the financial statements of the members of a group of companies[1] under common control is covered in general by the first major U.S. pronouncement on the subject, ARB No. 51 (AICPA, 1959), which remains the current major pronouncement on the subject. That pronouncement, quoted above, makes it appear that consolidation had always been with us.

Consolidation hasn't always been as firmly established everywhere else, however. For example, when International Accounting Standard No. 3, "Consolidated Financial Statements" (International Accounting Standard Committee, 1976), was issued by the IASC in 1976, countries such as France and Japan said it would cause a revolution in their financial reporting. And, before the *Seventh Council Directive Concerning Consolidated Accounts* of the European Economic Community was issued, "Consolidation was only legally required in a minority of Community member states" (Price Waterhouse, 1983, 2).

In its SFAS No. 94, "Consolidation of All Majority-Owned Subsidiaries" (FASB, 1987a), the FASB significantly revised the consolidation policy requirements of ARB No. 51. Consolidation policy, discussed below, consists of selecting the members of a group of related companies to include in the consolidated reporting entity. The FASB has had, off and on since 1982, a project to revise the entire Bulletin, including the possibility of an even more significant revision to consolidation policy by widening the concept of control. That project hasn't yet resulted in other significant changes to consolidation reporting.

---

1 Consolidated financial statements are called *group accounts* in the UK.

Should consolidated financial statements be presented?

> The question [of whether consolidated statements are necessary] has long since ceased to be asked.
>
> (Chambers, 1969, 631)

The first issue in consolidation is whether the financial statements of a group of related companies should be consolidated at all.

Most observers support consolidation. However, that practice shouldn't be beyond reconsideration, because no significant practice in financial reporting should be beyond reconsideration. Consolidation has never been comprehensively justified. A reconsideration likely would provide added confidence in its merits, but it's conceivable that it would provide convincing reasons to abandon the practice.

As indicated in Chapter 8 in the section "Selection of the reporting entity as classification," selection of the reporting entity is a purposeful activity. Reporting entities are selected because they are thought to best serve the purposes at hand. Consolidation is justifiable if it best serves the needs of the parties at interest in the parent company, the persons for whom consolidated financial statements are presented.

Chambers, Clarke, Dean, and Oliver made the most explicit arguments against ever presenting consolidated financial statements. Chambers acknowledged that he "has been guilty as anyone else in perpetuating the acceptance of the consolidation solution" (Chambers, 1969, 635), recalling that he had once written that "it is appropriate to consider the group as one entity ... This calls for a consolidation of the financial positions and results of all companies in a group" (Chambers, 1966, 288). But he repented:

> it now seems that the alternative is much more easy to defend on logical and practical grounds, and that the result is far more comprehensible and realistic than the product of the consolidation process ... annexures to the financial statements of the holding company, simple aggregative statements of the assets and liabilities and profit and loss account items of all the subsidiaries.
>
> (Chambers, 1969, 633, 635)

Clarke, Dean, and Oliver are implacably opposed:

> consolidated financial data cannot by any stroke of the imagination be considered a realistic reflection of the aggregative wealth and progress of the related companies ... aggregative representations of the outcome of the so-called group operations and its financial position are a financial nonsense.
>
> (Clarke *et al.*, 1997, 266, 267)

An objection to presenting consolidated financial statements comes from concerns about undisclosed restrictions on transfers of resources among members of consolidated groups. The control of a parent company over its subsidiaries isn't absolute. The parent company ordinarily may do nothing to prevent other entities that have interests in the subsidiaries from the full enjoyment of their rights. Major categories of such other entities are creditors and noncontrolling stockholders of the subsidiaries. Resources ordinarily may not be transferred from subsidiaries to the parent company or other subsidiaries under the direction of the parent company to harm those other entities, as intercompany transfers or otherwise. The assets of one member often may not be available to pay the liabilities of another member: "a consolidated balance sheet may be misleading because ... [l]egal distinctions between entities are often necessary to evaluate solvency..." (Heath, 1978, 140, 141). The consolidated balance sheet obscures that by merely listing all the assets and all the liabilities. Full disclosure can mitigate the problem, by indicating significant barriers to the movement of resources within the consolidated group of companies. Such disclosure isn't now required.

A related problem is the possibility that financial difficulties of some members of the group will be obscured by financial successes of other members of the group: "Critics of consolidated statements believe that the aggregation of data tends to hide and distort rather than inform" (Kam, 1990, 409). Full disclosure could mitigate that problem, too, though such disclosure is also not now required.

Most observers who support consolidation agree that those concerns are real, but they believe they can be overcome by disclosure and shouldn't be allowed to prevent users from receiving what they believe is the benefit of consolidation, which is reporting what they believe to be the substance of the relationships and events and not merely their forms.

Perhaps the FASB will provide a justification of consolidation in its project and give it added stature or, if the highly improbable happens and the FASB concludes that consolidation is on balance harmful, prohibit it.

Consolidation policy

If consolidated financial statements should be presented, consolidation policy needs to be determined. Consolidation policy should be determined by considering the needs of the users.

ARB No. 51 liberally excluded subsidiaries from the consolidated reporting entity. Beside excluding subsidiaries whose control by the parent is likely to be temporary or whose control doesn't rest with the majority stockholders (for example, a subsidiary in legal reorganization or bankruptcy), the Bulletin (in paragraph 2) permitted exclusion of subsidiaries in which the minority interests were so large in relation to the majority interests that presentation of separate financial statements for the companies were thought to be more meaningful and useful. It also gave (in paragraph 3) free choice in excluding subsidiaries. It said subsidiaries may be excluded simply

> if the presentation of financial information concerning the particular activities of such subsidiaries would be more informative to shareholders and creditors of the parent company than would the inclusion of such subsidiaries in the consolidation. For example, separate statements may be required for a subsidiary which is a bank or an insurance company and may be preferable for a finance company where the parent and the other subsidiaries are engaged in manufacturing operations.

Such exclusions seem to reflect less than complete allegiance to consolidation and likely seemed sensible at the time.

However, many began to object to the exclusion of subsidiaries whose control isn't in question, for several reasons. First, the practice resulted in consolidated financial statements that didn't aid comparisons of investment opportunities, because similar groups excluded subsidiaries diversely. Second, and perhaps more important, the exclusion of finance subsidiaries and similar subsidiaries kept many liabilities off consolidated balance sheets that would otherwise have been reported there. The reported debt-to-equity ratios were lower than they would have been had those subsidiaries been consolidated. Issuers believe the lower the reported debt-to-equity ratio is, the better, so they favored such exclusion:

> It would take too long to describe all of the other means available, within GAAP, to keep liabilities off the balance sheet, but one of them does deserve mention—that is, the nonconsolidated subsidiary ... The result ... is generally to maintain a lower debt-to-equity ratio...
>
> (Solomons, 1986, 124)

Information shouldn't be slanted that way to benefit the issuers to the detriment of the users.

For those reasons the FASB in its SFAS No. 94, in spite of considerable objection, especially from those who issued consolidated statements with large subsidiaries excluded at the time, terminated the exclusion from consolidation of any majority-owned subsidiary whose control by the majority stockholders of the parent company isn't in question.

The FASB has indicated that, in its project to reconsider consolidation, it's considering a requirement to consolidate minority-owned subsidiaries or even companies none of whose stock is owned by the parent company that the parent company controls by other means. If so, what has been known as minority interests could become noncontrolling majority interests for those consolidated reporting entities, with all the complications that portends. (Reporting on noncontrolling minority interests has been complicated enough, as discussed below.)

A fictitious reporting entity?

Because the reporting entities in consolidated financial statements transcend the legal boundaries of single member companies, the nature of the consolidated reporting entity is an issue, at least a terminological one (terminological issues are critical to financial reporting, whose terminology—such as "cost flows" and "expired cost," discussed in Chapter 10—has regularly led it astray). Authoritative financial reporting bodies have defined it in fictitious ("as if") terms. For example, ARB No. 51 (AICPA, 1959) stated in paragraph 1 that consolidated financial statements "present . . . the results of operations and the financial position of a parent company and its subsidiaries essentially *as if* the group were a single company with one or more branches or divisions" (emphasis added). International Accounting Standard No. 27 (International Accounting Standards Committee, 1990) defined consolidated financial statements in paragraph 6 as "statements of a group presented as those of a single enterprise." Clarke, Dean, and Oliver did the same: "Consolidating the separate financial statements of the parent company and its subsidiaries in effect lifts the corporate veil *as if* the accounts of each were those of the mere branches of one" (Clarke *et al.*, 1997, 269, emphasis added). But a consolidated reporting entity isn't fictitious and it isn't a single enterprise. It's a group of companies united for economic activity by common control.

Defining the consolidated reporting entity as it is not, turns consolidated statements into pro forma information. It provides precedent for injecting other pro forma aspects into financial statements, which should be factual parts of financial reports. Such a tendency should be resisted wherever it's accepted or proposed. Pro forma information included in financial reports should be separated from the financial statements and labeled as such.

Treatment of noncontrolling stockholdings

Though observers have agreed that noncontrolling stockholdings should be reported separately on the right side of the balance sheet in the U.S., they don't agree on their nature and on where on that side they should be reported.

Three camps

Observers fell into three camps over much of the twentieth century: (1) those who believed noncontrolling stockholdings should be reported with the liabilities, (2) those who believed they should be reported as a separate component in equity, and (3) those who believed they should be reported in a separate category between the liabilities and equity. The debate took on the appearance of a comedy routine. Never did any of the observers acknowledge the differences of position or try to justify their own positions, which some of them changed without apology or defense, even without notice. The users deserve higher-quality financial reporting literature than that.

The camps and examples of their camp followers are as follows (emphasis is added in these quotations).

1   *Camp 1—Liability:*

The proper practice is to take up as a *liability* the par value of the outstanding stock [held by the minority stockholders] together with its relative share of surplus.

(Dickinson, 1917, 183)

Any minority interest in subsidiaries is shown as the last item of *liabilities*.

(Macleod, 1981, 4.15)

2   *Camp 2—Equity:*

Under *capital stocks* will be included ... such part of the stock of the subsidiary companies as are not owned by the holding company.

(Lybrand, 1908, 120)

Minority interests ... are part of *equity*.

(FASB, 1985a, par. 254)

3   *Camp 3—Between liabilities and equity:*

The minority interest should be shown as *a distinct element between the liabilities proper and the capital and surplus* attaching to the dominant interest.

(Paton, 1941, 803)

The minority interest in the equity of consolidated companies should be classified in the consolidated balance sheet as a *separate item* and *should not be shown as part of stockholders' equity*.
(International Accounting Standards Committee, 1976, par. 43)[2]

Whenever an issue in financial reporting remains unsolved for a long time, such as this one has, we should suspect that something is wrong with the way it's formulated. Alternative formulations should be sought and evaluated, as discussed at the beginning of Chapter 3. An alternative formulation here might be, for example, whether noncontrolling interests should be reported in consolidated financial statements at all.

2 Note that the IASC and the FASB disagree.

Two possible ways to keep noncontrolling interests off the statements are suggested below.

First way—facilitate financial analysis[3]

The discussion of equity in Chapter 8 in the section "The reporting entity's side of its transactions and relationships" suggests the first way. The point is made there that the reporting entity's relationships and transactions with others each has two sides, the reporting entity's side and the other party's side. Because the reporting entity can't report both sides of a relationship or transaction it has with another party, it has to choose which side to report. The reasonable answer is for it to report its own side.

A U.S. reporting entity therefore shouldn't report the interests of others in it on the right side of its consolidated balance sheet; it should report its duties to others there, to the extent that it can. Based on that, a consolidated reporting entity not only shouldn't report the controlling interest ("owners' equity"), as discussed in Chapter 9, but it also shouldn't report the noncontrolling interest. As stated in that chapter, it should merely report in its balance sheet its assets, its liabilities, and its equity in its assets, simply the excess of the stated amounts of its assets over the stated amounts of its liabilities. Its liabilities represent its duties to its creditors. The duties of the consolidated reporting entity to its noncontrolling interests can't be reported in the consolidated balance sheet any more successfully than can its duties to its controlling interests, as discussed in Chapter 9.

The problem of the existence of noncontrolling interests in a consolidated group of companies is that if, as, and when subsidiaries with noncontrolling interests declare dividends, the parent company will have to share them with those interests. The effect of such possible future sharing can't be determined currently; it's a matter that should be considered by financial analysis. Information should be disclosed in the notes to facilitate such analysis.

Second way—proportional consolidation

Proposals have been made to keep noncontrolling interests off consolidated financial statements a second way, by proportional (or proportionate) consolidation. Under proportional consolidation, the assets, liabilities, revenue, and expenses of a subsidiary with noncontrolling interests are included in the consolidated financial statements only to the extent of the controlling interest. If the parent owns 60 percent of the stock of a subsidiary, 60 percent of each of the assets, liabilities, revenue, and expenses of the subsidiary are included. The equity of the reporting entity is then said to pertain all to the controlling interest.

3 This discussion and the next are taken from Rosenfield versus Rubin, 1986.

Proportional consolidation has these things in its favor: (1) the consolidated balance sheet balances and articulates with the consolidated income statement, and (2) no amounts are reported for the interests of outsiders, the noncontrolling interest. But reporting, for example, 60 percent of a building held 100 percent by a member of the consolidated reporting entity gives at least some people pause:

> Proportionate consolidation ranks right there in my mind with computing per-share data on segments. I don't know what those numbers mean; I don't think anybody knows ... You lose information with proportionate consolidation. For example, do they have $54 million of cash they could spend or $41 million?
>
> (AICPA, 1994b, II, 6, 2)

I don't support proportional consolidation.

Debating points

1   Whether consolidated financial statements should ever be presented is a dilemma.
2   Companies not majority owned by the parent company, directly or indirectly, shouldn't be consolidated; the FASB has lost its collective mind even considering consolidating them.
3   All companies controlled by the parent company, regardless of percentage of ownership, should be consolidated.
4   I don't care how consolidated financial statements are described; fictitious-schmictitious.
5   Minority interests should be excluded from the number columns of balance sheets.
6   Minority interests shouldn't be excluded from the number columns of balance sheets.
7   Proportional consolidation is a jim-dandy idea.

Epilogue
The hijacking of GAAP

> The only reason that the FASB wins [its] arguments is a political one, to wit, the SEC requires public companies in the U.S.A. to follow the FASB's rules. Resolution of such debates should turn on relevance of information, logic, merit and substance, not political clout.
>
> (Schuetze, 2001, 25)

In the Prologue, I promised to attempt to be evenhanded in presenting the major issues in financial reporting and the solutions to those issues that have been offered in the financial reporting literature. I nevertheless said I would also state my own views forthrightly, including solutions and arguments not otherwise found in the literature. I urged you readers to think for yourselves, to challenge the proponents and opponents of every side of every issue, including me. In one place (see Chapter 12), I went so far as to warn you readers to beware of a fundamental conclusion of mine, because it disagrees with so much of the financial reporting literature.

In this Epilogue, I abandon the attempt to be evenhanded. I state my overall views based on my conclusions that I state throughout the book without offering possible conflicting overall views. I leave the task of developing conflicting views to you readers.

Defective foundation of corporate governance

> corporate accounting does not do violence to the truth occasionally and trivially, but comprehensively, systematically and universally, annually and perennially.
>
> (Chambers, 1991b, 17, quoted in Dean, 2003, i)

The foundation of the edifice of corporate governance is GAAP. The issuers of the financial statements of reporting entities that sell their securities in public markets are required to conform them with GAAP. Outside auditors are required to use GAAP as the standard by which to appraise the reporting in financial statements. Peer review and the Public Oversight Board of the

AICPA, which supervised peer review, used GAAP as an underpinning of their work. The Public Company Accounting Oversight Board uses GAAP as an underpinning of their work. The SEC reviews filings with it for conformity with GAAP. Negligence and fraud in preparing, issuing, and auditing financial statements are gauged at least partly by lack of sound conformity with GAAP. The entire edifice of corporate governance rests on the assumption that sound application of current GAAP leads to sound reporting. Problems, for the most part, are thought to be caused by violation or substandard application of current GAAP.

But the main source of the problems isn't violation or substandard application of current GAAP. It's current GAAP itself. This is explored in this book and in Rosenfield, 2000.

The incentives of the users of financial reports should be paramount. But, the incentives of the issuers and the incentives of the users of financial reports in the design of GAAP are opposed, the issuers currently have the most power and influence in the design of GAAP, and the outside auditors have an incentive to tilt toward the incentives of the issuers. The result is inevitable: sound application of current GAAP doesn't lead to sound reporting. Financial reports are consumer products. Consumer products should be reliable and safe. However, as they are currently designed they are unreliable and unsafe:

> Present accounting rules perpetuate—indeed institutionalize—the very deficiencies in the quality of accounting information that they are relied upon to remediate.
>
> (West, 2003, 110)

> audited financial reports are among the most highly regulated yet also the least reliable of commodities.
>
> (Richard Brief, series editor, in West, 2003, front matter)

> Accounting practice enjoys a peculiar insulation from the conventional idea in Western law that consumers may presume goods and services to possess the characteristics making them fit for the uses commonly made of them.
>
> (Clarke *et al.*, 1997, 242, quoted in West, 2003, 181)

Further, their amounts are unauditable. The problem isn't mainly violation or substandard application of current GAAP, as committed by Enron, WorldCom, and the like—it's that current GAAP itself is seriously defective and produces amounts that are to a large extent unauditable.

West concludes that "The future of accounting as a professional occupation is bleak" (West, 2003, 188).

Power struggle

> we [should] look at the progress of accounting in the context of a power
> struggle...
>
> (Sterling, 1973, 65)

At present, consideration of financial reporting standards isn't essentially an intellectual activity. It's a power struggle: "Perhaps the APB should ... be renamed ... the Accounting Principles–Political Action Board" (Horngren, 1972, 39). The users so far have lost in that struggle, because the issuers and their allies—the outside auditors, the regulators, and elected and appointed government officials—have the power and are to a considerable extent arrayed against the users. The issuers and their friends have hijacked GAAP to serve their own interests.

Is there a solution?

> Effectively meeting the expectations of investors and the public in [the current] environment requires a standards-setting process that has the independence to withstand the myriad of constituent pressures that it inevitably faces and to make the tough decisions that inevitably are required.
>
> (Sutton, 2002, 324)

Some hope that the FASB can lead to a solution. For example:

> It may well be that one of the roles of the FASB should be to first initiate and lobby for a social arrangement whereby, attestors to, and analyzers of accounting information find it in their self-interest to apply the standards that could be derived from the objectives specified in the conceptual framework. Unless this prior step is taken by the FASB, it is not likely to succeed in its effort.
>
> (Ronen and Sorter, 1989, 73)

Some hope that formulation of financial reporting standards by the federal government can lead to a solution: "Some ... support ... a government override or takeover if private-sector standard setting produces unacceptable answers" (Beresford, 1995, 56). Others have their doubts:

> Mr. Levitt called Mr. Reed's argument [to eliminate the FASB and have the SEC replace it] "rich with irony ... I wonder if the theory is Government officials would develop better rules because they are much more reasonable, practical, thoughtful and flexible than their rigid, insulated and unresponsive brethren in the private sector."
>
> (Hansell, 1997, D9, quoting a comment of Levitt, Chairman of the SEC, about an argument of Reed, Chairman of Citicorp)

My doubts are based on my suspicion that financial reporting standard-setting by the federal government would lean to the politically powerful and vocal, not to the users of financial reports. I don't feel the same about the possibility of the PCAOB replacing the FASB as the setter of financial reporting standards.

To cut through the military–industrial (issuer–outside auditor) type complex that skews financial reporting standards-setting today would require a revolution of thinking. Giving outside auditors real independence and terminating the influence of the issuers on the standard-setters, regulators, and other government officials may be most of what's needed. Those changes are easier said than done, but Glater saw a ray of hope:

> Over the long run, the collapse of Enron may bequeath auditors far more authority, making it possible for them to stand up more readily to companies whose executives fear the Houston energy company's fate.
>
> (Glater, 2002)

The Sarbanes–Oxley Act of 2002, enacted because of the financial reporting breakdowns described in the Preface, requires that only the audit committees of the boards of directors of companies that sell their securities in public markets be allowed to appoint and discharge the outside auditors of the companies. That's a change from the previous arrangement in which the audit committees had that power but management often in fact performed those functions. Only time will tell whether that change significantly enhances the independence of outside auditors and whether that will make financial reporting standard-setting less controlled by the issuers of financial reports. One result has already been that outside auditors have increasingly become the party that does the discharging: Browning reports that "auditors are increasingly choosy about the companies they keep" (Browning, 2005).

Dangerous ideas

> soon or late, it is ideas, not vested interests, which are dangerous for good or evil.
>
> (Keynes, 1935, 384, quoted in Sterling, 1989, 82)

A major reason for my offering this book is to present ideas. If they are sound, who will take up the cause of making them dangerous? Will the AICPA? Will the FASB?[1] Will the SEC?[2] Will the PCAOB? Will Congress?[3]

---

1 In 1999 I explained to Jenkins, the Chairman of the FASB, the direction of the conclusions of this book and offered to send him an early draft. He declined the offer.
2 In 1998, Levitt, the Chairman of the SEC, criticized the financial reporting profession for engaging in earnings management by distorting the application of

Will you?

The current state of financial reporting is shameful. My jawboning would do no more good here than it usually does anywhere by anyone. Only you, the future of financial reporting, and especially those of you who are students or are or will become leaders of the profession, or are statesmen, can end this shame. And only if you love the profession or the nation enough, and feel responsible enough to your sole real clients, the users of financial reports and the citizenry.

Debating points

1 Current GAAP resulted from a process of give and take over a long period and is now good enough.
2 Financial reports are now unreliable and unsafe.
3 The future of accounting as a professional occupation is bright.
4 The FASB is currently the best hope for the profession and the users it serves.
5 The PCAOB is currently the best hope for the profession and the users it serves.

GAAP. In 1999 I told him about a central conclusion of this book, which is that earnings are currently managed to far greater effect by the application of inherently faulty GAAP than by distortion of the application of GAAP. In 2000, Turner, the Chief Accountant of the SEC, told me that

> Your letter seems to advocate ... an immediate, complete overhaul of GAAP. That answer, however, may not be practical ... We would welcome your views on other actions that might be undertaken to address the issues raised in your letters.

(Turner, 2000)

I told Mr Turner that I was advocating only a gradual overhaul of GAAP. In response to Mr Turner's request for my "views on other actions that might be undertaken," I provided him and Mr Levitt with a then-current draft of this book and outlined its contents and conclusions. I urged the SEC to become active in this matter. I indicated that I suspected that partisan opposition would emerge but that the SEC shouldn't allow itself to be thereby thwarted. I indicated that the FASB would have to change direction, including fulfilling its 22-year-old as yet unfulfilled promise to evaluate GAAP based on the objectives and concepts in its Conceptual Framework, a task I attempt in Chapter 10. I offered to provide any assistance desired.

Mr Levitt and Mr Turner left the SEC in 2001 without acting on the matter.
3 The Sarbanes–Oxley Act of 2002, landmark legislation in the governance of the financial reporting profession, was the first direct Congressional result of the financial reporting breakdowns at Enron, WorldCom and the rest, discussed in the Preface. The effects of the Act, if any, on financial reporting standard-setting are as yet unknown.

6 The users and the citizenry deserve better from us than they are now getting.
7 This book is so destructive of everything that's good and just and beautiful about our profession that someone should issue a fatwah against the author.

Appendix

The author's favorite article

Some books like this one present copies of articles in addition to text. The extensive quotation from the literature in this book makes that unnecessary. However, readers might appreciate a taste of the literature without having to dig any out. I have therefore appended my favorite article, "In Defence of Accounting in the United States," by Bob Sterling, from *Abacus*, December 1966 (I refer to it on page 406).

Abacus (December 1966), pp. 180–183

Robert R. Sterling

In defence of accounting in the United States *

In "Financial Information and the Securities Market" (Abacus Vol. I, No. 1) Professor Chambers presented some figures which reflected unfavorably on U.S. accounting relative to U.K. accounting. Specifically, he asserted that there are 124,416 different ways of getting cost in the U.K. but only 9,100 different ways in the U.S. No direct comparisons were made but the figures are there for all to see and the clear implication is that U.K. accounting is richer in variety than that of the U.S. That is a slander of U.S. accounting and cannot be left unchallenged. This note will demonstrate that the figures are wrong and that the opposite is true: U.S. accounting is much richer than that of the U.K.

Two separate types of errors may be identified in Mr. Chambers's figures: (I) logical fallacies[1] and (2) inadequate research.

---

* The author would like to thank Mr Duns Scotus for reading this manuscript. Under some theories at least, that is impossible.

1 A recent article showed that logical consistency is a symptom of an illness called valuitis. It is well known that Chambers has been suffering from valuitis for a long time. This fallacy is evidence of the absence of the symptom and therefore we may hope that he is recovering his health. However, I do not wish to draw that conclusion since it might be logically valid and therefore it would indicate that I am ill. For the same reason, I do not wish to conclude that a valid conclusion of mine would indicate that I was ill because that might be valid and therefore it would indicate that I was ill. Thus, I must conclude a contradiction but then the conclusion that I must conclude a contradiction might be valid. This is a question I intend to research further at a later time.

Logical fallacies

Chambers listed the possibilities of valuing only inventory in the U.S. but he listed commodity stocks, fixed assets (three classes) and security investments (three classes) for the U.K. Obviously, a larger number of classes will yield a larger number of combinations, other things being equal. Thus, the comparison is grossly unfair because the U.K. figure was calculated from a larger number of classes.

Second, he erred in calculating the number of different costs to be derived from inventory methods. He is talking about a manufacturing operation in which there are four different classes of inventory: materials, supplies, work-in-process and finished goods. Even a modest firm will have several different kinds of materials, etc. Any one of the ten methods may be used for each inventory and the order of using them is important. For example, Lifo for finished goods and Fifo for materials will produce a cost different from Fifo for finished goods and Lifo for materials.

Thus, under the conservative assumption that there are only ten inventories in a given firm; the number of different costs is 10! not 10. This yields 3,628,000 different costs from a consideration of different rules for inventory alone. If we now take account of the other factors listed by Chambers we have $10! \times 7 \times 13 \times 3 \times 3 = 2,971,332,000$. The U.K. figure of 124,416 pales in comparison.

Inadequate research[2]

Evidently in getting the "10 rules" for inventory valuation, Chambers took a cursory look at the *Accountants' Handbook*. Had he bothered to look further he would have found that this is a highly abstract list and that each category contains a rich variety of methods. Neuner[3] for example, lists five different kinds of Lifo:

---

2   The results of the following are part of a two-stage study on accounting which is forthcoming. First, I am preparing a complete inventory of accounting practices. The second stage will be to weave together the practices into a coherent body of principles. In this way, the principles can be inductively derived out of the facts of accounting action in practice without relying on assumptions and premises except where assumptions are necessary because the data are not perceptible facts.

The study will take a little longer than originally planned because I have not yet finished with Lifo inventories. So far, I have observed 1,984 different methods of Lifo. It is too early to draw distinctions or perceive objectives or sense relevance but I can tentatively report a corroboration of the A.LC.P.A. definition of assets. All accounts with a debit balance after the books are closed except those that are contra liabilities are in fact assets. The reader is cautioned that this corroboration pertains only to Lifo inventories in only 1984 cases.

3   John W. Neuner, *Cost Accounting Principles and Practice*, 6th edn, p. 136ff.

1   Lifo – perpetual
2   Lifo –periodic
Increases in inventory under 2. may be valued at

3   earliest purchase price
4   latest purchase price
5   average purchase price.

Later he lists six areas "on which there is no uniform practice." Freight-in is one category for which there are three different methods, for example. Each of these six categories has at least three different methods.

Next, there is a list of four categories of "Debatable inventory costs" and each of these four has at least three different methods. There are others but I will conclude with the 3×3 cost-or-market rule which Chambers mentions. Thus, there are $5 \times (3 \times 6) \times (3 \times 4) \times (3 \times 3) = 9,720$ different costs for Lifo alone.

We could go through each of the ten methods with similar results. However, one case is sufficient to demonstrate the inadequate research upon which Chambers bases his figures. In the U.S. we have more different methods for Lifo alone than he gives us credit for in total!

These calculations have dealt only with actual costs. There are 9,720 different actual costs under the Lifo method. In the U.S. there is a regrettable trend toward recording standard costs in the accounts. "Standards" are useful for comparison purposes but they are fictitious and therefore they should not be entered in the accounts.[4] The accounts must be records of events that have actually occurred. not what might have occurred or what will occur. There is, of course, no objection to putting standard costs in a footnote.

The inclusion of standard costs would strengthen our case against Chambers since there are different times for isolating the variance, different methods of calculation and different methods of disposition. Thus, standards would extend the richness of U.S. accounting but this would be an unfair tactic since they are not actual costs.

Of course, the actual actual costs can be obtained only by the method of

---

4   In addition to being fictitious, standards are based solely on someone's projections and are not actual facts of economic experience. I can see no reason why anyone would want to put standards in the accounts when 9,720 different objective Lifo costs are available. Variance analysis is helpful to management but managerial desires should not be confused with sound financial accounting. Moreover, accountants have completely overlooked a fertile source of variance. We could calculate the difference between the costs of the particular method in use and the costs of the alternative methods. Thus, for Lifo we could calculate 9,719 variances and then we could extend the analysis to Fifo, averages and so forth. In this was we could generate an almost infinite number of variances without ever referring to standards. Such variances would be completely *objective* since they are differences in actual costs.

specific identification.[5] This is the only way to measure the actual income but unfortunately it is sometimes impossible to use. This method would also have strengthened the richness case. Observe that if we have a large number of items in an inventory at different actual costs, there are almost an infinite number of combinations and hence almost an infinite number of actual actual costs and actual incomes. I did not use this method in making the calculations for this note because it would have required an estimate of the bias introduced by the shipping clerk or an assumption of randomness and I wanted my figures to be objective and verifiable.

But, I digress. Theoretical issues are not pertinent here. The important point is that 1 have shown that U.S. accounting is much richer than Chambers has given us credit for and, using the figure of 124,416, it is richer than U.K. accounting. The actual facts demand an immediate retraction and apology.

Retraction and apology

I grant Mr Sterling's point, and apologize to all who may have been misled or misrepresented by my conservatism. We have it on the highest authorities that conservatism is virtuous, and gives a fair representation. Perhaps it is not, and does not. I have since raised the estimate ("A Matter of Principle," *The Accounting Review*, July 1966) but even then in the same wantonly cursory manner. My apologies on that score too.

R. J. Chambers

---

5 Specific identification avoids the subjectivity of assuming a flow and accounts for the real flow of the goods. Many people have noted this and the fact that accounting for the real flow prevents management from manipulating their profits by assuming an unrealistic flow. It is true that some managers might instruct their shipping clerks to ship the goods on a highest-in-first-out basis in order to reduce taxes. This is not a valid objection to the method because if the goods were shipped in this order, then this would be the real flow (hence the actual costs and actual income) but it does present an auditing problem. The auditor must insist that the goods he indelibly marked with their actual costs. Some managers may object to the added expense of this procedure and they are often too obtuse to understand the subtleties of actual costs and income. The auditor can then explain that the expenses incurred in marking the goods will further reduce the income and thus further reduce taxes in accord with the original goal. This can also be applied to the managers who ship their goods on a lowest-in-first-out basis in order to increase their income. The expense of marking the goods is a small price to pay for the increase in actual income.

Bibliography

Abelson, Reed, 2003. "With No Surprise, Chief Is Out at Tenet Healthcare," *New York Times*, May 28

Accountancy Today, 2002. July 22–August 4

_____, 2003. "FASB Votes to Expense Options," May 19–June 1

Adams, Scott, 2000. *Slapped Together* (New York: HarperBusiness)

Adkerson, Richard C., 1978. "Discussion of DAAM: The Demand for Alternative Accounting Measurements," *Journal of Accounting Research*, 16 (Suppl.)

Alter, Jonathan, 2002. "Which Boot Will Drop Next?" *Newsweek*, February 4

Altman, Daniel, 2002. "Enron Had More than One Way to Disguise Rapid Rise in Debt," *New York Times*, February 17

American Accounting Association, 1936. "A Tentative Statement of Accounting Principles Affecting Corporate Reports," *Accounting Review*, June

_____, 1966. *A Statement of Basic Accounting Theory*

_____, 1973. *A Statement of Basic Auditing Concepts*

_____, 1991. "Report of the American Accounting Association Committee on Accounting and Auditing Measurement, 1989–90," *Accounting Horizons*, September

American Accounting Association's Financial Accounting Standards Committee, 1997. "Response to FASB Exposure Draft, Proposed Statement of Financial Accounting Standards—Reporting Comprehensive Income," *Accounting Horizons*, June

_____, 1998. "Criteria for Assessing the Quality of an Accounting Standard," *Accounting Horizons*, June

_____, 2004. "Evaluation of the IASB's Proposed Accounting and Disclosure Requirements for Share-Based Payment," *Accounting Horizons*, March

American Institute of Certified Public Accountants (American Institute of Accountants until 1957), 1939a. Accounting Research Bulletin No. 1, "General Introduction and Rules Formerly Adopted"

_____, 1939b. Accounting Research Bulletin No. 2, "Unamortized Discount and Redemption Premium on Bonds Refunded"

_____, 1939c. Accounting Research Bulletin No. 4, "Foreign Operations and Foreign Exchange"

_____, 1940. Accounting Research Bulletin No. 7, "Reports of Committee on Terminology"

_____, 1944a. Accounting Research Bulletin No. 23, "Accounting for Income Taxes"

_____, 1944b. Accounting Research Bulletin No. 24, "Accounting for Intangible Assets"

_____, 1947. Accounting Research Bulletin No. 32, "Income and Earned Surplus"

_____, 1949. Accounting Research Bulletin No. 38, "Disclosure of Long-Term Leases in Financial Statements of Lessees"

_____, 1950. Accounting Research Bulletin No. 40, "Business Combinations"

_____, 1952. Accounting Research Bulletin No. 42, "Emergency Facilities—Depreciation, Amortization, and Income Taxes"

_____, 1953a. Accounting Terminology Bulletin No. 1, "Review and Résumé"

_____, 1953b. Accounting Research Bulletin No. 43, "Restatement and Revision of Accounting Research Bulletins"

_____, 1957. Accounting Research Bulletin No. 48, "Business Combinations"

_____, 1958a. Accounting Research Bulletin No. 44 (Revised), "Declining-balance Depreciation"

_____, 1958b. "Report to Council of the Special Committee on Research Program," *Journal of Accountancy*, December

_____, 1959. Accounting Research Bulletin No. 51, "Consolidated Financial Statements"

_____, 1961. *Accounting Research and Terminology Bulletins, Final Edition*

_____, 1962. APB Opinion No. 2, "Accounting for the Investment Credit"

_____, 1963. "Audits of Corporate Accounts" (reprinted February)

_____, 1964. APB Opinion No. 4, "Accounting for the 'Investment Credit'"

_____, 1965. APB Opinion No. 6, "Status of Accounting Research Bulletins"

_____, 1966a. APB Opinion No. 8, "Accounting for the Cost of Pension Plans"

_____, 1966b. APB Opinion No. 9, "Reporting the Results of Operations"

_____, 1967. APB Opinion No. 11, "Accounting for Income Taxes"

_____, 1968. APB Opinion No. 15, "Earnings per Share"

_____, 1969. APB Statement No. 3, "Financial Statements Restated for General Price-Level Changes"

_____, 1970a. APB Opinion No. 16, "Business Combinations"

_____, 1970b. APB Opinion No. 17, "Intangible Assets"

_____, 1970c. APB Statement No. 4, "Basic Concepts and Accounting Principles Underlying Financial Statements of Business Enterprises"

_____, 1971. APB Opinion No. 20, "Accounting Changes"

_____, 1972a. APB Opinion No. 23, "Accounting for Income Taxes—Special Areas"

_____, 1972b. APB Opinion No. 25, "Accounting for Stock Issued to Employees"

_____, 1972c. *Establishing Financial Accounting Standards: A Report of the Study on Establishment of Accounting Principles*

_____, 1973a. APB Opinion No. 29, "Accounting for Nonmonetary Transactions"

_____, 1973b. Study Group on the Objectives of Financial Statements, *Report of the Study Group on the Objectives of Financial Statements*

_____, 1974. Study Group on the Objectives of Financial Statements, *Report of the Study Group on the Objectives of Financial Statements*, Volume II

_____, 1982. AcSEC Issues Paper, *Accounting for Employee Capital Accumulation Plans*, November 4

_____, 1990. Statement of Position 90–7, "Financial Reporting by Entities in Reorganization under the Bankruptcy Code"

_____, 1991. Charge to the Special Committee on Financial Reporting

_____, 1994a. Special Committee on Financial Reporting, *Comprehensive Report of the Special Committee on Financial Reporting*, "Improving Business Reporting—A Customer Focus"

_____, 1994b. Special Committee on Financial Reporting, *Database of Materials on Users' Needs for Information*

_____, 1994c. Statement of Position 94–6, *Disclosure of Certain Risks and Uncertainties*, December 30

_____, 2000. Statement of Position 00–2, *Accounting by Producers or Distributors of Films*, June 12

_____, 2002. News Update, May 6

Andrews, Andrea R. and Simonetti, Gilbert, Jr, 1996. "Tort Reform Revolution," *Journal of Accountancy*, September

Armstrong, Karen, 1994. *A History of God* (New York: Alfred A. Knopf)

Armstrong, Marshall, 1977. "The Politics of Setting Accounting Standards," *Journal of Accountancy*, February

Arnold, Jerry L. (ed.) 1988. *Proceedings of the October 8, 1987. Roundtable Discussion on Generally Accepted Accounting Principles and Regulatory Accounting Practices* (SEC and Financial Reporting Institute, School of Accounting, University of Southern California)

Association for Investment Management and Research (AIMR—since May 2004, CFA Institute), 1993. *Financial Reporting in the 1990s and Beyond*

Auden, W. H. and Kronenberger, Louis, 1981. *The Viking Book of Aphorisms* (New York: Dorset Press)

Backer, Morton (ed.) 1955. *Handbook of Modern Accounting Theory* (New York: Prentice-Hall, Inc.)

_____, 1973. "Valuation Reporting in the Netherlands: A Real-Life Example," *Financial Executive*, January

Bailey, Herbert S., Jr, 1975. "Quoth the Banker, 'Watch Cash Flow'" published in *Publishers Weekly*, © by Xerox Corporation, January 13

Barden, Horace G., 1973. Accounting Research Study No. 13, *The Accounting Basis of Inventories* (New York: AICPA)

Barringer, Felicity, 2002. "10 Months Ago, Questions on Enron Came and Went with Little Notice," *New York Times*, January 28

Barth, Mary E. and Landsman, Wayne R., 1995. "Fundamental Issues Related to Using Fair Value Accounting for Financial Reporting," *Accounting Horizons*, December

———, and Murphy, Christine M., 1994. "Required Financial Statement Disclosures; Purposes, Subject, Number, and Trends," *Accounting Horizons*, December

Barton, A. D., 1974. "Expectations and Achievements in Income Theory," *Accounting Review*, October

Barzun, Jacques, 2000. *From Dawn to Decadence* (New York: HarperCollins Publishers, Inc.)

Baxter, W. T., Editor, 1950. *Studies in Accounting* (London: Sweet & Maxwell Ltd.)

Baxter, W. T., 1966. *Accounting Theory* (New York: Garland Publishing, Inc.)

_____, 1967. "Accounting Values: Sale Price versus Replacement Cost," *Journal of Accounting Research*, Autumn

_____ and Davidson, Sidney (eds) 1962. *Studies in Accounting Theory* (Homewood: Richard D. Irwin, Inc.)

Bayless, Robert A., 2001. Remarks at "The SEC Speaks in 2001," Sponsored by the Practicing Law Institute, Washington, D.C., March 2

Beaver, William H., 1991. "Problems and Paradoxes in the Financial Reporting of Future Events," *Accounting Horizons*, December

Beckett, Paul, 1998. "Citigroup to Cut 6% of its Work Force, Take a $900 Million Charge After Tax," *Wall Street Journal*, December 16

Bedford, Norton M., 1965. *Income Determination Theory: An Accounting Framework* (Reading: Addison-Wesley)

———, 1971. "The Income Concept Complex: Expansion or Decline," in Sterling, *Alternatives*

Bell, John, 1974. "Ideal for Lever's Bank," *Sunday Times* (London), November 3

Bell, Philip W., 1971. "On Current Replacement Costs and Business Income," in Sterling, Robert R. (ed.), *Asset Valuation and Income Determination: A Consideration of the Alternatives* (Lawrence, Kansas: Scholars Book Co.)

Benis, Martin, 1999. "Shareholders' Equity," in Carmichael D. R., Lilien, Steven, and Mellman, Martin (eds), *Accountants' Handbook*, 9th edn (New York: John Wiley & Sons)

Berenson, Alex, 2002. "The Biggest Casualty of Enron's Collapse: Confidence," *New York Times*, February 10

Beresford, Dennis R., 1990. "Notes from the Chairman," *FASB Status Report*, September 30

———, 1991. Chairman of the FASB, Letter to John D. Dingell, Chairman, U.S. House of Representatives Subcommittee on Oversight and Investigations, March 15

———, 1994. "FASB Agrees Not to Require Expense Recognition for Stock Options," *FASB Status Report*, December 27

———, 1995. "How Should the FASB Be Judged?" *Accounting Horizons*, June

———, 1997. "How to Succeed as a Standard Setter by Trying Really Hard," *Accounting Horizons*, September

———, 2001. "Unfair Value: New Accounting Policies May Distort What the Authors Were Trying to Clear Up," *Barron's*, May 21

Beresford, Dennis R. and Johnson, L. Todd, 1995. "Interactions Between the FASB and the Academic Community," *Accounting Horizons*, December

Berton, Lee, 1983. "Many Firms Hide Debt to Give Them an Aura of Financial Strength," *Wall Street Journal*, December 13

———, 1984. "FASB Proposal on Pension Accounting Seen Under Fire at Hearings Next Week," *Wall Street Journal*, January 5

———, and Ricks, Thomas E., 1988. "SEC, Reportedly Pressed by Business, Studies Need for an Overhaul of FASB," *Wall Street Journal*, August 3

Bevis, Herman W., 1965. *Corporate Financial Reporting in a Competitive Economy* (New York: The Macmillan Company)

Black, Homer A., 1966. Accounting Research Study No. 9, *Interperiod Allocation of Corporate Income Taxes* (New York: AICPA)

Blair, Margaret M. and Wallman, Steven M. H., Task Force Co-Chairs, 2001. *Unseen Wealth: Report of the Brookings Task Force on Intangibles* (Washington: Brookings Institution Press)

Blensly, Douglas L. and Plank, Tom M., 1985. *Accounting Desk Book*, 8th edn (Englewood Cliffs: Institute for Business Planning, Inc.)

Bline, Dennis M. and Cullinan, Charles P., 1995. "Distributions to Stockholders: Legal Distinctions and Accounting Implications for Classroom Discussion," *Issues in Accounting Education*, Fall

Bloomberg News Service, 2002. "Auditors Failed to Warn in More than Half of Big Bankruptcies," April 23

BNA Reports, 2004. "Political Interference with FASB Proposal 'Dangerous Precedent,' Sen. Fitzgerald Says," April 21

Bologna, Michael, 2003. "Glassman Says Corporations Must Focus on Clear, Compelling Financial Disclosures," BNA, *Daily Tax Report*, April 11

Bonbright, James C., 1937. *Valuation of Property* (New York, McGraw-Hill)

_____, 1961. *Principles of Public Utility Rates* (New York: Columbia University Press)

Boulding, Kenneth E., 1955. *Economic Analysis*, 3rd edn (New York: Harper & Bros., Inc.)

_____, 1962. "Economics and Accounting: The Uncongenial Twins," in Baxter, N.T. and Davidson, Sidney, *Studies in Accounting Theory* (Homewood: Richard D. Irwin, Inc.)

Brannigan, Martha, 1988. "Sunbeam's Accounting Is Investigated by SEC," *Wall Street Journal*, June 22

Bricker, Robert James and Previts, Gary John, 1992. "Changing the Orientation of Financial Reporting: An Information Rights Perspective," Working Paper, Department of Accountancy, Case Western Reserve University, April 13

Broad, William J., 2001. "Smaller, Cheaper, Stealthier, Deadlier," *New York Times*, February 11

Brown, Clifford D., 1993. "The Emergence of Income Reporting," in Coffman, Edward N., *Historical Perspectives of Selected Financial Accounting Topics* (Homewood: Richard D. Irwin, Inc.)

Brown, Ken, 2002. "Tweaking Results Is Hardly a Sometime Thing," *Wall Street Journal*, February 6

Brown, P. R., 1982. "FASB Responsiveness to Corporate Input," *Journal of Accounting, Auditing, and Finance*, Summer

Brown, R. Gene and Johnston, Kenneth S., 1963. *Paciolo on Accounting* (New York: McGraw-Hill Book Company, Inc.)

Brown, Victor H., 1991. "Accounting Standards: Their Economic and Social Consequences," in FASB, *Benefits, Costs and Consequences of Financial Accounting Standards*

Browning, Lynnley, 2005. "Sorry, the Auditor Said, but We Want a Divorce," *New York Times*, February 6

Bryant, Adam, 1998. "Feeding the New Work Ethic," *New York Times*, April 19

Buckman, Rebecca, 2002. "SEC Still Investigates Whether Microsoft Understated Earnings," *Wall Street Journal*, February 13

Buffet, Warren, 2000. Berkshire-Hathaway, Inc. Annual Report

Burton, John C., 1975. "Financial Reporting in an Age of Inflation," *Journal of Accountancy*, February

_____, 1989. "A Commentary on the Reflections of Homer," *Journal of Accounting, Auditing & Finance*, Winter

_____ and Sack, Robert J., 1989. Editorial: "Tax Allocation: Time for a Fundamental Change," *Accounting Horizons*, June

_____, 1991. "Editorial: Time for Some Lateral Thinking," *Accounting Horizons*, June

Burton, John C., Palmer, Russell E., and Kay, Robert S. (eds) 1981. *Handbook of Accounting and Auditing* (Boston: Warren, Gorham and Lamont)

Business Roundtable, Accounting Principles Task Force, 1998. "Results of Survey on Financial Accounting and Reporting Standard-Setting Process," September 28

Butler, Samuel 1981 (quoted in Auden, W. H. and Kroenberger, Louis, *The Viking Book of Aphorisms*) (New York: Dorset Press)

Butterworth, J. E., 1982. "Discussion," in Sterling, Robert R. and Lemke, Kenneth W., *Maintenance of Capital: Financial versus Physical* (Houston: Scholars Book Co.)

Byrne, John A., Lavelle, Louis, Byrnes, Nanette, Vickers, Marcia, and Borrus, Amy 2002. "How to Fix Corporate Governance," *Business Week*, May 6

Byrne, Robert, 1988. *1911 Best Things Anybody Ever Said* (New York: Fawcett Columbine)

Byrnes, Nanette, McNamee, Mike, Brady, Diane, and Lavelle, Louis, 2002a. "Accounting in Crisis," *Business Week*, January 28

_____, 2002b. "Five Ways to Avoid More Enrons," *Business Week*, February 18

Carlin, George, 1997. *Braindroppings* (New York: Hyperion)

Carman, Lewis A., 1956. "Non-Linear Depreciation," *Accounting Review*, July

Carmichael, D. R. and Rosenfield, Paul (eds) 2002. *Accountants' Handbook*, 10th edn (New York: John Wiley & Sons)

Carmichael, D. R., Lilien, Steven, and Mellman, Martin (eds) 1999. *Accountants' Handbook*, 9th edn (New York: John Wiley & Sons)

Carsberg, Bryan, 1982. "The Case for Financial Capital Maintenance," in Sterling, Robert R. and Lemke, Kenneth W., *Maintenance of Capital: Financial versus Physical* (Houston: Scholars Book Co.)

Castellano, James G., 2002. "Chair's Corner," *The CPA Letter*, May

_____ and Melancon, Barry C., 2002. Letter to AICPA Members, February 1

Catlett, George R. and Olson, Norman O., 1968. Accounting Research Study No.. 10, *Accounting for Goodwill* (New York: AICPA)

Chambers, R. J., 1966. *Accounting, Evaluation and Economic Behavior* [AEEB] (Englewood Cliffs: Prentice-Hall, Inc.)

_____, 1969. *Accounting, Finance, and Management* (Chicago: Arthur Andersen & Co.) [This is a collection of 52 articles by Professor Chambers between 1949 and 1968.]

_____, 1971. "Evidence for a Market—Selling Price—Accounting System," in Sterling, Robert R. (ed.), *Asset Valuation and Income Determination: A Consideration of the Alternatives* (Lawrence, Kansas: Scholars Book Co.)

_____, 1973. *Securities and Obscurities: A Case for Reform of the Law of Company Accounts* (Sydney: Gower)

_____, 1979a. "Second Thoughts on Continuously Contemporary Accounting," *Abacus*, September

_____, 1979b. "'The Taxi Company' Under COCOA," in Sterling, Robert R. and Thomas, Arthur L., *Accounting for a Simplified Firm Owning Depreciable Assets* (Houston: Scholars Book Co.)

_____, 1987. "Accounting Education for the Twenty-first Century," *Abacus*, 23 (2)

_____, 1989. "Time in Accounting," *Abacus*, Spring

_____, 1991a. "Metrical and Empirical Laws in Accounting," *Accounting Horizons*, December

_____, 1991b. "Accounting and Corporate Morality—the Ethical Cringe," *Australian Journal of Corporate Law*, 1 (1)

Cheeseman, Henry R., 1975. "How to Create an Inflation Neutral Tax System," *Journal of Accountancy*, August

Clarke, F. L., Dean, G. W., and Oliver, K. G., 1997. *Corporate Collapse: Regulatory, Accounting and Ethical Failure,* 2nd edn (Cambridge: Cambridge University Press)

Clarke, George W., 1957. "Early Action by Adjusters Can Prevent Many U&O Claims from Becoming Difficult," *The National Underwriter,* September 12

Clymer, Adam, 2002. "Never Have So Many Missed the Forest," *New York Times,* February 10

Coffman, Edward N. (ed.) 1993. *Historical Perspectives of Selected Financial Accounting Topics* (Homewood: Richard D. Irwin Inc.)

Collins, Lane. G. and Mock, Theodore. J., 1979. "Selection and Evaluation Accounting Measures for Decision Making," in Sterling, Robert R. and Thomas, Arthur L., *Accounting for a Simplified Firm Owning Depreciable Assets* (Houston: Scholars Book Co.)

Cook, J. Michael, Kangas, Edward A., Gladstone, William L., Kullberg, Duane R., Groves, Ray J., Scanlon, Peter R., and Homes, Larry D., 1986. "The Future Relevance, Reliability, and Credibility of Financial Information," Recommendations to the AICPA Board of Directors, April

Cottle, Sidney, Murray, Roger F., Block, Frank E., with the collaboration of Leibowitz, Martin L., 1988. Graham and Dodd's *Security Analysis,* 5th edn (New York: McGraw-Hill Book Company)

Coughlan, John W., 1965. *Guide to Contemporary Theory of Accounts* (Englewood Cliffs: Prentice-Hall Inc.)

———, 1957. "Two Approaches to the Problem of Changing Prices," *Journal of Accountancy,* August

Cowan, Alison Leigh, 1990. "Shutdown is Expected at Spicer & Oppenheim," *New York Times,* November 28

Coyne, Jerry A., 1996. "God in the Details: The Biochemical Challenge to Evolution," a review of Michael Behe, *Darwin's Black Box,* in *Nature,* September 19

Crain's Detroit Business, 1994. "Don't Put Heat on Stock Options," September 12

Cramer, Joe J., Jr and Sorter, George H., 1974. *Objectives of Financial Statements,* Vol. 2, Selected Papers (New York: American Institute of Certified Public Accountants)

——— and Neyhart, Charles A., Jr, 1979. "A Comprehensive Framework for Evaluating Executory Contracts," *Journal of Accounting, Auditing, and Finance,* Winter

Crooch, G. Michael and Upton, Wayne S., 2001. "Credit Standing and Liability Measurement," FASB, *Understanding the Issues,* June

Crook, Kimberley, 2000. *Accounting for Share-Based Payments,* Special Report (Norwalk: Financial Accounting Standards Board), July

Danos, Paul and Imhoff, Eugene A., Jr, 1986. *Intermediate Accounting* (New York: Prentice-Hall)

Dash, Eric, 2005. "Time Warner Stops Granting Stock Options to Most of Staff," *New York Times,* February 19

Davidson, Sidney and Anderson, George D., 1987. "The Development of Accounting and Auditing Standards," *Journal of Accountancy,* May

DeCaro, Frank, 1998. "Style over Substance, *New York Times,* November 1

Dechow, Patricia M. and Skinner, Douglas J., 2000. "Earnings Management: Reconciling the Views of Accounting Academics, Practitioners, and Regulators," *Accounting Horizons,* June

Defliese, Philip L., 1983. "Deferred Taxes—Forever," *Journal of Accountancy,* August

Delonis, Robert J., 1988. Participant in Arnold, *Proceedings*

Demski, Joel, 2003. "Endogenous Expectations," excerpts in *Accounting Education News* (Sarasota: AAA, Fall)

de Tocqueville, Alexis, 1969. *Democracy in America* (Garden City, New York: Doubleday & Company, Inc. [first published in French in 1835])

_____, 1979. *Recollections* (Garden City, New York: Doubleday & Company, Inc. [first published in French in 1893])

Deutsch, David, and Lockwood, Michael, 1994. "The Quantum Physics of Time Travel," *Scientific American*, March 1994

Devine, Carl Thomas, 1985a. *Essays in Accounting Theory*, Vol. I (American Accounting Association)

_____, 1985b. *Essays in Accounting Theory*, Vol. II (American Accounting Association)

_____, 1985c. *Essays in Accounting Theory*, Vol. III (American Accounting Association)

_____, 1985d. *Essays in Accounting Theory*, Vol. IV (American Accounting Association)

_____, 1985e. *Essays in Accounting Theory*, Vol. V (American Accounting Association)

_____, 1999. *Essays in Accounting Theory: A Capstone* (London: Garland Publishing, a member of the Taylor & Francis Group)

Dewing, Arthur Stone, 1953. *The Financial Policy of Corporations*, 5th edn, Vol. 1 (New York: The Ronald Press Company)

Diamond, Jared, 1992. *The Third Chimpanzee* (New York: HarperCollins Publishers)

Dickinson, Arthur Lowes, 1917. *Accounting Practice and Procedure* (New York: Ronald Press Company)

Dingell, John, D., 1988. Letter to the Chairman of the SEC, August 26

Drucker, Peter F., 1994. "The Age of Social Transformation," *The Atlantic Monthly*, November

Dugan, Ianthe Jeanne, 2002. "Did You Hear the One about the Accountant? It's Not Very Funny," *Wall Street Journal*, March 14

Durant, Will, 1926. *The Story of Philosophy* (New York: Simon & Schuster)

_____, 1935. *The Story of Civilization: Part I, Our Oriental Heritage* (New York: Simon and Schuster)

_____, 1939. *The Story of Civilization: Part II, The Life of Greece* (New York: Simon and Schuster)

_____, 1944. *The Story of Civilization: Part III, Caesar and Christ* (New York: Simon and Schuster)

_____, 1950. *The Story of Civilization: Part IV, The Age of Faith* (New York: Simon and Schuster)

_____, 1953. *The Story of Civilization: Part V, The Renaissance* (New York: Simon and Schuster)

_____, 1957. *The Story of Civilization: Part VI, The Reformation* (New York: Simon and Schuster)

_____, 1961. *The Story of Civilization: Part VII, The Age of Reason Begins* (New York: Simon and Schuster)

_____, 1963. *The Story of Civilization: Part VIII, The Age of Louis XIV* (New York: Simon and Schuster)

_____ and Ariel Durant, 1965. *The Story of Civilization: Part IX, The Age of Voltaire* (New York: Simon and Schuster)

_____, 1975. *The Story of Civilization: Part XI, The Age of Napoleon* (New York: Simon and Schuster)

Dyckman, Thomas R., Downes, David H., and Magee, Robert T., 1975. *Efficient Capital Markets and Accounting, A Critical Analysis*, 1st edn (Englewood-Cliffs: Prentice-Hall, Inc.)

Eccles, Robert G., Herz, Robert H., Keegan, Mary E., and Phillips, David M. H., 2001. *The Value Reporting™ Revolution: Moving Beyond the Earnings Game* (New York: John Wiley & Sons, Inc.)

Editors' Notebook, 1973. *Journal of Accountancy*, March

Edwards, Edgar O., 1975. "The State of Current Value Accounting," *Accounting Review*, April

_____ and Bell, Philip W., 1961. *The Theory and Measurement of Business Income* (Berkeley: University of California Press)

Eichenwald, Kurt, 2003. "Former Enron Executive Pleads Guilty," *New York Times*, October 31

_____ and Henriques, Diana B., Gerth, Jeff, Oppel, Richard A. Jr, Stevenson, Richard W., and Van Natta, Don Jr, 2002. "Enron Buffed Image to a Shine Even as It Rotted from Within," *New York Times*, February 10

Elliott, Robert K., 1992. Letter to Edmund L. Jenkins, Chairman, AICPA Special Committee on Financial Reporting, September 23

Emshwiller, John R., 2002. "Documents Track Enron's Partnerships," *Wall Street Journal*, January 2

Evans, John H. III and Sridhar, Sri S., 2002. "Disclosure-Disciplining Mechanisms: Capital Markets, Product Markets, and Shareholder Litigation," *Accounting Review*, July

Evans, Thomas, G., 2003. *Accounting Theory* (Mason: South-Western)

Financial Accounting Standards Board, 1975a. Statement of Standards No. 5, SFAS "Accounting for Contingencies"

_____, 1975b. Statement of Standards No. 6, "Classification of Short-Term Obligations Expected to Be Refinanced"

_____, 1975c. Statement of Standards No. 7, "Accounting and Reporting by Development Stage Enterprises"

_____, 1975d. Statement of Standards No. 8, "Accounting for the Translation of Foreign Currency Transactions and Foreign Currency Financial Statements"

_____, 1976a. Discussion Memorandum, *An Analysis of Issues Related to Conceptual Framework for Financial Accounting and Reporting: Elements of Financial Statements and Their Measurement*, December 2

_____, 1976b. Statement of Standards No. 13, "Accounting for Leases"

_____, 1977a. Statement of Standards No. 15, "Accounting by Debtors and Creditors for Troubled Debt Restructurings"

_____, 1977b. Statement of Standards No. 19, "Financial Accounting and Reporting by Oil and Gas Producing Companies"

_____, 1978. Statement of Concepts No. 1, CON1, "Objectives of Financial Reporting by Business Enterprises"

_____, 1979a. Statement of Standards No. 25, "Suspension of Certain Accounting Requirements for Oil and Gas Producing Companies"

_____, 1979b. Statement of Standards No. 33, "Financial Reporting and Changing Prices"

_____, 1980a. Statement of Standards No. 35, "Accounting and Reporting by Defined Benefit Pension Plans"

_____, 1980b. Statement of Concepts No. 2, CON2, "Qualitative Characteristics of Accounting Information"

_____, 1980c. Statement of Concepts No. 3, CON3, "Elements of Financial Statements of Business Enterprises"

_____, 1981. Statement of Standards No. 52, "Foreign Currency Translation"

_____, 1983. Statement of Standards No. 72, "Accounting for Certain Acquisitions of Banking or Thrift Institutions"

_____, 1984a. Statement of Concepts No. 5, CON5, "Recognition and Measurement in Financial Statements of Business Enterprises"

_____, 1984b. "Action Alert," September 19

_____, 1984c. Invitation to Comment, *Accounting for Compensation Plans Involving Rights Granted to Employees*, May 31

_____, 1985a. Statement of Concepts No. 6, CON6, "Elements of Financial Statements"

_____, 1985b. Statement of Standards No. 87, "Employers' Accounting for Pensions"

_____, 1985c. "The Mission of the Financial Accounting Standards Board"

_____, 1986. Statement of Standards No. 89, "Financial Reporting and Changing Prices"

_____, 1987a. Statement of Standards No. 94, "Consolidation of All Majority-Owned Subsidiaries"

_____, 1987b. Statement of Standards No. 95, "Statement of Cash Flows"

_____, 1987c. Statement of Standards No. 96, "Accounting for Income Taxes"

_____, 1990a. Statement of Standards No. 106, "Employers' Accounting for Postretirement Benefits Other than Pensions"

_____, 1990b. Technical Bulletin No. 90–1, "Accounting for Separately Priced Extended Warranty and Product Maintenance Contracts," December 17

_____, 1991a. Statement of Standards No. 107, "Disclosures about Fair Value of Financial Instruments"

_____, 1991b. *Benefits, Costs, and Consequences of Financial Accounting Standards*

_____, 1991c. EITF Issue No. 98–10, "Accounting for Contracts Involved in Energy Trading and Risk Management Activities"

_____, 1992. Statement of Standards No. 109, "Accounting for Income Taxes"

_____, 1993a. Statement of Standards No. 115, "Accounting for Certain Investments in Debt and Equity Securities"

_____, 1993b. Exposure Draft, Proposed Statement of Financial Accounting Standards, "Accounting for Stock-based Compensation," June 30

_____, 1995a. Statement of Standards No. 121, "Accounting for the Impairment of Long-Lived Assets and for Long-Lived Assets to Be Disposed Of"

_____, 1995b. Statement of Standards No. 123, "Accounting for Stock-Based Compensation"

_____, 1996. Statement of Standards No. 125, "Accounting for Transfers and Servicing of Financial Assets and Extinguishments of Liabilities"

_____, 1997a. Statement of Standards No. 130, "Reporting Comprehensive Income"

_____, 1997b. "Action Alert," January 29

_____, 1997c. Statement of Concepts, "Using Cash Flow Information in Accounting Measurements," exposure draft, June 11

_____, 1998a. "Action Alert," February 4

_____, 1998b. "Action Alert," June 10

_____, 1998c. "Action Alert," November 11

_____, 1998d. "Action Alert," November 25

_____, 1998e. *FASB Status Report*, December 31

_____, 1998f. Statement of Standards No. 133, "Accounting for Derivative Instruments and Hedging Activities"

_____, 1999a. Statement of Standards No. 135, "Rescission of FASB Statement No. 75 and Technical Corrections"

_____, 1999b. "Action Alert," April 23

_____, 1999c. "Action Alert," June 30

_____, 1999d. Preliminary Views, *Reporting Financial Instruments and Certain Related Assets and Liabilities at Fair Value*, December 14

_____, 2000a. Statement of Standards No. 140, "Accounting for Transfers and Servicing of Financial Assets and Extinguishments of Liabilities"

_____, 2000b. Statement of Concepts No. 7, CON7, "Using Cash Flow Information and Present Value in Accounting Measurements"

_____, 2000c. Interpretation No. 44, "Accounting for Certain Transactions Involving Stock Compensation"

_____, 2001a. Statement of Standards No. 141, "Business Combinations"

_____, 2001b. Statement of Standards No. 142, "Goodwill and Other Intangible Assets"

_____, 2001c. Statement of Standards No. 143, "Accounting for Asset Retirement Obligations"

_____, 2002a. Interpretation No. 45, "Guarantor's Accounting and Disclosure Requirements for Guarantees, Including Indirect Guarantees of Indebtedness of Others"

_____, 2002b. *FASB Status Report*, January 18

_____, 2002c. "Action Alert," September 25

_____, 2002d. "The FASB Report," September 30.

_____, 2003a. Statement of Standards No. 150, "Accounting for Certain Financial Instruments with Characteristics of both Liabilities and Equity"

_____, 2003b. Project Updates updated August 2

_____, 2003c. , "Action Alert," November 26, 2003

_____, 2004a. Statement of Standards No. 123 (revised 2004), "Share-Based Payment"

_____, 2004b. Exposure Draft, Proposed Statement of Financial Accounting Standards, "Fair Value Measurements," June 23

_____, 2005. Memo on the Joint Conceptual Framework Project to the Financial Accounting Standards Advisory Council, June

Financial Analysts Journal, 1984. "Editorial Viewpoint," March–April

Fink, Ronald, 2002. "What Must Be Done? The Experts Weigh in on How to Prevent Future Enrons," *CFO*, April

Flegm, Eugene H., 1984. *Accounting: How to Meet the Challenges of Relevance and Regulation* (New York: John Wiley & Sons)

_____, 1986. Letter to the Editor of *Barron's*, January 13

_____, 1989. "The Limitations of Accounting," *Accounting Horizons*, September

_____, 1990. "Reflections on the FASB Conceptual Framework," *Research in Accounting Regulation*, Vol. 4

_____, 2000. Letter to P. Rosenfield, August 5

_____, 2002. Letter to P. Rosenfield, March 16

Foster, John M., 2003. "The FASB and the Capital Markets," *The FASB Report*, June 30

French, Kenneth R., 1987. "Enhancing the Value of a Going Concern," *Journal of Accountancy*, August

Freud, Sigmund, 1939. *Moses and Monotheism* (New York: Vantage Books)

Freund, William C., 1993. "That Trade Obstacle, the SEC," *Wall Street Journal*, August 27

Friedman, Thomas L., 1998. "My China for Your Congress," *New York Times*, May 30

Gaylin, Willard, 1984. *The Rage Within* (New York: Simon and Schuster)

Gellein, Oscar S. 1992. "Primacy: Assets or Income?," in Previts, Gary John (ed.), *Research in Accounting Regulation*, Vol. 6 (Greenwich: JAI Press)

Gerboth, Dale L., 1987a. "The Conceptual Framework: Not Definitions, But Professional Values," *Accounting Horizons*, September

_____, 1987b. "Commentary on the Accounting Game," *Accounting Horizons*, December

_____, 1988. "Commentary: The Limits of Technique," *Accounting Horizons*, March

_____, 1989. "Don't Spit in the Wind: Nonpension Retirement Benefits," *CPA Journal*, September

Gilman, Stephen, 1939. *Accounting Concepts of Profit* (New York: The Ronald Press Company)

Glater, Jonathan D., 2002. "Audit Firms Await Fallout and Windfall," *New York Times*, March 14

_____, 2003. "Freddie Mac Understated Its Earnings by $5 Billion," *New York Times*, November 22

Goldberg, Louis, 1963. "Present State of Accounting Theory," *Accounting Review*, July

_____, 1965. *An Inquiry into The Nature of Accounting* (Iowa City: American Accounting Association)

Gordon, Myron J., 1971. "Critique: Return on Investment: The Continuing Confusion among Disparate Measures," in Sterling, Robert T. and Bentz, William F., *Accounting in Perspective* (Dallas: South-Western Publishing Co.)

Governmental Accounting Standards Board, 1987. Statement of Concepts No. 1, "Objectives of Financial Reporting"

_____, 1989. Statement of Standards No. 9, "Reporting Cash Flows of Proprietary and Nonexpendable Trust Funds and Governmental Entities that Use Proprietary Fund Accounting"

_____, 1999. Statement of Standards No. 34, "Financial Statements—and Management's Discussion and Analysis—for State and Local Governments"

Granof, Michael H. and Zeff, Stephen A., 2002. "Unaccountable in Washington," *New York Times*, January 23

Greenberger, Robert S., 2002. "Questioning the Books: Panel, in Enron's Wake, to Review Lawsuit Curbs," *Wall Street Journal*, February 6

Gribbin, John, 1999. *Almost Everyone's Guide to Science, the Universe, Life, and Everything* (New Haven: Yale University Press)

Grisham, John, 2001. *The Brethren* (New York: Random House, Inc.)

Groves, Ray J., 1994. "Financial Disclosure: When More is Not Better," *Financial Executive*, May/June

Gu, Feng and Lev, Baruch, 2004. "The Information Content of Royalty Income," *Accounting Horizons*, March

Hackney, William P., 1973. "Comments," in Melcher, Beatrice, *Stockholders' Equity* (New York: AICPA)

Hamilton, James, 2003. "Enzi Roundtable on Stock Options reveals Serious Divide," *PCAOB Reporter*, May 27

Hamilton, Virginia, 1988. *In the Beginning: Creation Stories from Around the World* (New York: Harcourt Brace Jovanovich)

Hanna, John R., 1982. "Discussion," in Sterling, Robert R. and Lemke, Kenneth W., *Maintenance of Capital: Financial versus Physical* (Houston: Scholars Book Co.)

Hansell, Saul, 1997. "S.E.C. Chief Defends Accounting Board," *New York Times*, October 9

Harmon, Amy, 2003. "Digital Vandalism Spurs a Call for Oversight," *New York Times*, September 1

Hatfield, Henry Rand, 1916. *Modern Accounting* (New York: D. Appleton and Company)

_____, 1927. "What Is the Matter with Accounting?" *Accounting Review*, October

_____, 1937. "A Critique of the Tentative Statement of Accounting Principles Underlying Corporate Reports," address at the annual meeting of the American Accounting Association, December 29

Hawking, Stephen W., 1988. *A Brief History of Time* (New York: Bantam Books)

Healy, Paul M. and Wahlen, James M., 1999. "A Review of the Earnings Management Literature and its Implications for Standard Setting," *Accounting Horizons*, December

Heath, Loyd C., 1978. Accounting Research Monograph No. 3, *Financial Reporting and the Evaluation of Solvency* (New York: AICPA)

_____, 1988. "Commentary on Accounting Literature," *Accounting Horizons*, March

_____, 1990. "How About Some Constructive Input to the FASB?" *Financial Executive*, September/October

Hector, Gary, 1989. "Cute Tricks on the Bottom Line," *Fortune*, April 24

Heilbroner, Robert L., 1972. *The Worldly Philosophers, The Lives, Times, and Ideas of the Great Economic Thinkers*, 4th edn (New York: Simon and Schuster)

Helyar, John and Lublin, Joann S., 1998. "Corporate Coffers Gush with Currency of an Opulent Age," *Wall Street Journal*, August 10

Hempel, Carl G., 1952. "Fundamentals of Concept Formation in Empirical Science," in *International Encyclopedia of Unified Science*, Vols I & II (Chicago, University of Chicago Press)

Henderson, Scott and Peirson, Graham, 1980. *Issues in Financial Accounting*, 2nd edn (Melbourne: Longman Cheshire Pty Limited)

Hendriksen, Eldon S. and van Breda, Michael F., 1992. *Accounting Theory*, 5th edn (Boston: Richard D. Irwin, Inc.)

Henriques, Diana B., 2002. "A Proposed New Way to Police Accounting Still Relies on Accountants," *New York Times*, January 21

Hepworth, Samuel R., 1953. "Smoothing Periodic Income," *Accounting Review*, January

_____, 1956. *Reporting Foreign Operations* (Ann Arbor: University of Michigan)

Herdman, Robert K., 2001. "Testimony before the Subcommittee on Capital Markets, Insurance and Government Sponsored Enterprises and the Subcommittee on Oversight and Investigation, Committee on Financial Services, U.S. House of Representatives," December 12

_____, 2002. "Testimony Concerning the Roles of the SEC and the FASB in Establishing GAAP" before the House Subcommittee on Capital Markets, Insurance, and Government Sponsored Enterprises, Committee on Financial Services, May 14

Hermanson, Dana R., 2002. Letter to the Editor of *Newsweek*, February 2

Herrick, Anson, 1944. "Current Assets and Liabilities," *Journal of Accountancy*, January

Hicks, Ernest L., 1965. Accounting Research Study No. 8, *Accounting for the Cost of Pension Plans* (New York: AICPA)

Hill, Henry P., 1987. *Accounting Principles for the Autonomous Corporate Entity* (New York: Quorum Books)

Hitt, Greg, and Schlesinger, Jacob M., 2002. "Stock Options Come under Fire in Wake of Enron's Collapse," *Wall Street Journal*, March 26

Holsen, Robert C., 1963. "Another Look at Business Combinations," in Wyatt, Arthur R., *A Critical Study of Accounting Business Combinations* (New York: AICPA)

Horngren, Charles T., 1971. "The Accounting Discipline in 1999," *Accounting Review*, January

_____, 1972. "Accounting Principles: Private or Public Sector?," *Journal of Accountancy*, May

Horrigan, James O., 1993. "A Short History of Financial Ratio Analysis," in Coffman, Edward N., *Historical Perspectives of Selected Financial Accounting Topics* (Homewood: Richard D. Irwin Inc.)

Ihlanfeldt, William J., 1991. "The Rule-Making Process: A Time for Change," in Previts, Gary John (ed.), *Financial Reporting and Standard Setting* (New York: AICPA)

Ijiri, Yuji, 1971a. "A Defense for Historical Cost Accounting," in Sterling, Robert R. (ed.), *Asset Valuation and Income Determination: A Consideration of the Alternatives* (Lawrence, Kansas: Scholars Book Co.)

_____, 1971b. "Logic and Sanctions in Accounting," in Sterling, Robert R. and Bentz, William F., *Accounting in Perspective* (Dallas: South-Western Publishing Co.)

International Accounting Standards Committee (IASC), 1975. International Accounting Standard No. 1, "Disclosure of Accounting Policies"

_____, 1976. International Accounting Standard No. 3, "Consolidated Financial Statements"

_____, 1983. International Accounting Standard No. 22, "Business Combinations"

_____, 1990. International Accounting Standard No. 27, "Consolidated Financial Statements and Accounting for Investments in Subsidiaries"

_____, 1989a. "Framework for the Preparation and Presentation of Financial Statements"

_____, 1989b. International Accounting Standard No. 29, "Financial Reporting in Hyperinflationary Economies"

Jackson, Mr Justice, 1954. "Federal Power Commission versus Hope National Gas Company" (Supreme Court January 3, 1944), 51 PUR (NS) 193–235, quoted in Pinger, R. W., "The Semantics of Accounting," *Accounting Review*, October

Jenkins, Edmund, 2000. "Chairman's Notes," *FASB Status Report*, March 24

Jenkins, Holman W., Jr, 1999. "Mean Old FASB: Forcing Us to Think," *Wall Street Journal*, June 2

_____, 2002. "Welfare Reform for Accountants," *Wall Street Journal*, January 16

Jensen, M. C., 1983. "Organization Theory and Methodology," *Accounting Review*, April

Jensen, Robert E., 1971. "Critique: Logic and Sanctions in Accounting," in Sterling, Robert R. and Bentz, William F., *Accounting in Perspective* (Dallas: South-Western Publishing Co.)

John, Lauren, 1994. "Regulating the Regulators," *CFO*, December 1994

Johnson, L. Todd, 1994. *Future Events, A Conceptual Study of Their Significance for Recognition and Measurement* (Norwalk: Financial Accounting Foundation)

_____ and Petrone, Kimberley R., 1999a. "Why Eliminate the Pooling Method?" *FASB Status Report*, August 31

_____, 1999b. "Why Not Eliminate Goodwill?" *FASB Status Report*, November 17

_____ and Such, Annette, 2002. "FASB's Revenue Recognition Project," *The FASB Report*, December 24

Johnston, David Cay, 2000. "Study Finds That Many Large Companies Pay No Taxes," *New York Times*, October 20

Jones, Stewart, Rahman, Sheikh F., and Wolnizer, Peter W., 2004. "Accounting Reform in Australia: Contrasting Cases of Agenda Building," *Abacus*, October

Journal of Accountancy, 1998. News Report, June

_____, 1998. News Report, November

_____, 1999a. "CPA Leads Financial Execs," April

_____, 1999b. News Report, November

Kadlec, Daniel, 2002. "WorldCon," *Time*, July 8

Kam, Vernon, 1990. *Accounting Theory*, 2nd edn (New York: John Wiley & Sons)

Kaplan, Abraham, 1964. *The Conduct of Inquiry: Methodology for Behavioral Science* (San Francisco: Chandler Publishing Company)

Kell, Walter G., 1953. "Should the Accounting Entity Be Personified?" *Accounting Review*, January

Kepler, Johannes, 1618–21. *Epitome of Copernican Astronomy*, Book Four

Kessler, Andy, 2000. "Creative Accounting," *Wall Street Journal*, July 24

Ketz, J. Edward and Wyatt, Arthur R., 1983. "The FASB in a World with Partially Efficient Markets," *Journal of Accounting, Auditing & Finance*, Fall

Keynes, J. M., 1935. *The General Theory of Employment, Interest, and Money* (New York: Harcourt, Brace and Company)

Kinrich, Jeffrey H., Reiss, M. Freddie, and Kabe, Elo R., 1999. "Forensic Accounting and Litigation Consulting Services," in Carmichael, D. R., Lilien, Steven B., and Mellman, Martin, *Accountants' Handbook*, 9th edn (New York: John Wiley & Sons)

Kirk, Donald J., 1983. Address to Financial Analysts, *FASB Viewpoints*, October 19

_____, 1986. Address to the Business Council in 1979, quoted in Solomons, David, *Making Accounting Policy* (New York: Oxford University Press)

_____, 1988. "Looking Back on Fourteen Years at the FASB: The Education of a Standard Setter," *Accounting Horizons*, March

_____, 1989a. "Commentary on The Limitations of Accounting—A Response," *Accounting Horizons*, September

_____, 1989b. "Reflections on a 'Reconceptualization of Accounting': A Commentary on Parts I–IV of Homer Kripke's Paper, 'Reflections on the FASB's

Conceptual Framework for Accounting and on Auditing,'" *Journal of Accounting, Auditing & Finance*, Winter

_____, 1990. "Commentary on Future Events: When Incorporated into Today's Measurements?" *Accounting Horizons*, June

_____, 1999. Letter to P. Rosenfield, May 6

Klein, Melissa, 2002. "Guilty Verdict Draws Mixed Reactions," *Accounting Today*, July 8–21

Knutson, Peter H., 1995. Remarks at the AICPA's Twenty-Second Annual National Conference on Current SEC Developments, January

Kopp, Brewster, 1973. "Some Further Comments..." *Financial Executive*, January

KPMG, 1998. Advertisement, *New York Times*, July 26

Kripke, Homer, 1989. "Reflections on the FASB's Conceptual Framework for Accounting and on Auditing," *Journal of Accounting, Auditing & Finance*, Winter

Krugman, Paul, 2001. "Herd on the Street," *New York Times*, January 3

Kuhn, T. S., 1970. *The Structure of Scientific Revolutions*, 2nd edn (Chicago: University of Chicago Press)

Kuttner, Robert, 1985. "The Poverty of Economics," *The Atlantic Monthly*, February

Lafferty, M., 1978. "New Standard Issued on Deferred Taxation," *Financial Times*, October 16

Lamden, Charles W., Gerboth, Dale L., and McRae, Thomas W., 1975. Accounting Research Monograph No. 1, *Accounting for Depreciable Assets* (New York: AICPA)

Larkin, Richard F., 1999. "Not-for-Profit Organizations," in Carmichael, D. R., Lilien, Steven, and Mellman, Martin (eds), *Accountants' Handbook*, 9th edn (New York: John Wiley & Sons)

Larson, Kermit, 2000. Letter to P. Rosenfield, March 21

_____ and Schattke, R. W., 1966. "Current Cash Equivalent, Additivity, and Financial Action," *Accounting Review*, October

Lee, T., 1979. "The Simplicity and Complexity of Accounting," in Sterling, Robert R. and Thomas, Arthur L., *Accounting for a Simplified Firm Owning Depreciable Assets* (Houston: Scholars Book Co.)

_____, 1982. "Current Cost Accounting and Physical Capital," in Sterling, Robert R. and Lemke, Kenneth W., *Maintenance of Capital: Financial versus Physical* (Houston: Scholars Book Co.)

_____, 1990. "A Systematic View of the History of the World of Accounting," *Accounting, Business and Financial History*, October

Leisenring, James, 1994. Vice-Chairman of the FASB, remarks at an open meeting of the Board on December 13

Lemke, Kenneth W., 1982. "Financial Versus Physical Capital Maintenance: A Review of the Arguments," in Sterling, Robert R. and Lemke, Kenneth W., *Maintenance of Capital: Financial versus Physical* (Houston: Scholars Book Co.)

Leonhardt, David, 2002. "The Race Is On for Tougher Regulation of Business," *New York Times*, February 10

Lev, Baruch, 2001. *Intangibles: Management, Measurement, and Reporting* (Washington, Brookings Institution Press)

Levitt, Arthur Jr, 1997. Speech at the Economic Club of Detroit, May 1997, quoted in "News Report," *Journal of Accountancy*, August

_____, 1998. "The Numbers Game," Speech at New York Center for Law and Business, September 28

_____, 2000. Speech at New York University Center for Law and Business, May 10

Liesman, Steve, 2002. "SEC Accounting Cop's Warning: Playing by Rules May Not Ward off Fraud Issues," *Wall Street Journal*, February 12

_____, Weil, Jonathan and Paltrow, Scot, 2002a. "When Rules Keep Debt Off the Books—Enron Crisis Puts Spotlight on the FASB," *Wall Street Journal*, January 18

_____, Weil, Jonathan and Schroeder, Michael, 2002b. "Dirty Books? Accounting Debacles Spark Calls for Change: Here's the Rundown—Suddenly Everyone Has a Fix for a Tarnished Industry; Some May Even Pan Out—Returning to the Priesthood," *Wall Street Journal*, February 6

Lipe, Robert C., 2002. "Fair Valuing Debt Turns Deteriorating Credit Quality into Positive Signals for Boston Chicken," *Accounting Horizons*, June

Littleton, A. C., 1933. *Accounting Evolution to 1900* (New York: American Institute Publishing Co.)

_____, 1953. *Structure of Accounting Theory* (American Accounting Association)

Lochner, Lauren Coleman, 1996. "Allied Lands $150 M Deal—A Wedge of the Pie—Will Design 'Brains' of Reusable Space Vehicle," *The Record*, July 4

Loebbecke, James K. and Perry, Raymond E., 1979. "Financial Statements for a Taxicab Company," in Sterling, Robert R. and Thomas, Arthur L., *Accounting for a Simplified Firm Owning Depreciable Assets* (Houston: Scholars Book Co.)

Loomis, Carol J., 1989. "The Killer Cost Stalking Business," *Fortune*, February 27

_____, 1999. "Lies, Damned Lies, and Managed Earnings: The Crackdown is Here," *Fortune*, August 2

Lorensen, Leonard, 1972. Accounting Research Study No. 12, *Reporting Foreign Operations of U.S. Companies in U.S. Dollars* (New York: AICPA)

_____, 1992. Accounting Research Monograph No. 4, *Accounting for Liabilities* (New York: AICPA)

_____ and Rosenfield, Paul, 1983. "Vested Benefits—A Company's Only Pension Liability," *Journal of Accountancy*, October

Lowenstein, Roger, 2002. "Auditor Independence: The SEC Chairman Doesn't Get It," *Wall Street Journal*, January 23

Lucas, Timothy S. and Hollowell, Betsy Ann, 1981. "Pension Accounting: The Liability Question," *Journal of Accountancy*, October

Lybrand, William M., 1908. "The Accounting of Industrial Enterprises," *Journal of Accountancy*, December

Lynch, Peter, 1989. *One Up on Wall Street: How to Use What You Already Know to Make Money in the Market* (New York: Simon and Schuster)

MacDonald, Elizabeth, 2000. "Many Firms Changed Revenue Booking as a Result of Heightened SEC Scrutiny," *Wall Street Journal*, March 15

_____ and Beckett, Paul, 1998. "SEC Lists Two in Seeking Chief of Accounting," *Wall Street Journal*, May 1

Macleod, Roderick K., 1981. "Financial Statements: Form and Content," in Seidler, Lee J. and Carmichael, D. R. (eds), *Accountants' Handbook*, 6th edn (New York: John Wiley & Sons)

MacNeal, Kenneth, 1970. *Truth in Accounting* (reprinted in Lawrence, Kansas, by Scholars Book Co.)

Marple, Raymond P., 1963. "Value-Itis," *Accounting Review*, July

Mathews, Shailer and Smith, Gerald Birney (eds), 1921. *A Dictionary of Religion and Ethics* (London: Waverly Book Company)

Mattessich, Richard, 1964. *Accounting and Analytical Method* (Homewood: Richard D. Irwin, Inc.)

Mautz, Robert K., 1973. "A Few Words for Historical Cost," *Financial Executive*, January

May, George O., 1951. *Financial Accounting: A Distillation of Experience* (New York: The Macmillan Company)

McConnell, Pat and Pegg, Janet, 1995. *Accounting Issues*, "Mexican Currency Translation and Inflation Accounting: A Review," Bear, Stearns & Co, Inc. February 10

McGee, Suzanne, 1997. "Technical Analysis Successfully Tests Old Resistance Level Of Fundamentalists," *Wall Street Journal*, October 13

McGregor, Warren, 1996. *Accounting for Leases: A New Approach* (Norwalk: Financial Accounting Standards Foundation)

McKnight, Benjamin A. III, 1999. "Regulated Utilities," in Carmichael, D. R., Lilien, Steven B., and Mellman, Martin, *Accountants' Handbook*, 9th edn (New York: John Wiley & Sons)

McLean, Bethany, 2001. "Why Enron Went Bust," *Fortune*, December 24

Melcher, Beatrice, 1973. Accounting Research Study No. 15, *Stockholders' Equity* (New York: AICPA)

Mencken, H. L., 1988, quoted in Byrne, Robert, *1911 Best Things Anyone Ever Said* (New York: Fawcett Columbine)

Meredith, Robyn, 1998. "G.M. Earnings Hint at Trouble Later this Year," *New York Times*, April 18

Merrett, A. J. and Sykes, Allen, 1974. Letter to the Editor, *Financial Times* (London), November 4

Merrill Lynch, 1998. "Valuing the New Economy: How New Accounting Standards Will Inhibit Economically Sound Mergers and Hinder the Efficiency and Innovation of U.S. Business," June

Micklethwait, John, and Wooldridge, Adrian, 2000. *A Future Perfect* (New York, Crown Business)

Milburn, J. Alex, 1982. "Discussion," in Sterling, Robert R. and Lemke, Kenneth W., *Maintenance of Capital: Financial versus Physical* (Houston: Scholars Book Co.)

Miller, Herbert E., 1964. "Audited Statements—Are They Really Management's?" *Journal of Accountancy*, October

Miller, Paul B. W., 1978. "A New View of Comparability," *Journal of Accountancy*, August

———— and Bahnson, Paul R., 2000. "Inspector Clouseau, Gnats, Camels, and Financial Reporting," *Accounting Today*, September 4–24

————, 2002a. "The Book Is Out on Quality Financial Reporting," *Accounting Today*, July 22–August 4

————, 2002b. *Quality Financial Reporting* (New York: McGraw-Hill Book Company)

————, 2004a. "Value-Based Accounting II: Timeliness and Reliability," *Accounting Today*, February 23–March 14

————, 2004b. "Will the Stock Options Debate Never Be Buried?" *Accounting Today*, April 19–May 2

———— and Flegm, Eugene H., 1990. "Should the FASB Be Neutral or Responsive?" *Journal of Accountancy*, March

Mills, John R. and Yamamura, Jeanne H., 1998. "The Power of Cash Flow Ratios," *Journal of Accountancy*, October

Moonitz, Maurice, 1961. Accounting Research Study No. 1, *The Basic Postulates of Accounting* (New York: AICPA)

_____, 1971. "Critique: Inflation and the Lag in Accounting Practice," in Sterling, Robert R. and Bentz, William F., *Accounting in Perspective* (Dallas: South-Western Publishing Co.)

_____, 1974. Studies in Accounting Research No. 8, *Obtaining Agreement on Standards in the Accounting Profession* (Sarasota: American Accounting Association)

_____ and Jordan, Louis H., 1963. *Accounting: An Analysis of its Problems*, Vol. I (revised edn) (New York: Holt, Rinehart and Winston, Inc.)

_____ and Staehling, Charles C., 1952. *Accounting: An Analysis of its Problems*, Vol. I (Brooklyn: The Foundation Press, Inc.)

Morgenson, Gretchen, 2002. "Scandal's Ripple Effect: Earnings Under Threat," *New York Times*, February 10

Morrissey, John, 2000. Speech at the General Audit Management Conference, New Orleans, Louisiana, March 21

Mosso, David, 1978. Speech reported in *FASB Viewpoints*, January 26

Muir, Frederick M., 1984. "Financial Corp. of American Says it Fired Auditor," *Wall Street Journal*, October 1

Muto, Shiela, 2002. "Firms Use Synthetic Leases Despite Criticism," *Wall Street Journal*, February 20

Myers, John H., 1962. Accounting Research Study No. 4, *Reporting of Leases in Financial Statements* (New York: AICPA)

Nailor, Hans and Lennard, Andrew, 2000. *Leases: Implementation of a New Approach* (prepared for the G4+1 organizations) issued by the Financial Accounting Standards Board, February

Nasuhiyah, Ashari, Hian, Chye Koh, Soh, Leng Tan, and Wei, Har Wong, 1994. "Factors Affecting Income Smoothing Among Listed Companies in Singapore," *Accounting and Business Research*, 24 (96)

National Commission on Fraudulent Financial Reporting, 1987. *Report of the National Commission on Fraudulent Financial Reporting* [Treadway Report], October

New York Times, 1998. "McDonald's Sets Stock Buyback," September 29

_____, 1999. April 22

_____, 1999. "Rothschild Treasures Set Records," July 9

_____, 2002. "Accounting Change Cuts Assets of AOL," January 8

Newsday, 2002. "Martha Stewart's Earnings Slump: But Company Touts Prospects," April 24

Noll, Daniel J. and Weygandt, Jerry J., 1997. "Business Reporting: What Comes Next?" *Journal of Accountancy*, February

Norby, William, 1973. "Some Further Comments. . ." *Financial Executive*, January

Norris, Floyd, 1994. "Accounting Board Yields on Stock Options," *New York Times*, December 15

_____, 1998. "Clues, but No Guarantees," *New York Times Book Review*, January 18

_____, 1999a. "Can Regulators Keep Accountants from Writing Fiction?," *New York Times*, September 10

_____, 1999b. "The S.E.C. Tries to Make Companies Take Smaller Baths," *New York Times*, November 11

_____, 2000a. "Levitt to Leave S.E.C. Early; Bush to Pick 4," *New York Times*, December 21

_____, 2000b. "The Fed's Challenge: How to Cope with a Burst Bubble," *New York Times*, December 22

_____, 2002a. "Will S.E.C.'s Needs Be Met? Not by Bush," *New York Times*, February 8

_____, 2002b. "Promises of a Nimbler Accounting Board," *New York Times*, April 25

_____, 2002c. "Accounting Reform: A Bright Line Vanishes," *New York Times*, June 7

_____, 2003. "SureBeam Revenue Policy Questioned," *New York Times*, August 27

O'Brien, Kevin J., 2004. "Infineon Sets Aside $229 to Cover Any Penalty on Pricing," *New York Times*, July 21

Omar Khayyám (*c*.1050–1122) *Rubáiyát* [translated by Edward Fitzgerald].

Pallais, Don M., 1999. "Prospective Financial Statements," in Carmichael, D. R., Lilien, Steven B., and Mellman, Martin, *Accountants' Handbook*, 9th edn (New York: John Wiley & Sons)

Parkinson, Roger, 1976. *The Fox of the North* (New York: David McKay Company, Inc.)

Paton, W. A., 1922. *Accounting Theory—With Special Reference to the Corporate Enterprise* (New York: The Ronald Press Company)

_____, 1924. *Accounting* (New York: Macmillan Company)

_____, 1941. *Advanced Accounting* (New York: Macmillan Company)

_____, 1971. "Introduction," in Stone, William E., *Foundations of Accounting Theory* (Gainesville: University of Florida Press)

_____, 1972. "Foreword," to Reissuance of Sprague, Charles Ezra, *The Philosophy of Accounts* (Scholars' Book Co.)

_____ and Littleton, A. C., 1940. *An Introduction to Corporate Accounting Standards* (American Accounting Association)

Peragallo, Edward, 1938. *Origin and Evolution of Double Entry Bookkeeping* (New York: American Institute Publishing Company)

Petersen, Melody, 1998a. "A New Rule to Turn the Annual Report into True Confessions," *New York Times*, March 4

_____, 1998b. "Greenspan Endorses Accounting Board Decision," *New York Times*, June 15

_____, 1998c. "Accounting Board Pulls Back on Stock Plans," *New York Times*, July 20

_____, 1998d. "Film Industry Is Confronting Likely Change in Accounting," *New York Times*, September 21

Pinger, R. W., 1954. "The Semantics of Accounting," *Accounting Review*, October

Pitt, Harvey L., 2001. "How to Prevent Future Enrons," *Wall Street Journal*, December 11

_____, 2002. "Remarks before the Investment Company Institute, 2002 General Membership Meeting," May 24

Plato, *Statesman*, 1995. (World Library, Inc. [Electronically Enhanced Text])

Plitch, Phyllis, 2001. "Global Accounting Faces Stock-Option Tiff," *Wall Street Journal*, August 28

Pope, Alexander (1688–1744). *Essay on Man*

Popkin, Richard H. and Stroll, Avrum, 1956. *Philosophy Made Simple* (Garden City: Doubleday & Company, Inc.)

Previts, Gary John (ed.) 1991. *Financial Reporting and Standard Setting* (New York: AICPA)

_____, 1992. *Research in Accounting Regulation*, Vol. 6 (Greenwich: JAI Press)

Price Waterhouse, 1983. EEC Bulletin No. 2, "Special Supplement on the EEC Seventh Directive, Consolidated Financial Statements"

Quindlen, Anna, 2002. "The Axis of Re-Election," *Newsweek*, March 4

Reingold, Jennifer, 2003. "CEOs Who Should Lose their Jobs," *Fast Company*, October

Rescigno, Jeanne, 2001. "The Standards Challenge," *Journal of Accountancy*, November

Research Committee of the Institute of Chartered Accountants of Scotland, 1988. *Making Corporate Reports Valuable* (London: Kogan Page Limited)

Revsine, Lawrence, 1973. *Replacement Cost Accounting* (Englewood Cliffs: Prentice-Hall, Inc.)

_____, 1982. "Physical Capital Maintenance: An Analysis," in Sterling, Robert R. and Lemke, Kenneth W., *Maintenance of Capital: Financial versus Physical* (Houston: Scholars Book Co.)

_____, 1991. "The Selective Financial Misrepresentation Hypothesis," *Accounting Horizons*, December

_____ and Weygandt, Jerry J., 1974. "Accounting for Inflation: The Controversy," *Journal of Accountancy*, October

Riahi-Belkaoui, Ahmed, 1993. *Accounting Theory*, 3rd edn (New York: The Dryden Press)

Richards, Bill, and Thurm, Scott, 2002. "Boston Chicken Case Mirrors Enron Failure," *Wall Street Journal*, March 13

Richtel, Matt, 1999. "Webvan Is Delaying Its Offering of Stock," *New York Times*, October 8

Robbins, Barry P., 1987. "A Question of Basis," *Journal of Accountancy*, March

Roberts, Michael L., Samson, William D., and Dugan, Michael T., 1990. "The Stockholders' Equity Section: Form Without Substance?" *Accounting Horizons*, December

Rohter, Larry, 1999. "Ecuador Pins Hopes on Shift to Dollar," *New York Times*, July 2

Romero, Simon, 2000. "Qualcomm's Shrinking Act Could Pay Off Big," *New York Times*, October 23

Ronen, Joshua, 1974. "Discounted Cash Flow Accounting," AICPA, Vol. II

_____ and Sorter, George, 1989. "Reflections on 'Reflections on the FASB's Conceptual Framework for Accounting and on Auditing,'" *Journal of Accounting, Auditing & Finance*, Winter

Rosenfield, Paul, 1969a. "Accounting for Inflation—A Field Test," *Journal of Accountancy*, June

_____, 1969b. "Reporting Subjunctive Gains and Losses," *Accounting Review*, October

_____, 1971a. "General Price-Level Accounting and Foreign Operations," *Journal of Accountancy*, February

_____, 1971b. "Critique: Inflation and the Lag in Accounting Practice," in Sterling, Robert R. and Bentz, William F., *Accounting in Perspective* (Dallas: South-Western Publishing Co.)

_____, 1972. "The Confusion Between General Price-Level Restatement and Current Value Accounting," *Journal of Accountancy*, October

_____, 1975. "Current Replacement Value Accounting—A Dead End," *Journal of Accountancy*, September

_____, 1981. "Correcting for Inflation and Value Changes," in Seidler, Lee J. and Carmichael, D. R., *Accountants' Handbook*, 6th edn, Vol. I (New York: John Wiley & Sons)

_____, 1987. "Accounting for Foreign Operations," *Journal of Accountancy*, August 1987

_____, 2000. "What Drives Earnings Management? It is GAAP itself," *Journal of Accountancy*, October

_____, 2003. "Presenting Discounted Future Cash Receipts and Payments in Financial Statements," *Abacus*, June

_____, 2005. "The Focus of Attention in Financial Reporting," *Abacus*, February

_____ and Dent, William C., 1983. "No More Deferred Taxes," *Journal of Accountancy*, February

_____, versus Rubin, Steven, 1986. "Minority Interest: Opposing Views," *Journal of Accountancy*, March

Rosenthal, A. M., 1995. "As California Goes," *New York Times*, February 17

Rossant, John, Ewing, Jack, and Bremner, Brian, 2002. "The Corporate Cleanup Goes Global," *Business Week*, May 6

Rousseau, Jean-Jacques, 1953. *The Confessions* (New York: Viking Penguin, Inc.) (first published in 1781)

Rubin, Steven, 1999. "Consolidation, Translation, and the Equity Method," in Carmichael, D. R., Lilien, Steven, and Mellman, Martin (eds), *Accountants' Handbook*, 9th edn (New York: John Wiley & Sons)

Sagan, Carl, 1988. "Introduction," in Hawking, Stephen W., *A Brief History of Time* (New York: Bantam Books)

Salwen, Kevin G. and Block, Sandra, 1990. "SEC Alarmed by Accounting Standards Industry Adopted for Financial Concerns," *Wall Street Journal*, September 17

Samuelson, Robert J., 2001. "The Illusion of Knowledge," *Newsweek*, May 21

Schattke, Rudolph Walter, 1960. "The Implications of Economic Concepts of Income and Profit for Accounting" (Abstract of dissertation), *Accounting Review*, October

Schipper, Katherine, 1989. "Commentary on Earnings Management," *Accounting Horizons*, December

_____, 1994. "Academic Accounting Research and the Standard Setting Process," *Accounting Horizons*, December

_____, 2003. "Principles-Based Accounting Standards," *Accounting Horizons*, March

Schmitt, Christopher H., 2001. "A Handicapper's Guide to the New SEC Chief," *Business Week*, May 21

Schroeder, Michael, 2002a. "Levitt Calls for New Laws on Accounting," *Wall Street Journal*, January 25

_____, 2002b. "As Pitt Launches SEC Probe of Himself, Criticism Mounts," *Wall Street Journal*, November 1

_____ and Hitt, Greg, 2002. "Accounting Industry is Taken to Task," *Wall Street Journal*, March 8

Schroeder, Richard G. and Clark, Myrtle W., 1998. *Accounting Theory* (New York: John Wiley & Sons, Inc.)

Schuetze, Walter, 1991. "Keep it Simple," *Accounting Horizons*, June

_____, 1992. "Relevance and Credibility in Financial Accounting and Reporting," Speech before the American Accounting Association, August 12

_____, 1994. "Independence Not a Suitable Case for Treatment," *Financial Times*, June 24

_____, 1998. Remarks to the Financial Accounting and Reporting Section of the American Accounting Association at its 1998 Annual Meeting.

_____, 2000. Letter to the FASB, June 15

_____, 2001. "What Are Assets and Liabilities? Where Is True North? (Accounting That My Sister Would Understand)," *Abacus*, February

_____, 2003. "Auditing: Objective Evidence vs. Subjective Judgments," speech to the Foundation for Accounting Education, New York State Society of CPAs, September 9

———, 2004. *Mark-to-Market Accounting* (London: Routledge)

Schwartz, Clifford, 1998. "Accounting in the Americas," *Emerging Markets Corporate Research*, Lehman Brothers, November

_____ and McElyea, Suzanne, 2002. "Real Estate and Construction," in Carmichael, D. R. and Rosenfield, Paul (eds), *Accountants' Handbook*, 10th edn (New York: John Wiley & Sons)

Schwarz, Alan, 1998. "A Blast From the Past Makes Baseball a Current Event," *New York Times*, September 13

Scott, Diana J. and Upton, Wayne S., 1991. "The Role of Cost–Benefit Considerations in the FASB's Standards-Setting Process," in FASB, *Benefits, Costs and Consequences of Financial Accounting Standards*

_____, 1998. "SEC's Earnings Management Initiative Fact Sheet," issued with SEC News Release 98–96, September 28

Scott, William R., 1997. *Financial Accounting Theory* (Upper Saddle River: Prentice-Hall, Inc.)

Securities and Exchange Commission, 1976. Accounting Series Release No. 190

_____, 1978. Accounting Series Release No. 253

_____, 1999a. Staff Accounting Bulletin No. 99, "Materiality," August 12

_____, 1999b. Staff Accounting Bulletin No. 100, "Restructuring and Impairment Charges," November 24

Seligman, Dan, 2000. "The Crusade against Smoothing," *Forbes*, June 12

Shearer, Derek, 2000. "The Big Store," review of Micklethwait, John and Wooldridge, Adrian, *A Future Perfect*, in *New York Times Book Review*, July 2

Sherer, Paul M., 2000. "Chase Digs in Its Heels, but Ally J.P. Morgan Embraces 'Fair Value,'" *Wall Street Journal*, October 11

Shirer, William L., 1960. *The Rise and Fall of the Third Reich* (New York: Simon and Schuster)

Silverberg, Robert, 1964. *Time of the Great Freeze* (New York: Holt, Rinehart and Winston, Inc.)

Silverman, Rachel Emma, 2002. "GE Annual Report Bulges with Data in Bid to Address Post-Enron Concerns," *Wall Street Journal*, March 11

Sinclair, Upton, 1945. *Between Two Worlds* (New York: The Viking Press)

Skinner, Ross M., 1982. "The Impact of Changing Prices: The Canadian Position," in Sterling, Robert R. and Lemke, Kenneth W., *Maintenance of Capital: Financial versus Physical* (Houston: Scholars Book Co.)

_____, 1987. *Accounting Standards in Evolution* (Holt, Rinehart and Winston of Canada, Limited)

Sloan, Allan, 1996. "Trend Surfing," *Newsweek*, July 1

_____, 2002. "Prepare to Deal with a Murky Market," *Newsweek*, December 31, 2001/January 7

Smith, John T., 1998. "Responding to FASB Standard-Setting Proposals," *Accounting Horizons*, June

Smith, L. Murphy, 2003. "A Fresh Look at Accounting Ethics (or Dr. Smith Goes to Washington)," *Accounting Horizons*, March

Smith, Randall, Lipin, Steven, and Naj, Amal Kumar, 1994. "How General Electric Damps Fluctuations in its Annual Earnings," *Wall Street Journal*, November 3

Snailum, Walter W., 1910. *Fifteen Studies in Book-keeping* (Cambridge: Cambridge University Press)

Solomons, David, 1966. Book Review of Raymond J. Chambers, *Accounting, Evaluation, and Economic Behavior*, in *Abacus*

———, 1971. "Asset Valuation and Income Determination: Appraising the Alternatives," in Sterling, Robert R. (ed.), *Asset Valuation and Income Determination: A Consideration of the Alternatives* (Lawrence, Kansas: Scholars Book Co.)

———, 1978. "The Politicization of Accounting," *Journal of Accountancy*, November

———, 1986. *Making Accounting Policy* (New York: Oxford University Press)

———, 1989. *Guidelines for Financial Reporting Standards* (London: The Institute of Chartered Accountants in England and Wales)

Sorkin, Andrew Ross, 2000. "Vodka and Caviar for Everyone!" *New York Times*, November 26

Sorter, George H., 1983. Review of Eldon S. Hendriksen, *Accounting Theory*, 4th edn (Homewood: Richard D. Irwin, Inc., 1982), in *Accounting Review*, July

———, Gans, Martin S., Rosenfield, Paul, Shannon, R. M., and Streit, Robert G., 1974. "Earning Power and Cash Generating Ability," in Cramer, Joe J. Jr and Sorter, George H., *Objectives of Financial Statements*, Vol. 2, Selected Papers (New York: AICPA)

Spiller, Earl A. and Virgil, Robert L., 1974. "Effectiveness of APB Opinion 19 in Improving Funds Reporting," *Journal of Accounting Research*, Spring

Sprague, Charles Ezra, 1908. *The Philosophy of Accounts* (New York: Charles Ezra Sprague)

Sprouse, Robert T., 1963. "Historical Costs and Current Assets—Traditional and Treacherous," *Accounting Review*, October

———, 1966. "Accounting for What-You-May-Call-Its," *Journal of Accountancy*, October

———, 1987. "Commentary on Financial Reporting—Economic Consequences: The Volatility Bugaboo," *Accounting Horizons*, March

———, 1993. "Developing a Conceptual Framework for Financial Reporting," in Coffman, Edward N., *Historical Perspectives of Selected Financial Accounting Topics* (Homewood: Richard D. Irwin, Inc.)

——— and Moonitz, Maurice, 1962. Accounting Research Study No. 3, *A Tentative Set of Broad Accounting Principles for Business Enterprises* (New York: AICPA)

Staubus, George J., 1959. "The Residual Equity Point of View in Accounting," *Accounting Review*, January

———, 1961. *A Theory of Accounting to Investors* (Berkeley: University of California Press)

———, 1967. "Current Cash Equivalent for Assets: A Dissent," *Accounting Review*, October

———, 1971a. "The Relevance of Evidence of Cash Flows," in Sterling, Robert R. (ed.), *Asset Valuation and Income Determination: A Consideration of the Alternatives* (Lawrence, Kansas: Scholars Book Co.)

———, 1971b. "Critique: Return on Investment: The Continuing Confusion among Disparate Measures," in Sterling, Robert R. and Bentz, William F., *Accounting in Perspective* (Dallas: South-Western Publishing Co.)

_____, 1972. "An Analysis of APB Statement No. 4," *Journal of Accountancy*, February

_____, 1977. *Making Accounting Decisions* (Houston: Scholars Book Co.)

_____, 1985. "An Induced Theory of Accounting Measurement," *Accounting Review*, January

_____, 2003. "An Accountant's Education," *Accounting Historians Journal*, June

_____, 2004a. "On Brian P. West's Professionalism and Accounting Rules," *Abacus*, June

_____, 2004b. "Ethics Failures in Corporate Financial Reporting," *Journal of Business Ethics*, Fall

Sterling, Robert. R., 1966. "In Defence of Accounting in the United States," *Abacus*, December

_____, 1967. "Conservatism: The Fundamental Principle of Valuation in Traditional Accounting," *Abacus*, December

_____, 1968. "The Going Concern. An Examination," *Accounting Review*, July

_____, 1970a. *Theory of the Measurement of Enterprise Income* (Lawrence: University Press of Kansas)

_____, 1970b. "On Theory Construction and Verification," *Accounting Review*, July

_____, (ed.) 1971. *Asset Valuation and Income Determination: A Consideration of the Alternatives* (Lawrence, Kansas: Scholars Book Co.)

_____, 1972. "Decision Oriented Financial Accounting," *Accounting and Business Research*, Summer

_____, 1973. "Accounting Power," *Journal of Accountancy*, January

_____, 1977. "Foreword," in Staubus, George J., *Making Accounting Decisions* (Houston: Scholars Book Co.)

_____, 1979. *Toward a Science of Accounting* (Houston: Scholars Book Co.)

_____, 1982. "Limitations of Physical Capital," in Sterling, Robert R. and Lemke, Kenneth W., *Maintenance of Capital: Financial versus Physical* (Houston: Scholars Book Co.)

_____, 1987. "An Essay on Recognition," *R. J. Chambers Research Lecture 1985* (Sydney: University of Sydney, Accounting Research Center)

_____, 1988. "Confessions of a Failed Empiricist," *Advances in Accounting*, Vol. 6

_____, 1989. "Teaching the Correspondence Concept," *Issues in Accounting Education*, Spring

_____, 1990a. "Teacher, Educate Thyself," *Journal of Accounting Education*, 8

_____, 1990b. "Positive Accounting: An Assessment," *Abacus*, 26 (2) 1990

_____ and Bentz, William F., 1971. *Accounting in Perspective* (Dallas: South-Western Publishing Co.)

_____ and Lemke, Kenneth W., 1982. *Maintenance of Capital: Financial Versus Physical* (Houston: Scholars Book Co.)

_____ and Thomas, Arthur L., 1979. *Accounting for a Simplified Firm Owning Depreciable Assets* (Houston: Scholars Book Co.)

Stewart, Jenice P., 1989. "The Significance of an Orientation Postulate," *Abacus*, 25 (2)

Stiglitz, Joseph E., 2002. "Accounting for Options," *Wall Street Journal*, May 3

Stone, Brad, 1998. "From Here to There: The Physics of Time Travel," *Newsweek*, March 16

Stone, Justice, 1953. "Clark's Will v The Supreme Court of Minnesota" (1939, 204 Minn. 574, 284 NW 867), quoted in Kell, Walter G., "Should the Accounting Entity be Personified?" *Accounting Review*, January

Stone, Marvin L., 1971. "'Tis the Age of Aquarius—Even for Accounting," in Sterling, Robert R. (ed.), *Asset Valuation and Income Determination: A Consideration of the Alternatives* (Lawrence, Kansas: Scholars Book Co.)

Stone, Willard E. (ed.) 1971. *Foundations of Accounting Theory* (Gainesville: University of Florida Press)

Storey, Reed K., 1959. "Revenue Realization, Going Concern and Measurement of Income," *Accounting Review*, April

———, 1960. "Cash Movements and Periodic Income Determination," *Accounting Review*, July

———, 1966. "Director's Statement," in Black, Homer A., *Interperiod Allocation of Corporate Income Taxes* (New York: AICPA)

———, 1973. "Comments of Director of Accounting Research," in Melcher, Beatrice, *Stockholders' Equity* (New York: AICPA)

———, 1999. "The Framework of Accounting Concepts and Standards," in Carmichael, D. R., Lilien, Steven, and Mellman, Martin (eds), *Accountants' Handbook*, 9th edn (New York: John Wiley & Sons)

——— and Storey, Sylvia, 1998. *The Framework of Financial Accounting Concepts and Standards* (Norwalk: Financial Accounting Standards Board)

Strom, Stephanie, 2002. "Even Last Year, Option Spigot Was Wide Open," *New York Times*, February 3

Strunk, William, Jr and White, E. B., 1979. *The Elements of Style*, 3rd edn (New York: Macmillan Publishing Co., Inc.)

Sunder, Shyam, 2002. "Knowing What Others Know: Common Knowledge, Accounting, and Capital Markets," *Accounting Horizons*, December

Sutton, Michael H., 1997. "Financial Reporting in U.S. Capital Markets: International Dimensions," *Accounting Horizons*, June

———, 2002. "Financial Reporting at a Crossroads," *Accounting Horizons*, December

Tabori, Paul, 1993. *The Natural History of Stupidity* (New York: Barnes & Noble Books)

Taper, Eugene G., 1981. "Leases and Off-Balance Sheet Financing," in Burton *et al.* (eds), *Handbook of Accounting and Auditing* (Boston: Warren, Gorham and Lamont)

Tedeschi, Bob, 1999. "Advertising," *New York Times*, August 18

The Record, 1997a. "Out of this World," April 1

———, 1997b. "Shareholders Sue Children's Place," October 18

Thomas, Arthur L., 1964. "Value-Itis—An Impractical Theorist's Reply," *Accounting Review*, July

———, 1969. Studies in Accounting Research No. 3, *The Allocation Problem in Financial Accounting Theory* (American Accounting Association)

———, 1974. Studies in Accounting Research No. 9, *The Allocation Problem, Part Two* (American Accounting Association)

———, 1975a. *Financial Accounting: The Main Ideas*, 2nd edn (Belmont: Wadsworth Publishing Company, Inc.)

———, 1975b. "The FASB and the Allocation Fallacy," *Journal of Accountancy*, November

———, 1979. "Matching: Up from Our Black Hole," in Sterling, Robert R. and Thomas, Arthur L., *Accounting for a Simplified Firm Owning Depreciable Assets* (Houston: Scholars Book Co.)

———, 1995. Letter to P. Rosenfield, January 28

Thomas, C. William, 2002. "The Rise and Fall of Enron," *Journal of Accountancy*, April

Thomas, Robert McG., Jr, 1998. "Harry Stanley Dies at 100; Master of Erudite Nonsense," *New York Times*, March 6

Thompson, George D., 1991. "The Paton and Littleton Monograph: Landmark or Folly?" *Accounting History*, 3 (2)

Tradewell International, 1998. Advertisement, *American Way*, November 1

Turner, Lynn, 1999. Letter to P. Rosenfield, October 27

_____, 2000. Letter to P. Rosenfield, January 18

_____, 2001. "Past, Present, and Future," remarks at Securities Regulation Institute, Northwestern University, School of Law, January 24

UK Research Committee, 1988. *Making Corporate Reports Valuable—The Literature Surveys* (Edinburgh: The Institute of Chartered Accountants of Scotland)

United Nations Economic and Social Council, 1977. Group of Experts on International Standards of Accounting and Reporting, Commission on Transnational Corporations, *International Standards of Accounting and Reporting* (E/C. 10/33), October 18

U.S. Steel Corporation, 1947. *Annual Report*

Van Riper, Robert, 1986. "'Due Process' and the Decision-Making Process," *FASB Viewpoints*, October 31

Vatter, William J., 1947. *The Fund Theory of Accounting and its Implications for Financial Reports* (Chicago: University of Chicago Press)

_____, 1955. "Corporate Stock Equities—Part I," in Backer, Morton (ed.), *Handbook of Modern Accounting Theory* (New York: Prentice-Hall, Inc.)

_____, 1971. "Current Issues about Current Costs," in Sterling, Robert R. (ed.), *Asset Valuation and Income Determination: A Consideration of the Alternatives* (Lawrence, Kansas: Scholars Book Co.)

Veblen, Thorstein, 1899. *The Theory of the Leisure Class* (New York: Macmillan Company)

_____, 1904. *The Theory of Business Enterprise* (Charles Scribners' Sons)

Wade, Nicholas, 1998. "From Ants to Ethics: A Biologist Dreams of Unity of Knowledge," *New York Times*, May 12

Wall Street Journal, 1990. "Spicer & Oppenheim to Disband, Merge Offices with Others," November 29

_____, 1999. "Senators Call for Hearings on Accounting Changes," July 16

_____, 2002. "Too Bad for Andersen, But Good for Accounting," May 1

Wallace, Robert, 1969. *The World of Van Gogh* (Alexandria: Time-Life Books)

Walsh, Mary Williams, 2003. "Failed Pensions: A Painful Lesson in Assumptions," *New York Times*, November 12

Walters, Ralph, 2002. Letter to P. Rosenfield, November 7

Watts, Ross L., 1994. "Positive Research in Accounting," Working Paper for inclusion in *The Foundations of Modern Financial Accounting Thought*, October 13

_____, 1999. Letter to P. Rosenfield, March 3

_____, 2003. "Conservatism in Accounting Part I: Explanations and Implications," *Accounting Horizons*, September

_____ and Zimmerman, Jerold L., 1978. "Towards a Positive Theory of the Determination of Accounting Standards," *Accounting Review*, January

_____, 1986. *Positive Accounting Theory* (Englewood Cliffs: Prentice-Hall, Inc.)

_____, 1990. "Positive Accounting Theory: A Ten Year Perspective," *Accounting Review*, January

Wechsler, Dana, 1990. "Numbers Game: The Bankers' New Headache," *Forbes*, January 8

Weetman, Pauline and Gordon, Paul D., 1988. "The Philosophy and Objectives of External Corporate Reporting, Including Users and Their Information Needs," in *Making Corporate Reports Valuable—The Literature Surveys* (Edinburgh: The Institute of Chartered Accountants of Scotland)

West, Brian P., 2003. *Professionalism and Accounting Rules* (New York: Routledge)

Weston, Frank T., 1971. "Response to Evidence for a Market—Selling Price—Accounting System," in Sterling, Robert R. (ed.), *Asset Valuation and Income Determination: A Consideration of the Alternatives* (Lawrence, Kansas: Scholars Book Co.)

Westwood, Mark and Mackenzie, April, 1999. *Accounting by Recipients for Non-Reciprocal Transfers, Excluding Contributions by Owners: Their Definition, Recognition and Measurement* (Norwalk: Financial Accounting Standards Board)

Wheeler, John Archibald, 2000. "A Practical Tool, but Puzzling, Too," *New York Times*, December 12

White, Gerald I. and Sondhi, Ashwinpaul C., 1999. "Analyzing Financial Statements," in Carmichael, D. R., Lilien, Steven, and Mellman, Martin (eds), *Accountants' Handbook*, 9th edn (New York: John Wiley & Sons)

White, Morton, 1957. *The Age of Analysis* (New York: George Braziller, Inc.)

Whitehead, Alfred North, 1938. *Modes of Thought* (New York: The Macmillan Co.)

Wilke, John R., 1998. "Greenspan Questions Antitrust Efforts," *Wall Street Journal*, June 17

Willens, Robert and Phillips, Andrea J., 1995. "The Contract with America," *Journal of Accountancy*, April

Williams, Harold, 1989. Address to the 1983 Arthur Young Professors Roundtable at Arden House, quoted in Kripke, Homer, "Reflections on the FASB's Conceptual Framework for Accounting and on Auditing," *Journal of Accounting, Auditing and Finance*, Winter

Williams, Jan R., 1999. "Financial Statements: Form and Content," in Carmichael, D. R., Lilien, Steven, and Mellman, Martin (eds), *Accountants' Handbook*, 9th edn (New York: John Wiley & Sons)

Williams, Paul F., 2001. Book Review of Carl Thomas Devine, *Essays in Accounting Theory: A Capstone, the Accounting Review*, October

Wolk, Harry I., Francis, Jere R., and Tearney, Michael G., 1992. *Accounting Theory, A Conceptual and Institutional Approach*, 3rd edn (Cincinnati: South-Western Publishing Co.)

Wolnizer, Peter W., 1987. *Auditing as Independent Authentication* (Sydney: Sydney University Press)

World Accounting Report, 1989. "Harmonising Goodwill," July

Worthy, Ford S., 1984. "Manipulating Profits: How it's Done," *Fortune*, June 25

———, 1992. "The Battle of the Bean Counters," *Fortune*, June 1

Wyatt, Arthur R., 1963. Accounting Research Study No. 5, *A Critical Study of Accounting for Business Combinations* (New York: AICPA)

———, 1983. "Efficient Market Theory: Its Impact on Accounting," *Journal of Accountancy*, February

———, 1988. "Professionalism in Standard-Setting," *The CPA Journal*, July

———, 1989a. "Commentary on Interface Between Teaching/Research and Teaching/Practice," *Accounting Horizons*, March

———, 1989b. "Commentary on Accounting Standards and the Professional Auditor," *Accounting Horizons*, June

_____, 1997. "Review: The Accounting Profession—Major Issues: Progress and Concerns," *Accounting Horizons*, June

_____, 2004. "Accounting Professionalism—They Just Don't Get it!," *Accounting Horizons*, March

Yager, Charles R., 1988. Participant in Arnold, Jerry L. (ed.), *Proceedings of the October 8, 1987 Roundtable Discussion on Generally Accepted Accounting Principles and Regulatory Accounting Practices* (School of Accounting: University of California)

Zakaria, Fareed, 2001. "New Dangers Amid the Ruins," *Newsweek*, March 5

Zeff, Stephen Addam, 1961. *A Critical Examination of the Orientation Postulate in Accounting, with Particular Attention to its Historical Development*, PhD dissertation, University of Michigan

_____. 1982. *"Truth in Accounting*: The Ordeal of Kenneth MacNeal," *Accounting Review*, July

_____, 1987. "Leaders of the Accounting Profession: 14 Who Made a Difference," *Journal of Accountancy*, May

_____, 1994. "A Perspective on the U.S. Public/Private-Sector Approach to Standard Setting and Financial Reporting," Inaugural Lecture, State University of Limburg, June 3

_____, 1995. Letter to P. Rosenfield, April 25

_____, 2002. "'Political' Lobbying on Proposed Standards: A Challenge to the IASB," *Accounting Horizons*, March

_____, 2003a. "How the U.S. Accounting Profession Got Where It Is Today, Part I" *Accounting Horizons*, September

_____, 2003b. "How the U.S. Accounting Profession Got Where It Is Today: Part II" *Accounting Horizons*, December

Zuckerman, Laurence, 1998. "$1.4 Billion Boeing Charge to Force First Yearly Loss Since '47," *New York Times*, January 22

Author index

Subject index

eBooks – at www.eBookstore.tandf.co.uk

A library at your fingertips!

eBooks are electronic versions of printed books. You can store them on your PC/laptop or browse them online.

They have advantages for anyone needing rapid access to a wide variety of published, copyright information.

eBooks can help your research by enabling you to bookmark chapters, annotate text and use instant searches to find specific words or phrases. Several eBook files would fit on even a small laptop or PDA.

NEW: Save money by eSubscribing: cheap, online access to any eBook for as long as you need it.

Annual subscription packages

We now offer special low-cost bulk subscriptions to packages of eBooks in certain subject areas. These are available to libraries or to individuals.

For more information please contact webmaster.ebooks@tandf.co.uk

We're continually developing the eBook concept, so keep up to date by visiting the website.

www.eBookstore.tandf.co.uk